A CENTURY OF CI[
The Centenary Histor
of Hull City A.F.C.
1904 ~ 2004

By Mike Peterson

Published by:
Yore Publications
12 The Furrows, Harefield,
Middx. UB9 6AT.

© Mike Peterson 2005

British Library Cataloguing-in-Publication Data.
A catalogue record for this book
is available from the British Library.

Reprinted in paperback form: August 2011
(Formerly ISBN 0954783077)

ISBN   9780956984814

Printed and bound by:
4 Edge Ltd.

Foreword

In the context of Hull City's history, my time as chairman to date is relatively brief when compared with others who have previously held the post, but I think you would agree that much has happened since I took up the position in March 2001. At times it has felt like I have been here a lifetime! Perhaps that's why I was invited to write the foreword to 'A Century of City'? Whatever the reason, I am pleased to have this opportunity to provide a few words of introduction before you turn the subsequent pages and start what I hope will be an enjoyable and enlightening trip down memory lane.

I do not profess to be an expert on the history of the Tigers but from what I've heard and read previously, the issue of finance – particularly the lack of it – has been a recurring theme throughout the club's first 100 years. That was certainly the case when I became involved. To my mind though, the financial problems did not obscure the tremendous potential I believed this club possessed and that is why I was keen to become involved. Gradually, that potential is now starting to be realised and the success we have enjoyed in recent years has been due to a lot of hard work from everyone associated with Hull City: players, management, staff and supporters. This foreword, therefore, also gives me the opportunity to say a big thank you to everyone connected with this club for that outstanding commitment.

However, for this club to progress further – and I sincerely believe it will – it is essential that everyone continues to put in the maximum effort. I can assure you that I, and everyone else at Hull City, am committed to that aim and I know that the supporters share that commitment. I don't know about you but I'm getting a little weary of being reminded that Hull is the largest city in Europe never to have played host to domestic football at the highest level. Together, I believe we can do something about trying to rectify that anomaly during the Tigers' second century.

I hope you enjoy reading 'A Century of City' and that in looking back over the years it revives some happy personal memories for you. Equally, I hope you enjoy looking forward to what we can achieve together in the future.

Adam Pearson
Hull City AFC Chairman

ACKNOWLEDGEMENTS

Without the efforts, earlier this century, of Hull City's chairman, Mr Adam Pearson, it is quite possible there wouldn't have been a Hull City, never mind 'A Century of City' to write about. For that alone, I and many thousands of other people who hold the Tigers dear to their hearts have much to thank him for. In addition, I am most grateful for his kindly agreeing to this book being written and also for providing the Foreword. There are others at the club to whom I am indebted for their assistance and in particular I would like to thank Rob Smith for his help and support throughout the project.

For their help in compiling the words, pictures and statistics I must express my gratitude to Ray Tupling, Trevor Bugg, Alan Moor, Chris Elton, Tony Brown, Jim Creasey and my wife Angela. Whether my query was about names, games, goals or grammar, they never failed to answer my call for assistance. I am particularly grateful to John Wilson and Nick Turner, who granted me the freedom of their respective picture collections. I must also express my appreciation to Dave Lofthouse, the Yorkshire Post and the Hull Daily Mail for providing various pictures and granting permission for their use throughout the book.

For his professional expertise in designing the cover for this book, my grateful thanks to Dominic Love. Modestly, he told me it was a favour he didn't mind doing. It is a favour I will not forget. Thanks Dom.

During the course of my research I visited the Local Studies library in Hull on a number of occasions. Each time the help and courtesy I received from the staff was of their usual high standard; my thanks to them for that and my apologies for testing their patience to the limit on how to use the machinery!

My gratitude goes to Peter Holme at the National Football Museum for his assistance in gaining access to the Football League's early records. Also my thanks are extended to Alan Mabbutt and Doug Saunders who kindly lent me some of their City ephemera, thus ensuring that the Tigers' story would be as comprehensive as possible.

Finally, I would like to recognise the tremendous help I received from Dave Twydell and all at Yore Publications for turning my raw script into the finished article.

CONTENTS

Although the birth of Hull City was announced on 28th June 1904, its conception, it could be argued, can be traced back to a meeting some 25 years earlier, in a hotel room in Hull. It was not a sordid liaison – the intentions of the participants were strictly honourable – neither, however, was it an immaculate conception and as events unfolded the evidence suggests that the development of Hull City football club had echoes more of Charles Darwin than Mary and Joseph about it.

The location in question was the Crown and Cushion Hotel, situated at No.3 Land of Green Ginger in the centre of Hull. On the 4th October 1879 a gathering of twelve men, all members of the Hull Town Cricket Club, met to discuss how they could best occupy their leisure time during the winter months. In a city that had a strong Rugby Union set up, it would not have been unexpected if they had chosen to chase the oval ball around the sporting fields of Hull.

Yet these men were passionate and talented cricketers – amongst their number was Lamplough ('Lamp') Wallgate, the club professional, who had played for Yorkshire CCC during the mid 1870s – and it may well have been their affection for the round cricket ball that influenced the ensuing discussion that evening. Eventually, they chose a ball of the same shape but just bigger in circumference, and the resolution arising out of that meeting was "That a Football Club be formed in connection with the Hull Town Cricket Club under Association Rules."

Membership of this new club would be restricted to Hull Town members only, and further restrictions were imposed in that the "…football club would not use the square, or do any damage to the cricket ground." It was also agreed that management of the club would be carried out by a sub-committee of Hull Town Cricket Club members and membership subscription to the football club would cost half-a-crown (12½p).

Mr T.W. Hearfield was elected president and 'Lamp' Wallgate elected vice-president, with Messrs Kendall and Walker elected Treasurer and Secretary respectively. Also elected onto the committee were Messrs Hicks, Summers, Hart, Middleton and Milner.

A list of rules was drawn up, one of which offers a tantalising glimpse of the evolutionary process that eventually resulted in the formal creation of Hull City Football Club nearly a quarter of a century later. Rule 11 stated that: "The club colours shall be Amber and Black".

The minutes of Hull Town's inaugural meeting show the club colours will be Amber and Black - over a century later the same colours are still predominant in the city

By the early 1880s Hull Town football club had developed into a strong member of the local football scene, which had gone from strength to strength during the same period. However, towards the end of that decade the fortunes of Hull Town football club waned and by 1887 the club had been disbanded. All was not lost though, for within two years the club had been reformed but it proved to be only a temporary resurrection and by the end of 1889 the demise of Hull Town was permanent…or so it seemed.

Although the fortunes of Hull Town had fluctuated and eventually failed, the name resurfaced in 1896 but this time the driving force behind the continuing development of association football within the city was not cricket but rugby. A year previously rugby had undergone a major reorganization: prior to 1895 the sport had existed under one code, Union, but in 1895 the Northern Union sides had set up their own 'League' competition and were gaining both local and regional support.

The situation in the city of Hull reflected that elsewhere in the North and one of the local Union clubs initially refusing to cross the great divide within the oval ball sport was Hull Kingston Rovers.

Unable to run a successful 'A' team, they amalgamated with a local soccer club by the name of Albany, and the new club was called Hull Town Association Club.

The date of amalgamation was 25th August 1896 and the team captain was W. Robson with J.F. Haller acting as club secretary. The newly formed club was allowed to use Rovers' ground on alternate Saturdays to fulfil their fixtures. Their first fixture was at Bradford on 5th September 1896, a game they lost 2-1, but that early setback did not prevent the 'reborn' Hull Town from enjoying success, reaching the final of the Scarborough and East Riding Cup.

Match ticket (priced at 3d) for Hull Town's fixture against the Black Watch from York in December 1896

Within a couple of years though, the initial enthusiasm had apparently worn off and Hull Town went the way of its namesake from previous years and disbanded during the summer of 1898. From that disbandment both players and officials went their various ways without, however, completely severing their soccer connections within the city. They remained influential in the continuing development of soccer locally and some were also instrumental in the creation of an amateur club by the name of Hull City who had a brief but impressive season-long existence at Dairycoates.

Despite such setbacks the enthusiasm amongst these early pioneers of association football was not dampened and many still entertained a bold vision: the creation of a professional football club within the city. That vision was nearing reality when the Annual General Meeting of the East Riding of Yorkshire Football Association was held in the Manchester Hotel on 23rd June 1904.

In his address to the assembled gathering, reported in the Hull Daily Mail, the President, Mr Alfred E. Spring, made reference to the strong possibility of there being "a 'class' team in the city before the end of next season." Now Alfred Spring was highly regarded amongst soccer people and his words were not mere idle speculation.

Spring expanded on his statement by explaining that although some initial problems had been encountered, the group of businessmen had not lost their enthusiasm for a venture that they believed would incur an initial start-up cost of approximately £2,500 - £3,000.

One of the major stumbling blocks concerned the acquisition of a suitable playing venue. One possibility, the ground already in existence in the Dairycoates area of the city, was not felt to be of the required standard, but Spring advised the meeting that he was confident the project would have a successful outcome. Spring's confidence was well-placed, for he had been heavily involved in discussions with the consortium looking to bring professional soccer to Hull. In addition, there were others on the committee: namely the Association's Treasurer (John Bielby) and committee member, Jack Fuller – who had been Secretary of Hull Town back in 1896 – involved in the discussions.

The excitement that Spring's announcement generated had not died down before the official announcement about the creation of "Hull City Association Football Club Co. Ltd" was made on 28th June 1904 and adverts were placed nationally to recruit players. Listed amongst the club's directors were Alf Spring, as well as Ben Crompton and Fred Levitt who had been involved in the 'amateur' version of Hull City as well as other clubs, including the various models of Hull Town.

The timing of the official announcement meant there was no chance of the fledgling Hull City being elected to the Football League, but this was not of major concern to the directors for they had been assured by football's authorities that the club's articles of association would be passed.

The directors realised that the club's first season of existence would be one of building a firm foundation leading, hopefully, to a successful application for League membership in the spring of 1905. They were also well aware that such a venture would not come cheaply. The anticipated costs for the season would be in the region of £1,500 with wages accounting for a substantial portion of that figure. What was not so easily quantifiable was the income such a venture would generate.

Drawing up a suitable list of fixtures also had potential difficulties. As a new club their attraction to well established clubs was limited, and few were overly enthusiastic at the prospect of hosting a fixture against an 'unknown' quantity. The Directors, however, had been encouraged by the fact that a number of clubs had promised to bring "their best elevens" to Hull throughout the season and games already promised against Grimsby and Bradford would generate local interest and rivalry.

By the end of July the directors were well on their way to compiling an attractive list of fixtures throughout the coming months, and a number of established League clubs, such as Notts County, Middlesbrough, Barnsley, Bradford City, Leicester Fosse and Glossop, had already committed themselves to visiting the latest soccer outpost. As each week passed, the list grew.

It was envisaged that most Saturday afternoons would be taken up with a fixture and several Thursday afternoons as well. As Saturday morning working was an established norm for a substantial section of the city's working community, with Thursday also widely recognised as being only a half-day on the work front, the directors were obviously keen to encompass the widest possible spectating spectrum.

Where those fixtures would be played was resolved when the directors entered into an agreement with the chairman of Hull RLFC, W.F.B. Eyre, to share their ground on alternate Saturdays for a planned period of three years, although the City directors were searching for a more permanent home.

As for acquiring players, substantial headway was being made. By early August a decent squad was being assembled, combining some useful local talent together with players possessing substantial League experience with clubs such as Grimsby Town, Preston North End and West Bromwich Albion. In today's terms such acquisitions would not have come cheaply, but because Hull City were not a League team they were not required to pay transfer fees, and as for the weekly wage bill, the Directors were not expecting it to exceed £25 per week.

When pre-season training began, in early August, the temperature in the city was touching 90 degrees. It may have been traditional cricketing weather, but the attention of the sporting public of Hull was becoming increasingly drawn towards the forthcoming football season and the prospects of the new professional club. With the opening fixture against Notts County – a decent side and founder members of the Football League – set for 1st September, excitement matched the local temperature.

With a couple of public practice matches to whet the appetite – the last of these, played on the 30th August and generating a crowd in excess of 1,000 – all looked set to launch Hull City into the ocean of Association football some 48 hours later. The game against Notts County was timed to start at 5 pm, with Hull FC's Boulevard ground providing the venue. Heavy rain during the night threatened to put a dampener on proceedings, but the morning of Thursday 1st September dawned dry but dull.

Spectators started to arrive at the ground just after 3pm. At 4.10pm the opposition had arrived in the city and were conveyed to the ground by open wagonnette. Perhaps it was this strange sight that encouraged the previously uninterested to take a peek at history being made, although they probably would not have recognised it as history at the time.

When the advertised kick-off time (5pm) arrived, the crowd was estimated at well in excess of 3,000. Not all of them were committed soccer men. There was more than a sprinkling of the curious as well, and it was perhaps for their sake that the Directors had had the foresight to place around the ground boards outlining the major points of the game and these were also printed on the back of the programme of the teams. It was a gesture well received.

There was not so much a football match occurring that day as a civic occasion. As well as spectators in their thousands, there was a substantial group of official guests, headed by the mayor, Alderman Jarman, whose reception as he stepped onto the field was almost as warm as that which had greeted the emergence of both sets of players. As Alderman Jarman officially 'kicked off', spectators were still streaming into the ground and when the game was properly started, with the new Hull City having first touch of the ball, that initial estimate of 3,000 was being revised to nearer 5,000.

They had much to cheer about in the opening minutes as the local XI showed no fear of their more experienced opponents and threatened the Notts goal on a couple of occasions during the early exchanges. The confidence of the Hull team and the exuberance of the spectators increased when a goal was scored before the game was very old and it was George Rushton, receiving a pass from McKiernan, who had the honour of opening Hull City's scoring account. Although Notts responded well to this setback, and put heavy pressure on the home side's goal, the scoreline remained unchanged when the referee, Mr Plastow of Grimsby, blew for half-time.

After an interval of 10 minutes the second half got underway in front of a crowd that had grown to some 6,000 in number, and who were coming to terms with the finer points of this seemingly strange sport. Notts County, having ended the first half in more dominant fashion over their opponents, began the second in similar vein. The home defence held firm, however, and somewhat against the run of play increased their lead with Rushton adding to his earlier strike.

Perhaps Notts now realised that this was no longer exhibition football and upped their game by another gear. Their pressure eventually paid off as the game reached the three-quarter mark with a melee in the Hull goal area resulting in a penalty kick being awarded to the visitors:

Green driving a firm kick past Whitehouse. As Notts pressed for the equaliser the Hull defence still held firm, with Leiper in particular making a number of timely tackles and clearances. With only minutes left Notts still trailed and it was only in the final minute of the game that Wainman managed to salvage their honour with the equalising goal.

Any disappointment the crowd may have felt at seeing their own team denied at the death was well hidden as they warmly applauded both sets of players off the field. They had witnessed a good game and the prospects for the Hull side looked bright if they could maintain this good start.

Indeed that was a view shared by one of the visiting Notts officials who, when asked for his thoughts on the new City team responded: "Good! Very good." When asked for his opinion on the prospects of Association football becoming established within the city, he was equally positive. "Rather" he replied, "look at the enthusiasm of the crowd, and the attendance for an evening match. Oh yes, the prospect looks bright."

That positive outlook was shared by the City Directors as well. Even though the crowd, assessed at around 6,000, contained many whose primary allegiance was to Hull FC and who were season ticket holders of the rugby club, which allowed them free access to the Association games, the attendance receipts amounted to a respectable £80. It looked as if the Directors' innovative investment would prove sound.

Fears that the first game would turn out to be just a novelty seemed groundless as similar numbers turned up regularly for City's home fixtures and for the visits of Preston North End and Sheffield United, the attendance figures pushed 8,000 and 10,000 respectively according to the local media. They compared favourably with many established League sides; in fact Liverpool, who finished champions of Division Two for the 1904/05 season played a number of games during their League campaign in front of fewer spectators.

That the attendances at City's home fixtures were so encouraging perhaps lay, in part, with the deal City's directors had struck with their Rugby counterparts and landlords at the Boulevard. It had been agreed that all of Hull FC's passholders – numbering some 1400 at the time – would be entitled to free admission for the Association game that Hull City were pioneering. Many took up that offer and whilst the City Board feared their initial reaction might be unfavourable, in the words of one City director the eventual outcome of this plan was deemed a success as "…many who originally came to jeer, stopped to cheer."

It seemed Association football was becoming accepted in the city. Perhaps one of the things that made it so was the fact that entertainment and goals were almost guaranteed. Of the 46 games played, only one finished goalless…and that was the home fixture on 25th March 1905 against Manchester City, then current FA Cup holders, so that result was an achievement in itself given the status of the two clubs at the time. The game was also memorable for another reason in that it produced the club's third different venue for home fixtures during their first season in existence. Although the bulk of City's home games thus far had been played at the Boulevard, the week prior to Manchester City's visit they'd entertained Scarborough at the Dairycoates ground that had been used by a previous incarnation of Hull City.

It was intended to revert to the Boulevard for the Manchester game. However, Hull FC had fallen foul of the Rugby League authorities because of crowd trouble at Hull's Challenge Cup match against Hunslet. As a punishment, Hull FC were ordered to close the Boulevard for their next two home fixtures, and the Rugby League authorities also refused permission for the ground to be used to stage City's fixtures during that period. Unable to make use of Dairycoates, it was the local Cricket Club who came to their rescue and offered City use of the Circle to stage the fixture. So began the club's association with a piece of land that would span its century of existence as the club's current home, the Kingston Communications Stadium is built on part of that same ground.

With over 100 goals to their credit from their 46 games during that first season, it was clear that Hull City were an attacking force with forwards who knew where the goal was, as Rushton (29), Spence (25) and Smith (17) demonstrated. It must have given the directors great encouragement as they continued to prepare their campaign for election to the Football League.

That campaign took an interesting turn in April 1905 with the announcement of changes to the club's board of Directors. In order to give the club some gravitas, Sir Seymour King, one of the city's members of Parliament, was appointed president. There was also a change in the position of chairman with William Gilyott, who had held the position of chairman since the club's formation, standing down to take the role of vice-chairman with Alwyn Smith taking the senior post. The Board was also strengthened with three new appointments made: J. Bainton, H. Ostler and K. Wilson.

Bainton and Ostler had strong sporting links within the city, the former being president of Hull Town Cricket Club, whilst Ostler was the Hull representative on Yorkshire County Cricket club's committee. As well as arrivals, there were also departures:

James Ramster, one of the club's original directors, and who had taken a 'hands on' role in team affairs during their inaugural season, announced his departure not only from the club but also the city, due to business commitments.

To strengthen their forthcoming application for membership of the Football League, the Directors sent a letter seeking support to each of the League's existing members. The document, endorsed by the city's council, contained many statistics reinforcing the merits of the club's application and made its intent clear from the start: "As you are aware, it is the intention of Hull City FC to make application…to be admitted to the Second Division of the League. The subject of this letter is therefore to bring to your notice, several of the many points the directors of the Hull club think should weigh very considerably with you and, we trust, convince you that we are worthy of your support and vote."

The letter went on to state how association football in Hull had grown in popularity over the previous decade – local clubs had grown from 7 to 96 during that time; in support of which the letter pointed out that spectator interest in the Hull club had been substantial, both in terms of numbers and finance. Attendances had remained in four figures throughout the season and revenue from those fixtures had exceeded £1,000. Offset against that income were guarantees, amounting to over £500, which the directors had paid to encourage the visit to Hull of many first class clubs.

The Directors pointed out that whilst they had agreed a three-year lease for use of the Boulevard ground they had also purchased what they described as "one of the finest sporting venues in the county", namely that of Hull Cricket Club which, according to the directors, had "ample accommodation for a big crowd and a pitch par excellence." This ground – currently occupied by the East Riding Amateurs – had already been used to stage a fixture (the visit of Manchester City) and it was proposed to provide accommodation for 4,000 spectators as an interim measure before another part of the plot would be laid out specifically for the use of the Hull Club.

They also made it their clear intention to run not one but two teams, with the second perhaps known as the 'Tiger Cubs' as one director suggested, participating in the Midland League. The director's reference to the 'Tiger Cub' nom de plume seemed to cement the acceptance of the club's new nickname of the Tigers that had been suggested a few weeks earlier by 'Athleo', a reporter for the Hull Daily Mail. He had suggested that the club's colours of black and amber – chosen by one of the original directors, Ernest Morison and perhaps a throwback to the creation of Hull Town in 1879 – leant themselves to an animal link, similar to the two major rugby clubs in the city (Hull and Hull KR). From that suggestion arose the nickname of 'The Tigers' which has stuck with the club throughout its history.

Whilst the directors had produced a detailed document in support of their application, they did not rest there. Within two weeks of that document being drafted, they gave further evidence of their determination to be successful in their application by announcing the appointment of Ambrose Langley as player-manager on 28th April 1905.

Langley was an experienced footballer – he had served Sheffield Wednesday as a resolute full-back for more than a decade and during that time established a then League record of 85 consecutive appearances. Although aged 35 at the time of his joining the Tigers, it was a commonly held opinion that he still had plenty to offer on the playing front. Given that the Tigers had conceded more than 60 goals during that inaugural season, a little tightening up at the back would be needed if their dream of League football was to become a reality.

If there was no doubting his talent as a player, what might have caused some confusion to the 21st century football supporter was the managerial aspect of Langley's appointment; he was not a player-manager in the sense that today's supporters would understand. In the early days of Association football it was the norm for team selection to be the remit of the Board of Directors, or at least a directors' sub-committee and in this respect Hull City adhered to the norm; in fact it would be some 20 years before any manager of Hull City would have complete control over playing matters.

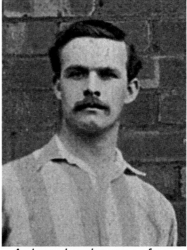

Ambrose Langley moves from Sheffield Wednesday to become Hull City's first player-manager.

In modern terms, Langley would have been seen as more of a player-coach, with a fair chunk of today's club secretary's role thrown in as well for good measure. Langley would be heavily involved in identifying talent, determining tactics and involving himself in team training matters, but his role in team selection would be more participating than patriarchal. Yet such issues would be somewhat redundant should the club's application for membership of the Football League fail.

The outcome of that application was known within a month of Langley's appointment. At the League's Annual General Meeting on 29th May 1905 the Tigers application, together with those of Chelsea, Leeds City, Clapton Orient, Stockport County, Burslem Port Vale, Burton United and Doncaster Rovers was considered, with the latter three clubs applying for re-election. Only three places were available. By 12 noon the votes had been cast as follows: Leeds City (25), Burslem Port Vale (21), Chelsea (20) and Hull City (18).

Disaster! Or was it?

The next item on the management committee's agenda was the consideration of a proposal by Mr C.E. Sutcliffe of the Burnley club that the League be extended.

That motion was passed, and when the applications of the previously unsuccessful clubs were reconsidered, only Doncaster Rovers found themselves still out in the cold.

It seems strange that the League's management committee had chosen to consider the above items in that particular order. Had the expansion of membership been considered first, then only one vote would have been needed and the 'drama' that surrounded Hull City's entrance into the Second Division of the Football League would have been avoided.

Whatever the circumstances surrounding their election, however, it did not alter the fact that the Directors of Hull City had achieved their objective and that within months of that momentous decision League football would be taking place in Hull.

Hull City's Board of Directors at the start of the 1905-06 season: Back Row (left to right): Mr. F.G. Stringer, Mr. A.B. Glossop, Mr. A. Langley (Manager), Mr. G.J. Kennington;Middle Row: Mr. J.F. Haller (Secretary), Mr. E. Morison, Mr. Jas. Spring, Mr. A.E. Spring, Mr. J. Barraclough, Mr. J.W. Locking;Front Row: Mr. J.M. Bielby, Mr. W. Gilyott (Vice-Chairman), Mr. Alwyn D. Smith (Chairman), Mr. G.W. Lilley, J.P, Mr. E. K. Wilson.

*W*ith only three months to complete their preparations before the opening fixture of the 1905/06 season kicked off on 2nd September there was much to do. However, issues relating to where the club would play were pretty much under control. Work was in hand to develop the piece of land acquired on Anlaby Road and it was anticipated that it would be operational before the end of the season. In the interim the club had the use of The Circle and could also fall back on using Hull FC's ground as they had done during their first season.

What took up most of the Directors' and Ambrose Langley's time was putting together a squad of players capable of not only cementing the club's new found standing, but also taking them one stage further into the top division. With the club no longer of amateur status, acquiring players would be a lot more expensive than it had been a year earlier: fees would have to be paid and the squad would need to be much bigger with greater depth.

Langley was an experienced professional in the art of association football: his playing career had spanned nearly 20 years before he joined the Tigers. As such, he was better equipped than many within the club to appreciate the calibre of player required. His trawling of the transfer market brought in the likes of Martin Spendiff, Davy Gordon, 'Soldier' Wilson, George Browell and Jackie Smith; not household names at the time of their joining perhaps, but many of them would go on to take their place in the Tiger pantheon of legends.

As a result of Langley's 'shopping expedition', it was a different looking Hull City from some twelve months previously that reported for pre-season training on 10th August 1905. It was also a different training regime than would be recognised by all of today's football professionals. According to the Hull Daily Mail the first day's activities were taken up with "skipping and jumping" in the morning, then "a long walk" in the afternoon.

The programme of practice matches was also somewhat different to today. Only two practice games were played and one of those was an 'in-house' affair, when the 'Probables' took on the 'Possibles' in a game open to the public on 26th August. This latter fixture became something of a regular occurrence in the Tigers' pre-season preparations over the years and it was well into the 1960s before it disappeared from City's 'fixture list'.

By the time the first Saturday in September arrived – the traditional point for the football season to start – the Tigers were ready to take on their first League opponents: Barnsley.

Barnsley had been elected to the Football League at the start of the 1898/99 season and whilst never threatening the promotion places they had, over the seasons, made steady progress up the Division and had finished the previous campaign (1904/05) in seventh place. It would be a stern, but not daunting test of Hull City's League mettle. Whilst all of the Tigers on show that September Saturday afternoon were making their Hull City League debuts, nearly half were wearing the club's colours for the first time in any meaningful match; in all, five players were on show for the first time. For the record, let it be stated now that the following team was responsible for putting Hull City on the Football League map: Spendiff, Langley, Jones, Martin, Robinson, Gordon, Rushton, Spence, Wilson, Howe and Raisbeck.

If the emergence of good quality association football had captured the interest of the sporting public of Hull a year previously, the step up to League status did not pass unnoticed within the city as early attendances indicated. The accurate recording of football attendances did not commence until the 1920s. As such, it was the opinion of those reporting the matches that gave any guide as to the attendance on the day. In the club's very first game (v Notts County) in September 1904, the attendance had been estimated at some 6,000; for the game against Barnsley, it was estimated at 8,000. Whatever the actual number, there could be no doubting that they got their money's worth.

A delayed kick-off, due to transport problems encountered by Barnsley en-route to the East Riding, meant a heavier than anticipated workload for the band providing the pre-match entertainment. They cannot have done too bad a job for those who had paid waited patiently and in good humour. For those whose affections lay in the direction of the home team, it was not long after the game finally kicked off that they had something to cheer about. Clearly inspired by the pre-match pep-talk of club chairman, Alwyn Smith, Langley's Tigers set about their task with relish and within two minutes 'Geordie' Spence had cemented his place in the Hull City record book by scoring the opening goal of the game. It was a lead and a joy short-lived however, because before the 10 minute mark had passed Barnsley had equalised through Jack Bell.

Play settled down into an even contest that reflected the scoreline but shortly before half-time one of City's debutants, Davy Gordon, re-established the Tigers lead. Their position was strengthened as the match weaved its way through the second 45 minutes with another new boy, 'Soldier' Wilson adding a third and Davy Gordon crowning a memorable personal performance with his second, and the Tigers' fourth goal of the afternoon.

If there had been any doubts about Hull City's ability to compete at this level, the final scoreline of 4-1 in their favour did much to ease such misgivings.

Davy Gordon scored twice on his and the club's Football League debut against Barnsley on 2nd September 1906.

Buoyed by the conviction of their opening performance, Langley and his team set off for the capital in good heart to fulfil their next two fixtures against fellow League newcomers: Clapton Orient and Chelsea respectively. In the first the Tigers had a narrow but comfortable 1-0 win over Orient; in fact the weather – the game was played in a rainstorm – probably presented the Tigers with more problems than their opponents did, if newspaper reports of the game are to be believed.

City's next fixture was planned for 48 hours later, against Chelsea, so it was decided that the club would spend the weekend in London resting and preparing rather than travelling. The Chelsea fixture would prove historic, as it was the first League fixture ever staged at Stamford Bridge.

Although newcomers to League football like City, Chelsea had recruited an expensive group of players from all over the country. Included in their ranks was Bill Foulkes, the former Sheffield United and England goalkeeper whose reputation between the sticks was as considerable as his physique.

Given the array of talent against them on the evening, defeat for the Tigers, and its margin (5-1), perhaps came as no surprise. Chelsea were well fancied to gain promotion at their first attempt – although come the season's end they found themselves one place short, with Manchester United and Bristol City taking the two promotion places on offer. And if it was any consolation, when Chelsea visited the Tigers' lair in February 1906, revenge of sorts was gained with a 4-3 victory.

If the result at Stamford Bridge offered a reality check on City's prospects for the season, it was quickly followed by similar results that showed life in the League would not be without its disappointments. More than a month passed after the Orient game before the Tigers claimed another League victory: a 3-0 win over Chesterfield on 11th October.

By the end of October the Tigers had completed 10 League fixtures. Four wins, four defeats and two draws clearly indicated that they would not have things all their own way, a fact never better illustrated by their final two games of the month, which were both played on the same day.

The first of these games was the home League encounter with early pacesetters Manchester United. The date for this game was 28th October, a date that coincided with the second qualifying round of matches for the FA Cup. Despite their League status City were not excused the qualifying process, and victory over Grimethorpe Utd in the previous qualifying round meant that the Tigers were scheduled to play Denaby Utd on 28th October in the next round.

In addition to the fixture clash, there was a problem with the club using The Circle. This was not insurmountable as the club could call on the assistance of their previous landlords, Hull FC, to make use of the Boulevard. What remained unresolved however was the drain the day would place on the club's playing resources.

The Football Association refused City permission to postpone the Denaby game so they were left with no option but to play their first string against the League leaders from Manchester, whilst the Reserves were dispatched to Denaby with the aim of gaining a draw and allowing the first team to complete the task in the replay. The script, however, was not fully adhered to. Whilst the Tigers' First XI, not unexpectedly, lost to United – although the margin of victory (1-0) emphasised how close the game was – the Reserves compensated for that disappointment by returning to the East Riding having defeated Denaby 2-0. It was scant consolation that this sequence of events led to a subsequent change in the rules of the Cup competition thus preventing a repetition.

Hull City's involvement in rewriting the competition rules did not end there, however. In the next round the Tigers were paired at home to Leeds City and whilst the weather put paid to the original date for the fixture, when the game was played the Tigers were trailing 1-0 with not much time left on the referee's watch. They were rescued by an injured player, George Rushton, who was being attended to by City's trainer (Jim Leach) on the touchline. Whilst receiving treatment, Rushton spotted a scoring opportunity; he dashed back onto the field, seized control of the ball and ran through an astonished Leeds defence to score the equaliser.

In those days, a player did not require the referee's permission to re-enter the field of play. Needless to say Rushton's action, plus similar occurrences in other matches, soon brought about a rewording of the rules to prevent future 'unauthorised invasions'.

The Tigers won the replay with Leeds (2-1), went on to beat Oldham Athletic in the 4th Qualifying Round and finally went out, 1-0, to Reading in the first round proper on 13th January 1906.

Their exploits in the Cup, however, were not at the expense of progress in the League. By the time Christmas arrived the Tigers had already registered large victories over Bradford City (5-2) and Lincoln City (4-1) and their Christmas fixtures provided them with four victories in four games (including a friendly against Wigan) – all of which were away from home. It was a sequence of festive results that would take nearly a century to be matched.

As a consequence of their fine form in League and Cup, the Tigers found themselves handily placed to lay claim to one of the promotion places to Division One. That they found themselves in this position was primarily due to their ability to score goals. With the likes of Gordon, Rushton, Howe and the two Smiths regularly contributing to City's scoresheet, they had even been able to allow one of their pre-season forward acquisitions, 'Soldier' Wilson, to move on to near rivals Leeds. His stay there would be short: ending in the most tragic of circumstances with his death during Leeds' home game against Burnley in October 1906.

The Tigers had a wealth of talent in the forward line, worth their weight in gold even though they were paid only in pennies. Yet despite their ability to score goals, the Tigers had yet to master the art of not conceding them, and a sequence of bad results in February and March – including a heavy 5-0 defeat away to Manchester Utd – meant their push for promotion faltered and then fell away such that come the season's end, they finished in fifth place.

Amongst the unfolding disappointment of their fading promotion hopes lay a significant piece of Hull City history. It came on the 24th March 1906 in the home game against Blackpool. The scoreline (2-2) may have been disappointing in the context of City's promotion intentions, but the venue had huge importance: it was the club's first game at their new Anlaby Road home, just a few hundred yards from the Circle.

Although their new surroundings failed to provide them with the necessary impetus to mount a late promotion challenge, for a first attempt finishing fifth that season was not a bad effort – of the other new boys in that Division, only heavy spending Chelsea finished higher, and even their expenditure was not enough to grant them promotion. On the subject of expenditure, the Directors had slightly miscalculated their budget for staging professional football in the city, and in the words of one Director, Ernest Morrison, they had to revert to the occasional "whip round" to pay the week's expenses.

If you had to sum up that first season in one word it would be goals. Whilst City had little trouble in scoring them (67), what let them down was their inability to prevent them (54). A goal difference of plus 13 for the season fell well short of that achieved by the teams above them: their figures ranged from 43 to 62. If the Tigers were to mount a serious attempt on promotion during their second campaign, they would have to continue their good work up front whilst tightening up at the back.

If the significance of maintaining a healthy gap between 'Goals For' and 'Goals Against' was recognised, the next couple of seasons suggested that the lesson wasn't learnt. Of the seven players Langley gave League debuts to during the 1906-07 season, only two had defensive leanings. As a consequence the Tigers' season followed a similar pattern: there were games when they scored and shipped plenty of goals. Sometimes the balance was in their favour, sometimes it favoured the opposition. Come the end of the 1906/07 season, City's goals tally had fallen to 65, whilst those conceded had risen to 57. The combination of results that provided those figures meant the Tigers finished the season in ninth place.

In the following season (1907/08), the price of a Season Pass rose to 7/6d (37$\frac{1}{2}$p) and the first official programme ever produced by the club appeared for the home game against Barnsley on 7th September. If the introduction of a matchday programme was a sign that the club were moving with the times, then come the end of that season there were also signs that the club was again moving in the right direction: their final League placing improved slightly to 8th and the number of goals they scored rose to 73; unfortunately, so did the number of goals they conceded (62). Whilst the home game against Clapton Orient showed them at their best – a 5-0 win – other matches, such as the away fixtures at Glossop and Burnley (1-5 and 0-5 respectively) highlighted the darker side of Hull City.

Yet for all the frustration that such diversity in results must have generated amongst supporters, they at least had the pleasure and privilege of seeing two of the greatest ever players to have been associated with the club develop and progress. In today's game they would have been worshipped and revered by the home fans, whilst other clubs' supporters would have undoubtedly coveted them but at the same time, perhaps, considered one a 'sporting freak'.

The players in question were Gordon Wright and Jackie Smith. Given that the Tigers' apparent early League strength lay in their ability to attack rather than defend, it will come as no surprise to learn that both were forwards. Both made their debuts in the Tigers' inaugural League season, but it was in the subsequent seasons of that opening decade of the 20th Century that they cemented their places in Tiger legend.

Edward Gordon Dundas Wright – Arguably Hull City's only Full England international, although the record books insist on maintaining otherwise.

To describe Gordon Wright as a 'sporting freak' may be considered derogatory, but no personal slight is intended; his appearance and demeanour certainly gave no offence and his skills were at times mercurial but on average just magnificent. What generates the freakish reference is the fact that he was an amateur. Football in the 21st century would have valued Wright in millions and his annual salary would have been in the same ballpark. Yet money – even the pitiful wage that a professional footballer earned in those days – was of no apparent interest to him; he played the game for fun and expenses, and those expenses were always conservative, never liberal.

The son of an East Riding clergyman, Wright had equal amounts of talent at both top and bottom of his body. Educated at Cambridge he played for both the University – he won his 'Blue' at football in 1903/04, 1905/06 and 1906/07, scoring once in the 5-0 defeat of Oxford on his debut – and Corinthians, an exalted amateur club of its day with a status akin to Arsenal, or Manchester United in the modern professional era. His talent was also recognised at national level and it is in this context that his place in the Tigers' history is at its most contentious.

Although an amateur in status, there was nothing in the rules of the game that prevented him from playing for a professional club. It was considered something of a coup therefore when the Tigers acquired his agreement to turn out for them during university vacations and when other commitments allowed. Having registered his signature with the Football League on 29th December 1905, it was some months before he made his debut for the club in the 4-0 home victory over West Bromwich Albion on 7th April 1906; not unsurprisingly, he was amongst the goalscorers.

Some three weeks previously Wright had made his debut for England in the senior international against Wales at Ninian Park Cardiff on 19th March. What has always remained a bone of contention has been the fact that the Football Association minutes referring to that game, together with the vast majority of reference books written

since, have always allocated Wright's full international appearance to Cambridge University, rather than Hull City.

The 'discrepancy' has never been officially rectified, despite the efforts of many students of the Tigers' history. So whilst Tigers' fans throughout the world remain convinced that EGD Wright is Hull City's one and only full England international – and technically the League's files would suggest this is the case, the record books continue to display a different story.

The mystery surrounding that discrepancy has never been fully solved; I doubt it ever will be. Yet perhaps a plausible explanation appeared in an article about Gordon Wright in the January 1949 edition of "TIGER MAG" – a publication that offered regular stories about, and interviews with, both past and present Tigers.

In that article the writer stated the allocation of Cambridge University as his 'international club' was at the behest of Wright who felt it was his "duty" as they, together with the Corinthian club had "brought him forward" and "helped to gain his cap..." Certainly such a sentiment seems in keeping with Wright's sporting ethos as to how one should play the game. Whether it is the truth, or whether it just adds another layer to the mystery and myth that surrounds the Tiger career of Gordon Wright must be left to the individual to decide. As compensation, there is the fact that Wright represented his country at Amateur level – in the early 1900s many would have considered that a higher accolade – for England on twenty occasions, and participated in the 1912 Olympic games in Stockholm, but I suspect any City fan of whatever era would trade all that for official resolution of his solitary full honour.

If Wright was regarded as the artist in City's forward line during the opening decade of their history, then Jackie Smith was undoubtedly the artisan. The name Smith was not unfamiliar to those early followers of the Tigers' fortunes. As well as Jackie, there would be Joe – often called 'Stanley' to avoid confusion – and Wallace. For many of their games in the latter years of the 1900s it was not unusual to find three Smiths in the Tigers' forward line, but in only one – the 5-1 victory over West Bromwich

Albion on 23rd April 1910 – did all three appear on the scoresheet, sharing City's five goals between them: Jackie with a hat-trick, 'Stanley' and Wallace claiming one apiece. It was probably an accurate reflection of where they stood in the pecking order of Tiger strikers.

Jackie Smith may not have enjoyed the benefits of upbringing and education that helped develop Gordon Wright into the Tiger legend that he undoubtedly is, but he has every right to sit on the same pew in the Tiger pantheon. Where Wright built his reputation on character, craft and charisma, Jackie Smith built his on graft, grit and goals…and plenty of them.

John 'Jackie' Smith: City's first goalscoring hero, who also topped the League's goalcharts twice during his stay with the Tigers

Born and raised in the North East, Smith's football education was carried out in the streets of Wardley and the playing fields of Hebburn. At 5' 7" he was small for an inside or centre-forward, but displayed enough potential for the Tigers to take a chance on him. That potential took a little time to develop in the black and amber stripes. His first season with the club (1905/06) brought the acceptable, but not exceptional, return of five goals in 20 League outings.

In subsequent campaigns the pendulum swung the other way. In the next four seasons he was the club's leading goalscorer on three occasions – niggling injuries during the 1908/09 season prevented a clean sweep. In two of those three seasons, Smith not only topped his club's goalscoring charts, he also finished top of the pile for the entire League:

in 1907/08 with 31 goals in 37 appearances; in 1909/10 with 32 goals in 35 outings. Such a talent would have commanded a king's ransom in today's transfer market.

On the scoring front, however, the Tigers were not a one-trick pony. As well as Jackie Smith's namesakes, Joe (Stanley) and Wallace, the club also had the likes of Alf Toward and Arthur Temple. All were not shot-shy in front of goal, and providing the ammunition for them to fire past the opposition's "custodian of the leather" was Gordon Wright.

Arthur Temple was City's leading goalscorer in the 1908/09 season and joint top – with Tom Browell – in the 1911/12 season.

Squad rotation had not even been developed to the concept stage by the time the 1909/10 season opened with a 2-1 win for the Tigers at Barnsley on 2nd September 1909. As such, with six outstanding forwards competing for five positions something had to give, and before the season was two months old, it was Alf Toward who had given way to his colleagues, moving on to fellow Division Two opponent Oldham Athletic.

The decision of Ambrose Langley to realise his asset and sell Toward – he cost Oldham the princely sum of £350 – appeared to have no detrimental effect on the way his remaining charges performed.

Before Toward departed, the Tigers had already topped the table and a 7-0 thrashing of Birmingham, during the month of Toward's departure suggested nothing amiss in the forward line, or defence for that matter. Although their fortunes ebbed and flowed throughout the winter months, the Tigers were never far off the promotion pace. Come the end of February 1910 they kicked on, putting together a string of 12 results that produced 11 wins and a draw. With one game of the season left the top of the Second Division table looked like this:

	P	W	D	L	F	A	Pts	GoalAvge
Manchester City	37	23	8	6	79	37	54	2.13
Hull City	37	23	7	7	80	43	53	1.86
Derby County	37	22	8	7	72	47	52	1.53
Oldham Athletic	37	22	7	8	76	39	51	1.94

With only two teams being promoted, Manchester City were already home and dry – their goal average was better than Derby's and Oldham couldn't catch them. The contest for the remaining place rested between the Tigers, Oldham and Derby, with the Tigers holding the strongest hand: a draw would be sufficient to move them up with Manchester and achieve their dream. Derby's last fixture of the season was away to West Bromwich Albion; the Tigers were away to Oldham Athletic. A draw would be enough. When those last games of the season were completed the Second Division table appeared thus:

	P	W	D	L	F	A	Pts	GoalAvge
Manchester City	38	23	8	7	81	40	54	2.03
Oldham Athletic	38	23	7	8	79	39	53	2.03
Hull City	38	23	7	8	80	46	53	1.74
Derby County	38	22	9	7	72	47	53	1.53

There is little point dwelling on the details of that encounter with Oldham, it is the result that mattered and the result is burnt in the memory of every Tigers' fan, whatever their age; but for the record, the final result was a 3-0 victory for Oldham. What adds more misery to the melancholy is that it was Alf Toward who opened the scoring for 'The Latics', his 13th League goal for the Lancastrian outfit since moving across the Pennines from Anlaby Road. Unlucky 13 for the Tigers, but £350 well spent for Oldham. It earned them the second promotion spot at the Tigers' expense by the margin of 0.29 of a goal.

In their five year membership of the Football League, it was the closest the Tigers had come to joining the top clubs. In a century of City they have never been closer.

There was no change in the Tigers fortunes the following season (1910/11); no heroic comeback, no spectacular disintegration. The Tigers finished fifth in the table, a placing not previously unfamiliar to them and an end of season residency in the Second Division's Top 10 would be their lot for the remaining five seasons of League competition – with one exception (1912/13) – before it was suspended due to Word War One.

There were changes in the Tigers' playing ranks however. Within months of that Oldham disappointment, Jackie Smith had moved on to First Division Sheffield United, and within a couple of seasons his namesakes also departed: 'Stanley' to Everton and Wallace retiring through illness. There were others who came in to take their places, however: Stan Fazackerley, Thomas 'Boy' Browell and Sammy Stevens.

All three carved their niche in the Tigers' history: Fazackerley for his scoring exploits on home and foreign soil – 19 goals in 27 appearances during the 1912/13 season and 22 goals in five games on the club's end of season tour to Scandinavia in 1912, including 11 in one game. 'Boy' Browell displayed tremendous youthful talent: a debut at the age of 17, joining his two brothers in the same team; a goal every other game in the League during 1910/11 and bettered in the following season with 16 goals in 16 League appearances before Everton stole him for £1,500. Sammy Stevens could match both Fazackerley and Browell for the quantity of goals they scored, his Tiger statistics confirm that. He also lasted the pace better, staying with the Tigers until the early 1920s although what should have been his prime time was lost to World War One.

The fluctuations in City's forward line were also mirrored in the half-backs and defence. Roughley gave way to Hendry in goal, and whilst Nevins and McQuillan held a firm grip on the full back slots, other defensive and creative positions had regular changes to the personnel performing the tasks.

Jock McQuillan (left) and Tommy Nevens formed a formidable full-back pairing during the early 1900s

Those changes were reflected in results and one week during the 1911/12 season encapsulated their efforts better than most: concede eight goals in one game, score four in the next.

The 'Trondhjem Tigers' – *City's end of season tour to Scandinavia in May saw Stan Fazackerley set a club record for goals in a game by scoring 11 times in the 16-1 victory over a Trondheim & District XI.*
Back Row: W. Glossop (Director), F. Stringer (Director), N. Hendry, P. O'Connell, A. Temple, E. Roughley, J. Houghton, A. Fenwick, S. Stevens, A. Langley (Manager);
Front Row: W. Wright, W. McDonald, C. Best, J. McQuillan, S. Fazackerley, E. Neve.

In the space of seven days the Tigers were beaten 8-0 away to Wolves – the worst defeat in their history – and seven days later they put four past Leicester Fosse with Tom Browell scoring all four.

Tigers in training: The Tigers prepared for their FA Cup tie against Newcastle Utd on 1st Feb 1913 by spending a few days in Bridlington. Shown here are (left to right): N. Hendry, H. Goode, J. Boyton, S. Fazackerley. W. McDonald, H. Taylor (trainer) and P. O'Connell.

In one sense the Tigers' team was evolving but in another, an era was coming to an end. The timescale may have been a tad on the short side, but in defining an era events can be just as important as time. If any evidence was needed to support the hypothesis you need look no further than the 1912/13 season. For the first time in their short history the Tigers struggled. Only a quartet of victories in their final four games of the campaign provided an end of season placing of twelfth: nothing spectacular compared with previous performances but without that late flourish, applying for re-election could well have been on the cards.

If that season was unexceptional in the League, at least the FA Cup offered a crumb of comfort. Their progress halted in Round 2 – defeated by Newcastle United after a replay – but at least it included their first ever away victory in the 'proper' stages of the competition rather than the qualifying rounds. That victory came at Fulham on 11 January 1913, and in preparation for the tie the Tigers had spent the week in Worthing. Part of their pre-Cup training involved following the local hunt, an event that would have evoked some strong reaction today, but back then the estimated 10 miles that they tramped merely represented an unusual variation to their training programme. Whatever, it worked. In a game initially under threat from fog of "a pea soup variety", the Tigers withstood the attacks of a vigorous Fulham forward line and left the capital with a 2-0 victory to savour, their goals coming from Fazackerley and Stevens; "...dogged defence with an attack avidly willing to accept opportunities..." were the qualities that earmarked their performance that day and "which gained the Tigers their great victory", according to a newspaper reporter at the game.

Yet it was not just performances that suggested an era in the Tigers' history was coming to an end, events involving personnel also offered the clearest evidence. In the course of that season the Tigers lost their chairman, vice-chairman, secretary, manager and captain. For the latter two the parting of the ways followed the final game of the season: at home to Leicester Fosse.

The game itself had some minor historical significance in that the scoreline has changed over the years – what initially started as a 2-1 win for the Tigers has subsequently been fine tuned to a 2-0 Tiger victory. Of major historical significance from a City supporter's perspective is the fact that it was Gordon Wright's last game in City's colours and that within days of that final game of the season Ambrose Langley tendered his resignation.

Langley had been in charge from the beginning of the club's League career whilst Wright had captained the side ever since his appearance in the Tigers' debut League season. Splitting his working week between being a master at Hymers College and the captain of Hull City, Wright had been inspirational during his spell in the East Riding.

Langley's spell was more astute than inspiring. His dealings in the transfer market had, on numerous occasions, produced the maximum talent at the minimum of cost, but he had been unable to produce the end product; reverting to modern parlance he had probably taken the Tigers as far as he could. He returned to Hillsborough – the setting for the bulk of his playing career prior to moving to Hull. Wright moved further afield, pursuing an engineering career that took in South America and Africa.

When the Tigers began the 1913/14 season it was fresh faces all round. "Jim" Spring was appointed Chairman; Harry Chapman, who had stepped up from the Tigers' playing ranks to assume the role of Secretary earlier in the year, added the managerial role to his portfolio with Davy Gordon, the last remnant of the Tigers' inaugural League team, taking over the captaincy.

That first season 'under new management' saw an upturn in the Tigers' fortunes. By the turn of the year the Tigers headed the table, on goal difference, from Notts County and Woolwich Arsenal, having games in hand on their nearest rivals as well. If Sammy Stevens and new signing Bill Halligan could maintain the fine run of scoring that had taken the Tigers to the top, then the prospects of promotion looked hopeful. A narrow defeat at home to Arsenal in the middle of January dropped the Tigers down to third and their chances of recovering the lost ground were further hampered by a poor sequence of results that saw them gain three wins in fifteen games. This meant that by time the Easter programme of fixtures had been completed they were in ninth place, leaving them six points off the promotion places with only four points left to play for.

Their League position at Easter, however, was the least of their problems. Hours after they had lost at home to Bury on 13th April 1914, their Anlaby Road ground was badly damaged by fire. Looking back on the incident City's chairman wrote some time later about "...that sad day when we (the directors) stood among the ruins." The directors approached a local businessman, Bob Mungall, for a loan of £1,000 to carry out the necessary repairs. "What security can you offer?" asked Mungall, "All this", said one director, pointing to a ton of scrap – the remnants of the stand – piled on the field. Mungall must have appreciated the 'irony' of the director's response, for he gave the Tigers the money and work commenced on building a new main grandstand capable of holding 5,000 people.

In the end the Tigers finished in seventh place, due in the main to ever-present Sammy Stevens' return of 26 goals in 38 League appearances. If the season had offered the prospect of a new era beginning in the Tigers' history, there was little prospect of it developing as Chapman was forced to resign because of serious illness in September 1914. By then the country was at war and football was being overshadowed; but when the fog of war was lifted over Europe, financial clouds remained over Hull City.

*Some of City's players pose before their admirers during a home game in the 1913/14 season.
Left to right are: J. Lee, W. 'Tim' Wright, D. Morgan, S. Stevens, J. Lyons, J. Pattison,
N. Hendry, H Taylor jnr (trainer's son) and J. McIntosh.*

## CHAPTER 3

WAR AND PEACE

The 1914/15 season was a strange campaign, not just for the Tigers but for every other club as well. By the time the League programme kicked off, on 3rd September 1914, the country had been at war for almost a month and during that time much consideration and debate had taken place as to how sport in general, and football in particular, should respond. There was no shortage of those willing to offer advice and it will come as no surprise to learn that the advice offered spanned a wide range of opinions.

At one end of the spectrum there was the strong moral view that suggested it was disrespectful for people to be enjoying themselves, by either playing or watching sport, when the country's armed forces were fighting, and dying, on their behalf. In support, others suggested that whilst professional sport was being pursued the country's war effort was being detrimentally affected: recruitment was restricted and industrial output reduced as people were engaged in other activities. Such opinions were countered with the view that football matches offered an aid rather than an obstruction to recruitment as large gatherings of spectators could be canvassed more easily to "join up for the colours".

What weighed heavily on the minds of football's authorities however was the legality of suspending the competition when players had already signed contracts for the season before War had even been declared. These would still have to be honoured even if there were no fixtures, and without fixtures there would be little, if any, income for clubs to offset against their various expenses.

The government offered limited assistance on the matter. The possibility of them banning football could not be discounted, especially as they had already applied restrictions on cricket and racing.

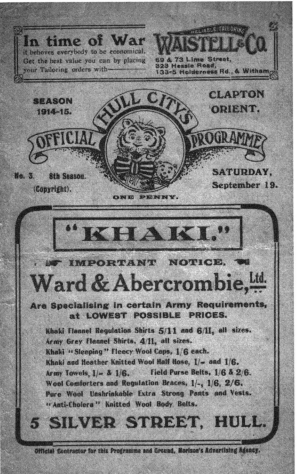

The programme for City's home game against Clapton Orient on 19th September 1914.

Yet for some reason they fought shy of a total ban, and although the mood of the debate frequently changed amongst those engaged in the debate, it was perhaps this apparent reluctance of the Government to interfere that encouraged football's authorities to press ahead and continue with the season's programme of fixtures.

With the sport reprieved it was on 3rd September 1914 that the Tigers played their first fixture of the campaign: at home to Stockport County. The match provided debuts for James Medcalf and Charlie Deacey; it also provided City with a 1-0 win, their goal coming from Sammy Stevens. Shortly after the season started the Tigers found themselves in need of a new manager. Harry Chapman had suffered a lengthy illness and was unable to continue. In the early days of his ill-health, it had been one of the Directors, Fred Stringer, who had assisted Chapman with his duties. When Chapman formally resigned the Directors asked Stringer to step up and take full control. Stringer was happy to do so and resigned his seat on the Board and took over the vacant seat in the Manager's office.

Stringer's first season in charge saw the Tigers finish in seventh place. That was due in the main to the scoring talents of Sammy Stevens; his tally from 37 League outings amounted to 24, ably supported by Bill Halligan's contribution of 17 goals from the same tally of games in the League. For the second season in a row the Tigers had reason to be grateful that Sammy Stevens did not let them down. A centre-forward of "total resolve and commitment; inactivity was against his nature..." was how one sports commentator of the time assessed his talent. Stevens had struck a rich vein of goalscoring form (26 goals in 38 League games) in the previous season (1913/14) and it was clear he had retained his form as the 1914/15 season unfolded.

It was form that attracted attention not only from opposing defenders, but also international selectors who, unfortunately, hesitated in selecting him for a full cap, but named him as reserve on one occasion; but for the War that hesitation would have surely been overcome.

In the context of what was happening in Europe, City's end of season placing in the Football League was of little relevance. However, when that 1914/15 season ended it was clear that things could not continue in the way they had done over the last nine months. Recognising that the nation's eyes were being diverted from the football fields to the fighting fields, the Football League suspended their competition for the remainder of the War's duration. In its place they organised a more regionalised structure, much reduced in size and comprising two groups – the Lancashire section and Midlands section – with the Tigers being allocated to the Midlands section.

By a strange coincidence the Tigers began their fixtures in this new competition by playing the same opponents who had introduced professional football to the city just a day over 11 years earlier: Notts County. This time the venue was reversed and the score line had nothing marked down for the Tigers, County winning 2-0. The attendance was slightly down from the previous encounter, which was not surprising given that recruitment to the colours was very much the order of the day and that many of the nation's men were answering the call.

At the forefront of that recruitment campaign was the emphasis on friends doing their duty together. As such, numerous 'Pals' regiments were mustered and the city of Hull responded magnificently with four such battalions been formed in a matter of weeks. One of those four battalions was formally called the 12th Battalion East Yorkshire Regiment, although it became more popularly known as the 'Sportsmen and Athletes Battalion'. It comprised those who enjoyed 'the game', whatever its rules; amongst their number were, no doubt, Hull City supporters and players.

With one of the main recruitment centres – Wenlock Barracks – situated just a few hundred yards from City's Anlaby Road ground, it was only natural that the club would feel the impact. Although the ground still staged training on Monday through to Friday the emphasis of that training fluctuated between football and fighting, with many of the new recruits reporting to Wenlock Barracks finding themselves practising drills etc on the very field where City's players had been playing soccer the previous Saturday.

Some of those new recruits may even have played on the Anlaby Road surface. An article in The Times newspaper of 30th November 1914 reported that "many professional footballers were responding to the call to arms", and mentioned that included in that number were 20 from Hull City. Established first-teamers McIntosh and Lyon had joined up almost immediately following the declaration of war; however, a look through the various teamsheets at that time suggests that a vast majority of the number referred to in The Times article were probably reserves and/or amateurs, as the nucleus of the side changed little during that 1914/15 season. That didn't mean though that the Tigers were comfortably off in terms of playing resources – on one occasion, in December 1915, they took to the field with only 10 men. City, as with just about all the other teams operating during the war, had to function with a reduced squad; it often meant that those first team players who remained were regularly expected to play out of their normal position to allow the club to field a team each Saturday. There was no better example of that flexibility than Joe Edelston.

Some of the 'Hull Pals' commence their military training at City's Anlaby Road ground

Edelston had joined the Tigers in March 1913 and quickly made the right-half berth very much his own. He continued to do so throughout much of the Tigers' wartime campaigns, but he was also regularly called upon to take over the goalkeeping role whenever Nick Hendry was unavailable. Only once, in his 17 wartime competition appearances in goal for the Tigers, did Edelston suffer what could be considered an embarrassing result for a goalkeeper. That came on the 12th February 1916 against Bradford City, when he had cause to retrieve the ball from the Tigers' goal on eight occasions, whilst his opposite number in the Bradford team was beaten on just the four.

The restricted wartime competition meant that City found themselves as the most northerly members of the Midlands section, which contained 13 other teams. Even with fixtures restricted to Saturdays only, their programme of games was completed by the end of February – they finished in 11th place. To fill in the remaining weeks of what would have been considered a normal season, a Subsidiary competition was staged during March and April with the Division being split into three Groups: North, South and Midlands. The Tigers, placed in the Northern group, finished 4th of the six teams participating.

During the summer of 1916, other business commitments forced Fred Stringer to stand down from his role as City's manager. Maintaining their recent policy of 'in-house' appointments the Directors elevated David Menzies to the post of manager – Menzies had joined the Tigers' coaching staff on the 5th July 1914. Menzies and his team faced a similar structure of fixtures for the 1916/17 season, although this time the Division had expanded to 16 teams. In the Primary competition the Tigers again finished 11th, and in the process suffered a couple of heavy defeats: 8-2 away to Barnsley, and 7-1 at Notts County on Boxing Day 1916; a strange result given the Tigers had beaten County at home 2-0 the previous day. Although the Subsidiary fixture list was restricted to home and away games against Chesterfield, Lincoln and Grimsby, an intricate method of combining results from both competitions gave City a final placing of 9th of the 16 competing teams.

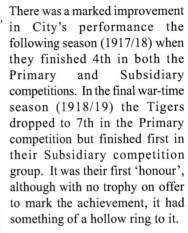

Joe Edelston, normally a half-back in City's team, often found himself having to play in goal during their wartime fixtures

There was a marked improvement in City's performance the following season (1917/18) when they finished 4th in both the Primary and Subsidiary competitions. In the final war-time season (1918/19) the Tigers dropped to 7th in the Primary competition but finished first in their Subsidiary competition group. It was their first 'honour', although with no trophy on offer to mark the achievement, it had something of a hollow ring to it.

City's performance in those last two seasons was quite impressive given that for both they were frequently without the services of Sammy Stevens. The responsibility for goalscoring, however, was accepted with some relish by Robert Hughes and David Mercer – particularly during the first of those two seasons.

If anybody had come close to filling the void left by Gordon Wright's departure, it was probably Bobby Hughes. Although not signing officially for the Tigers until July 1919, Hughes had played regularly for the club during the war-time competition. Capable of playing on either wing, he was perhaps seen at his best on the left and it was from that position he scored 25 goals in 32 appearances during the 1917/18 season. However, he was pipped as City's leading goalscorer that season by David Mercer, who scored 26 in 34 outings – including six in six games during the Subsidiary competition.

Yet if it was close in the goalscoring stakes, Mercer left his team-mates trailing in his wake as far as appearances went. Add up the Tigers' total number of war-time competition games and you'll arrive at the figure of 142. Add up the number of appearances made by David Mercer for City during that time and you'll arrive at exactly the same number: 142. From the opening game of the 1915/16 season to the closing fixture of the 1918/19 season, Mercer's name was never once missing from the teamsheet.

Top and tail that sequence of appearances with another 40 between April 1914 – April 1915 and 30 between August 1919 and April 1920 and you had a grand total of 218 consecutive games in the Tigers' colours. Included in that run were 69 goals. No wonder they called him 'Magical Mercer': as much for his stamina as his skill.

The history books tell us that at the 11th hour on the 11th day of the 11th month of 1918, the guns fell silent in Europe. Not strictly true, but certainly by the time the Tigers had played out a 2-2 draw away to Rotherham County on Saturday 16th November 1918 the foundations of peace were established. That peace had come at a significant cost, not least in terms of lives lost and in that respect neither the city of Hull nor Hull City were exempt.

Of the four local battalions of the East Yorkshire Regiment raised in the city, the number of soldiers either killed, missing in action, or dying of their wounds was measured in thousands; included in their number were nearly 400 from the 12th Battn: the Sportsman's Battalion. The losses sustained by those with a closer connection to Hull City approached nowhere near that figure and in comparison to other League clubs of the time, the Tigers were perhaps fortunate that their 'First team' losses, both past and present, were restricted to single figures. Nevertheless, included in that number were names that evoked strong memories of happier times.

Perhaps the most famous of those names was Jackie Smith, who had regularly topped the Tigers' list of goalscorers during their early seasons, although his career had never reached the same peaks since leaving the club for Sheffield United in 1910. Smith enlisted in the York and Lancaster Regiment in the early stages of the conflict and was killed in action on 7th September 1916.

Jackie Smith had signed for City at the beginning of their Football League journey in 1905. One of his team-mates that season was Patrick Lavery. City was Lavery's only League club and prior to his joining the Highland Light Infantry, he had played for a variety of Northern non-League outfits. Like Smith, Lavery answered the call to arms quite early in the conflict and was killed on the 25th September 1915.

During the 1913/14 season the Tigers' squad contained a couple of Lyons: Sam and Jack who were brothers. Sam had made his debut in December 1912, whilst Jack arrived on the scene some 10 months later in October 1913. Jack remained with the Tigers during the conflict, whilst Sam, after a short spell with Barnsley, joined up, serving in the famous Middlesex Regiment, one of whose battalions was nicknamed the Footballers' battalion. Sam was killed on the first day of the Battle of the Somme on 1st July 1916.

A team-mate of the Lyons brothers during the 1913/14 season was Douglas Morgan. A successful player in the Scottish Junior soccer scene – he had captained Inverkeithing Utd to victory in the Scottish Junior Cup in 1913, Morgan stayed with the Tigers until the last game of the 1914/15 season, a 4-1 home win over Grimsby Town.

Within weeks Morgan had enlisted in the Royal Garrison Artillery (168th Siege Battery). He was critically wounded on 31st December 1916. Initial research suggested he died the following day from his wounds. However, further research by his relatives confirms that Morgan died on the day he was wounded.

'Jock' Taylor played nine times for the Tigers between 1908-09, before moving on to Gillingham and finally returning 'home' to play in Scotland for Leith Athletic. When war was declared he enlisted in the 13th Battalion Royal Scots. Like Sam Lyon, Taylor fought and died in the first Battle of the Somme: killed in action on 15th September 1916.

The Treaty of Versailles was signed in June 1919. It brought a formal end to the war that was supposed to end all wars and established the League of Nations. Within three months the Football League re-established its normal programme of games. David Menzies remained in charge and he brought in some new faces to swell the Tigers' squad.

Their team for the opening game of the 1919-20 season showed five changes from the last time the Tigers had played peace-time football; on the goalscoring front, however, little changed. Stevens scored in the opening game – they lost 4-1 away to Birmingham – and Stevens continued to score as the Tigers made a decent start to the campaign; by the beginning of December they were fourth in the table, just one point off the promotion places. At the beginning of the month they had a convincing 5-2 home victory over Lincoln City, but seven days later lost the return fixture 2-0. The remaining four games during December began and ended with away and home fixtures against Wolverhampton Wanderers; both games highlighted the Jekyll and Hyde image that illustrated City's season. In the away fixture (20th December), City lost 4-2 to a Wolves team who were struggling at the bottom of the table. Seven days later, in the return fixture at home, the Tigers recorded the biggest League win of their history thus far, destroying Wolves 10-3 with David Mercer scoring four and Sammy Stevens netting a hat-trick. Such Jekyll and Hyde performances continued into the second half of the season and put paid to any promotion aspirations the Tigers may have held.

As the season was meandering towards a moderate conclusion it flared into life, for all the wrong reasons, when the Tigers played Coventry City twice within a week. The first game, at Coventry on 21st February 1920, was a bad-tempered affair that City won 1-0. The ill-feeling resurfaced in the return fixture a week later. Coventry, who employed some pretty physical tactics, took a first-half lead through a disputed penalty from Walker.

The visitors continued with their rough play into the second-half and it came as no surprise that they were reduced to 10 men when Walker was sent off for serious foul play – in the opinion of both reporters and spectators a reduction in Coventry's numbers should have occurred much earlier in the game.

With City holding a man advantage, they pressed for the equaliser whilst Coventry continued to take no prisoners in defending their lead. Another bad foul, this time on City's Bobby Hughes, caused the referee to issue Coventry's Blair with his marching orders. Then, to the amazement and annoyance of the crowd, he dismissed Hughes who had merely been the victim. Incensed, some of the crowd came onto the pitch to try and get to Blair, but were held back by the police. At the end of the game the crowd trouble flared up again and as the players were leaving the field, Coventry's captain (Copeland) was hit in the face by a stone thrown from one of the spectators. Again the police had to intervene and there were serious repercussions for the club.

City concluded the 1919-20 season in 11th place; it was not the finish that the Directors and supporters had hoped for. Although seemingly united in disappointment, it did not prevent either faction from engaging in lively debate as to where the fault lay. In the view of the fans it was the apparent poor standard of players acquired before and during the season that was the root of the trouble. With the benefit of hindsight, it is difficult to see the logic of that particular argument. During the period in question, the likes of Tom Bleakley, Matt 'Ginger' Bell, Jimmy Lodge – who originally arrived under the pseudonym of 'Barras' – and Jackie Crawford were signed.

Bleakley and Bell would each go on to accrue over 400 League and Cup appearances in stays with the club that lasted more than a decade. Lodge had an association with the club, in various capacities, that spanned half a century and took in all of the Tigers' championship-winning years (1933, 1949 and 1966), whilst Jackie Crawford went on to play for England, admittedly after he had departed the Tigers.

The fact that the debate took place at a time when the club had just sold Sammy Stevens to Notts County for less than £2,000 only served to inflame the fans' feelings and probably coloured the supporters' thinking about the ambitions of the Directors. Those feelings were expressed forcefully and freely, and not surprisingly were picked up by the media. One such reporter, under the 'nom de plum' of "Veritas" annoyed the Directors so much in giving publicity to the supporters' views that one of them issued a public challenge to the reporter to find a left-back for whom the club "will pay up to £2,000 if he satisfies our manager he is class enough."

Responding to the challenge, "Veritas" replied that "When the director sends his cheque along we will talk business." Apparently warming to his task, "Veritas" went on to enquire of the City Board whether it was true that the club "…are paying over £4 10s a week to a player whom the club signed without seeing him play, but whom they simply dare not play having once see him?" The player in question was never identified and the challenge never pursued.

Again, with hindsight, what was emerging were the financial facts of life that faced Hull City throughout much of the 1920s and 30s. The club had never been what you would call financially secure. In their early League years the shortfall between income and expenditure had frequently been met out of the Directors' pockets and the fire damage to the club's ground had needed 'external' financial assistance, which was still being paid for. From the Directors' viewpoint the books had to be balanced and if that meant cashing in on the playing assets, such as Sammy Stevens, then they felt they had no option but to take the opportunity when it arose and rely on their manager and scouting network to find replacements of at least the same standing, if not better. A risky business.

In some respects that policy appeared initially to be vindicated. The acquisition of George Morrall at the beginning of that first post-war season had paid off handsomely. Acquired initially on amateur terms, his first season haul of 17 League goals was just one short of Stevens's return and within months of Stevens's departure they had acquired another goalscorer, Paddy Mills, who would outshine the memory of Stevens with his goals.

Earlier acquisitions in that 1920-21 season included Mick Gilhooley and Tom Brandon. Both would make their name in the Tigers' history book, but for the present they were merely part of a team that often flattered to deceive. A draw at West Ham and a heavy defeat away to Birmingham at the start of the season were followed by three consecutive victories. From then on the sequence of draws and defeats grew longer whilst the wins reduced dramatically, not helped by the departure of David Mercer to Sheffield United. The fee received, at over £4,000 a League record, did little to assuage the feelings of the supporters even if it did calm the Tigers' Bank manager. Only once more during the 1920-21 season did the Tigers muster back to back victories in the League.

By the time the Christmas fixtures arrived, the Tigers were lying fourth from bottom in the table. It was a position they still occupied come Easter, and it was only one defeat in the remaining 11 games of the season that saw them eventually move away from the re-election zone. Analysis of the final table showed 10 wins and 20 draws. As a foundation for promotion, it wasn't good enough.

Mick Gilhooley was a stalwart in City's defence during the early 1920s.

Tom Brandon's versatility meant he was comfortable at either full-back or inside-forward.

Yet sandwiched within the frustration of that season was a glimpse of what City were capable of; it came in the third round of the FA Cup when Burnley visited Anlaby Road on February 19th 1921.

The Tigers shocked the football world when they ended Burnley's 26 match unbeaten record in February 1921. Standing: D. Menzies (Manager), J. Collier, S. Cheetham, W. Mercer, M. Bell, J. Barrass, J. Beck (Trainer), [Inset: J. Crawford]; Sitting: D. McKinney, T. Brandon, M. Gilhooley, H. Sergeaunt, H. Wilson. Mascot: Baby Brandon.

The Tigers were languishing in the lower reaches of Division Two, whilst Burnley were sitting proudly at the top of Division One and had been unbeaten in their last 26 games. Victory number 27 seemed a formality, especially as the Tigers were fielding a player in their forward line – Tom Brandon – who was far more comfortable at left-back. However, when the final whistle blew the Tigers had won 3-0 and it was debateable who was more surprised: the crowd or Burnley. Adding to the incredulity was the fact that Brandon had scored twice: one a header from feet in front of goal, the other a shot from over 25 yards out from goal. City's other goal, from Henry Wilson, just put the cherry on top of the icing. That game and the game a week later, at home against Sheffield Wednesday which ended 1-1, summed up the Tigers in all their frustrating glory: victory against the best in the League and a draw against a team below them in the Division.

The frustrations of that 1920/21 season came to a head during the close season. However, it was not on the terraces that boiling point was reached, it was much closer to home: in the manager's office. Working on the basis of having to find inexpensive talent to replace that already found and sold at substantial fees, and then seeing that replacement talent go the same way was proving to be something of a vicious circle for David Menzies. He broke it by accepting an offer to manage First Division outfit Bradford City.

The financial environment within which the club was operating appeared not to deter the applicants to succeed Menzies. Nearly 100 submitted their CVs for the Directors' consideration and their choice, Harry Lewis, was a man of great experience: as a player, a referee and an administrator. However, by his own admission the early part of his first season (1921/22) in charge was not a great experience. Before the season was a month old, and having played just six games the Tigers were bottom of the Division with one win and a draw – dumped there courtesy of a 6-0 thumping at

Ex Newcastle Utd and Ireland international, Bill McCracken was appointed as City's manager in March 1923

Fulham on 17th September. Five wins and one loss in the next six games moved them up to seventh place in the table and from that point they mounted an encouraging challenge for promotion that was hampered by poor results over Christmas and Easter and finally saw them finish in fifth place – on the morning of Christmas Eve they were third, just one point away from the promotion places.

To improve, Lewis knew he would have to buy. The Directors, however, had different ideas. They sanctioned the sale of Mick Gilhooley to Sunderland – at £5,250 another League transfer record – and Bobby Hughes to Sheffield United, thus depriving him of two of his main assets for the forthcoming season. Lewis's replacements were nowhere near the required standard and the opening months of the 1922/23 season were not happy ones. Seven wins from 23 games meant that on 1st January 1923 the Tigers were eleven points off the promotion spots, whilst six points separated them from those teams con-templating relegation. The season could go either way; within days it was Lewis who went.

Paddy Mills opens the scoring with this header in the 2-0 victory away to Crystal Palace (January 1922)

With his hands tied as far as transfers were concerned, his authority was also being persistently under-mined by the Directors who insisted on their say in team selection. Another defeat, this time away to Man-chester United on 6th January 1923 – although the Tigers had beaten the Red Devils a week earlier – was the final straw for Lewis. He gave the Directors full rein to choose the team for the next game, an FA Cup tie against West Ham at Anlaby Road, because two days before that fixture he resigned. Now with undisputed control of team selection, the Directors' selection committee brought in Bob Coverdale for Tom Eccles and in what was a close encounter, the Tigers lost 3-2.

The Tigers had prepared for this tie by spending a few days in Filey and the sea air must have had an invigorating effect on them as the game kicked off at a cracking pace, with four goals being scored in the opening 25 minutes of the game and all five goals scored before half-time. West Ham got off to an ideal start by netting twice within 10 minutes: Moore sent Ruffell away for the Hammers and City's full-back Gibson was forced to give away a corner; from it Moore headed the ball past Mercer. West Ham's defence rather desperately cleared a couple of City attacks, but then, after 10 minutes, increased their lead when Kay sent the speedy Watson racing past 'Ginger' Bell to fire a low shot wide of Mercer.

Mills pulled a goal back for the Tigers after 23 minutes, beating four men before smashing the ball past Hufton as three West Ham defenders fell in a heap on top of him. Two minutes later Crawford put City level and it was all to play for once more, although the 15,000 City fans, who'd produced gate receipts for the match of £1,250, were beginning to get worried about fog forcing the tie to be abandoned. West Ham fought back and after Moore had hit the crossbar, the London side re-gained the lead just before the interval: Watson, whose speed worried the Tigers throughout the game, forced his way past

Jackie Crawford (left) with City's trainer Joe Beck.

Bew and Gibson and then Mercer let the centre-forward's shot slip through his hands, the ball having just enough momentum left to trickle over the line.

The second half saw City bombard the West Ham goal, but the Hammers defended successfully in an exciting game that, on the heavy ground, became a test of stamina as much as skill. Only once was the Hammers' goal breached, but the 'goal' was disallowed by Manchester referee H. W. Andrews. City's players crowded around him to protest, but to no avail. When the final whistle blew, it was West Ham who continued their Cup journey – a journey that finally ended in the first ever Wembley Cup Final, losing out to Bolton Wanderers. The Tigers were left to rue their luck and concentrate on appointing their next manager.

The Directors were clear who they wanted to replace Harry Lewis and that was Irish international Bill McCracken; the only problem was that McCracken, even at the age of 40, was still playing regularly for club (Newcastle United) and country. Protracted negotiations for his release took nearly two months to complete and it wasn't until the beginning of March 1923 that he was finally able to watch a City fixture as their manager.

A run of seven games unbeaten at the start of his spell as City's boss suggested that the Director's had been right in persisting with their negotiations. A mid-table finish offered encouragement for the future, but if McCracken did not fully appreciate the financial environment he would have to work in, the point was forcibly made when one of the leading lights of the forwards, Jackie Crawford, was sold to Chelsea at the end of the season. The sale may have soothed the accountant's fevered brow, but it was just another headache for McCracken.

Crawford had joined the Tigers from non-League Jarrow Town in December 1919 and waited patiently for his chance in the first team, which did not arrive until the away fixture at Huddersfield in March 1920. From then on though, Crawford became very much a permanent fixture in the side, predominantly on the right wing. At £3,000 Crawford would prove to be a bargain for Chelsea, notching up over 400 appearances for the London club and gaining international recognition for England against Scotland in 1931.

Perhaps his greatest game in City's colours came in the 5-0 thrashing of First Division Middlesbrough in the first round of the FA Cup in January 1922. In preparation for the tie, City had spent a few days at Ilkley, where it was reported, "they found the air fresh and bracing." When the game started, Middlesbrough discovered how fresh and bracing the Tigers were, for in the early stages Flood hit an upright and Mills hit the bar. Boro' left Wilson upfield and tried to crack City's defence with long passes aimed at him, but when centre-half Gilhooley failed to subdue him, full-back Lodge was there to cover so that keeper Mercer was well protected. After a number of near misses the Tigers took the lead in the 40th minute. It was a move in which Bell, Gilhooley, Bleakley, Mills and Hughes took part before Crawford, who had given his marker the runaround throughout the half, scored.

Minutes into the second half Coverdale scored from a pass by Hughes. City, who were "fit and fighting", then had to weather a brief Middlesbrough fightback before storming back. In the 74th minute Mills got the third; five minutes from the end, Mills and Flood set up a goal for Bleakley and, in the last minute, a shot by Mills rebounded off the keeper to Coverdale, who lobbed the ball home.

With none of the Crawford money at his disposal McCracken would have to rely on developing young talent; it was a strategy that would require time, but in any manager's career time is often the scarcest of commodities. McCracken brought in young new faces for the start of the 1923/24 season, but any hopes of mounting a serious promotion campaign were more optimistic than realistic. In his favour, at least, was an experienced defensive line-up: Mercer, Gibson and Bell had occupied positions one to three on the teamsheet for a couple of seasons and had developed a good understanding. McCracken built on this and developed the trio into an effective unit that took full advantage of the offside rule as it stood then, much to the frustration of opposition forwards and fans. Where the frustration lay for City fans and manager alike, was in the lack of a proven goalscorer. Heavy expectation rested on the shoulders of 'Paddy' Mills but he struggled to deliver in the opening months of the campaign – his first goals of the season didn't arrive until Boxing Day 1923.

One win in the opening ten games confirmed the suspicion that the Tigers' defence would be hard pressed that season and left them third from bottom in the table at the start of October. During that month there was also as much unrest off the field as on it. The interference by the Directors that had hastened Harry Lewis's departure continued during McCracken's early days; it came to a head during October with McCracken finally getting his way. Now with sole responsibility for team matters, he would stand or fall by results.

For much of the remaining season (1923/24) those results offered little encouragement. At the beginning of December 1923 the Tigers were still third from bottom in the table, but only one defeat in six games brought McCracken some relief: a three place rise in the table and the first goals of the season from Paddy Mills (two hat-tricks in three games). The month of December proved to be deceptive however. It was the middle of February before the Tigers tasted victory again in the League and their proximity to the relegation places caused more than a little anxiety as game after game through March and early April produced only defeats or draws. Two wins over Easter finally secured the club's Second division status, with a finishing position of 17th.

Programme for City's 3rd round FA Cup tie against the Cup holders Bolton Wanderers in January 1924

The start of the 1924/25 season followed a similar pattern to the previous campaign. It was seven games before the team had a win bonus to enjoy and by the time the Tigers visited Old Trafford in the middle of November – where they lost to Manchester United 2-0 – they were uncomfortably positioned in the table: two places and three points from the relegation spots. The one crumb of comfort available to McCracken was the fact that his goalscoring problems had eased. The potential that had been seen in Paddy Mills was starting to be realized. With eight goals to his credit after 14 League games, a brace in fixture number 15 – a 2-1 win over eventual champions Leicester City – left him one short of his previous season's total with less than half of the current campaign's fixtures completed.

In the space of one week, in the middle of January, Paddy Mills provided ample evidence that he had found his shooting boots, to such an extent that it even encouraged his fellow forwards to get their name on City's scoresheet as the Tigers put together consecutive 5-0 home victories over Crystal Palace and Portsmouth – City's goalscorers in both games were the same: Mills, Hamilton and Martin, with just the distribution of goals differing in each game. The Palace game was a dress rehearsal for the FA Cup tie between the two teams scheduled for the end of the month. In between those two fixtures was the first-ever visit to Hull by Portsmouth, who had finished the previous season as Division Three (S) champions.

Leading by example for the Tigers that day was Paddy Mills, even though he played for only a little over half the game. He scored his 20th goal of the season after six minutes and then got another in the 29th minute, following a dazzling piece of football by team-mate Martin. "Then," says the report on the game, in a style of prose that was as eloquent as it is antiquated by today's reporting standards, "H. Foxall contributed to the fall of his side through hopelessly failing to arrest the career of the ball which Hamilton coolly annexed, making headway before passing to Martin, who scored from 20 yards".

Shortly before half time Mills was badly injured after a tackle by Foxall, and though he was carried off he was able to return, but went off again for good shortly after halftime. The Tigers, however, held on to their 3—0 lead even though they had been reduced to ten men and in the last ten minutes Hamilton broke through the Pompey defence and drove the ball past the advancing Kane and then Martin scored from a free-kick by Gibson.

Mills was in fine scoring form. It was a good job too, for as the season unfolded the Tigers never strayed far from mid-table and Mills's final tally of 25 League goals represented exactly half of the club's total for the season. Although the responsibility for scoring had rested very

much with Mills during the season, a young forward by the name of Sammy Hamilton had broken into the first team and a return of seven goals from 27 League outings offered potential, as did the partnership he formed with Mills during that time. If they could carry that sort of form into the next season things looked promising. Unfortunately that promise never had the opportunity to develop. Suffering from nose and throat problems, Hamilton was operated on during the close season but died in a local nursing home during his recovery.

Such tragedy implied the sporting Gods were conspiring against the Tigers. A promising start to the 1925/26 season suggested the implication was ill-founded. Again the Tigers were reliant on Paddy Mills for their goals and in the opening games he did not disappoint. Together with new signing Pat Lee, their goals helped the Tigers to five wins in the opening seven games and fifth place in the division. Receiving help on the scoring front from Andy Thom and George Whitworth, City continued to register victories, but as 1925 moved into 1926 the balance of results favoured defeats rather than victories and a downward spiral in the League table. A resounding win over Bradford City (5-0) on 16th January 1926 reversed the trend and returned the Tigers to the top half of the table. It proved to be only a temporary upturn in their fortunes as their next victory in the League did not occur until March and from then until the end of the season they added only another four wins in twelve games, not helped by the transfer of Paddy Mills to Notts County for just over £3,000.

The sale of Mills, and another mid-table finish to the season rekindled the debate that had smouldered through much of the decade about the club's ambitions and financial stability. The unrest on the terraces had conveyed itself to the Directors at just about every annual general meeting held during the 1920s thus far and there had been frequent calls for the board to resign en bloc to make way for fresh blood. Persistent press speculation about the Tigers' finances, and even their continued existence, merely added further pressure to a board of Directors that was beginning to fragment into factions and cliques. Fragmentation turned to disintegration during the close season of 1926. Jasper Spring, who had been the club's chairman for a decade, and had grown increasingly troubled at the lack of harmony amongst the directors, resigned. Dr C.D. Pullan took over the chair, stating publicly his intention to revive the club's fortunes and elevate them to Division One.

Pullan's rhetoric and McCracken's moulding of his young charges seemed to pay off in the opening games of season 1926/27. The scoring mantle passed from Paddy Mills to George Whitworth – with support from McLaughlin and Lee – and all three played their part in the early success, but closer inspection revealed where the credit really lay: in defence. The full-back partnership of 'Jock' Gibson and team captain 'Ginger' Bell had remained solid for just about all of the decade thus far. Initially in partnership with Billy Mercer as the custodian apex of the defensive triangle, Mercer had subsequently given way to George Maddison who was well on his way to establishing legendary status in the Tigers' cause. Such was their ability that one First Division club reputedly offered the Tigers an open cheque to sign all three! Despite their financial predicament, the club's directors commendably declined the offer.

In City's first twelve games that season (1926/27) they conceded just four goals; an impressive statistic but not a record as Manchester United had restricted their concession to four in fourteen games at the start of the 1924/25 season. Irrespective of the statistical significance, it was sufficient to give the Tigers leadership of the Division after their 1-0 win over Grimsby Town and keep them there for the next two weeks. For the remainder of 1926 they never dropped below third place, and even consecutive losses to Chelsea in the Christmas Day and Boxing Day fixtures still left them in second place behind Middlesbrough when the Tigers travelled to play South Shields on New Year's Day.

A surprising 3-1 defeat knocked the Tigers' confidence and it received a further blow in the next game when they suffered a heavy 5-2 defeat away to Wolves. It meant they dropped down to fifth and although they returned to winning ways at home to Notts County and remained undefeated during February, it had little impact on their League placing.

At the beginning of March they had moved up one place, but three defeats in five matches during that month saw them slip down to seventh and that's where they finished the season – the club's highest during McCracken's tenure. The reserves hadn't done too badly either, ending their season as champions of the Midland Combination league.

It appeared that McCracken's youth policy was finally starting to pay dividends as the youngsters breaking through into the team were benefiting from playing alongside the wiser heads of Gibson, Bell, and Bleakley. New talent was added in the shape of Jimmy Howieson, who had cost the Tigers £4,000 when they signed him in February 1927, and a youngster by the name of Stan Alexander was blooded in the forward line.

McCracken had the nucleus of a decent team and much was expected of the Tigers when they started the 1927/28 campaign as one of the favourites for promotion. By the end of October that promotion favourite tag looked somewhat presumptuous as they were lying seventh from bottom in the table. Inconsistency did not help their cause and by the beginning of March they were well out of the promotion race. Realising that their chance was gone, McCracken began blooding some of the youngsters again, perhaps with an eye to the future and one in particular who caught the eye during the latter weeks of that season was Ronnie Starling.

Starling had been a precocious talent in his schooldays and when tested in the hard non-League arena of the North East with Washington Colliery, had not been found wanting.

City's championship winning reserves from the 1926/27 season:
Standing: P. Lee, J. Roy, J. Campbell, F. Gibson, W. Cowan, J. McLoughlin, G. Wilson;
Sitting: J.W. Alexander, S. Alexander, J. Morris, J. Murray.

Sent to Hull for a trial whilst only sixteen, McCracken was so impressed that he travelled back with Starling to Durham and persuaded his parents to let the lad work in City's office and play for the club as an amateur; when he turned 17 he was offered a professional contract.

As well as blooding the youngsters during the final weeks of the 1927/28 season, McCracken was acquiring them from the amateur game. Perhaps one of his finest acquisitions within this category was Sammy Weaver, who was signed from junior football at 19 for a fee of £100, and who, two seasons later, brought much needed revenue into the Tigers' bank account when he was sold to Newcastle United.

Both Starling and Weaver would play influential roles in the 1928/29 season, but in the early part of that campaign the spotlight was very much on another of McCracken's signings, Ken McDonald. Just turned 25 when joining the Tigers, he was no McCracken babe but he was a goalscorer of some pedigree, as 136 goals from 145 League outings for his previous club, Bradford Park Avenue, confirmed. If he could repeat that scoring rate then McCracken had a bargain.

A goal on his Tiger debut in the opening game of the 1928/29 season, as City drew 2-2 at home to Southampton, augured well for McCracken's judgement and as each game passed the wisdom of that judgement increased. In the opening 22 games of the season, McDonald's name was missing from the scoresheet only eight times. By the end of Christmas Day 1928, McDonald had scored 22 goals in 22 games, including all five in City's 5-1 victory over Bristol City on 17 November. He was on course to rewrite City's goal-scoring records. However, an injury sustained in the early days of January drastically reduced his effectiveness and appearances during the second part of the campaign. By the end of the season his tally of 23 goals from 32 games was impressive by normal standards, but disappointing by the early pace he had set.

Ken McDonald scored 22 goals by Christmas during the 1928/29 season.

Another of McCracken's pre-season signings, who displayed signs of becoming something special during the campaign, was Douglas 'Dally' Duncan. Signed on the strength of an impressive performance during a pre-season trial match, Duncan, aged only 18, had played in the trial game under the surname of Dunn and it was only when his signature was penned on the contract that his true identity and pedigree was revealed. Duncan was, in fact, a highly rated Scottish winger who had represented his country at Schoolboy level and been coveted and chased by a number of senior Scottish clubs; it was something of coup therefore for the Tigers to steal him from them. Duncan made his debut early in the season and drew admiring glances from spectators and visiting scouts alike. Finishing his first season of professional football with 20 appearances and three goals, many informed observers considered him to be the 'find' of the season.

Also emerging during the season were the young bucks, Starling and Weaver. Both managed a higher appearance tally than McDonald, although their combined goal tally of seven fell well short of his. Given that both still had some time to go before the traditional 'key of the door' entitlements were theirs, they could be satisfied with their efforts, as could McCracken and the crowd, even if that satisfaction was tempered with disappointment at finishing only 14th in the League.

What did cheer up the faithful was McCracken's re-acquisition of former star, Paddy Mills. Having been transferred to Notts County some three years earlier, Mills had subsequently moved on to Birmingham, although his time deep in the Midlands had proved somewhat unproductive and unhappy. He did not take too much persuading to return, therefore, to the scene of his former glories and the supporters greeted the news gleefully and received him back into the Tigers' lair like a prodigal son; only the fatted calf was missing, times were still hard after all.

If club and supporters had high hopes for the final season (1929/30) of the 1920s, they would be met and dashed in varying degrees and by the cruellest manner. It would be a season to remember and forget, probably in equal measures. McCracken probably had as good a collection of players as at any time during his previous six seasons in charge, and although he brought in some new faces during the summer they were essentially to strengthen the squad, with only Phil Cartwright and Bill Gowdy being regulars in the starting line-up throughout the season. City opened the campaign with a 1-0 win over Swansea and not surprisingly the goal came from Ken McDonald. Four wins in the opening five games put City in second place, one point behind Oldham Athletic. Heavy defeats against Bristol City and Wolverhampton Wanderers, plus only one win from the next ten games meant that by the middle of November the Tigers had slipped down to 14th in the table and anxiety as to how the season would evolve began to emerge. That anxiety was further increased when one of their bright young stars, Sammy Weaver, was sold on to Newcastle United – money worries were rearing their head again.

(Above) Stan Alexander scored a hat-trick against Plymouth Argyle to set the Tigers off on an epic Cup run in 1930.

(Below) Douglas 'Dally' Duncan was a star for the Tigers during the late 1920s and early 30s

Injuries and suspension forced McCracken to delay naming his side until just before the kick-off, a highly unusual practice in those days. In the end he plumped for a side that leant heavily on experience with Starling being brought in to replace the suspended Howieson. It was Starling who opened the scoring for the Tigers and Alexander added another before Blackpool's leading goalscorer, Hampson, pulled one back for the Tangerines. Any anxiety amongst the 23,000 home supporters was quelled when Walsh, Starling and Taylor worked a good move between them, allowing Paddy Mills to restore a two-goal cushion for the Tigers that remained when the game ended.

The anxieties on the playing front were eased slightly with a decent string of results in December that moved them a couple of places up the table and then attention turned to the FA Cup, with the Tigers facing new opponents in the shape of Plymouth Argyle. Many within the club fancied their chances of a good showing in the competition that season; such a showing would probably help their financial predicament as well. Matt Bell, the Tigers' inspirational skipper of many years standing went so far as to publicly state that the Tigers "would go far" in this season's competition. Whether it was an assessment of the journey to Devon, or a prophecy on their chances in the competition only time would tell.

Although Plymouth played in a Division below the Tigers, they were in fact leading the Southern section so the result was not a foregone conclusion. That assessment was confirmed by the closeness of the final scoreline (4-3), City coming out narrowly on top in a game of seven goals thanks to a hat-trick from Stan Alexander and a solitary strike from 'Dally' Duncan. That victory earned the Tigers a home tie against fellow Division Two opponents Blackpool, who were at the top of the table when the draw was made. Added spice was brought to the tie by the renewal of an acquaintance with an early legend in the Tigers' history: Tom 'Boy' Browell.

The draw for Round 5 gave the Tigers a trip to either First Division Manchester City or Southern Section Swindon Town. In the end it was to Maine Road that the Tigers travelled, and if that prospect wasn't daunting enough they has to make it without the help of their injured skipper, Matt Bell. McCracken chose Jimmy Howieson as Bell's replacement, both as left-back and skipper, and Ronnie Starling retained his place.

In front of a crowd exceeding 60,000 the Tigers came under early pressure and within 10 minutes it paid off for Manchester as Toseland scored. After half an hour the Tigers were back on level terms, Paddy Mills heading home a Billy Taylor cross. Parity remained until just into the second half when Billy Taylor capped a fine performance with a goal that put the Tigers ahead and probably reflected the merits of both teams' performance on the afternoon. For the remainder of the game Manchester City lay siege to the Tigers' goal, but the defence held firm and Gibson was not required to repeat his heroics of the first half.

It is said that the further you travel in the Cup, the harder it gets; not necessarily so in City's case when the draw for the next round was made. Having just overcome a side at the top end of Division One, the Tigers' next opponents in the Cup (Newcastle United) were of a similar calibre but their location in Division One was at the bottom of the table; even the venue, St James' Park, was insufficient to worry McCracken and his charges unduly. For McCracken it would be a contest of mixed emotions. A Newcastle player for over 20 years before moving to Anlaby Road, he had led the Magpies to FA Cup and League glory; now he was charged with plotting their downfall. And just like the earlier Blackpool tie, there were former Tiger connections to contend with, this time of more recent history in the shape of Sammy Weaver, who had moved between the clubs just a matter of months earlier. As in the previous tie against Manchester City, McCracken would be without one of his star performers. Although Matt Bell was fully fit and capable of taking up his usual left-back station, the forward line was depleted by the absence of Paddy Mills; Howieson therefore reverted to a more attacking role.

In front of a crowd of 63,486, with many more locked out, the early pattern of play was pretty even. It wasn't until the half-hour mark approached that the deadlock was broken, with Lang's strong header from Boyd's cross giving City's custodian, Fred Gibson, no chance. Rather than unsettle the Tigers, the set-back merely increased their resolve and an equalizing header from Stan Alexander was thoroughly deserved. From that point on, if either side looked capable of finishing the tie at the first attempt, it was the Tigers. However, a draw was indeed the final outcome and battle would recommence five days later at Anlaby Road.

With no new injuries to contend with – although Paddy Mills was still unfit – McCracken fielded an unchanged side for the replay that attracted a then club record attendance of 32,930. Newcastle, however, had four different faces in their line-up. A quiet goalless first half was instantly forgotten when Taylor set off on a mazy run down the Newcastle left wing before delivering a strong cross into the path of Jimmy Howieson. The easy and sensible options looked to be a return ball to Taylor or a pass out to Dally Duncan on the Tigers' left.

He chose neither. Instead he drove a fierce shot towards the top left hand corner of the Newcastle goal that their keeper, McInroy, could only help on its way. For the first time in the tie the Tigers were ahead. It signalled a major onslaught on their own goal by the Newcastle forwards but the experienced Tigers' defence held firm and the final whistle produced an historic result. The Tigers had reached an FA Cup semi-final for the first time in their history. Perhaps that prophecy of Bell's had something to it?

As the only lower division team remaining in the competition, the other semi-finalist, Arsenal, Huddersfield and Sheffield Wednesday, were no doubt hoping to be paired with the Tigers as the easier route to Wembley. It was Arsenal upon whom Lady Luck smiled and the date and venue for the game would be Elland Road, Leeds on 22nd March. Given the distances to be travelled by the teams and their respective supporters, the game was akin to a home fixture for the Tigers. Certainly their colours seemed more predominant amongst the 47,549 spectators crowded into Elland Road when both teams emerged onto the pitch that afternoon. The Tigers made only one change from the side that had defeated Newcastle: Mills returning in place of Taylor. As for Arsenal, they were at full strength with such legendary names as James, Jack, Bastin and Hapgood wearing their traditional red and white shirts.

Undeterred by the talent arrayed against them the Tigers started confidently and took the lead after 15 minutes. A poor clearance by the Arsenal goalkeeper (Lewis) was seized upon by Jimmy Howieson who lobbed it into the Arsenal penalty area; Lewis misjudged the flight and the ball ended up in the Arsenal net via the crossbar. If that was a jolt to Arsenal's ambitions they received another one a few minutes later when Duncan sent in a "fast slanting shot" towards the Arsenal goal that beat Lewis all ends up and gave City a two goal lead with the game barely 30 minutes old.

City's squad that battled through to the semi-finals of the FA Cup in 1930 where they eventually lost to Arsenal after a replay.
Left to right: M. Bell, F. Gibson, G. Goldsmith, A. Childs, J. Walsh, W. Gowdy, D. Duncan, R. Starling, A. Rodgers, S. Alexander, W. Taylor, B. Mills, T. Bleakley, J. Howieson.

There was no change to the scoreline in the remainder of that half even though the Tigers lost Matt Bell to injury, although he came back early in the second half. With less than half-an-hour to go Arsenal pulled a goal back through Jack. It caused unease on the Tigers' terrace, though not panic, but as the last quarter of the game was played out it was Arsenal who started to take the ascendancy, aided by their rough tactics that reduced the effectiveness of Bell, Goldsmith, Mills and Walsh.

With eight minutes remaining the London side's mounting pressure and physical approach paid off. Cliff Bastin evaded the tackle of the injured Paddy Mills and had a clear route to goal before unleashing a fierce shot from the edge of the Tigers' penalty area that left Fred Gibson helpless.

Arsenal had survived to fight another day and one couldn't help feeling that the Tigers had missed their chance.

The programme for City's FA Cup semi-final
tie against Arsenal at Elland Road
on 22nd March 1930

The reply was scheduled for Villa Park four days later and the Tigers were forced into changes with the veteran Tom Bleakley and Phil Cartwright coming in to replace the injured Jimmy Walsh and Stan Alexander. Arsenal too made a change, although theirs was more tactical, replacing Hulme with Williams.

The programme for City's FA Cup semi-final replay against Arsenal at Villa Park on 26th March 1930

The replay was not a thrilling spectacle. This time only one goal was needed and it was scored by Arsenal's Jack, although the Tigers felt hard done by in that they believed the ball had crossed the dead-ball line before Williams had managed to cross it into Jack's path. Their cause was further hampered by the dismissal of Arthur Childs for a misdemeanour that apparently only the referee saw – it gave Childs the unenviable record of being the first player ever to be dismissed in an FA Cup semi-final. In what was generally considered by the assembled reporters to be a poor and niggardly game, what praise there was on offer was generally directed in the Tigers' direction for the way they had fought – sometimes literally – with ten men. Arsenal were no doubt happy to concede their share of any praise, they were through to the final and plaudits were of no comfort to McCracken's Tigers.

City's centre-half, Arthur Childs, made Cup history when he became the first player ever to be dismissed in an FA Cup semi-final. He was 'red carded' in the replay against Arsenal at Villa Park

With all the excitement of the Cup run, it was perhaps understandable that attention to League matters may have slipped. When they began their adventure in the FA Cup the Tigers were 12th in the table; by the time the adventure ended at Villa Park they had dropped six places to 18th, two points away from the relegation places. However, with at least two games in hand on the teams below them, they had every opportunity to put daylight between themselves and trouble.

They did not seize the first opportunity, losing 3-0 at home to Blackpool. A 1-0 win over Oldham two days later eased their situation a little by moving them a couple of places up the table away from danger. Danger, however, fought back and landed the Tigers right in the relegation zone with a string of six games without a win that included a

heavy 7-1 defeat at West Bromwich Albion. The lack of points from those games was serious enough without compounding the problem further by damaging their goal average.

A 2-0 win at home over Tottenham Hotspur offered the Tigers encouragement and with two games left in City's fixture list the table looked so:

	P	W	L	D	For	Agst	Pts	Goal Avge
Bradford City	41	11	18	12	57	76	34	0.75
Hull City	40	13	20	7	49	77	33	0.64
Notts County	42	9	18	15	54	70	33	0.77
Bristol City	40	12	20	8	58	81	32	0.72

With Notts County already down, a win in their penultimate fixture would guarantee the Tigers Second Division football next season, because the fixture in question was at home to Bristol City. As they blew their chance in the big game against Arsenal, so they did against Bristol. A solitary goal, scored by Bristol's Williams settled the game in their favour and left City in even more trouble, although all was still not lost as the table showed before the start of the last round of fixtures on 3rd May:

	P	W	L	D	For	Agst	Pts	Goal Avge
Bristol City	41	13	20	8	59	81	34	0.73
Barnsley	41	13	20	8	54	70	34	0.77
Bradford City	41	11	18	12	57	76	34	0.75
Hull City	41	13	21	7	49	78	33	0.63
Notts County	42	9	18	15	54	70	33	0.77

The final fixtures had Bristol away to Preston North End; Barnsley at home to Oldham; Bradford away to Charlton and the Tigers at home to Wolverhampton Wanderers. A win for the Tigers and defeat for either Bristol, Barnsley or Bradford would do. What happened was a 2-0 win for Tigers, a 3-1 win for Bradford and a 2-1 victory for Barnsley. City's fate rested on Bristol City's result, and when it came through it was not good news. They had drawn 2-2 at Preston and so the bottom of the table had the following look about it:

	P	W	L	D	For	Agst	Pts	Goal Avge
Reading	42	12	19	11	55	67	35	0.82
Bristol City	42	13	20	9	61	83	35	0.73
Hull City	42	14	21	7	51	78	35	0.65
Notts County	42	9	18	15	54	70	33	0.77

Twenty years earlier goal average had denied the Tigers entry to Division One, now that same mathematical mechanism despatched them to the Northern Section of Division Three.

## CHAPTER 4

The summer of 1930 was a time for taking stock within Hull City football club. Their rapid decline in the latter weeks of the recently ended season had been a shock and the consequential relegation, for the first time in their history, had been a big blow. Yet once the inquest began the recriminations were perhaps not as strong as might have been expected. The backlog of fixtures generated by the Cup run had placed great demands on McCracken's squad and injuries to Goldsmith and Bell, plus the suspension of Arthur Child following his dismissal in the semi-final replay against Arsenal, not only robbed City of valuable experience for important games, but also meant a number of players having to play outside of their normal positions.

Again the calls for the club's management at all levels to be replaced were heard, and there was a change at the highest level in the Boardroom, with the club's chairman, Dr Pullan, stepping down and making way for Jim Barraclough. His first task would be to help his manager plan for an early departure from Division 3(N). Aware that some of his squad were capable of much better than the Northern section and therefore likely to move on, whilst others were coming towards the end of their careers, McCracken increased his resources across the board, bringing in fresh faces at the back, in the middle and up front. Departures from Anlaby Road included Ronnie Starling to Newcastle United, for a fee of £4,000, and 37-year old Tom Bleakley who dropped down into the local non-League scene by joining Goole Town.

Life in the Northern section of the Football League would not be easy. With only the champions being promoted, the Tigers would be competing with 21 other teams for one promotion slot in a division that had a reputation for being more rugged in its play than Division Two. Consequently, the type of player needed required strength and courage just as much as skill and craft. There was no doubting that many of McCracken's young stars possessed those latter qualities – their subsequent careers would confirm it – what was in question was whether they possessed sufficient quantities of the former.

If the Tigers were in any doubt as to what faced them during the 1930/31 season, those doubts were quickly dispelled in the opening fixture: a 3-2 defeat away to Stockport County. To their credit the team responded positively and only three defeats in the next 15 games had them in sixth place at the end of November and three points adrift of the top team, Wrexham. Included within that run were plenty of goals from City: only twice did they fail to get on the scoresheet, and the vast majority of those goals came from the usual source of Paddy Mills,

Dally Duncan and Stan Alexander – the latter making his best start to a season for City with 12 goals in the first sixteen games. December and January followed a similar pattern on the goals front but were frustratingly inconsistent results wise. Heavy defeats at Tranmere (0-4) and Lincoln (0-3) were countered by even heavier wins over Halifax (10-0), Doncaster (8-2), Southport (5-1) and Chesterfield (4-0). Whilst Alexander and Duncan contributed their share of goals, the bulk of them came from a small young forward by the name of Simon Raleigh, who McCracken had signed from Huddersfield at the start of the season. Raleigh's heavy bout of scoring in the Reserves prompted McCracken to promote him to the first team and he did not disappoint, contributing five in the win over Halifax and a hat-trick in the Doncaster game.

For all their goals the Tigers' position in the table remained unchanged at sixth by the end of January, with the points gap from top spot increasing to ten. They had it all to do if promotion was to be gained. A poor string of results throughout February and March made that task virtually impossible and even a sequence of five consecutive wins in April – with Mills contributing seven goals during that run – merely moved them up to fifth place. Four games after that run, the season had ended and the Tigers had dropped to sixth. It was a disappointing first season in the Northern section, the disappointment being compounded by the fact that City's relegation partner from the previous season, Notts County, had won promotion at the first time of asking

Although the goals of Raleigh (15 from 15 games), Alexander (24 from 41), Duncan (18 from 40) and Mills (12 from 30) provided a positive aspect to the campaign, it was insufficient to appease either supporter or Director.

———————

Simon Raliegh scored 5 goals in City's 10-0 defeat of Halifax Town on Boxing Day 1930. His 15 League outings during the 1930/31 season brought him 15 goals

Whenever such a situation arises it is inevitably the manager who suffers the consequence and it was no different for the Tigers. Having been given the chance to restore City to their former home of Division Two, and failed, the announcement of McCracken's resignation, after lengthy discussion with club chairman Jim Barraclough, came as no surprise.

George Maddison (left) and Matt 'Ginger' Bell.
Two legends in the lifetime of Hull City

When the Tigers had beaten Manchester City in the previous season's FA Cup, McCracken had been quoted as saying: "No, I am not saying anything about what we expect to do in the next round yet... one thing I don't mind saying though, and that is if we haven't some young players who are on the way to make a big name for themselves in football I am a bad judge."

McCracken was not a bad judge of playing talent. The fact that such acquisitions as Starling, Duncan, Weaver and others went on to either play at a much higher level or gain international honours confirmed that. What was McCracken's downfall was the fact that due to circumstances not always within his control – the financial constraints that regularly required the selling on of budding talent being one – he was never able to harness that talent into one team for a period of time sufficient for them to achieve their potential in black and amber shirts.

McCracken wasn't the only departure of note during the close season of 1931. Matt 'Ginger' Bell had been a virtual ever-present in the Tigers' ranks since joining them in 1919. After the departure of Mick Gilhooley, Bell took over the captaincy and for nine years he led the Tigers by example. His leadership was exemplary; his versatility was almost on a par. Although the left-back spot was his without question, the occasional injury to City's goalkeeper during matches often required Bell to take over between the sticks; he was no mean performer in the art of goalkeeping. When, in January 1925, George Maddison was injured in the first half of City's 1-1 home draw against Wolves in the FA Cup, Bell had taken over for the entire second-half. For the replay Bell was selected in goal and did a sterling job, denying Wolves at one end whilst Paddy Mills sneaked the winner during extra-time at the other.

Bell's time at Hull produced over 400 League and Cup outings, plus one goal. It earned him a club record which remained until the outbreak of World War Two. It was no more than he deserved.

In appointing Mc-Cracken's successor, the Directors were seeking a man with experience of operating in the lower Leagues on a limited – some said non-existent – budget. Haydn Green was their choice, based primarily on his previous experience as assistant manager at Lincoln City and manager of Ebbw Vale in the extremely strong Southern League.

From the beginning Green demonstrated that he understood what was needed to compete and succeed in the Northern Section. He brought in seasoned, hardened pros such as ex-England internationals Jack Hill and Russell Wainscoat to bolster defence and attack; in addition to supplementing the existing old heads in City's squad, they also complemented the legacy of youthful talent that McCracken had left.

Early results during Green's first season in charge (1931/32) offered promise. Three wins in the first three games had City joint top with Gateshead. Two wins from the next ten games brought the task facing Green into much sharper focus: it would be a season of rebuilding and reshaping tactics as well as personnel. So it proved as the season unfolded, and whilst City's fixtures again provided plenty of goals – a 6-3 win at Rochdale, a 4-4 draw with Stockport and 4-1 wins over Walsall, Darlington, Doncaster, New Brighton and Lincoln – there were was never much chance of them attaining top spot and keeping it. The season should have been a useful learning curve for Green, and a final position of 8th not a bad foundation for him to build on for the future. Whether he had learnt from the experience would be closely monitored by the occupants of terrace and boardroom alike at Anlaby Road.

Having lost Dally Duncan to Derby County, Green brought in Cliff Sargeant as his replacement; it would prove a wise buy. To strengthen the half-back line he brought in a little known player from Grimsby by the name of Tom Gardner. Strong in the tackle and accurate in his distribution,

Gardner's football armoury had the added bonus of a substantial throw-in for the forwards to feed off. If he was little known when he arrived, his name was on everyone's lips, and in all of the scouts' notebooks 12 months later. However, Green's most inspired acquisition, in preparation for the 1932/33 campaign, was the signing of Bill McNaughton.

Like many of Green's signings, McNaughton was mature in years and experienced in the ways of League football. In McNaughton's case, he also had a stack of goals to support his credentials as a proven goalscorer. Green intended pairing him up front with Russell Wainscoat in the hope that if they clicked he would have a powerful strike force. They clicked.

Defeats at Walsall and Wrexham in the first two months of the 1932/33 season did not worry Green unduly. Sandwiched in between them was a string of victories, and by the time City lost for the third time in the season, it was well into October. Wainscoat and McNaughton were regular names on City's scoresheet and they were fifth in the table and two points off the leaders; by the end of October they were in second place behind Chester. By the time City suffered their fourth defeat of the season – on 1st February 1933 away to Darlington – another 13 games had passed and City were still in second place behind Chester. Three days later a 6-1 win over Doncaster Rovers took them to the top of the table, one point ahead of Chester.

Their position in the table was due to a combination of factors. A solid defence of Maddison, Goldsmith and Woodhead had come together at the beginning of October and remained unchanged throughout the winter – in fact it remained unchanged for the rest of the season. The half-backs gave solid support both in defence and attack and whilst goals were coming from all areas of the forward line, it was the contributions of Wainscoat and McNaughton that caught the eye.

Whilst McNaughton was taking the lead on the goalscoring front, Wainscoat did not disappoint in that department and besides, his role within the team was as much creator as finisher. Although Jack Hill was the captain, Wainscoat was the General, marshalling the troops to expose the weaknesses he'd identified in the opposition's defensive line and prompting half-backs and wingers to take full advantage; if, in the process, he managed to get his name on the scoresheet it was considered a bonus.

Having scaled the Northern section mountain in the early days of February, defeat away to Barnsley on the eighteenth of the month dropped them down to second.

However, by the end of the month they had regained their place at the summit and retained it for much of March and halfway into April, thanks in no small measure to a 2-0 home win over Chester. A 2-0 loss to Tranmere on Good Friday (14th April) allowed Chester to leapfrog City into top spot, but by Easter Monday the places were reversed and as the month end approached the points gap between City and the chasing duo of Chester and Wrexham showed a little more daylight. The finishing line was in sight, and it was reached on 1st May 1933 when promotion and the championship were wrapped up in the 2-1 home win against York City: two Bill McNaughton goals crowning a great season for both club and player.

Programme from the game against York City on 1st May 1933 when City claimed the Div 3(N) championship

With one game left the Tigers could relax. In fact they relaxed a little too much, suffering a 3-2 reverse at second from bottom Rochdale. The result was of no consequence, but again, McNaughton was responsible for both of City's goals; it took his tally to 41 in the League out of a Tiger total of 100. No City player before him had scored so heavily for the club in a single season and no City player since has come anywhere near to matching his achievement.

Although Green had entered his name in the club's history book as the first manager to win either promotion or a championship, his task was far from over. The team that had won promotion was heavy on experience but more importantly, age; if the club was to progress further Green would need players, patience and a loosening of the purse strings.

Bill McNaughton's 41 goals in the 1932/33 season set a new club record that still remains unbeaten

history so Green was aware that life would get no easier in the higher division. New players were brought in, but they were very much on the fringe of the first team and for much of that first season back in Division Two, Green relied heavily on the players who had won the Northern Section championship.

Season 1933/34 ill-ustrated how good that Northern Section team had been. With only minor changes they held their place in the higher Division without too much trouble at all. By the middle of March, with ten games left, they were in 15th place with a 12 point cushion between them and bottom team Lincoln City. By the end of the month the safety gap was still being maintained but Haydn Green had gone. At a board meeting on 20th March, Haydn Green tendered his resignation.

The latter was not really an option. In addition to the financial restrictions within which the club had been operating for many years, the recent acquisition of a piece of land to develop into a permanent home for the Tigers had placed an additional financial burden on their resources. City's Anlaby Road ground did not belong to them, they merely leased the land.

Mindful that the council were looking at various infrastructure proposals for the city that could jeopardise the feasibility of Anlaby Road, the directors had sought alternative accommodation. They had identified a piece of land no more than a couple of miles up the road from their present ground which they had subsequently bought and started to develop. It was one of the few far-sighted decisions the directors had taken for many a year, but in the short term it was proving to be a huge drain on their limited resources.

Patience had never been a commodity in abundant supply amongst those connected with Hull City thus far in their

Little was ever made public about the detail of that board meeting, but as the season had progressed it was apparent from many of his pre and post match comments the he was growing increasingly frustrated at the perceived lack of support he'd received in developing the team. What had probably brought matters to a head had been the recent sale of Tommy Gardner to Aston Villa for a fee of £4,5000. To the Directors it represented a substantial return on their initial investment, but to Green it was the loss of another young Tiger starlet. It was the last straw.

If there was surprise at the announcement of Green's departure, it was probably only over the timing. With nine games and seven weeks of the season left, Green's request for his immediate release implied that he either had another League club lined up or that his working relationship with the Board had reached such a low point it was impossible to carry on. Green did move on to another managerial position, but it was in the non-League arena with Guildford – hardly a career enhancing move, even if the Tigers were financially strapped.

Reading between the lines of the chairman's (Jim Barraclough) statement announcing Green's departure, there is evidence to suggest that the directors had become as unhappy with Green as he had with them. In accepting Green's resignation Barraclough referred "...to the successful connection the manager had had with the club and on behalf of the Board...expressed good wishes for his future". They were hardly words of fulsome praise for the club's first-ever manager to have achieved promotion ...with a Championship to boot.

As was the case when Green had been appointed some three years earlier, there was no shortage of applicants to fill the vacancy and this time the Tigers were a Second Division, rather than Northern Section, outfit. The unanimous choice of the Directors was Jack Hill, a seasoned ex-international footballer who Green had signed in November 1931, and who'd skippered the Tigers to the Northern Section championship of 1932/33. I wonder whether Green had any idea at the time of signing Hill that he was getting more than a captain, he was acquiring his successor.

The Directors' thinking behind the appointment of Jack Hill was that his experience as team captain would mean he'd already be well acquainted with the players and their strengths and weaknesses. Those weaknesses were painfully clear as Hill began his tenure by taking charge of the team from the touchline for the remaining four games of the season – all four were lost and amongst them was a humbling 7-0 defeat at Oldham Athletic. In the home game against Preston North End, on 21st April, attention was briefly diverted from the pitch to the terraces, however, when a poor performance by the referee incited the crowd to violence with repercussions in the form of ground closure at the start of the following season.

With deficiencies in City's playing squad clearly evident, Hill was allowed to spend some money during the Summer of 1934 in an effort to build up a squad of players that would not only be capable of holding its own in the division, but also of moving up a step. Hill cast his net wide for players: from Scotland to Southampton.
Included in their number were his replacements, both as centre-half and captain: they being Bill Tabram and Dave Wright respectively; the former cost a substantial fee and gave good value during his three year stint at Anlaby Road, whilst the latter lasted just a season.

Hill's first full season in charge (1934/35) could not have had a worse start. Their opening fixture was the long journey to Devon to face Plymouth Argyle, a replay of their opening game in that FA Cup run some four years previously. Like that game, this opening match had plenty of goals – ten in all – but the outcome was nowhere near as memorable.

With seven League debutants in the side the Tigers scored four goals, unfortunately Plymouth scored six. Three more defeats and a draw followed before the Tigers registered their first win of the campaign, a 4-0 thumping of West Ham. It set the pattern for the season, and although there were some memorable victories – 3-2 against Manchester United and 2-1 victories over both of the clubs eventually promoted, Brentford and Bolton Wanderers – there were far too many defeats for everyone's liking, one of which was the 5-1 defeat at home to Newcastle United in the FA Cup on 12 January 1935. For all of Hill's surgery to the team they improved their end of season position by just a couple of places, finishing 13th compared to 15th in the previous campaign.

At least Hill's acquisitions in the forward line had shown promise. Hutchison and Acquroff were largely responsible for most of City's goals during the season and helped soften the blow of the loss of their goalscoring machine of the championship season, Bill McNaughton. McNaughton had never really adapted to life in the higher division and by the end of October had returned to the Northern Section, joining Stockport County and rediscovering his knack of goalscoring in the process.

If Hill's first season as manager had proved something of a disappointment, the following season (1935/36) turned out to be an unmitigated disaster. Again, Hill's summer had been taken up with recruiting on a large scale. For the opening game of the season, therefore, it was a new look Hull City that took on Fulham at Anlaby Road. Not only were there five new faces in the side: Ken Cameron, Gordon Dreyer, Leo Dunne, Maxey Holmes and Bob Yorke, there were also eleven new shirts. For the first time in their history the club changed their strip from the traditional black and amber shirts with black shorts to a light blue shirt and white shorts. It would prove to be an ill-advised choice.

The Tigers drew 1-1 with Fulham and Ken Cameron marked his debut by scoring City's goal. However, from that promising start things deteriorated rapidly so by the time game three had been completed, on the 7th September, the Tigers were bottom of the table and that slot became their regular resting place for much of the season.

Two wins in the opening ten games had moved them up slightly to third from bottom by the middle of October, but by the end of the month they had returned from whence they came and were still there when the return fixture with Fulham was played on 28th December 1935. Of the 22 games played thus far in the League the Tigers had won just four, drawn five and conceded 56 goals in the process, whilst scoring less than half that number (25).

City's players enjoying pre-season training (1935/36), There was little to smile about at the end of the season, however, as they were relegated.

The second half of the season saw them fare no better, and for much of it they had to do without Jack Hill. With 1936 less than two weeks old the Tigers had cemented their position at the foot of the table and made an early exit from the FA Cup to boot. Five days after that FA Cup defeat away to West Bromwich Albion, Jack Hill announced his resignation. In an interview with the Hull Daily Mail, in which he confirmed his departure, Hill attributed the team's poor performance in the season thus far to "...a long chapter of mishaps and sickness among the players." He went on to state that although "...much worried by the position of the team in the League" he still believed that they "...will steer clear of relegation."

With City rooted at the bottom of the table, it is doubtful there were many fans who shared that optimism, and as the rest of the season was played out, they were proved right. They had to wait until 8th February to witness City's first win of 1936; by then the Tigers were well adrift from the safety zone. That victory in early February was one to savour for City fans, because between then and the end of the season in May, there was not another one to enjoy.

There are very few men in football who choose to abandon the safe waters of Division Two for the plughole of that same division, especially when the plug is only half inserted. That, however, was the choice of one man, made all the more imponderable by the fact that the team he was joining had just been thrashed 6-1 by the team he was leaving. The man in question was David Menzies, and he could hardly say he was unprepared for life at Anlaby Road; after all, he had been in residence there as the Tigers' manager some 15 years previously.

Since leaving the Tigers in 1921 Menzies had built a reputation for building decent teams at a diminutive cost. The club he was leaving, Doncaster Rovers, was living proof. The previous season they had been promoted as champions from the Northern Section and, at little cost to the club's bank account, were sitting comfortably in seventh place in Division Two having just recorded their biggest victory of the season thus far by putting six goals past the Tigers, with only Jimmy Nicol's goal registering a token protest.

Even after a 15 year gap Menzies still retained happy memories of the club which had given him his chance in football management.

It was that affection which stoked his desire to try and turn things around at a club who were drifting back into the Northern Section, laden with debts that could quite easily sink them without trace. Yes, the debts that had started to bubble to the surface shortly after Menzies had swapped one City (Hull) for another (Bradford) were still around and growing ever bigger.

Menzies had ten games left in the 1935/36 season to achieve the seemingly impossible: preserve the Tigers' Division Two status. It was impossible, and well before the season's end the Tigers' return to the Northern section of Division Three had been confirmed; a final record of:

P42 W5 D10 L27 F47 A111 Pts 20

was the worst end of season figures they'd produced in their history.

The task facing Menzies for the 1936/37 season was akin to making the proverbial silk purse from a sow's ear, and then having made that silk purse, he needed to fill it with gold. The Tigers were in debt to the tune of nearly £20,000 – a significant sum at the time. A lack of funds had brought the development of their new stadium on Boothferry Road to a virtual standstill, and money to spend on players was not available.

As he had done before, Menzies scoured football's basement to unearth some treasure. It looked as if he might have found it when the season kicked off on 29th August 1936. Reverting to their traditional black and amber stripes, a 3-1 victory away at Port Vale got the Tigers off to the winning start they desperately needed, with two of City's goals coming from one of Menzies's bargain buys, making his debut in the game, John Mayson.

By the time the Tigers had completed a 3-2 victory at home to Gateshead on 10th October, things were definitely looking up. They sat third in the Northern section table, three points behind the leading club (Chester) but with a game in hand. Equally promising was the fact that after nine games they remained unbeaten – no other team in the League could boast a similar start to the season, and no other team in the League had conceded fewer goals (six) than City in those opening fixtures. A tantalizing glimpse of a bright future lay on the horizon after that Gateshead game. Two days later (12th October) that vision was destroyed when David Menzies suffered a heart attack and died.

In trying circumstances life went on for Hull City. Not unsurprisingly, their unbeaten record went in the next game, losing 5-2 away to Mansfield on 17th October and in the closing months of 1936 the Tigers struggled to come to terms with the loss of Menzies after just 20 games of his second coming.

Whilst the directors looked for a replacement, the team managed to sustain a promotion challenge; given the circumstances it was a remarkable achievement. By the end of December they were lying second in the table, two points behind Chester; by the end of December they also had a new manager.

The Directors' choice to succeed David Menzies was Ernie Blackburn, who had managed Wrexham since January 1932. Blackburn was not a total stranger to Hull; during World War One he had served with one of the 'Hull Pals' battalions in France. When the war ended he began his professional career with Aston Villa, playing at the highest level within the Football League. In 1922 he was transferred to Bradford City and although his career was cut short by injury, there was time for him to play at right-back for Bradford in both the home and away fixtures against the Tigers during the 1922/23 season. Moving from the playing side to the dug-out side of the white line presented no problem to him, and during his time at Wrexham he'd acquired a strong reputation for shrewdness in judging a player and juggling the pennies; a fact not lost on City's directors.

Although Blackburn made a few alterations to the playing strength and tactics during the remainder of the season, too many defeats against fellow promotion contenders, and an inability to dominate lesser teams, in terms of standings in the table, proved to be City's undoing in the promotion race. By the end of the season they had dropped down to fifth, with a substantial points gap (14) between them and eventual champions, Stockport County. The season may have ended disappointingly but the prospects remained encouraging. With time to prepare and plan and with a full season within which to operate, both Directors and supporters had high hopes of Ernie Blackburn and his charges for the 1937/38 campaign.

By a strange quirk of footballing fate the fixture list pitched the Tigers at home to Blackburn's former club, Wrexham, in the opening game of that campaign. There was no room for sentiment however, with the Tigers overcoming the Welsh outfit 3-2. Two of Blackburn's new acquisitions also overcame any first-day fretting by sharing City's three goals between them: Jack Fryer netting twice and Hamilton McNeill scoring the other.

That pair, with support from their fellow forwards, regularly got their names on City's scoresheet as the season progressed through the autumn of 1937. Fryer and McNeill accounted for all of City's goals in the 4-0 win over Barrow on 6th September; this time with McNeill in the ascendancy, scoring a hat-trick. That game meant City were in fourth place, just a point behind joint leaders: Lincoln City, Rotherham United and Oldham Athletic.

Hamilton McNeil – who scored on his League debit against Wrexham on 28th August 1937.......

......Jim Blyth didn't miss a single League game during the 1937/38 season.

City next repeated that 4-0 scoreline in their last game in December. Darlington were the opponents and Fryer and Pears were the scorers with a brace apiece. The Tigers were still a point off the joint leaders, but whilst they had overtaken Lincoln and Oldham in the table, they still had Rotherham and now Tranmere Rovers ahead of them.

Having started the season with a home win over Wrexham, they started the New Year with an away win against the same team. It moved them up into second place and after an honourable defeat away to Huddersfield Town in the FA Cup they made their promotion intentions clear by thrashing Southport 10-1, their goals being shared between all the forwards that afternoon: Pears (3), Hubbard (2), Davies (2), McNeill (2) and Fryer. That result gave them joint leadership of the Division on points, with only goal average allowing Rotherham to keep their nose in front.

By Easter things still looked good. They'd seen off Rotherham's challenge and were tussling for supremacy at the top of the table with Tranmere, again it was only goal average giving Tranmere the edge. Two draws and a win from that Easter programme was not quite what City were looking for, but it didn't look too serious and with two games to go the Tigers had finally claimed top spot in their own right after a 3-1 home win over York City.

Their final two games were at home: first against Tranmere and then Crewe Alexandra. That Tranmere game was the big one: win that and they'd have one hand on the championship trophy. They didn't win. In a game that most commentators agreed was dominated by the Tigers, a combination of woodwork and inaccuracy kept the Tranmere goal intact, whilst at the other end Tranmere's Billy Eden took his chance and scored the only goal of the game. That was it. City's chance of glory, promotion and the championship had gone. When the season ended City had finished third and Tranmere took top spot and all that went with it.

Disappointed at missing out on promotion, Hull City almost disappeared during the summer of 1938. With virtually no income during the close season their financial problems almost buried them. Resignations from the Board of Directors, including Chairman Jim Barraclough, placed a heavy financial burden on the remaining directors. It was a burden the club's creditors were unwilling to tolerate and only skilful negotiation and pleading from those who remained, and the appointment of Alderman Shepherd as chairman prevented the closure of the club. As had happened in the past, the Tigers' survival to compete in the Football League came at the cost of selling part of the 'family silver' with some of their best talent moving on to other clubs.

Against the odds, the Tigers lined up with the rest at the start of the 1938/39 season. That they finished in seventh place may have been disappointing in some respects; but that they finished at all was considered a miracle, given the albatross placed around their necks by the abacus that constantly failed to count more income than expenditure. Even their all time record League victory – 11-1 at home to Carlisle United on 14th January 1939 – failed to lift the gloom over Anlaby Road.

Part of that gloom concerned the lack of progress on the development of the new stadium. Despite grants totalling nearly £10,000 to assist with the early costs of building the ground it was clear the Tigers were struggling to raise the additional funding required to meet their anticipated completion deadline of the summer of 1940. Aware of the club's difficulties, property developers tried to take advantage by bidding to buy the land from the Tigers' directors to progress their own plans for a major sports development on the site, which included provision for football and a variety of other sports.

The bid made to the Directors reflected little more than half of the land's value. To their credit, City's directors rejected the offer and despite their financial problems chose to press ahead with their own plans for the new stadium.

However, it was not just finances that soured the atmosphere of that 1938/39 season. As it wound its way from August to May football decreased in relevance as events elsewhere attracted attention. The conflict of 1914-18 was described as the war to end all wars. It failed. As the 1938/39 season ran its course there was another World War brewing. Many doubted there would be another season of League football. Within the city boundaries of Hull many suspected there might not be a Hull City.

There was another season of League football and Hull City lasted the pace. However, that 1939/40 League season lasted just two games.

Somewhat against the odds the Tigers kicked off the new season on Saturday 26th August 1939 with a 2-2 home draw against Lincoln. A week later (2nd September) they travelled to Southport and drew 1-1; in both games, new signing Richard Lowe scored. Within twenty-four hours of the Southport game concluding, Britain was at war with Germany.

This time, there was no repetition of the dithering that had marked the previous outbreak of hostilities between the two countries back in 1914. The imposition by the government of a ban on large numbers of people congregating in one place meant the Football League had no option but to abandon the season's programme of fixtures, with the results of those games already played being expunged from official records – quite annoying for Richard Lowe as he never played for the Tigers in any competitive fixture again.

Within a few weeks the ban was relaxed and permission granted for friendly matches to be arranged, provided that the number of spectators admitted to such games did not exceed 8,000 or half the ground's capacity. It allowed, therefore, the Football League to draw up plans to create a regional competition with teams split into eight geographical groups. The Tigers were allocated to the North East Regional League for the 1939/40 season along with ten other clubs.

The problem of getting a team together was one that troubled City just as much as any other club throughout the war. The League was keen to avoid excessive use of 'Guests' in matches, insisting that they be used "only in emergencies." Conditions were such that "emergencies" became the norm and as a result many unfamiliar faces were to be found in City's colours during the wartime campaigns.

Although City had a core of players who had been with the club before the war such as Bly, Cunliffe, Meens and Woodhead etc, it was not possible to field a full team of regulars for each game. As such many 'local amateurs' were given their chance and players from other clubs who were based in the area whilst on service with the armed forces were invited to play.

Their first season (1939/40) in the wartime league saw them finish a creditable seventh. The following season (1940/41) the structure of the league was amended and the Tigers competed in the North Regional League, which consisted of 36 clubs, a figure two short of the number of players City used to fulfil their fixtures. Only once that season did they field the same team for consecutive games.

Perhaps it was that constant chopping and changing that accounted for a final finish of 33rd, a finish decided not by points awarded for wins and draws, but by goal average. That being the case, heavy defeats against Middlesbrough (0-8), Grimsby (2-8) and Barnsley (0-5) did not help their cause.

For both of these seasons the Tigers continued at their Anlaby Road ground. It was a venue that would not be available for much longer, courtesy of the Luftwaffe as they pounded the "East coast town" – as Hull was referred to in radio broadcasts – mercilessly. City's ground was badly damaged and combined with the constant problems they faced in raising a team, as well as the financial problems that refused to go away, it was decided that the club would "close down" for the duration. The Tigers returned to the wartime competition in 1944, joining the Northern Section. The fixtures were split between a First Championship, which ran from August to December, and a Second Championship that occupied the months of March and April. Sandwiched in between was a qualifying competition for the Football League War Cup (North).

With City's Anlaby Road ground unfit for use due to damage inflicted on it by the Luftwaffe, and their 'new stadium' having temporarily been requisitioned by the military, the Tigers utilized Hull FC's ground (The Boulevard) to stage all but one of their home games that season – the exception being the game against Newcastle United on 11th November 1944, which was played at Bootham Crescent.

From a City supporter's perspective the season had little to offer. The team was, more often than not, unrecognizable due primarily to the fact that in all competitions they employed a total of 85 different players. Not unsurprisingly there was little cohesion and understanding amongst those in black and amber shirts, reflected in some horrible results that began in the first game of the season: an 8-1 defeat at home to Doncaster Rovers. Scorelines of 8-2, 7-1, 7-0, 6-3, 6-2 and 6-1 littered City's fixtures that season, and every one of them went against the Tigers.

The club was clearly struggling, and it came as no surprise when the Tigers elected not to participate in the following season (1945/46). Their obvious problems on the field were merely a reflection of the financial troubles that still afflicted them off it. Abstaining from that season was a signal to many that the sun was setting on Hull City, and that the end was in sight for the club. In hindsight it was merely the dawning of a new era.

Despite having been bomb damaged during 1940/41, The Boulevard (the home of Hull F.C.) was still capable of staging City's fixtures during the 1944/45 season.

## CHAPTER 5

A FALSE DAWN?

lthough the Wartime competition suggested the dying throes of Hull City football club, behind the scenes of this apparent sporting tragedy much activity was taking place to ensure the Tigers' future.

Hull City's new Board of Directors at the start of the 1946/47 season
Back Row: F.R. Metcalf, J. Needler, W.R. Smith, R. Buttery, G.H. Needler;
Front Row: K. Percival (President), H. Needler (Chairman), Major FC Buckley (Secretary-manager).

For some time a local builder by the name of Harold Needler had held the ambition to bring First Division (now known as the Premiership) football to the city of Hull. In pursuing this dream, his initial idea of creating a new team based at a new sporting complex on the northern outskirts of the city was thwarted by the Football League's refusal to grant membership of this proposed new team to their League.

Undeterred, Needler, together with a number of like-minded business men, resolved to achieve his aims by acquiring Hull City and completing the Tigers' new stadium project on Boothferry Road. In a series of meetings between the existing Directors of Hull City, and those looking to acquire the same status, a deal was finally struck in December 1945 which saw Harold Needler assume ownership of the club. Taking the position of Chairman, Needler invited the then Sheriff of Hull, Kenneth Percival, to become President of the club. Joining both on the board were, amongst others, Harold Needler's brothers, John and George, plus Dick Smith who had been instrumental in negotiating the purchase.

Rather than bearing the full financial burden of running Hull City, the Directors made an appeal to the public of Hull to buy shares in the club, at five shillings (25p) each, with a view to raising £50,000. Within a month the sum raised had reached £60,000. It was a clear indication that the supporters of Hull City were right behind Needler and his fellow Directors. With a sound financial foundation on which to build, the Directors set about building a team and completing the new stadium.

Needler and his brothers put their experience as builders to good use to ensure that the new ground – now referred to as Boothferry Park – would be ready for the start of the Football League in August 1946.

The aftermath of World War Two meant many commodities, especially building materials, were in short supply. Consequently the new club was only granted permission to build one complete stand – the West Stand – and to cover the central section of the North Stand; the rest of the ground remaining as open terracing. Even this restricted amount of building work was subjected to stringent cost restrictions by the Government, and full use had to be made of the building materials already in place on the site.

Many of the existing structures, left over from the land's former use as a golf club and then a military depot, were carefully dismantled and re-used, wherever possible, to provide the new structures and facilities for spectators. Seating in the West Stand was nothing more than benches and it would be some years before Boothferry Park would compare with the futuristic plans outlined by the new Board of Directors. They envisaged a stadium with a capacity approaching 80,000 with subways to car parks and a dedicated railway service

It was not only the accommodation that required substantial work to prepare it for the new season, but also the pitch. Boothferry Park's wartime use as a tank building and storage depot had left the ground in a sorry state, and it fell to an army of volunteers – responding to an appeal by the Directors – to carry out a variety of tasks such as weeding, painting and labouring to ensure that City's first home game would go ahead; indeed that 'army' was still working on the pitch just hours before it made its debut.

That debut arrived on 31st August 1946 with a local derby, of sorts, against Lincoln City. In the souvenir programme issued for the game, the chairman opened his notes with the words: "Saturday, 31st August, 1946, will always be a Red Letter day in my life as it is the culmination of an idea which originated in my mind some years ago." It was a sentiment that would have been shared by many in the crowd of 25,586.

A new ground and a new Board of Directors, however, were not the only changes that signalled the emergence of a new Hull City. The directors' original intention was to have a completely new kit, consisting of orange shirts, with the city's three crown crest, white shorts and orange and blue socks. Problems in obtaining the necessary materials meant them having to settle for a strip similar to that of some eleven years previously (light blue shirts and white shorts). It was a strip that did not receive universal approval and by the time the following season (1947/48) commenced, tradition had won the day and amber and black became the Tigers' hallmark colours, although a compromise of sorts was reached with the stripes of old being replaced by a plain amber shirt with black trim and black shorts.

In addition to the aforementioned 'innovations' the club also appointed a new secretary-manager, Major Frank Buckley, who'd had a distinguished career in the game as a player and as manager – notably with Wolves. It was Wolves to whom Harold Needler had initially turned in seeking a manager before the start of the 1946/47 season, his target being 29-year old Stan Cullis. His performances for Wolves and England, in addition to his overall approach to the game, suggested he was ideal management material. It was Buckley who acted as the go-between and when Harold Needler spoke to Cullis he made him an attractive offer: a salary far in excess of a player's maximum wage, and a luxury house as well.

Cullis was tempted; he even went so far as to inform the Wolves' Directors that he would be retiring from playing. Their chairman, Joe Baker, persuaded him to stay at Molineux however – the promise of an assistant-manager's job when he retired helped, and Cullis still wanted to win some major honours in the game as a player. He changed his mind again and stayed with Wolves. Buckley's new role, therefore, leant more towards the managerial than the secretarial.

That opening game against Lincoln City was not the scintillating soccer exhibition which would have put the seal on such a momentous occasion. It was a dour affair, played in conditions more akin to October than August and the lack of fluency shown by both teams was perhaps due to the fact that of the 22 players on the field, 17 were making their League debut, eight of them for the Tigers.

Lincoln took the honours in the first half, but in the second the Tigers came back and had the opportunity to take both points when City's centre-forward, Herbert Knott, managed to put the ball into the Lincoln net. Any joy was short-lived however, as the referee indicated a foul had been committed in the process.

Under those circumstances, a 0-0 scoreline came as no surprise. Neither did the news that the Tigers' goalkeeper, Billy Bly, was injured during the game; it would prove to be a common occurrence throughout Billy's career with the Tigers. It might have restricted his outings for the club, but it had no impact on the standard of performances he produced during his Boothferry Park years.

It was not until the 12th October that the home supporters were able to cheer a victory at their new ground and the season had the feel of transition about it, demonstrated by the fact that during its course Major Buckley used 43 players. In that context, a mid-table position was a respectable outcome and the new Board of Directors could draw comfort from other areas when analysing their first season's performance.

Total revenue for the season, consisting only of gate receipts, transfer fees, car park receipts and programme sales, amounted to just under £59,000 – a figure some five times greater than in the last full season of peacetime football (1938/39). A net profit of £6,686 8s 1d was made on the season of which £916 13s 4d was offered to shareholders as a dividend (equating to roughly 2d a share). At the Annual General Meeting this offer was unanimously rejected by the shareholders, who voted instead to plough the money back into the club.

That first season also placed a heavy demand on the Boothferry Park pitch. The playing area had not been treated kindly during the war: the parking of tanks is not the ideal use for a football pitch. That damage was accentuated by the severe winter of 1947 – one of the worst on record. It meant that Boothferry Park was often 'off limits.' From the beginning of January through to the beginning of March, only one City fixture in the League was played on home soil. As Andy Davidson – the club's record appearance holder – remembers from his first day at Boothferry Park, it was "...a pitch that looked like a mud heap." It meant that City's first season after the war was the longest ever in their history: it began with a home fixture in August 1946 and ended with a home fixture in June 1947. Much of the ensuing close season was used to dig up the pitch – the labour force consisted essentially of the ground staff (including the apprentices) – and deep drains were laid.

The following season (1947/48) saw an improvement in the pitch as well as progress on it by the team. After 18 matches the Tigers headed the table on goal average and remained involved in promotion issues until Easter – despite only winning twice in 11 games during February and March – before finally ending the season in fifth place, still a marked improvement on the previous season's effort. Buckley was not so profligate in his use of players this time – he used only 35 – but whilst the quantity had dropped, there was an increase in quality, demonstrated by one of his new signings, Norman Moore, who displayed early promise as a prolific goalscorer – his 24 League outings bringing a return of thirteen goals.

In hindsight, however, overshadowing all of those events was a signing, not of Buckley's making, which would have a major impact on both club and city. It involved an ex-England international whose career had blossomed on either side of the war, a man who brought national recognition to the Tigers and, in the opinion of many Hull City supporters, one of the club's greatest players. He was Raich Carter.

Having received similar offers from Leeds Utd and Notts County to take up an assistant manager's role, there was some surprise when Carter chose the Tigers. Carter's logic for accepting the post was twofold: he believed he could learn from the vastly experienced Major Buckley and that Buckley's advancing years offered him a quicker route to management. As it turned out, his thinking was spot on. Within days of his arrival Buckley, obviously unhappy at the way the Directors had acted, resigned. Carter would have to learn his new job quickly and without the benefit of Buckley's experience and guidance. One got the impression that Carter was undaunted by the prospect.

Carter's Tiger debut was in the home game against York City on 3rd April 1948. A disastrous Easter had seen City slip out of the promotion race and it would have come as no surprise if attendances at Boothferry Park for the remainder of the season had taken a nosedive. It did not happen; in fact the reverse was very much the case. By the time Raich Carter stepped on to the Boothferry Park pitch to commence his City career, a new stadium record crowd (32,466) was in attendance; it helped boost the average attendance for the season to 24,642, setting a new club record.

Raich recalled the occasion in his book entitled 'Footballer's Progress': "…I led my new team-mates out on to the field at Boothferry Park and was greeted by a terrific roar of welcome that was a foretaste of the life that lay before me in Hull." He was right; over the next few years the Boothferry Roar would be a regular feature of City's home games and attendance records would regularly crumble.

With Carter's arrival came expectation; there was a buzz in the city that big things were about to happen at Hull City. Carter was aware of it and used the remainder of the 1947/48 season and the close season to analyse the merits of the squad he'd inherited and plan to fill any gaps he identified. He had done his job well and his first full season in charge saw the Tigers get off to a record breaking start, and set further records as the season progressed.

Victory against Accrington Stanley on 28th September 1948 gave City their ninth straight League win at the start of the 1948/49 season, setting a new Football League record.

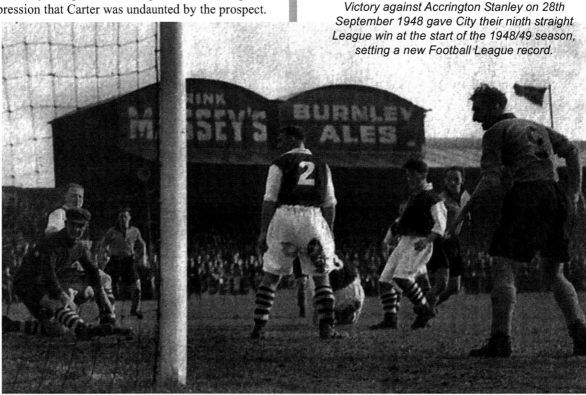

They were unbeaten in their first eleven League matches – victory in each of the first nine set a new League record that stood for twelve years until beaten by Tottenham Hotspur in 1960 – and new attendance records were set in each of the first three home fixtures. From early September until Christmas Day, the race for the Northern Section championship was dominated by two teams: Rotherham United and the Tigers. For all of that time Rotherham held pole position with the Tigers tucked in behind, the points gap never rising above five, and the Tigers with games in hand.

Let Battle Commence – Opposing captains, Jack Shaw (Rotherham Utd) and Raich Carter (Hull City) exchange festive greetings before the start of the 1948 Christmas Day top of the table clash at Boothferry Park . City won 3-2

He did not spurn it and from five yards put the ball firmly into the Rotherham net with their keeper, Bolton, well beaten. The goal gave City added confidence in their play and they were unfortunate to reach half-time with nothing further to show for their growing supremacy.

At the start of the second half, Rotherham took the game to the Tigers in search of an equalizer, but City's defence held firm and on the hour mark they increased their lead when Harrison set off on a long run

When the two teams first met that season, it was at Boothferry Park on Christmas Day 1948. Rotherham were still top with a five points advantage. It was match of the day, not just in the Northern Section, but the entire Football League, an impression strengthened by the fact that it produced the highest attendance (49,655) of the day in all four Divisions; in actual fact the game had been made all ticket and the ticket sales reported to the Football League were recorded as 54,652, a figure that the League's records still regard as the official attendance. Whatever happened to the missing 5,000?

Wherever they were, they missed a belter of a game. The early exchanges were even, but City opened the scoring in the 19th minute when a neat interchange between Harrison and Jensen provided a scoring opportunity for Willie Buchan.

down the wing. He put in a fine cross to Carter who played the ball on to the unmarked Bloxham and his shot found the net before Rotherham's keeper had chance to react. Three minutes later the Tigers moved further ahead when a poor clearance from Rotherham's left-back, Radford, was picked up by Carter. He played a tantalising ball into the goalmouth which Buchan bundled into the net. Rotherham protested strongly that Buchan had fouled their keeper in the process but the Referee waved their protests aside and the Tigers were very much in the driving seat.

Five minutes from the end Rotherham reduced the deficit when Lowder took full advantage of a defensive slip by City's Meens and Taylor, his low shot beating a despairing dive from Billy Bly. With a minute left the score margin narrowed even more, when Shaw finished off good work from Guest and Ardon. The final score of 3-2 in City's favour did no justice to the dominance they had enjoyed over the Division's leaders for much of the game.

The two teams met again 24 hours later at Millmoor. This time it was a much tighter affair with both defences dominating a game that finished goalless in front of a crowd less than half that which had watched the Boothferry Park encounter. From being five points adrift on Christmas Eve the Tigers had reduced the deficit to three and served notice on Rotherham that they would not have things all their own way in the quest for promotion and the championship.

January 1949 saw both teams involved in League and Cup; by the end of the month Rotherham's interest in the latter had ended, whilst the Tigers maintained their challenge on both fronts. At the beginning of February, Rotherham United were still top with City two points behind in second. Results-wise, February was a bad month for the Tigers; they lost twice within the space of a week. The first defeat came at Bradford City (2-4) on 19th February – it turned out to be the Tigers only defeat on their League travels that season. A week later they lost in the FA Cup, their fine run ended at the quarter final stage as a result of a narrow 1-0 defeat at home to Manchester United in front of a new club record home attendance of 55,019 – a record that still stands.

At the beginning of March the League positions remained unchanged, but Rotherham had extended their lead to four points, although the Tigers had four games in hand. Out of the Cup, City were now able to concentrate on the League and set about catching Rotherham with a vengeance. Playing six games during March, and undefeated in all of them, they overtook the South Yorkshire outfit and opened up a two point gap, with two games still in hand

over their rivals. It was all over by the end of April. The Tigers finished the month with a 6-1 demolition of Stockport County, whilst Rotherham could only draw 1-1 at home to Carlisle.

With two games left, it meant the Tigers were promoted as champions of the Northern section. They had been champions before (back in 1932/33) but that previous experience fell somewhat short when compared to the class of 1948/49. Granted, Haydn Green's boys had scored more goals and remained unbeaten at home during their season of triumph, but in every other aspect – points gained, wins, draws, defeats and goals conceded – Carter's Tigers took the honours.

Programme for City's home game against Stockport County on 30th April 1949. A 6-1 victory for the Tigers saw them promoted from Division Three (North) as champions

It wasn't just on the pitch that the post-war City held sway either. For the first time in their history the Tigers played to five figure gates for every single League and Cup encounter of that campaign;

A Funny Old Game – Hull City lost only once on their League travels during the 1948/49 season: Bradford City beat them 4-1 on 19th Feb 1949. The Tigers' team that day was:
Back Row: J. Taylor, T. Berry, W. Bly, V. Jensen, H. Meens, K. White; Front Row: K. Harrison, H. Carter, W. Price, W. Buchan, A. Mellor. At the end of the season, City topped the Div. 3(N) table, whilst Bradford City finished bottom.

for the first time in their history more than a million people passed through the turnstiles to watch Hull City home and away. Whatever the deprivations that still remained within the city, following the end of World War Two, people still found the funds to follow the Tigers' fortunes.

With an attack that had more than proved its worth in winning the championship, it was in defensive areas that Carter tweaked his squad for the new season, bringing in Gerrie Bowler from Portsmouth. The mass of support that had helped carry the club to arguably their best season thus far in their history returned in greater numbers for the 1949/50 season. An opening day crowd of over 42,000 attended Boothferry Park for City's first game in Division Two; a 3-2 victory over Bury saw them depart anticipating another successful crusade towards the holy grail of Division One.

The reality check on that dream, however, was just around the corner: two days later the Tigers' were beaten 4-2 away to Blackburn Rovers. Similar reverses were suffered as the season unfolded. A 6-2 defeat at Sheffield Wednesday, a 5-0 troun-cing at Southampton and a 4-0 defeat against Sheffield United at fortress Boothferry brought

At a cost of £20,000, Don Revie's arrival from Leicester City set a new transfer record for the Tigers in November 1949.

Programme for the Tottenham Hotspur vs Hull City game on Friday 7th April 1950. The game was watched by 66,889 spectators: the highest ever attendance for a League match involving the Tigers.

home to City's supporters that life in Division Two would be no fast-track to Division One.

Initially their challenge was strong. Despite the early setbacks at Blackburn and Sheffield Wednesday, the Tigers had climbed up to second place in the table behind a Tottenham Hotspur side starting to edge away from the rest. No expense was spared to maintain City's position: a club record transfer fee of £20,000 was paid to acquire the services of a talented young footballer from Leicester City by the name of Don Revie. Seen as the potential successor to Carter on the playing field, Revie quickly settled in and for the remainder of 1949 the Tigers held second place for much of the time on the strength of 14 wins from 24 games.

From January 1950, however, they struggled to keep up with the hot pace set by Spurs. As the second half of the season progressed the Tigers' challenge faded, not helped by the transfer of Norman Moore to Blackburn Rovers on Transfer deadline day in March. Finishing the season in seventh place, they were left with the small consolations that the attendance for their home game against Sheffield Wednesday (50,103) set a new League attendance record for Boothferry Park and that they were the only club to avoid defeat, both home and away, against eventual Divisional champions, Tottenham Hotspur – the Easter holiday fixtures between the two sides had seen a 0-0 draw at White Hart Lane in front of a crowd of 66,889 – the largest ever League attendance for a game involving the Tigers – and a 1-0 victory at Boothferry Park.

To the neutral observer, an end of season final placing of seventh would be regarded as an excellent outcome for City's first season in a higher grade of football, but within the confines of Boothferry Park there was no such satisfaction. A second consecutive promotion had been expected, at least by those on the terraces, and its failure to materialise put something of a dampener on the season.

Having lost his main source of goals (Norman Moore), Carter went north of the border during the close season and signed South African born Alf Ackerman, from Clyde. His impact was immediate, scoring twice in the 3-3 draw at West Ham which opened the Tigers' 1950/51 campaign; Carter scored City's third. Both players were on the mark again in the next game, another 3-3 draw, this time at home to Barnsley. In the opening 11 games of the season the Tigers never failed to score, amassing 25 goals but only a disappointing 13 points. The early loss, through injury, of goalkeeper Billy Bly plus a season-long struggle to find a settled defensive and midfield blend meant that the Tigers never threatened to affect the promotion race.

Although it was defensive matters that seemed to be causing the most trouble, Carter's first mid-season move into the transfer market was to strengthen his forward line again, returning to Scotland to acquire the services of Syd Gerrie from Dundee. It wasn't until January 1951 that he made a move to shore up his defence, but when he did, he set a new transfer record for the Tigers when signing ex-England international, Neil Franklin, from Stoke City for £22,500.

January also had a major significance as far as off the field matters were concerned, as the FA Cup Third Round tie at home to Everton, on 6th January 1951, provided the setting for the opening of the club's new railway platform. It meant that the Tigers were the only club in the League with a direct rail link from city centre to stadium terrace. In tandem with that work was the development of the eastern terrace: it was covered and offered accommodation to some 15,000 spectators. It was not on the grand scale that the directors had originally envisaged, but it was, nevertheless, a clear sign that they still had grand designs for Hull City.

On the field the season comprised 16 League victories, evenly spread either side of the New Year, 15 defeats and 11 draws. It meant an end of season placing of 10th, and although a total of 74 goals were scored (including one own goal), they were shared amongst just six City players, the most frugal distribution of all 92 League clubs that season.

Overall it was another frustrating outcome for those who occupied either terrace or boardroom. Whilst the latter would have been pleased to see the average home attendance for the season reach just short of 32,000, they would be well aware that any further delay in achieving success would merely result in dwindling support. The excitement and euphoria generated by the new stadium and promotion had not proved to be the catalyst for further glories. Having been starved of success for so long, the appetite of all had been whetted by the late 40s. When the main course arrived, in the shape of the opening years of the 50s, it proved to be somewhat disappointing.

That disappointment intensified dramatically as the 1951/52 season got under way. Before the season was half a dozen games old, Raich Carter announced his resignation on 5th September 1951. "The reason I have resigned" he explained, "is not because of interference in team selection matters, as I have been given full responsibility for those throughout, but it is because of disagreement on matters of a general nature in the conduct of the club's affairs."

Raich Carter announces his resignation as Hull City's manager on 5th September 1951. Three months later he had been persuaded to return to the club on a playing basis only.

Having already lost the previous season's leading goalscorer, Alf Ackerman, to Norwich City, the departure of Carter was an extremely bitter blow. Within weeks of his departure the quality and morale of the squad was further depleted by the sale of his protégé, Don Revie, to Manchester City in an exchange deal that saw Ernie Phillips move in the opposite direction. In total the transfer was valued at £25,000 with Phillips accounting for £13,000 of that sum. In purely cash terms there was a substantial deficit on the sale; from a playing perspective the loss was even greater. Such action gave sustenance to the seeds of doubt already sown in the minds of some supporters' minds regarding the capabilities of Harold Needler and his colleagues.

That doubt blossomed as the last months of 1951 were endured. Whilst Carter kept himself fit by training at the Boulevard, team selection and day to day management of the club fell to the Directors, with contributions from various members of the coaching staff. Not unsurprisingly the team suffered. By the beginning of December, City had won only twice in the 15 games since Carter's departure. As a consequence their League position was becoming perilous; only Blackburn Rovers were below them in the table. Something had to be done; thankfully it was.

After delicate negotiations that required some manoeuvring from both parties, agreement was reached in early December for Carter to return to Boothferry Park in a purely playing capacity. It had an immediate effect: for the first time in nearly three months Tigers' fans had a League victory – 2-0 at home to Doncaster on 8th December – to savour. With Carter back in the team, their fortunes revived dramatically. Victories rather than defeats became the norm, and a 2-0 win at Old Trafford, against Manchester United in the FA Cup – who would finish the season as champions of Division One – provided brief but glorious respite from the grind of the League as the Tigers fought to get themselves away from the relegation zone. Nothing startling when compared with what had gone on in recent years, but much better than appeared likely at the halfway point of the season.

Contributing substantially towards that 'mini revival' were the fourteen goals from Syd Gerrie, and eight from Raich Carter. Despite their hard work, however, by the time City's last game of the season arrived – away to Doncaster on 26th April 1952 – their Second Division status was by no means secured. One of six clubs capable of filling the two relegation spots, ideally they needed a win to be safe, although a point might be enough if results elsewhere went their way. Thankfully, the win was achieved with Raich Carter scoring the only goal of the game; it was his parting gift to the supporters of Hull City. Shortly after the season ended he announced he'd played his last game for the Tigers.

But even at the age of 38 there was still some football left in him, as frequent trips across the Irish Sea and an Irish FA Cup winner's medal with Cork Athletic in 1953 confirmed.

Since Carter's resignation as manager in September 1951, the Directors and coaching staff had selected the team each week. An end of season finish of 18th place suggested they were perhaps not best suited to the task. A new managerial appointment was needed, sooner rather than later, if the Tigers were to have any chance of progressing. That new appointment came in June 1952 when Bob Jackson, who had taken Portsmouth to the League championship in 1949 and 1950, was offered and accepted the position of manager.

Despite a heady start to the new season (1952/53), which saw the Tigers joint top of the division at the end of August, Jackson's first season in charge was neither definitive nor distinguished in the annals of Hull City. A run of seven consecutive defeats throughout October and November saw the Tigers plummet down the division towards the relegation zone again. A lack of goals from City's forwards, together with a leaky defence, gave the Tigers a hard season. Syd Gerrie's output was only half that of the previous season and he lacked support in attack, with only Ken Horton managing to reach double figures. A repetition of the previous season's final placing (18th) was all Jackson had to show for his efforts.

His cause was not helped by injuries to key players, with the services of such experienced stars as Neil Franklin and Alan Mellor being denied him. Franklin's season was over before September was out, requiring a second knee operation within 12 months, whilst persistent cartilage trouble brought Mellor's playing career to an end. Even Jackson's philosophy of giving youth its chance was hampered by the injury jinx. One such player was Andy Davidson. Making his debut in September 1952, his season was finished by February (1953) when he broke his leg. For Davidson, broken limbs would be a hazard of his profession but it was a testimony to his resolve as much as to his recuperative powers that he eventually went on to make 579 League and Cup appearances for the Tigers, setting a record that still stands today, and is unlikely ever to be beaten.

Off the field, the development of Boothferry Park continued apace. In November 1952 the club was granted approval for the installation of floodlights. Hull City were amongst the pioneers as regards floodlit football. Boothferry Park's first set was installed by January 1953, and was christened with a game against Dundee on 19th January 1953; it was a game watched by a crowd of 31,702 spectators who saw the visitors win 4-1.

City played a number of games under floodlights – all friendlies; it would be another three years before the Football League sanctioned the use of floodlights for league fixtures.

For the first time since they returned to the post-war Second Division, the Tigers were able to point to a better playing record than the previous season, finishing the 1953/54 season in 15th place, three places higher than in the previous campaign. Whilst the number of victories in the League rose by two to 16, the defeats remained unchanged at 20, merely strengthening the im-

(Above) Plymouth's goalkeeper, Bill Shortt, just beats City's Syd Gerrie to the ball in the game at Home Park on 14th March 1953, which the Tigers won 2-1.

(Below) F.A.Cup February 1954: City's keeper, Billy Bly, blocks a shot from Tottenham's Walters as Viggo Jensen (Hull City) and Les Bennett (Tottenham) watch on.

Time, however, was an unaffordable luxury for Jackson as he discovered in March 1955. By that time the Tigers' season was developing into their worst since the war. Despite having their defence strengthened by the return of a fully fit Neil Franklin, much of the season was again spent hovering around the relegation zone. The trouble lay up front, rather than at the back as they suffered badly from a lack of firepower in front of goal. Even the acquisition of ex-England striker, Wilf Mannion, failed to bring any relief. In nearly 50% of their League games that season they failed to register a goal.

pression amongst supporters that inconsistency was the only consistent aspect of the Tigers. The number of goals scored increased and that was due primarily to the return of a former goalscoring star Alf Ackerman who added 19 in League and Cup, including four in the 8-0 annihilation of Oldham Athletic at Boothferry Park.

Whilst the League offered little but frustration throughout the season, at least a lengthy FA Cup run – that finally ended in a fifth round replay defeat away to Tottenham Hotspur – did something to maintain interest and boost attendance figures which had dropped by more than a third on those achieved only five years previously. Jackson persisted with his policy of giving extended runs to young players and whilst they undoubtedly benefited from it, such an option always requires time before any benefits accrue.

The lack of success on the field was having a detrimental effect on the club as a whole. Attendances were averaging below 20,000 and if the Tigers were going anywhere, then a return to Division Three (North) looked the best bet. If that state of affairs wasn't bad enough, Jackson allowed his then leading goalscorer, Alf Ackerman, plus right-winger Ken Harrison to depart for a joint fee of just over £6,000 to fellow relegation candidates, Derby County. The news was received badly by City supporters and the directors appeared equally unimpressed.

On 17th March – just days after the departure of Ackerman and Harrison – Jackson was gone as well, the directors announcing that he'd been given "leave of absence" with former Birmingham City manager, Bob Brocklebank, appointed to take his place.

Jackson's response to the news was relaxed to say the least. When asked to comment on the directors' announcement he smiled and replied: "I have nothing to say. According to the board I am on leave of absence, but my contract does not expire until June 30th 1957." When asked about his immediate plans, his response was even more languid: "I am just clearing up my things and having a comfortable smoke." If Jackson gave the impression of being unconcerned about his dismissal, it was probably due to the fact

Neil Franklin welcomes City's new signing, Wilf Mannion to the club.

that he knew he had employment law on his side. To confirm it, he had quickly instigated a claim against the club for unfair dismissal that dragged on for many months, and only a settlement between the two parties, hours before the court case began, avoided some embarrassing publicity for Hull City and their directors.

With 11 games left in the season, Brocklebank's immediate priority was to secure the Tigers Second Division status. Although the club dropped three places in the table during that time, a final resting place of 19th was the right side of the trapdoor, and a six-point breathing space between themselves and the relegated teams – Ipswich and Derby – meant City's last fixture of the season – away to Derby County – could be 'enjoyed' without the added pressure of relegation resting on the result.

It was the same for both teams: With Derby already relegated, the fact that they beat the Tigers 3-0 was of little significance, and the fact that their goals were scored by the most recent of ex-Tigers, Ackerman (2) and Harrison, merely provided one of those little ironies in football that make the game so interesting. Imagine, however, what the reaction would have been if that result had sent City down. Would Bob Jackson have been so languid? I suspect not; he would probably have gone into hiding!

Although the Tigers had comfortably avoided relegation, they did not have a long wait before the dreaded drop occurred; it came in the following season (1955/56). Luck was against them from the start of that campaign. An injury to Dennis Durham in the first half of the campaign's opening game – against Leicester City on 20th August 1955 – meant them playing with 10 men for much of the match, eventually losing 4-2. That defeat, rapidly followed by others against Lincoln City and Liverpool put the Tigers 22nd in the table – bottom. Victory in the return fixture with Lincoln at the end of the month temporarily lifted them off the bottom of the table, but they soon returned

they stayed there for much of the season. More importantly, that's were they were come the end of the season. Even the acquisition of forwards of the calibre of Bill Bradbury, Doug Clarke and ex-England international Stan Mortensen, were insufficient to overcome the inadequacies elsewhere in the team.

Unhappiness with events on the field were clearly signalled off it by the fact the average home attendance for the season set a new low for Boothferry Park: 15,419. In what seemed to be their darkest season for many a year, there were a couple of small chinks of light. One offered brief diversion from their troubles in the League and temporarily restored pride, whilst the other had a sting in its tail.

The first came in the form of a floodlit friendly against the all-conquering Vasas club side from Hungary on 17th October 1955. Having gone undefeated during their tour of the United Kingdom, Vasas against the Tigers – firmly rooted to the bottom of Division Two - was considered by the national Press to be one of those potential "Lambs to the slaughter" stories; there was pressure for the game to be cancelled. It went ahead however, and against the expectations of just about everyone the Tigers emerged victorious 3-1, with City's new boy, Bill Bradbury, scoring a hat-trick.

The second occasion came some months later, in April 1956. Additional work to Boothferry Park's existing floodlights meant they reached the necessary standard and the Football League gave their approval for League fixtures to be staged at night. The first such fixture was against Doncaster Rovers. What should have been a glittering event, and a landmark in the club's history was completely overshadowed by the result. The 1-1 draw against their South Yorkshire rivals – City's goal being scored by Doug Fraser – confirmed the Tigers' relegation to Division Three (North), with four matches of the season still remaining.

Compounding that disaster was City's last fixture of the month. On 28th April Leeds United, managed by the former Tiger messiah of the post-war era, Raich Carter, beat City 4-1 a Boothferry Park and secured promotion to the First Division. Carter had achieved his dream; the Tigers, however, were not part of it. For all the vision of the directors, the impetus of the new stadium and the enthusiasm of the supporters, a decade on the 'new' Hull City found themselves back at square one.

## CHAPTER 6

UPS AND DOWNS

$\mathscr{B}$rocklebank's first full season in charge of the Tigers had not been the most promising of starts to his managerial stint at Boothferry Park: relegation is not the obvious way to seek the approval and support of those on the terraces. His second season (1956/57), therefore, needed to be much better: an immediate return to Division Two would have been the ideal response, but at the very least a decent attempt at promotion would be expected.

With the minimum of transfer activity during the summer, and defeat in the opening game of the season (vs. Halifax on 18th August 1956), Brocklebank's prospects did not look promising. Three wins on the bounce during the remainder of August though put the Tigers in second place – a point behind Hartlepools United – and gave Brocklebank some breathing space. However, as late summer moved through autumn and into early winter, the Tigers found that the Northern section was no less competitive than when they had last been there.

By New Year's Day 1957, when City and Hartlepools shared six goals at the Victoria ground, Hartlepools were still top of the table – albeit jointly with Bradford City – whilst City had dropped to 12th, some nine points off the pace. From that point they were always playing catch-up. They did, to some extent, but only improved to eighth by the season's end: too many defeats (15) spoiling the benefits that their 21 victories and consistent scoring from Bill Bradbury and Doug Clarke – both finished the season with 18 goals apiece – might have brought.

The Northern Section would be their 'playing field' for another season, although it would be the last as the Football League had already announced plans to replace the Northern and Southern sections with a Third and Fourth Division for the start of the 1958/59 campaign.

For much of the season, Brocklebank had placed a heavy reliance on the same squad that had seen the Tigers relegated: only six players made their League debuts. To a large extent that policy was foisted on him by financial circumstances. Attendances were still on a downward spiral – for the season just completed (1956/57) the average home attendance just managed to keep its head above the 12,000 mark. With none of the commercial diversity common in football clubs of the 21st century, each departed spectator had a significant impact on the accounts – less than five years earlier the average was more than double, so in that respect the club's income, theoretically, had been more than halved, but with nowhere near the same reduction in costs. It came as no surprise, therefore, that when the accounts revealed a loss in the region of £13,000 – a mere trifle when compared with the financial quagmire in which the club found themselves in the latter decades of the 20th century – a vote of no confidence in the directors by the shareholders was proposed, but defeated, at the Annual General Meeting.

Against that background, and in the knowledge that a poor showing in the forthcoming 1957/58 season would see the Tigers 'relegated' to the new 4th Division, a vastly improved performance was certainly called for.

Doug Clarke beats Halifax Town's keeper (Arthur Johnson) to the ball during the game at Boothferry Park on 7th September 1957. The Tigers won 5-2 and Clarke scored four of City's goals.

Brian Bulless scores the goal – against Bury on 25th April 1959 – that confirms City's promotion from Division Three.

In the opening half of the season the call was not answered. By the time their first fixture of 1958 was complete – a 2-2 draw at Halifax Town on 11th January 1958 – more than half their fixtures had been completed and the Tigers were in 13th place; the prospect of being founder members of the League's new basement division (Division Four) was turning into an alarming probability.

Thankfully, although a young squad in years they did not let the pressure get to them, and by the end of March thoughts of Division Four had turned into aspirations about Division Two as a series of fine performances moved the Tigers steadily up the League and in with a chance of promotion. Lying fourth in the table, and having recently beaten top of the table Scunthorpe Utd 2-0 on their own patch, it was not beyond the realms of possibility that sustaining such form would bring its reward.

That belief was strengthened even further when the opening game of April produced a 9-0 thrashing of Oldham Athletic at Boothferry Park – rewriting the stadium's goalscoring record book in the process. Unfortunately, however, the Tigers had peaked too soon. Two victories in the remaining seven fixtures saw them miss out on pro-

motion with a final placing of fifth, but having comfortably retained their Third Division status. Collectively it was a disappointing end to the season for the team, although for certain individuals there was some reward for their efforts. Billy Bly and Johnny Stevens were selected to represent the Northern Section against their Southern counterparts and Stevens' fine form was recognised with an Under-23 Cap for Wales against England.

Relegation looked to be on the cards during the early games of the 1958/59 season. Only one victory in the first seven games, culminating in a 6-1 defeat at Southampton on 13th September, had the Tigers last but one in the table, to the disquiet of just about everyone associated with the club: Directors, Manager, players and spectators. Bill Bradbury, Brian Bulless and Brian Cripsey all made transfer requests; all were granted by the Directors.

Brocklebank, who's playing career had been built on a foundation of fair play and good manners – traits he carried with him into management – publicly made his feelings clear. Whether or not it was the shock of seeing their normally mild mannered manager ripping them to shreds in the press, it certainly had the desired effect on the players.

In the game following the Southampton debacle the team did some ripping to shreds themselves: demolishing Notts County 5-0.

From that point on it was a vastly different Hull City that played out the rest of the season with startling success. Differences within the team were resolved, transfer requests were withdrawn and the goals started to flow from a forward line that remained unchanged for 23 consecutive games, with Bill Bradbury and Colin Smith in particular to the fore. From that Notts County game until the end of season fixture at Wrexham on 29th April 1959 – a total of 38 League games – only nine times was City's scoresheet lacking either name.

By the end of November the Tigers had moved from second from bottom to second from top, and there they stayed for pretty much the remainder of the season. A 2-0 win over Bury in their last home game of the season confirmed the Tigers promotion and Boothferry Park was a much happier place once more. The last game of the season – away to Wrexham – gave them the chance to go up as champions, but a heavy 5-1 defeat scuppered that as well as costing the players money: 'Talent money', to be shared between the players of the club finishing top, was set at £550 with the runners-up receiving £440.

Not surprisingly Bill Bradbury's name was on City's scoresheet for that Bury game. It had turned out to be something of a momentous season for Bradbury, setting a new post-war League and Cup goalscoring record for the Tigers: his 30 goals beating the previous record set by Norman Moore (28 in 1948/49). There was no doubt that on such form he would cause a lot of trouble in Division Two.

Bill Bradbury didn't cause a lot of trouble in Division Two as neither his nor the Tigers' occupation of that division lasted long enough; Bradbury departed during the season, whilst the Tigers' tenancy lasted but a season (1959/60), as they plummeted straight back down to Division Three. City's opening day fixture of the 1959/60 season was at

Over four decades of service, Billy Bly made more than 400 League and Cup appearances for the Tigers.

Bill Bradbury set a club post-war record with his 30 goals during the 1958/59 promotion season.

Boothferry Park against fellow promotion partners, Plymouth Argyle; it went City's way (3-1). However, heavy defeats away to Sheffield United (0-6), Liverpool (3-5), Charlton Athletic (0-4) and Middlesbrough (0-4), quickly brought home to Brocklebank and his players, that the task they faced in surviving the step up in status would not be easy. Again, finances had given Brocklebank little room for manoeuvre in the transfer market, and although he brought in new forwards in Ralph Gubbins (from Bolton), Jackie Sewell (Aston Villa) and Roy Shiner (Sheffield Wednesday) none were capable of dovetailing with Bradbury, or reaching double figures on the goalscoring front.

Following the Middlesbrough defeat the Tigers found themselves in 21st place and for the rest of the season they struggled to move away from that spot; in fact more often than not they found themselves at the foot of the table. With only six goals from 22 appearances in the League, Bradbury was allowed to move on to Bury in February. It was a sad comment on the state of City's forwards that his tally for the season left him in third place in the Tigers' goalscoring chart: only Roy Shiner (8) and David King (7) – a promising youngster who had risen through youth and reserve ranks – fared better.

A 1-1 draw at fellow strugglers Portsmouth in the penultimate fixture of the campaign sealed the Tigers' fate and it was back to Division Three. One notable absentee from City's retained list at the end of the season was Billy Bly. His association with the Tigers had spanned four decades and for nearly 25 years he had been the Tigers' regular keeper. During that time he'd amassed over 450 appearances, equalling the club record for a keeper, first set by 'Geordie' Maddison.

There was an unappealing balance to the Tigers' first season back in Division Three (1960/61): played 46, points 46; won 17, lost 17, goals scored 73, goals conceded 73. Only draws and end of season table placing disturbed the symmetry: 12 and 11th respectively.

Unrest at the lack of progress was demonstrated by average home attendances for the season falling well below 10,000 (8,434) and ten players were transfer-listed well before the season ends. Only two events disrupted the ordinariness of the entire campaign: the FA Cup Second Round tie against Darlington required five attempts before the Tigers finally progressed further – a club record in that competition – and the emergence of a raw young local lad (Chris Chilton) who would, before the decade was out, have written his own chapter in the history of Hull City.

Even though Brocklebank was less than half way through a five-year contract, it came as little surprise to anyone when the announcement of his removal from the manager's office was made shortly after the end of that 1960/61 season. A track record of more relegations than promotions and no discernable prospect of things improving in the immediate future caused the Board to act. A few weeks later, on 12th July 1961, his replacement was announced: Cliff Britton.

Cliff Britton - City's longest serving manager (1961-1970)

Britton was an ex-England international who possessed a solid rather than spectacular record as manager during spells at Burnley, Everton and Preston. His early days in charge at Boothferry Park tended to confirm that reputation, and it wasn't long before the patience of the supporters had been exhausted and calls for his removal, and that of the directors, were heard at the annual gathering of shareholders. But the chairman and his colleagues on the Board did not succumb to the pressure and gave Britton the time to develop his philosophy and team. It paid dividends, for over the next ten years Hull City experienced some of the most exciting and successful times in its history, and not all that excitement was confined to playing matters.

Starting with a squad that numbered less than 20, of which only 14 could be classed as full-time professionals, the expectations of City's fans for the prospects for the new season (1961/62) erred heavily on the cautious side. An opening day defeat (2-3) at newly promoted Peterborough, followed by a more convincing dismantling (0-4) at the hands of Port Vale offered evidence aplenty for such caution. A 1-0 victory over Northampton, and a 3-1 avenging result over Port Vale – both games at Boothferry Park – raised the spirits a little, and they were increased even further when City's next defeat was not experienced until a further five games, during which two of Britton's new signings, Ray Henderson and John McSeveney, offered plenty of evidence that they had an eye for taking a goal as well as making one.

By the end of September they held a top ten place in the table, well within striking distance of the promotion front runners, but between October and the end of December that distance had been extended almost out of the Tigers' reach. Lying 16th in the table on New Year's Day 1962 – 12 points off the promotion places and 12 points off the bottom of the table – unless there was either a spirited resurgence or a spectacular collapse, their season was realistically over. Neither event materialised, but there was sufficient progress made for them to end the season in 10th place. At least the 'balance sheet' of victories and defeats, goals (for and against) and points had a more positive look about it than that of the previous season.

Having brought new faces in during his first season in charge, Britton continued the strategy during the close season and it was a new look Hull City that took to the field at the start of the 1962/63 season. That new look was immediately apparent in the shirts they wore: for the first time in nearly a quarter of a century, the Tigers reverted to amber and black striped shirts.

Within those shirts were new players and as the season unfolded the likes of Chris Simpkin, Len Sharpe, Billy Wilkinson and Mike Williams would be introduced to the City fraternity on the terraces. As in the previous season the new campaign got off to a quiet start. Early victories were matched by early defeats, with the only compensation for spectators being the almost certain guarantee of goals – even if, on occasions many more ended up in the Tigers' net than the opposition's.

Only one game in the first half of the season ended goalless (Crystal Palace at home on 20th September); indeed that game was the only instance in the Tigers' entire League programme.

Again, inconsistency bedevilled the Tigers' season with the home and away games against Millwall and Queen's Park Rangers illustrating the point emphatically. Within the space of ten days the Tigers lost 5-1 away to Millwall and then beat them 4-1 at Boothferry Park. As for QPR, the time-frame between the home and away encounters may have been measured in months rather than days but the unpredictability of their performance remained unaltered. Away to Queen's Park Rangers the Tigers were convincingly beaten 4-1; at home to Queen's Park Rangers the Tigers emerged victorious by exactly the same scoreline (4-1).

With such diverse performances producing a 'no man's land' of a season, at least both Cup competitions generated some exciting and entertaining distractions. In the recently created Football League Cup the Tigers, at the third attempt, produced a minor 'giant-killing' performance to dispose of Second Division Middlesbrough. In the FA Cup, it was the Tigers who nearly played 'Goliath' to Crook Town's 'David'. Leading 4-1 at one stage early in the second-half, the non-League side had the whiff of glory in their nostrils. Fortunately, goals from McSeveney (2), Henderson (2) and Chilton spared City's blushes in what history may well regard as the most exciting Cup game ever staged at Boothferry Park.

Whatever encouragement those exploits in the Cup may have provided to City, mother nature conspired to nullify the effect by producing one of the severest winters of the 20th century; it meant that Boothferry Park didn't stage a City fixture between 29th December 1962 and 13th March 1963.

By the time the season's end arrived in the last week of May 1963, memories of Cup exploits were fading fast and City's fans were left to spend the close season mulling over the implications of another mid-table finish (10th). They had little time for deep thought however. Within days of the season's end, Harold Needler announced a substantial personal financial injection into the club that offered renewed hope for a higher grade of football, as well as substantial improvements to the stadium.

Needler's business interests had progressed at a much faster rate than his ambitions for Hull City. As such he was in a position to make the club a gift of £200,000 worth of shares in his company, Hoveringham Gravel, which quickly doubled in value on the stock exchange. With a bank balance that was the envy of many a First Division outfit, Cliff Britton now had the ammunition to mount a serious pro-

motion assault with sufficient funds left over to enhance the stadium's facilities to a level much more in keeping with the sporting status to which the club aspired.

As ever, in such circumstances, whenever Britton tried to spend some money on players the fees demanded were astronomical. Those who knew Cliff Britton were well aware that he would not be rushed into spending money unwisely. As a consequence, and much to the frustration of the fans, the only substantial development they could see involved Boothferry Park rather than the team. Work began almost immediately on building a new gymnasium. One had been included in the initial plans for developing the East Stand, but now it was decided to site the new building at the rear of 'Bunkers Hill'. Built at a cost of £53,000 the gym was over 150 ft in length and provided plenty of opportunities for the full range of tactical training.

During the summer of 1963 Britton did purchase new players – Ron Rafferty, Maurice Swan and Dennis Butler – names which would attain a greater prominence in the near future. But rather than rebuffing the overtures of those managers keen to sell players to the Tigers, Britton spent almost as much time rejecting the enquiries of those managers eager to acquire one of his 'home-grown' talents, Chris Chilton. At just 20 years of age, Chilton already had over 100 appearances and numerous goals, including two hat-tricks, on his Hull City CV. His reputation as a goalscorer was spreading rapidly and as the 1963/64 season got underway, Chilton was quickly enhancing that reputation with all four of City's goals in their 4-2 defeat of Wrexham in October. The frequency and quantity of enquiries about Chilton's availability increased, and each enquiry was politely rebuffed by Britton; he was buying, not selling.

Again, erratic form in the League proved to be City's downfall as far as their promotion aspirations were concerned. The early promise of Rafferty was negated after only three games, when a broken foot, suffered in the home draw with Colchester at the end of August, kept him out of the side until February. By then the Tigers were in the lower half of the table and although they rallied to eventually finish the season in eighth place, in many people's eyes that was a disappointing outcome. That disappointment was reflected at the Club's Annual General Meeting; neither manager nor chairman had an easy ride.

During the summer of 1964 work began on replacing the floodlight system with the most modern available – the old lights continued in service for many years with Scarborough - and the latest addition to Hull's skyline gave the club the best floodlights in any football stadium in Britain. Whilst substantial progress was being made on Boothferry Park's structures and facilities, the pace was more sedate on the playing front.

Terry Heath, a £12,000 signing from Leicester, and Alan Jarvis – a free signing from Everton – were added to City's squad for the start of the 1964/65 season, but neither had a significant impact on City's opening games. By the end of September, with 10 League games already under their belt, a total of nine points and 15th place in the table suggested that the season was heading in the same nondescript direction as its immediate predecessors.

The first sign that the future might be starting to look a little brighter came on 7th October 1964, when the Tigers entertained Barnsley in an evening game that saw the new floodlights in use for the first time. It also saw City score their best home win for nearly six years when four goals from Chris Chilton and a hat-trick from Ray Henderson meant Barnsley were battered to the tune of 7-0. Chilton's quartet was his second in just over a year, and for one so young he was developing into a fine goalscoring prospect. If only Britton could find someone to work in tandem with Chilton and ease the burden on his young shoulders.

Britton found someone the following month. It meant parting with a substantial sum of money (£40,000) for the time, but when analysed under the microscope of history, it turned out to be money well spent; in fact it was tantamount to theft. Britton's acquisition was Ken Wagstaff – "Waggy".

Ken Wagstaff

Like Chilton, Waggy was still 21 years old and had developed a reputation for scoring goals with Mansfield Town. Signing professional forms for Mansfield at just 17½ years old.

Wiggy had learnt his trade under the managerial guidance of the then Stag's manager and former City legend, Raich Carter. He arrived at Boothferry Park with impressive Mansfield statistics of 93 goals from 181 appearances. Those figures, coupled with the transfer fee, suggested to the patrons of Boothferry Park that he was something special. He did not disappoint them.

Scoring on his League debut (Exeter City 21st November 1964) Waggy soon struck up a good understanding with his new strike partner and both scored consistently through November and December in a run that saw City steadily climb up the table. By the beginning of January 1965, the Tigers had moved up to sixth place in the table and had the promotion places in their sights. By the end of the month they occupied one of those places and Cliff Britton had been spending some more of Harold Needler's money – another £80,000 to be precise and for that sum he'd acquired two players from Rotherham United: a cultured playmaker in Ken Houghton, and a wizard winger in Ian Butler.

With all three new signings settling in quickly the Tigers maintained a healthy run of results that saw them lose only once in 12 games between New Year's Day 1965 and 20th March. Yet despite such a good run (7 wins and 4 draws), City were still locked in a fierce struggle with five other clubs for the two promotion places. The upcoming Easter fixtures would be crucial in deciding whether it would finally be City's season, or just another frustrating one.

Three games in four days over the Easter Holiday weekend proved to be disastrous as far as the Tigers were concerned. A 2-1 defeat on Good Friday at Southend was followed, 24 hours later, by a 2-1 defeat at home to Mansfield. The return fixture against Southend, on Easter Monday, produced a 0-0 draw and gave the Tigers but a solitary point from a possible six. It left them in fourth place and a point off the promotion places with one game left. That final game was at home to Brentford, and although they won it (2-1) the teams above them also won and promotion was denied yet again. Although disappointed, the supporters were not unduly harsh. They had seen enough to suggest that things would be different next season. They were proved right, and how!

As the expectation built up during the summer of 1965, so did the building work at Boothferry Park. Construction of a new cantilever stand and terracing began on what had always been known as Bunkers Hill. Ever since Boothferry Park had opened, Bunkers Hill had been just an open expanse of terracing, with an almost sheer drop in the southwest corner. So deep was it that a high barrier had to be erected to prevent spectators falling over the edge and disappearing into what were then allotments.

Bulldozers cleared the existing terracing and dozens of deep piles were sunk to provide the new stand's foundation. Built at a cost of just over £125,000, it had 3,000 seats, and terracing – which was interspersed with 67 crush barriers – for a similar number. It was a sight to behold. The new stand was ready for the start of the 1965/66 campaign and 18,829 spectators witnessed the Tigers begin what would turn out to be a momentous season with a 3-2 victory over local rivals Scunthorpe United.

By the beginning of September the Tigers had hit the top of the table. A few hiccup results in that month (3-1 and 4-1 defeats at home to QPR and York respectively) dropped them down a few places but October and November saw them recover handsomely; by Christmas they were jostling for top spot with Millwall. The Boxing Day encounter between the two teams at Boothferry Park attracted a crowd in excess of 40,000; it had been nearly fifteen years since a similar attendance.

The Tigers won the game 1-0 and moved to the top of the table; the following day the return fixture was played in London with the Lions coming out on top (3-0). It meant that leadership of the Division changed hands twice in 24 hours. It would happen again as the campaign moved into the second half of the season. As the New Year began, City set off on a sequence of fourteen League games from 15th January that produced thirteen victories and a draw. Running in parallel was their best FA Cup run for over 30 years. Opposition from higher divisions was met and mastered, and it took a replay at Boothferry Park before Chelsea – eventually beaten themselves in the final – overcame the Tigers.

Any disappointment from the Chelsea game, understandable though it may have been, did not linger long; there was still a consolation prize of promotion and a possible championship to be secured. The promotion was achieved with three games to spare: goals from Waggy and Chillo gave City a 2-1 win at Bristol Rovers on 6th May 1966. With promotion secured, they could now concentrate all their attention on securing the divisional championship.

Ian Butler's goal against Southend on 20th May 1966, confirmed City as champions of Division Three for the 1965/66 season

That task was completed at Boothferry Park on the evening of 20th May 1966. A goal from Ian Butler produced a 1-0 victory over Southend in a game that was more tense than entertaining. Yet when the final whistle went 30,371 Tigers' fans went mad, many rushing onto the pitch and demanding their heroes present themselves to receive the adulation due to them. It was a scene reminiscent of some seventeen years earlier, when Carter's boys stood in the Directors' box and enjoyed the same experience.

During the season not a single home match attendance dropped below 14,000; many of those fans used the shuttle train service to get to Boothferry Park. In previous seasons there had only been the need for three trains to make the journey, transporting approximately 3,000 fans to the ground. Now the demand had risen such that seven trains capable of carrying up to 1,000 people at a time were often required. Throughout the 1965/66 season over 100,000 spectators used the train.

The euphoria of that evening lingered in the minds of City fans throughout the summer of 1966, enhanced by the fact that England won the World Cup and the Tigers had played a small part in that achievement as well. As part of England's preparations, a strong Football League side – managed by Alf Ramsey – had played against their Irish counterparts at Boothferry Park in October 1965. In preparation for that game, the Football League side – which contained many of England's eventual World Cup winners – played a short practice match against the Tigers; it was a 'game' the Tigers won, 2-0.

There seemed hardly enough time to draw breath before the 1966/67 season was ready to start and the Tigers eager to continue their progress. In all the excitement, a lack of squad strengthening by Cliff Britton went seemingly unnoticed. It was understandable that Britton, apart from signing a goalkeeper and a young full-back, showed loyalty to those players who had served him so well in the previous 12 months; the significance would be felt over the subsequent months and years, and with the benefit of hindsight was probably the first serious mistake of his Tigers' tenure. Whilst Britton had little to worry about as far as attack and midfield were concerned, the defence was nowhere near as secure.

Whilst there may have existed a belief and confidence in the team's ability always to score more than the opposition during their Division Three days, the higher division would not be so generous.

As the new season (1966/67) got underway, the Tigers made a steady start. By the end of September it was showing signs of becoming spectacular: three home wins in the space of eight days gave the Tigers six points, thirteen goals and temporary leadership of Division Two. It seemed they were preparing to scale new heights; what it actually meant was that they'd already peaked and for the remainder of the season they fell gently down from that autumnal pinnacle and landed softly in mid-table. Whilst the goals flowed generously from Chilton, Wagstaff and others, unfortunately the defence was equally as generous, even with the steel of Andy Davidson.

Further development of Boothferry Park during the summer of 1967 brought the ground to its peak in terms of facilities. It could accommodate over 40,000 with nearly 10,000 of those seated. The pitch was impressive and the floodlights were in a league of their own. In recognition of its status international fixtures returned: in the next six years Boothferry Park would stage more prestigious games than it had done in its previous twenty years of existence. Boothferry Park was a First Division stadium waiting for a First Division team. Unfortunately that team never turned up.

It was clear to almost everyone except, apparently, Cliff Britton, that there was a need for further team strengthening if the momentum of the mid 60's was not to be lost. That strengthening never really happened. Britton stuck strictly to his managerial policies of loyalty to those players who'd served him well in earlier seasons and giving youth its chance when the circumstances required. Admirable principles granted, but very few promotions have been won on such principles and the Tigers and their fans paid the price for Britton's perceived stubbornness: in the remaining seasons of the 'swinging 60s' the club hovered very much in the no-man's land of mid-table.

With the team that had promised so much gradually growing old, any replacements Britton brought in came predominantly from the reserves. Admittedly, many of them had the talent to play at such a level, but what they lacked was the experience. That latter characteristic requires time, and time was not really on Britton's side if the step up to the top flight of the Football League was to be made.

Only once in the next three seasons (1967/68–1969/70) did Britton make a significant purchase of a player not only of similar expertise, but also experience to those already present in the squad, and that was Tom Wilson at a cost of £18,000 – it hardly made a dent in his cash reserves.

Britton still had money to spend, yet he hesitated and that hesitancy finally cost him his job.

Andy Davidson. His 579 League and Cup appearances for the Tigers is an all-time club record.

As the team grew old it was only to be expected that some would disappear altogether. The most significant of those departures was Andy Davidson, Britton's inspirational skipper of the Tigers for so many years. Davidson's departure, like his debut, came in an away fixture; he lasted barely ten minutes in the League game at Aston Villa in November 1967 before injury forced his substitution. He never played for the Tigers' first team again. Davidson's playing career had begun back in September 1952. In the subsequent sixteen years he recorded 579 games in League and Cup competitions – a club record. He started at centre-forward and finished at right-back. If another chapter in the history of Hull City was coming to an end, then Andy Davidson's exit from first team action was the opening sentence of the final paragraph.

As the 1960's drew to a close, the Tigers were near permanent residents of Division Two's mid-table. A 6-0 defeat at Cardiff at the beginning of November 1969 brought matters to a head. If Harold Needler was to see his First Division dream come true then something would have to be done. It was. Within a week of that Cardiff defeat the Board announced that Britton's role would change: moving from team manager to general manager. A younger player-manager would be sought to take the Tigers into a new era.

## CHAPTER 7

NEW BROOMS

The 'younger player-manager' to replace Cliff Britton was appointed on 19th May 1970. It was Terry Neill, a centre half with Arsenal and captain of Northern Ireland. At 28-years old he certainly fitted the 'younger player' criteria and was still capable of playing at a higher level than the Tigers currently operated. The only doubt lay in the 'managerial' element. As a manager, Neill was an unknown quantity. He'd captained Arsenal, and virtually all of his time at Highbury had been under the managerial guidance of Bertie Mee, so the background was promising, but if the Board of Directors at Boothferry Park were looking for a new brush to sweep clean, the question still remained: had they got the right brush?

Terry Neill.

Neill's entrance at Boothferry Park was nothing if not grand. He arrived in an E-type Jaguar – part of the package offered by Harold Needler that persuaded Neill to take a near £5,000 per annum drop in salary to move from Highbury to Hull. At an age younger than some of the players he was managing, perhaps the E-type was his way of making a statement to his new charges. Some statement. It could have backfired, but his early performances in the team soon showed that he had the aptitude to back up the apparent attitude.

Those early pre-season performances – in the newly created Watney Cup – allowed Neill to assess the strengths and weaknesses of his squad. The 4-0 beating of Fourth Division Peterborough would merely confirm what riches he possessed in strikers – Waggy and Chillo got a brace apiece – but it was the next game, at home to Manchester United, which would give him a more detailed assessment of the task he faced. To their credit the players did not let their new boss down. Against a side that contained such legends as Best, Charlton, Law and Stiles, the Tigers were only beaten on penalties (4-3) after normal time and extra time had seen the score remained unchanged at 1-1. What Neill saw must have both pleased and worried him.

He knew the team were capable of promotion, but what concerned him was time: much of his squad were mature in

City's Malcolm Lord prepares to tackle Bobby Charlton during the Watney Cup semi-final against Manchester United on 5th August 1970 – the first competitive game in English football to be settled by a penalty shoot-out.

years and if there was to be a push for promotion it would have to be a quick one.

Their start to the League campaign (1970/71) was a decent one. By mid October, and with nearly a third of the season's fixtures completed, the Tigers were top of the table; but it was close: a point reinforced three games later when they had dropped to fourth. By the time the home game against Sheffield Wednesday on Boxing Day kicked off City had recovered some of the lost ground – moving up to third – and a win over the Owls would move them further up the table. With less than 10 minutes of that game remaining, any thoughts of further progress up the table lay with the discarded wrapping paper from the previous day's Xmas gifts: in tatters. Trailing 4-1 to a moderate Wednesday side, only a supreme recovery inspired by goals from Chris Chilton – captain on the day – and the two Kens (Wagstaff and Houghton) saw City snatch a draw and prevent any further loss of ground.

With the New Year came the FA Cup and for the first couple of months of 1971 the Tigers managed to juggle League and Cup games without either seriously hampering the other. At the beginning of March the Tigers were fifth in the table, but only a point behind the leaders, Sheffield United. They were also through to the quarter-finals of the Cup and were paired at home to First Division Stoke City. In front of a crowd of 41,452 – their highest home attendance for nearly 20 years – the Tigers came off worst in a five goal thriller that was only settled in Stoke's favour (3-2) thanks to a controversial decision from a linesman and a legitimate claim for a goal by Terry Neill being ignored by the Referee.

Chris Chilton (9) and Ian Butler cause panic in the Stoke defence during the FA Cup quarter-final tie at Boothferry Park on 6th March 1971

to record a famous 2-1 victory. The added bonus was that the result took them joint top of the table in terms of points, but a slightly inferior goal average put them in second place.

Any joy produced by the result at Bramall Lane was not long for the savouring. A comparatively easy home fixture against Oxford United, which offered the chance of establishing a firm grip on one of the promotion places, turned into a terribly disappointing home defeat to the tune of 1-0. Although not disastrous on its own – there were still ten games left – it was a result that had a seemingly damaging impact on the team's confidence. From that point on they lost their way and faded badly to finish fifth. It may have been their best League performance for nearly sixty years, but it did little to assuage the disappointment felt by all associated with the club. That disappointment lingered long in the system.

Logically, Terry Neill and his coaching staff knew that their only realistic chance of getting promoted with the current squad had gone; the quick push for promotion had failed. The prospect of squeezing another attempt out of the same group of players would be optimistic to say the least. The effectiveness of the championship-winning squad of some five years earlier was diminishing rapidly through a combination of age, injury and transfers. Realistically, another promotion attempt would be some time in the making because first Neill would have to rebuild.

With any type of construction, there is always an element of initial destruction, and Hull City was no different. Within weeks of the new season (1971/72) beginning the first stage of that rebuild was seen in the sale of Chris Chilton to Coventry City for a fee of £92,000. What might have seemed a strange decision at the time – selling your previous season's leading goalscorer is rarely perceived as the act of a rational man – probably turned out, in hindsight, to be good business from a commercial viewpoint, because within a couple of seasons Chilton's League career was ended by injury.

There was little time for the Tigers to lick their wounds; three days after the Stoke game they were back on the promotion trail and facing a trip to Sheffield United. In what has gone down in Hull City folklore as the "Battle of Bramall Lane", the Tigers – fielding two new signings in Ken Knighton and Bill Baxter – fell behind to an early United goal but lived up to their nickname and fought back

Chris Chilton celebrates the 209th goal of his Tiger career in the 1-1 draw against QPR in November 1970.

What may have eased Neill's decision was his belief that he already possessed a successor to the Tigers' all-time leading goalscorer in Stuart Pearson – like Chilton, a local lad who'd scored heavily at reserve level and who, within five years, would be scoring at international level for England, alas with Manchester United rather than Hull City as his parent club.

Whilst the shock of Chilton's departure was still fresh in the memory, another of the mid-sixties stalwarts, Chris Simpkin, was allowed to move on. Add the fact that Chilton's strike partner of old, Ken Wagstaff, struggled with injury and also struggled to find his goal touch, plus Ken Houghton's absence for more than half the season, it was no surprise to find the Tigers in the lower end of Division Two. Only a maximum point Easter finally pushed them away from the relegation scrap and into the calmer waters of mid-table come the end of the season.

Now if the words give the impression that the season (1971/72) was one of dismantling and departures it would be false; there were arrivals and advances. The arrivals came in the shape of John Kaye and Jimmy McGill – who provided grit in defence and midfield respectively – whilst the advances came in the development of Stuart Pearson and Roy Greenwood; in Pearson's case he developed quickly enough to finish the season as leading goalscorer. The rebuilding was taking place; it was just that it would take time. That requirement of time extended into the following season (1972/73); yet despite further signings being made and the development of the home-grown talent continuing, the end of season position (13th) suggested otherwise.

With further signings, in the shape of Steve Deere and Chris Galvin, and the continued development of Stuart Pearson and Roy Greenwood, that rebuilding process looked to be nearing completion as the Tigers produced a more competitive showing during the 1973/74 season. Being losing finalists in the Watney Cup was supplemented by their longest ever journey in the League Cup – they eventually lost to Liverpool in Round 4 after a replay. As for the bread and butter of the League, they spent much of the season in the top ten positions and occasionally threatened the promotion places. A final placing of 9th suggested that Neill was on track to revive the Tigers fortunes and the following campaign was anticipated eagerly.

Whether Neill's blueprint for reconstruction would have materialised remained unknown. Despite the departure of Stuart Pearson to Manchester United for a fee of £170,000 – a then club record – the Tigers got off to a decent start in the League and at the end of the first month (August) of the season were well up with the pack jostling for the promotion places. But before the middle of September had been reached, the Tigers were without a manager. Terry Neill had succumbed to what football in general would have perceived to be a much greater challenge: an ex-Arsenal man taking over the managerial reigns of Tottenham Hotspur, the Gunners' arch-enemy.

City's Roy Greenwood about to be tackled by Martin Buchan during the Tigers' 2-0 victory over Manchester United at Boothferry Park on 23rd November 1974.

Whilst the negotiations over Terry Neill's departure were coming to their conclusion, Neill suggested to Harold Needler that he need look no further than City's own coaching staff for Neill's successor: the man he had in mind was John Kaye. Neill had signed Kaye in 1971 to bring strength and determination to the Tigers' defence. He achieved that, and a useful centre-back partnership of Neill and Kaye was starting to develop until Neill's retirement brought it to a premature end. Kaye continued as the senior partner alongside new signing Steve Deere, but within 12 months that partnership was broken up when injury curtailed Kaye's playing career. At the invitation of Terry Neill, Kaye remained at the club and was appointed first-team coach during the summer of 1974. Accepting Neill's advice, Needler offered John Kaye the chance to occupy the manager's chair; Kaye accepted but only on the understanding that it would initially be on a trial basis of four games. Kaye wanted to be sure that he could do the job rather than just think he could.

That caution looked well placed following Kaye's managerial debut: an away trip to Nottingham Forest on 14th September 1974. It finished 4-0 to Forest and meant Kaye's debut was worse – in terms of margin of defeat – than any of his Tiger predecessors. Despite no win during his four game 'trial' – the remaining three games were all drawn – there was sufficient reassurance from the performances for the chairman to repeat his offer of the manager's job and for Kaye to accept it. Initially, Kaye's appointment coincided with an upturn in the Tigers' fortunes: following the defeat at Forest, the team suffered only one further defeat in the next eight games as Kaye's awareness of defensive matters was reflected in the team's performances during that spell: strong, uncompromising and parsimonious in the concession of goals.

Returning to Nottingham some six weeks later (2nd November 1974), this time to take on Notts County, City's defensive frailties returned and they departed Meadow Lane very much on the wrong end of a 5-0 drubbing. That game apart, November went well for the Tigers: they were undefeated in the remaining games that month and in doing so captured the scalp of runaway table leaders, Manchester United (2-0) in the process. By the time they'd beaten Bristol City on the last day of November the Tigers had propelled themselves into fourth place and Kaye's efforts were acknowledged with him being awarded the divisional 'Manager of the Month'.

If November had provided a springboard for the Tigers to mount a serious promotion challenge, December proved to be more of a plank: no wins in five games, a blank Christmas in terms of points and a descent in the table to 10th place. Having lost so much ground in such a short time, recovering the deficit proved beyond them; and whilst an end of season placing of eighth showed a minor improvement on the previous season, the feeling of what might have been dominated the emotions of both club and supporters over the subsequent summer months.

Such disappointment, however, was put into perspective with the announcement of Harold Needler's death on 24th July 1975. Known as "Big 'Aitch" amongst the employees of Hull City, his passing was a massive blow and one from which the club didn't recover as the new season (1975/76) progressed. It had been Needler's vision and backing – both financially and emotionally – that had taken the Tigers so far, and when one considers the history of Hull City one of its most positive aspects was Needler's stewardship. Often referred to as the 'Father of Hull City', it was an accolade deeply deserved. Although four decades have passed since his demise, and the subsequent history of the Tigers has taken many a twist and turn, whenever his name has been mentioned it has always been in the most respectful and almost reverential of terms.

The Needler family maintained their Tiger link when Harold's son, Christopher, took over as chairman on 7th August. Christopher stated that a fitting memorial to his father's memory would be for the Tigers to gain promotion in the forthcoming season. Whilst everyone connected with the club empathised with the sentiment, sentiment has never been the strongest of foundations upon which to build a promotion campaign.

Harold Needler, the 'father' of Hull City.

The defensive capabilities of the Tigers, under Kaye's guidance, were not in doubt; what caused concern was the scoring of goals, rather than the preventing of them. Although he could still call on the services of Ken Wagstaff, the last remaining playing link with the championship-winning side of 10 years previously, injuries were starting to take their toll on 'Waggy' and he was no longer the potent scoring force of old. In fact, before the year (1975) was out, injury brought an end to his Hull City career.

The strikers that Kaye had brought in whilst manager, such as Alf Wood and Dave Sunley, always faced an uphill task in trying to emulate the efforts of Chilton and Wagstaff. Not unsurprisingly, the pretenders to the Waggy and Chillo throne failed to live up to the billing of their predecessors; neither were they able to provide the necessary strike rate on which successful promotion campaigns are based. Although they flirted throughout the season with the relegation zone, realistically they were too good to go down; unfortunately, they were not good enough to go up. Ending the season in 14th place was not an unfair reflection of their efforts.

Even the signing of Billy Bremner, early into the 1976/77 season, failed to provide the catalyst for the

Billy Bremner.

promotion push so desperately wanted by the fans. Although in the autumn of his career Bremner still had some talent left in his body, and his appetite for the game was far from sated. That point was illustrated by a goal on his debut at home to Nottingham Forest. The game also illustrated how desperate City fans were to experience some success: they came in their droves, boosting the attendance on the afternoon to over 16,000 in a season where the average home attendance hovered around the 7,000 mark. Yet for all Bremner's experience and enthusiasm the Tigers still failed to progress, ending the season in exactly the same place in the table (14th) as they had in the previous season.

There's an old saying that goes something along the lines of "bad news comes in threes." The Tigers provided their own variation on that theme during the 1977/78 season: during it they had three managers… and the bad news was that at the end of it they were relegated. Essentially, the season revolved around two games against one team: the home and away fixtures against Mansfield Town on 1st October 1977 and 25th February 1978 respectively. In the intervening months between those two dates, the Tigers went through three managers and two Chairmen.

The ever increasing volume of disquiet on the terraces over the lack of success in the previous two seasons was eventually heard in the Boardroom. Before the season had even started Kaye had been told that things must improve, or else. A 3-0 home win over Sunderland on the opening day of the season (20th August 1977) suggested the message had got home, and a goal on his debut from new signing Bruce Bannister offered some hope that a solution may have been found to the lack of goals. Both premises proved false. Seven games later the Tigers lost 2-0 at home to Mansfield; they were in 16th place in the table and moving in the wrong direction. After the return fixture, some five months later at Field Mill, which also saw City beaten (1-0), they were three places lower in the table and still heading in the wrong direction.

The initial consequence of that first Mansfield game was the dismissal of John Kaye. Nearly a month before that match, however, Kaye had signed another striker, Alan Warboys. He'd hoped that Warboys would recreate the profitable partnership he'd enjoyed with Bruce Bannister during their days together with Bristol Rovers. Then, they'd achieved national notoriety for their scoring exploits. In the three games they played together before Kaye's departure, neither troubled the scoresheet and offered little to suggest a rekindling of their previous understanding.

The fan's favourite to replace Kaye was Billy Bremner. According to the experts on the terraces the main reason the ex-Leeds legend had crossed into enemy territory was the understanding that the manager's job was his when the opportunity arose. As is so often the case, the experts were wrong. Kaye's successor, however, was an internal appointment and there was more than a trace of Elland Road in his provenance. Bobby Collins – a former Leeds colleague of Bremner – stepped up from coach to chief within a matter of weeks; a route remarkably similar to Kaye's appointment some three years earlier.

Collins' tenure began well: a 2-0 home win over high-flying Tottenham Hotspur, with Alan Warboys – Kaye's last signing before his sacking – adding a little irony to the occasion by opening his scoring account for the Tigers with both goals. An opening sequence of seven games undefeated lulled those on the terraces into thinking that perhaps the directors had made the right choice in Collins over Bremner. That theory was blown out of the water during the next fourteen fixtures as the Tigers won only once. In the middle of that run came a change in the board-room.

Having taken over as chairman following the death of his father in the summer of 1975, Christopher Needler announced he was stepping down in December 1977. In taking such action Needler hoped that new leadership might bring about a change in the club's fortunes.

The mantle of chairman passed to local businessman Bob Chapman, although Christopher Needler remained on the Board. Despite the change at the top the club's fortunes continued to deteriorate on the pitch; and although not immediately apparent at first, the club's balance sheet started to take a turn for the worse as well.

It was the playing side that caused most consternation initially. Hull City directors had been criticised in the past for their sluggishness in removing underachieving managers from their posts. This newly amended board could not be tarred with that brush; they showed Collins the door despite his being only four months into a two-year contract. Again, Billy Bremner's name was in the frame as Collins' successor, and again Bremner missed out. The directors' choice was Ken Houghton – former playing legend at Boothferry Park and currently in charge of a developing and successful youth set up at the club. With only fifteen matches left – the first of which was away to Mansfield Town – Houghton, together with his assistant Andy Davidson, another Tiger legend, faced a tall order if the season was to be rescued and the club to survive in Division Two.

Although beaten at Mansfield, Houghton's home debut produced a rare victory: 3-2 against Millwall with all three of City's goals coming from Alan Warboys. That victory proved rare indeed: it was City's last at home that season and together with a further win, at Charlton, provided the briefest of respites as the Tigers settled into the relegation spots during April. Their fate was sealed with a 2-1 defeat away to Leyton Orient on the 22nd of that month.

After more than a decade of striving to reach the top level in English football, the Tigers went backwards rather than forwards. The optimists on the terraces, whilst acknowledging the disappointment of relegation, suggested it could be a blessing in disguise: the club could regroup, sort out their problems on and off the field and come back much stronger for the experience. The pessimists, not unsurprisingly, took a different view. To them, relegation was just the thin edge of the wedge. The pessimists won that particular philosophical debate. In fact the pessimists held sway for some considerable time, as over the next couple of decades the club experienced some of the lowest points ever in its history and on more than one occasion was close to extinction.

## CHAPTER 8

TROUBLED TIMES

$\mathscr{H}$aving been handed what was commonly believed to have been 'Mission Impossible' during the closing weeks of the previous season (1977/78), Ken Houghton was virtually fireproof when the recriminations over relegation began amongst the supporters. The players and directors were not so lucky.

In an attempt to lower the temperature the directors gave Houghton the go-ahead to acquire new players during the summer, although with the Tigers' coffers dwindling day by day, there was a 'but': provided some revenue was brought in through departures. On the departures front the names of Peter Daniel, John Hawley and Dave Roberts appeared quite quickly, with the sum total of their fees amounting to more than £250,000; another departure, and not totally unexpected, was that of Billy Bremner. Moving in to Boothferry Park were John Farley, Micky Horswill and Keith Edwards. The latter cost in the region of £60,000 but as the ensuing months confirmed it was a bargain. Also arriving was ex-Manchester United boss, Wilf McGuiness, to help Houghton and Davidson on the coaching side.

All told, the summer of 1978 was one of the busiest in recent years for City and as the new season (1978/79) approached the activity seemed to please everyone and an aura of tranquil optimism hovered over the club. Undefeated in their first four League games, the Tigers headed the table in the early days of September. Thoughts of an early return to Division Two began to germinate in the minds of those associated with the club. Such thoughts did not last long, however, as the Tigers' traditional trait of inconsistency returned to see them go without a victory in October.

The season thus followed a similar pattern to previous ones with wins at a premium and draws and defeats occurring too regularly. With the prospect of another relegation growing ever stronger after a run of four consecutive defeats during February and March, the Tigers confounded everyone by producing an 11 game unbeaten run – underwritten by regular goalscoring from Keith Edwards – which not only moved them away from the relegation places, but brought the promotion spots tantalizingly into view. Unfortunately they proved to be just out of reach and the Tigers had to settle for eighth place – Keith Edwards, however, took pole position in the goalscoring charts, not only for City, but also for the Division. It augured well for the future, if only they could crack the consistency conundrum.

During the summer of 1979 the directors announced plans to redevelop Boothferry Park. They were nothing spectacular; essentially they were just a rehash of the original board's thinking some 30 years earlier. In tandem with the stadium development there was further development on the squad front. An influx of new players saw Paul Moss, Trevor Phillips and Mick Tait – the latter's fee of £150,000 setting a new club record – brought in to provide additional bite and creativity in midfield. Both off-field and on-field activity suggested that a philosophy of 'speculate to accumulate' was being adopted by the Hull City hierarchy. It wasn't too long before it became apparent that 'last throw of the dice' was a more apt description.

Neither development came to much. The plans for the ground faded gently into the background and the Tigers' start to the 1979/80 campaign offered little in the way of encouragement. It was five games into the new season before they recorded a victory, and as the halfway point of the campaign approached they were nearer the relegation region than the promotion places. Things came to a head at the end of the first week of December 1979: a 7-2 thrashing away to Brentford on 8th December cost Houghton his job and the directors were looking for their fourth manager in as many years.

Their previous three selections – Kaye, Collins and Houghton – had all been people who'd enjoyed an impressive professional playing career, but who'd had little or no managerial experience before their Boothferry Park appointments. For their next choice the Directors changed tack and went for someone whose professional playing pedigree was non-existent but who'd impressed on the managerial front...with the Welsh national team. Welcome to Hull, Mike Smith.

Smith's signature did not come cheap; neither did he arrive alone, bringing with him his entourage of Cyril Lea, as his assistant, and Bobby Brown to assist with youth development and scouting. If the board saw Smith as the fresh face to bring new hope at the start of a new decade – Smith's first game in charge was away to Plymouth Argyle on 1st January 1980 – then they were in for something of a rude awakening as the result of that game ended 5-1 in Argyle's favour.

Now if that result was just a blip, it lasted a long time. The rest of the season was a continual struggle to avoid being sucked into a relegation dogfight: only 'fortress' Boothferry Park - where the Tigers won eight out of their remaining eleven games – and the goals of Keith Edwards saved them from relegation and the Directors from extremely red faces.

Those eight home victories, during the early months of Smith's reign, proved somewhat prophetic; for during his first full season in charge (1980/81) the Tigers won only eight games (seven at home, one away) and were firmly entrenched in the relegation places for much of the campaign. It was a pitiful season and relegation was confirmed well before the season ended. For the first time in the club's history they faced life in the basement division of the Football League. It was not what Boothferry Park had been built for. After such a disastrous season, it was inevitable that changes would be made. Yet, surprisingly, those changes came not in the boss's office, but the boardroom. Chairman Bob Chapman and fellow director Ian Blakey resigned, with Christopher Needler taking over as chairman again.

Now if dropping down into the Fourth Division was perceived as the lowest point in the history of Hull City, the perception was wrong. There was much worse to come.

A moderate start to the 1981/82 campaign saw any promotion prospects disappear by Christmas. A decent FA Cup run, ended by Chelsea in a Third-round replay at Boothferry Park, offered some consolation, and cash, but

in February 1982 events on the field paled into insignificance when it was announced that the Tigers had been put into receivership.

The landscape of Hull City's history has never been the easiest of terrains for supporters to traverse. The promotion peaks are few and far between and travelling between them has necessitated the navigation around numerous pot-holes – both financial and football in their origin. Such pot-holes, however, were of inconsequential significance when compared to the crater that resulted when the following announcement was made on 25th February 1982: "…Mr Needler, who has supported the club over the past years to the extent of some £325,000 with further bank guarantees of £225,000, has been advised that he should not, in all the circumstances, continue funding the club." Although wrapped in the finest of financial speak, the message was frighteningly simple: Hull City had run out of cash.

It was an unwanted first for the Tigers. Although English football had been suffering a financial crisis for years, unfortunately it fell to Hull City to be the first to be admitted into the intensive care unit, with all indicators suggesting little chance of resuscitation, never mind recovery. Clubs had gone to the wall before – Accrington Stanley and Bradford Park Avenue were recent examples – but at least they'd managed to survive until the end of a season before giving up the ghost.

City's players learn of the club's financial difficulties in February 1982.

Whilst Christopher Needler had promised to continue providing funds until a buyer was found, there was no guarantee that his money would see the Tigers through to the end of the season.

A firm of chartered accountants, Casson Beckman, was appointed to oversee the Tigers' finances in the short term and one of their partners, Martin Spencer, was appointed as administrator and manager, with the aim of restructuring the club on a sound financial basis that would allow it to be sold as a going concern. Purchasing Hull City in its present plight did not offer an attractive prospect to a sane man. According to Christopher Needler he had already lost more than £500,000 keeping the Tigers afloat and the club was still losing money at the rate of about £9,000 a week – in today's game the weekly wage of a decent championship player or premiership reserve – when the decision to sell was made.

Initially, restructuring meant dismantling. As any civil engineer worth his salt will tell you, it's always best to start at the top. First to go therefore was manager Mike Smith, followed almost simultaneously by his assistant Cyril Lea. Day-to-day management of the team was placed in the hands of Bobby Brown and Chris Chilton.

Next, the administrator turned his attention to the playing staff. With just enough nous to realise that whilst sacking the entire squad might save on wages, it would present something of a problem as far as playing football was concerned, Spencer placed all 23 players on City's books on the transfer list. Thus, whenever they played they were in the shop window: one of the incentives used by Brown and Chilton to keep up the spirits of their players. After all, if a P45 is more likely than a pay packet, it's better to have caught the eye of a watching scout. Not the best of circumstances in which to be fulfilling League fixtures, but difficult circumstances often bring out the best in people.

Whilst the shock was still being absorbed within the city, Mr Spencer called on the people of Hull to demonstrate their support for the club by attending home matches. He argued it would act as a signal to potential buyers that there was still a wish for professional football to remain within the city. The call was answered as 5,220 turned up at Boothferry Park – nearly double the previous home game's attendance – for the home game against Mansfield. Fighting funds were created, survival plans developed and various action groups sprang up to support the club and its players in the battle to survive.

Under Brown and Chilton the players displayed a resolve worthy of the club's nickname and strung together a series of results that moved them steadily up the table; and as the results on the pitch improved, so spectator numbers rose.

Once the Administrator (Mr Spencer) realised the calibre of talent available within the club, the 'Free Transfer' sign was quickly taken down. One player in particular almost seemed to thrive on the pressure. That player was Les Mutrie, who set a new club record for goalscoring in consecutive games: fourteen goals in nine games.

Les Mutrie

The Tigers ended the season in eighth place, a more than creditable achievement given the circumstances. The players had done their bit to ensure League football was still a possibility for the following season. Yet despite that the players, like the supporters, were still unsure as to where the future of the club lay. The spotlight returned to Mr Spencer and his efforts to find a buyer.

His efforts came to fruition on 15th May 1982 when Christopher Needler revealed that a buyer had been found and the sale of the club had been completed. The buyer was Don Robinson, a leisure-business millionaire and former Rugby League player for Hull KR; he'd also been chairman of the highly successful non-League football club Scarborough. The deal involved the sale of some of Needler's shares to Robinson with Boothferry Park being purchased by a "recreational foundation" set up by the Needler family, thus "ensuring that it is available for the playing of soccer in particular, but also for other recreational and community activities for the people of Hull." Robinson invited Christopher Needler to join the new board, which also included Clifford Waite as Vice-Chairman and James Johnson, the then MP for Hull West. The supporters, however, whilst overjoyed that their club had been saved, were still keen to know what was going to happen on the pitch.

Who would be manager? Would players be sold? Would any new players be brought in? Robinson quickly addressed the first of those questions by appointing Colin Appleton to take over as manager from the 'caretaker' duo – Chris Chilton and Bobby Brown – who were still retained to assist Appleton: Chilton became Appleton's assistant whilst Brown eventually took over the role of club secretary.

Colin Appleton led the Tigers to promotion during his first season in charge.

Robinson also confirmed that no more players in addition to those who had already moved on, such as Nick Deacey and Micky Horswill, would need to be sold and as for new players Robinson confirmed that Appleton would be allowed to boost the squad. Included amongst those new arrivals was ex-Tiger Peter Skipper.

Even before the new season (1982/83) started, there were doubts being expressed as to the wisdom of Appleton's appointment. Although he had enjoyed some managerial success in the non-League game, he was untested in the professional arena. Defeat on the opening day of the new season – 2-1 away to Bristol City – did not ease the doubts. However, Appleton was not so easily disheartened.

Relying heavily on the efforts of those who had done the club proud during the opening months of 1982, his team went undefeated in the next nine games. In fact they only suffered a total of six defeats in the League all season and promotion was achieved with a 0-0 draw at Chester City on 30th April 1983. What doubts had existed at the start of the campaign had been well and truly dispelled, and by the end of the season the attendances at Boothferry Park were more than double those at the start.

The Robinson and Appleton partnership had confounded their critics. Robinson was the rumbustious charismatic showman. Appleton, in contrast, was quiet and resilient. An unworkable combination at first glance perhaps, yet it must not be forgotten that they had worked successfully together at Scarborough.

Appleton's team selections may not have matched the flamboyance of his chairman, but they were effective, and promotion in his first season was a pretty impressive response to those who doubted. Although stepping up a grade, a 4-1 home victory over Burnley in the opening game of the new season (1983/84) suggested to City fans that the Tigers would not be relegation fodder in Division Three. A brace of goals from new signing Steve Massey in that opening game also suggested that for all his apparent inclination for rugged defensive teams, Appleton was not clueless when it came to signing strikers.

The Tigers went through the opening 11 League games undefeated and a 0-0 draw at Bolton Wanderers on 18th October saw them hit the top of the table. Included within that run were big home wins over Millwall and Sheffield United (5-0 and 4-1 respectively). In parallel with the performances was an improvement in the attendances – nearly 15,000 people had watched the home win over Sheffield United.

A home defeat to Plymouth Argyle on 22nd October knocked the Tigers off the top of the table and took a little wind out of their sails. But they soon got back on track and in the run up to Christmas they continued to keep up with the other promotion hopefuls. Three consecutive 1-0 victories in the last week of 1983 – which included the defeat of Scunthorpe, who had England cricket legend Ian Botham in their team, in front of a crowd of 15,461 – added substance to the hopes of consecutive promotions.

Bad weather at the beginning of 1984 meant the Tigers went nearly a whole month without a game, managing just two away games during January. When normal service was resumed, the months of February and March saw City still hovering around the top four positions. Unfortunately, however, as the scrap intensified City failed to take advantage whenever their rivals slipped up; when they lost City tended to lose as well. In the end their chance of promotion rested on the final game of the season – a rearranged fixture at Burnley, with the top of the table looking like this:

	Team	P	W	L	D	F	A	Pts	GD
1	Oxford Utd	46	28	7	11	91	50	95	41
2	Wimbledon	46	26	11	9	97	76	87	21
3	Sheffield Utd	46	24	11	11	86	53	83	33
4	Hull City	45	22	9	14	69	38	80	31

Oxford and Wimbledon were already promoted. The final promotion place rested between Sheffield United and the Tigers. To secure the last promotion place the Tigers needed to win by three clear goals; they only managed two. Thus promotion slipped away from them by the agonisingly slim margin of one goal – the same goal difference meant Sheffield United's superior 'goals for' tally secured the final promotion slot:

Team	P	W	L	D	F	A	Pts	GD
1 Oxford Utd	46	28	7	11	91	50	95	41
2 Wimbledon	46	26	11	9	97	76	87	21
3 Sheffield Utd	46	24	11	11	86	53	83	33
4 Hull City	46	23	9	14	71	38	83	33

Again, mathematics had shaped their destiny. If that wasn't bad enough, within hours of the Burnley game finishing it was revealed that Colin Appleton had resigned to take the manager's job at Swansea. Amidst the disappointment came the opportunity to rescue something from the season. Whilst pursuing promotion, the Tigers had enjoyed some success in the newly introduced Associate Members Cup – a competition open to the bottom two divisions of the Football League. They managed to win through to the final, against Bournemouth. In later years the competition would have some prestige in the football calendar, with the final played at Wembley and subsequently the Millennium Stadium, Cardiff. In 1984 however, the competition was still finding its feet and City won the toss to stage the Final at Boothferry Park – the one and only time that Boothferry Park would stage a national senior final. Chris Chilton was in charge of the team for this game, but with the Tigers still suffering from the disappointment of missing promotion it came as no major shock to find them on the wrong end of a 2-1 scoreline.

Without a manager and with nothing tangible to show for their efforts, it was a somewhat downcast squad who departed for Florida to undertake the shortest of end of season tours – they played in the second leg of the Arrow Cup. It was basically nothing more than a home and away set of friendly games against the Tampa Bay Rowdies. City had won their home game (3-0) and despite losing 1-0 in Tampa, the Tigers won the competition to give them some silverware at the end of a long campaign.

Of more significance, however, was the announcement during the tour concerning the appointment of Appleton's successor. It was Brian Horton, whose reputation as a natural leader had been built during his playing days with Port Vale, Brighton and Luton. He had enjoyed success at all three clubs and served under some astute managers so he could not fail to have learned from those experiences. He put that knowledge to good use in his first season in charge (1984/85).

Horton's face wasn't the only new one around Boothferry Park by the start of the new season. On the playing front Mike Ring, Neil Williams and Lawrie Pearson were brought in, but there was no straight replacement for Brian Marwood, City's leading goalscorer for the past two seasons, who'd been transferred to Sheffield Wednesday.

In the boardroom Don Robinson boosted his squad by inviting Harold Bermitz and Mike Thorpe to become directors. Horton's League debut, as both manager and player, came in the 0-0 draw at Lincoln. A week later he celebrated his first Tiger win in the 3-0 home victory over Bournemouth.

Brian Horton receives his Manager of the Month Award ifor March 1985.

That latter result offered some measure of revenge for the Cup defeat some three months earlier; if anything, the result was more meaningful as League points were at stake.

The opening weeks of the League programme produced a sedate rather than spectacular start to Horton's reign, but between October and January the Tigers embarked on a thirteen match unbeaten run that put them firmly in the promotion frame – by the time they'd drawn 1-1 away to Bournemouth, they were in second place in the table. Although the next five matches brought three defeats, another unbeaten run, this time encompassing nine matches, steered the Tigers towards promotion. A 1-0 victory at Walsall confirmed their return to Division Two after a seven-year absence.

Horton had already made one astute signing in anticipation of the Tigers operating at a higher grade, when he signed Richard Jobson – although in Jobson's early days the wisdom of his acquisition was doubted. Horton also added two more promising youngsters to his squad. Returning to one of his former clubs, Luton, Horton acquired the signatures of Frankie Bunn and Gary Parker. Both would prove more than capable of operating at Division Two level, and both went on to make their names at a much higher level, albeit with other clubs.

If City's supporters thought that their first season in Division Two (1985/86) would be one of consolidation, they were in for a pleasant surprise, and many of the Tigers' opponents got quite a shock. Although it took them seven games to claim their first League win, from that point on they rapidly adjusted to life at the higher grade and mounted a credible and consistent challenge for promotion. They ended the season in sixth place, their highest League placing for over a decade.

It proved to be a memorable season, both on and off the field. Their first ever League game at home on a Sunday (22nd December 1985) produced a 2-1 win over fierce local rivals, Leeds United, and a new club record for a transfer fee received was established, when centre-forward Billy Whitehurst was sold to Newcastle United for in excess of £¼ million.

That Billy Whitehurst was the reason for rewriting this record would have surprised many who watched him during his early Tiger days. Signed from Mexborough Town for less than a tenth of what he was eventually sold for, his early performances suggested that City had been robbed. His strength, attitude and commitment were never in doubt, it was just the apparent lack of skill, ability and craft that caused concern on the terraces. Eventually 'Big Billy' came good, and for that much of the credit must go to THE Hull City centre-forward of all time, Chris Chilton. Under Chillo's coaching Billy mastered the art of forward play and gave the Tigers' attack a cutting edge. In Billy's case it was more broadsword than rapier, but it was effective and many's the time that an opposing manager offered to take him off the Tigers' hands. It took big money from a big club to finally persuade City to let Bill move on.

After all the positives that had come out of the season just ended and despite the loss of their hero, the following campaign was eagerly anticipated. As has often been the case with Hull City, they flattered to deceive. Undefeated during the opening month (August), they slumped in September – one win and five defeats – recovered slightly in October and November but had a disastrous December and New Year that saw them suffer heavy defeats. They were slipping into the relegation battle before they finally got their act together and produced a string of strong performances in the closing weeks to settle just below mid-table.

The reasons for such sharply contrasting efforts in consecutive seasons is a subject that has exercised the minds of many City fans throughout their history, and to my knowledge no satisfactory answer has yet been found. From one season to the next, they were the perennial Jekyll and Hyde of the Football League and it was anyone's guess as to which one would be wearing a Hull City shirt at the start of each new season.

When the 1987/88 campaign got under way, early results suggested that Dr Jekyll was in residence. By the time the Christmas fixtures got underway the Tigers were in sixth place and well placed to challenge for promotion. It soon became apparent, however, that Dr Jekyll had been drinking from the wrong bottle during the festivities, and as the New Year unfolded, Mr Hyde had replaced him. After a run of sixteen matches without a win, stretching from the middle of January to the middle of April, the 4-1 home defeat by Swindon Town on 12th April brought about Horton's dismissal. Moments after the game ended, Don Robinson told Horton his services were no longer required; only months earlier he'd invited Horton to join the Board of Directors in recognition of his achievements. Football, a funny game? Whatever gives you that impression?

Having had time to think about his outburst, Robinson, realising that his decision had been based more on rage than reason, tried to revoke Horton's dismissal. Horton refused his overtures, taking a philosophical view about the decision. "It was not a surprise. I have been in this game long enough to see the signs. You go into management knowing that unless you are consistently successful you will be sacked." For the remainder of the season, Tom Wilson and Dennis Booth shared the role of caretaker manager and guided the Tigers through their last four games of the season without defeat.

Don Robinson drew up a shortlist from which to select Brian Horton's successor. It contained just three names: Eddie Gray, Peter Reid and Terry Yorath. In the end he plumped for Gray, whose managerial experience was the greater and who had done well at Rochdale under difficult financial circumstances. In announcing his decision Don Robinson revealed that he had admired Gray's managerial qualities for some time, in fact he admitted that if he had been looking for a manager three years previously, then Eddie Gray would have been his choice.

Gray had been manager at Rochdale for two years having previously been player manager at Leeds United. His spell at Rochdale had been successful in terms of keeping them in the League, on a budget that made the money available to him at Boothferry Park look like a lottery rollover win – and Don Robinson was renowned for being prudent with the pounds!

Gray retained Dennis Booth as his assistant. Many had expected Booth to be given the job of manager but rather than take umbrage at being overlooked, Booth was willing to help Gray put the Tigers in Division One. "Naturally I'm a little disappointed not to get the job," he said "but my ambition for Hull City is the same as it has always been. That is to help them into the First Division and I would like to see that through."

Gray got his Tigers off to the best possible start in the new League season (1988/89) with a 1-0 home victory over Manchester City. It was a somewhat fortuitous victory as the Tigers spent much of the game under pressure from the Manchester midfield and attack. It also proved to be a rare victory in the first half of the season as the Tigers only gained another four wins in the League. It meant that they were in relegation trouble for much of the time and the signs didn't look good when the Tigers sold Tony Norman to Sunderland in the last week of 1988.

Throughout the history of Hull City there have been many good goalkeepers charged with the responsibility of guarding the Tigers' net. Spendiff, Roughley, Hendry, Mercer,

Tony Norman – Hull City's greatest ever goalkeeper?

Maddison, Bly, McKechnie, Wealands, Fettis and Carroll all had records that withstand scrutiny. Tony Norman was up there with them, and in many respects his statistics put him ahead of them all. Norman arrived as a relative unknown from Burnley in February 1980. He was a Mike Smith signing – one of the few things that the former Welsh manager got right in his unhappy spell with the Tigers. Norman soon demonstrated a level of competency and consistency that became his hallmark. Between August 1983 and September 1988, Norman never missed a single League or Cup match. In doing so he set a new club record for consecutive appearances. Running concurrently with that ever-present attribute were two promotions for the Tigers and international recognition with Wales.

His move to Roker Park involved the return of a former City favourite, Billy Whitehurst, and a replacement goal-

keeper in Iain Hesford. Whitehurst scored on his 'second' debut for the Tigers, whilst Hesford made a more modest contribution to the game: a 1-1 draw at Boothferry Park. As the remainder of the season unfolded City continued flattering to deceive. Four wins in five games took them to the middle of February. From then until the end of the season in mid May they won only one further game in the League.

Some respite came in the shape of a lucrative FA Cup run that included a 2-1 victory at Bradford City. That game resulted in the dismissal of Bradford's management team Terry Dolan and Stan Ternent – both would go on to make their mark in the history of Hull City before the century was out. The cup run ended on 18th February when the Tigers entertained Liverpool in the fifth round before a crowd of over 20,000 – the last time the Tigers would play at Boothferry Park in front of a crowd of such size.

A potential 'Cup shock' was on the cards at half-time as City led 2-1, but the final score of 3-2 in favour of Liverpool left the remainder of the season somewhat barren. Their only victory in those remaining weeks came against Plymouth Argyle on March 25th. The game also provided the debut for two new Tigers: Ian McParland and Peter Swan. At a combined cost in excess of £350,000 – Peter Swan becoming, at the time, the Tigers most expensive signing at £200,000 – it was a desperate last throw of the dice to resurrect a disappointing season. It failed.

Eddie Gray spent some serious money to acquire the services of Ian McParland.....

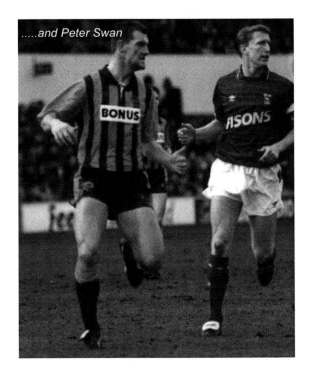
.....and Peter Swan

After eleven months in charge Eddie Gray was sacked. Explaining his decision Robinson said "It is a very sad day, Eddie is one of the nicest people I have ever had the privilege of meeting…but it is just a matter of things not having worked out." Dennis Booth was also shown the door, ending a playing and coaching association with the Tigers that had spanned some nine years.

To whom would Robinson turn now to revive the flagging fortunes of Hull City? In an attempt to recreate the success enjoyed in the early years of his chairmanship, Robinson reappointed Colin Appleton as manager. In stark contrast to his earlier spell at the club, Appleton's six-month reign at Boothferry Park was nothing short of disastrous, with the team winning only one match out of fifteen.

It came as no surprise, therefore, that when Don Robinson announced his own resignation on 30th October 1989, the new incumbent, Richard Chetham, sacked Appleton almost immediately and replaced him, temporarily, with Tom Wilson. Wilson's spell in charge was a short one as the new chairman soon made a permanent appointment: Stan Ternent, who at the time was a coach with Crystal Palace.

The task facing Ternent was a daunting one. So far, during the 1989/90 season, the team had managed no victories in the first sixteen League games but Ternent managed one in his first match, ironically a 3-2 victory at one of his old clubs, Bradford City.

Ternent's strategy, throughout his time at Boothferry Park, appeared to be based on acquiring players of experience such as Dave Bamber, Malcolm Shotton, and Leigh Palin, plus youngsters with potential such as Paul Hunter. Such a strategy did not come cheap, but it seemed to have the desired effect on results and by the end of the 1989/90 season Ternent had steered the Tigers to a respectable midtable spot that had seemed unimaginable six months earlier.

Whilst the Tigers were making steady progress towards Second Division safety, City's new chairman announced plans for a share issue aimed at raising £1 million. The last time such a move had been proposed was when the club had been reformed straight after World War Two. At that time the response by the public of Hull raised over £50,000. Much more was needed this time if the Tigers were to remain secure at Boothferry Park. Take up of the share offer was modest in the extreme and the £1 million was never raised. A sign of the times it may have been, but in hindsight it was more a sign of things to come as far as the Tigers were concerned.

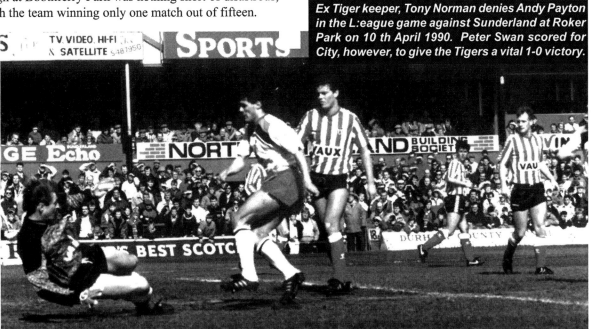
Ex Tiger keeper, Tony Norman denies Andy Payton in the L:eague game against Sunderland at Roker Park on 10 th April 1990. Peter Swan scored for City, however, to give the Tigers a vital 1-0 victory.

## CHAPTER 9

THE DARK AGES

1990 - 1998

During the summer of 1990, Ternent continued his spending spree: acquiring David Mail for £160,000 from Blackburn Rovers and Tony Finnigan for a more modest £30,000 from the same club; a further £80,000 went on acquiring the services of Russ Wilcox from Northampton Town. Ternent was clearly intent on mounting a major assault on the promotion front for the 1990/91 season.

City's new signings for the start of the 1990/91 season (left to right): Russ Wilcox, Tony Finnigan and David Mail.

first half of the season they won only five of the 23 League games played. Included amongst them was a fine 2-1 victory over Newcastle United and a 5-2 thumping of Leicester City. Offset against those, however, was the 7-1 thrashing at Upton Park by West Ham, a 4-1 bashing from Bristol City and a 2-1 home defeat against Barnsley on the 29th December that saw the Tigers rooted to the bottom of the table. Could things get worse? Would they get worse? They could; they would. They did.

That assault fell pretty much at the first hurdle when just two games into the season came the announcement that Richard Jobson had been sold to Oldham Athletic in a deal worth nearly £½ million. Even before that news the season hadn't started well, with both of those games ending in 2-1 defeats: at home to Notts County and away to Blackburn Rovers. If that wasn't bad enough, whilst Jobson was making his debut for Oldham in a 3-1 victory over Portsmouth that took them to the top of the Second Division, the Tigers suffered a 5-1 humiliation away to Sheffield Wednesday that left them at the bottom of the same table.

In hindsight it would probably have been kinder if the season had ended there and then. It would have saved City's fans a lot of suffering; it would have saved City some cash and it wouldn't have made much difference to the business ends of the final League table. Nine months later, that final League table for the 1990/91 season still showed Oldham at the top and City rock bottom. Jobson's Oldham went to Division One; Ternent's Tigers went to Division Three. Well the latter part of that statement wasn't strictly true. The Tigers did go to Division Three, but Ternent had been sacked well before the "I's and T's" of the season had been dotted and crossed.

The departure of Jobson was a blow from which neither Ternent nor the team seemed to recover. Victories were sporadic during the rest of 1990: it took the Tigers eight attempts before they recorded a League win and in the

On New Year's Day 1991, the Tigers travelled to Fratton Park and were trounced by Portsmouth – the 5-1 scoreline in Pompey's favour could have been much worse. The reaction of the travelling supporters left the chairman, Richard Chetham, in no doubt as to what action was needed, and two days later he took it. Ternent was sacked.

Ternent departed insisting that he had not been given the backing promised him by the Board. In the local press (Hull Daily Mail) he was quoted: "We have made some progress since I came here but I don't feel I have had the backing that I was promised…I kept the club in the Second Division last season and I would have done it again this season but unfortunately the Chairman and the Board of Directors feel a change is in the best interest of Hull City…"

Whether the promises referred to by Ternent were kept or not was something the supporters were not privy to. All they knew was that when Ternent had taken over the Tigers in November 1989 the club were bottom of Division Two; thirteen months later they were still bottom of Division Two. In between Ternent's wheeling and dealing had involved expenditure on players of approximately £750,000, and income from player sales of approximately £745,000. Where was the progress he referred to?

Tom Wilson again assumed the mantle of caretaker manager. His first game in charge was the FA Cup Round Three tie against Notts County at Boothferry Park on 5th January 1991. City lost 5-2. Next came Sheffield Wednesday at home in the League on the 12th January. City lost 1-0. Seven days later the Tigers travelled to Swindon for their next game; they lost 3-1. Before the Tigers took to the field again, the weather had called time-out and the rest of January was a fallow period. However, Richard Chetham put the time to good use and appointed a new manager. On 30th January Terry Dolan's nameplate was affixed to the manager's door at Boothferry Park.

In announcing the appointment the chairman stated: "…I am very confident that his (Terry Dolan) appointment as Hull City's new manager will bring about a change in our fortunes." He went on: "We hope that this will be the start of a long period of stability at Hull City." If only his crystal ball had been working when he made that statement, perhaps he might have chosen his words more carefully.

Dolan's debut began with a defeat and for the rest of the season he presided over a long battle against relegation. It was one he lost. Three victories in the remaining 21 games were insufficient for the team to avoid demotion for the second season in succession. The only light that shone in the dark days of 1990/91 were the goals of Andy Payton and Peter Swan, and both departed within months of Dolan's arrival.

Like Ken Houghton some two decades earlier in similar circumstances, Dolan was absolved of much of the blame for another relegation. Yet whilst the disappointment of demotion dominated the close-season conversations, attention was briefly diverted to the future of Boothferry Park. Plans were announced to build a new all-seater North Stand. The idea was to convert the terracing into seats, as well as installing further seats on the roof of the supermarket; the intention was for the work to be completed by the close of the 1991/92 season.

The plan was a "priority as far as ground improvements at Boothferry Park are concerned", according to vice-chairman Martin Fish, who fronted the press conference. He went on to explain that restricting away fans to the North Stand would make 500 seats in the West Stand available for home supporters and it would also cut down on policing costs. The plan never materialised however, and the only tangible alteration to Boothferry Park during that season was the removal of the perimeter fencing.

From an accountant's viewpoint relegation was perhaps a blessing for the Tigers. The Taylor Report – produced to look at football stadium safety following the Hillsborough disaster – had insisted that all First and Second Division clubs would be required to make their grounds all-seating by 1994. Those clubs in Divisions Three and Four had until the year 2000 to comply. Thus, City had a 6-year breathing space – assuming they weren't promoted during that time. It turned out to be a safe assumption.

The additional time was important; for as well as the terracing on the North Stand there was also the East Stand, which was completely terraced, and the terracing in front of the South and West Stand seating areas. To make the East Stand all-seating would cost in the region of £4m; converting the South and West Stands would not be cheap either. The plans were ambitious but the costs, given City's current plight, made them unaffordable. Not surprisingly, therefore, none of the planned developments took place.

That the plans for developing Boothferry Park had been announced by the club's vice-chairman, Martin Fish, was no great surprise. Fish was an accountant by profession and brought those skills with him when invited into the boardroom during the summer of 1987. In addition, at the time of the announcement Richard Chetham was not in the best of health.

The severity of Chetham's illness became apparent later in the summer when he announced that he was standing down as chairman and handing over control of the club to Martin Fish. The responsibility for improving the club's fortunes on and off the pitch now lay in the hands of Martin Fish and Terry Dolan. History does not look kindly on their efforts and for the squeamish amongst you it is recommended that the next few pages are skipped.

Martin Fish took over as chairman of Hull City in the summer of 1991

To place the blame entirely at the feet of Fish and Dolan for the depths to which Hull City plummeted throughout the rest of the 90s may seem unfair. But some do. In their defence and, in an attempt to take a rational and dispassionate approach to understanding the causes and reasons for the Tigers' decline, it could be argued that their starting base was not the best.

The club had been in decline for many years; their descent of the League and a perusal of the accounts during that time suggested little else. Financial trouble was prevalent. Within months of Fish and Dolan's reign beginning Peter Swan and Andy Payton had been sold to Port Vale and Middlesbrough respectively for a combined sum in excess of £1 million. None of that money was made available for team strengthening; virtually all of it went on keeping the Tigers in business. In one respect therefore you could argue that Fish and Dolan were instrumental in keeping the Tigers alive. Not many did, however.

Dolan's first full season in charge (1991/92) saw the Tigers put together a frustrating sequence of results – classic examples being the 4-1 defeat at Brentford on 17th September, followed four days later by the 4-1 home victory over Torquay. As a consequence they got a little too close to the relegation zone for comfort on more than one occasion during that season, and only a sequence of four consecutive victories in the last four games of the campaign banished any prospect of a second consecutive relegation and left them in 14th place.

Decent runs in both FA and League Cup competitions offered temporary respite and revenue, though the future looked anything but bright as worsening financial circumstances dictated that what ability there was at the club soon found itself in some other team, and any money generated from the sale was used solely to keep Hull City going.

Despite their mid-table finish, the Tigers found themselves in Division Two at the start of the 1992/93 season. It came about through a restructuring of the Football League (FL) that saw the First Division clubs breaking away to form the Premier League and the remaining divisions within the FL stepping up in name, though not necessarily in quality. However, City's start to the season was reasonable, with four victories in the opening five League games.

Andy Payton's transfer to Middlesbrough for £750,000 set a new club record.

It was a young team – illustrated by the fact that Matt Edeson, whose debut against Fulham on 10th October 1992, made him City's youngest ever League debutant – bolstered by loan signings. This meant that nearly 30 players were used throughout the season and the frequent changes to the team line-up did not help; neither did the sale of Leigh Jenkinson to Coventry, but finances dictated. Relegation was avoided, but only just.

Things were bad at Boothferry Park, and they were deteriorating. Money was scarce and that meant there was little hope of things improving on the field. The prospects of the ground being developed were pretty much zero and diminishing further as each month passed. Whichever way you looked, it didn't look good. "No cash and no ambition" was the headline in the Hull Daily Mail when they carried out the post-mortem on City's season. It was a damning but accurate assessment.

Against that backdrop, the following season (1993/94) was a pleasant surprise. Injuries and limited resources created a strike partnership that proved an instant success. Linton Brown – a rare purchase at the beginning of 1993 courtesy of money from the Supporters fund – and Dean Windass – a local lad getting a second chance at making the grade in professional football – set about scoring goals with a regularity not seen since the days of Swan and Payton.

The rag, tag and bobtail collection of free transfers, loan signings and promising youngsters gelled into a team that actually threatened the play-offs and promotion; in the end they finished ninth. In the context of Hull City's history, it was perhaps nothing to get excited about, but in the current climate it was worth savouring. As the following season (1994/95) unfolded, it promised to be even better as the Tigers' eclectic squad maintained their improvement and again flirted with the play-offs until the last few games, eventually having to settle for eighth place.

Terry Dolan's efforts in this 'revival' were recognised when he won the Manager of the Month award for October (1994) after the club had enjoyed a seven match unbeaten run. Given the resources at his disposal and the financial constraints under which the club were operating, it was a worthy achievement.

Whilst October 1994 was good news week for City fans in one sense, in another it was a melancholy month. Raich Carter, the original post-war hero of Hull City died after a long illness. His cortege called at Boothferry Park and the current squad, plus many of the spectators who had hailed Carter in his Tiger playing days were there to pay their respects. The team paid their tribute on the field by thrashing Crewe 7-1 in the first home fixture after Carter's death.

History reveals that the peak of Dolan's popularity as City's boss was reached during the 1994/95 season. From that point on, until his departure in the summer of 1997, he carried out his duties amidst an atmosphere of acrimony and anguish for the dwindling band of supporters.

If the promise displayed in the previous two seasons had raised the supporters hopes that the corner had been turned and the good times might be returning, then season 1995/96 shattered those illusions without mercy. For the second time in Dolan's reign the Tigers were relegated. It was an horrendous season. It began with a home defeat; it ended with a home defeat. In between the Tigers won only five of their 46 League fixtures, made little progress in any of the cup competitions and sold two of their prized assets – Dean Windass and Alan Fettis – for something in the region of £1 million.

Terry Dolan receives his Manager of the Month award for October 1994.

Dean Windass City's 'Local Hero' in the mid 1990s

The selling of these two stars may have disposed of City's debt, but it also disposed of any chance City had of avoiding relegation.

From the spectator's perspective it was a disaster and what compounded the disaster was the insult perpetrated on the supporters in the aforementioned final home game of the season on 4th May 1996. The game in question was a local derby against Bradford City. The Tigers were already relegated but Bradford needed a win to secure a place in the play-offs, and interest in the match was high amongst their supporters with large numbers expected to attend. Boothferry Park's poor state of repair meant that the part of the ground normally allocated to visiting supporters would not be big enough. The chairman announced that the South Stand – both seats and terracing – would be given over to accommodate the Bradford fans, with the regular South Stand supporters being moved into the North Stand terracing and West Stand seats. The decision was not well received.

For many City supporters it was the cardinal sin and final straw combined. The chairman's explanation that the decision had been made on the advice of the Police was essentially a waste of breath. It cut no ice with the fans and any prospects of forgiveness were on a par with City's chances of avoiding relegation: non-existent.

The anticipated trouble occurred with pitch invasions, fighting amongst supporters and the consequential interruptions to play. The battle lines between Tigers' fans and Martin Fish had been drawn.

Whilst this particular Boothferry Park battle was being fought, the whole question of the ground's future was very much in the spotlight. A couple of months before the Bradford game the directors had admitted that they were considering leaving the stadium. The ground was in desperate need of repair and development. Either approach would cost substantial sums of money, which the club did not have.

Although Boothferry Park came under the organisational umbrella of Hull City football club, exactly whose name was on the title deeds was an intricate question that probably required the skills of an accountant rather than an estate agent to answer it fully. In the process of any such investigation, the name of Central Land Holdings (CLH) would have eventually emerged. The chairman of CLH was former Hull City chairman and currently a director of the club, Christopher Needler. CLH had received an offer for Boothferry Park in the region of £5 million. If the directors were to accept it, they would need to find an alternative home.

Alternative sites and options were on offer: either a new location such as Costello Stadium, or Priory Park, or the club could ground share with one of the city's rugby league clubs – it had happened before, back in the early days of the Tigers' existence – but ground sharing appeared to be neither an economical nor politically acceptable option. Building a new ground would cost a minimum of £8m and only provide accommodation for about 8,000 spectators – hardly in keeping with the vision put forward some fifty years earlier by Christopher Needler's father, Harold.

In the end the Directors opted to remain at Boothferry Park and work towards developing the ground themselves. Given the alternatives, it was not a difficult decision to take. Again, various options were to be considered as to which parts would be developed and when. The issue of the ground's future and ownership would take on even greater significance in the coming years, but for the time being it was put on the back burner as more immediate issues demanded attention. First of all was the fact that the club was again operating in the basement division of the Football League.

It was that issue, amongst others, that caused some disgruntled supporters to create an organisation called 'Tigers 2000'. Their apparent 'raison d'etre' was to remove the existing boardroom regime from Boothferry Park. 'Tigers 2000' wanted success to return to Hull City, and they saw little chance of that happening whilst Martin Fish

remained as chairman, particularly since he'd extended the contract of Terry Dolan and his assistant (Geoff Lee) almost immediately after the club's recent relegation.

In his defence Fish argued that but for his efforts, combined with those of Dolan and Lee, there would have been no Hull City to be arguing over; the club could have folded more than once under their stewardship. This was true; in fact Fish was probably as familiar with the courtroom as he was with the boardroom, having frequently visited the former to stave off various winding up orders against the club from a number of organisations, including the Inland Revenue.

Such an explanation did little to appease the aggrieved supporters and it was in such an atmosphere that the 1996/97 season commenced. An opening sequence of ten games undefeated in the League gave City a more than respectable start to the campaign. The run included the home fixture against Barnet on 31st August 1996, 50 years to the day since Boothferry Park had staged its first fixture. Even though half a century separated the games, they were linked by the same 0-0 scoreline.

Despite the undefeated sequence and the Golden Jubilee celebrations, the relationship between supporters and club remained one of simmering resentment. One almost got the feeling that certain sections of the fans were patiently waiting, even hoping, for City to lose so that hostilities against the management, at all levels, could be resumed and intensified. That opportunity came on 5th October 1996, a home game against local rivals Scunthorpe United. The 2-0 reverse suffered by City ignited a large protest.

During the game the pitch was invaded and a sit-down protest staged in the centre circle. After the game the protests continued. Adopting a siege mentality, Fish remained defiant. "I am not going and Terry Dolan will not be going," he said. "We will work our way through this." Defiant but buoyant words from a defiant but beleaguered chairman.

Fish's optimism proved to be unfounded. As the season unfolded, following that Scunthorpe game, so the results deteriorated and assets disposed of – the latest being Roy Carroll, sold for a fraction of his worth for the sake of cash flow. From the remaining 35 League games, only nine victories were recorded. A final finishing position of seventeenth may have looked disappointing but if it hadn't been for the strong start, the final position would have been much worse. But in the midst of that disappointment shone the dim glow of a new club record. The FA Cup replay at Boothferry Park on 26th November 1996, produced the most goals scored by a City player in a single League or Cup game when Duane Darby scored a double hat-trick in the Tigers' 8-4 victory over non-League Whitby Town, which was only sealed in extra time.

Less than a week before that Whitby game, another entry had been made in the Tigers' record book. The midweek home fixture against Torquay United produced an attendance of 1,775, the lowest ever officially recorded home attendance for the Tigers in either League or Cup. A number of factors conspired in its creation: a midweek visit from Torquay brought few opposition supporters; a cold and dreary winter's evening at Boothferry Park was not an enticing prospect when live Champions League football was on the telly; one win from City's previous ten League games offered little to whet the supporter's appetite and supporter dissatisfaction with the present regime was on the increase.

Little wonder, therefore, that the club's AGM held a few weeks later did not strictly adhere to the Biblical commandment "Love thy Neighbour".

In the run-up to that meeting, the issue of the future location of the Tigers' lair had resurfaced. It was becoming increasingly apparent that Boothferry Park was unlikely to remain their home for much longer. Having being denied assistance from the Football Trust to develop the ground, and having given the cold shoulder to a proposal to share a multi-use stadium on the banks of the Humber, made by a local property developer, there were still other options to be considered by the directors. One was an approach from a former chairman and owner of the club, Don Robinson.

It was no secret that the club was up for sale, and Robinson tabled an offer of £1.5 million for the club. The response of the directors was to offer Robinson control of the football side of the club for the princely sum of £1, with the existing board retaining the short term ownership of the ground. Not surprisingly Robinson rejected the offer.

Another option was the proposal from Needler for local government and businesses to work with the club in providing and developing a new ground, or 'super stadium' as he referred to the project. The initial response from the council did not look promising when council leader, Pat Doyle, stated: "We have neither the capital nor revenue to spend on a super stadium. But we do have land and we do have the ability to access lottery funds and talk to the sports council."

Picking up on Councillor Doyle's comments Christopher Needler called on the council to provide land for a new stadium.

Duane Darby scored a double hat-trick in City's 8-4 victory over Whitby Town in the FA Cup 1st round replay on 26th November 1996

Needler also offered to assist by applying for grants to support this project. There was no mention of money forthcoming from the Needler family, but his choice of words was interesting and somewhat prophetic. "Discussions about a super stadium with the city council is the future for Hull City," He was right, it would prove to be the future for the Tigers but there were still many twists and turns to be taken first.

Initial discussions between City's directors and the Council did not progress smoothly. In rejecting the club's initial proposal, a statement issued by the council suggested that: "A project of this magnitude will inevitably require substantial financial backing…it will also take some time to develop an appropriate financial package…and also to appraise the many planning and environmental issues once a potentially suitable site can be identified." It went on "The current proposal … unfortunately does not yet satisfy the council's principal objectives." The council were looking for a project that would serve the community as well as providing a home for at least one of the city's three professional sports clubs.

At the Tigers' AGM, held just a month after the debate over the concept of a super stadium began, Needler spelled out in stark terms what the future held for Hull City if something wasn't done soon. He re-iterated the explanation of the Directors' rejection of Robinson's original offer, that to accept would have been unfair to existing shareholders. He also confirmed that the decision had been made to sell Boothferry Park, and again called on local government and businesses to help provide and develop a new ground. Needler warned that unless the super stadium became a reality the Tigers would more than likely be heading for receivership again. The club's debts were mounting (including £750,000 still owed to Needler) and the bank was pressing for repayment of its financial assistance.

The only asset available to resolve the problem was Boothferry Park, for which the earlier offer of £5m was still valid. By the time the AGM was held (mid-December 1996) the Tigers' performances on the field were clearly indicating that promotion at the first time of asking would not be happening. For the remainder of the season it was where the Tigers would reside in the future – if they still had one – that tended to dominate the headlines, and as the season wore on the odds on the club having new owners shortened.

Not pitch advertising, just a clear message to club chairman, Martin Fish, from a certain section of City's fans

Whilst this debate raged a seemingly unconnected event was taking place many miles away from the East Riding that would have a significant impact not only on Hull City, but also on sport in the city. The event in question was a round of golf involving two businessmen with sporting backgrounds: one was Tim Wilby, an ex-Rugby League professional; the other was David Lloyd, a successful entrepreneur who had also enjoyed a fruitful career as a tennis professional – by British standards anyway.

During the game Wilby, whose Rugby career had taken in a spell with Hull FC, explained to Lloyd the untapped sporting and business potential that existed within the city of Hull and surrounding area. Lloyd's interest was aroused and by April 1997 he was actively involved in negotiations to purchase the Tigers, having already taken a major financial interest in Hull F.C. – that interest would extend to full control before very long.

Whilst negotiations to buy Hull City were in full swing, the Tigers were limping towards the end of another dreadfully disappointing season. The football had been so poor that little attention had been paid to it as all the action seemed to be taking place off the pitch with the talk of new owners, a new stadium and a new manager accounting for the majority of newspaper column inches. Yet whilst all this 'new' talk was going on, there was no let up in the campaign to remove the old regime. The protests against Fish and Dolan continued both inside and outside the ground. At times it got nasty.

Towards the end of June the negotiations concerning the sale of Hull City appeared to be complete, with David Lloyd acquiring control. Tim Wilby was immediately installed as the Tigers' new chairman and one of his first tasks was to advise Terry Dolan that his services were no longer required.

The 'sacking' of Dolan was a little premature, however, as technically the club was still under the control of Fish and Needler due to a delay in the paperwork at the Takeovers and Mergers Commission.

Thus when pre-season training began at the beginning of July 1997, it was Fish who recalled Dolan to Boothferry Park to supervise the initial training programme until the takeover was completed. That took a few days longer than expected but by 11th July the deal was finally and formally completed. Lloyd and Wilby were in charge; Fish and Dolan had departed Boothferry Park. From the perspective of City's supporters their initial aspirations had been achieved: the Tigers had been saved; regime change had taken place at Boothferry Park, and there was the promise of a new manager, new players and before too long a new home.

Lloyd's plans centred on the sale of both Boothferry Park and the Boulevard, with a new stadium being built on land he hoped the Council would donate. In the interim, because of the conditions placed on the sale by Christopher Needler, the Tigers' immediate future would rest at Boothferry Park. However, before too long Lloyd hoped to have moved the Tigers out of their present home to share the Boulevard with Hull FC until the new stadium was built…wherever that might be.

Within a couple of days of formally taking control, Tim Wilby was introducing the Tigers' 'big name' manager to the media. It was Mark Hateley, who'd had a successful playing career for a variety of big British clubs, and some foreign ones as well, together with over 30 international appearances for England. On the playing front he was indeed a big name, but as far as management went he was an unknown quantity. Still, even the greatest of football's bosses had started their managerial careers somewhere, why not Boothferry Park for Mark Hateley?

Mark Hateley - appointed as City's new manager in July 1997

Spirits were revived slightly a few days later with a 0-0 draw away to Macclesfield Town in the First Round, First Leg, of the Coca Cola League Cup so that when the Tigers staged their first League fixture at Boothferry Park on 16th August there was something of a carnival atmosphere about the place.

Adding to the occasion was the first visit to Boothferry Park of City's new owner David Lloyd. A crowd of over 7,400 attended the Notts County game – more than double the previous season's average. Lloyd received a warm reception from the home supporters before the start of the game, but it would turn out to be one of the very few times that owner and supporters were in mutual appreciation mode. Looking back, the relationship between the two was peaking early. It would only be a matter of months before it spiralled down into mutual loathing. If City's fans had thought the club's problems were over and a new era was dawning, they were wrong.

What didn't help was City's erratic form. Their first League victory of the season came at the fourth time of asking. When it arrived, on 30th August, it set a record: the highest number of goals seen in a League fixture at Boothferry Park, with Swansea City beaten 7-4. Any hope it gave was short-lived and so was the chairman's reign. By mid September Wilby had 'resigned' and David Lloyd had taken over. Now the fun started.

With less than a month before the start of the new season Hateley, together with his assistant, Billy Kirkwood, had little opportunity to put too many plans in place for the new campaign. However, from the way the pre-season friendlies had gone there were grounds for optimism and despite their recent actions, Hull City fans were never short of optimism, especially as the off the field problems appeared to be in the process of being resolved; it meant they could divert their full attention to playing matters.

Such optimism received a dash of reality when the 1997/98 League season opened with a 2-0 defeat away to Mansfield Town on 9th August 1997.

City's Mark Greaves (4) challenges Newcastle's John Barnes during the Coca-Cola Cup tie at St James' Park on 15th October 1997.

Although Hateley was allowed by Lloyd to bring in some players– such as ex-England international David Rocastle on loan from Chelsea, and Chris Bettney from Sheffield United, and to spend a small sum on acquiring Matt Hocking, also from Sheffield United, the Tigers League form continued to be erratic. It was tolerated on the terraces whilst they maintained their progress in the Coca-Cola League Cup.

Having disposed of Macclesfield in Round One, the Tigers gained a notable scalp in Premier League newcomers Crystal Palace in Round Two. That set up another encounter with Premiership opposition: a trip to face Newcastle United. Although not disgraced by the 2-0 defeat, the Tigers were never in with a shout of delivering another shock result. They therefore returned to League matters and continued along their erratic way – three days after a decent display against Newcastle they lost 2-0 at Barnet.

That result left City second from bottom in the table and facing a relegation fight. Three days after the Barnet trip they were at Cambridge United, where they recorded their first away League victory of the season. Rather than congratulating his manager on a good result, after the game Lloyd allegedly berated Hateley for spending money unnecessarily on hotel facilities for the players before the game. It seemed the chairman was more concerned about pounds than points.

Lloyd's bank statements probably told him he had good reason to be. Negotiations over the sale of Boothferry Park were not progressing well, and every day's delay cost him money. Neither were his plans for a new super stadium going smoothly.

Problems with the sitting tenants (Kwik Save) at Boothferry Park, failure to acquire a site for the new stadium, poor relations with the city council and mounting debts were putting pressure on Lloyd and his bank account. Thus, it was imperative, in Lloyd's view, that the Tigers move from their home and lodge at the Boulevard as quickly as possible.

Whilst the League Cup had offered the supporters some hope for the season, the FA Cup merely provided humiliation. For the first time in City's post-war history they lost at home to a non-League outfit, Hednesford Town, by a 2-0 margin on 15th November. It was back to the League therefore and a battle to avoid the drop for the remainder of the season. Further loan signings – Brian McGinty and Steven Boyack from Hateley's former club, Rangers – helped the cause, but it was the lack of effort from others, that finally saved their season. The early confirmation of Doncaster's relegation to the Conference prevented Hateley and Lloyd's first season in charge from being a total embarrassment.

Lloyd's plans for both Hull City and Hull FC, as regards their future accommodation arrangements, continued to go badly. Opposition to his plans grew with each passing day. If City moved, and Boothferry Park was sold, the fans believed the club would never find a home and the one remaining asset would be gone. Lloyd's relationship with the council was deteriorating rapidly and the early love affair with both club's supporters was well and truly over. The Annual General Meetings of both clubs were stormy events – after the meetings he publicly accused the people of Hull of "…living in the dark ages." With Lloyd's help, they would get darker.

## CHAPTER 10

FROM NADIR TO NIRVANA

*A*gainst a background of simmering hostility between supporters and sole shareholder, the 1998/99 season got under way. So far the 90's had not been nice for Tigers' fans. The merest sniff of success had occurred in the earlier years of the decade but now, as it drew towards its close, the aroma around Boothferry Park certainly wasn't Calvin Klein; it was more decay and decline. But there was worse still to come.

Hateley brought in new faces – such as David D'Auria, Jon French, Stevie Hawes and Neil Whitworth – and some not so new (David Brown) before the season started; he even made the traditional pre-season optimistic noises about promotion. The season began, however, pretty much as the previous one. Two defeats in the opening two games set the tone. After the 2-1 home defeat against Darlington, Lloyd was critical of both team and fans. All the signs were that he'd had enough and was looking for a way out – before too long it was common knowledge that Lloyd's representatives were in discussion with prospective buyers for Hull City.

Although Lloyd rejected early offers for the club, after the Worthington Cup game at Bolton Wanderers on 15th September nobody was in any doubt that David Lloyd and Hull City would not remain an item for any longer than absolutely necessary. The scoreline in that game was 3-1 to Bolton, not a surprise given the League positions of both teams at the time: Bolton were eighth in Division One, City were second from bottom in Division Three. Yet the game still caught the media's attention.

What generated the interest was the protest mounted at the Reebok Stadium by the travelling City fans. It was loud; it was sustained and in one respect it was novel. There was the traditional request for the chairman to take his leave – although the words used were slightly more Anglo-Saxon in their meaning. Lloyd's intentions to move the Tigers to the Boulevard were dealt with in an equally forthright manner, but what made the point more graphically than any chanting was the tennis ball protest, involving hundreds of tennis balls being thrown onto the pitch by City fans. It was their way of advising Lloyd to stick to what he knew best.

The point was well made. Hours after the game, Lloyd apparently instructed his representatives to contact the prospective buyer of Hull City, whose offer had again been rejected just hours before the game at Bolton. Lloyd had changed his mind. The offer was accepted.

Aware that the pendulum of negotiation had swung their way, the consortium – headed by former Scunthorpe United chairman, Tom Belton – tried to alter the terms of the offer and the timescale of payments. Whilst Lloyd was keen to offload Hull City from his investment portfolio, he would not do so on the terms suggested and the consortium's revised offer was rejected, much to everyone's frustration: Lloyd's, the consortium, and the fans. Negotiations continued, as did the fans' protests. The pressure mounted and Lloyd was the first to crack: rather spectacularly so on national radio.

By then the Tigers had slumped to the bottom of the table and the ire of the fans on the subject was matched by the invective of Lloyd when interviewed on Radio 5 Live on 3rd October 1998. He pulled no punches in apportioning blame for the Tigers' plight. "I'm the only person in the history of Hull who's put his hand in his pocket and paid the bills," was one of his more restrained comments. It was a statement that clearly demonstrated his lack of knowledge about the history of Hull City: Harold Needler had been a generous benefactor for more than a quarter of a century, and his family had maintained the tradition long after his death. David Lloyd had been 'paying the bills' for less than 18 months.

In what many regarded as an act of revenge for his treatment, three days after that interview, on Tuesday 6th October, Lloyd announced that unless a buyer for the club was found by the weekend, he would close the club down. "I will not put the club into receivership or administration. I don't have to do that because it's my debt," he said. In a newspaper interview he stated: "I have had my fill of certain people in Hull and am going. It will be the end of professional football in the city." In one respect the feeling was mutual: there were plenty of Hull City supporters who'd had their fill of David Lloyd.

City's next fixture was scheduled for Friday 9th October, when they were due to play Cardiff City at Boothferry Park. Lloyd's comments initially put the game in doubt, but as the hours passed the risk receded. It did however take on the mantle Boothferry Park's 'last match ever'. It was a billing that had been posted previously throughout the Tigers' recent history and had been defied. So it would prove again.

The largest crowd of the season so far (8,594) turned up for the game. Many held signs handed out by the local newspaper that stated: "HULL CITY AFC WE'LL SUPPORT YOU EVERMORE." That support would be needed more than ever as the Tigers lost the game 2-1.

As part of the supporters' campaign to save the club, they had formed a Co-operative, partly to oppose Lloyd's plans and partly to have a greater say in how their club was run. The danger was that unless somebody bought out Lloyd, and soon, there would be no Hull City.

For the rest of October the future of Hull City seemed to be the only topic of conversation within the city. Such conversations bred rumour and counter rumour. Prospective buyers, both real and imagined, were identified from near and far. Don Robinson made another attempt to gain control of the club but it came to nothing; other local consortiums were mentioned and consortiums with no connections to the area also made an appearance and then melted into the background. Survival hopes rose and fell as each day passed.

Finally, at the beginning of November, a deal was done. The buyers were Tom Belton's consortium. For approximately £200,000 they bought Hull City football club. What they didn't get was Boothferry Park; that still remained in the hands of David Lloyd and would lead to problems in the coming months.

Tom Belton, who fronted the consortium that bought the Tigers from David Lloyd in November 1998.

The new owners promised money for new players and also guaranteed that the Tigers would stay at Boothferry Park. Under the terms of the deal the new owners had agreed an eight-year lease with Lloyd and would develop a plan allowing them eventually to buy the ground from Hull City's former owner. But first there was a far greater problem to be resolved. The Tigers were still at the foot of the Football League and in grave danger of relegation to the Conference.

Initially Mark Hateley remained as manager. However, the wave of enthusiasm and improved performances that usually runs concurrent with new owners was not apparent in that first game, at home to Leyton Orient; the result was a familiar: defeat. The new owners did not dither. Within the week the Tigers had a new boss: Warren Joyce. It was rumoured he was not the unanimous choice of the new directors. Neither, initially, was it greeted with universal approval on the terraces. You see, there was history between Warren Joyce and Hull City fans.

"Cometh the hour, cometh the man". As far as the 1998/99 season was concerned, for the Tigers that man was Warren Joyce.

Joyce had been assisting Hateley since Billy Kirkwood – Hateley's original assistant – had left the club to return to Scotland. The irony though lay in the fact that Terry Dolan had originally signed Joyce, and when Dolan had come under fire from the fans, Joyce had come out in support of Dolan. For that 'crime' he had endured an uneasy relationship with City's supporters. The relationship had reached rock-bottom during the home game against Brighton and Hove Albion on 15th March 1997. City won 3-0 and Warren Joyce scored twice. After each goal he ran not to the City fans to celebrate, but instead to the closed and deserted East Stand and stood there with arms aloft in front of…nobody. The message was clear: "You don't love me, I don't care."

There were bridges to be built between Warren Joyce and some Hull City fans.

To help him, Joyce brought in former Nottingham Forest and Derby County playing legend, John McGovern. They had been at Bolton Wanderers together in the early 1980s: Joyce as a player and McGovern as manager. The task they faced was huge. Early results suggested it might be beyond them; by the end of 1998 the Tigers were still bottom of the League, six points adrift from the team above them and safety. The siren call of the Conference could be heard.

Although City struggled in the League, inexplicably they progressed in the FA Cup. It was a diversion that provided some relief to the supporters, and cash to the club, but the Cup wasn't the priority. Fortunately the diversion came to a lucrative end in Round Three away to Aston Villa. A 3-0 defeat wasn't a disgrace and Joyce could turn his full attention to preserving the Tigers' League status.

The first opportunity came just a week after the trip to Villa Park. City were at home to Rotherham United, who were on the fringe of the promotion and play-off places. Making their City debuts were Gary Brabin (signed from Blackpool) and Mark Bonner (on loan from Cardiff City). It was the game that proved to be the catalyst for City's recovery. The Tigers won 1-0; Mark Bonner scored the goal. It proved to be his only goal and only game in City's colours – injury forced his early return to Cardiff, but I doubt a single player has ever made a greater contribution to the Tigers' cause in just 90 minutes.

From that game the Tigers never looked back. They battled, fought, clawed – use whatever verb you like, it will scarcely do justice to the effort the team put into escaping the relegation trapdoor that had, at one point, been creaking under the Tigers' weight and threatening to give way. In the 22 games they played from Rotherham onwards, the Tigers lost only three times. With games to spare they secured their League status and avoided relegation. It was their 'Great Escape'. The bridges between Warren Joyce and Hull City's fans had been built.

In recognition of this achievement both Joyce and McGovern were offered three-year contracts, and noises from the Directors – but not the management – suggested that the following season would be a promotion campaign. They weren't the only noises from that quarter; soon the sound of infighting could be heard from within the confines of the Boardroom.

The man who fronted the consortium that had purchased the Tigers from David Lloyd was Tom Belton; he'd also taken the boardroom lead as the 'Great Escape' season unfolded. It earned him admiration and respect from the terraces; it also earned him the 'Supporter of the Year' award for that season. Whilst the fans feted Belton, some of his fellow consortium members were plotting his downfall. In May 1999 he was ousted as chairman and fellow consortium partner, David Bennet, was also removed from the Board of Directors. Another consortium member, Nick Buchanan, took over as chairman.

However, arousing even greater interest was Buchanan's ally and fellow consortium member, Steven Hinchliffe, who owned just over a third of the shareholding in the club. Already banned from holding any directorships in companies, as a result of previous business dealings, his precise role at Boothferry Park was shrouded in mystery – officially, Hinchliffe was described as a vice-president offering advice to Buchanan and his fellow Directors. That mystery deepened following a lengthy article by Hinchliffe in the matchday programme for the Worthington cup-tie against Liverpool in September 1999; it appeared to be more than just advice. It prompted investigations into the club by football's authorities, and it wasn't long before other authorities – both financial and legal – were taking more than a passing interest in the affairs of Hull City.

Whilst the fallout from the battle between Belton, Bennet and Buchanan was still settling in the confines of Boothferry Park, taking place elsewhere within the City was an equally interesting event; one that would impact on both Boothferry Park and its present landlord and tenants, although the impact would take a year or so to make its mark. In July the council-owned telephone network was floated on the stock exchange. Almost immediately its value was placed in the billion pounds bracket and Hull City Council became a cash rich council. With money now available, the prospect of a new super stadium became more of a reality.

This brought added spice to the relationship between landlord (David Lloyd) and tenant (Buchanan et al) at Boothferry Park. It was a relationship that was already deteriorating rapidly, caused in the main by unpaid rent. Despite this apparent disagreement, the new directors continued to make noises that a deal was being struck to buy Boothferry Park from David Lloyd – even though Lloyd frequently poured scorn on the idea – but just occasionally Buchanan and his cohorts would make references to the prospect of the super stadium being the Tigers' future residence. The two viewpoints, as with the two protagonists, didn't appear to sit comfortably together.

It wasn't the best of backdrops against which to provide the promotion winning performance alluded to some months earlier by the Directors. It came as no surprise therefore that as the 1999/2000 season progressed, neither the performance nor the promotion materialised – even the introduction of Jamaican internationals Ian Goodison and Theo Whitmore failed to ignite a push for promotion. Diversions, in the shape of attractive cup-ties against Liverpool and Chelsea, helped to ease the disappointment – and boost the club's bank balance – but as the season wore on expectations were revised from promotion to play-offs and then from play-offs to acceptance of mid-table indifference.

Supplementing the inconsistency on the field was the growing uncertainty about the club's future and its growing debts. Negotiations about where the Tigers would call home in the next century only added to the intrigue. One minute it was a case of Boothferry Park is all but bought;

the next minute, negotiations to move into the new community stadium – being built by the city council, and to be shared with Hull FC – were well underway. Confusing? Oh yes. It was like being in the Hall of Mirrors at Hull Fair. Look in one mirror and you found the image of Buchanan committed to Boothferry

Ian Goodison (left) and Theo Whitmore notched up over 50 international appearances between them for Jamaica whilst with the Tigers. Whitmore's 28 appearances makes him the club's most capped Tiger. Ian Goodison is just behind him with 26 outings

———

Park; look in another and there was Buchanan, bags packed and ready to move to the Super Stadium.

There was no doubting that Joyce's squad of players was capable of much better, but the flashes of good football they produced were not sufficient to provide the results needed. Murmurings about his managerial ability started to increase in volume and, exactly twelve months from having secured the club's League status, City's manager went from Joyce the divine, to Joyce the dismissed.

You had to feel some sympathy for Warren Joyce. And many did. Having successfully guided the Tigers through probably the most traumatic season in their history, it didn't seem unreasonable for him to be given some time to establish a foundation and build from that. Time however, was as scarce a commodity at Boothferry Park as money. Neither was available in any quantity. His masters needed solutions to their problems – many of which were of their own making – and when Joyce couldn't bail them out by producing a successful team that generated interest and income on demand, he was cast away whilst his employers went in search of the next quick fix.

That 'fix' came quickly – almost indecently so. Within 24 hours of Joyce's sacking leaks to the press suggested that the Tigers already had a new manager signed up: Brian Little. Within the week that leak had turned into fact and Brian Little was indeed paraded before the assembled media as City's new saviour. Having experienced one blockbuster – 'The Great Escape' – under Warren Joyce, the main feature now on show at Boothferry Park was 'The Life of Brian'.

With nothing at stake for the Tigers in the closing games of the season, Little was able to carry out a watching brief from the touchline assessing the strengths and weaknesses of his squad in readiness for the next season. Within a month of him taking over, he couldn't even watch from the touchline as the club's landlord, David Lloyd, had called in the bailiffs and locked the gates to Boothferry Park; unpaid rent, to the tune of over £100,000 being the cause.

On top of that was the transfer embargo placed upon the club by the football authorities as a result of the PFA having had to bail the club out on numerous occasions and pay the players' wages. 'The Life of Brian' was an apt summary title for the situation the club found itself in…again: 'Pythonesque' in its creation, except it wasn't funny.

Eventually, solutions were found to unlock the gates of Boothferry Park, but the events of the close-season signalled trouble ahead; and as the 2000/01 season got underway it was spelt out in capital letters. Debt after debt started to emerge. There was anger and frustration on the terraces; there were continuing investigations by the FA and the police over the way the club was being run. There seemed to be no future for Hull City. It was being stripped of its dignity – there were no assets left; they were long gone.

Yet despite that, the team had still managed to keep themselves on the fringe of the play-off places; at the beginning of February 2001 they were in 10th place, just eight points off the play-off pace. Then City's world fell in.

Having failed to learn the lessons from the spring and summer of 2000, the Directors were behind with the rent again;

they also owed the Inland Revenue somewhere in the region of £500,000. The club was shipping money at the rate of about £30,000 a week. Despite the money coming in through the turnstiles, despite the money banked from lucrative home games against Premiership opposition in the previous season's Cup competitions; despite the more than £½ million pound received from the transfer fees for Adam Bolder and Andy Oakes and the early redemption of sell-on clauses for players already sold, the club was going bust. Even the Directors' allegedly unpaid restaurant bills were attracting media attention. Yet City's fans weren't overly concerned with identifying who'd eaten all the pies. What they wanted to know was who'd consumed the cash?

The Tigers were due in the High Court on 7th February 2001 to face a winding up order by the Inland Revenue over unpaid taxes. Twenty-four hours earlier (6th February) David Lloyd's bailiffs returned to Boothferry Park and locked the club out again. With a home game against Leyton Orient scheduled on the 10th, the prospects of it being fulfilled looked remote in the extreme. At the winding up hearing, however, the club were granted a 14 day stay of execution having successfully applied to enter administration, with Kroll Buchler Phillips appointed as administrator.

On the day of the court hearing the club's chairman, Nick Buchanan, fell on his sword and resigned. Some of his fellow directors swiftly followed his example. Buchanan explained his departure thus: "I've fought and tried and fought and tried again to turn this club around but decided it's better if someone else has a go."

You would have struggled to have found a City fan sorry to see him depart, and if he hadn't fallen on his sword, there would have been no shortage of volunteers from those same supporters to push him onto it.

The administrator's first task was to get City back into Boothferry Park. After some delicate negotiating they achieved it in time for the Tigers to take to the field against Leyton Orient on the appointed day at the appointed time. The players would have been forgiven if they'd declined to take part, however, as they'd not been paid for five weeks. They didn't though, and on an emotional afternoon a goal from Rodney Rowe earned the Tigers a 1-0 victory.

Brian Little receives his Manager of the Month award for February 2001

City's Board of Directors at the start of the 2000-01 season (left to right): D. Capper, P Webster, N. Buchanan, R. Ibbotson and A. Daykin Before the season was finished, all had departed.

Whilst the administrator unravelled the financial mess the club was in and sought to find a creditable buyer, the players continued to do City proud and strung together a sequence of results that edged them closer to the play-offs. In the process Brian Little deservedly won the Third Division Manager of the Month award for February.

A number of prospective purchasers held talks with the administrator, including former director and chairman Tom Belton. Don Robinson was also a possibility and the consortium – led by Mel Griffin – that would eventually purchase Boothferry Park from David Lloyd also held exploratory discussions about buying the club. With debts of approximately £1.8 million, any negotiations to sell the club would be complex.

The complexity of those negotiations meant that the uncertainty over the club's future lasted for nearly a month, and during that time the full extent of the debt and mismanagement emerged. By the first week in March the Administrators were in a position to put forward a proposal to the creditors that would see the club sold to a "party who wishes to remain anonymous." This was the phrase used in the Proposed Company Voluntary Arrangement document that detailed the debts and outlined the proposed method of settling them – in essence the club would be sold for £360,000.

For the agreement to be accepted, both the creditors and the shareholders had to approve it. On the morning of Thursday 8th March 2001, the creditors attended a meeting to discuss and vote on the proposal. It was a quiet meeting with the proposal being passed without much fuss. Whilst that meeting was going on however potential trouble from the shareholders – due to meet in the afternoon – was brewing.

The major shareholder, and recently resigned chairman, was Nick Buchanan. Concerned at not knowing who the new owner of Hull City would be, he intimated that his approval of the proposal could not be taken for granted. However, when the shareholders meeting was held he voted in favour of the proposal and the club had been saved – again. All that remained was to discover the identity of the Tigers' saviour.

The conjecture and intrigue went on for four days. It wasn't until the following Monday (12th March) that a press conference was called and the new owner revealed. Speculation had spanned the globe in trying to reveal his identity and when the secret was finally solved, it turned out to be a former director of Leeds United: Adam Pearson.

In announcing his purchase Adam Pearson made clear he was the sole owner of the new company that would trade under the name of: The Hull City AFC (Tigers) Ltd.

"The financial commitment, the overall risk involved, is mine alone" he confirmed. He demonstrated that he had done his preparatory work when he announced that sponsorship deals were in place and that "the new stadium is an integral part of the overall plan…and we are confident of striking a deal with the council for the new stadium. This was a major part of the attraction of taking over."

Adam Pearson

Adam Pearson confirmed that money would be made available for signing players and that Brian Little would be given the fullest support in continuing the good work carried out on the playing side during the traumatic opening months of 2001. New players were brought in and a play-off place was secured.

By coincidence, the Tigers were paired with Leyton Orient in the play-off semi-final. It had been Leyton Orient who had visited earlier in February in a game considered by some to be Boothferry Park's 'last game ever;' a phrase not unfamiliar to City fans in recent years.

The atmosphere inside the ground was much brighter than during the previous meeting, almost carnival in nature. It was the first time the Tigers had ever been involved in the play-offs and there was a lot at stake; that was reflected in the game. It was one of those occasions where the result was perhaps more important than the performance. Consequently it was a tense affair but, like that February encounter, a single goal settled it in the Tigers' favour.

The second leg at Brisbane Road did not produce a fairy tale ending; perhaps City had already used up their ration of good fortune prior to that fixture. A 2-0 victory for Orient saw them go through to the final at the Millennium Stadium in Cardiff, leaving the Tigers to prepare for their last full season at Boothferry Park – their new home was scheduled for completion in December 2002.

During the summer of 2001, Boothferry Park resembled a giant revolving door with the comings and goings occurring so frequently it was hard to keep up. The departures included Johnny Eyre, Gary Brabin, Jason Perry, David Brown, Jon Whitney, Steve Wilson, Jason Harris, Mark Atkins, Gary Fletcher, Kevin Francis, Steve Swales and Jamie Wood. In each case no fee was recouped; their replacements did not come as cheaply.

Nearly £¾million pounds went on acquiring the signatures of Lawrie Dudfield, Gary Alexander, Andy Holt and Ryan Williams. In addition Matt Glennon, Julian Johnsson, David Kerr, Scott Lee, Matt Bloomer, David Beresford, Nicky Mohan, Michael Price and Ben Petty all signed with modest fees being involved in some cases.

Boothferry Park's final full season was one of anticipated glory as the first League game of the 2001/02 season approached. When it came the side contained seven debutants – a Tiger event last seen some 70 years previously. Early season form – undefeated in the opening eight games – suggested that the anticipation was not without authentic basis.

Throughout the opening months of the new season the Tigers' lair proved to be a footballing fortress. Its future may have been limited, its 'walls' crumbling through age, but they still offered stout resistance to visiting invaders. As the Tigers maintained a heavy involvement in promotion matters in the closing months of 2001, so the uncertainty over the lifespan of Boothferry Park was resolved with the signing of the contracts that would see City play in their new home in December 2002.

It was a landmark in the history of the club. Yet reaching that landmark triggered off a chain of events that would see a season of promise disintegrate into a season of disappointment and dismissal. City's impeccable home form had distorted the dangers of indifferent performances and results on their travels, and come the turn of the year their away form came home to haunt them.

Defeat in the first home game of 2002 set the alarm bells tinkling and as the victories dried up so the Tigers dropped down the table. Where previously on the terraces there had been songs of praise, these were now replaced by murmurings of discontent and whispers over the future of the manager. Such whispers grew in volume throughout January and February as each game passed and victory proved elusive. The volume did not diminish even when the chairman, Adam Pearson, publicly backed Brian Little in the latter days of January 2002.

To a football manager, a vote of confidence from the chairman can mean only one thing: it's time to start clearing your desk and perusing the 'Situations Vacant' pages of the national newspapers. By the end of February 2002 Brian Little had cleared his desk and said goodbye to Hull City. Billy Russell – City's youth coach – took over temporary control.

Russell's tenure – his second such spell in two years – lasted roughly a month before a new managerial appointment was made. At the beginning of April Little's successor was announced; it was Jan Molby. Molby's Tiger debut, at home to Luton Town on 6th April 2002 was not the most auspicious of starts; Luton put four goals past the Tigers, without reply. It was the worst home debut by a new manager in the club's history and merely emphasised how badly the season had disintegrated.

With just four games remaining in the season, and the Tigers involved in neither promotion nor relegation issues – it was just as well for they won none of those four games – Molby had the luxury of using them to observe the talent within his squad. His end of season statements to the press and the fans suggested he was not overly impressed with what he saw. It meant that the summer of 2002, like the summer of 12 months previously, was likely to be a busy one for the Tigers.

The anticipated activity on the transfer front started within days of the season ending. The first arrival was Stuart Green, an exciting 20-year old midfield player who joined on a year long loan. It wasn't long before he was joined by others, including John Anderson, Ian Ashbee, Ben Burgess, Greg Strong and Stuart Elliott, the latter's signature acquired at what was initially believed to be for a fee approaching the club record, but later investigation revealed the value to be somewhat short of £200,000. A decent performance in the pre-season friendly games suggested that Molby's new model army was capable of marking what would be a big season for the Tigers – the move to their new home was only months away – with promotion; certainly the bookmakers thought so.

The money men looked to be on the button as the Tigers appeared comfortable in their opening League fixture of the 2002/03 season, at home to Southend United. Debut goals from Green and Elliott confirmed their class and a debut red card for Ian Ashbee confirmed his temperament. Even so, at 2-1 to the Tigers and with less than a minute of the game remaining, it looked a promising start. With virtually the last kick of the game, Southend equalised. It appeared to take the wind out of the Tigers' sails. City's next two League games ended in draws; City also ended both games with 10 men, Strong and Green being dismissed against Bristol Rovers and Exeter City respectively.

Still looking for his first League win as City's manager seemed to affect Molby more than his extrovert and forthright personality suggested it would.

*Indifferent performances and results put
increasing pressure on Jan Molby*

That pressure seemed to be transferred to the players and it showed in their performances. His attitude and statements in the press suggested there was little harmony within the Tigers' ranks.

The bringing in of additional loan resources smacked of desperation by Molby and did little to boost his squad's confidence or the team's performances. Defeat at Hartlepool and another home draw – this time against Leyton Orient – increased that pressure; it also increased the criticism Molby levelled at his players.

Finally, that elusive win arrived: 2-1 away to Cambridge United on 7th September. It saved Molby from equalling an unwanted record; for that win arrived 156 days after he'd had taken charge, one day short of the 157 it had taken Major Frank Buckley to achieve his debut win back in the 1946/47 season. A comprehensive 4-0 home defeat of Carlisle United, in City's next game, suggested that the Tigers had got the early season nerves out of their system and would move on apace to join the promotion frontrunners. Three days later that theory was horribly dispelled when City put in a miserable performance at home to lose 3-1 to Macclesfield. If City were to be considered promotion contenders, then they should have been disposing of the likes of Macclesfield without any trouble at all, especially at home.

That they didn't piled ever more pressure on Molby's shoulders. The fans were getting restless and it was clear that Adam Pearson, although not putting Molby under any public pressure, was clearly concerned that his substantial investment in players was not reaping the rewards that everyone seemed to anticipate.

Two more draws – against Oxford United and Swansea City – only increased the unease and added to the pressure. It was still early days as far as the League campaign was concerned, but two wins out of eleven games was nowhere near promotion form. When, in the next game, the Tigers lost to Molby's former team, Kidderminster Harriers, the parting of the ways followed swiftly.

Where Brian Little's departure had been preceded with a vote of confidence, Molby's departure was, in the main, preceded by silence. Little public comment came from the boardroom: either in support or to condemn. Instead, Adam Pearson acted swiftly to end conclusively what had looked like a good idea in appointing Molby, but had turned out not to be so.

Molby's departure, two days before City's next game – at home to Rochdale (12th October) – gave Billy Russell his third spell as City's caretaker manager. It would be a cameo role, covering only that Rochdale fixture, because before that game kicked off City's new manager was introduced to the crowd. Peter Taylor, with experience of gaining promotion at Brighton and Gillingham, plus international management experience with England at Full and Under-21 levels, became the Tigers' third manager in less than nine months.

Although not taking over officially until the following Monday, Taylor watched his new charges put on their best display of the season thus far, beating Rochdale 3-0 with some classic football and clinical finishing. However, in the post-match interviews Billy Russell confirmed that the team that had just run Rochdale ragged had in fact been selected by Molby earlier in the week. It confirmed how thin the dividing line can be between success and failure.

Time would also confirm that some of Molby's acquisitions – Elliott, Ashbee and Green for example – would prove astute buys. His skills in the transfer market were not in question; it appeared however, that the same could not be said of his man-management skills.

Peter Taylor had nowhere near as long to wait as Molby to record his first League win as City's manager. His first game in charge came at Torquay United; the Tigers walked it 4-1 and triggered off a seven match unbeaten run in the League that was only spoilt by an FA Cup defeat at home to Macclesfield Town.

With both results and morale seemingly on an upward trend, attention was diverted briefly from football to history, when the last ever match at Boothferry Park was staged on 14th December 2002. It was a billing that had been posted on many a previous fixture at the Tigers' lair in recent years, due in the main to the mismanagement of the club by many of both Adam Pearson and Peter Taylor's predecessors. Yet now it had finally arrived, it did so with the blessing of everyone.

That the result did not go the Tigers' way – they lost 1-0 to Darlington – did not seem to unduly disappoint the near 15,000 crowd. The future promised too much excitement to be dampened by the disappointment of one result. Besides, within four days there would be another home game to watch, in the much more majestic surroundings of the Kingston Communications Stadium.

Despite the euphoria over their new surroundings and the improvement in the team's performances, neither were sufficient to get City within grasping distance of either promotion or the play-offs. Although Taylor had a good pedigree, he was no miracle worker and perhaps he'd been left with too much to do. However, although the Tigers finished the season in mid-table, Taylor used the time to prepare for a concentrated assault on promotion in his first full season in charge.

That assault was based on acquiring players he was familiar with and whom he believed could carry out the tasks necessary to achieve the objective. He had already signalled such a policy with his early signings, such as Damien Delaney, Stuart Melton and Martin Reeves – some were short term solutions, others held a longer tenancy in Taylor's plans.

Ready for action, the new stadium

On 18th December 2002 the Tigers christened their new home with a friendly game against Premiership side Sunderland. To add prestige to the fixture, at stake was the Raich Carter Trophy – a playing legend for both clubs. From his seat in the celestial grandstand, Carter would have looked on with approval that things were looking better for his Tigers. A crowd of 22,467 saw City gain ownership of the trophy with a 1-0 win thanks to a goal from Steve Melton.

Eight days later (26th December), another 22,000 plus crowd watched the Tigers at their new home. This time, however, the game had League points at stake rather than trophies. The visitors were League leaders, Hartlepool United. Goals from Dean Keates and Stuart Green – celebrating the fact that his loan deal had just been converted into a permanent move – gave the Tigers a memorable 2-0 victory. It added to the growing confidence amongst the fans that promotion, in this memorable season, was still within their grasp.

However, it wasn't just a policy of 'Friends Reunited'; Jon Walters had no 'previous' with Taylor, but he could score goals, as the brace on his debut at Carlisle on 1st March 2003 demonstrated.

Neither was it a policy that gained universal acceptance amongst the supporters, but the overwhelming majority were willing to give him the benefit of the doubt. If promotion was achieved those doubts would disappear; if it wasn't, the likelihood was that it would be Taylor doing the disappearing.

During the summer of 2003 Peter Taylor supplemented his squad in all departments; acquiring Alton Thelwell, Andy Dawson, Richard Hinds, Jason Price and Danny Allsopp gave him options in defence, midfield and attack. To ease the wage bill some of the existing squad were allowed to move on.

The fixture list provided a succinct summary of the Tigers' life in the basement division of the Football League. For seven years they'd occupied the same Division but during that time life had been anything but dull. They'd started their tenure with a home game against Darlington; seven years on their first fixture of the new campaign (2003/04) was a home game against Darlington. Using a biblical analogy, the intervening time between those two fixtures could certainly have been classified as 'seven lean years'. Were they on the brink of reversing that trend?

A comfortable 4-1 defeat of Darlington at the KC Stadium on 9th August 2003 got City off to just the start they needed. A mixed bag of results throughout the rest of August and well into September raised a few concerns but on the last evening of that latter month a 1-0 home victory over Swansea City in front of a crowd just under 21,000 – with many more locked out of the stadium – took the Tigers to the top of the table.

A 1-0 defeat at home to Torquay on 21st February 2004 dropped the Tigers down to second in the table, and there they stayed for the rest of the season. As each game passed the possible permutations to prevent promotion dwindled. Come April and the Tigers had the chance to wrap it all up with games to spare.

Nerves played their part and probable victories were turned into either draws or defeats, but if the nerves were jangling, an outstanding victory in the return fixture with Swansea City confirmed that their grip on promotion would not be loosened; it was just a matter of time before the party could begin.

The home game against Huddersfield Town on 24th April set a new stadium attendance record (23,495) for a League fixture, and victory would have sealed promotion. The subsequent 0-0 draw was disappointing enough, but com-

Stuart Elliott (7) celebrates his goal against Swansea City on 30th September 2003 that took the Tigers to the top of Division Three.

There they stayed throughout all of October and well into November. Performance and results wobbled in the run up to Christmas, but even so they comfortably maintained a stronghold in the play-off places and by the time they'd beaten York City at Bootham Crescent on Boxing Day, they'd clawed their way back to the top.

The York victory was followed by a 2-0 home victory against Cambridge United, the Tigers' first game in their centenary year. By the time the return game against York was staged, and won, at the KC stadium on 7th February City had strung together seven consecutive League victories – a run only once before either matched or surpassed in the Tigers' history, and that had been by Raich Carter's championship-winning side of 1948/49. Was history about to repeat itself in other respects?

pounding that disappointment was a serious injury to Ben Burgess, whose 18 goals in the season had put the Tigers on the brink, meant they would have to do it without his assistance. They did.

Seven days after the Huddersfield game the Tigers travelled to Yeovil and won 2-1. They were promoted. The 'seven lean years' had come to an end; in fact it was exactly 19 years since the Tigers had tasted such success. After that wait, the final game of the season, at home to Bristol Rovers, was not just a promotion party, it was a carnival. The players did their bit, winning 3-0 and the supporters did theirs by cheering their team on before, during and after the game. Many thousands more repeated the performance some 24 hours later when the Tigers'

AT LAST! *After a wait of 19 years the Tigers can celebrate promotion at the end of the 2003/04 season*

squad paraded through the city on open top buses, alighting at the city hall and taking further plaudits on the balcony from the sea of black and amber clad fans below.

With another promotion under his belt, there were very few left claiming an allegiance to the Tigers who still doubted Taylor's tactics and talent; those who did were massively outnumbered. Not unexpectedly, Taylor's name was linked with every managerial vacancy going, but he declared he was happy at Hull and still had things to do there: another promotion for a start, something never before achieved in the Tigers' history.

Close season transfer activity was not so hectic as in previous years, and although money was still spent on bringing in the likes of Michael Keane and Aaron Wilbraham, the most significant signing involved a local lad coming home. Nicky Barmby had played football at the highest level for much of his career. A CV that included England, Spurs, Middlesbrough, Liverpool, Everton and Leeds United confirmed he was of premier quality. Throughout that career, however, he had never lost his love of Hull City and when the opportunity arose for him to move the short distance down the M62 from Leeds to Hull, he took little persuading.

To have somebody of his calibre and still the right side of 30 in your squad suggested that the club were willing to have a good crack at another promotion campaign, despite the words of caution from both chairman and manager. The fixture list for the forthcoming season also of-fered some encouragement to the superstitious. Prior to the promotion just achieved, the last time the Tigers had been promoted had been back in the 1984/85 season when they'd begun their home fixtures with a visit from Bournemouth and ended the season with an away game against Brentford. When the fixture list was published for the 2004/05 season the Tigers were scheduled to start at home against Bournemouth and end the campaign at Brentford; history in the remaking?

Nicky Barmby comes home

Victory over Bournemouth on the opening day set the Tigers on their way. The early months saw a mixture of wins, draws and defeats that kept them in the play-off places without too much trouble, but they never really showed in the promotion slots. That changed when a magnificent 4-2 victory at Hillsborough against Sheffield Wednesday, in front of a crowd of 28,701 – the highest attendance to witness an away victory for the Tigers in a League game since the 'Battle of Bramall Lane' back in March 1971 – moved the Tigers into second place behind Luton Town – who they'd comprehensively beaten 3-0 at home some six weeks earlier.

City held on to second place for the rest of the calendar year, and as they'd begun their centenary year with a victory, so they ended it with one and in the process set a new stadium attendance record of 24,117 as they overcame Doncaster Rovers on 28th December 2004.

Their centenary year might have ended, but their centenary season was still underway and seemingly going well. A 2-1 home victory over Huddersfield Town on New Year's Day was followed 48 hours later by a 3-1 away win at Stockport County. The significance of that latter result was twofold. Firstly, it took the Tigers to the top of League One (the new name for what in effect was the old Division Three in the days of pre-sponsorship football) for the first time in the campaign.

Secondly, it gave the Tigers a sequence of eight straight wins in the League, surpassing their achievement of the previous campaign and making Peter Taylor the only manager in the club's history to have put two such runs together.

City's time at the top was brief. A home draw against Peterborough, twelve days after the Stockport game, dropped them down to second and set off a comparatively poor run that saw them win only once in seven games. Despite that, however, they retained their hold on second place and strengthened it with an impressive win at Tranmere, their nearest rivals for automatic promotion, on 5th March 2005. It opened up a seven point gap between City and the chasing promotion pack, which was stretched to ten points three days later after a 1-0 home win over Hartlepool.

Ten points ahead with ten games to go gave the Tigers the breathing space they needed to achieve what none of their predecessors had: back to back promotions. Confirmation of that new paragraph in the club's history came in the home game against Swindon Town on 16th April. The point gained from a 0-0 draw proved enough when news came through that Tranmere had achieved the same result against Blackpool and thus run out of games to pass the Tigers' already accumulated points total. City were promoted. Again.

BACK-TO-BACK *Twelve months after celebrating promotion from Division Three, City's players are at it again, this time it's promotion from Division Two at the end of the 2004/05 season.*

Taylor's Tigers had delivered the goods. Whilst it had undoubtedly been a collective effort, for one player in particular, Stuart Elliott, it had been a magnificent year. Although regarded more as a wide midfield player than an out and out forward, his 29 League and Cup goals was the best strike return from a City player for nearly two decades; he would surely have threatened City's seasonal scoring record book but for a six week injury absence. Not unsurprisingly he was voted City's player of the year.

The scenes after that Swindon game were a repeat of those nearly twelve months previously – and any neutral observer at the match was left in no doubt what this meant for a club who had been on the edge of extinction nearly as many times as their nickname's namesake. If the closing decade of the 20th century had been their nadir, then the opening decade of the 21st century was developing into nirvana.

Perhaps understandably, there was an after-effect following the effort put in to achieving promotion in consecutive seasons. Although the last home game of the season rewrote the KC stadium's attendance record for a City game (24,227 vs. Sheffield Wednesday on 30th April), defeat in that fixture, plus defeats in the away games either side of it – Walsall and Brentford respectively – produced City's worst results run of the season. Nobody was complaining too much. In the context of what had been achieved, it would have been somewhat churlish to expect cream, icing and cherry on the promotion cake.

There can surely be no better way to celebrate any soccer season than by gaining promotion or winning a trophy of some importance; to do so in your centenary season just adds greater significance to the achievement and celebration. Throughout the century of City, their fans have rarely had reason to celebrate: three championships and five promotions is a sparse diet for your allegiances to survive on; but survive they have, often against the odds. Yet even as the events of the past century fade, its significance will not be lost on Hull City supporters and there are lessons to be learnt, perhaps the most significant being that is best not to look back with regret, but rather to look forward with relish.

THE BOULEVARD

The home of Hull FC rugby club, the Boulevard also offered a home to Hull City in their early days. City's first ever match – against Notts County on 1st September 1904 – was staged there, and in the Tigers' inaugural season (1904/05), the Boulevard was the venue for all but two of City's home fixtures. When making their application to join the Football League, the Tigers had already acquired land which would be converted into their own stadium, but declared the Boulevard as a reserve option. Even though the Tigers took up residency at their new home during their inaugural League season (1905/06) it wasn't unusual for the Boulevard to come to City's rescue and host a home fixture on occasions when circumstances required; that hospitality extended right through until the mid 1940s. The idea of the Tigers relocating back to the Boulevard was resurrected during the 1990s. David Lloyd, who owned both Hull City and Hull FC, proposed that the Tigers return to the Boulevard on a temporary basis to ground-share with their Rugby League neighbours whilst a new home for both clubs was negotiated. It was a proposal not well received by either set of supporters and before it could become a reality, Lloyd had relinquished his business interest in the Tigers.

Competition	P.	W.	D.	Lost	For	Against
League	3	1	0	2	4	4
Other Comps	17	8	2	7	32	41
Other	28	17	6	5	73	44
Total	48	26	8	14	109	89

DAIRYCOATES

Owned by the East Riding County Football Association, Dairycoates was in regular use by local amateur teams in the late 1800s and early 1900s. It was used once by City in their first season (1904/05) as an association football club, when they entertained Scarborough on 18th March 1905. It was one of a number of ground options that the club's directors considered when looking for a permanent home as part of their application to join the Football League, but they eventually decided that neither the facilities nor pitch were up to the required standard.

Competition	P.	W.	D.	L.	For	Against
Other Matches	1	1	0	0	6	0

THE CIRCLE

Although only a temporary home for the Tigers, it still takes its place in the club's history for being the venue for City's inaugural Football League home fixture – against Barnsley on 2nd September 1905. Owned by Hull Cricket club, it was loaned to the Tigers whilst they developed a piece of land adjacent to the Circle which had been acquired by the club to provide them with a more permanent residence, and which would not be ready for occupation until later in the 1905/06 League season.

Competition	P.	W.	D.	L.	For	Against
League	11	6	3	2	23	12
FA Cup	4	2	1	1	11	4
Other	1	0	1	0	0	0
Total	16	8	5	3	34	16

ANLABY ROAD

On land leased – from Hull Cricket Club – rather than bought, Anlaby Road was the first ground that City could genuinely call home, and which remained so until just after the outbreak of World War Two. The ground was christened, on 24th March 1906, by the visit of Blackpool in a League encounter that ended all square (2-2) with Peter Howe scoring both goals. Severely damaged by fire over the Easter weekend in 1914, at one stage it looked likely that the Tigers would have to seek an alternative venue, but the necessary finance was found amongst local businessmen to rebuild it. Serious crowd trouble in February 1920 and April 1934 had repercussions for both club and ground, in what were generally troubled times for the Tigers, with financial troubles dominating their tenure. That said, Anlaby Road was the stage for some of the Tigers' more notable performances in their history: the FA Cup giant-killings of Burnley and Middlesbrough in the early 1920s; the victory over York City on May day 1933 that gave the Tigers their first ever promotion and the Third Division (North) championship trophy to boot; and the 11-1 defeat of Carlisle United in January 1939 that set a club record for their largest ever League victory.

The outbreak of World War Two sealed the ground's fate, and almost killed off the club as well. Still constrained by a lack of money, bomb damage to the ground proved too expensive to repair and for a short while the Tigers reverted back to their first-ever lair, the Boulevard, before

The Circle Ground, and the adjoining Anlaby Road Ground

going into 'hibernation' for the remainder of the Wartime competition. When peacetime football resumed it was a new Hull City that returned to the Football League. The club had been bought by a local businessman (Harold Needler) who also completed the construction of the stadium that the previous directors had started but been unable to complete. Whilst Anlaby Road's last Football League fixture was staged on 22nd April 1939 – although it did host a League game against Lincoln at the start of the abandoned 1939/40 season – the ground was used for training and as the venue of reserve and junior fixtures until the mid 1960s

Competition	P.	W.	D.	L.	For	Against
League	595	328	147	120	1199	597
FA Cup	37	18	11	8	61	36
Other Comps	100	58	15	27	212	150
Other	34	17	6	11	69	49
Total	766	421	179	166	1541	832

BOOTHAM CRESCENT

Necessity forced the Tigers to use Bootham Crescent – the home of York City – to fulfil a wartime competition home fixture against Newcastle United on 11th November 1944. With their Anlaby Road ground having been 'bombed out', the Tigers were lodging at the Boulevard during the 1944/45 season.

However, on the date in question Hull FC had been drawn at home to Dewsbury in the Rugby League Cup. As landlord they obviously had first call, so the Tigers were required to look elsewhere; fortunately York City were happy to oblige. In front of a crowd of approximately 2,000 the Tigers held a strong Newcastle side to a half-time scoreline of 2-2, although their resistance weakened in the second-half and City were soundly beaten: 3-6.

Competition	P.	W.	D.	L.	For	Against
Other Comps	1	0	0	1	3	6

BOOTHFERRY PARK

From concept to completion, the construction of Boothferry Park spanned three decades. It was worth the wait. Although work had started on its creation well before the start of World War Two (WW2), a severe lack of funds had caused the directors to mothball the project, with very little prospect of it ever being completed, although during WW2 it was commandeered for use by the military. Also during that time the club was bought by Harold Needler and included in the sale was the part finished ground. A master builder by trade, Needler was able to bring the ground up to the required standard by the start of the 1946/47 season, although it was a close run thing, not helped by the strict rules governing the use of building materials at the time. To circumnavigate this particular problem, a lot of materials from the old buildings – in its previous life, the land had formed part of Hull Golf club – were used.

Boothferry Park

The long term aim was for the ground to have a capacity of 80,000 with its own railway station and 'en-suite' car parking. The capacity aim was never reached, but the railway platform was – the only ground in the country to have such a facility. Over time Boothferry Park's facilities were gradually built up. By the mid 1960s, and after a further substantial input of cash from Harold Needler, Boothferry Park was considered to be one of the top grounds in the Football League: with six floodlight towers, its own gymnasium, a magnificent playing surface and a capacity of approximately 45,000 – although in the late 40s, over 55,000 had watched the Tigers lose 1-0 to Manchester United in the quarter-finals of the FA Cup.

By the early 70s Boothferry Park was in its prime, and hosted international and representative football and rugby league matches; during its lifetime Boothferry Park hosted a variety of sports from baseball to show jumping. It was a ground fit for the First Division; unfortunately the setting was never quite matched by its playing occupants. From the late 70s onwards the ground went into a gradual decline with money, as ever, at the root of its problems. With little money to develop it further, the capacity was reduced and during its latter years various sections of the ground were closed off for safety reasons. Moving to a new home was an option considered by a succession of the club's owners during the 1990s.

However, it was only when the Tigers' current owner, Adam Pearson, acquired the club that the move was guaranteed and the Tigers were all set to relocate to the purpose built community stadium built by the city council and which would be shared with Hull FC. That move occurred in December 2002.

Competition	P.	W.	D.	L.	For	Against
League	1248	609	346	293	2073	1292
FA Cup	84	31	21	32	132	125
FL Cup	52	23	12	17	71	63
Other Comps	38	21	6	11	53	35
Other	129	57	37	34	284	186
Total	1551	741	422	387	2613	1701

KINGSTON COMMUNICATIONS STADIUM

At a cost of more than £43 million, and financed by the city council following the public flotation of the council owned telephone company on the stock exchange, a magnificent 25,400 capacity all-seater stadium was constructed in West Park in the opening years of the 21st century. The exact location touched the sites of two of the Tigers' former homes, and is but a stone's throw from the Boulevard where they began their sporting life over a century ago.

The Kingston Communications Stadium

Sharing the facilities with Hull FC Rugby League club, the Tigers have gone from strength to strength in their new setting, which is more popularly known as the KC stadium. The Tigers have won promotion in each of the two full seasons they've been tenants at the KC – a feat never before achieved in the club's history – and the stadium has been internationally acclaimed and has already staged international football and rugby league fixtures as well as hosting a number of top level concerts.

Competition	P.	W.	D.	L.	For	Against
League	58	37	14	7	109	47
FA Cup	3	2	0	1	7	4
FL Cup	1	0	1	0	2	2
Other Comps	1	0	0	1	1	3
Other	8	2	1	5	6	16
Total*	71	41	16	14	125	72

* Games cover the period up until the end of the 2004-05 season.

'Last and First'
League Match programmes for the last at Boothferry Park and the first at Kingston Communications

By the end of the 2004-05 season, well over 100 players had each made a century or more League appearances for Hull City. Brief biographies, together with their appearances statistics, for each of those 'Tiger Centurions' follows. The abbreviations relating to each player's appearance details are as follows:

The years following the player's name represent the first year of the first and last season with the club.
Appearances: Total number of appearances in that competition (with substitute appearances in brackets), followed by goals scored. Under 'debut', this relates to a Football League match; (h) is a home game, and (a) is an away match.
Abbreviations: LGE (Football League), FAC (FA Cup), FLC (Football League Cup), OC (Other Competitons).

ABBOTT, Gregory Stephen   (1992-1996)
Born:14.12.1963, Coventry
Debut: 19.12.92 AFC Bournemouth (a) 0-0
Appearances: LGE: 120 (4) - 15; FAC: 3 (1) - 0:
FLC: 5 - 1; OC: 6 (2) - 2.

Having been successful at Bradford City when Terry Dolan was at the helm – 281 League appearances and captain during their Division Three championship winning season (1984/85) – Abbott was probably hoping for a repeat performance when Terry Dolan brought him to Boothferry Park in December 1992. It didn't happen, however, even though Abbott quickly established himself in the team and became captain. For much of his time in a City shirt relegation rather than promotion was on the agenda; and when relegation finally arrived, at the end of the 1995/96 season, Greg was released as part of a major clear-out by Dolan.

ALLISON, Neil James   (1991-1996)
Born:20.10.1973, Hull
Debut: 11.05.91 Newcastle Utd (a) 2-1
Appearances: LGE: 95 (11) -3; FAC: 3 -0; FLC: 7 (1) -1;
OC: 6 (1) -0

Allison made his debut in the final game of the 1990/91 season, by which time the Tigers' relegation to Division Three had been confirmed. He showed great promise in the away victory over Newcastle United – the Tigers' first ever League victory at St James' Park – and went on to show great promise in subsequent seasons, but never reached the level of consistency that such promise required. Injuries did not help his cause; neither did the troubles that plagued the Tigers throughout the 90s. Both meant he never really established himself as a permanent fixture in the side and even his best season at the club, in terms of appearances (1995/96), was marred by relegation.

ASHBEE, Ian   (2000 -   )
Born: 06.09.1976, Birmingham
Debut: 10.08.02 Southend Utd (h) 2-2
Appearances: LGE: 110 (0) - 4; FAC: 4 - 0; FLC: 3 -1;
OC: 1 -0

Ian Ashbee wrote his name in Hull City's record book when his goal at Yeovil in May 2004 confirmed the Tigers' first promotion for nearly 20 years. Some twelve months later he was making a further entry when the Tigers achieved back-to-back promotions for the first time in their history and Ashbee became only the second City player to captain the club to more than one promotion. Always determined and wholehearted in his displays, he's also demonstrated stirring leadership qualities which will put him in the front rank of contenders whenever the subject of identifying City's all-time greatest captain is raised.

ASKEW, William 'Billy'   (1982 – 1989)
Born: 02.10.1959, Great Lumley (Co. Durham)
Debut: 28.08.82 Bristol City (a) 1-2
Appearances: LGE: 247 (6) -19; FAC: 19 -0; FLC: 14 -0;
OC: 12 (2) -1.

Unknown when he arrived for a trial at Boothferry Park in the summer of 1982, Askew soon made his mark as a bustling all action midfield player – with the ability to take a more defensive role when required. Helping the Tigers to promotion during his first season (1982/83) he was ever present, two seasons later (1984/85), when the Tigers gained a further promotion to Division Two. Each step up in grade did not prove insurmountable for Askew's talents and he continued to shine to such an extent that First Division Newcastle United were willing to part with serious money to acquire his signature.

ATKINSON, Graeme   (1989-1994)
Born:11.11.1971, Hull
Debut: 09.12.89 Port Vale (h) 2-1
Appearances: LGE: 129 (20) -23; FAC: 4 (1) - 1; FLC: 6 (3) - 2; OC: 7 -0.

Impressive schoolboy form prompted the Tigers to take Atkinson on as a YTS trainee and his development progressed at a rapid pace. Shortly after his 18th birthday he had broken into the first team and made sporadic appearances over the next couple of seasons in a variety of positions stretching from right-back to left-wing, which emphasised his versatility and didn't hamper his knack of scoring goals. Ever-present throughout the 1992/93 season, Atkinson started to attract the attention of other clubs. With the Tigers in dire financial straits, it came as no surprise when an offer of £80,000 from Preston North End was accepted and Atkinson's talents were transported to the other side of the Pennines.

BANKS, Francis Stanley (1966-1975)
Born:21.08.1945, Hull
Debut: 26.08.67 Blackburn Rovers (a) 0-2
Appearances: LGE: 284 (4) - 6; FAC: 22 - 0; FLC: 14 - 1;
OC: 10 - 0

Freed by Southend United, Banks wrote to numerous clubs asking for a trial. Hull City was the only club that responded positively. A successful trial resulted in a contract offer from the Tigers, which Banks accepted. Gradually establishing himself in City's defensive line-up, he occupied a variety of positions before settling in at right-back following the retirement of Andy Davidson.

Despite being troubled by injuries, Frankie still displayed sufficient talent to notch up over 300 League and Cup appearances whilst in the Tigers' colours. That talent even extended to grabbing the occasional goal whenever he ventured upfront in support of an attack.

BEARDSLEY Donald Thomas   (1962-1972)
Born: 23.10.1946, Alyth
Debut: 07.09.66 Portsmouth (a) 1-0
Appearances: LGE: 128 (2) - 0; FAC: 6 - 0; FLC: 3 - 0;
OC: 5 - 0

Having turned professional within 12 months of joining the Tigers as an amateur in 1962, Beardsley had to wait more than three years before making his first team debut in the early weeks of the 1966-67 season. A full back equally comfortable on either flank, such talent and dexterity should have made him a regular selection. Not so. From his debut onwards, Beardsley always faced strong competition from others within the Tigers' squad to occupy either berth. It was testimony to his talent that in the face of such competition, his seasonal appearances regularly extended into double figures.

BELL, Matthew 'Ginger'   (1919 – 1930)
Born: 08.07.1897, West Hartlepool
Died: 27.01.1962
Debut: 08.09.19 Stoke City (a) 1-3
Appearances: LGE: 393 - 1; FAC: 30 - 0

A legendary figure in the history of Hull City, Matt Bell came to prominence during the inter-war years as a talented and courageous full-back, plus a captain of inspirational proportions. His striking red hair accounted for his nickname and exemplified his approach to the game: passionate, powerful and plucky. He made his first Tiger outing in the first season following World War One, and his association with the Tigers went on to span three decades, during which time he pretty much made the left-back spot his personal fiefdom, although his versatility allowed him to cover other positions as circumstances dictated. Moving to right-back, when required, presented no problem, and in an era of no substitutes he was always first on call to take over in goal whenever the Tigers' custodian of the net was indisposed during a game. During the 1929-30 season he led the Tigers to the semi-finals of the FA Cup, where they lost to Arsenal after a replay. His disappointment was compounded when in the same season the Tigers were relegated for the first time in their history. Before the following season (1930-31) was concluded, Bell, with much regret, was transferred to First division Nottingham Forest. In nearly 400 League outings for the Tigers, Bell scored only once – against Port Vale in April 1924 – a testament to his defensive vocation.

BERRY, Thomas   **(1947-1957)**
Born: 31.03.1922, Clayton-le-Moors
Died: Sept 2003
Debut: 06.09.47 Rotherham Utd. (a) 0-0
Appearances: LGE: 275 - 1; FAC 20 - 0

Berry joined the Tigers in the summer of 1947 after his early career had been disrupted by service in the RAF during World War Two. Within weeks he found himself in the first team and during the 1948/49 season Berry missed only three of the Tigers' 49 League and Cup games – all through injury. He provided the cornerstone of a Tigers' defence that proved to be the most miserly in the club's history: conceding only 28 League goals in a season that saw them finish as champions of Division Three (North). In the eight seasons following promotion, only once did his appearances fail to reach double figures, and that was due to a serious injury sustained during the 1954/55 season.

BLEAKLEY, Thomas   **(1918 – 1929)**
Born: 16.05.1893, Little Hulton
Died: 01.10.1951
Debut: 30.08.19 Birmingham City (a) 1-4
Appearances: LGE: 368 - 5; FAC: 21 - 2; OC: 13 - 0

At 5' 6" Bleakley would not be considered a giant in the ranks of Hull City. Convert the criteria to ability and consistency, however, and there will not be many in front of Tom Bleakley. Like Matthew Bell, Bleakley's career with the Club spanned three decades and, throughout that time, his technique and tactical awareness, coupled with his consistency, affords him renowned eminence. Together with Mike Gilhooley, Bleakley provided City with a half-back partnership that was generally acknowledged as the best that they had ever had up to that point – it could be argued that there have been none better since.

BLY, William 'Billy'   **(1938-1960)**
Born: 15.05.1920, New Houghton
Died: 24.03.1982
Debut: 01.04.39 Rotherham Utd (a) 2-0
Appearances: LGE: 403 - 0; FAC 35 - 0; OC: 18 - 0

Ask any City fan to name the club's top three goalkeepers of all time, and Billy Bly's name will be included more often than not. Joining the club as an apprentice in August 1937, it wasn't long before he was pushing for a first team outing; that came in April 1939. With the prospect of establishing himself in the first team for the start of the next season, it was a sporting tragedy that the outbreak of World War two robbed him of the chance and reduced his time in the Tigers' ranks by some six years. When peacetime football resumed, the Tigers had moved to their new home at Boothferry Park and Bly had the honour of being a member of that inaugural team; he went on to be a regular during the rest of the 40s, was the regular first choice throughout the 50s and was still holding down his place in the team as the 60s began. In all, his four decades with the Tigers produced 456 League and Cup outings in goal, a figure that equalled that of his early mentor, George Maddison and one which means that both share top spot in the club's records book as far as goalkeeping appearances are concerned – but for the war that record would surely have been his alone. Any Tigers team that took to the field with Bly between the posts was enriched by his talent and courage. It is just a shame that circumstances dictated to deny him the international recognition his talents deserved.

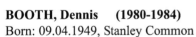

BOOTH, Dennis   (1980-1984)
Born: 09.04.1949, Stanley Common
Debut: 16.08.80 Millwall (a) 1-1
Appearances: LGE: 121 (2) - 2; FAC: 12 - 0; FLC: 7 - 0;
OC: 9 - 0
Div. 4, 1977/78

In the dark administration days of 1982, when the Tigers' very existence was in doubt, nobody epitomised a Tiger's spirit better than Dennis Booth. Having achieved success with both Lincoln City and Watford, it must have come as something of a shock for Booth – who joined the Tigers for what proved to be a bargain £40,000 in the summer of 1980 – to have his early years at Boothferry Park dominated by events off the field rather than on it.

Success was not far away however, and he was an important member of the teams that won promotion in seasons 1982/83 and 1984/85, both as a player – primarily he was a defender – and coach. At the end of his playing career, he remained with the Tigers, filling both coaching, assistant and caretaker manager roles.

BRADBURY, William   (1955-1959)
Born: 03.04.1933, Matlock
Died: Aug. 1999
Debut: 15.10.55 Bury (h) 2-3
Appearances: LGE: 178 - 82; FAC: 12 - 7

Derbyshire born, Bill Bradbury spent his early years in football in the midlands: first as an apprentice with Coventry City, for whom he made 24 League appearances (7 goals) and then Birmingham City (3 Appearances, 2 goals). His manager at Birmingham had been Bob Brocklebank, and when Brocklebank moved to Boothferry Park to assume managerial duties, one of his first tasks was to persuade Bill Bradbury to join him. A goal on his debut set the tone for Bradbury's tenure with the Tigers and he either shared top billing in the Tigers' scoring charts, or held it in his own right in each of his first four seasons with the club. His peak came during the 1958-59 promotion season when his 30 League goals set a new post-war club record and his career statistics with City demonstrates a goal nearly every other game.

BROWELL, Anthony 'Andy'   (1908-1911)
Born: 17.09.1888, Wallbottle Northumberland
Died: 07.03.1964
Debut: 21.11.08 Birmingham City (a) 2-1
Appearances: LGE: 101 - 5; FAC: 8 - 0

'Andy' was the second in the trio of Browell brothers who wore the City's colours during the early years of the Tigers' history. He arrived two years after his elder brother (George) and developed into a useful centre-half, regularly playing alongside George for more than two years. Although his League appearances just creep over the century mark, the tally would have been greater but for a serious leg injury that meant he missed much of the opening half of the 1910/11 season. When he did resume playing he quickly demonstrated that the injury had not impeded his ability and a move to First Division Everton swiftly followed, although he enjoyed nowhere near the regularity of appearances with the Merseysiders that he had with the Tigers.

BROWELL, George   (1905-1910)
Born: 1884, Wallbottle Northumberland
Died: 1951
Debut: 30.09.05 Burton Utd. (h) 1-1
Appearances: LGE: 194 - 3; FAC: 14 - 0

George was the eldest of the Browell brothers and was a member of the Tigers' first League campaign. He didn't break into the first team until the end of September 1905, but from that point on he was regular member of City's half-back line for the rest of the decade, including the 1909/1910 season which saw the Tigers come agonisingly close to promotion to the top flight. Together with brother Andy, and Davy Gordon, he gave the Tigers a solid rather than spectacular half-back formation. Determined in his tackling as he was accurate with his distribution, George proved a great servant to Hull City in their formative years, and when he moved onto Grimsby Town in 1911, he displayed the same qualities for them.

BROWN, David Alistair   (1997-2000)
Born: 02.10.1978, Bolton
Debut: 28.03.98 Macclesfield Town (h) 0-0
Appearances: LGE: 108 (23) - 23; FAC: 10 - 3; FLC: 9 (1) - 5; OC: 5 (1) – 0

Initially on Oldham Athletic's books as a schoolboy, Brown was at the centre of controversy when he was allegedly poached by Manchester United. Whatever the circumstances, he never made the grade at Old Trafford and was recommended to the Tigers by Warren Joyce, who although on City's playing staff, did some coaching at Old Trafford. Not a hit straight away, Brown soon demonstrated he had an eye for goal and the ability to unsettle defenders. That latter talent often rebounded on him and reduced the effectiveness of his game on occasions. Yet despite letting his frustrations get the better of him, he still scored regularly rather than frequently and was City's leading League goalscorer in his first full season with the club.

BROWN, Linton James   (1992-1995)
Born: 12.04.1968, Hull
Debut: 09.01.93 Preston North End (a) 2-1
Appearances: LGE: 111 (10)-24; FAC: 4 (1) - 1; FLC: 6-0; OC: 4-0

At a time when money was almost non-existent, never mind tight at Boothferry Park, the arrival of Linton Brown came about from money raised by the club's fans as part of the 'Put a Tiger in your Team' campaign. His acquisition brought a new meaning to the phrase '…a fans' player."

Prior to joining City, Brown's footballing career had been predominantly non-League based, where he acquired a reputation for pace and goalscoring. Both were in evidence during his time with the Tigers. The partnership he formed with Dean Windass – perhaps more by necessity than nous on the part of the management at the time – proved surprisingly fruitful, especially during the 1994/95 season.

BULLESS, Brian   (1952-1963)
Born: 04/09.1933, Hull
Debut: 18.04.53 Southampton (h) 1-0
Appearances: LGE: 326 - 30; FAC: 24 - 5; FLC: 7 - 0

One of the most versatile players ever to have been on the club's books, Bulless joined the Tigers straight from school turning professional early in 1951. Very much at home on the left flank of the team, Bulless was comfortable in filling either a defensive, midfield or attacking role with ease. Despite a goal on his debut he was still used sparingly in the early seasons of his professional career, and it wasn't until the latter part of the 1950s that he became a regular member of the first team. However, once he did his consistency of performance and effort meant that very few in the squad bettered his seasonal tally of appearances and provided him with a tally of League appearances that exceeded 300 and would probably have breached the 400 barrier but for injuries that required lengthy recovery time. Highly regarded by both fans and team-mates, his loss was a major blow to the Tigers: players of his calibre, consistency and flair were just as hard to come by in those days as they are now.

BURBANKS, William Edwin   (1948-1952)
Born: 01.04.1913, Bentley
Died: 26.07.1983
Debut: 21.08.48 Tranmere R. (a) 2-1
Appearances: LGE: 143 - 21; FAC: 10 - 1

When Eddie Burbanks joined the Tigers, he was already in what many experts would describe as the twilight of his career – making his Tiger League debut at over 35 years of age had him pushing club records at the more mature edge of the debut timeline. Yet his new manager and former playing colleague, Raich Carter, had no qualms about the implications of Burbank's birth certificate on his ability to do a job for the Tigers. A championship medal at the end of his first season with City confirmed Carter's confidence. A left-winger of undoubted class, Burbank's experience and expertise in that role allowed the likes of Moore, Carter and Ackerman to benefit. Staying with City for five years, his departure did not announce his retirement, rather just another debut, this time for Leeds United, at the tender age of 41.

BUTLER, Dennis Michael   (1963-1969)
Born: 07.03.1943, Fulham
Debut: 24.08.63 Watford (a) 3-3
Appearances: LGE: 215 (2) - 0; FAC: 20 - 0; FLC: 9 - 0.

Throughout his career Dennis Butler amassed over 400 League and Cup appearances; that more than 50% of them were made on behalf of Hull City in just over six years gives you an idea of the tremendous service he gave the club. With limited opportunities at Chelsea, a move to the Tigers offered him more opportunity to progress. He grasped that opportunity almost immediately, establishing himself in the first team at left back and making the position very much his own for the next five years. During that time he forged a solid full-back relationship with Andy Davidson. Very rarely did the Tigers take to the field without them and both were influential in the club's championship-winning season of 1965/66.

BUTLER, Ian   (1964-1972)
Born: 01.02.1944, Darton
Debut: 02.01.65 Colchester Utd. (h) 5-1
Appearances: LGE: 300 (5) - 66; FAC: 22 - 4; FLC: 9 - 0; OC: 3 - 0.

The 1960s are often referred to as the 'swinging sixties' in the history books. If that's true, then during that same decade Boothferry Park was often rocking. Contributing his fair share to bringing about that state of affairs was Ian Butler.

Already in possession of proven credentials as a left-winger of unbridled talent when he joined the Tigers in January 1965, he went on to enhance his reputation during the remainder of that decade. Many an opposing full back must have dreaded a trip to Boothferry Park, aware that Ian Butler's name was on the teamsheet; such a trip offered only the prospect of torment during the game, followed by nightmares on the journey home. No slouch himself when it came to scoring goals, Butler was at his best when providing scoring opportunities for others: notably Chris Chilton and Ken Wagstaff. Whilst others might have monopolised the limelight for their goalscoring performances, it was Ian Butler, more often than not, who provided them with the stage, and somewhat fittingly it was Ian Butler that scored the goal that secured the Tigers the Division Three championship during those swinging sixties.

CARTER, Horatio ('Raich') Stratton   (1947-1951)
Born: 21.12.1913, Hendon, Sunderland
Died: 09.10.1994
Debut: 03.04.48 York City (h) 1-1
Appearances: LGE: 136 - 57; FAC: 14 - 5

Even before Raich Carter joined Hull City his career in football had all the trappings of a superstar: a Football League Championship winner's medal (with Sunderland), FA Cup winner's medals (with Sunderland and Derby County – and the only player to win such medals either side of World War Two) plus a tally of England caps that was limited only by events outside of his control. Football fans throughout the world admired his ability and achievements, but those in the East Riding held him in special affection for what he achieved with Hull City. Winning the Division Three (North) championship may have seemed somewhat modest when set alongside his other triumphs, but as far as the occupants of the Boothferry Park terraces were concerned it was the style with which it was achieved that cemented Carter forever in their affections.

Within weeks of joining the Tigers as a player, and also assistant-manager, Carter found himself elevated to player-manager. Such a step did not perturb him. Instead he planned for his first full campaign in sole charge assiduously. He brought in new faces, changed the roles of some of those already under his charge and by the start of the 1948/49 was ready to lead the Tigers on a journey that would hopefully end with promotion. It was an imperious journey. Along the way he and his team set new records in terms of victories and attendances and by its end the objective had been achieved with games to spare. The Tigers were champions of Division Three (North) and the questions posed of this rookie manager had been answered in emphatic style.

Just one remained: could he take them to the First Division. Sadly, the answer was no; yet it did not diminish what he had already achieved and had no effect whatsoever on the status of Raich Carter in the annals of Hull City.

CHILTON, Christopher Roy   (1960-1971)
Born: 25.06.1943, Sproatley
Debut: 20.08.60 Colchester Utd (a) 0-4
Appearances: LGE: 415 - 193; FAC: 39 - 16; FLC: 21 - 10; OC: 2-3.

Whether you consider Chris Chilton to be the greatest ever player to have worn the Tigers' colours is a matter of opinion. Some supporters will plump for Chillo, whilst others will opt for alternative names from the same era, or some other section of the Tigers' timeline. However, there can be no argument over the Tigers' greatest ever goalscorer; it is Chris Chilton. He sits atop the club's all time scoring list and will probably remain there for the next century and beyond. The record books prove it beyond a shadow of a doubt, and on that score the rest will forever remain in his shadow. To score over 200 goals whilst trying to survive against defenders who had no qualms about whether they marked you or maimed you, illustrates just how good Chillo was and why, whenever the history of Hull City is recounted, the name of Chris Chilton will be frequently mentioned in the telling. He joined the Tigers as a raw youngster; yet if he arrived in the raw, he rapidly developed into the finished article.

Making his League debut whilst still in his teens, his start was not the most auspicious – the Tigers lost 4-0 to Colchester United on 20th August 1960 – but his potential, having been recognised, was persevered with. It wasn't long before that perseverance paid off. At the end of his first season he had played 49 League and Cup games and was the club's leading scorer with 20 goals; he was not yet 18 years old. Although struggling in his second season, he returned to form from thereonin and by the time he'd reached the age of 21 he'd made more than a century of appearances and scored over 50 goals. There are others in City's 'Who's Who' of forwards who would have got nowhere near that goal tally had they played in the Tigers' colours for 21 years! His was a special talent: as comfortable with scoring goals, as making them for others.

When he was joined by the equally talented Ken Wagstaff (Waggy), in the 1964/65 season, their partnership became legendary; but as their reputation grew so did the attention. Chillo's ability to register nearly a goal every other game, even before Waggy's arrival, made him a marked man. On occasions it was literally so as defenders grew desperate in trying to deal with his threat in the air and strength on the ground. Yet if defenders concentrated on Chillo, it left Waggy with space aplenty to wreak havoc, but then having switched their attention to Waggy, Chillo took full advantage. It was a dilemma defenders never solved. When the Tigers won the Third Division championship in the 1965/66 season Chillo and Waggy scored over 50 goals between them. Even the step up in standard to Division Two did not hamper their scoring exploits and for the rest of the decade either one or the other led City's goalscoring charts.

In the 1970/71 season it was Chilton's 21 goals that brought the Tigers agonisingly close to fulfilling the long held dream of playing First Division football. Close, but no cigar. Those goals rekindled the interest of other clubs in Chilton and shortly into the start of the 1971/72 season Chris Chilton left the Tigers for Coventry and began a journey that took in three continents, brought him some success and recognition and eventually brought an end to his playing career. When that aspect of his career ended however, he returned to his roots both geographically and spiritually. Joining the Tigers' coaching squad in the latter half of the 1970s, at the invitation of his former teammate and then current Hull City boss, Ken Houghton, he coached the Tigers juniors, with no little success. That success was overshadowed as the 1980s developed with the club facing bankruptcy and closure. Asked to take the helm on a caretaker basis, Chilton helped keep the Tigers afloat and also played his part in what success they enjoyed during that decade – he was assistant manager during both of the seasons (1982/83 & 1984/85) that the Tigers won promotion.

CLARKE, Douglas   (1955-1964)
Born: 19.01.1934, Bolton
Debut: 12.11.55 West Ham (h) 3-1
Appearances: LGE: 368 - 79; FAC: 31 - 6; FLC: 12 - 2.

Arriving at Boothferry Park in the midst of a poor season for the Tigers, it was hoped Clarke's past scoring record – an average of one in just over two games – would help the club escape the relegation trouble they were slipping into.

A goal on his debut raised hopes, but sadly his return of six goals from 26 League outings was one of the more modest efforts in his career – the same could be said of the Tigers that season as they were relegated. The following season (1956/57) saw him return to something like his old self and he shared top spot in the club's League goals chart that season, but took top spot when his efforts in the FA Cup were included. Forming a useful partnership with Bill Bradbury, their goals were a major part of the club's mini revival during the remainder of the 50s, ably demonstrated during the 1958/59 season when the Tigers were promoted. The goals of Bradbury (30), Smith (26) and Clarke (12) represented over 75% of the Tigers' League goals during that campaign. By that time Clarke's role in the team had switched from poacher to provider and it was as a right winger, rather than an inside forward, that his remaining seasons at Boothferry Park were spent.

COLLIER, John. 'Jock'   (1920-1925)
Born: 01.02.97, Dysart
Died: 27.12.1940
Debut: 28.08.20 West Ham Utd. (a) 1-1
Appearances: LGE: 168 - 0; FAC: 14 - 0

'Gritty', would be an apt description of Collier's style of play. Signed from Scottish junior football just after World War One, Collier quickly established his place in the first team and was a regular – injuries permitting – in five of the six seasons he spent with the club. During that time the Tigers held the middle ground of Division Two with one exception, season 1921/22, when they finished fifth and missed out on promotion by four points. But for a poor start to that campaign – one win in their opening six games – things might have been different; that Collier was missing from the team during that sequence may have been more than just coincidence as regards its eventual outcome.

COLLINSON, Leslie   (1956–1966)
Born: 02.12.1935, Hull
Debut: 24.11.56 Bradford City (h) 1-0
Appearances: LGE: 296 (1) - 14; FAC: 26 - 0; FLC: 9 - 2

Collinson was originally on the Tigers' books as an amateur for some three years before finally turning professional in the latter part of the 1950s. From that point on, however, he swiftly moved into the first team and held down a regular slot in the half-back line with little difficulty. His ability during a game to switch from defensive duties to being a more creative character meant he was a useful player to have in the side.

The fact that he possessed a powerful shot was a bonus and gave opposition keepers cause for concern when he was in full flight towards them with the ball at his feet. Very much a regular choice during his first team career and rarely did his seasonal League appearances tally drop below 40. When they did it was during the more successful spells in the club's history: injury forced him out of much of the promotion winning season of 1958/59 and when the Tigers won the Third Division Championship, Collinson's place in the pecking order of midfielders had been usurped by the likes of Ken Houghton, Chris Simpkin and Alan Jarvis. Nevertheless, those disappointments will not distract from the fact that he is one of the few locally born Tigers to have breached the 300 appearances mark.

CRAWFORD, John Forsyth 'Jackie'   (1919-1922)
Born: 26.09.1896, Jarrow
Died: 27.07.1975
Debut: 13.03.20 Huddersfield Town (a) 0-2
Appearances: LGE: 126 - 9; FAC: 8 - 4

Although signed from junior football, it was soon apparent that Crawford had all the attributes to become a major talent, and so it proved during his three and a bit seasons with the Tigers. One of the smallest players ever to have been on City's books, Crawford had pace aplenty to keep him out of trouble whenever it appeared; allied to that pace was a range of close ball skills that often left his opposing fullback flummoxed. Capable of playing on either wing he made the switch whenever required with no perceived drop in performance. Such a talent was obviously going to attract the attention of higher placed clubs, and with the 1920s being an austere decade on the financial front for the Tigers, the supporters recognised that it would not be long before other clubs would be talking the financial language that the Tigers' directors found hard to ignore. Sold to Chelsea in May 1923, Crawford spent over a decade with the Pensioners and earned one full cap for England, a paltry return for such a talent.

CRIPSEY, Brian Samuel   (1952-1958)
Born: 26.06.1931, Hull
Debut: 03.01.53 Brentford (a) 0-1
Appearances: LGE: 145 - 19; FAC: 14 - 1.

Another diminutive winger who emerged from local junior football, Cripsey spent the bulk of his League career with the Tigers. During that time he had what must have seemed a perpetual battle to establish and hold down a regular first team place; eventually he gained the upper hand.

With a clear preference for the left-wing berth, Cripsey had tussles with Burbanks and Bulless to occupy that berth. In the case of the latter, it was very much a local affair – both were Hull lads by birth – and for much of the 50s they were in evidence on the Tigers' left flank, Bulless's versatility allowing him to fill either full-back, half-back or inside forward positions. Cripsey's talents during his time at Boothferry Park were formally recognised when he was selected for the annual representative fixture between the Northern and Southern sections of Division Three.

CROFT, Stuart Dunbar   (1972-1980)
Born: 12.04.1954, Ashington
Debut: 09.05.73 Cardiff City (a) 2-0
Appearances: LGE: 187 (3) - 4; FAC: 12 - 2; FLC: 9 - 0; OC: 4 - 0.

"Ability with attitude" is one description that has previously been applied to the career of Stuart Croft. An undoubted talent in his youth, Croft managed to break into the first team with seemingly little trouble and alongside Paul Haigh formed one of City's more solid defensive centre-back partnerships for many a year. Captaining the Tigers for one season during the managerial reign of Ken Houghton, Croft looked set for a lengthy spell in the Tigers' colours but it did not happen; and although his League and Cup appearances for the Tigers exceeds 200, there lingers a feeling that it could have been much higher.

DANIEL, Peter William   (1974-1977)
Born: 12.12.1955, Hull
Debut: 18.09.74 West Bromwich Albion (a) 2-2
Appearances: LGE: 113 - 9; FAC: 8 - 0; FLC: 2 - 0; OC: 5 - 0.

Following in the footsteps of Andy Davidson and Frank Banks – who between them had dominated the right-back berth for well over a decade, – Daniel had much to live up to when he broke into the first team during the opening weeks of the 1974/75 season. A couple of games at right-back were followed by a lengthier spell at left-back before making the former position his own part way through the following season (1975/76) and retaining it until his departure to Wolverhampton Wanderers three years later. Comfortable on the ball, Daniel was cultured in his defensive work and possessed sufficient pace to frequently join the attack without compromising those defensive duties. Add to that a talent for taking a decent penalty and it was not surprising when his abilities were recognised at international level with the England Under-21 team.

DAVIDSON, Andrew 'Jock'   **(1952-1967)**
Born: 13.07.1932, Douglas Water
Debut: 08.09.52 Blackburn Rovers (a) 0-2
Appearances: LGE: 520 – 18; FAC: 43 – 1; FLC: 16 – 0.

For approximately fifteen years Andy Davidson's name regularly appeared on the Tigers' First XI teamsheet. It tells barely half the story. He arrived at Boothferry Park as a 14-year old junior in 1947 and departed the club as assistant manager in 1979. For over 30 years 'Jock' Davidson was associated with Hull City on a daily basis. History, however, will forever have him firmly planted within the annals of Hull City for amassing more appearances for the club than any other player; a record, like that of Chris Chilton's scoring achievements, that's unlikely to be surpassed during the club's remaining lifetime.

Born in Douglas Water in 1932, Davidson developed into a more than useful schoolboy player. An unspoken mutual appreciation between himself and Glasgow Celtic failed to retain his talents north of the border, and it was to join his brother at Boothferry Park that Andy Davidson's footballing journey began. By the time he was 16 Andy had made sufficient progress to be on the fringe of the first team – occasionally travelling as non-playing reserve. It also generated interest from clubs closer to his home – including Celtic – but he rejected those, despite bouts of homesickness in his early days with City, to carve out a career in the Football League.

That career began in earnest in the early 1950s when he finally broke into the first team, making his debut in the 2-0 defeat at Blackburn Rovers in September 1952. Given that his name, to many City fans, is synonymous with the 'Number Two shirt' – in those days the traditional identification of a right full-back – it may surprise some to learn that the shirt he wore on his debut bore the number nine on its back. It was an early indication of the versatility of his talent. As time passed, Andy travelled through the Tigers' formation filling positions on both the left and right flank, in the forward and half-back line, before laying claim to the right-back spot – even though in his own opinion he was better suited to playing on the left, and at half-back, where he could be more involved. Anyone privileged to witness Davidson 'in the flesh' would never dream of questioning his involvement and commitment to the club's cause from right-back, and the imagination can only speculate as to what he would have achieved had he not spent so many years playing out of position!

Yet any self-perceived shortcomings were irrelevant as far as his team-mates and managers were concerned. He was their leader and inspiration, week in week out, and led the Tigers through one of their more successful and glamorous seasons (1965/66) when they won the Third Division Championship and reached the quarter-finals of the FA Cup – only eliminated from that competition, in Andy's opinion, by poor refereeing, for which he has sill refuses to forgive the man responsible. The man in question went on to referee the 1974 World Cup Final and was generally acclaimed for his performance. You can see, therefore, why Andy's commitment could never be doubted.

Andy Davidson was not just another player. Three times he suffered a broken leg; each time he fought back to full fitness and it epitomises his character as much as his condition that there was never any detrimental effect on his game when he returned. Injury, however, did finally curtail his playing days in November 1967, by which time he had posted 520 League appearances. No one since has come close.

DAVIES, David Daniel 'Dai'   **(1935-1946)**
Born: 05.12.1914, Aberdare
Died: 13.10.1984
Debut: 02.09.35 Tottenham H. (a) 1-3
Appearances: LGE: 141- 30; FAC: 8 - 3; OC: 40 - 7.

Davies joined the Tigers at the start of the 1935/36 season and had just nine outings in what was one of the most miserable campaigns the Tigers have ever mounted during their Football League membership: relegation, over a century of goals conceded and just five victories; their points tally (20) still remains their lowest ever for a season. From that inauspicious start Davies's fortunes picked up, and for the next three seasons he missed just 12 League games from a possible 126 – he was ever-present in the last of those campaigns.

His ratio of goals also improved with each season and his talent was on the verge of international recognition before World War Two intervened and robbed him of what should have been his prime years.

DELANEY, Damien   (2002-)
Born: 20.07.1981, Cork
Debut: 19.10.02 Torquay Utd (a) 4-1
Appearances: LGE: 119 – 4; FAC: 5 – 0; FLC: 2 – 0.

Delaney was the first of Peter Taylor's signings when he took over as City's manager in October 2002; Taylor was well aware of Delaney's capabilities from their time together at Leicester City. At £50,000 many City fans were starting to doubt the wisdom of their new gaffer when Delaney, playing predominantly at left-back, did not have the happiest of starts. However, when switched to the centre of defence his performances were a revelation: commanding and consistent. A vital cog in the promotion-winning team of season 2003/04, Delaney capped an impressive season by convincingly winning the player of the year award. Maintaining that form in the following campaign (2004/05), Delaney forged a good partnership with Leon Cort that helped the Tigers to another promotion – the first ever back to back promotions in the club's history.

DENBY, Stanley   (1932-1936)
Born: 19.06.1912, Goole
Died: 12.1995
Debut: 01.10.32 Southport (h) 4-0
Appearances: LGE: 124 - 3; FAC: 6 - 0.

Signed from Goole Town towards the end of the 1931/32 season, Denby played a supporting role in the Tigers' first-ever championship winning season (1932/33). When asked to step up in class to Division Two though, he made the transition with apparent ease, playing in all but three of the season's League fixtures in the left-half berth and gave every impression of making the position his own for years to come. Injuries then intervened and he was forced to miss substantial parts of the next three seasons, by which time others had laid claim to his preferred berth and Denby was forced to mix and match between both flanks in order to get a game.

de VRIES, Roger Stuart   (1970-1979)
Born: 25.10.1950, Hull
Debut: 15.08.70 Swindon Town (a) 1-1
Appearances: LGE: 314 (4) - 0; FAC: 12 - 0; FLC: 18 - 1; OC: 14 - 0.

To make your senior club debut against arguably the most famous club side in the world, and face a forward line that contained such legendary soccer surnames as Charlton, Law and Best must have been a daunting prospect for someone still in his teens. Yet that was the test that faced Roger deVries, and it was a test that he passed – against Manchester United in the Watney Cup – with flying colours. Within a fortnight he was making his League debut and retained his place for the bulk of the 1970/71 season: one of the most glorious and galling to have emerged during the club's century existence. A dedicated club man, quiet and unobtrusive, deVries displayed little in the way of frills in his play, he was just a solid, dependable full-back who averaged over 30 games a season during his first team career at Boothferry Park.

DEWHURST, Robert Matthew   (1993-1998)
Born: 10.09.1971, Keighley
Debut: 06.11.93 Rotherham Utd: (h) 4-1
HULL CITY: LGE: 132 (6) - 13; FAC: 8 - 1; FLC: 8 - 0; OC: 7 - 0.

Dewhurst achieved almost cult like status during his time at Boothferry Park, without ever enjoying any success with the club. Displaying the characteristics of endeavour, energy and an ability to exploit his height in the opposition's penalty box at set pieces, he quickly endeared himself to those on the terraces, who accepted that he was never going to reach the top in football, but he was always going to try his best. Although never the quickest of players on the club's books, his speed was diminished even further when he returned to the side after breaking his leg just before Christmas 1995. Whilst remaining commanding in the air, he was susceptible to a nippy forward on the ground, which partly explained the reason behind his departure in 1998. Yet when he returned to Boothferry Park in the opposition's colours, the warmth of his welcome matched that of his 'home side' days.

DUNCAN, Andrew (1930-1934)
Born: 25.01.1911, Renton
Died: 10.10.1983
Debut: 28.03.31 Wrexham (a) 0-2
Appearances: LGE: 105 - 31; FAC: 9 - 0.

Whilst the early years of the Tigers' history were dominated by the name Smith on the goalscoring front, in the opening years of the 1930s, it was the surname of Duncan that held a similar ascendancy amongst City's forwards. For a couple of seasons it was a double act: 'Dally' and Andy. Andrew was the youngest by a couple of years and a similar time-span separated their respective City debuts.

In Andy's case it came towards the end of March 1931 and although the game in question produced a defeat for the Tigers, it provided strong evidence that Bill McCracken had unearthed another potentially fine talent from non-League football. Possessed of substantial pace, Andy Duncan also had an eye for goal, as his statistics confirm.

DUNCAN, Douglas 'Dally'   (1928-1931)
Born: 14.10.1909, Aberdeen
Died: 02.01.1990
Debut: 03.09.28 Oldham Athletic (a) 1-0
Appearances: LGE: 111 - 47; FAC: 11 - 3.

A much admired talent in local Scottish football, City boss, Bill McCracken, pulled off a master-stroke when he obtained the signature of Douglas Duncan at the start of the 1928/29 season. Whilst his namesake (Andy Duncan) was deceptively fast, Douglas was deceptively slow, inducing his opposing full-back into a sense of false security, that more often than not resulted in said full-back's demise as Duncan was away and moving towards goal with the option of either creating an opportunity for his fellow forwards, or seizing the chance himself. This apparent lethargy in his play earned him the nickname 'Dally' but it was a 'nom de plum' dripping in contradiction; there was nothing lethargic about Dally Duncan.

DURHAM, Raymond Dennis   (1946-1958)
Born: 26.09.1923, East Halton
Debut: 24.05.47 Oldham (h) 0-1
Appearances: LGE: 267 - 7; FAC: 22 - 0.

Durham's versatility was both a blessing and a curse during his early Hull City years. Capable of operating in defence, midfield or attack, he was a useful player to slot in whenever injuries or tactics dictated, yet he was never allowed to establish any one position as his own. Injuries and illness did not aid his cause on this matter either, and it is as much a testimony to his tenacity as his talent that he refused to allow the footballer's curse to prevent him from forging a career with the Tigers that spanned more than a dozen years. During that time he notched up nearly 300 League and Cup appearances yet only once did he achieve an unbroken seasonal tally of appearances; that was during the 1952/53 season. It contrasted sharply with the 1955/56 season when his name appeared in the opening game of the season and then injury condemned him to miss the remainder. That the Tigers were relegated that season may just have been a coincidence; it may not. However, such disappointments were balanced by the joys of two promotions: 1948/49 and 1958/59. Those two seasons illustrate Durham's durability perfectly; only one other player could match Durham's achievement, and that was Billy Bly.

EDELSTON, Joseph   (1912-1919)
Born: 27.04.1891, Appleby Bridge
Died: 10.03.1970
Debut: 29.03.13 Fulham (h) 0-1
Appearances: LGE: 109 - 0; FAC: 8 - 0; OC: 130 - 1.

But for World War One, Joe Edelston would probably have doubled his count of League outings for the Tigers, rather than just creeping over the qualification mark; he was that good. Tactically aware at any stage in the game, Edelston had the ability to transfer his thoughts into action and change the course of a game. Although the war did not mean the Tigers losing the services of Edelston, it did mean that his appearances were of a slightly lesser standing in the statistical field, although his performances on the field rarely dropped from the high standards he'd set in those earlier League campaigns. The war-time competition also brought a new dimension to Edelston's talents. On many an occasion he captained the Tigers and on almost the same number he demonstrated his versatility by either playing at inside-forward, half-back, centre-half or full-back. If that wasn't an impressive enough range of positions, he also started at least one game per wartime season in goal.

EDWARDS, Keith   (1978-1981 & 1987-1989)
Born: 16.07.57, Middlesbrough
Debut (1): 19.08.78 Carlisle Utd (h) 1-1
Debut (2): 26.03.88 Leicester City (a) 1-2
Appearances: LGE: 185 (2) - 86; FAC: 13 - 8; FLC: 12 (1) - 2; OC: 5 (2) - 1.

In two spells with the Tigers Edwards set, and maintained, the highest of standards as a goalscorer. For that he was adored from the terraces. His ability to score goals, from chances of varying degrees of difficulty, puts him in the same category as other Tiger scoring legends from the past. Edwards had pace, possessed a powerful shot and had the predatory instinct that distinguishes a great striker from merely a good one. During his first spell, his debut season's goal tally (25) was the nearest anyone had come to matching either Bradbury or Wagstaff's seasonal records. Such talent meant he was destined for better things and so it came about, but 10 years later he was back. Whilst he'd probably not enjoyed the level of success during his time away, as soon as he donned a City shirt again, he found his goalscoring touch – a goal on his second 'debut' removed any doubts that he'd lost his touch and whilst that second spell covered only 59 games, he still managed 33 goals including 26 League goals during the 1988/89 season that not only helped the Tigers avoid relegation, but also made him Division Two's leading scorer for that campaign. Such a record reignited the interest of other clubs, and for a second time the Tigers lost a rare and precious talent. They came to regret it.

EDWARDS, Michael   (1997-2002)
Born: 25.04.1980, North Ferriby
Debut: 28.12.97 Rotherham Utd: (a) 4-5
Appearances: LGE: 165 (13) - 6; FAC: 11 - 2; FLC: 8 (1) - 0; OC: 9 (1) - 0

Aged just 17, Edwards was given his chance in the senior game at Rotherham during Christmas 1997. Whether he enjoyed it – the Tigers lost out by the odd goal in nine – is a moot point, but the experience did not harm his progress as he kept his place in the side for all but two of the remaining games in that season. Despite his youth he continued to hold down a regular place in the side, even though it often meant playing out his preferred position (central defence). Consequently his appearances total quickly mounted up and he passed the 50, 100 and 150 appearances landmarks at a very young age. At times, Edwards was the most experienced Tiger – in terms of appearances made for the club – in the side, and it certainly gave him an 'old head', it was just perched on young shoulders that's all.

ELLIOTT, Stuart   (2002-)
Born: 23.07.1978, Belfast
Debut: 10.08.02 Southend Utd (h) 2-2
Appearances: LGE: 107 (7) – 53; FAC: 2 (2) – 1: FLC: 1 (1) – 0; OC: (1) – 1

Although the name Stuart Elliott appears twice in the playing ranks of Hull City, rest assured there is only one Stuart Elliott. A strike record, thus far, of nearly a goal every other game is sufficient to confirm that Stuart Elliot is ca-

pable of scoring whoever is placed in front of him. If he cannot beat them for speed and ball control, he is more than capable of beating them in the air – at times he appears to defy gravity and seemingly has as much power in his forehead as his feet. A key member of the Tigers' back to back promotion winning squads of 2003/04 and 2004/05, his worth to the side was never better illustrated than in that latter season when he scored 27 League goals, even though he missed nearly six weeks of the season through injury. Without that he would surely have threatened the Tigers' post-war seasonal scoring record and may well have had a tilt at the all time landmark to boot. If you consider that fanciful thinking, then consider his record between the away and home fixtures against Swindon Town in that 2004-05 season. In the intervening period, Elliott made the starting line-up on 17 occasions. In that time the Tigers won all 17 games and Elliott scored 17 goals – on the scoring front, the last City player to produce such a record was Sammy Stevens some 90 years previously.

FEASEY, Paul Cedric   (1952-1964)
Born: 04.05.1933, Hull
Debut: 21.02.53 Barnsley (h) 2-2
Appearances: LGE: 271 - 0; FAC: 25 - 0; FLC: 8 - 0.

Standing at well under six feet tall, few coaches or managers would immediately think centre-half material when setting eyes on Paul Feasey. Yet it was in the centre-half role that Feasey made his League debut during the 1952/53 season. When his next League appearance occurred nearly three years later, during the relegation season of 1955/56, it was again the centre-half role he undertook. Holding down a regular spot in the team during that first season after relegation, Feasey went on to become a first team regular for the remainder of the 1950s. During that time, only injury kept him out of the side and during the 1958/59 season he missed but a single League game throughout the whole campaign and led City to promotion from Division Three. His time with the Tigers lasted until the mid-60s by which time he had accumulated over 300 League and Cup outings – but no goals.

FETTIS, Alan William   (1991-1995 & 2002-2003)
Born: 01.02.1971, Newtonards
Debut (1): 17.08.91 Reading (a) 1-0
Debut (2): 01.02.03 Southend Utd (a) 0-3
Appearances: LGE: 151 (4) - 2; FAC: 5 - 0; FLC: 8 (1) - 0; OC: 9 - 0

Another player with two Hull City spells on his CV. In his first he arrived as an unknown goalkeeper and left having more than made his mark. His second spell, unfortunately, was something of a mirror image as he never managed to match his achievements of the previous decade. Plucked from Irish football, his solid and sometimes spectacular performances brought admiration and international recognition. Although signed to prevent goals, his ability to score them – as he demonstrated in the games against Oxford Utd and Blackpool during the 1993/94 season – proved he had more than one string to his bow.

FISHER, James Bernard   (1955-1962)
Born: 23.02.1934, York
Debut: 22.10.55 Swansea Town (a) 1-4
Appearances: LGE: 126 - 0; FAC: 11 - 0; FLC: 5 - 0.

A muscular keeper who commanded his box well, Fisher would have been the regular choice at any other club during his professional career. At Hull City, however, Fisher had Billy Bly to contend with. As such, for much of his early Tiger life Fisher had to be content with an understudy role. However, as Bly was often blighted with injuries, the need for Fisher to step into the breach was not as infrequent as he might have first feared.   Bly was not Fisher's only obstacle to making the first team, the Tigers had other decent young keepers on their books, but when Billy Bly's time at Boothferry Park was called, it was Fisher who got first shot and he did not disappoint, being City's regular goalkeeper for two seasons before moving on to Bradford City.

FLOUNDERS, Andrew John   (1980-1986)
Born: 13.12.1963, Hull
Debut: 04.10.80 Oxford Utd: (h) 0-1
Appearances: LGE: 126 (33) - 54; FAC: 10 (3) - 4; FLC: 6 (2) - 3; OC: 6 (5) - 2.

Flounders never had the look of a striker - slight of build and relatively short of inches – but his record at Hull City – and elsewhere – confirms that he has every justification to be described as such. At Boothferry Park, during the time of such as Keith Edwards and Billy Whitehurst, Flounder's opportunities were initially limited but when those more recognised forwards departed, Flounders didn't waste his opportunities in the first team and he contributed fully to the Tigers' two promotions seasons whilst he was with them.

GALVIN, Christopher   (1973-1978)
Born: 24.11.1951, Huddersfield
Debut: 25.08.73 Oxford Utd: (h) 0-0
Appearances: LGE: 132 (11) - 11; FAC: 9 - 1; FLC: 11(1) - 1; OC: 8 - 1

A five year spell with Leeds Utd had yielded only seven League outings – understandable, given he was competing with Billy Bremner and Johnny Giles for a midfield place – so Galvin's move to Hull City offered him the chance of regular first team football. After a relatively quiet first season, Galvin did achieve regular first team football with the Tigers during his five year spell at Boothferry Park. Renowned for his 'two-step shuffle', it bemused supporters and baffled opponents. Versatile in that he was capable of playing in either midfield or defence, the only attribute missing from his game was a regular goalscoring record, which was partly responsible for his being allowed to move on to Stockport.

GARVEY, Brian   (1957-1964)
Born: 03.07.1937, Hull
Debut: 01.03.58 Bury (a) 1-1
Appearances: LGE: 232 - 3; FAC: 17 - 0; FLC: 9 - 0

On occasions, in the latter part of the 1950s and early 1960s, over half of the Tigers' team would consist of locally born players, and Brian Garvey was frequently one of them. Garvey's forte was defence; he was capable of playing in any of the defensive positions, be it at full-back or half-back, and whether it was on the right or left flank he would invariably produce an honest and workmanlike performance. After a solitary outing in the 1957/58 season, he became a regular member of City's promotion-winning side of 1958/59. From that point, until his departure to Watford in the summer of 1965, Garvey's seasonal appearances tally never fell below 30 – with the exception of his final season.

GERRIE, Sydney   (1950-1956)
Born: 14.06.1927, Aberdeen
Debut: 11.11.50 Cardiff City (a) 1-2
Appearances: LGE: 146 - 59; FAC: 6 - 3

With a proven track record for scoring goals, Gerrie did not come cheap when the Tigers signed him from Dundee in October 1950. That track record was quickly verified with three goals in his first five games. In tandem with Alf Ackerman – another forward recruit from the Scottish League – the pair scored regularly in their first season (1950/51) together. When Ackerman departed before the start of the following season, the onus for goals fell on Gerrie, and he did not disappoint – 24 from 38 League games. Powerfully built, he led the line for City, upsetting the opposition's rearguard and creating chances for others, as well as taking them himself. Averaging two goals every five games, Gerrie's scoring statistics puts him in the Tigers' top 20 goalscorers, and rightly so.

GIBSON, Frederick William   (1927-1932)
Born: 18.06.1907, Somercoates
Debut: 03.12.27 Stoke City (a) 1-3
Appearances: LGE: 101 - 0; FAC: 9 - 0

There have been periods in the Tigers' history when they have been blessed with not one good goalkeeper, but two. One such period was between 1927 and 1932 when they had the legendary 'Geordie' Maddison and they also had Fred Gibson. Both possessed an imposing physique and both battled it out for possession of the Tigers' green woolly jumper. Whilst Maddison held sway in the early years, it was Gibson who guarded the Tigers' net when they came to national prominence during their epic FA Cup run of 1929/1930. With relegation following quickly, Gibson was edged out by Maddison and by the time City had been crowned as champions of Division Three (North) in 1933, Gibson had been sold on, at a handsome profit, to first division Middlesbrough.

GIBSON, John Rutherford 'Jock'   (1922-1928)
Born: 23.03.1898, Philadelphia (USA)
Died: July 1974
Debut: 26.08.22 Bury (a) 0-1
Appearances: LGE: 210 - 0; FAC: 8 - 0

Although a native of North America, Gibson's early years were shared between England and Scotland. His early football career was spent with Sunderland but his opportunities there were restricted.

However, when he moved to Hull he settled into the right-back position with no trouble at all and formed, for many a year, a strong partnership with 'Ginger' Bell – of Gibson's 210 League outings for the Tigers, 179 were in partnership with Bell. It was a partnership that did not concede goals lightly: in over 50 of those games the Tigers' goal was never breached. Whilst the pairing attracted much interest from other clubs, it was only Gibson who was allowed to move on to Sheffield United and in doing so his transfer fee of £5,000 – substantial for the time – provided the cash-strapped Tigers' directors with much needed revenue.

GOLDSMITH, George   (1928-1933)
Born: 11.03.1905, Loftus
Died: Sept. 1974
Debut: 29.12.28 Southampton (a) 2-3
Appearances: LGE: 172 - 0; FAC: 18 - 0

Interestingly, George Goldsmith follows 'Jock' Gibson in this alphabetical list of Tiger centurions, for it was Goldsmith who followed Gibson into the Tigers' first team when the latter was transferred to Sheffield United. Lithesome in appearance Goldsmith possessed speed and a feisty tackle, but his attributes were not all defensively inclined: his distribution and vision made him a valuable addition to the Tigers' ranks. After a useful partnership with Matt Bell, that took in FA Cup glory and Football League disaster (relegation), he went on to form a similarly formidable partnership with Cliff Woodhead that provided a solid foundation for City's championship season of 1932/33.

GORDON, David S.   (1905-1913)
Born:1883, South Leith
Debut: 02.09.05 Barnsley (h) 4-1
Appearances: LGE: 274 - 17; FAC: 21 - 0

Davy Gordon was the mainstay of the Tigers during their early years. Signed from Scottish amateur football just prior to City's entrance into the Football League, Gordon took to the professional game like the proverbial duck to water. Whilst there were others in the team that perhaps enjoyed a higher profile there were very few, if any, that could match Gordon's consistency or versatility. Capable of playing at half-back or inside-forward, he regularly caught the eye for his performances and whenever his name was missing from the Tigers' teamsheet, it was due more to a lack of physical fitness than a loss of form.

GREAVES, Mark Andrew   (1996-2002)
Born: 22.01.1975, Hull
Debut: 05.10.96 Scunthorpe Utd. (h) 0-2
Appearances: LGE: 152 (25) - 10; FAC: 11 - 1; FLC: 8 -
1; OC: 6(2) - 0

Having being a member of Brigg Town's successful trip
to Wembley in the 1996 FA Cup Vase Final, Mark Greaves
signed for his hometown club and began a professional
career at Boothferry Park that was initially blighted with
injuries and a requirement to appear in positions not best
suited to his talents. Eventually settling into his more favoured central defensive role, for the remainder of his time
with the Tigers he displayed a level of consistency and
commitment that endeared him to the fans and earned him
the 'Player of the Year' award for the 1999/2000 season.

GREENHALGH, James Radcliffe   (1946-1950)
Born: 25.08.1923, Manchester
Debut: 31.08.46 Lincoln City (h) 0-0
Appearances: LGE: 148 - 5; FAC: 19 - 2

Greenhalgh made his debut for the Tigers in their inaugural League match at Boothferry Park in August 1946. It
was a season City's manager used in excess of 40 players
in trying to find the right Tiger blend. He obviously had
no worries regarding Greenhalgh, for no player exceeded
Greenhalgh's tally of games (41) that season. Diminutive
in size he may have been but determined in style was his
trademark. Missing only one game during the 1948/49
championship-winning season, Greenhalgh's performances provided the foundation for that success and he
maintained his wholehearted approach to the game during
his time with the Tigers.

GREENWOOD, Patrick George   (1965-1971)
Born: 17.10.1946, Hull
Debut: 08.01.66 Swindon Town (a) 1-3
Appearances: LGE: 137 (12) - 3; FAC: 7 (1) - 0; FLC: 4 (1) - 0

Greenwood made his debut for the Tigers during their successful 1965/66 season. It was nearly another twelve
months before he appeared in the first team again, but when
he did he gradually built up his number of outings, enjoying a prolonged run in the team between 1967-1969. Although never fully establishing himself as a first team regular in one position, his ability to operate effectively in a
variety of roles meant Greenwood frequently made the
side to replace others who were injured. Such versatility
saw him fill roles from right-back to left-wing and whilst
his performances rarely earned the description of spectacular, they rarely deviated from dependable and solid.

GREENWOOD, Roy Thornton   (1971-1975)
Born: 26.09.1952, Leeds
Debut: 29.09.71 Swindon Town (h) 2-0
Appearances: LGE: 118 (8) - 24; FAC: 11 - 0; FLC: 9 - 4;
OC: 9 - 2

A talented youngster with speed and trickery in his feet,
Greenwood was a more than adequate successor to the
mantle of Ian Butler, who had made the left-wing berth
his own for over half a decade. Complementing his ability to beat his opponent and deliver a threatening ball into
the opposition penalty area, was his aptitude for scoring a
more than adequate number of goals in his own right.
Admired by Terry Neill, City's manager at the time, when
Neill moved on to higher graded clubs he endeavoured to
persuade Greenwood to join him. It never worked out,
but Greenwood did eventually play at a higher level and
didn't look out of place.

HAIGH, Paul   (1974-1980)
Born: 04.05.1958, Scarborough
Debut: 26.04.75 Sheffield Wednesday (h) 1-0
Appearances: LGE: 179 (1) - 8; FAC: 7 - 1; FLC: 13 - 2;
OC: 9 - 1

Haigh joined the Tigers as an apprentice and made such
quick progress that his first team debut came whilst he
was still only 16 years old. A defender, both good in the
air and on the ground, Haigh was capable of playing in
any position across the back four, although it was at the
centre of defence where his talents were best utilised. That
talent was recognised with a single appearance for the
England Under-21 side. With sufficient skill and speed to
play himself out of the trickiest of situations, he formed a
useful partnership with Stuart Croft. Both players, however, soon came to the attention of visiting scouts and both
were sold, through financial necessity, enjoying varying
degrees of success with their subsequent clubs.

HARRIS, William Charles   (1949-1953)
Born: 31.10.1928, Swansea
Died: Dec. 1989
Debut: 29.04.50 Sheffield Utd (a) 0-5
Appearance: LGE: 131 - 6; FAC: 14 - 1

From a team perspective, Harris's debut was not the most
auspicious, but he soon adapted to the rigours of professional football without too much trouble and occupied a
variety of roles within the team before eventually settling
into the right-half berth. His vision in spotting an attacking opportunity, and taking advantage of it, earned him
rave reviews from the press and admiring glances from

visiting scouts. Having cost the Tigers just £2,000 when signing him from welsh amateur side Llanelly, his subsequent transfer to Middlesbrough for £15,000 represented good business for City and demonstrated the progress he had made whilst with the Tigers. That progress was maintained with Middlesbrough, as Harris made over 350 appearances for them and gained international recognition.

HARRISON, Francis John   (1952-1959)
Born: 12.11.1931, Gateshead
Died:. Nov. 1981
Debut: 08.09.52 Blackburn Rovers (a) 0-2
Appearances: LGE: 199 - 0; FAC: 15 - 0

Although primarily a defender, Harrison would have fitted comfortably into the modern day role of wing-back, as coupled with his defensive attributes was an ability to instigate attacking moves. Such an aptitude did not conform to the stereotype defender of his era, and therefore was not always fully appreciated by those on the terraces who preferred their defenders to defend pure and simple. Those responsible for team selection, however, held no such misgivings and regularly picked him to do duty on the Tigers' behalf. Consequently, his tally of outings rose steadily during his stay and whilst his total of League outings fell one short of a double century, that barrier would have undoubtedly been breached with ease had he not suffered the misfortune of breaking his leg in December 1954.

HARRISON, Kenneth   (1946-1954)
Born: 20.01.1926, Stockton-on-Tees
Debut: 10.05.47 Tranmere Rovers (h) 1-0
Appearances: LGE: 238 - 47; FAC: 25 - 4

A player possessing impressive pace, Harrison was a member of City's free-scoring forward line that set the Division Three (North) scene alight during the 1948/49 season. In tandem with his wing partner, Eddie Burbanks, Harrison provided plenty of ammunition for his fellow forwards but still managed to help himself to the occasional goal when the chance came. He adapted well to life in Division Two and attracted attention on a regular basis. Like his namesake from the same era, his appearances for City would have been greater but for breaking his kneecap in the opening minutes of the high profile FA Cup tie at home to Tottenham Hotspur. He recovered and returned to sufficient form for Derby County to pay a significant sum for his services during the 1954/55 season.

HASSALL, Wilfred   (1946-1952)
Born: 23.09.1923, Manchester
Died: 26.06.1998
Debut: 16.09.46 Gateshead (h) 1-2
Appearances: LGE: 141 - 3; FAC: 16 - 0

A member of the original Boothferry Park squad first recruited by Major Frank Buckley, Harris had just started to establish himself as a useful right full-back when a serious injury put him out of action for some 18 months. As a consequence, he missed the opportunity to win a championship winner's medal in the 1948/49 season. It wasn't until the end of September 1950 that Hassall was able to reclaim the Number 2 shirt, which he retained almost permanently until the latter part of his final season with the Tigers, before departing to Worcester City in the summer of 1953.

HAWLEY, John East   (1972-1977 & 1982)
Born: 08.05.1954, Withernsea
Debut (1): 21.04.73 Sunderland (h) 0-2
Debut (2): 04.12.82 Blackpool (a) 1-1
Appearances: LGE: 104 (13) - 23; FAC: 5 - 1; FLC: 10 (1) - 2; OC: 5 (2) - 0

Not since the early days of E.G.D. Wright in Hull City's history had a player of amateur status possessed such talent to capture the imagination of Tigers' fans, but John Hawley's first spell at Boothferry Park evoked such emotions. Naturally gifted, Hawley spent his early days with City playing for expenses only and it took the club some four years before they finally persuaded him to sign professional terms. Within a couple of seasons of joining the professional ranks, Hawley was moving in higher circles – Leeds, Sunderland and Arsenal – with varying degrees of success and enjoyment. His second spell at Boothferry Park was a brief month's loan to assist the Tigers in their promotion season of 1982/83; he played only three games, but still managed a goal to revive the memories of what he'd achieved before.

HENDERSON, Raymond   (1961-1967)
Born: 31.03.1937, Wallsend
Appearances: LGE: 226 (3) - 54; FAC: 22 (1) - 6; FLC: 12 - 1

Five goals in nine games during his time at Middlesbrough persuaded Cliff Britton to spend £2,000 to sign Ray Henderson. It turned out to be money well spent. Whilst capable of playing as a winger or inside forward, it was probably in the former role that City fans will have the clearest recollection of Henderson's efforts.

Whilst probably the least well-known of City's 'Famous Five' forward line of the mid 60s, Henderson was no slouch at either supplying chances or scoring goals. His three substitute appearances in the League hold special place in the Tigers' history, for he was the first City player to be utilised as a substitute in 1965 when the rules were changed, and just for good measure he also became the first City player to score when coming on as a substitute. Both achievements were accomplished in the same game: away to Brighton & Hove Albion on 20th August 1965.

HENDRY, Conal Nicholson 'Nick'   **(1911-1919)**
Born: 1887, York
Died: 09.04.1949
Debut: 23.03.12 Gainsborough Trinity (h) 1-1
Appearances: LGE: 140 - 0; FAC: 11 - 0; OC: 115 - 0

During City's early years they were fortunate to be able to call on the services of some extremely good goalkeepers. Included in their number was Nick Hendry: a goalkeeper of safe handling with both shots and crosses. Taking over on a regular basis at the start of the 1912/13 season, Hendry retained his place for a consecutive run of 103 games before injury forced him to miss the away fixture at Clapton Orient in January 1915. Returning in the following game he kept his place up to the outbreak of World War One and during the war-time competition he was between the Tigers' stick for the vast number of those fixtures.

HOBSON, Gary   **(1990-1995)**
Born: 12.11.1972, North Ferriby
Debut: 10.04.91 West Bromwich Albion (a) 1-1
Appearances: LGE: 135 (7) - 0; FAC: 2 (2) - 0; FLC: 13 (1) - 0; OC: 6 - 0

A product of City's youth system, Hobson made his League debut whilst still a teenager and displayed a maturity in his performances that frequently belied his years. By preference his best position was on the left of central defence, but City's circumstances during Hobson's stay often required him to play out of position. Whenever asked to do so his endeavour and commitment to the Tigers' cause never diminished. Although hampered by injuries on more than one occasion, Hobson's talent remained constant and attracted interest from a number of clubs. Given the financial straits the club were operating in, bids for his services were not exactly discouraged and his move to Brighton in March 1996 at least helped ease City's debt, even if it did not offer Hobson a higher grade of football.

HOUGHTON, Kenneth   **(1964-1972)**
Born: 18.10.1939, Rotherham
Debut: 09.01.65 Bournemouth (a) 3-2
Appearances: LGE: 253 (11) - 79; FAC: 22 (1) - 9; FLC: 10 (2) - 2; OC: 5 - 1

In the space of two months during the mid 60s, Cliff Britton spent £120,000 in purchasing three players. By modern-day standards such expenditure would be considered no big deal, yet back then it was a sum of money not to be sniffed at. However, it turned out to be money well spent as Britton at last had found the remaining pieces to solve his Tigers' promotion puzzle. One of those missing pieces was Ken Houghton. Houghton's move to Boothferry Park brought to an end a long and patient pursuit of the midfield general that Britton had been seeking. It soon became clear that Britton was right to be patient. Houghton became that midfield general and helped mould those around him into an effective attacking force and and in conjunction with Chris Simpkin and Alan Jarvis, also provided an effective first line of defence against any opposition attack. With Houghton's prompting and vision, the Tigers were an attacking force of some power.

HUBBARD, Clifford   **(1933-1938)**
Born: 1911, Worksop
Died: Nov. 1962
Debut: 02.09.33 Swansea Town (a) 1-1
Appearances: LGE: 183 - 56; FAC: 12 - 5; OC: 8 - 1

Hubbard joined the Tigers from Scunthorpe Utd in readiness for their first season back in Division Two (1933/34). Initially intended to be introduced into the first team gradually, injury to Andy Duncan hastened the plan's timetable; fortunately it worked. Hubbard made a good impression and went on to miss only six games after his introduction that season and towards the end of it settled in on the right wing. With regularity of appearance there also came an improvement in his strike rate, such that by the time the last peacetime season (1938/39) had concluded he'd scored 19 goals from 40 outings.

JACOBS, Wayne Graham (1987-1991)
Born: 03.02.1969, Sheffield
Debut: 26.03.88 Leicester City (a) 1-2
Appearances: LGE: 127 (2) - 4; FAC: 8 - 0; FLC: 7 - 0; OC: 6 - 0

Signed from Sheffield Wednesday on transfer deadline day in March 1988, Jacobs was one for the future according to Stan Ternent. He was right, except that Jacob's future did not lie too long with the Tigers, more's the pity. Although displaying all the talent and enthusiasm that suggested Ternent's assessment was correct, Jacob's suffered a serious knee injury in January 1992. By that time he'd already notched up over a century of outings and was proving to one of the brighter lights in the Tigers' dark days. The injury sidelined him for over a year and the financial climate at Boothferry Park resulted in his being released – a classic example of short-term economics over long-term investment. Jacob's resurrected his career and went on to play at the highest level in English football, whilst the Tigers drifted down to the basement

JARVIS, Alan Leslie (1965-1970)
Born: 04.08.1943, Wrexham
Debut: 22.10.65 Workington (a) 0-3
Appearances: LGE: 148 (11) - 12; FAC: 12 - 0; FLC: 5 (1) - 0

Plucked from Everton's reserve ranks by Cliff Britton, Jarvis went on to repay Britton's faith by becoming one of the most consistent and productive members of City's championship winning side of 1966, if not necessarily the most prominent. A thinking player, Jarvis provided a useful balance to the Tigers' midfield during the latter part of the 60s and his talents did not go unnoticed. He was rewarded with his first full cap for Wales whilst on the Tigers' books and thus became the first player from the club to represent the principality.

JENKINSON, Leigh (1987-1992)
Born: 09.07.1969, Thorne
Debut: 27.02.88 Sheffield Utd. (h) 1-2
Appearances: LGE: 95 (35) - 13; FAC: 6 (1) - 0; FLC: 7 (2) - 1; OC: 9 (2) - 1

A player with pace, Jenkinson's League debut came some 16 months after his senior debut in the Associate Members Cup game away to Southampton in November 1986. Combined with his pace was his 'trick' of double bluffing his opponent with footwork not seen since the days of Chris Galvin. Always a useful asset to the side, for his speed and attacking attributes, if not always his defensive work-rate, his century plus of appearances is aided by substitute appearances that set a club record – subsequently surpassed by Neil Mann. His pace and talent were destined for a bigger stage than the Tigers could offer, and although his career never reached the heights once thought possible, he nevertheless acquitted himself in the highest divisions on both sides of Hadrian's wall.

JENSEN, Hans Viggo (1948-1956)
Born: 29.03.1921, Skagen (Denmark)
Debut: 30.10.48 New Brighton (h) 4-1
Appearances: LGE: 308 - 51; FAC: 27 - 3

A Danish amateur international and Olympian, the Tigers were fortunate that work commitments in the autumn of 1948 brought Jensen into contact with the club.

Fortunate indeed, for after a short spell with City on amateur terms – due to immigration requirements – Jensen signed professional forms two years later. In the interim, however, Jensen had already established himself as a firm favourite with the fans for his outstanding talent and versatility – and earned himself a Division Three (North) championship-winner's medal in the process. Capable of playing anywhere on the left-side of the team, he always gave good value – both in terms of effort and goals – whether it was at left-back, left-half or left-wing

JOBSON, Richard Ian (1984-1990)
Born: 09.05.1963, Cottingham
Debut: 09.02.85 Burnley (h) 2-0
Appearances: LGE: 219 (2) - 17; FAC: 13 - 1; FLC: 12 - 0; OC: 9 - 0

After a shaky start, Richard Jobson went on to become one of the best central defenders ever to have played for the Tigers in the latter half of the 20th century. Cool, calm and collected personified a Jobson display in amber and black. Never seemingly under pressure, Jobson possessed the pace and skill to get himself out of trouble, and when he ventured into the opposition's penalty area at set pieces, he was capable of causing trouble and nicking a goal. A bargain at £40,000 when signed from Watford, his talent deserved a much higher valuation, and so it proved when he was sold to Oldham Athletic: his transfer out fee was more than ten times what the Tigers paid.

JOYCE, Warren Garton (1994 & 1996-1999)
Born: 20.01.1965, Oldham
Debut (1): 21.01.95 Brentford (h) 1-2
Debut (2): 17.08.96 Darlington (h) 3-0
Appearances: LGE: 146 (1) - 15; FAC: 8 - 1; FLC: 7 (1) - 1; OC: 7 - 2

That Hull City were able to celebrate their centenary as a Football League club is, it could be argued, down to Warren Joyce. A surprising statement perhaps, given that during Joyce's playing days his relationship with the fans was not always the warmest. After a brief loan spell in 1995 Warren Joyce eventually joined the Tigers on a permanent basis in the summer of 1996. Made captain, his perceived closeness to Terry Dolan did not endear him to the fans. Joyce, however, was his own man and he did not let such antipathy affect him. Within a couple of seasons, that antipathy had turned to adoration as in the role of player-manager he guided the Tigers through the 'Great Escape' season of 1998/99: when relegation from the Football League had seemed inevitable. If ever there was a right man at the right time in Hull City's history, it was Warren Joyce.

LEE, Christopher (1993-1995)
Born: 18.06.1971, Halifax
Debut: 21.08.93 Plymouth Argyle (h) 2-2
Appearances: LGE: 104 (12) - 5; FAC: 3 (1) - 0; FLC: 4 - 1; OC: 5 - 0

Being the son of City's assistant-manager, Jeff Lee, heaped added pressure on the shoulders of Chris Lee during his time at Boothferry Park. That Lee senior was Terry Dolan's assistant did not endear Lee junior to those on the terraces; he was frequently the target of the boo boys. He did not let it affect him unduly and whilst not blessed with an abundance of skill, he compensated by offering endeavour, commitment and determination. That his century of Tiger outings was accumulated in just three seasons suggests he was also consistent in his performances – in his first two seasons, he topped the appearances list in one, whilst in the other only one player exceeded his outings tally.

LORD, Malcolm (1966-1978)
Born: 25.10.46, Driffield
Debut: 27.03.67 Birmingham City (a) 1-2
Appearances: LGE: 271 (27) - 24; FAC: 14 - 0; FLC: 8 (1) - 1; OC: 11 (2) - 1

"A professional's professional" was manager Cliff Britton's assessment of Malcolm Lord in the early days of his career.

It was in response to the criticism Lord attracted from the terraces during those early days in the Tigers' first team. That Lord went on to make nearly 350 League and Cup outings during a lengthy Tiger career confirms that Britton – and his successors – knew a decent player when they saw one; and Mally Lord was a decent player. Rarely flamboyant in his displays, Lord's game was all inconspicuous industry: he did the hard graft to provide the platform for others more creative to display their talents; yet he was not without ability on the goals front. Whilst his style was not immediately appreciated by Tigers' fans, they were eventually won over by his industry and commitment and made him their player of the year at the end of the 1973/74 season.

MADDISON, George 'Geordie'   (1924-1937)
Born: 14.08.1902, Birtley
Died: 18.05.1959
Debut: 08.11.24 Stockport County (h) 3-0
Appearances: LGE: 430 – 0; FAC: 24 – 0; OC: 2 - 0

Only five players in the history of Hull City have made over 400 League appearances for the club; 'Geordie' Maddison was the first. Joining City from Tottenham Hotspur in the early 1920s Maddison, despite his youth, displayed a maturity in his performances that had not been seen in a Tigers' keeper for many a year. Physically imposing, Maddison commanded his area and was equally as proficient on the ground as in the air. Taking over from Billy Mercer at the start of the 1925/26 season, Maddison did not miss a League game until November 1927.

Then, he was replaced by Fred Gibson and from that point on both battled for City's goalkeeping shirt. It was an awesome contest with one, then the other, holding the upper hand; but for that competition Maddison would surely have pushed his appearances tally well over the 500 mark and probably nearer to 600. Even so, he still set a club appearance record that stood for over 30 years and in the process took the standard of City goalkeeping to another level, a level few of his successors have matched.

MAIL, David   (1990-1994)
Born: 12.09.1962, Bristol
Debut: 25.08.90 Notts County (h) 1-2
Appearances: LGE: 140 (10) – 2; FAC: 4 – 0; FLC: 5 – 0; OC: 9 (1) – 0

Signed during the summer of 1990 for the not inconsiderable sum of £160,000, the intention of pairing Mail with Richard Jobson at centre-back was scuppered almost immediately with the sale of Jobson to Oldham. It meant that Mail would take on the senior role within City's back four. With over 200 League appearances for Blackburn Rovers, it was a task within his capabilities and one he performed well, whether he was required to play at centre-back or on the flanks. Not the quickest player on City's books at the time, Mail compensated for this deficiency with both tactical and positional awareness, plus strength in the tackle and ability in the air.

MANN, Neil   (1993-2000)
Born: 19.11.1972, Nottingham
Debut: 14.09.93 Wrexham (a) 0-3
Appearances: LGE: 138 (37) – 9; FAC: 6 (2) – 1; FLC: 12 (4) – 0; OC: 8 (2) – 1

From his early days in the Tigers' team, 'Manny' became something of a cult hero amongst City fans who took him to their hearts for the 'never say die' spirit encompassed in his performances. Plucked from non-League football he made the transition to the League game without too much trouble and offered an attacking outlet even when employed in a defensive role. Full of character his career was cruelly cut short by two serious knee ligament injuries. Having overcome the first – suffered against Scunthorpe in November 1998 – he suffered a reoccurrence nearly a year later against Liverpool in the League Cup. It effectively ended his playing career but he remained with the club in a youth coaching capacity.

MARTIN, George Scott   (1922-1927)
Born: 14.07.1899, Bothwell
Died: 06.11.1972
Debut: 28.10.22 Rotherham County (h) 2-3
Appearances: LGE: 204 – 55; FAC: 14 – 3

A goal on his debut augured well for Martin's time with the Tigers, and so it proved as he was a regular member of City's front line for much of the 1920s. Capable of leading the attack, or supporting it from either of the inside-forward positions, Martin was a useful partner to City's more prolific scorers of that time, such as 'Paddy' Mills and Charlie Flood. Yet if Martin was more comfortable providing scoring chances for others, he was not averse to taking the responsibility for scoring them himself when required, and whilst his strike rate with the Tigers was acceptable rather than exceptional, he did attract interest from other clubs and played at the top level with Everton.

MARWOOD, Brian   (1979-1983)
Born: 05.02.1960, Seaham Harbour
Debut: 12.01.80 Mansfield Town (h) 3-1
Appearances: LGE: 154 (4) – 51; FAC: 16 – 1; FLC: 4 (1) – 0; OC: 12 – 1

Rising through the youth and reserve ranks, Marwood established himself as one of the finest post-war players on City's books. Fleet of foot and masterful at close ball control, he presented a permanent threat whenever he appeared on the Tigers' right wing. A more than decent ratio of goals to games was augmented by his role as penalty taker during his time at Boothferry Park. He scored more often than not from the penalty spot but some of those misses proved crucial, especially during the 1983/84 season when promotion was denied to the Tigers by the margin of a single goal. There was no need for recriminations however, Marwood's contribution to City's cause will forever be in credit. Taking his leave at the end of the 1983/84 season, Marwood's career continued on an upward spiral gaining League championship honours with Arsenal and international recognition with England.

McCLAREN, Stephen   (1979-1984)
Born: 03.05.1961, Fulford
Debut: 05.05.80 Bury (h) 0-1
Appearances: LGE: 171 (7) – 16; FAC: 16 – 3; FLC: 7 (2) – 0; OC: 11 (1) - 1

McClaren's spell with the Tigers encompassed the good and the bad of Hull City's history. One of the many excellent youngsters that broke into the first team in the early 1980s, he endured the hardship of administration followed by the happiness of two promotion winning seasons (1982/ 3 & 1984/5) to which he made a valuable contribution. Skilful on the ball, he also had energy in abundance and was perpetual motion in most games. From a central midfield position McClaren carried out his defensive and attacking duties with little trouble and popped up with a crucial goal on more than one occasion. Taking up coaching and then management at the end of his playing career, McClaren has acquired the highest of reputations in these fields at both club and international level.

McEWAN, Stanley   (1983-1987)
Born: 08.06.1957, Cambuskenneth
Debut: 10.03.84 Newport County (a) 1-1
Appearances: LGE: 113 – 25; FAC: 6 – 1; FLC: 10 – 2; OC: 11 – 3

An extremely competent defender, McEwan arrived at Boothferry Park to form an impressive partnership with Peter Skipper. That partnership covered more than a century of games and formed the foundation for the Tigers' promotion from Division Three in 1985. In addition to his defensive abilities, McEwan also posed a threat in attack. With a venomous shot, he was a near certainty from the penalty spot and deadly accurate from free-kicks within a 30 yard radius of the opposition's goal meant his name regularly appeared on the scoresheet during that aforementioned promotion campaign.

McGILL, James Morrison   (1971-1975)
Born: 27.11.1946, Glasgow
Debut: 30.10.71 Preston North End (a) 1-3
Appearances: LGE: 141 (6) – 2; FAC: 11 – 1; FLC: 8 (1) – 0; OC: 10 – 1

The nicknames of McGill's first two League clubs – Huddersfield Town (Terriers) and Hull City (Tigers) – are appropriate in describing McGill's style of play. To the opposition he was a nuisance, never letting them settle into their rhythm and never one to shirk a confrontation. With over 160 League outings for Huddersfield already under his belt by the time he joined the Tigers, he brought experience as well as energy to a City midfield that had guile aplenty from Ken Houghton and Ken Knighton but was often short on grit. By concentrating on the necessities of football, rather than the niceties, McGill did not always endear himself to fan or foe, and the occasional run-in with the referee was not unusual. Yet to harness that aspect of his play would have diminished the contribution he made to the Tigers' cause.

McKECHNIE, Ian Hector   (1966-1973)
Born: 04.10.1941, Lenzie
Debut: 20.08.66 Coventry City (a) 0-1
Appearances: LGE: 255 – 0; FAC: 17 – 0; FLC: 7 – 0;
OC: 5 – 0

One of the great characters in the last 50 years of the Tigers' history, but of greater relevance was the fact that he was also one of the great Tiger keepers from that same era. Combine the two and you need look no further to explain why 'Kekkers' was adored by Tigers' fans. They loved him so much they pelted him with oranges whenever he made an appearance before them. It was an act of kindness, however, related to his dietary requirements rather than any assessment of his performances. Joining the Tigers on a free transfer from Southend United, McKechnie made the keeper's jersey practically his own following his debut and he was virtually ever-present in the Tigers' goal from November 1967 to April 1971. In possession of a powerful kick, his clearances from the Tigers' penalty area often found their way into the oppositions' same location without bouncing. Such a feat was not his only claim to fame. In the Tigers' Watney Cup semi-final fixture against Manchester United, McKechnie became the first goalkeeper in the Football League to save a penalty during a penalty shoot-out.

McMILLAN, Eric   (1960-1963)
Born: 02.11.1936, Beverley
Debut: 20.08.60 Colchester Utd (a) 0-4
Appearances: LGE: 150 – 3; FAC: 14 – 1; FLC: 10 – 0

Making his debut in the same game as Chris Chilton, McMillan more than matched his fellow debutant for appearances – at least in their early days. Between September 1961 and October 1963, McMillan notched up 127 consecutive outings: a testimony to his consistency as much as his capability; during the same period Chilton only mustered 85 outings. On the goals front though, it was a different story: Chilton scored 34 goals from his 85 appearances, whilst McMillan's 127 games were goal barren. Scoring goals, however, was Chilton's province rather than McMillan's, whose duties were more defensively orientated and which were performed diligently.

McNEIL, Robert Muirhead   (1980-1984)
Born: 01.11.1962, Bellshill
Debut: 13.09.80 Blackpool (a) 2-2
Appearances: LGE: 135 (3) – 3; FAC: 17 – 0; FLC: 5 – 0;
OC: 8 - 1

McNeil was another of the good youngsters on the Tigers' books during the 1980s who made it through to the first team and stayed there. Of that crop McNeill was perhaps the least prominent: he did his job at right-back without any fuss and was rarely found wanting against his opponent. His appearances rose with each passing season – he was ever-present during the 1983/84 campaign – and consequently so did his confidence. It was surprising therefore that he was allowed to leave at a time when he was approaching his prime, and the consequential problems the club faced in finding an adequate replacement suggested that the decision had been somewhat premature.

McQUILLAN, John   (1906-1913)
Born:1888, Boldon
Debut: 17.11.06 Lincoln City (a) 1-0
Appearances: LGE: 239 – 2; FAC: 18 – 1; OC; 31 – 2

McQuillan spent eight years with the Tigers. During that time he was consistency and reliability personified. Making his debut at left-back, that position became his own over the ensuing seasons. Not short of pace, he timed his tackles well and was never rash in his distribution of the ball. Such qualities brought him respect from friend and foe alike; it also brought frequent enquiries from other clubs as to his availability. All were rebuffed until the summer of 1914 when he was allowed to move on to Leeds.

McSEVENEY, John Haddon   (1961-1964)
Born: 08.02.1931, Shotts
Debut: 31.08.61 Port Vale (h) 3-1
Appearances: LGE: 161 – 60; FAC: 12 – 8; FLC: 10 – 2

Although never the tallest player on the field, opponents soon realised that McSeveney was not easily knocked off the ball. For his size he was tremendously strong and when in possession of the ball he was extremely dangerous. Operating mainly on the left wing, his close control was excellent, his pace took him past many an opponent and then left him clear to either deliver an accurate cross or go for goal himself. A glance at his record with City suggests that when the latter option was taken the right result was usually achieved. He headed the club's goalscoring chart in his first season at the club, and repeated the feat the following season before the scoring prodigy that was Chris Chilton finally got into his stride.

MEENS, Harold   (1938-1951)
Born: 05.10.1919, Doncaster
Died: Sept 1987
Debut: 18.02.1939 Darlington (a) 1-0
Appearances: LGE: 146 – 0; FAC: 15 – 0; OC: 49 – 3

Meens spent only a few months with the Tigers as an amateur before finally being persuaded to turn professional. It was nearly three years, however, before he broke through into the first team. Having done so, and before he could fully establish himself in the side, his career was put on hold for the duration of World War Two. When peacetime football resumed, so did his career with City. For a couple of seasons he alternated between left-back and centre-half, but it was during the championship-winning season of 1948/49 that he became established in the latter role and made an extremely good job of it. Missing only two games throughout the entire season, he led a miserly defence that conceded only 28 goals in the League – a club record that remains intact to this day.

MELLOR, John Allan   (1947-1951)
Born: 16.10.1921, Droylsden
Died: Aug 1997
Debut: 13.09.47 Stockport County (a) 0-0
Appearances: LGE: 104 – 4; FAC: 13 – 0

After consistently impressing during his non-League career – both pre and post World War Two – Mellor signed for the Tigers in the summer of 1947. Breaking into the first team just weeks into the new season (1947/48), Mellor's outings during the remainder of that season came in spurts. He fared better in the following campaign and helped the Tigers win the Division Three (North) title, playing at left-half for much of that campaign and continued in the same position when the Tigers moved up to Division Two. Although capable of destroying opposition attacks, he was equally adept at constructing City's attacks and his ability to prompt such raids with accurate long passing made him an important element of City's team during that era.

MERCER, William Henry 'Billy'   (1914-1922)
Born: 1888, Prescot
Died: 05.06.1956
Debut: 23.01.15 Clapton Orient (a) 3-0
Appearances: LGE: 193 – 0; FAC: 10 – 0; OC: 4 – 0

One of the abiding features of Hull City during the inter-war years was the succession of superb goalkeepers that played for them; included in that number was William (Billy) Mercer. Starting his career as an outfield player with non-League Prescot, an injury crisis led to his volunteering to go in goal. He took to it like a duck to water, although the serious injuries he sustained during World War One threatened to end his career entirely. Fortunately he overcame those and resumed his career with the Tigers. Taking over from Nick Hendry part way through

the 1919/20 season, he missed only six League games out of a possible 198. His quiet but assured performances attracted the attention of the top clubs and his transfer to Huddersfield Town at least allowed a wider audience to witness his talent.

MILLS, Bertie Reginald 'Paddy' (1920-1925&1929-1932)
Born: 23.02.1900, Multan (India)
Died: 22.01.1994
Debut (1): 11.12.20 Nottingham Forest (a) 0-2
Debut (2): 04.01.30 Cardiff City (h) 2-2
Appearances: LGE: 269 – 101; FAC: 22 – 9

A natural goalscorer, Paddy Mills had two spells with the Tigers and he was admired throughout both. In the first spell he was approaching his prime and announced his arrival on the football scene with consistently heavy scoring. Unable to resist the opportunity to cash in on his talent, City's directors sold him on to Notts County. Unfortunately the move didn't work out; neither did his subsequent transfer to Birmingham. Within four years of his departure, therefore, he was back in the Tigers' colours and whilst not reaching the heights of his previous spell, he showed he still had the ability to score goals and did so at a rate that set a club record that stood for many years until beaten by Chris Chilton.

MILNER, Michael   (1959-1967)
Born: 21.09.1939, Hull
Debut: 30.03.59 Tranmere Rovers (h) 1-0
Appearances: LGE: 160 – 0; FAC: 12 – 0; FLC: 4 – 0

Milner had to wait four years from signing professional forms for the Tigers – in July 1958 – before establishing himself as City's first choice centre-half. It was a position that early performances suggested he would hold on to for some while. Unfortunately, injury intervened and during his absence another local lad, Brian Garvey, did so well that Milner struggled to regain his place. Eventually he did, towards the end of the 1963/64 season, and this time he held on. Rarely conspicuous but inevitably consistent in his performances Milner missed just four games during the 1964/65 season, and was ever-present in the championship-winning season of 1965/66.

MUTRIE, Leslie Alan   (1980-1983)
Born: 01.04.1952, Newcastle
Debut: 26.12.80 Rotherham (h) 1-2
Appearances: LGE: 114 (1) – 49; FAC: 8 – 1; FLC: 5 (1) – 0; OC: 3 – 0

On the strength of three impressive performances for Blyth Spartans against the Tigers in the FA Cup, Mike Smith risked a small sum of money on buying Les Mutrie. It turned out to be money well spent. Mutrie had tried full-time football before – at Carlisle United – without success, but he did not let this second chance slip by. In his first full season he notched 27 League goals from 43 outings and formed a more than useful partnership with Billy Whitehurst. Whilst Billy battered opposing defences, Mutrie mugged them. Included in that season's statistics was a sequence of nine game during which he scored in every one: 14 goals in total. In doing so he set a new club record that still exists and firmly cemented Mutrie in Tiger folklore.

Whilst he never matched that scoring feat in his subsequent seasons, he did play his part in helping the Tigers to promotion in the 1982/83 season and was included in the PFA Division Four Team for that season as well as winning the Supporters' Player of the Year award.

NEILL, William John Terence   (1970-1972)
Born: 08.05.1942, Belfast
Debut: 15.08.70 Swindon Town (a) 1-1
Appearances: LGE: 103 – 4; FAC: 11 – 0;FLC: 2 – 0; OC: 6 – 0

After 11 successful years at Arsenal, Terry Neill moved into management at an age (28) when he still had a few good playing years ahead of him. An authoritative defender who could tackle and compete in the air with the best of them, Neill had formed an impressive partnership with Frank McClintock whilst at Highbury and captained his country (Northern Ireland) on numerous occasions. Initially taking a player-manager role when moving to Boothferry Park, Neill brought steel and skill to the Tigers' back four and took the Tigers to their best League finish for nearly sixty years – just missing out on promotion to Division One and an unlucky quarter-final exit in the FA Cup.

NEVE, Edwin   (1906-1911)
Born: 03.05.1885, Prescot
Died: Aug. 1920
Debut: 08.09.06 Clapton Orient (h) 2-0
Appearances: LGE: 102 – 12; FAC: 2 – 0

As a natural left-winger Neve faced the strongest of competition, in the shape of the legendary E.G.D. Wright, for a regular place on the Tigers' left-flank. Under normal circumstances therefore, Neve's count of outings would have been nowhere near the centurion qualification mark. As an amateur, however, Wright had numerous commitments outside of those to the Tigers and consequently Neve was frequently called upon to stand in. Whenever he did so his performances were of a good standard; indeed some supporters preferred Neve to Wright; unfortunately for Neve, City's manager at the time, Ambrose Langley, did not share that opinion.

NEVINS, Thomas   (1907-1913)
Born: 1886, Washington (Co. Durham)
Died: 1950
Debut: 18.01.08 Burnley (a) 0-5
Appearances: LGE: 130 – 0; FAC: 10 – 0

Nevins was a defender in the classic mould of his era: stocky and strong, but perhaps just a tad short of pace. Capable of playing on either flank in the full-back spot, he gradually established himself in the right-back berth and had his best spell in the 1912/13 season missing only five games. His lack of pace found him out occasionally but it wasn't every week he came up against a flier and more often than not he had enough talent to keep his opposing wingman quiet.

NISBET, Gordon James Mackay   (1976-1980)
Born: 18.09.1951, Wallsend-on-Tyne
Debut: 11.09.76 Bolton Wanderers (a) 1-5
Appearances: LGE: 190 (3) – 1; FAC: 10 – 1; FLC: 11 – 0; OC: 6 – 0

Nisbet's started his football life as a goalkeeper, but he was eventually converted to full-back with some success, gaining international recognition, at Under-23 level, in this role. Moving to the Tigers in the early part of the 1976 season his early outings were in a more attacking role: operating on the right side of midfield or attack. When Peter Daniel was transferred to Wolves the Tigers had a natural replacement at right-back in Nisbet, and he immediately made that position his own, displaying assurance and aptitude in each performances. He was ever-present in the in the number two shirt for seasons 1978/79 and 1979/80 before being allowed to move on to Plymouth Argyle with whom he maintained the same high standards.

NORMAN, Anthony Joseph   (1979-1988)
Born: 24.02.1958, Mancot
Debut: 16.02.80 Millwall (h) 1-0
Appearances: LGE: 372 – 0; FAC: 26 – 0; FLC: 22 – 0; OC: 22 – 0

Of all the great goalkeepers the Tigers have been associated with throughout their existence, it could be argued that Tony Norman is the greatest. It is an opinion that can be substantiated with statistics. Ranked third in terms of goalkeeping appearances, his 'clean sheet' and goals conceded per game is bettered by no other Tiger custodian of similar longevity in the Tigers' colours. Signed from Burnley in the opening weeks of 1980, there was little to suggest that Norman would go on to achieve the legendary status he did whilst at Boothferry Park. However, the signs soon materialised that Norman would be something special. Quiet and unassuming in appearance he may have been, but put him between the Tigers' sticks and he became commanding and assured. He played a major part in City's two promotions during his residency and to say he made the goalkeeping shirt his own is an understatement given that between August 1983 and September 1988, he never missed a single League or Cup match. It set a new club record and it's unlikely to ever be bettered.

NORTON, David Wayne   (1990-1993)
Born: 03.03.1965, Cannock
Debut: 12.01.91 Sheffield Wednesday (h) 0-1
Appearances: LGE: 149 – 5; FAC: 7 – 1; FLC: 7 – 0; OC: 9 – 1
Debut: 12.01.91 Sheffield Wednesday (h) 0-1

From a medical viewpoint Norton's arrival at Boothferry Park, initially on loan and then permanently a few months later, should never have occurred. The physicians had discovered that Norton's pelvis was apparently crumbling and recommended that he retire. That he ignored that advice, went on to make well over a century of appearances for the Tigers and continued his career long after he'd departed Boothferry Park tells you much about the man. Stubborn? Perhaps. Determined and steel-willed? Definitely. Those latter qualities were what he brought to a Hull City team throughout his time with the Tigers. Not unsurprisingly he captained the team and led by example on many an occasion.

PAYTON, Andrew Paul   (1986-1991)
Born: 23.10.1967, Whalley
Debut: 04.04.87 Stoke City (a) 1-1
Appearances: LGE: 116 (27) – 55; FAC: 8 – 0; FLC: 9 (2) – 2; OC: 3 – 0

Payton's strike rate with the Tigers was admirable under any circumstances, but given that much of his Tiger time was spent in a side that struggled, his ability to conjure goals from mere scraps of chances speaks volumes for his ability. Possessing blistering pace undoubtedly helped him escape the clutches of cumbersome defenders, and with Peter Swan he formed a strike partnership that would have been better suited to a side regularly pressing for promotion rather than regular battles against relegation. Any striker with a proven track record of scoring goals will attract attention and Andy Payton was no different. In need of cash just as much as League points, the club did not stand in his way and his to move to Middlesbrough set a club transfer record.

PEACOCK, Richard John   (1993-1998)
Born: 29.10.1972, Sheffield
Debut: 16.10.93 Fulham (h) 1-1
Appearances: LGE: 144 (30) – 21; FAC: 7 (1) – 1; FLC: 12 (3) – 2; OC: 5 (1) – 0

A goal within minutes of coming on as a substitute in his League debut against Fulham did much to endear Richard Peacock to City fans. It looked as if Terry Dolan had unearthed another potential star from the non-League scene. Although somewhat slight in build, Peacock had skill and speed in abundance, and he was seen at his best when employed on the wing harnessing his speed with good close bal control. Occasionally, however, circumstances required him to take a more central forward role, but it was a position he never appeared fully comfortable in, and at times it seemed to affect his confidence.

PEARSON, James Stuart   (1969-1973)
Born: 21.06.1949, Hull
Debut: 15.05.70 Portsmouth (h) 3-3
Appearances: LGE: 126 (3) – 44; FAC: 7 – 0; FLC: 7 – 1; OC: 6 (1) – 0

Pearson's early days as a striker at Boothferry Park were spent in the shadows of Chris Chilton and Ken Wagstaff. He faced a daunting task, therefore, in trying to force his way into the first team. He managed the occasional outing whilst Chillo and Waggy were still around, but it was Chilton's departure to Coventry City that offered Pearson his best chance of making a name for himself. The chance did not go begging. Although smaller than Chillo, Pearson had similar ability and characteristics, he also started to score goals with almost the same regularity. Such performances earned him a dream move to Manchester United and the chance to test himself at the highest level. It was a test he passed with flying colours.

ROBERTS, Garreth William   (1978-1990)
Born: 15.11.1960, Hull
Debut: 10.03.79 Bury (h) 4-1
Appearances: LGE: 409 (5) – 47; FAC: 28 – 5; FLC: 24 – 2; OC: 19 (2) – 5

Garreth Roberts had over eleven years in the Tigers' first team. During that time he made over 400 League appearances, scored nearly 50 goals, captained the team to two promotions – the first player to do so in the club's history – and when he staged his testimonial game against

Tottenham Hotspur in May 1992, the attendance was more than double the season's average. Although he was one of the smallest players ever to have worn the Tigers' shirt, his contribution to the Tigers' cause was huge. It was a contribution built on commitment, determination and a never say die spirit that blended in well with his talent and versatility.

ROBERTS, James. Dale   (1979-1984)
Born: 08.10.1956, Newcastle
Died: 05.02.2003
Debut: 16.02.80 Millwall (h) 1-0
Appearances: LGE: 149 (4) – 6; FAC: 10 – 0; FLC: 8 – 1; OC: 11 – 0

Having failed to establish himself in the first team at Ipswich Town, Roberts tried his luck with Hull City. His luck changed as his pace, poise and positional play made an immediate impact and brought him a regular spot in the Tigers' defence. He made over 150 League appearances for the club in quick time, and that figure would have been greater but for injury misfortunes, one of which ended his playing career. After a short spell out of the game, Roberts returned to Boothferry Park to take up a youth coaching role and displayed an aptitude for that aspect of the game. He subsequently took up coaching posts with Ayr United and Ipswich Town, and it was whilst enjoying a successful spell at that latter club that his life was tragically cut short through cancer.

ROBINSON, William Samuel   (1905-1908)
Born: 01.01.1880, Prescot
Died: 1926
Debut: 02.09.05 Barnsley (h) 4-1
Appearances: LGE: 119 – 6; FAC: 12 – 1

A member of the Tigers' inaugural League team, Robinson's staple football diet before joining City had been in the reserves of Manchester City. With the Tigers, however, it was very rare for Robinson not to be sampling first team fare as he quickly developed into a commanding centre-half and was a dependable lynchpin in their defence, rarely missing a game and rarely letting a centre-forward get the better of him.

ROUGHLEY, Edward   (1906-1911)
Born: 1880, Prescot
Died: 1948
Debut: 01.04.07 Burslem Port Vale (h) 4-1
Appearances: LGE: 157 – 0; FAC: 9 – 0

Roughley spent a couple of seasons as goalkeeping understudy to the splendid Martin Spendiff. When he eventually claimed the goalkeeping spot as his own, however, it was soon apparent that Spendiff's standards would be maintained by Roughley. Safe in his handling and sound in his positioning, Roughley missed only five games in his four seasons as the Tigers recognised number one. Yet despite such consistency, he also holds the unenviable record of being the Tigers' custodian to have conceded most goals in a single League game – the 8-0 defeat against Wolves in November 1911. A perusal of the match reports of that game, however, suggest that the blame for the size of that defeat was not laid at the feet – or hands – of Roughley.

SAVILLE, Andrew Victor   (1983-1988 & 1998)
Born: 12.12.1964, Hull
Debut (1): 31.12.83 Port Vale (h) 1-0
Debut (2): 19.09.98 Halifax Town (h) 1-2
Appearances: LGE: 77 (27) – 18; FAC: 3 (2) – 1; FLC: 6 – 1; OC: 4 (2) – 0

Initially joining the Tigers on non-contract terms from local football, Saville turned professional within months. His debut followed on the last day of 1983, but it was some time before his next outing occurred and a couple of seasons before he made the first team on a regular basis. However, when he did finally establish himself his role was more in fashioning chances for others than finishing them himself. Allowed to leave, Saville fashioned a decent career for himself with a number of clubs higher placed than City, but his association with the Tigers was briefly rekindled when he spent a short period on loan during the 1998/99 campaign.

SIMPKIN, Christopher John   (1962-1971)
Born: 24.04.1944, Hull
Debut: 18.08.62 Bristol Rovers (h) 3-0
Appearances: LGE: 284 (1) – 19; FAC: 18 – 1; FLC: 9 – 1; OC: 2 – 0

A product of local football, Simpkin's early outings for the Tigers was as an inside-forward and they were not always successful outings – square pegs and rounds holes? Yet when Cliff Britton moved him into a midfield role the transformation was startling; it showed him at his best: utilising his ability to stop the opposition's attacks before they fully developed and also prompting his own forwards. With those attributes Simpkin's name was rarely missing from a Britton teamsheet, and whilst he might not have enjoyed the public eye that hovered more over the likes of

Houghton, Chilton, Butler and Wagstaff, those same players knew that their job was easier because Chris Simpkin was very effective at doing his job.

SKIPPER, Peter Dennis   (1978-1979 & 1982-1988)
Born: 11.04.1958, Hull
Debut (1): 02.03.79 Swansea City (a) 3-5
Debut (2): 28.08.82 Bristol City (a) 1-2
Appearances: LGE: 286 (2) – 19; FAC: 17 – 1; FLC: 16 – 1; OC: 16 (1) – 0

Cut Pete Skipper in half and you'll probably find the words "Hull City" running through his flesh and bones. In two spells he epitomised all that is good about local lads representing their hometown club. His first spell with the Tigers arose from sterling displays in the local leagues, but when allowed to leave after only making a handful of appearances it seemed that Skipper's association with City was ended. Wrong. His second spell coincided with one of the rare successful periods in the Tigers recent history, and that success was due in no small way to Skipper's talents as a fearsome central defender with a warrior-like approach to the game – the fact that he scored the Tigers' goal away to Walsall, that secured their promotion to Division Two in May 1985 is a more tangible record of his contribution to the Tigers' cause.

SMITH, John 'Jackie'   (1905-1910)
Born: 1886, Wardley
Died: Sept. 1916
Debut: 23.09.05 Leeds City (a) 1-3
Appearances: LGE: 156 – 98; FAC: 12 – 4

Every generation of City fans will have their own goal-scoring hero. That being the case, there is little doubt that the very first generation would nominate 'Jackie' Smith as their hero. Although somewhat small (5' 7") for a striker, Jackie did not let size prevent him from racking up a hugely impressive tally of goals during his time with City. Regularly topping City's goalscoring charts, Smith twice achieved the same feat for the entire Football League, with 31 and 32 goals in seasons 1907/08 and 1909/10 respectively. That the latter of those achievements was not rewarded with promotion for the Tigers was a tragedy, as was his death, in 1916, during World War One.

SMITH, Joseph E. 'Stanley'   (1905-1911)
Born: 1886, Stanley
Debut: 30.09.05 Burton Utd (h) 1-1
Appearances: LGE: 213 – 46; FAC: 18 – 6: OC: 34 - 4

They were the same height and shared the same initials. They even shared the same surname and their time with the Tigers coincided. Two things, however, separated 'Jackie' Smith from Joseph Smith. One was the quantity of goals they each scored for City, and the other is that Joe was given the differentiating nom de plume of 'Stanley'. Whilst Stanley's goal count falls well short of Jackie's, he more than makes up for it in the number of appearances he accrued in City's colours. And that shortfall in goals by comparison, takes nothing away from Stanley's efforts because many of Jackie Smiths goals were forged from the efforts of 'Stanley' Smith. Capable of playing anywhere in the forward line, Stanley was a useful player to have and when paired with Jackie they made many an opposing defence look utterly foolish.

SPENDIFF, Martin Nelson   (1905-1907)
Born: 24.06.1880, North Shields.
Died: 18.10.1943
Debut: 02.09.05 Barnsley (h) 4-1
Appearances: LGE: 104 – 0; FAC: 11 – 0

The first of over a century of players to have kept goal for the Tigers throughout their history, and Spendiff set a high standard for his successors to match. Already vastly experienced – he'd played over 100 games for Grimsby Town – when he joined the Tigers, he put that experience to good use in a fledgling Tiger outfit when they embarked on their first season of League football. Ever-present in that first season, his tidy handling and accurate distribution offered his colleagues assurance in defence and the advantage when initiating a counter attack.

STEVENS, Samuel   (1911-1919)
Born: 18.11.1890, Netherton
Died: 1948
Debut: 10.02.12 Fulham (h) 2-3

Appearances: LGE: 150 – 84; FAC: 11 – 9; OC: 30 - 23
The successor to the goalscoring feats of 'Jackie' Smith, Stevens accepted the responsibility with no qualms and produced a highly satisfactory ratio of goals to games. Acquiring those goals took skill, determination and courage. Often targeted by opposition defenders, his stocky physique meant he was difficult to knock off the ball and any confrontation between him and his marker often went in favour of Stevens. Scoring in seven consecutive games during the 1913/14 season, he set a club record that lasted for over half a century and during the same season managed to score 17 goals in 17 games, an achievement unmatched in Tiger history for more than 90 years.

SWAN, Maurice Michael George   (1963-1967)
Born: 27.09.1938, Drumcondra
Debut: 16.09.63 Southend (a) 1-1
Appearances: LGE: 103 – 0; FAC: 14 – 0; FLC: 5 – 0

Despite his slight build, Swan was capable of looking after himself in the rough and tumble of the penalty area, and his handling both in the air and on the ground marked him out as a competent goalkeeper. Signed from Cardiff City for the start of the 1963/64 season, Swan faced early competition from Mike Williams for the Tigers' 'green jersey' but eventually established himself such that he made the majority of appearances as City's keeper during his time at the club and was first choice during their championship-winning season of 1965/66.

SWANN, Gary   (1980-1986)
Born: 11.04.1962, York
Debut: 23.08.80 Exeter City (h) 3-3
Appearances: LGE: 176 (10) – 9; FAC: 11 – 1; FLC: 9 (1) – 0; OC: 11 (2) - 0

In his early days in the first team, it was Swann's versatility and industry that maintained his place in the side, and his career in the Tigers' colours is probably measured more in terms of grit than glamour. Eventually settling in at left-back, Swann was sufficiently competent to rack up a decent tally of outings without ever catching the eye from the terraces; although the fact that he had a decent career with each of his subsequent League clubs suggested that his talents were more appreciated by those within the game, rather than those who just watch it.

TABRAM, William David   (1934-1936)
Born: 19.01.1909, Swansea
Died: 15.04.1992
Debut: 29.08.34 Plymouth Argyle (a) 4-6
Appearances: LGE: 106 – 5; FAC: 3 – 0; OC: 1 - 0

Tabram was a colossus of a centre-half during his time with City, if not in physique then certainly in performance and the consistently high standard thereof. In joining the Tigers at the start of the 1934/35 season, Tabram became the second costliest signing at that point in their history. Once he had adjusted to life in the East Riding and familiarised himself with his new colleagues there was little doubt that the money had been well spent. As the lynchpin in the Tigers' back line, he orchestrated City's defensive tactics comfortably and frequently made himself a nuisance in the opposition's penalty at corners and set pieces.

TAYLOR, William   (1926-1930)
Born: 05.06.1898, Langley Green
Debut: 28.08.26 Wolverhampton W (h) 1-0
Appearances: LGE: 152 – 17; FAC: 13 – 1

Prior to joining the Tigers, Taylor's career had been relatively quiet and conducted mainly in the non-League game. With City, however, that career was revitalised. Ever present on the left-wing in his first full season, he provided useful service to his forward colleagues. Having demonstrated his talents on the left, he demonstrated his versatility by reproducing those same talents on the right flank. Instrumental in the Tigers progress to the only FA Cup semi-final appearance in their history, injury robbed him from making the big game, and said injury was also instrumental in his eventual departure.

TEMPLE, George Arthur   **(1907-1913)**
Born: 1887, Newcastle
Died: 1959
Debut: 02.09.07 Clapton Orient (a) 0-1
Appearances: LGE: 173 – 77; FAC: 11 – 4

Although Temple's time was early in the Tigers' history, his output was still sufficient to place him in the 'Top 10' of City's all-time scoring greats. At a time when City had an apparent abundance of free-scoring forwards, Temple regularly kept his place on merit. His speed and ability to score from even the tightest of angles made him a handful for defenders to deal with. Their job was no easier when they tried to contain him in the air and his tally of goals was distributed pretty evenly between head and feet.

THOM, Alexander   **(1922-1925)**
Born: 11.10.1890, Ardrossan
Died: 01.10.1973
Debut: 23.09.22 Fulham (h) 1-0
Appearances: LGE: 131 – 18; FAC: 9 – 0

Signed from Scottish football, Thom's speed and close ball control on the wing quickly made him a favourite on the Anlaby Road terraces. The occasional goal in his own name only added to his reputation as a skilful provider of goalscoring opportunities for others. Each of his four seasons with the Tigers produced appearance totals in excess of thirty and given that he was well into his thirties when he joined, it emphasised his fitness and conditioning just as much as his flair and consistency.

WAGSTAFF, Kenneth   **(1964-1975)**
Born: 24.11.1942, Langworth
Debut: 21.11.64 Exeter City (h) 3-1
Appearances: LGE: 374 (4) – 173; FAC: 29 – 14; FLC: 19 – 6; OC: 7(1) – 4

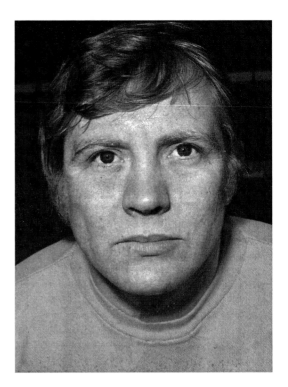

In recent years there have been a number of polls to identify the Tigers' greatest ever player. Ken Wagstaff has topped every one; and for good measure he's topped similar polls at his former club, Mansfield Town. He was that sort of player. Just under 200 goals from just over 400 appearances is a terrific return from over a decade of service in the Tigers' cause. It suggests a player of stamina, a player of skill and a player with a predator's instinct for goal. That was Waggy. A goal on his debut set the scene for Waggy's stay at Boothferry Park and a goal just about every other game over the next eleven seasons is a statistic that sets him apart from many others who have dared to call themselves Tiger strikers; with one exception; and that one exception was his strike-partner for much of his time at City: Chris Chilton. Together they terrorised defences and when you total the number of games they played together, you'll find their goal count from those games is greater. That neither played for their country was a travesty. That both played for Hull City was thrilling.

WARREN, Lee   **(1988-1993)**
Born: 28.02.1969, Manchester
Debut: 27.08.88 Manchester City (h) 1-0
Appearances: LGE: 141 (12) – 1; FAC: 5 (1) – 0; FLC: 8 – 0; OC: 4 (1) – 1

Warren Lee was Eddie Gray's first signing when Gray took over as City's manager in the late 1980s. Described as promising young midfield player, Lee built up over a century of Tiger outings not just from midfield but from all over the pitch.

Versatile in the extreme, Warren turned out in attack, midfield and defence – and just for good measure he made more than the occasional appearance as an emergency goalkeeper during a game. Whether such versatility helped or harmed his development is open to debate, but whilst mangers came and went during Lee's stay at Boothferry Park, all were willing to utilise his talents.

WEALANDS, Jeffrey Andrew   **(1971-1978)**
Born: 26.08.1951, Darlington
Debut: 11.03.72 Fulham (h) 4-0
Appearances: LGE: 240 – 0; FAC: 11 – 0; FLC: 19 – 0; OC: 12 – 0

Initially signed to understudy and provide competition for City's established goalkeeper at the time, Ian McKechnie, it wasn't long before Wealands had taken over the number one position and went on to make it his own for the bulk of the 1970s. His height enabled him to deal comfortably with crosses and he was rarely found wanting on ground shots: his tremendous reflexes being a feature of his ground play. Talented enough to play at a higher level, he did so with both Birmingham City and Manchester United before a back injury threatened to end his career. Fortunately, dropping down into the non-League scene prolonged it sufficiently for him to earn Cup honours with Altrincham and maintain his reputation.

WHITTLE, Justin Phillip   **(1998-2003)**
Born: 18.03.1971, Derby
Debut: 28.11.98 Carlisle Utd (h) 1-0
Appearances: LGE: 184 (9) – 2; FAC: 8 (2) – 0; FLC: 9 – 0; OC: 7 – 1

WHITEHURST, William   **(1980-1985 & 1988-1989)**
Born: 10.06.1959, Thurnscoe
Debut (1): 25.10.80 Gillingham (a) 0-2
Debut (2): 31.12.88 Ipswich Town (h) 1-1
Appearances: LGE: 212 (17) – 52; FAC: 13 (1) – 5; FLC: 11(1) – 6; OC: 16 – 6

One of the undoubted cult heroes of the latter part of the Tiger century, Whitehurst was a raw talent when he first arrived at Boothferry Park. So raw in fact, that many on the terraces doubted whether he possessed any. Yet those earning a living from the game saw the potential and under the tutelage of Chris Chilton, Whitehurst finally blossomed into a bustling centre-forward in the classic mould, packing pace, power and the ability to pummel defences into his big frame – he also won over his terrace critics completely. Numerous enquiries were made for his services and it was Newcastle who eventually acquired them, but repeating his Tiger successes at a higher level proved difficult. After spells with numerous clubs, Whitehurst returned for a second spell with City and forged a useful scoring partnership with Keith Edwards before both moved on to different clubs.

Mr Dependable or, given his military background, Sergeant Steadfast. Either description would adequately summarize Whittle's wholehearted commitment and consistency during his spell with the Tigers following his transfer from Stoke City in November 1998. At a time when City were facing the prospect of being dumped out of the Football League, it was Whittle who tightened up City's rearguard and provided the backbone to their revival and avoidance of relegation. Winning the 'Player of the Year' award in his first season was a just and accurate reflection of his performances during that campaign. Consistency and commitment continued to hallmark his performances throughout his spell and he was undoubtedly the fans' favourite.

WILCOX, Russell   (1990-1992)
Born: 25.03.1964, Hemsworth
Debut: 08.09.90 Swindon Town (h) 1-1
Appearances: LGE: 92 (8) – 7; FAC: 5 – 1; FLC: 5 – 0; OC: 5 (1) – 0

After experiencing mixed fortunes with his previous clubs, Wilcox's transfer to the Tigers, for a fee in excess of £100,000 reflected the progress he had made during that time and the reputation he'd earned as a useful but uncompromising defender. Those qualities were quickly demonstrated in the Tigers' colours as he became a regular fixture, as well as captain, in City's team. Although his League outings just match the 'Tiger Centurion' criteria, there would have been many more outings but for injuries that produced more than his fair share of absences, each of which were felt.

WILKINSON, William 'Billy'   (1962-1972)
Born: 24.03.1943, Stockton-on-Tees
Died: July 1996
Debut: 12.04.63 Halifax Town (h) 2-0
Appearances: LGE: 208 (15) – 34; FAC: 16 (1) – 5; FLC: 10 – 2; OC: 2 – 0

Wherever Billy Wilkinson was asked to play in a Tigers' shirt, you could rest assured that nothing less than total commitment and endeavour would be produced. That he was asked to play in a variety of positions was testament to his undoubted ability and impressive versatility: at various times throughout his Tiger career he had regular spells in defence, midfield or attack.

During each of those periods his individual performance was rarely found wanting. When in the forward line he would score his share of goals; in midfield he provided opportunities for others to score and in defence his attitude was one of "they shall not pass." On leaving the Tigers Wilkinson continued his career on a global scale, eventually settling in Australia where his premature and poignant demise was brought about through a heart attack whilst out jogging.

WILSON, Stephen Lee   (1990-2000)
Born: 24.04.1974, Hull
Debut: 04.05.91 Plymouth Argyle (h) 2-0
Appearances: LGE: 180 (1) – 0; FAC: 13 – 0; FLC: 13 – 0; OC: 11 (1) – 0

Of all the locally born goalkeepers to have turned out for Hull City, Steve Wilson is probably the most successful, in terms of appearances at least, and certainly none have worked as hard to achieve that success. Making his debut at the start of the 1990s – one of the least successful decades in the Tigers' history – Wilson faced strong competition throughout his stay from other challengers intent on bedoming City's regular shot-stopper. Each time his determination not to be ousted won through and the gloves and jersey returned into his possession.

WINDASS, Dean   (1991-1995)
Born: 01.04.1969, Hull
Debut: 11.10.91 Swansea City (a) 0-0
Appearances: LGE: 173 (3) – 57; FAC: 6 – 0; FLC: 11 – 4; OC: 12 – 3

Although Windass had been on City's books as a YTS trainee, he was released and moved into the local soccer scene. There his performances were of such a standard that he was offered another chance with City, one that had a much happier outcome. Operating in either midfield or attack, Windass never held back in his displays, and City fans loved him for it. Grit and goals marked his second Tiger spell, and such characteristics were also marked on the cards of many a visiting scout drawn to watch this warrior like Tiger score goals and terrorise opponents. The need for cash meant the Tigers had to cash in on their one true asset and Windass moved onwards and upwards, although he never lost his love for the Tigers.

WOODHEAD, Clifford   **(1930-1938)**
Born: 17.08.1908, Darfield
Died: June 1985
Debut: 20.12.30 Southport (h) 5-1
Appearances: LGE: 305 – 0; FAC: 18 – 0; OC: 52 – 0

Following in the footsteps of legendary Tigers Matt Bell and Jock McQuillan, Cliff Woodhead maintained the high standards set by his aforementioned predecessors in the Tigers' number three shirt. Although making his debut on the opposite flank, it was at left-back that Woodhead's name appeared most often on a City teamsheet and the reason for such frequency was his consistent mastery of the art of full-back play. A key member of City's championship-winning team of 1932/33, Woodhead took the consequential divisional step up with no problems whatsoever. A player of his talent could operate at any level, and it was the Tigers' good fortune that Woodhead chose Hull City as the sole beneficiary of that talent during his professional League career.

WRIGHT, Edward Gordon Dundas   **(1905-1912)**
Born: 03.10.1884, Earlesfield Green
Died: 05.06.1947
Debut: 07.04.06 West Bromwich Albion (h) 4-0
Appearances: LGE: 152 – 14; FAC: 16 – 0

Wright had educational and sporting talent in equal quantity, and both were generous measures. Educated at Cambridge, he gained his football 'blue' there and if the record books are to be believed, his only full international cap as well – although the Football League's registration book for 1905 provides a similarly convincing case for the Tigers. Family ties with the East Riding brought him into contact with Hull City and whilst he remained an amateur throughout the length of his playing career, his appearances on the Tigers' left-flank, as well as England's, never fell short of thoroughly professional. Combining his duties of teaching at Hymers College with captaining the Tigers, he juggled both occupations comfortably and proved to be an inspirational individual to both student and colleague.

WRIGHT, William J. 'Tim'   **(1908-1920)**
Born: 1891, Patrington
Died: 21.12.1951
Debut: 24.10.08 Chesterfield (a) 4-0
Appearances: LGE: 153 – 5; FAC: 13 – 0; OC: 78 - 15

Wright was on of the first 'local products' to be displayed in the early Tiger teams and his durability over imported talent can be demonstrated that his displays on the Tigers' behalf spilled over into three decades. Whilst some of his League career was lost to World War One, Wright still turned out for the club regularly in the replacement competition. A formidable performer, predominantly in the left-half berth, Wright possessed few of the tricks that his namesake on the left-wing was wont to display, but that wasn't Wright's game. His was tough-tackling, and good distribution – more often than not to Gordon Wright so that he could weave his magic. In League games his goals were rare, but during the wartime competition his versatility paid off on the goals front as he was frequently required to occupy a more forward berth and his strike rate during those times was much more impressive.

APPLETON, Colin (1982-1984 & 1989)

Although untried as a manager in League football, Colin Appleton had enjoyed success in the non-League game with Scarborough, and in his first spell at Boothferry Park he showed why he had enjoyed that success. With shrewd signings and an attention to detail over tactics and opponents, Appleton guided the Tigers to promotion in his first season (1982/83). He then followed that up with an agonisingly close effort in his second season – promotion being missed by just one goal. His second spell, at the start of the 1989/90 season, was in stark contrast: one win in 16 matches meant that when Richard Chetham took over as chairman, his first task was to sack Appleton.

Competition	Played	Won	Drawn	Lost	For	Agst
League	105	48	37	20	160	92
FA Cup	4	1	1	2	4	5
FL Cup	6	2	1	3	4	8
Other Comps	7	5	1	1	9	3
Total	122	56	40	26	177	108

BLACKBURN, Ernest (1936-1946)

Blackburn's spell as City's boss was bedevilled with financial troubles. Consequently his era is marked more by events off the field rather than on it, although in two seasons (1936/37 & 1937/38) he moved the Tigers within spitting distance of promotion. He was in charge of the club at the outbreak of World War Two, when the club was in serious danger of folding, but by the time the war had ended the club was in the hands of new owners and their plans did not include Ernie Blackburn as manager.

Competition	Played	Won	Drawn	Lost	For	Agst
League	106	44	29	33	199	164
FA Cup	6	3	1	2	13	8
Other Comps	91	30	10	51	145	242
Total	203	77	40	86	357	414

BRITTON, Clifford (1961-1970)

One of the all-time greats in the managerial annals of Hull City, Britton presided over a team and a stadium that was the envy of many. After a sluggish start, Britton's plans finally fell into place during the mid 60s and the Tigers roared to the Third Division championship and quarter finals of the FA Cup in the 1965/66 season.

With some strengthening in defence, the team would undoubtedly have had a better than evens chance of reaching the First division, but Britton's loyalty to his 'boys of 66' probably resulted in his eventual 'elevation' to general manager. One of the greats, but missed his chance to be the greatest.

Competition	Played	Won	Drawn	Lost	For	Agst
League	398	165	101	132	680	577
FA Cup	29	11	9	9	51	40
FL Cup	19	6	4	9	29	33
Total	446	182	114	150	760	650

BROCKLEBANK, Robert (1955-1961)

Relegation in his first season (1955/56) was not the best of starts to Brocklebank's Tiger career. He also struggled to establish his authority over the players in those early days but eventually he prevailed, and to his credit restored the Tigers to Division Two in 1958/59. A hesitancy in spending money to strengthen that promotion squad had immediate consequences as the Tigers went straight back to Division Three in the following season, and didn't look like retrieving the situation under Brocklebank's guidance; hence his dismissal at the end of the 1960/61 season.

Competition	Played	Won	Drawn	Lost	For	Agst
League	279	105	64	110	434	460
FA Cup	20	7	7	6	34	29
FL Cup	2	0	1	1	1	5
Total	301	112	72	117	469	494

BUCKLEY, Franklin C (1946-1948)

A distinguished career, both on the football field and on Flanders field was the precursor to Buckley's journey into management which reached similar heights, especially with Wolves. It made him a great name in the game and his arrival to lead the 'new' Hull City suggested great things. They never materialised. For one with such vast experience of the game, his tenure at Boothferry Park exhibited uncertainty: both in team selection and tactics. Those early seasons after the war were not the easiest, but given Buckley's background that is when you would have expected him to have been at his best: possessing the know-how to determine his tactics and team, and stick to them. He didn't, and his performance during his near two-year tenure tends to confirm that. The fact that the Directors brought in 'assistance' (Raich Carter) without apparently involving Buckley, suggests that they'd realised their mistake before Buckley realised his.

Competition	Played	Won	Drawn	Lost	For	Agst
League	80	31	19	30	100	95
FA Cup	9	4	3	2	14	14
Total	89	35	22	32	114	109

CARTER, Horatio S. (Raich) (1948-1951)

As a player Carter inspired both Sunderland and Derby County to League and Cup glory. As a player-manager with Hull City he displayed the same characteristics: leading the Tigers – in many a game by personal example – to the Third Division (North) championship in 1948/49, and breaking records along the way. Whilst Carter was on the field the Tigers were a difficult proposition for anyone – sometimes too difficult. When he moved to the dug-out side of the white line, the inspiration seemed somewhat diluted; his players seemed to lose direction, and the Tigers' march to the 'Promised Land' suffered the same fate. Yet when he left the club altogether, following a dispute with the club's Directors in September 1951, the full impact of Carter's influence became all too apparent. The team were completely lost, and his return – as a player only – was a major contributory factor to City avoiding the relegation that seemed almost certain. That Carter never took the Tigers to the top flight of English football detracts not one iota from his achievements whilst associated with Hull City: his record puts him on the front row in City's managerial pantheon. However, he was capable of taking a side to the top flight – he did it with Leeds United just two seasons after his departure from Hull City; but if he'd done it with the Tigers, giving him the keys to the city would not have been enough. They would have had to have given him the city.

Competition	Played	Won	Drawn	Lost	For	Agst
League	137	65	36	36	250	188
FA Cup	14	8	3	3	21	11
Total	151	73	39	39	271	199

CHAPMAN, Henry 'Harry' (1913-1914)

Chapman rose through the Tigers' ranks to assume the manager's job following the resignation of Ambrose Langley at the end of the 1912/13 season – it had been Langley who'd signed Chapman as a player some two years earlier. A more than competent forward, injury prematurely curtailed Chapman's playing career; but he remained with the Tigers, however, moving into an administration role at which he proved equally adept. With Langley's departure he seemed the obvious choice to step up and this he did, initially with some success.

Yet whilst injury had shortened his playing days, so illness dogged his managerial stint and after only a season in charge he was forced to resign on ill-health grounds; within two years of his resignation that illness claimed his life.

Competition	Played	Won	Drawn	Lost	For	Agst
League	38	16	9	13	53	37
FA Cup	2	0	1	1	1	2
Total	40	16	10	14	54	39

COLLINS, Robert Y. (1977-1978)

The reign of Bobby Collins as Hull City's manager holds the dubious distinction of being the briefest in the club's history, as well as being the 'meat' in the managerial sandwich that was the 1977/78 season. That particular campaign started with John Kaye in charge and ended with Ken Houghton in the hot seat as the Tigers slid through the relegation trapdoor into Division Three. Collins's contribution to that season lasted all of 22 games, and started off quite well with victory over Tottenham Hotspur, and a sequence of only one defeat in seven games. From that point on, however, it deteriorated rapidly and defeat away to Mansfield in February 1978 brought about his managerial exit; ironical really, as it was defeat at home to Mansfield in the same season that had brought about his managerial employment.

Competition	Played	Won	Drawn	Lost	For	Agst
League	19	4	7	8	19	22
FA Cup	1	0	0	1	0	1
FL Cup	2	1	0	1	3	5
Total	22	5	7	10	22	28

DOLAN, Terence. (1991-1997)

If ever there was a sweepstake held to determine Hull City's greatest manager and you drew the ticket with Terry Dolan's name on it, be advised to dispose of it there and then; you will not win. In the opinion of many City fans the Dolan years were dour, dull and disastrous: producing two relegations and little else. Yet there were times when Dolan's efforts were not totally derided, and the 'Manager of the Month' award for October 1994 suggested some ability. Admittedly, the financial constraints he was required to operate in were not conducive to good times, but there were a number of 'bargain basement' players he spotted and developed who went on to better things and brought in much needed revenue to the club. What the supporters wanted more than anything, however, was success. On that particular front, Dolan failed to deliver…and paid the price.

Competition	Played	Won	Drawn	Lost	For	Agst
League	295	91	89	115	328	379
FA Cup	13	5	2	6	15	16
FL Cup	16	4	3	9	19	30
Other Comps	16	6	2	8	15	21
Total	340	106	96	138	377	446

GRAY, Edwin 'Eddie' (1988-1989)

When appointed, just before the beginning of the 1988/89 season, Eddie Gray was lauded by City's chairman (Don Robinson) as the man for the job of getting the Tigers into English football's top flight. According to Robinson, Gray was a man he'd admired for a long time and who, if he'd been available at the time, would have been appointed some four years earlier in preference to Brian Horton. At the end of the 1988/89 season Don Robinson sacked Eddie Gray. Results at the start of the season, comings and goings throughout it and a near FA Cup shock against Liverpool suggested success. One victory in the last eighteen games of the season confirmed that suggestion was suspect, and also confirmed Gray's going.

Competition	Played	Won	Drawn	Lost	For	Agst
League	46	11	14	21	52	68
FA Cup	3	2	0	1	6	5
FL Cup	2	0	0	2	1	5
Other Comps	1	0	0	1	1	2
Total	52	13	14	25	60	80

GREEN, Haydn (1931-1934)

Haydn Green's place in Tiger history was guaranteed when he led the club to their first promotion and championship trophy, all in the same season (1932/33). Having built a team to get them that far, Green recognised that he would need to build another if they were to progress further. Such a task required patience and money; neither commodity was available in the quantity Green required. Thus he faced an unenviable undertaking that left him in the middle of a long running dispute between directors and supporters over the club's future direction and ambitions. Growing ever more frustrated by the impasse, Green resigned with the task incomplete – but not for the want of trying on his part.

Competition	Played	Won	Drawn	Lost	For	Agst
League	115	56	24	35	228	149
FA Cup	10	5	2	3	23	16
Total	125	61	26	38	251	165

HATELEY, Mark W. (1997-1998)

Produced as the 'Big Name' manager to match the big plans new owner David Lloyd and his associate Tim Wilby had for the Tigers, it soon became apparent to many on the Tigers' terraces that it was just a big mistake. Hateley's lack of managerial experience showed and the results his teams produced came nowhere near to matching the expectations that had been built up. Avoiding relegation in his first season, Hateley's second campaign saw the club heading in a similar direction after only a few games. When ownership of Hull City changed hands in the autumn of 1998, one of the first things the new owners did was to change managers.

Competition	Played	Won	Drawn	Lost	For	Agst
League	63	14	11	38	71	114
FA Cup	1	0	0	1	0	2
FL Cup	9	2	3	4	9	13
Other Comps	2	1	0	1	2	2
Total	75	17	14	44	82	131

HILL, John H. (1934-1936)

Signed by Haydn Green to help the Tigers gain promotion, Hill stepped up into the Tigers' managerial chair as Green's successor. Respected by all within the club, as well as those who supported it, Hill tried to continue the rebuilding process that Green had started. However, the problems that had frustrated Green remained to haunt Hill and whilst his first season was one of consolidation, his second (1935/36) was a constant battle against relegation. Spending much of the season rooted at the foot of Division Two, and leaking goals at an alarming rate, Hill's resignation before the season was complete came as no surprise; neither did the ensuing relegation.

Competition	Played	Won	Drawn	Lost	For	Agst
League	69	20	13	36	90	144
FA Cup	2	0	0	2	1	7
Total	71	20	13	38	91	151

HORTON, Brian (1984-1988)

Although a managerial virgin, Horton's appointment as player-manager saw him inherit a squad from Colin Appleton that had narrowly failed to gain back-to-back promotions. His managerial inexperience was more than counterbalanced by his tremendous leadership qualities and playing experience, qualities which saw him take the Tigers up into Division Two at his first attempt in the 1984/85 season.

That early success brought added pressure to continue the march upwards, and valiantly though he tried the journey time was taking much longer than the patience of both supporters and directors were willing to endure. Sacked more out of frustration than judgment after a 4-1 home defeat against Swindon Town in April 1988, Horton was offered his job back hours later, but refused.

Competition	Played	Won	Drawn	Lost	For	Agst
League	170	68	52	50	233	217
FA Cup	12	5	3	4	16	15
FL Cup	13	4	3	6	17	23
Other Comps	9	5	2	2	17	13
Total	204	82	60	62	283	268

HOUGHTON Kenneth (1978-1979)

Successful as the man in charge of City's juniors, it was Houghton the Directors turned to when the club were deep in relegation trouble during the 1977/78 season; he thus became the club's third manager during that sorry season. Relegation was inevitable and Houghton therefore concentrated on building a promotion side, bringing in a number of players – and breaking club transfer records in the process – to restore the Tigers' fortunes. The best of those was Keith Edwards, whose goals often hid deficiencies in other areas of the team's play. Defensive frailties and inconsistency eventually proved to be Houghton's downfall, culminating in a 7-2 defeat at Brentford in December 1979 that resulted in his dismissal.

Competition	Played	Won	Drawn	Lost	For	Agst
League	83	25	25	33	100	117
FA Cup	4	1	1	2	5	9
FL Cup	5	1	1	3	4	6
Total	92	27	27	38	109	132

JACKSON, J. Robert (1952-1955)

Having led Portsmouth to back-to-back League championships earlier in his managerial career, Jackson appeared to be a sound choice to replace Raich Carter as City's manager. Initially hampered by injuries to key players, Jackson's efforts produced little in the way of progress and merely served to sour relations between him and the Directors. After just over two seasons in charge, and with the club spending too much time at the wrong end of the table for the directors and supporters liking, the directors' patience ran out and Jackson was given 'leave of absence' – a novel way of describing his dismissal.

Competition	Played	Won	Drawn	Lost	For	Agst
League	115	40	22	53	157	181
FA Cup	10	3	4	3	16	15
Total	125	43	26	56	173	196

JOYCE, Warren G. (1998-2000)

Having endured an uneasy relationship with Tigers' fans as a player, Joyce's selection as the man to rescue the Tigers from the rapidly increasing probability of relegation to the non-League game may have seemed somewhat strange – especially as Joyce had no experience of management. With clear daylight between the Tigers and League safety at the time of his appointment, Joyce had it all to do; but he did it. Bringing in experienced and seasoned professionals, Joyce built a team that battled its way up the table to avoid the relegation spot with room and time to spare. The season (1998/99) became known as the 'Great Escape'. Having achieved so much in such a short space of time, the pressure on Joyce to gain promotion mounted. With the resources available to him it proved too much and the cruelty of the beautiful game was blatantly exposed when within twelve months of saving the Tigers, he was sacked.

Competition	Played	Won	Drawn	Lost	For	Agst
League	71	25	22	24	70	67
FA Cup	8	4	2	2	14	14
FL Cup	4	2	0	2	6	9
Other Comps	5	3	1	1	5	2
Total	88	34	25	29	95	92

KAYE, John (1974-1977)

Appointed on the recommendation of outgoing manager, Terry Neill, the wisdom of that appointment was questioned when Kaye – who had ended his playing days at Boothferry Park – marked his managerial debut with a 4-0 defeat at Nottingham Forest – the worst debut by a Tigers' boss in the club's history. From that poor start, however, things picked up and within a couple of months of his appointment Kaye was being feted as the Manager of the Month for November 1974. Kaye's teams were forceful in defence but suffered from fragility in attack. It meant that the club hovered in mid-table for much of Kaye's time in charge. When the fragility up front worked its way towards the back Kaye's days were numbered, and a 2-0 home defeat to Mansfield in October 1977 made up the directors' minds to call time on John Kaye's spell in charge.

Competition	Played	Won	Drawn	Lost	For	Agst
League	128	40	41	47	130	150
FA Cup	8	1	4	3	10	11
FL Cup	6	3	1	2	10	7
Other Comps	9	1	3	5	5	11
Total	151	45	49	57	155	179

LANGLEY, Ambrose (1905-1913)

The Tigers' first manager and one who, in terms of margin, took the club closest to the top flight of English football; missing out by 0.29 of a goal at the end of the 1909/10 season. Astute in the transfer market, Langley brought many good players to Hull City at very little cost, but was unable to blend them together into a successful promotion-winning side. He resigned at the end of the 1912/13 season and returned to his former club, Sheffield Wednesday, to take up an administrative role.

Competition	Played	Won	Drawn	Lost	For	Agst
League	304	143	60	101	517	404
FA Cup	24	8	8	8	28	22
Total	328	151	68	109	545	426

LEWIS, Harold (1921-1923)

Taking over from David Menzies, Lewis had a rocky start to his spell in charge of the Tigers. Having overcome that handicap, however, a sustained run of form in his first season in charge saw City finish fifth in Division Two, with the basis of a good young side capable of doing better in the future. Unfortunately, financial pressures meant the future was marked more by selling than success. Whilst Lewis was forced to abide by the Directors' willingness to convert skill into cash, it was not a policy conducive to maintaining good relations between the two parties. His frustration eventually boiled over in January 1923 when he tendered his resignation.

Competition	Played	Won	Drawn	Lost	For	Agst
League	66	26	17	23	73	67
FA Cup	2	1	0	1	5	3
Total	68	27	17	24	78	70

LITTLE, Brian (2000-2002)

A talented manager, achieving success at a much higher level than the Tigers were languishing in at the time of his appointment, Little still had his work cut out to bring success to a club that was on the financial critical list.

Restricted in the transfer market and being locked out of the ground on more than one occasion characterised his early management days at Boothferry Park. Even the threat of bankruptcy and closure did not deflect him from his task and miraculously his first full season in charge (2000/01) ended with the Tigers making the play-offs. With a new owner and a much more settled financial state of affairs, Little set about building on the foundations he'd already laid. The good start was not maintained though, and he paid the ultimate price when relieved of his duties towards the end of what had turned into a frustrating season (2001/02).

Competition	Played	Won	Drawn	Lost	For	Agst
League	82	34	27	21	95	77
FA Cup	4	1	1	2	7	6
FL Cup	4	2	0	2	4	7
Other Comps	6	3	0	3	6	5
Total	96	40	28	28	112	95

McCRACKEN, William R. (1923-1931)

One of the longest serving members of the Tigers' managerial ranks, McCracken's spell in charge illustrated perfectly how outrageously fickle football fortune can be. Arriving on the back of a distinguished playing career, McCracken's early days in the hot seat matched those of his immediate predecessors: no money to spend and always facing the possibility of losing any developing talent should the right bid be made. That said, McCracken preserved and showed he was his own man. Gradually, under his guidance, the Tigers' fortunes on the field improved – even though their fortunes off it remained parlous. Astute at recognising and developing young talent, many a player started their career with Hull City as a result of McCracken's eye for talent, but usually that career ended elsewhere – and often at a higher level. The peak and trough of McCracken's Tiger spell collided in one season – 1929/30. A modestly developing season in the League was enlivened by a cracking FA Cup run that took the club to their first ever semi-final appearance, and just 15 minutes away from the final before Arsenal snatched an equaliser and took the replay honours. The disappointment of missing out on that glory was compounded by subsequent poor League form during the remainder of the season, which produced their first ever relegation. The effect on McCracken was one he never recovered from and just over a year later he had departed.

Competition	Played	Won	Drawn	Lost	For	Agst
League	348	125	95	128	487	476
FA Cup	24	8	8	8	33	39
Total	372	133	103	136	520	515

MENZIES, David L. (1916-1921 and 1936)

Menzies is one of only two managers to have had more than one spell in charge of Hull City. His first spell came in the midst of World War One, when League football was suspended and replaced by a wartime competition that offered only moderate success. When peacetime football resumed the Tigers ploughed a mid-table furrow for the remaining two seasons of Menzies stay – due in no small measure to the inconsistency of their performances from one week to the next. Perhaps it was frustration at such variance that Menzies did not hang about when the chance to manage Bradford City was offered to him; perhaps he thought it best to jump before he was pushed. Fifteen years later, and having built up a useful managerial reputation, Menzies returned to help the Tigers survive both on the field and off it. He joined too late to prevent the Tigers' relegation, but appeared to be tuning things around when he suffered a fatal heart attack in October 1936.

Competition	Played	Won	Drawn	Lost	For	Agst
League	103	33	34	36	144	155
FA Cup	6	3	1	2	10	7
Other Comps	107	46	22	39	189	180
Total	216	82	57	77	343	342

MOLBY, Jan (2002)

The arrival of Jan Molby as Brian Little's replacement was not the best kept of secrets, and his tenure at Boothferry Park was not the longest: having arrived in April 2002, by October of that year he had departed. Although adept in the transfer market – the Tigers undoubtedly benefited from some of the players he acquired – he appeared to display no such talent when it came to man-management, and there seemed little enthusiasm amongst the players whilst Molby was in charge. Perhaps that's why it took nearly six months for Molby to register his first League victory – from the ranks of previous Tiger bosses only Frank Buckley had waited longer. Five games after that debut victory and Molby was gone. Few tears were shed.

Competition	Played	Won	Drawn	Lost	For	Agst
League	16	2	8	6	18	25
FL Cup	1	0	0	1	2	4
Total	17	2	8	7	20	29

NEILL, W.J. Terence (1970-1974)

Aged 28 when appointed as the Tigers' player-manager in the summer of 1970, Neill was actually younger than some of his charges. None of his players, however, could match Neill's experience of international and top flight domestic football. He put that experience to good use in his first season in charge, which produced the Tigers' nearest finish to joining Division One for many a decade. It was achieved with an ageing team, however, and another crack was unlikely to be successful, and so it proved. Neill, therefore, had to start a rebuilding programme that would take time. Having to continue to wait for another crack at promotion tested the patience of all at Boothferry Park, but Neill's efforts obviously impressed someone, because before the task was anywhere near complete he was head-hunted by Tottenham Hotspur.

Competition	Played	Won	Drawn	Lost	For	Agst
League	174	61	55	58	218	212
FA Cup	13	7	2	4	18	13
FL Cup	10	3	2	5	14	17
Other Comps	9	5	2	2	13	6
Total	206	76	61	69	263	248

SMITH, Michael (1980-1982)

An impressive stint as manager of the national Welsh football team prompted City's directors to entice Mike Smith to taker over as City's manager following the dismissal of Ken Houghton in December 1979; the fact that Smith had no managerial experience at League club level seemed of little consequence. Time would tell. Whilst his initial efforts helped stave off the threat of relegation, it was only postponed as in the following season City were relegated to Division Four for the first time in their history. There is a huge gap between managing Wales vs. England and Torquay Utd vs. Hull City. It was a gap that Smith never successfully bridged, but that gap became immaterial because events off the field were gathering momentum and exploded during Smith's first season of sampling basement football. Financial hardship caused the Tigers to be placed into receivership and one of the cost cutting measures implemented by the Receiver was to relieve Mike Smith of his managerial duties.

Competition	Played	Won	Drawn	Lost	For	Agst
League	94	25	28	41	107	142
FA Cup	12	5	5	2	15	13
FL Cup	4	0	1	3	1	11
Other Comps	6	2	1	3	5	6
Total	116	32	35	49	128	172

STRINGER, Frederick G. (1914-1916)

When illness prevented Harry Chapman fulfilling his duties as City's manager, Fred Stringer was asked by his fellow directors to help out. The request was not made out of desperation, because Stringer was an experienced football administrator. When Chapman was forced to resign because of his illness, it was Stringer that stepped up to fill the breach. His first season in charge (1914/15) was a strange season as the country was at war, but despite his inexperience in certain areas Stringer still managed to guide the club to seventh place in Division Two. From then on Stringer's problems lay in putting out a team as the War took precedence and League football was replaced by a regionalised competition. He did not make too bad a job of it though, but the demands of his own business interests forced him to relinquish his position with City without a blemish on his reputation.

Competition	Played	Won	Drawn	Lost	For	Agst
League	31	15	5	11	55	46
FA Cup	5	3	1	1	11	7
Other Comps	36	15	3	18	60	85
Total	72	33	9	30	126	138

TAYLOR, Peter (2002-   )

Experienced at both club and international level, it was considered something of a coup to attract a manager of Taylor's calibre to manage a club in the Football League's basement division. And so it proved. Having acclimatised himself to the requirements for success at that level, Taylor set about the task of providing City's first promotion for nearly twenty years with determination. That determination paid dividends and with a game to spare season 2003/04 ended with the Tigers moving onwards and upwards. Reproducing that performance in the following season proved to be within his capabilities and the club celebrated their centenary season with another promotion – the first time in their history that back-to-back promotions had been achieved. In the process Taylor matched or bettered a number of other Tiger managerial records – and did so whilst also managing the England Under-21 side on a part-time basis. As the Tigers enter their second century of existence, the journey continues with Peter Taylor at the helm.

Competition	Played	Won	Drawn	Lost	For	Agst
League	125	62	32	31	203	134
FA Cup	5	2	0	3	8	10
FL Cup	2	0	1	1	2	4
Other Comps	4	1	1	2	8	10
Total	136	65	34	37	221	158

TERNENT, F. Stanley (1989-1991)

Inheriting a team part way through the 1989/90 season that had gone 16 League games without victory, Ternent had an immediate impact by gaining success at his first attempt. He followed that by steering the Tigers away from the relegation zone and ended the campaign in the safe harbour of mid-table. His strategy for success seemed centred around acquiring experienced players, who didn't always come cheap. It seemed to be paying dividends but for a club still plagued by money troubles, any acquisitions had to be balanced with disposals and some of those arrivals were nowhere near the quality of those who departed. As a consequence results suffered, and a run of heavy defeats in the opening months of the 1990/91 season turned up the pressure on Ternent as the patience of directors and supporters evaporated. When another big defeat was suffered on New Year's Day 1991, the Directors had little hesitation in putting an end to Ternent's tenure.

Competition	Played	Won	Drawn	Lost	For	Agst
League	55	19	13	23	84	106
FA Cup	1	0	0	1	0	1
FL Cup	3	0	2	1	1	4
Other Comps	2	0	0	2	2	5
Total	61	19	15	27	87	116

Caretaker Managers:

Competition	Played	Won	Drawn	Lost	For	Agst
League	115	41	23	51	145	167
FA Cup	7	1	1	5	12	22
FL Cup	0	0	0	0	0	0
Other Comps	2	1	0	1	5	3
Total	124	43	24	57	162	192

Players Who's Who (Key see sheet 11)

Name		D.O.B	Place of Birth	Died	First Season	Last Season	Previous Club	Next Club	Appearances					Goals			
									L.Full	L.Sub	FAC	FLC	Oth.	Lge	FAC	FLC	Oth.
Abbott GS	Greg	14/12/1963	Coventry		1992	1995	Guiseley	Guiseley	120	4	4	5	8	15	0	1	2
Ablett GI	Gary	19/11/1965	Liverpool		1986		Liverpool (loan)		5	0	0	0	0	0	0	0	0
Ackerman AAE	Alf	05/01/1929	Pretoria, S. Africa	1988	1950		Clyde	Norwich City	92	0	11	0	0	49	2	0	0
					1953	1954	Norwich City	Derby County									
Acquroff J	Jack	09/09/1911	Chelsea	1987	1934	1936	Folkestone	Bury	70	0	1	0	1	25	0	0	0
Adey TW	Thomas	22/02/1901	Hetton-le-Hole	1986	1923		Bedlington United	Swindon Town	16	0	0	0	0	0	0	0	0
Ainsworth EW	Edgar	1910	Hull	1952	1932		Juniors (Hull)	York City	2	0	0	0	0	0	0	0	0
					1935		York City	Released									
Alberry WE	Ted	21/07/1922	Doncaster	1978	1946		Leeds United	Gainsborough Trinity	1	0	0	0	0	0	0	0	0
Alcide CJ	Colin	14/04/1972	Huddersfield		1998		Lincoln City (loan)		27	2	2	3	0	4	0	2	0
					1998	1999	Lincoln City	York City									
Alexander GG	Gary	15/08/1979	Lambeth		2001	2002	Swindon Town	Leyton Orient	64	4	3	3	4	23	2	2	3
Alexander S	Stan	17/09/1905	Percy Main	1961	1926	1931	Percy Main Amateurs	Bradford City	98	0	10	0	0	41	5	0	0
Allen MJ	Mervyn	16/10/1909	Bargoed	1976	1931	1933	Gilfach FC (Glam)	Carlisle United	15	0	0	0	0	1	0	0	0
Allison NJ	Neil	20/10/1973	Hull		1990	1996	YTS	Swindon Town	95	11	3	8	7	3	0	1	0
Allsopp D	Danny	10/08/1978	Melbourne		2003	2004	Notts County	Melbourne Vistory (Aus)	45	19	2	1	0	22	0	0	0
Anderson J	John	02/10/1972	Greenock		2002	2003	Livingston	Bristol Rovers	42	1	1	1	0	1	0	0	0
Angus S	Stevland	16/09/1980	Westminster		2004		Cambridge United (loan)		1	1	1	0	0	0	0	0	0
Annables W	Wally	31/10/1911	Swinton	1979	1936	1938	Grimsby Town	Carlisle United	62	0	1	0	3	1	0	0	0
Appleby R	Richie	18/09/1975	Middlesbrough		2002	2003	Kidderminster Harriers	Released	6	0	0	1	0	0	0	0	0
Ashbee I	Ian	06/09/1976	Birmingham		2002		Cambridge United		110	0	4	3	1	4	0	1	0
Askew W	Billy	02/10/1959	Great Lumley		1982	1989	Gateshead	Newcastle United	247	6	19	14	14	19	0	0	1
Atkins M	Mark	14/09/1968	Doncaster		2000		Doncaster Rovers(loan)		8	0	0	0	2	0	0	0	0
Atkinson C	Charlie	17/12/1932	Hull		1953	1955	Juniors (Hull)	Bradford PA	37	0	2	0	0	2	1	0	0
Atkinson G	Graeme	11/11/1971	Hull		1989	1994	YTS	Preston NE	129	20	5	9	7	23	1	2	0
Atkinson GA	Arthur	30/09/1909	Goole	1983	1933		Lincoln City	Mansfield Town	5	0	0	0	0	0	0	0	0
Atkinson P	Peter	13/02/1924	Middlesbrough	1972	1946	1947	Billingham Synthonia	Released	6	0	0	0	0	0	0	0	0
Atkinson T	Trevor	19/11/1928	Barnsley		1946		Hull Amateurs	Barnsley	2	0	0	0	0	0	0	0	0
Baker M	Matthew	12/12/1979	Harrogate		1999		YTS	Hereford United	0	2	0	1	1	0	0	0	0
Baldry GW	George	26/05/1911	Cleethorpes	1987	1933		Grimsby Town	Scunthorpe Utd	5	0	0	0	0	2	0	0	0
Bamber JD	Dave	01/02/1959	St Helens		1989	1990	Stoke City	Blackpool	25	3	0	2	0	5	0	0	0
Banks FS	Frank	21/08/1945	Hull		1967	1975	Southend United	Southend United	284	4	22	14	10	6	0	1	0
Bannister BI	Bruce	14/04/1947	Bradford		1977	1979	Plymouth Argyle	Un.Sportive Dunkerque	79	6	4	9	3	20	0	4	0
Barker GA	Geoff	07/02/1949	Hull		1968	1970	Apprentice	Darlington	29	1	0	2	0	0	0	0	0
Barley HF	Harry	01/02/1905	Grimsby	1958	1931		Grimsby Town	New Brighton	13	0	0	0	0	2	0	0	0
Barmby NJ	Nicky	11/02/1974	Hull		2004		Leeds United		38	1	2	0	0	9	0	0	0
Barnes PS	Peter	10/06/1957	Manchester		1987		Manchester City	Sporting Farensa (Por)	11	0	0	0	0	0	0	0	0
Barraclough W	Billy	03/01/1909	Hull	1969	1927		Bridlington Town	Wolves	9	0	0	0	19	0	0	0	2
					1940		Doncaster Rovers(Guest)										
Baxter WA	Bill	23/04/1939	Edinburgh		1970	1971	Ipswich Town	Northampton Town	20	1	2	0	0	0	0	0	0
Beardsley DT	Don	23/10/1946	Alyth		1966	1972	Apprentice	Grimsby Town	128	2	6	3	5	0	0	0	0
Bell DK	Doug	05/09/1959	Paisley		1988		Shrewsbury T (loan)		4	0	0	0	0	0	0	0	0
Bell E	Ernie	22/07/1918	Hull	1968	1936	1937	Juniors (Hull)	Mansfield Town	27	0	0	0	27	5	0	0	4
					1946		Aldershot	Scarborough									
Bell M	Matt	08/07/1897	West Hartlepool	1962	1919	1930	West Hartlepool	Nottm. Forest	393	0	30	0	0	1	0	0	0
Bell WT	William	17/03/1905	North Seaton		1932		Grimsby Town	Released	4	0	0	0	0	0	0	0	0
Bennett RM	Reuben	21.12.1913	Aberdeen	1989	1935		Aberdeen East End	Queen of the South	3	0	0	0	0	0	0	0	0
Bennion JR	John	02/04/1934	Burnley		1957	1959	Burnley	Stockport Co.	35	0	1	0	0	1	0	0	0
Bennyworth IR	Ian	15/01/1962	Hull		1979		Apprentice	Gainsborough Trinity	1	0	0	0	2	0	0	0	0
Bentley KJ	Keith	27/07/1936	Hull		1957		Apprentice	Scarborough	4	0	2	0	0	0	0	0	0
Beresford D	David	11/11/1976	Middleton		2001		Huddersfield Town	Plymouth Argyle	33	8	1	2	3	1	0	0	0
Berry T	Tom	31/03/1922	Clayton-le-Moors	2003	1947	1957	Great Harwood	Buxton	275	0	20	0	0	1	0	0	0
Best C	Charles	1888	Boosbeck	1965	1911	1912	Eston United	Retired (Injury)	35	0	2	0	0	4	1	0	0
Best J	Jerry	23/01/1901	Mickley	1975	1936		Darlington	Retired	31	0	1	0	0	11	0	0	0
Betsy K	Kevin	20/03/1978	Seychelles		1999		Fulham (loan)		1	1	0	0	1	0	0	0	0
Bettney CJ	Chris	27/10/1977	Chesterfield		1997		Sheffield United (loan)		28	2	0	2	1	1	0	0	0
Betts AC	Charlie	02/01/1886	Scunthorpe	1967	1914	1919	Derby County	Scunthorpe Utd	51	0	6	0	107	0	0	0	0
Bew DC	Danny	1896	Sunderland	1951	1922		Sunderland	Swindon Town	11	0	1	0	0	0	0	0	0
Blackburn EH	Eddie	18/04/1957	Houghton-le-Spring		1974	1979	Apprentice	York City	68	0	5	2	1	0	0	0	0
Blampey SL	Stuart	13/06/1951	North Ferriby		1969	1974	Apprentice	Scarborough	61	11	1	4	1	1	0	0	0
Bleakley T	Tommy	16/05/1893	Little Hulton	1951	1919	1929	Armed Services	Goole United	368	0	21	0	13	5	2	0	0
Blenkinsop E	Ernie	20/04/1902	Cudworth	1969	1921	1922	Cudworth United	Sheffield Wed.	11	0	0	0	0	0	0	0	0
Bloomer J	Jimmy	10/04/1926	Rutherglen		1947		Strathclyde	Grimsby Town	4	0	0	0	0	2	0	0	0
Bloomer MB	Matthew	03/11/1978	Grimsby		2001	2002	Grimsby Town	Lincoln City	0	3	0	1	0	0	0	0	0
Bloxham JA	Alec	02/07/1923	New Houghton	1982	1947	1949	Ollerton Colliery	Boston Utd	33	0	5	0	0	2	0	0	0
Bly W	Billy	15/05/1920	Newcastle	1982	1938	1959	Walker Celtic	Weymouth	403	0	35	0	18	0	0	0	0
Blyth JB	Jim	09/08/1911	Edinburgh	1979	1937	1938	Tottenham H	Heart of Midlothian	72	0	6	0	2	0	0	0	0
Bolder A	Adam	25/10/1980	Hull		1998	1999	YTS	Derby County	18	2	0	0	3	0	0	0	0
Bonner M	Mark	07/06/1974	Ormskirk		1998		Cardiff City (loan)		1	0	0	0	0	1	0	0	0
Booth D	Dennis	09/04/1949	Stenley Common		1980	1984	Watford	Retired	121	2	12	7	9	2	0	0	0
Bound MT	Matthew	09/11/1972	Bradforn-on-Avon		1993		Southampton (loan)		7	0	0	0	0	0	0	0	0
Bowering M	Mike	15/11/1936	Hull		1958	1959	Juniors (Hull)	Chesterfield	45	0	1	0	0	7	0	0	0
Bowler GC	Gerry	08/06/1919	Londonderry		1949		Portsmouth	Millwall	38	0	4	0	0	0	0	0	0
Bown HA	Herbert	03/05/1893	East Ham	1959	1924		Halifax Town	Retired	4	0	1	0	0	0	0	0	0
Boyack S	Steven	04/09/1976	Edinburgh		1997		Glasgow Rgrs (loan)		12	0	0	0	0	3	0	0	0
Boyton J	John	1891	Glasgow		1912	1913	Kilsyth Emmett Rov.	Linfield	13	0	1	0	0	1	0	0	0
Brabin G	Gary	09/12/1970	Liverpool		1998	1999	Blackpool	Boston Utd	89	6	5	6	3	9	0	0	0
Bracey L	Lee	11/09/1968	Ipswich		1999	2000	Ipswich Town	Ossett Town	19	1	3	6	1	0	0	0	0
Bradbury W	Bill	03/04/1933	Matlock	1999	1955	1959	Birmingham City	Bury	178	0	12	0	0	82	7	0	0
Bradford B	Bernard	13/02/1906	Walker	1975	1929		Walker Park	Walsall	1	0	0	0	0	0	0	0	0
Bradshaw G	Gary	30/12/1982	Hull		1999	2003	YTS	Hall Road Rangers	10	12	1	0	1	1	0	0	0
Branch M	Michael	18/10/1978	Liverpool		2002		Wolverhampton Wanderers (loan)		6	1	0	0	0	3	0	0	0
Brandon WT	Tom	28/05/1893	Blackburn	1956	1920	1921	West Ham United	Bradford	56	0	5	0	0	3	2	0	0
Brayson JH	Joe	12/12/1902	Newcastle	1970	1926		Juniors (N. East)	Released	3	0	0	0	0	0	0	0	0

Name		D.O.B	Place of Birth	Died	First Season	Last Season	Previous Club	Next Club	Appearances					Goals			
									L.Full	L.Sub	FAC	FLC	Oth.	Lge	FAC	FLC	Oth.
Bremner WJ	Billy	09/12/1942	Stirling	1997	1976	1977	Leeds United	Doncaster Rovers	61	0	3	4	0	6	0	1	0
Brentano SR	Stephen	09/11/1961	Hull		1984	1986	North Ferriby United	Bridlington Town	11	1	2	0	3	0	0	0	0
Bridges B	Ben	03/02/1937	Hull		1957		Apprentice	Scarborough	1	0	0	0	0	0	0	0	0
Brien AJ	Tony	10/02/1969	Dublin		1996	1997	West Bromwich Albion	Stalybridge Celtic	43	4	3	7	2	1	0	0	0
Briggs AL	Arthur	27/05/1900	Newcastle		1922	1923	Walker Celtic	Manchester City	5	0	0	0	0	0	0	0	0
Briggs J	James	1893	West Moor, Newcastle		1912		Craghead United	Released	2	0	0	0	0	0	0	0	0
Brightwell D	David	07/01/1971	Lutterworth		2000		Carlisle United	Darlington	24	3	2	2	1	2	0	0	0
Browell A	Andy	17/09/1888	Walbottle	1964	1908	1911	Newburn Juniors	Everton	101	0	8	0	0	5	0	0	0
Browell G	George	1884	Walbottle	1951	1905	1910	West Stanley	Grimsby Town	194	0	14	0	0	3	0	0	0
Browell T	Tommy	19/10/1892	Walbottle	1955	1910	1911	Newburn Grange	Everton	48	0	4	0	0	32	0	0	0
Brown AS	Andrew	11/10/1976	Edinburgh		1996	1997	Leeds United	Clydebank	7	22	2	2	0	0	0	0	0
Brown DA	David	02/10/1978	Bolton		1997	2000	Machester United	Torquay United	108	23	10	10	6	23	3	5	0
Brown HS	Henry	23/05/1918	Workington	1963	1946		Wolves	Retired	22	0	5	0	0	0	0	0	0
Brown LJ	Linton	12/04/1968	Driffield		1992	1995	Halifax Town	Swansea City	111	10	5	6	4	24	1	0	0
Brown MJ	Mick	11/07/1939	Walsall		1959	1965	Gloucester Schools	Lincoln City	8	0	1	0	0	0	0	0	0
Brown NL	Nicky	16/10/1966	Hull		1985	1991	YTS	Released	80	6	6	4	2	3	1	0	0
Brown R	Ron	20/03/1923	Ballymoney		1946		Plymouth Argyle	Linfield	7	0	0	0	0	3	0	0	0
Brownsword NJ	Jack	15/05/1923	Campsall		1946		Frickley Colliery	Scunthorpe Utd	10	0	1	0	0	0	0	0	0
Brumwell P	Phil	08/08/1975	Darlington		2000		Darlington	Darlington	1	3	0	2	0	0	0	0	0
Buchan WRM	Willie	17/10/1914	Grangemouth		1947	1948	Blackpool	Gateshead	40	0	6	0	0	12	1	0	0
Buckley NA	Neil	25/09/1968	Hull		1986	1991	YTS	Guiseley	55	5	5	3	1	3	1	0	0
Bulless B	Brian	04/09/1933	Hull		1952	1963	Hull Schools	Retired	326	0	24	7	0	30	5	0	0
Bullock A	Arthur	1909	Hull		1932	1934	Hull Schools	York City	18	0	0	0	0	3	0	0	0
Bunn FS	Frank	06/11/1962	Birmingham		1985	1987	Luton Town	Oldham Athletic	89	6	5	6	6	23	1	2	4
Burbanks WE	Eddie	01/04/1913	Bentley	1983	1948	1952	Sunderland	Leeds United	143	0	10	0	0	21	1	0	0
Burdett T	Thomas	07/07/1912	Hetton-le-Hole	1984	1933		Wheatley Hill	Fulham	3	0	0	0	7	0	0	0	5
					1940		Bury (Guest)										
Burgess B	Ben	09/11/1981	Buxton		2002		Stockport County		51	2	1	1	0	22	0	0	0
Burnett DH	Dennis	27/09/1944	Bermondsey		1973	1974	Millwall	Brighton & HA	46	0	5	1	0	2	0	0	0
Bursell JC	Cliff	16/01/1935	Hull	1973	1952		Juniors (Hull)	Goole Town	2	0	0	0	0	2	0	0	0
Burton S	Steve	10/10/1982	Hull		2002	2003	YTS	Kidderminster Harriers	2	9	1	0	2	0	0	0	0
Butler DM	Dennis	07/03/1943	Fulham		1963	1969	Chelsea	Reading	215	2	20	9	0	0	0	0	0
Butler I	Ian	01/02/1944	Darton		1964	1972	Rotherham United	York City	300	5	22	9	3	66	4	0	0
Butler LS	Lee	30/05/1966	Sheffield		1990		Aston Villa (loan)		4	0	0	0	0	0	0	0	0
Byrne A	Andrew		Dublin		1913		Shelbourne	(Ireland)	3	0	0	0	0	0	0	0	0
Bywater S	Steven	07/06/1981	Manchester		1999		West Ham (loan)		4	0	0	0	0	0	0	0	0
Caceres AA	Adrian	10/01/1982	Buenos Aries (Arg)		2001		Southampton	Perth Glory	1	3	0	0	0	0	0	0	0
Calvert M	Mark	11/09/1970	Newcastle-upon-Tyne		1988	1992	YTS	Scarborough	24	6	0	2	3	1	0	0	0
Cameron K	Ken	01/01/1905	Hamilton		1935		Bolton Wanderers	QPR	30	0	0	0	0	12	0	0	0
Cameron WS	William'Kilt	1884	Mossend	1958	1913	1914	Bury	Bury	47	0	5	0	1	10	2	0	0
Campbell AF	Austen	05/05/1901	Hamsterley	1981	1935		Huddersfield T	Retired	11	0	0	0	0	0	0	0	0
Campbell J	Joe	31/10/1903	Walker	1981	1925	1926	Walker Park	Bradford City	11	0	0	0	0	0	0	0	0
Capewell R	Ron	26/07/1929	Sheffield		1954		Sheffield Wed.	King's Lynn	1	0	0	0	0	0	0	0	0
Carroll RE	Roy	30/09/1977	Enniskillen		1995	1996	YTS	Wigan Ath.	46	0	1	2	1	0	0	0	0
Carruthers MG	Martin	07/08/1972	Nottingham		1992		Aston Villa (loan)		13	0	0	0	3	6	0	0	0
Carter HS	Raich	21/12/1913	Sunderland	1994	1947	1951	Derby County	Retired	136	0	14	0	0	57	5	0	0
Carter J	Joe	23/04/1920	Bingley	1978	1946		Notts County	Bournemouth	5	0	1	0	0	0	0	0	0
Cartwright HP	Phil	08/02/1908	Scarborough	1974	1929		Bradford PA	Lincoln City	20	0	1	0	0	0	0	0	0
Cassidy J	Joe		Glasgow		1935	1936	Glasgow Ashfield	Released	8	0	0	0	0	1	0	0	0
Chadwick C	Cliff	26/01/1914	Bolton		1946		Middlesborough	Darlington	23	0	4	0	0	7	1	0	0
Chapman H	Henry	1879	Kiveton Park	1916	1910	1911	Sheffield Wed.	Retired	32	0	2	0	0	7	0	0	0
Charlesworth AL	Arthur	1898	Hull	1966	1919	1920	Juniors (Hull)	Worksop Town	15	0	0	0	1	7	0	0	0
Charlton W	Bill	04/06/1912	South Stoneham		1934		Southampton	Wimbledon	3	0	1	0	0	1	1	0	0
Cheetham S	Samuel	03/12/1896	St Helens	1967	1920	1921	Matt's Heath FC	Bradford City	28	0	5	0	0	1	0	0	0
Childs JA	Arthur	25/04/1899	Acomb	1964	1928	1930	Darlington	Exeter City	74	0	10	0	0	8	0	0	0
Chilton CR	Chris	25/06/1943	Hull		1960	1971	Juniors (Hull)	Coventry City	415	0	39	21	2	193	16	10	3
Clark W	William				1919		Juniors (Tyneside)		1	0	0	0	0	0	0	0	0
Clarke D	Doug	19/01/1934	Bolton		1955	1964	Bury	Torquay United	368	0	31	12	0	79	6	2	0
Cleland JH	James				1914		(Southern League)	Released	1	0	0	0	7	0	0	0	1
Coates DP	David	11/04/1935	Newcastle		1956	1959	Shiny Row FC	Mansfield Town	62	0	1	0	0	13	0	0	0
Collier JC	Jock	01/02/1897	Dysart	1940	1920	1925	Inverkeithing United	QPR	168	0	14	0	0	0	0	0	0
Collinson L	Les	02/12/1935	Hull		1956	1966	Juniors (Hull)	York City	296	1	26	9	0	14	0	2	0
Conway A	Andy	17/02/1923	South Shields	1996	1947	1948	North Shields	Dartford	6	0	0	0	0	5	0	0	0
Cook PH	Peter	01/02/1927	Hull	1960	1946	1947	Juniors (Hull)	Scarborough	5	0	2	0	0	0	1	0	0
Cooke A	Albert	11/04/1908	Royston, Yorkshire	1988	1930	1931	Scunthorpe United	Halifax Town	35	0	0	0	0	0	0	0	0
Corbett AM	Alex	20/04/1921	Saltcoats		1947		New Brighton	Dartford	8	0	0	0	0	0	0	0	0
Corkain S	Steve	25/02/1967	Stockton		1986		Juniors (Hull)	Billingham Synthonia	5	0	0	0	1	1	0	0	0
Corner JN	Norman	16/02/1943	Horden		1963	1966	Horden Colliery Wel.	Lincoln City	5	0	1	2	0	4	0	0	0
Cort LTA	Leon	11/09/1979	Bermondsey		2004		Southend United		43	1	3	1	0	6	0	0	0
Coverdale WR	Robert	16/01/1892	West Hartlepool	1959	1915		Sunderland (Guest)		63	0	3	0	5	5	2	0	0
					1921	1923	Sunderland	Grimsby Town									
Cowan W	William	28/11/1900	Gateshead	1979	1925	1926	High Fell FC	Blackpool	11	0	1	0	0	8	1	0	0
Cox PR	Paul	06/01/1972	Nottingham		1994		Notts County (loan)		5	0	0	0	0	1	0	0	0
Crawford JF	Jackie	26/09/1896	Jarrow	1975	1919	1922	Jarrow Town	Chelsea	126	0	8	0	0	9	4	0	0
Crawshaw CB	Cyril	02/03/1916	Barton-on-Irwell		1946		Stockport County	Retired	2	0	0	0	0	2	0	0	0
Crickmore CA	Charlie	11/02/1942	Hull		1959	1961	Juniors (Hull)	Bournemouth	53	0	2	3	0	13	0	1	0
Cripsey B	Brian	26/06/1931	Hull		1952	1958	Juniors (Hull)	Wrexham	145	0	14	0	0	19	1	0	0
Croft SD	Stuart	12/04/1954	Ashington		1972	1980	Apprentice	Portsmouth	187	3	12	9	4	4	2	0	0
Crosbie RC	Bob	02/09/1925	Glasgow	1994	1953	1954	Bradford	Grimsby Town	61	0	7	0	0	22	4	0	0
Crozier JPL	James	29/10/1906	Miton		1927		Glasgow Ashfield	Glasgow Celtic	3	0	0	0	0	0	0	0	0
Cubie NG	Neil	03/11/1932	South Africa		1957		Bury	Scarborough	4	0	0	0	0	0	0	0	0
Culkin N	Nick	06/07/1978	York		1999		Manchester United (loan)		4	0	0	0	0	0	0	0	0
Cummins GP	George	12/03/1931	Dublin		1962	1963	Cambridge City	Retired	21	0	3	1	0	2	0	0	0
Cumner RH	Horace	31/03/1918	Cwmaman		1937		Margate (loan)	Arsenal	12	0	0	0	0	4	0	0	0
Cunliffe A	Arthur	05/02/1909	Blackrod	1986	1938		Burnley	Rochdale	42	0	3	0	32	20	1	0	10

Name		D.O.B	Place of Birth	Died	First Season	Last Season	Previous Club	Next Club	Appearances					Goals			
									L.Full	L.Sub	FAC	FLC	Oth.	Lge	FAC	FLC	Oth.
Curran E	Edward 'Terr	20/03/1955	Kinsley		1986		Panionis (Greece)	Sunderland	4	0	0	1	1	0	0	0	1
Dagnall W	Walter	1883	Prescot		1906		St Helens Rec.	Retired	8	0	0	0	0	2	0	0	0
Dakin SM	Simon	30/11/1974	Nottingham		1993	1995	Derby County	Arnold Town	29	7	2	2	2	1	0	0	0
Daley AJ	Alan 'Digge	11/10/1927	Mansfield	1975	1947		Mansfield Town	Bangor City	7	0	0	0	0	0	0	0	0
Daniel PW	Peter	12/12/1955	Hull		1974	1977	Apprentice	Wolves	113	0	8	2	5	9	0	0	0
Daniel RC	Ray	10/12/1964	Luton		1986	1988	Luton Town	Cardiff City	55	3	1	1	1	3	0	0	0
Darby DA	Duane	17/10/1973	Birmingham		1995	1997	Doncaster Rovers	Notts County	79	7	4	5	4	27	6	1	2
					1998		Notts County (loan)										
Darling BS	Ben	23/03/1916	South Shields	1974	1938		South Shields	Retired	2	0	1	0	0	0	0	0	0
D'Auria DA	David	16/03/1970	Swansea		1998	1999	Scunthorpe United	Chesterfield	52	2	5	7	2	4	0	0	1
Davidson A	Andy	13/07/1932	Douglas Water		1952	1967	Apprentice	Retired	520	0	43	16	0	18	1	0	0
Davidson DC	David	19/03/1926	Douglas Water	1996	1946	1947	Douglas Water Thistle	Scarborough	22	0	1	0	0	4	0	0	0
Davidson I	Ian	31/01/1947	Goole		1966	1967	Juniors (Goole)	York City	5	1	0	0	0	1	0	0	0
Davies DD	Dai	05/12/1914	Aberdare	1984	1935	1946	Aberaman Ath.	Scunthorpe Utd	141	0	8	0	40	30	3	0	7
Davies GA	George	19/01/1897	Prescot	1956	1920	1921	Prescot FC	Merthyr Town	11	0	0	0	0	0	0	0	0
Davies HJK	Harry				1963	1905	1906	Doncaster Rovers	Leicester Fosse	34	0	4	0	0	0	0	0
Davies JG	John	18/11/1959	Llandyssil		1980	1982	Cardiff City	Retired (Injury)	24	0	2	1	0	0	0	0	0
Davin M	Martin		Dumbarton		1930		Bolton Wanderers	Yeovil & Petters Utd	8	0	0	0	0	1	0	0	0
Davis I	Ian	01/02/1965	Hull		1981	1982	Apprentice	Scarborough	25	3	0	0	4	1	0	0	0
Davison AJ	Aidan	11/05/1968	Sedgefield		1996		Bolton Wan. (loan)		9	0	0	0	1	0	0	0	0
Davison R	Bobby	17/07/1959	South Shields		1995		Rotherham United(loan)		11	0	0	0	1	4	0	0	0
Dawson A	Andy	20/10/1978	Northallerton		2003		Scunthorpe United		66	1	4	1	0	3	0	0	0
De Mange KJPP	Ken	03/09/1964	Dublin		1987	1990	Leeds United	Released	48	20	4	2	2	1	0	0	0
Deacey C	Charlie	06/10/1889	Wednesbury	1952	1914	1920	West Bromwich Albion	Grimsby Town	75	0	6	0	15	4	1	0	2
Deacy NS	Nick	19/07/1953	Cardiff		1979	1981	Vitesse Arnhem (Hol)	Happy Valley (HK)	80	7	12	1	5	7	1	0	1
Dearden KC	Kevin	08/03/1970	Luton		1990		Tottenham H. (loan)		3	0	0	0	0	0	0	0	0
Deere SH	Steve	31/03/1948	Burnham Market		1973	1974	Scunthorpe United	Bridlington Town	65	1	6	6	6	2	0	0	0
Delaney D	Damien	20/07/1981	Cork		2002		Leicester City		119	0	5	2	0	4	0	0	0
Denby S	Stanley	19/06/1912	Goole		1932	1936	Goole Town	Guildford City	124	0	6	0	0	3	0	0	0
Dennison CR	Bob	12/09/1932	Hull		1954	1957	Juniors (Hull)	Scarborough	24	0	1	0	0	1	0	0	0
deVries RS	Roger	25/10/1950	Hull		1970	1979	Juniors (Hull)	Blackburn Rovers	314	4	12	18	14	0	0	1	0
Dewhurst RM	Bob	10/09/1971	Keighley		1993	1998	Blackburn Rovers	Exeter City	132	6	8	8	7	13	1	0	0
Diamond JJ	Jack	30/10/1910	Middlesbrough	1961	1931		Juniors (E. Riding)	Shelbourne	1	0	0	0	0	0	0	0	0
Dickinson PJ	Patrick	06/05/1978	Vancouver (Canada)		1996	1997	YTS	Vancouver 86ers	2	2	0	1	0	0	0	0	0
Dickinson W	Billy	18/02/1906	Wigan		1938		Southend United	Retired	18	0	0	0	1	5	0	0	0
Dimbleby S	Stan	27/11/1916	Killingholme	1992	1935	1936	Killingholme FC	Port Vale	20	0	0	0	0	0	0	0	0
Dixon E	Edward	1884	Easington		1906		Lincoln City	Released	3	0	0	0	0	0	0	0	0
Dixon ES	Stan	26/05/1894	Choppington	1979	1926	1929	Blackburn Rovers	Retired	99	0	6	0	0	3	0	0	0
Dobson I	Ian	03/10/1957	Hull		1975	1979	Apprentice	Hereford United	86	6	4	7	3	7	0	0	0
Dodds LS	Les	20/09/1912	Portishead	1967	1933	1934	Grimsby Town	Torquay United	20	0	0	0	0	4	0	0	0
Don RP	Robert		Glasgow		1935	1936	Glasgow Perthshire	Galston (S. Africa)	21	0	0	0	0	0	0	0	0
Donaldson C	Clayton	07/02/1984	Bradford		2002	2004	YTS	York City	0	2	0	0	3	0	0	0	1
Doncel-Varcarcel	Antonio	31/01/1967	Lugo (Spain)		1996	1997	Ferrol (Spain)	Released	30	8	2	5	1	2	0	0	0
Dowen JS	Jack	1914	Wolverhampton	1994	1938		Wolves	Wolves (Ass. Trainer)	39	0	3	0	2	0	0	0	0
					1944		Wolves (Guest)										
Downes P	Percy	12/09/1905	Langhold		1931		Blackpool	Stockport Co.	11	0	0	0	0	3	0	0	0
Downie JD	Johnny	19/07/1925	Lanark		1944		Bradford PA (Guest)		27	0	1	0	1	5	0	0	0
					1954		Luton Town	Kings Lynn									
Doyle DP	Dermot		Dublin		1921	1922	Pontypridd	Released	6	0	0	0	0	0	0	0	0
Doyle R	Bobby	27/12/1953	Dumbarton		1985	1986	Portsmouth	Retired (Injury)	43	0	3	3	4	2	0	0	0
Doyle SC	Steve	02/06/1958	Neath		1989	1990	Sunderland	Rochdale	47	0	1	5	1	2	0	0	0
Dreyer G	Gordon	1914	Sunderland	2003	1935		Hartlepools United	Hartlepools United	5	0	0	0	0	0	0	0	0
Dryburgh TJD	Tom	23/04/1923	Kirkcaldy		1954		Leicester City	King's Lynn	23	0	1	0	0	3	0	0	0
Dudfield LG	Lawrie	07/05/1980	Southwark		2001	2002	Leicester City	Northampton Town	39	20	2	2	3	13	2	0	0
Dudley CB	Craig	12/09/1979	Ollerton		1998		Notts County (loan)		4	3	0	0	0	2	0	0	0
Duke M	Matt	16/06/1977	Sheffield		2004		Burton Albion		1	1	0	1	1	0	0	0	0
Duncan A	Andy	25/01/1911	Renton	1983	1930	1934	Renton Thistle	Tottenham H	105	0	9	0	0	31	0	0	0
Duncan D	Dally	14/10/1909	Aberdeen	1990	1928	1931	Aberdeen Richmond	Derby County	111	0	11	0	0	47	3	0	0
Duncan JR	James	02/04/1938	Hull		1955	1959	Juniors (Hull)	Bradford City	26	0	0	0	0	3	0	0	0
Dunne L	Leo		Dublin		1935		Manchester City	Released	8	0	0	0	0	0	0	0	0
Durham RD	Denis	26/09/1923	East Halton		1946	1958	East Halton United	Bridlington Trinity	267	0	22	0	0	7	0	0	0
Duthie J	Jim	23/09/1923	Trumperton		1951	1952	Grimsby Town	Southend United	17	0	0	0	0	3	0	0	0
Dyer AC	Alex	14/11/1965	West Ham		1986	1988	Blackpool	Crystal Palace	59	1	4	2	0	14	1	0	0
Eccles TE	Thomas	1900	Hull	1968	1921	1922	Juniors (Hull)	Bridlington Town	9	0	0	0	0	2	0	0	0
Eccleston SI	Stuart	04/10/1961	Stoke-on-Trent		1980	1981	Stoke City	Port Vale	22	1	0	2	3	0	0	0	0
Edelston JH	Joe	27/04/1891	Appley Bridge	1970	1912	1919	St Helens Rec.	Manchester City	109	0	8	0	130	0	0	0	1
Edeson MK	Matt	11/08/1976	Beverley		1992	1994	YTS	Guiseley	0	5	0	0	1	0	0	0	0
Edge R	Roland	25/11/1978	Gillingham		2004		Hibernian		13	1	0	1	1	0	0	0	0
Edwards EC	Edmund	1912	Spennymoor		1936		Clapton Orient	Mossley	10	0	0	0	1	1	0	0	1
Edwards K	Keith	16/07/1957	Middlesbrough		1978	1981	Sheffield United	Sheffield United	185	2	13	13	7	86	8	2	1
					1987	1989	Aberdeen	Stockport Co.									
Edwards M	Michael	25/04/1980	North Ferriby		1997	2002	YTS	Colchester United	165	13	11	9	10	6	2	0	0
Ellington LS	Lee	03/07/1980	Bradford		1996	1998	YTS	Altrincham	7	8	3	3	3	2	0	0	0
Elliott H	Harvey	21/01/1922	Middleton	1996	1946		Juniors (Manchester)	Mossley	4	0	0	0	0	0	0	0	0
Elliott ST	Stuart	27/08/1977	London		1996		Newcastle U (loan)		3	0	0	0	0	0	0	0	0
Elliott ST	Stuart	23/07/1978	Belfast		2002		Motherwell		107	7	4	2	1	53	1	0	1
Ellis J	John	25/01/1908	Tyldesley	1994	1938		Bristol Rovers	Clapton Orient	32	0	2	0	1	0	0	0	0
Ellison K	Kevin	23/02/1979	Liverpool		2004		Chester City		11	5	0	0	0	1	0	0	0
Eyre J	John	09/10/1974	Hull		1999	2000	Scunthorpe United	Oldham Athletic	43	9	5	5	5	13	2	3	1
Facey D	Delroy	22/04/1980	Huddersfield		2004		West Bromwich Albion	Oldham Athletic	12	9	2	1	1	4	2	0	0
Fagan C	Craig	11/12/1982	Birmingham		2004		Colchester United		11	1	0	0	0	4	0	0	0
Fagan F	Fionan 'Padd	07/06/1930	Dublin		1951	1953	Transport FC (Dublin)	Manchester City	26	0	0	0	0	2	0	0	0
Farley JD	John	21/09/1951	Middlesbrough		1978	1979	Wolves	Bury	59	1	4	3	0	5	0	0	0
Farquharson H	Hugh	1913	Glasgow		1934	1935	Renfrew Juniors	Dunfermline Ath	7	0	0	0	0	0	0	0	0

Name		D.O.B	Place of Birth	Died	First Season	Last Season	Previous Club	Next Club	Appearances					Goals			
									L.Full	L.Sub	FAC	FLC	Oth.	Lge	FAC	FLC	Oth.
Faulconbridge C	Craig	20/04/1978	Nuneaton		1998		Coventry City (loan)		4	6	1	0	2	0	0	0	0
Fawcett RE	Robert	31/07/1903	Usworth	1972	1929	1930	Usworth Colliery	Released	6	0	0	0	0	0	0	0	0
Fazackerley SN	Stan	03/10/1891	Preston	1946	1911	1912	Accrington Stanley	Sheffield United	29	0	3	0	0	19	1	0	0
Feasey PC	Paul	04/05/1933	Hull		1952	1964	York Railway Institute	Goole Town	271	0	25	8	0	0	0	0	0
Fenwick AR	Austin 'Alf'	26/03/1891	Hamsterley	1975	1911	1913	Cragheart United	West Ham United	17	0	0	0	0	7	0	0	0
Ferguson JB	Brian	14/12/1960	Irvine		1980	1981	Newcastle United	Goole Town	24	4	3	2	3	2	0	1	0
Fettis AW	Alan	01/02/1971	Newtownards		1991	1995	Ards	Nottingham Forest	151	4	5	9	9	2	0	0	0
					2002	2003	York City	Macclesfield Town									
Fewings PJ	Paul	18/02/1978	Hull		1994	1997	YTS	Hereford Utd	32	25	3	7	2	2	0	1	1
Fidler RM	Richard	26/10/1976	Sheffield		1995		Leeds United	Ashfield United	0	1	0	0	0	0	0	0	0
Finnigan A	Tony	17/10/1962	Wimbledon		1990		Blackburn Rovers	Swindon Town	15	3	0	3	0	1	0	0	0
Fisher JB	Bernard	23/02/1934	York		1955	1962	Juniors (York)	Bradford City	126	0	11	5	0	0	0	0	0
Flannigan T	Tommy	27/05/1908	Edinburgh	1981	1929		Stoke City	Loughborough Cor's	2	0	0	0	0	0	0	0	0
Fletcher P	Peter	02/12/1953	Manchester		1974	1975	Manchester United	Stockport Co.	26	10	3	2	3	5	1	1	1
Flood CW	Charlie	18/07/1896	Newport, Isle of Wig	1966	1920	1921	Plymouth Argyle	Bolton Wanderers	54	0	2	0	0	25	0	0	0
Flounders AJ	Andy	13/12/1963	Hull		1980	1986	Apprentice	Scunthorpe United	126	33	13	8	11	54	4	3	2
Folan C	Caleb	26/10/1982	Leeds		2001		Leeds United (loan)		0	1	0	0	0	0	0	0	0
Forgan TC	Tommy	12/10/1929	Middlesbrough		1953		Juniors (Middlesbro')	York City	10	0	1	0	0	0	0	0	0
Forrester JM	Jamie	01/11/1974	Bradford		2002	2003	Northampton Town	Bristol Rovers	17	15	1	0	1	7	0	0	1
Forward FJ	Fred	08/09/1899	Croydon	1977	1932		Portsmouth	Margate	39	0	4	0	0	6	2	0	0
Foster T	Thomas	1913	Hull		1934	1936	Juniors (Hull)	Guildford City	25	0	1	0	1	1	0	0	0
Fowler HN	Norman	03/09/1919	Stockton	1990	1946	1949	Middlesbrough	Gateshead	52	0	1	0	0	0	0	0	0
France DB	Darren	08/08/1967	Hull		1991	1992	North Ferriby United	Doncaster Rovers	19	24	3	2	4	7	0	0	0
France R	Ryan	13/12/1980	Sheffield		2003		Alfreton Town		29	30	2	1	2	4	1	1	0
Francis KMD	Kevin	06/12/1967	Birmingham		2000		Stockport County	Hednesford Town	22	0	0	0	2	5	0	0	0
Franklin CF	Neil	24/01/1922	Stoke-on-Trent	1996	1950	1955	Stoke City	Crewe Alexandra	95	0	1	0	0	0	0	0	0
Fraser DM	David	06/06/1937	Newtongrange		1955	1957	Arniston Rangers	Mansfield Town	11	0	0	0	0	7	0	0	0
French JC	Jon	25/09/1976	Bristol		1998	1999	Bristol Rovers	Barry Town	9	6	1	3	2	0	0	0	0
Frost WB	Ben		Hessle		1905		Hessle FC	Released	1	0	1	0	0	0	0	0	0
Fry R	Russell	04/12/1985	Hull		2002		YTS		1	0	1	0	2	0	0	0	0
Fryer JL	Jack	23/09/1911	Widnes		1937		Wrexham	Nottm. Forest	40	0	3	0	0	23	1	0	1
Gage KW	Kevin	21/04/1964	Chiswick		1997	1998	Preston North End	Released	10	3	2	1	1	0	0	0	0
Gallacher C	Con	24/02/1922	Londonderry		1947		Middlesbrough	Rochdale	18	0	3	0	0	3	1	0	0
Galvin C	Chris	24/11/1951	Huddersfield		1973	1978	Leeds United	Stockport Co.	132	11	9	12	8	11	1	1	1
Gardner T	Tommy	28/05/1910	Huyton	1970	1932	1933	Grimsby Town	Aston Villa	66	0	7	0	0	2	0	0	0
Garratt S	Syd	1899	Hull		1920	1922	Juniors (Hull)	Goole Town	8	0	0	0	0	0	0	0	0
Garvey B	Brian	03/07/1937	Hull		1957	1964	Juniors (Hull)	Watford	232	0	17	9	0	3	0	0	0
Gaynor LA	Len	22/09/1925	Ollerton		1950		Eastwood Colliery	Bournemouth	2	0	0	0	0	0	0	0	0
Gerrie S	Syd	14/06/1927	Aberdeen		1950	1956	Dundee	Retired	146	0	6	0	0	59	3	0	0
Gibson A	Alex	25/01/1925	Glasgow		1949	1950	Clyde	Stirling Albion	21	0	0	0	0	0	0	0	0
Gibson D	David	14/02/1958	Seaham		1975	1977	Apprentice	Scunthorpe United	19	5	0	1	3	0	0	0	0
Gibson FW	Fred	18/06/1907	Somercotes		1927	1932	Dinnington Colliery	Middlesbrough	101	0	9	0	0	0	0	0	0
Gibson JR	Jock	23/03/1898	Philadelphia, USA	1974	1922	1928	Sunderland	Sheffield United	210	0	8	0	0	0	0	0	0
Gibson PR	Paul	01/11/1976	Sheffield		1998		Manchester U (loan)		4	0	0	0	0	0	0	0	0
Gibson RH	Bob	05/08/1927	Ashington	1989	1949		Aberdeen	Ashington	12	0	0	0	0	5	0	0	0
Gilbert KR	Kenny	08/03/1975	Aberdeen		1995	1996	Aberdeen	Ross County	21	11	1	1	2	1	0	0	0
Gilberthorpe AE	Alfred 'Teddy'	01/01/1886	Bolsover	1960	1908		Chesterfield	Released	18	0	2	0	0	4	0	0	0
Gilhooley M	Mike	26/11/1896	Glencraig, Edinburgh		1920	1921	Clydebank	Sunderland	65	0	7	0	0	1	0	0	0
Gill G	Gary	28/11/1964	Middlesbrough		1983		Middlesbrough (loan)		0	1	0	0	0	0	0	0	0
Glennon M	Matt	08/10/1978			2001	2002	Bolton Wanderers	Carlisle United	35	0	2	3	2	0	0	0	0
Goldsmith G	George	11/03/1905	Loftus	1974	1928	1933	Loftus Albion	Tottenham H	172	0	18	0	0	0	0	0	0
Goodall EI	Edward	13/10/1913	South Shields	1978	1937		North Shields	Bolton Wanderers	26	0	3	0	1	0	0	0	0
Goode HJ	Bert	01/04/1887	Chester	1951	1912		Aston Villa	Wrexham	28	0	2	0	0	10	0	0	0
Goodin W	Walter	1883	Hull		1905		Juniors (E. Riding)	Released	1	0	0	0	0	0	0	0	0
Goodison I	Ian	21/11/1972	Kingston (Jam)		1999	2001	Olympic Gardens (Jam)	Seba Utd (Jam)	67	3	7	2	5	1	0	0	0
Gordon D	Dan	1883	West Calder		1909	1910	Bradford PA	Southampton	11	0	0	0	0	0	0	0	0
Gordon DS	Davy	1883	Leith		1905	1913	Leith Athletic	Leith Athletic	274	0	21	0	0	17	0	0	0
Gordon KG	Gavin	24/06/1979	Manchester		1995	1997	YTS	Lincoln City	22	16	0	5	2	9	0	1	0
Goulden JT	John	26/12/1903	Sunderland	1981	1924		Juniors (Hull)	Released	2	0	0	0	0	0	0	0	0
Gowdy WA	Bill		Belfast		1929	1931	Ards	Sheffield Wed.	65	0	8	0	3	1	0	0	0
					1940		Aldershot (Guest)										
Graham J	Jimmy	05/11/1969	Glasgow		1994	1995	Rochdale	Guiseley	63	0	1	4	2	1	0	0	0
Granger M	Mick	07/10/1931	Leeds		1962		York City	Halifax Town	2	0	0	0	0	0	0	0	0
Greaves MA	Mark	22/01/1975	Hull		1996	2002	Brigg Town	Boston United	152	25	11	8	8	10	1	1	0
Green L	Les	17/10/1941	Atherstone		1961		Atherstone Town	Nuneaton Borough	4	0	0	0	0	0	0	0	0
Green M	Mel	20/10/1951	Hull		1971	1972	Apprentice	Cambridge United	10	0	0	0	0	0	0	0	0
Green S	Stuart	15/06/1981	Carlisle		2002		Newcastle United		91	8	4	2	1	20	1	0	1
Greenhalgh JR	Jimmy	25/08/1923	Manchester		1946	1950	Newton Heath Loco	Bury	148	0	19	0	0	5	2	0	0
Greenwood PG	Paddy	17/10/1946	Hull		1965	1971	Apprentice	Barnsley	137	12	8	5	0	3	0	0	0
Greenwood RT	Roy	26/09/1952	Leeds		1971	1975	Apprentice	Sunderland	118	8	11	9	9	24	0	4	2
Grimes V	Vince	13/05/1954	Scunthorpe		1973	1977	Apprentice	Scunthorpe United	84	5	5	5	5	9	1	0	1
Gubbins RG	Ralph	31/01/1932	Ellesmere Port		1959	1960	Bolton Wanderers	Tranmere Rovers	45	0	6	2	0	10	2	1	0
Guyan GW	George	05/04/1901	Aberdeen		1926	1927	South Shields	Connah's Quay	19	0	3	0	0	9	2	0	0
Haigh P	Paul	04/05/1958	Scarborough		1974	1980	Apprentice	Carlisle United	179	1	7	13	9	8	1	2	1
Hall E	Ellis	22/06/1889	Ecclesfield	1949	1905	1906	Juniors (Sheffield)	Stoke City	8	0	0	0	2	0	0	0	0
					1915		Goole Town (Guest)										
Hall G	George		Errington		1922	1923	Juniors (N. East)	Durham City	12	0	0	0	0	4	0	0	0
Hall H	Harry	1887	Ecclesfield		1905	1906	Juniors (Sheffield)	Rotherham Town	2	0	0	0	0	0	0	0	0
Halligan W	Billy	1886	Athlone	1950	1913	1914	Wolves	Preston NE	65	0	7	0	1	28	0	0	0
Hamilton S	Samuel	01/01/1902	Belfast	1925	1924		Ebbow Vale	Died	27	0	4	0	0	7	1	0	0
Hamilton T	Tommy		Stevenston		1923		Llanelly	Released	2	0	0	0	0	0	0	0	0
Hannaby C	Cyril	11/10/1923	Doncaster		1946	1947	Wolves	Halifax Town	17	0	2	0	0	0	0	0	0
Hardy JH	Jack	15/06/1910	Chesterfield	1978	1937	1938	Chesterfield	Lincoln City	65	0	6	0	2	0	0	0	0
Hargreaves C	Chris	12/05/1972	Cleethorpes		1993	1994	Grimsby Town	West Bromwich Albion	34	15	3	1	4	0	1	0	0

Name		D.O.B	Place of Birth	Died	First Season	Last Season	Previous Club	Next Club	Appearances					Goals			
									L.Full	LSub	FAC	FLC	Oth.	Lge	FAC	FLC	Oth.
Harper S	Steve	03/02/1969	Newcastle-under-Lyme		1999	2000	Mansfield Town	Darlington	63	2	7	5	3	4	0	0	0
Harris A	Albert	16/09/1912	Horden		1930		Hetton United	Blackhall Colliery	5	0	0	0	0	0	0	0	0
Harris J	Jason	24/11/1976	Sutton		1999	2000	Preston North End	Southend United	19	19	1	3	3	4	0	0	0
Harris WC	Bill	31/10/1928	Swansea	1989	1949	1953	Llanelly	Middlesbrough	131	0	14	0	0	6	1	0	0
Harrison FJ	Frank	12/11/1931	Gateshead	1981	1952	1959	Juniors (Hull)	Margate	199	0	15	0	0	0	0	0	0
Harrison GR	Gerry	15/04/1972	Lambeth		1998		Sunderland (loan)		11	0	0	0	0	0	0	0	0
					1999		Sunderland (loan)										
Harrison K	Ken	20/01/1926	Stockton		1946	1954	Billingham FC	Derby County	238	0	25	0	0	47	4	0	0
Harron J	Joe	14/03/1900	Langley Park	1961	1920		Langley Park FC	Northampton Town	2	0	0	0	0	0	0	0	0
Hart J	Jimmy	02/01/1903	Glasgow		1926		Vale of Clyde	Flint Town United	2	0	0	0	0	0	0	0	0
Hassall W	Wilf	23/09/1923	Manchester		1946	1952	R.M. Alsager	Worcester City	141	0	16	0	0	3	0	0	0
Hateley MW	Mark	07/11/1961	Wallasey, Liverpool		1997	1998	Glasgow Rangers	P/Mgr (dismissed)	12	9	0	6	0	3	0	0	0
Havelock PHW	Harry	20/01/1901	Hull	1973	1923		Juniors (Hull)	Lincoln City	9	0	0	0	0	2	0	0	0
					1931		Crystal Palace	Folkestone									
Hawes SR	Steven	17/07/1978	High Wycombe		1998		Sheffield United	Altrincham	18	1	2	4	1	0	0	0	0
Hawker D	David	29/11/1958	Hull		1977	1979	Apprentice	Darlington	33	2	4	3	0	2	0	0	0
Hawley JE	John	08/05/1954	Patrington		1972	1977	Juniors (E. Riding)	Leeds United	104	13	5	11	7	23	1	2	0
					1982		Arsenal (loan)										
Haworth R	Ronald	10/03/1901	Lower Darwen	1973	1924	1925	Blackburn Rovers	Manchester United	36	0	1	0	0	10	0	0	0
Head M	Mike	13/04/1933	Hull		1954		Juniors (E. Riding)	Wisbech Town	3	0	0	0	0	0	0	0	0
Heard TP	Pat	17/03/1960	Hull		1985	1987	Middlesbrough	Rotherham United	82	2	5	5	3	5	0	0	0
					1992		Hall Road Rangers	Hall Road Rangers									
Heath RT	Terry	17/11/1943	Leicester		1964	1967	Leicester City	Scunthorpe United	27	6	3	1	0	1	3	0	0
Hedley F	Foster	06/01/1908	Monkseaton	1983	1928		Jarrow	Nelson	2	0	0	0	0	0	0	0	0
Hedley GT	George 'To	1882	Co Durham	1937	1905	1907	Hearts	Leicester Fosse	78	0	6	0	0	2	0	0	0
Hedley RB	Ralph	1897	Byker	1969	1923		Newburn	Crystal Palace	9	0	0	0	0	0	0	0	0
Hedley T	Thomas	1890	Jarrow		1911		Juniors (N. East)	Released	2	0	0	0	0	0	0	0	0
Helsby T	Tom	1904	Runcorn	1961	1934		Swindon Town	Newport County	22	0	1	0	0	0	0	0	0
Hemmerman JL	Jeff	25/02/1955	Hull		1973	1976	Apprentice	Port Vale	45	14	3	1	2	10	1	0	0
Henderson R	Ray	31/03/1937	Wallsend		1961	1967	Middlesbrough	Reading	226	3	23	12	0	54	6	1	0
Hendry CN	Nick	1887	York	1949	1911	1919	Darlington	York City	140	0	11	0	115	0	0	0	0
Henzell WH	William	1897	Newcastle		1920		Walker Celtic	Retired	2	0	0	0	0	1	0	0	0
Hesford I	Iain	04/03/1960	Zambia		1988	1990	Sunderland	Maidstone United	91	0	5	4	2	0	0	0	0
Hessenthaler A	Andy	17/08/1965	Gravesend		2004		Gillingham (loan)		6	4	0	0	0	0	0	0	0
Hewitson R	Robert	1888	Newburn	1957	1912		Newburn FC	Released	1	0	0	0	0	0	0	0	0
Hickton J	John	24/09/1944	Brimington		1976		Middlesbrough (loan)		6	0	0	0	0	1	0	0	0
Higgins W	William		Scotland		1934		Rutherglen Glencairn	Released	5	0	0	0	0	0	0	0	0
Hill JH	Jack	02/03/1897	Hetton-le-Hole	1972	1931	1933	Bradford City	Appointed Manager	94	0	8	0	0	2	2	0	0
Hinds R	Richard	22/08/1980	Sheffield		2003	2004	Tranmere Rovers	Scunthorpe United	40	5	1	1	2	1	0	0	0
Hobson G	Gary	12/11/1972	North Ferriby		1990	1995	YTS	Brighton & Hove A.	135	7	4	14	6	0	0	0	0
Hockaday D	David	09/11/1957	Billingham		1990	1992	Swindon Town	Shrewsbury Town	72	0	3	4	4	2	0	1	0
Hocking MJ	Matthew	30/01/1978	Boston		1997	1998	Sheffield United	York City	55	2	4	6	4	2	0	0	0
Hodges GP	Glyn	30/04/1963	Streatham		1997		Sin Tao (Hong Kong)	Nottingham Forest	13	5	1	1	2	4	0	0	0
Holah ET	Eric	03/08/1937	Hull		1960		Juniors (Hull)	Bradford City	1	0	0	0	0	1	0	0	0
Holbrook S	Steve	16/09/1952	Richmond, Yorkshire		1970	1971	Apprentice	Darlington	2	1	0	0	0	0	0	0	0
Hollifield M	Mike	02/05/1961	Middlesbrough		1983	1984	Wolves	Tranmere Rovers	45	0	2	2	4	1	0	0	0
Holme PC	Phil	21/06/1947	Briton Ferry		1972	1973	Swansea City	Retired	29	9	6	2	3	11	0	3	0
Holmes MM	Max	24/12/1908	Pinchbeck		1935	1936	Grimsby Town	Mansfield Town	29	0	1	0	0	10	0	0	0
Holt A	Andy	21/04/1978	Stockport		2000	2003	Oldham Athletic	Wrexham	45	26	1	1	6	3	0	0	0
Hood D	Derek	17/12/1958	Washington		1977	1979	West Bromwich Albion	York City	20	4	4	3	0	0	0	0	0
Hoolickin SJ	Steve	13/12/1951	Moston, Manchester		1980	1981	Carlisle United	Retired	31	0	2	1	2	0	0	0	0
Horne A	Alf	1903	Birmingham	1976	1925	1926	Stafford Rangers	Southend United	25	0	1	0	0	2	0	0	0
Horswill MF	Mickey	06/03/1953	Annfield Plain		1978	1981	Plymouth Argyle	Happy Valley (HK)	82	2	3	8	5	6	0	0	0
Horton B	Brian	04/02/1949	Hednesford		1984	1986	Luton Town	Dismissed as Manager	38	0	4	4	1	0	0	0	0
Horton JK	Ken	26/08/1922	Preston		1952	1954	Preston NE	Barrow	76	0	10	0	0	16	4	0	0
Hotte TA	Tim	04/10/1963	Bradford		1987	1988	North Ferriby United	Goole Town	1	4	0	0	0	0	0	0	0
Houghton J	Jack	1888	Wallsend	1950	1910	1912	Wallsend Park Villa	Fulham	28	0	0	0	0	3	0	0	0
Houghton K	Ken	18/10/1939	Rotherham		1964	1972	Rotherham United	Scunthorpe United	253	11	23	12	5	79	9	2	1
Hoult AJ	Alan	07/10/1957	Burbage, Leics		1977		Leicester City (loan)		3	0	0	0	0	1	0	0	0
Howe P	Peter	1884	Co Durham		1905	1906	Reading	Released	32	0	5	0	0	15	4	0	0
Howieson J	Jimmy	07/06/1900	Rutherglen	1974	1926	1927	St Mirren	America	67	0	7	0	0	12	2	0	0
					1929		America	Shelbourne									
Hubbard C	Cliff	1911	Worksop	1962	1933	1938	Scunthorpe United	West Ham United	183	0	12	0	8	56	5	0	1
					1944		West Ham U (Guest)										
Hughes EW	Emlyn	28/08/1947	Barrow	2004	1982		Rotherham United	Mansfield Town	9	0	0	0	0	0	0	0	0
Hughes R	Bobby	05/08/1892	Pelaw	1955	1919	1921	Northampton Town	Sheffield United	66	0	3	0	62	9	0	0	31
Humphries G	Glenn	11/08/1964	Hull		1995		Golden Valley (HK)	North Ferriby Utd	9	3	1	2	1	0	0	0	0
Hunter P	Paul	30/08/1968	Kirkcaldy		1989	1992	East Fife	Cowdenbeath	37	31	3	4	3	11	1	0	0
Hutchison D	Duncan	03/03/1903	Kelty	1972	1934		Derby County	Dundee Utd	38	0	1	0	0	8	0	0	0
Huxford H	Harold	02/02/1916	Grimsby		1938		Grimsby Town	Boston Utd	10	0	1	0	3	1	0	0	0
							Grimsby Town	Guest									
Inwood GF	Gordon	18/06/1928	Kislingbury		1950		West Bromwich Albion	Kettering Town	3	0	0	0	0	0	0	0	0
Iremonger J	James	05/06/1901	Wilford	1980	1924		Clifton Colliery (Nottm)	Released	1	0	0	0	0	0	0	0	0
Jacketts GA	George	1887	Hull	1957	1919		Juniors (Hull)	Ebbw Vale	2	0	0	0	95	0	0	0	3
Jacobs WG	Wayne	03/02/1969	Sheffield		1987	1991	Sheffield Wed.	Released	127	2	8	7	6	4	0	0	0
Jarvis AL	Alan	04/08/1943	Wrexham		1965	1970	Everton	Mansfield Town	148	11	12	6	0	12	0	0	0
Jenkinson L	Leigh	09/07/1969	Thorne		1987	1992	YTS	Coventry City	95	35	7	9	11	13	0	1	1
Jensen HV	Viggo	29/03/1921	Skagen, Denmark		1948	1956	Esbjerg Forende (Den)	(Denmark)	308	0	27	0	0	51	3	0	0
Jevons P	Phil	01/08/1979	Liverpool		2002		Grimsby Town (loan)		13	11	1	1	0	3	0	0	0
Jobson JW	John	29/07/1908	Burradon	1974	1930		Hatfield Main	Released	2	0	0	0	0	0	0	0	0
Jobson RI	Richard	09/05/1963	Cottingham		1984	1990	Watford	Oldham Athletic	219	2	13	12	9	17	1	0	0
Johnson S	Sam	10/02/1919	Barnton		1946	1947	Northwich Victoria	Scarborough	10	0	1	0	0	0	0	0	0
Johnson S	Simon	09/03/1983	West Bromwich		2002		Leeds United (loan)		4	8	0	1	0	2	0	0	0
Johnson W	William				1919		Juniors (E. Riding)	Bridlington Town	5	0	0	0	0	0	0	0	0

Name		D.O.B	Place of Birth	Died	First Season	Last Season	Previous Club	Next Club	L.Full	L.Sub	FAC	FLC	Oth.	Lge	FAC	FLC	Oth.
Johnson W 'Bill'	Bill	1900	Seaton Delaval		1923	1925	Seaton Delaval	Blyth Spartans	46	0	2	0	0	0	0	0	0
Johnsson J	Julian	24/02/1974	Denmark		2001		Sogndal (Nor)	Bóltfelagið B36 (Far. Is)	38	2	2	2	3	4	1	0	0
Jones DB	David	03/07/1964	Harrow		1992		Bury	Non Contract	11	1	0	0	0	1	0	0	0
Jones E	Ellis	05/04/1900	Spennymoor	1972	1925		Spennymoor United	Annfield Plain	8	0	0	0	0	1	0	0	0
Jones G	Glanville	27/02/1921	Merthyr Tydfil		1946		Merthyr Tydfil	Bournemouth	7	0	0	0	0	0	0	0	0
Jones JM	James	1925	Manchester		1946		Juniors (Lancashire)	Released	1	0	0	0	0	0	0	0	0
Jones T	Tom	1877	Newport, Shropshire		1905		Bristol Rovers	Wigan Town	27	0	7	0	0	2	0	0	0
Jordan AR	Alf		Belfast		1924	1925	Stoke City	Bristol Rovers	9	0	0	0	0	0	0	0	0
Jordan D	David		Belfast		1932	1935	Ards	Wolves	24	0	1	0	0	15	0	0	0
Joseph ME	Marc	10/11/1976	Leicester		2002		Peterborough United		79	5	3	1	1	1	1	0	0
Joyce WG	Warren	20/01/1965	Oldham		1994		Burnley (loan)		146	1	8	8	7	15	1	1	2
					1996	1990	Burnley	Released									
Kaye J	John	03/03/1940	Goole		1971	1973	West Bromwich Alb.	Appointed Coach	71	1	5	4	6	9	0	0	0
Keane MJT	Michael	29/12/1982	Dublin		2004		Preston NE	Rotherham United	12	8	3	1	1	3	1	1	0
Keates DS	Dean	30/06/1978	Walsall		2002	2003	Walsall	Kidderminster Harriers	45	5	0	2	2	4	0	0	0
Keen JF	James	25/11/1897	Walker	1980	1924		QPR	Darlington	17	0	0	0	0	0	0	0	0
Keers JM	John	1900	Tow Law	1963	1925		Tow Law FC	Annfield Plain	8	0	0	0	0	1	0	0	0
Kelly GJ	Gavin	29/09/1968	Beverley		1988	1989	YTS	Bristol Rovers	11	0	0	1	1	0	0	0	0
Kelly NAO	Tony	14/02/1966	Meriden		1991		Stoke City (loan)		6	0	0	0	0	1	0	0	0
Killgallon MC	Mark	20/12/1962	Glasgow		1980		Ipswich Town	Released	0	1	0	0	0	0	0	0	0
King DJ	Dave	24/10/1940	Hull		1959	1962	Juniors (Hull)	Kings Lynn	65	0	1	1	0	24	1	0	0
King G	George	05/01/1923	Warkworth		1947	1948	Newcastle United	Port Vale	3	0	0	0	0	0	0	0	0
Kirman H	Harold	03/12/1930	Hull		1955		F. Akew Y.C	Gillingham	2	0	0	0	0	0	0	0	0
Kitchen JE	Joe	1886	Brigg	1962	1921	1922	Sheffield United	Scunthorpe United	30	0	0	0	0	5	0	0	0
Kitchen N	Norman	26/07/1911	Sunderland	1998	1935		Eden Colliery	Southport	4	0	0	0	0	1	0	0	0
Knight R	Richard	03/08/1979	Burton		1999		Derby County (loan)		1	0	0	0	0	0	0	0	0
Knighton K	Ken	20/02/1944	Barnsley		1970	1972	Blackburn Rovers	Sheffield Wed.	79	1	5	3	4	9	0	1	2
Knott H	Bert	05/12/1914	Goole	1986	1946		Brierley Hill Alliance	Released	6	0	1	0	22	1	0	0	25
Koffman SJ	Jack	03/08/1920	Prestwich	1977	1946		Manchester United	Congleton Town	4	0	0	0	0	0	0	0	0
Kuipers M	Michel	26/06/1974	Amsterdam		2003		Brighton & Hove Albion (loan)		3	0	0	0	0	0	0	0	0
Kynman DJ	David	20/05/1962	Hull		1980	1981	Apprentice	Bridlington Trinity	11	0	0	0	0	0	0	0	0
Langley A	Ambrose	10/03/1870	Horncastle	1937	1905		Sheffield Wed.	Appointed Manager	13	0	2	0	0	0	0	0	0
Lavery P	Patrick	1884	Hebburn	1915	1905		Gateshead	West Stanley	2	0	1	0	0	0	0	0	0
Lawford CB	Craig	25/11/1972	Dewsbury		1994	1995	Bradford City	Liversedge	45	17	2	6	5	3	0	0	1
Lawrance RS	Ray	18/09/1911	Gainsborough	1987	1933	1935	Gainsborough Trinity	Newport County	34	0	0	0	0	1	0	0	0
Lawrence M	Matt	03/04/1909	Cefn-y-Bedd		1937	1938	Wrexham	Released	25	0	0	0	1	1	0	0	0
Lee C	Chris	18/06/1971	Halifax		1993	1995	Scarborough	Guiseley	104	12	4	4	5	5	0	1	0
Lee DJF	David	28/03/1980	Basildon		2001		Southend United	Brighton & Hove Albion	2	9	1	1	1	1	0	0	0
Lee James	Jimmy	26/01/1926	Rotherham		1949		Wolves	Halifax Town	3	0	0	0	0	1	0	0	0
Lee John	John	1890	Sheffield	1955	1913	1919	Juniors (Sheffield)	Chelsea	75	0	8	0	67	19	3	0	28
Lee PF	Pat	20/01/1903	Uddingston	1981	1925	1926	Vale of Clyde	Accrington Stanley	25	0	1	0	0	6	0	0	0
Lees N	Norman	18/11/1948	Newcastle		1966	1970	Apprentice	Darlington	4	1	0	1	0	0	0	0	0
Lester AB	Ben	10/02/1920	Sheffield		1946	1947	Selby Town	Lincoln City	27	0	4	0	0	17	2	0	0
Lewis H	Harry	19/12/1893	Birkenhead	1976	1923	1924	Liverpool	Mold Town	36	0	2	0	0	5	0	0	0
Lewis K	Karl 'Junior	09/10/1973	Wembley		2003	2004	Leicester City	Released	44	8	2	0	1	3	0	0	0
Lightbourne KL	Kyle	29/09/1968	Bermuda		2001		Macclesfield Town (loan)		3	1	0	0	0	0	0	0	0
Lill DA	David	17/02/1947	Aldbrough		1966	1969	Apprentice	Rotherham United	16	2	0	0	0	2	0	0	0
Linaker JE	Johnny	14/01/1927	Southport		1951	1952	York City	York City	26	0	1	0	0	3	0	0	0
Livingstone AM	Allan	02/12/1899	Alexandria	1970	1922		Dumbarton Harp	Released	1	0	0	0	0	0	0	0	0
Llewellyn GL	George	1916	Abercwmboi		1936		Caerphilly	Scarborough	4	0	0	0	1	0	0	0	0
Lloyd CF	Charlie	27/09/1906	North Shields	1979	1926		Percy Main Colliery	Southend United	7	0	0	0	0	0	0	0	0
Lloyd EH	Edward	25/07/1905	Oldham	1976	1933		Stockport Co.	Carlisle United	1	0	0	0	0	0	0	0	0
Lodge JW	Jimmy	11/01/1895	Felling	1971	1919	1923	Newburn	Halifax Town	81	0	2	0	0	0	0	0	0
Longden E	Eric	18/05/1904	Goldthorpe	1983	1930		Leeds United	Blackpool	88	0	5	0	0	12	0	0	0
					1932	1934	Blackpool	Scarborough									
Lord B	Barry	17/11/1937	Goole		1958	1960	Goole Buchanan FC	Goole Town	5	0	0	0	0	0	0	0	0
Lord M	Malcolm	25/10/1946	Driffield		1966	1978	Apprentice	Scarborough	271	27	14	9	13	24	0	1	1
Loughran J	James	1898	Seaham Colliery		1922	1923	Easington Colliery	Barrow	4	0	0	0	0	0	0	0	0
Lowthorpe A	Adam	07/08/1975	Hull		1993	1997	YTS	Gainsboro' Trinity	70	11	2	5	5	3	0	0	0
Lund GJ	Gary	13/09/1964	Grimsby		1992		Notts County (loan)		22	0	0	0	0	6	0	0	0
					1994		Notts County (loan)										
					1994		Notts County (loan)										
Lyall G	George	04/05/1947	Wick		1975	1976	Nottm. Forest	Scarborough	42	0	5	1	3	5	0	0	1
Lyon J	Jack	03/11/1893	Prescot	1975	1919	Prescot FC	Leeds United	37	0	2	0	15	6	0	0	7
Lyon S	Sam	20/11/1890	Prescot	1977	1912	1913	Prescot FC	Barnsley	6	0	0	0	0	1	0	0	0
Mackay W	William		Ireland		1937		Swansea Town	Released	12	0	0	0	2	0	0	0	0
MacKenzie GD	George (D	27/01/1908	Queens Park		1974	1933	Queens Park	Stockport Co.	9	0	1	0	0	4	0	0	0
Mackie J	John		Baillieston		1960	1934	1935	Bridgeton Waverley	Bradford City	14	0	0	0	0	0	0	0	0
Maddison G	George	14/08/1902	Birtley	1959	1924	1937	Tottenham H	Retired	430	0	24	0	2	0	0	0	0
Mail D	David	12/09/1962	Bristol		1990	1994	Blackburn Rovers	Brigg Town	140	10	4	5	10	2	0	0	0
Major JL	Jack	12/03/1929	Islington		1946		Juniors (Hull)	Sunderland	13	0	0	0	0	0	0	0	0
					1955	1956	Bishop Auckland	Goole Town									
Mann N	Neil	19/11/1972	Nottingham		1993	2000	Grantham Town	Retired (Injury)	138	37	8	16	10	9	1	0	1
Manning JT	Jack	1886	Boston	1946	1905	1906	Boston Town FC	Bradford P.A.	54	0	8	0	0	9	0	0	0
Mannion WJ	Wilf	16/05/1918	South Bank		1954		Middlesbrough	Poole Town	16	0	1	0	0	1	0	0	0
Marcelle C	Clint	09/11/1968	Port of Spain		2000		Goole Town	Darlington	16	7	1	1	0	2	0	0	0
March HJ	Harold	30/01/1904	Gamston	1977	1929		Armed Services	Lincoln City	8	0	0	0	0	0	0	0	0
Marks J	Jamie	18/03/1977	Belfast		1995	1996	YTS (Leeds United)	Linfield	11	4	2	0	1	0	0	0	0
Marshall JM	James	1897	Bishop Auckland		1920		St Peters Albion	Preston Colliery	1	0	0	0	0	0	0	0	0
Marshall LK	Lee	21/01/1979	Islington		2003		West Bromwich Albion (loan)		10	1	0	0	0	0	0	0	0
Martin F	Frank	1887	Gateshead	1967	1910		Juniors (N. East)	Grimsby Town	29	0	3	0	0	0	0	0	0
Martin GS	George	14/07/1899	Bothwell	1972	1922	1927	Hamilton Academicals	Everton	204	0	14	0	0	55	3	0	0
Martin JJ	James	28/11/1908	Patricroft	1980	1935		Bacup Borough	Accrington Stanley	4	0	0	0	0	1	0	0	0
Martin T	Tommy	21/12/1924	Glasgow		1955	1956	Nottm. Forest	Rothes FC	32	0	0	0	0	2	0	0	0

Name		D.O.B	Place of Birth	Died	First Season	Last Season	Previous Club	Next Club	L.Full	L.Sub	FAC	FLC	Oth.	Lge	FAC	FLC	Oth.
Martin WTJ	Bill	1883	Poplar	1954	1905		Millwall Athletic	Clapton Orient	4	0	3	0	0	0	0	0	0
Marwood B	Brian	05/02/1960	Seaham Harbour		1979	1983	Apprentice	Sheffield Wed.	154	4	16	5	12	51	1	0	1
Mason AJ	Andy	22/11/1974	Bolton		1995	1996	Bolton Wanderers	Chesterfield	14	12	0	4	3	4	0	0	0
Mason TE	Thomas	26/07/1893	Hull	1969	1919	1920	Armed Services	Rotherham Town	3	0	0	0	0	0	0	0	0
Massey S	Steve	28/03/1958	Denton		1983	1984	Northampton Town	Cambridge United	34	8	2	5	4	9	1	1	0
Matthews M	Mike	25/09/1960	Hull		1991		Scarborough	Halifax Town	10	6	1	0	3	2	0	0	1
Matthews R	Rob	14/10/1970	Slough		2000	2001	Stockport Co.	Northwich Victoria	17	6	2	1	4	3	1	0	0
Maxfield S	Scott	13/07/1976	Doncaster		1995	1997	Doncaster Rovers	Doncaster Rovers	23	12	1	2	1	0	0	0	0
Mayson JD	Jackie	24/10/1908	Southport	1991	1936		Clapton Orient	Tranmere Rovers	23	0	1	0	1	8	1	0	0
McAinsh J	James	13/10/1913	Clackmannan	1978	1933		Juniors (Scotland)	Gateshead	7	0	0	0	0	0	0	0	0
McClaren S	Steve	03/05/1961	Fulford		1979	1984	Apprentice	Derby County	171	7	16	9	12	16	3	0	1
McCorry H	Henry	1888	Felling		1913		Newburn	Chesterfield Town	10	0	0	0	0	4	0	0	0
McCunnell B	Barry	20/09/1948	Hull		1969		Juniors (Hull)	Barton Town	0	1	0	0	0	0	0	0	0
McDonald K	Ken	24/04/1898	Llanwrst		1928	1929	Breadford P.A.	Halifax Town	41	0	2	0	0	29	2	0	0
McDonald RR	Rob	22/01/1959	Hull		1976	1979	Apprentice	Wageningen (Holland)	17	8	0	3	0	2	0	0	0
McDonald WW	Billy	1892	Quebec, Co Durham	1948	1911	1913	Craghead United	Chesterfield	69	0	5	0	0	5	0	0	0
McEwan S	Stan	08/06/1957	Cambuskenneth		1983	1987	Exeter City	Wigan Ath.	113	0	6	10	11	25	1	2	3
McGee J	Jock	1902	Rothesay		1922	1926	Harrogate	Retired (Injury)	70	0	10	0	0	0	0	0	0
McGifford GL	Grahame	01/05/1955	Carshalton		1976		Huddersfield T	Port Vale	1	0	0	0	1	0	0	0	0
McGill JM	Jimmy	27/11/1946	Glasgow		1971	1975	Huddersfield T	Halifax Town	141	6	11	9	10	2	1	0	1
McGinty B	Brian	10/12/1976	East Kilbride		1997	1998	Glasgow Rangers	Scarborough	43	10	3	4	4	6	1	1	0
McGorrighan FO	Frank	20/11/1921	Easington	1998	1946 1947		Carlisle United Blackburn Rovers	Blackburn Rovers Southport	26	0	7	0	0	1	1	0	0
McIntosh JB	James	25/05/1886	Glasgow	1959	1910	1913	Glasgow Celtic	Released	92	0	4	0	0	2	0	0	0
McIntosh JW	Jim	19/08/1950	Forfar		1975	1976	Nottingham Forest	Dundee United	20	0	1	0	1	1	0	0	0
McKechnie IH	Ian	04/10/1941	Lenzie		1966	1973	Southend United	Goole Town	255	0	17	7	5	0	0	0	0
McKinney D	Daniel	09/11/1898	Belfast	1956	1920	1922	Belfast Celtic	Bradford City	55	0	5	0	0	12	0	0	0
McLaughlin G	George	18/01/1904	Bridgeton		1926		Darlington	Accrington Stanley	8	0	1	0	0	2	0	0	0
McMillan E	Eric	02/11/1936	Beverley		1960	1963	Chelsea	Halifax Town	150	0	14	10	0	3	1	0	0
McMurray C	Campbell		Glasgow		1920	1921	Juniors (Glasgow)	Workington	4	0	0	0	0	0	0	0	0
McNaughton WF	Bill	08/12/1905	Poplar	1980	1932	1934	Gateshead	Stockport Co.	85	0	7	0	0	57	2	0	0
McNeill HJ	John		Glasgow		1937	1938	Ayr United	Bury	52	0	6	0	2	27	2	0	0
McNeil RM	Bobby	01/11/1962	Hamilton		1980	1984	Apprentice	Blackpool	135	3	17	5	8	3	0	0	1
McParland IJ	Ian	04/10/1961	Edinburgh		1988	1990	Notts County	Dunfermline	31	16	1	4	2	7	1	0	0
McPheat J	John	25/08/1911	Longriggend	1979	1935		Rutherglen Glencairn	Guilford City	9	0	0	0	0	0	0	0	0
McQuillan J	Jack	1888	Boldon		1906 1915	1913	Everton Leeds City (Guest)	Leeds City	239	0	18	0	31	2	1	0	2
McSeveney JH	John	08/02/1931	Shotts		1961	1964	Newport County	Retired	161	0	12	10	0	60	8	2	0
Medcalf JT	James		Newark		1914		Notts County	Released	2	0	0	0	0	0	0	0	0
Meens H	Harold	05/10/1919	Doncaster	1987	1938	1951	Shepherds Road	Retired (Injury)	146	0	15	0	49	0	0	0	3
Mellor JA	Allan	16/10/1921	Droylsden	1997	1947	1951	Ashton United	Retired (Injury)	104	0	13	0	0	4	0	0	0
Melton S	Steve	03/10/1978	Lincoln		2002	2003	Brighton & Hove Albion	Boston United	19	11	0	1	2	0	0	0	0
Melville D	David		Glasgow		1913		Juniors (Glasgow)	Clyde	5	0	0	0	0	0	0	0	0
Melville J	Jim	15/03/1909	Barrow	1961	1933		Blackburn Rovers	Northampton Town	14	0	2	0	0	1	0	0	0
Mercer DW	Dave	20/03/1893	St Helens	1950	1913	1920	Skelmersdale	Sheffield United	91	0	6	0	142	26	0	0	48
Mercer WH	Billy	1892	Prescot	1954	1914	1924	Prescot Athletic	Huddersfield T	193	0	10	0	4	0	0	0	0
Metcalfe V	Vic	03/02/1922	Barrow		1958	1959	Huddersfield T	Retired	6	0	0	0	0	3	0	0	0
Middlehurst JH	James	1892	Prescot	1954	1914	1919	St Helens Rec	Released	9	0	0	0	0	0	0	0	0
Middlemas JR	John	17/01/1896	Easington	1984	1922		Blyth Spartans	York City	10	0	1	0	0	0	0	0	0
Miller AH	Alforth	27/09/1914	Gainsborough	1987	1934		Gaindsborough Trinity	Barrow	4	0	0	0	0	0	0	0	0
Miller RJ	Robert	03/11/1972	Manchester		1992	1993	Oldham Athletic	Released	22	6	3	0	2	0	0	0	0
Mills BR	Bertie 'Paddy'	23/02/1900	Multan, India		1920 1929	1925 1932	Barton Town Birmingham	Notts County Scunthorpe Utd	269	0	22	0	0	101	9	0	0
Mills J	James	30/09/1915	Dalton Brook	1994	1946	1947	Rotherham United	Halifax Town	42	0	5	0	0	1	0	0	0
Milner M	Mike	21/09/1939	Hull		1958	1967	Juniors (Hull)	Stockport Co.	160	0	12	4	0	0	0	0	0
Mitchell A	Andrew	20/04/1907	Coxhoe	1971	1933		Manchester United	Northampton T	8	0	0	0	0	0	0	0	0
Mitchell CB	Brian	30/07/1963	Stonehaven		1993		Bristol City	Retired (Injury)	9	0	0	2	1	0	0	0	0
Mitchell R	Ronald	1902	Birkenhead		1924	1925	Liverpool	Nelson	27	0	0	0	0	1	0	0	0
Mohan N	Nicky	06/10/1970	Middlesbrough		1992 2001	2002	Middlesbrough (loan) Stoke City	Gateshead	31	1	0	2	1	2	0	0	0
Montgomery SW	Stan	07/07/1920	West Ham		1946		Romford	Southend United	5	0	0	0	10	0	0	0	4
Mooney EP	Peter	22/03/1897	Walker		1927		Newcastle United	Scunthorpe Utd	11	0	0	0	0	0	0	0	0
Moore A	Alan	07/03/1927	Hebburn		1951		Chesterfield	Nottm. Forest	13	0	0	0	0	4	0	0	0
Moore J	John	01/10/1966	Consett		1988		Sunderland	FC Utrecht (Holland)	11	3	0	2	1	1	0	0	0
Moore JE	John	1912	Newcastle		1934		Hebburn Colliery	Gateshead	5	0	0	0	0	0	0	0	0
Moore NW	Norman	15/10/1919	Grimsby		1946	1949	Grimsby Town	Blackburn Rovers	81	0	11	0	0	46	7	0	0
Moran SJ	Steve	10/01/1961	Croydon		1993		Exeter City	Retired (Injury)	11	5	1	1	2	5	0	0	0
Mordue T	Thomas	22/07/1905	Horden	1975	1923		Herrington Swifts	Horden Athletic	6	0	0	0	0	0	0	0	0
Morgan D	Doug	1890	Inverkeithing	1917	1913	1914	Inverkeithing Thistle	Killed in WW1	52	0	6	0	0	0	0	0	0
Morgan S	Steve	19/09/1968	Oldham		1999		Wigan Athletic	Halifax Town	17	2	4	0	2	1	0	0	2
Morley B	Ben	22/12/1980	Hull		1997	1999	YTS	Boston United	7	19	2	3	3	0	1	0	0
Morrall GA	George	1893	Birmingham	1964	1919	1920	Blackheath Town	Grimsby Town	37	0	1	0	2	17	0	0	1
Morris CJ	Chris	12/10/1939	Spilsby		1958	1960	Juniors (Hull)	York City	17	0	0	0	0	4	0	0	0
Morris J	John		Newarthill		1926		Newarthill FC	Bradford City	1	0	0	0	0	0	0	0	0
Morrison J	John	1886	Jarrow		1908		Jarrow FC	Swindon Town	4	0	0	0	0	0	0	0	0
Morrison JO	Owen	08/12/1981	Londonderry		2002		Sheffield Wednesday (loan)		1	1	0	0	0	0	0	0	0
Mortenson SH	Stan	26/05/1921	South Shields	1991	1955	1956	Blackpool	Southport	42	0	4	0	0	18	2	0	0
Moss PM	Paul	02/08/1957	Birmingham		1979	1980	Wolves	Scunthorpe United	53	1	3	2	3	7	0	0	1
Mudd PA	Paul	13/11/1970	Hull		1988		YTS	Scarborough	1	0	0	0	0	0	0	0	0
Munnings CE	Eddie	06/07/1906	Boston	1995	1931		Swindon Town	Swindon Town	31	0	3	0	0	7	2	0	0
Murphy G	George 'Spud'	22/07/1915	Cwmfelinfach	1983	1947		Bradford City	Scunthorpe Utd	15	0	1	0	0	9	1	0	0
Murray J	Joseph	28/08/1908	Hull	1988	1925	1930	Juniors (Hull)	Lincoln City	17	0	0	0	0	1	0	0	0
Murray M	Malcolm	26/07/1964	Buckie		1988	1989	Hearts	Mansfield Town	9	2	0	2	0	0	0	0	0
Murray, Terry	Terry	22/05/1928	Dublin		1951	1953	Dundalk	Bournemouth	32	0	1	0	0	6	0	0	0

Name		D.O.B	Place of Birth	Died	First Season	Last Season	Previous Club	Next Club	Appearances					Goals			
									L.Full	L.Sub	FAC	FLC	Oth.	Lge	FAC	FLC	Oth.
Murray, Thos.	Thomas	07/04/1889	Middlesbrough	1976	1913		Bradford City	Retired (Injury)	2	0	0	0	0	0	0	0	0
Musgrave A	Archibald	1883	Carlisle	1964	1909	1910	Workington	Grimsby Town (trial)	7	0	0	0	0	0	0	0	0
Musselwhite P	Paul	27/12/1968	Portsmouth		2000	2003	Port Vale	Scunthorpe United	94	1	4	0	5	0	0	0	0
Mutrie LA	Les	01/04/1952	Newcastle		1980	1983	Blyth Spartans	Colchester Utd	114	1	8	6	3	49	1	0	0
Myhill GO	Glyn 'Boaz	09/11/1982	Modesto (USA)		2003			Aston Villa	68	0	3	0	1	0	0	0	0
Neal J	John	03/04/1932	Silksworth		1949	1955	Silsworth Juniors	Kings Lynn	60	0	2	0	0	1	0	0	0
Needham J	Jack	04/03/1887	Newstead		1919	1920	Wolves	Released	18	0	0	0	0	1	0	0	0
Neill WJT	Terry	08/05/1942	Belfast		1970	1972	Arsenal	Tottenham Hotspur(Mgr)	103	0	11	2	6	4	0	0	0
Neish J	John	1910	Elgin		1935		Partick Thistle	Released	1	0	0	0	0	0	0	0	0
Nelson A	Arthur	15/05/1909	Darnall	1977	1927	1928	Sheffield Woodhouse	Scarborough	21	0	1	0	0	8	0	0	0
Neve E	Ned	03/05/1888	Prescot	1920	1910	1911	St Helens Rec.	Derby County	102	0	2	0	0	12	0	0	0
Nevins T	Tommy	1886	Washington	1950	1907	1913	Washington Athletic	Blyth Spartans	130	0	10	0	0	0	0	0	0
Newton W	Billy	14/05/1893	Cramlington	1973	1931		Stockport Co.	Stockport Co.	24	0	3	0	0	0	0	0	0
Ngata H	Henry	24/08/1971	New Zealand		1989	1991	YTS	South Shore (NZ)	8	17	1	1	0	0	0	0	0
Nicholson PW	Peter	11/12/1936	Hull		1960		Juniors (Hull)	Barton Town	1	0	0	0	0	0	0	0	0
Nicklas C	Charlie	26/04/1930	Sunderland		1951		Silksworth Colliery	Darlington	6	0	0	0	0	1	0	0	0
Nicol JC	John	26/01/1911	Edinburgh		1935		Burton Town	York City	6	0	0	0	0	2	0	0	0
Nielson NF	Norman	06/11/1928	Johannesburg, SA		1956	1957	Bury	Corby Town	25	0	3	0	0	0	0	0	0
Nisbet GJM	Gordon	18/09/1951	Wallsend		1976	1980	West Bromwich Albion	Plymouth Argyle	190	3	10	11	6	1	1	0	0
Norman AJ	Tony	24/02/1958	Mancot		1979	1988	Burnley	Sunderland	372	0	26	22	22	0	0	0	0
Norrie CT	Craig	22/07/1960	Hull		1978	1981	Apprentice	Wageningen (Holland)	22	9	8	2	6	4	2	0	0
Norris D	Dave	22/02/1981	Stamford		2001		Bolton Wanderers (loan)		3	0	0	0	0	1	0	0	0
Norton DW	David	03/03/1965	Cannock		1990	1993	Notts County	Northampton Town	149	0	7	7	9	5	1	0	1
Oakes A	Andy	11/01/1977	Crewe		1998		Winsford United	Derby County	19	0	0	0	1	0	0	0	0
O'Brien MT	Mick	10/08/1893	Kilcock	1940	1924	1925	Leicester City	Brooklyn Wan. (USA)	74	0	6	0	0	0	1	0	0
O'Connell P	Pat	1887	Dublin		1912	1913	Sheffield Wed.	Manchester United	58	0	5	0	0	1	0	0	0
O'Riley PJ	Paul	17/10/1950	Prescot		1968	1973	Apprentice	Barnsley	19	11	1	3	0	2	0	0	0
Ormondroyd I	Ian	22/09/1964	Bradford		1994		Leicester City (loan)		10	0	0	0	0	6	0	0	0
Ostemobor J	Jon	23/03/1983	Liverpool		2002		Liverpool (loan)		8	1	0	0	0	3	0	0	0
Owen G	Gordon	14/06/1959	Barnsley		1987		Bristol City (loan)		3	0	0	0	0	1	0	0	0
Owen GL	Griffith	28/07/1897	Liverpool		1924		Liverpool	Chester	2	0	0	0	0	0	0	0	0
Pace A	Arthur	1885	Newcastle	1968	1908	1909	Hebburn Argyle	Rotherham Town	5	0	0	0	25	0	0	0	0
					1915	1917	Worksop Town (Guest)										
Palin LG	Leigh	12/09/1965	Worcester		1989	1991	Stoke City	Released	57	0	3	4	3	7	0	0	1
Palmer CA	Charlie	10/07/1963	Aylesbury		1986	1988	Derby County	Notts County	69	1	3	3	2	1	0	0	0
Parker GS	Garry	07/09/1965	Oxford		1985	1987	Luton Town	Nottm. Forest	82	2	4	5	2	8	0	0	1
Parker WD	David	27/05/1915	Liverpool	1980	1937		Marine	Wolves	30	0	3	0	1	0	0	0	0
Parkinson KJ	Keith	28/01/1956	Preston		1981		Leeds United (loan)		0	1	0	0	0	0	0	0	0
Patterson GT	George	15/09/1924	Castleton, Yorkshire		1954	1955	Silksworth Juniors	Kings Lynn	7	0	0	0	0	1	0	0	0
Pattison JM	John	03/05/1889	Bedlington	1978	1912	1914	Bedlington Colliery	Scunthorpe Utd	48	0	3	0	46	0	0	0	0
Payton AP	Andy	23/10/1967	Burnley		1986	1991	YTS	Middlesbrough	116	27	8	11	3	55	0	2	0
Peach J	Jack	04/04/1923	Barnsley		1946	1947	Selby Town	QPR (trial)	19	0	4	0	0	2	1	0	0
Peacock RJ	Richard	29/10/1972	Sheffield		1993	1998	Sheffield FC	Lincoln City	144	30	8	15	6	21	1	2	0
Peacock T	Terry	18/04/1935	Hull		1955		Juniors (Hull)	QPR	2	0	0	0	0	0	0	0	0
Pearce TH	Herbert	1889	Bethnal Green	1961	1910	1911	Juniors (London)	Portsmouth	3	0	0	0	0	0	0	0	0
Pears J	Jack	23/02/1904	Ormskirk		1937		Swansea Town	Rochdale	30	0	3	0	2	8	3	0	0
Pearson F	Frank	18/05/1884	Manchester		1906		Chelsea	Luton Town	13	0	0	0	0	6	0	0	0
Pearson JS	John	01/09/1963	Sheffield		1991		Barnsley (loan)		15	0	0	0	2	0	0	0	1
Pearson L	Lawrie	02/07/1965	Wallsend		1984	1986	Gateshead	Bristol City	58	1	6	8	2	0	0	0	0
Pearson SJ	Stuart	21/06/1949	Hull		1969	1973	Juniors (E. Riding)	Manchester United	126	3	7	7	7	44	0	1	0
Peat N	Nathan	19/09/1982	Hull		2000	2004	YTS	York City	0	2	1	0	3	0	0	0	0
Perry J	Jason	02/04/1970	Caerphilly		1998	2000	Lincoln City	Newport County	14	1	2	0	4	0	0	0	0
Pettit RJ	Ray	11/12/1946	Hull		1966	1971	Apprentice	Barnsley	78	1	1	4	0	0	0	0	0
Petty BJ	Ben	22/03/1977	Solihull		2001	2002	Stoke Ciity	Stafford Rangers	24	5	2	2	3	0	0	0	0
Phillips E	Ernie	29/11/1923	North Shields		1951	1953	Manchester City	York City	42	0	3	0	0	0	0	0	0
Phillips T	Trevor	18/09/1952	Rotherham		1979		Rotherham United	Chester	22	0	0	2	0	3	0	0	0
Philpott L	Lee	21/02/1970	Barnet		2000	2002	Lincoln City	Weymouth	45	9	2	1	3	2	0	0	0
Pinkerton H	Henry		Glasgow		1934		Juniors (Scotland)	Port Vale	2	0	0	0	0	1	0	0	0
Porteous T	Trevor	09/10/1933	Hull	1997	1951	1955	Juniors (Hull)	Stockport Co.	61	0	2	0	0	1	0	0	0
Potter CB	Cecil	14/11/1888	West Hoathly	1975	1919		Norwich City	Hartlepools United	10	0	0	0	22	0	0	0	7
Potts JF	Joe	25/02/1889	Newcastle		1912	1913	Ashington	Portsmouth	5	0	0	0	0	0	0	0	0
Price AJW	Billy	10/04/1917	Hadley	1995	1948		Reading	Bradford City	8	0	0	0	0	5	0	0	0
Price J	Jason	12/04/1977	Pontypridd		2003		Tranmere Rovers		35	25	3	2	2	11	1	0	1
Price M	Michael	29/04/1982	Wrexham		2001	2002	Everton	North Ferriby United	1	3	0	2	2	0	0	0	0
Price TD	Dudley 'Dug	17/11/1931	Swansea		1960	1962	Southend United	Bradford City	76	0	8	6	0	26	3	1	0
Prince A	Arthur	08/12/1902	Bucknall	1980	1928		Sheffield Wed.	Walsall	5	0	0	0	0	0	0	0	0
Quantick JH	John	06/07/1909	Cwm	1972	1933	1936	Dudley Town	Retired	88	0	2	0	0	1	0	0	0
Quigley MAJ	Mike	02/10/1970	Manchester		1995	1997	Manchester City	Altrincham	36	18	3	7	3	3	0	1	0
					1999		Altrincham	Bradford Park Avenue									
Rafferty R	Ron	06/05/1934	South Shields		1963	1964	Grimsby Town	Aldershot	16	0	0	0	0	6	0	0	0
Raisbeck A	Andrew		Scotland		1905	1906	Liverpool	(Canada)	47	0	7	0	0	5	1	0	0
Raleigh S	Simeon	1909	Rotherham	1934	1930	1931	Huddersfield T	Gillingham	31	0	2	0	0	21	0	0	0
Ranby S	Sam	1897	Hull	1958	1920		Juniors (E. Riding)	Released	1	0	0	0	0	0	0	0	0
Reagan CM	Martin	12/05/1924	York		1946	1947	York City	Middlesbrough	18	0	4	0	0	1	2	0	0
Reddy M	Michael	24/03/1980	Kilkenny		2001		Sunderland (loan)		1	4	0	0	0	4	0	0	0
Reeves ML	Martin	07/09/1981	Birmingham		2002		Leicester City (loan)		5	3	0	0	0	1	0	0	0
Regan CA	Carl	09/09/1980	Liverpool		2002	2003	Barnsley	Droylsden	33	5	1	1	1	0	0	0	0
Revie DG	Don	10/07/1927	Middlesbrough	1989	1949	1951	Leicester City	Manchester City	76	0	6	0	0	12	1	0	0
Richards SC	Steve	24/10/1961	Dundee		1979	1982	Apprentice	Grantham Town	55	3	4	3	5	2	0	0	0
Richardson G	George	12/12/1912	Worksop	1968	1938	1947	Sheffield United	Bangor City	36	0	5	0	10	15	4	0	0
Richardson GEH	George	04/12/1891	Seaham Harbour	1969	1923	1925	Huddersfield T	Bradford City	40	0	6	0	0	2	0	0	0
Ring MP	Mike	13/02/1961	Brighton		1984	1985	Brighton & H.A.	Aldershot	17	7	4	4	2	2	1	1	0
Rintanen M	Mauno	28/04/1925	Finland		1956		HJK (Helsinki)	Released	4	0	0	0	0	0	0	0	0
Rioch GJ	Greg	24/06/1975	Sutton Coldfield		1996	1998	Peterborough United	Macclesfield	86	5	5	7	3	6	1	3	0

Name		D.O.B	Place of Birth	Died	First Season	Last Season	Previous Club	Next Club	Appearances					Goals			
									L.Full	L.Sub	FAC	FLC	Oth.	Lge	FAC	FLC	Oth.
Roberts DF	David	26/01/1949	Southampton		1974	1977	Oxford United	Cardiff City	86	0	3	5	4	4	0	0	0
Roberts GW	Gareth	15/11/1960	Hull		1978	1990	Apprentice	Released	409	5	28	24	21	47	5	2	5
Roberts JD	Dale	08/10/1956	Newcastle	2003	1979	1984	Ipswich Town	North Ferriby Utd	149	4	10	8	11	6	0	1	0
Roberts JG	John	11/09/1946	Abercynon		1980		Wrexham	Oswestry	26	0	3	2	0	1	0	0	0
Roberts N	Neil	07/04/1978	Wrexham		2001		Wigan Athletic (loan)		3	3	0	0	0	0	0	0	0
Robertson LV	Len	01/03/1916	Middlesbrough	1979	1946	1947	Watford	Accrington Stanley	9	0	0	0	0	2	0	0	0
Robinson C	Charles	20/08/1905	Rotherham	1972	1937	1938	Plymouth Argyle	Released	68	0	6	0	4	4	0	0	0
Robinson J	Joe	04/03/1919	Morpeth	1991	1948	1952	Blackpool	Wisbech T (p/m)	70	0	7	0	0	0	0	0	0
Robinson WS	William	01/01/1880	Prescot	1926	1905	1908	Manchester City	Bolton Wanderers	119	0	12	0	0	6	1	0	0
Robson CL	Leslie	01/11/1931	South Shields		1951		Juniors (Hull)	Darlington	3	0	0	0	0	1	0	0	0
Robson JC	Jack	24/03/1906	Birtley	1966	1924		Juniors (N. East)	Reading	1	0	0	0	0	0	0	0	0
Robson W	William		West Stanley		1910	1911	Hebburn Argyle	Released	8	0	0	0	0	0	0	0	0
Rocastle DC	David	02/05/1967	Lewisham	2001	1997		Chelsea (loan)		10	0	0	1	0	1	0	0	0
Rodgers A	Arthur	08/02/1907	Frickley		1928	1932	Denaby United	Doncaster Rovers	67	0	3	0	0	0	0	0	0
Roughley E	Ed	1880	Prescot	1948	1906	1911	St Helens Rec.	Chesterfield Town	157	0	9	0	0	0	0	0	0
Round LF	Len	21/05/1928	Wallheath		1957		Ayr United	Sittingbourne	17	0	0	0	0	0	0	0	0
Rowe R	Rodney	30/07/1975	Huddersfield		2000	2001	Gillingham	Wakefield & Emley	19	16	0	1	2	8	0	0	0
Rumney J	John	01/05/1898	Dipton	1969	1922	1923	Preston Colliery	Chesterfield	13	0	0	0	0	4	0	0	0
Rushton G	George	07/10/1880	Stoke-on-Trent	1964	1905	1906	Brighton & Hove Albion	Swindon Town	29	0	9	0	0	14	1	0	0
Russell S	Simon	19/03/1985	Hull		2002	2003	YTS	Kidderminster Harriers	0	1	0	0	1	0	0	0	0
Ryley HS	Henry	1894	Hull		1920		Barrow (On Trial)	Not offered contract	1	0	0	0	0	0	0	0	0
Salvidge GB	George	1912	Hull	1941	1938		Juniors (E. Riding)	Burton Town	4	0	0	0	0	1	0	0	0
Sansam C	Christian	26/12/1976	Hull		1996		Bradford City	Barton Town	2	1	1	0	1	0	0	0	0
Sargeant C	Charlie	02/02/1909	Cornsay	1988	1932	1933	Bristol City	Chester	60	0	6	0	0	16	2	0	0
Savage JA	John	14/12/1929	Bromley		1950		RAF	Halifax Town	4	0	0	0	0	0	0	0	0
Saville AV	Andy	12/12/1964	Hull		1983	1988	Apprentice	Walsall	77	27	5	6	6	18	1	1	0
					1998		Cardiff City (loan)										
Schofield J	Jon	09/03/1965	Barnsley		1999		Mansfield Town	Lincoln City	13	12	4	4	2	0	0	0	0
Scorer R	Bob	05/10/1898	Felling	1971	1921	1922	Juniors (N. East)	Bristol Rovers	5	0	0	0	0	0	0	0	0
Scott H	Henry	04/08/1897	Newburn		1926	1927	Wolves	Bradford P.A.	29	0	5	0	0	8	2	0	0
Seddon FO	Frank	01/05/1928	Stockton		1949		Notts County	Halifax Town	3	0	0	0	0	0	0	0	0
Sergeaunt TH	Harry		Newcastle		1920	1921	Felling Colliery	Brighton & Hove A.	19	0	5	0	0	8	1	0	0
Sewell J	Jackie	24/01/1927	Kells, Whitehaven		1959	1960	Aston Villa	Lusaka City (Zambia)	44	0	5	1	0	8	1	0	0
Sharman SJ	Sam	07/11/1977	Hull		1996		Sheffield Wed.	Gainsboro' Trinity	2	2	0	0	0	0	0	0	0
Sharp A	Alex		Dundee		1935		Blackburn Rovers	Raith Rovers	18	0	1	0	0	4	0	0	0
Sharpe LT	Len	29/11/1932	Scunthorpe		1962	1965	Scunthorpe United	Goole Town	58	0	7	6	0	4	0	0	0
Shaw A	Alan	09/10/1943	Preston		1961	1963	Preston NE	Goole Town	15	0	3	0	0	1	1	0	0
Shaw FE	Frederick	1891	Newcastle		1911	1912	Wallsend	Portsmouth	9	0	0	0	0	1	0	0	0
Shaw JF	Joe	1882	Durham		1907	1908	Sunderland	Grimsby Town	46	0	2	0	0	20	2	0	0
Shaw RE	Richard	11/09/1968	Brentford		1989		Crystal Palace (loan)		4	0	0	0	0	0	0	0	0
Sheen J	John	30/08/1920	Airdrie	1997	1946		Sheffield United	Kettering Town	5	0	0	0	0	1	0	0	0
Shelton T	Tom	1907	Nottingham		1931	1933	Juniors (Mansfield)	Released	5	0	0	0	0	1	0	0	0
Shepherd E	Ernie	14/08/1919	Wombwell		1948	1949	West Bromwich Albion	QPR	15	0	0	0	0	3	0	0	0
Sherwood CH	Clifford	1914	Wolverhampton		1938		Wolves	Released	4	0	0	0	0	0	0	0	0
Shiner RAJ	Roy	15/11/1924	Seaview, Isle of Wi	1988	1959		Sheffield Wed.	Cheltenham Town	22	0	1	0	0	8	0	0	0
Shotton M	Malcolm	16/02/1957	Newcastle		1989	1991	Barnsley	Ayr United	58	1	4	2	2	2	0	0	0
Simmon H	Harry	1879	Bearpark	1951	1905	1907	Leadgate Park Col.	Retired	17	0	1	0	11	0	0	0	2
Simms S	Sydney		West Yorkshire		1934		West Bromwich Albion	Scarborough	3	0	0	0	0	0	0	0	0
Simpkin CJ	Chris	24/04/1944	Hull		1962	1971	Apprentice	Blackpool	284	1	18	9	2	19	1	1	0
Skipper PD	Peter	11/04/1958	Hull		1978	1979	Juniors (Hull)	Darlington	286	2	17	16	17	19	1	1	0
					1982	1988	Darlington	Oldham Athletic									
Slater H	Harold	1900	Bradford		1921	1922	Harrogate	Castleford Town	3	0	0	0	0	0	0	0	0
Smales K	Ken	03/05/1932	Hull		1956		Juniors (Hull)	Scarborough	1	0	0	0	0	0	0	0	0
Smith A	Alan				1946		Juniors (Hull)	Released	1	0	0	0	0	0	0	0	0
Smith D	Dennis	22/08/1925	Nelson		1956	1959	Frickley Colliery	Accrington Stanley	15	0	0	0	0	0	0	0	0
Smith EA	Edwin	1884	Birmingham		1946		Brierley Hill Alliance	Crystal Palace	9	0	0	0	0	0	0	0	0
Smith EC	Colin	03/03/1936	Doncaster		1910	1911	Juniors (Hull)	Rotherham United	65	0	1	0	0	39	0	0	0
Smith FA	Fred	14/02/1926	Aberdeen		1949	1950	Aberdeen	Sheffield United	17	0	0	0	0	1	0	0	0
Smith HR	Ray	13/09/1934	Hull		1954	1955	Juniors (Hull)	Peterborough United	23	0	0	0	0	2	0	0	0
Smith I	Ian		Langley Park		1920		Juniors (Hull)	Released	1	0	0	0	0	0	0	0	0
Smith J	John	1886	Wardley		1905	1910	Hebburn Argyle	Sheffield United	156	0	12	0	0	98	4	0	0
Smith JE	Joe 'Stanle	1886	West Stanley	1916	1905	1911	West Stanley	Everton	213	0	18	0	34	46	6	0	4
					1916	1917	Bury (Guest)										
Smith MK	Mike	19/12/1968	Hull		1988	1990	YTS	Ayr Utd	14	5	0	1	0	1	0	0	0
Smith S	Shaun	09/04/1971	Leeds		2002	2003	Crewe Alexandra	Rochdale	17	5	1	1	1	1	0	0	0
Smith SJW	Sam	07/09/1904	Stafford	1988	1928		Port Vale	Millwall	14	0	0	0	0	2	0	0	0
Smith TP	Thomas Pott	??/07/1901	Newcastle	1978	1923		Merthyr Town	Hartlepools Utd	8	0	0	0	0	2	0	0	0
Smith W	Wally	1883	Allerton	1917	1908	1911	Leicester Fosse	Worksop Town	91	0	6	0	0	32	0	0	0
Sneekes R	Richard	30/10/6/	Amsterdam		2001		Stockport Co.	Released	17	5	1	0	2	0	0	0	0
Speed F	Fred	1909	Newcastle		1930	1933	Newark Town	York City	49	0	3	0	0	15	3	0	0
Spence G	George	1876	Rothesay		1905		Southampton	Clyde	19	0	4	0	0	2	2	0	0
Spendiff MN	Martin	24/06/1880	North Shields	1943	1905	1907	Grimsby Town	Bradford City	104	0	11	0	0	0	0	0	0
Spivey R	Dick	18/08/1916	Hull	1973	1934	1936	Juniors (Hull)	Torquay United	21	0	0	0	17	5	0	0	2
					1939	1940	Southport (Guest)										
Staniforth G	Gordon	23/03/1957	Hull		1973	1976	Apprentice	York City	7	5	0	0	0	2	0	0	0
Stansfield J	Jack	14/07/1896	Bradford	1980	1921		Castleford Town	Castleford Town	12	0	0	0	0	1	0	0	0
Starling RW	Ronnie	11/10/1909	Pelaw	1991	1927	1929	Washington Colliery	Newcastle United	78	0	8	0	0	13	1	0	0
Stephens WJ	Johnny	26/06/1935	Cardiff	1992	1952	1957	Juniors (Cardiff)	Swindon Town	94	0	9	0	0	20	2	0	0
Stephenson W	William	1888	Whitburn		1907	1909	Whitburn FC	Tottenham Hotspur	64	0	2	0	0	0	0	0	0
					1919		Tottenham H	Hartlepools United									
Stevens S	Sammy	18/11/1890	Netherton		1911	1919	Cradley Heath	Notts County	150	0	11	0	30	84	9	0	23
Stewart DC	Dave	20/05/1958	Belfast		1974	1978	Bangor City	Chelsea	46	5	3	5	4	7	0	0	0
Stockdale RK	Robbie	30/11/1979	Middlesbrough		2004		Rotherham United		12	2	0	0	0	0	0	0	0
Stocks JR	Joe	27/11/1941	Hull		1959	1960	Juniors (Hull)	Millwall	9	0	1	0	0	1	0	0	0
Stoddart GG	George		Fife		1920		Raith Rovers	Released	7	0	0	0	0	0	0	0	0
Stoker G	Gareth	22/02/1973	Bishop Auckland		1991	1992	YTS (Leeds United)	Hereford United	24	6	3	3	2	2	0	0	0
Stokes A	Archer	1920	West Ella		1938		Juniors (Hull)	Released	1	0	0	0	0	0	0	0	0

Name		D.O.B	Place of Birth	Died	First Season	Last Season	Previous Club	Next Club	L.Full	L.Sub	FAC	FLC	Oth.	Lge	FAC	FLC	Oth.
Storey E	Ernest	1888	Birtley		1908		Juniors (N. East)	Spennymoor United	3	0	0	0	0	0	0	0	0
Stott GRB	George	31/01/1906	North Shields	1963	1932		Bradford City	Released	4	0	0	0	0	0	0	0	0
Stowe DD	Dean	27/03/1975	Burnley		1992		YTS	Released	0	1	0	0	0	0	0	0	0
Strong G	Greg	05/09/1975	Bolton		2002	2003	Motherwell	Boston United	3	0	0	0	2	0	0	0	0
Sullivan C	Con	06/06/1903	Tynemouth		1926	1928	Newburn	Bradford P.A.	65	0	5	0	0	3	0	0	0
Summers GTF	Gerry	04/10/1933	Birmingham		1963	1965	Sheffield United	Walsall	59	0	3	3	0	1	1	0	0
Sunley D	David	06/02/1952	Skelton		1975	1977	Sheffield Wed.	Lincoln City	58	11	3	5	6	11	0	0	0
Surrey TH	Thomas	31/10/1907	Gateshead	1976	1929		Scotswood	Released	1	0	0	0	0	0	0	0	0
Swales SC	Steve	26/12/1973	Whitby		1998	2000	Reading	Halifax Town	57	11	1	5	3	0	0	0	0
Swan CS	Chris	04/12/1900	Byker	1979	1925	1928	Stockport Co.	Crystal Palace	73	0	4	0	0	8	0	0	0
Swan MMG	Maurice	27/09/1938	Drumcondra, Dublin		1963	1967	Cardiff City	Dundalk	103	0	14	5	0	0	0	0	0
Swan PH	Peter	28/09/1966	Leeds		1988	1990	Leeds United	Port Vale	76	4	2	5	1	24	0	1	0
Swann G	Gary	11/04/1962	York		1980	1986	Apprentice	Preston NE	176	10	11	10	13	9	1	0	0
Tabram WD	William	19/01/1909	Swansea	1992	1934	1936	Port Vale	South Shields	106	0	3	0	1	5	0	0	0
Tait MP	Mick	30/09/1956	Wallsend		1979		Carlisle United	Portsmouth	29	4	1	0	0	3	1	0	0
Tait P	Paul	24/10/1974	Newcastle		2001		Crewe Alexandra (loan)		0	2	0	0	0	0	0	0	0
Tarrant JE	Ted	12/02/1932	Stainforth		1950	1953	Juniors (Doncaster)	Walsall	30	0	0	0	0	2	0	0	0
Taylor AD	Alan	14/11/1953	Hinckley		1983		Vancouver Whitecaps	Burnley	13	1	0	0	6	3	0	0	4
Taylor AM	Arthur 'Archie	07/11/1939	Dunscroft		1962		Goole Town	Halifax Town	1	0	0	0	0	0	0	0	0
Taylor J	Jock		Scotland	1916	1947	1949	Parkhead FC	Gillingham	72	0	14	0	0	0	0	0	0
Taylor, John	John	15/02/1914	Barnsley	1978	1907	1908	Norwich City	Weymouth	9	0	0	0	0	3	0	0	0
Taylor W	Billy	05/06/1898	Langley Green		1926	1930	Aberdare Ath.	Norwich City	152	0	13	0	0	17	1	0	0
Taylor-Fletcher G	Gary	04/06/1981	Liverpool		2000		Northwich Victoria (loan)		1	4	0	0	0	0	0	0	0
Teasdale T	Tom				1946		Trialist	Released	1	0	0	0	0	0	0	0	0
Teece DA	David	01/09/1927	Middleton, Manchester		1953	1955	Hyde United	Oldham Athletic	25	0	0	0	0	0	0	0	0
Temple GA	Arthur	1887	Newcastle	1959	1907	1913	Wallsend Park Villa	Blyth Spartans	173	0	11	0	0	77	4	0	0
Terry SG	Steve	14/06/1962	Clapton		1988	1989	Watford	Northampton Town	62	0	1	4	2	4	0	0	0
Thelwell A	Alton	05/09/1980	Islington		2003		Tottenham Hotspur		24	5	0	1	1	1	0	0	0
Thom A	Alec	10/10/1894	Androssan	1973	1922	1925	Airdrieonians	Swindon Town	131	0	9	0	0	18	0	0	0
Thomas AC	Alf	1895	Hetton-le-Hole		1923	1924	Merthyr Town	South Shields	36	0	2	0	0	4	0	0	0
Thomas DG	Gwyn	26/09/1957	Swansea		1989	1990	Barnsley	Carlisle United	21	1	0	1	0	0	0	0	0
Thompson D	Denis	10/04/1924	Whitburn		1946	1947	Whitburn Welfare	South Shields	9	0	0	0	0	8	0	0	0
Thompson JWJ	Jimmy	19/04/1898	West Ham	1984	1931		Fulham	Tunbridge Wells Rgs	1	0	0	0	0	0	0	0	0
Thompson LA	Les	23/09/1968	Cleethorpes		1987	1990	YTS	Maidstone United	31	4	1	3	1	4	0	0	0
Thompson N	Neil	02/10/1963	Beverley		1981	1982	Nottm. Forest	Scarborough	29	2	0	0	3	0	0	0	0
Thomson RW	Bob	24/10/1905	Falkirk		1934		Newcastle United	Racing Club de Paris	4	0	0	0	0	0	0	0	0
Thomson S	Scott	08/11/1966	Edinburgh		1997		Raith Rovers	Airdrieonians	9	0	0	3	0	0	0	0	0
Thorley E	Ernest 'Cliff	12/11/1909	West Melton		1934	1935	Sunderland	Kidderminster Harriers	34	0	2	0	0	5	0	0	0
Thornton W	Billy	1883	West Yorkshire	1966	1903		Doncaster Rovers	Denaby Utd	1	0	1	0	0	0	0	0	0
Todd PR	Paul	08/05/1920	Middlesbrough		1951	1952	Blackburn Rovers	Kings Lynn	27	0	3	0	0	3	0	0	0
Toward AV	Alf	1882	Castleside	1962	1908	1909	Leadgate Park Col.	Oldham Athletic	10	0	0	0	0	6	0	0	0
Townend HV	Vincent	1889	Selby	1958	1909	1911	Selby Town	Goole Town	12	0	0	0	0	1	0	0	0
Treanor JL	Jim	11/10/1913	Heap	1966	1936	1938	Accrington Stanley	Released	44	0	1	0	1	1	0	0	0
Trevitt S	Simon	20/12/1967	Dewsbury		1995	1997	Huddersfield T	Guiseley	50	1	0	3	1	1	0	0	0
Tucker DC	Dexter	22/09/1979	Pontefract		1997		YTS	Gainsborough Trinity	1	6	0	0	0	0	0	0	0
Tulloch R	Ron	15/07/1932	South Africa		1954		S. African Football	S. African Football	3	0	0	0	0	0	0	0	0
Turner A	Bert	03/09/1907	Sheffield		1928	1930	Denaby United	Walsall	19	0	0	0	0	2	0	0	0
Turner H	Henry		Wallsend		1914		Wallsend Elm Villa	Released	6	0	0	0	0	3	0	0	0
Turner RF	Bobby	14/02/1910	Leicester	1978	1931		Cockfield	Southport	1	0	0	0	0	0	0	0	0
Turner RP	Robbie	18/09/1966	Littlethorpe		1996		Cambridge United (loan)		5	0	0	0	0	2	0	0	0
Van Blerk J	Jason	16/03/1968	Sydney (Aus)		2001		Stockport County	Shrewsbury Town	10	0	0	0	0	1	0	0	0
Varney J	John	27/11/1929	Oxford		1950		Oxford City	Lincoln City	9	0	1	0	0	0	0	0	0
Vickers J	Jack	07/08/1908	Auckland Park	1980	1928		Bishop Auckland	Darlington	2	0	0	0	0	0	0	0	0
Wadsworth EA	Eric	1894	Goole		1919		Juniors (Yorkshire)	Hornsea Town	1	0	0	0	0	0	0	0	0
Wagstaff K	Ken	24/11/1942	Langwith		1964	1975	Mansfield Town	George Cross (Aus)	374	4	29	19	8	173	14	6	4
Wainscoat WR	Russell	28/07/1898	Maltby	1967	1931	1933	Leeds United	Retired	79	0	6	0	0	42	8	0	0
Waites P	Paul	24/01/1971	Hull		1989	1990	YTS	North Ferriby	11	0	1	0	1	0	0	0	1
Walden G	George	1889	London		1909		Juniors (London)	Rotherham Town	2	0	0	0	0	1	0	0	0
Walker JW	William	1889	High Spen		1923		Langly Park FC	Leadgate Park FC	5	0	0	0	0	1	0	0	0
Wallace RG	Ray	02/10/1969	Lewisham		1994		Stoke City (loan)		7	0	0	0	0	0	0	0	0
Walmsley DG	David	23/11/1972	Hull		1990	1991	YTS	Guiseley	5	5	2	2	1	4	0	0	0
Walsh JA	Jimmy	15/05/1901	Stockport	1971	1925	1930	Liverpool	Colwyn Bay	82	0	7	0	0	9	0	0	0
Walters J	Jon	20/09/1983	Birkenhead		2002		Bolton Wanderers (loan)										
					2003	2004	Bolton Wanderers	Wrexham	20	28	2	1	1	7	1	0	0
Walters PL	Peter	08/06/1952	Whickham		1970	1971	Juniors (N. East)	Corby Town	2	0	0	0	0	0	0	0	0
Warboys A	Alan	18/04/1949	Goldthorpe		1977	1978	Fulham	Doncaster Rovers	44	5	1	0	0	9	0	0	0
Warren LA	Lee	28/02/1969	Manchester		1988	1993	Rochdale	Doncaster Rovers	141	12	6	8	5	1	0	0	1
Wassell KD	Kim	09/06/1957	Wolverhampton		1983		Australia	Bradford City (N/C)	1	0	0	0	0	0	0	0	0
Watson AE	Arthur	12/07/1913	South Hiendley	1995	1946		Chesterfield	Retired	35	0	5	0	25	2	0	0	0
Watson JI	John		Aberdeen		1927	1930	Aberdeen Richmond	Suspended Sine Die	47	0	1	0	0	0	0	0	0
Watson TR	Tommy	29/09/1969	Liverpool		1995		Grimsby Town (loan)		4	0	0	0	1	0	0	0	0
Wealands JA	Jeff	26/08/1951	Darlington		1971	1978	Darlington	Birmingham City	240	0	11	19	12	0	0	0	0
Weaver S	Sam	08/02/1909	Pilsley	1985	1928	1929	Sutton Town	Newcastle United	48	0	2	0	0	5	0	0	0
Webb D	Daniel	02/07/1983	Poole		2002	2003	Southend United	Cambridge United	4	12	0	0	2	0	0	0	1
Weldon A	Tony	12/11/1900	Croy, Glasgow		1930		Everton	West Ham United	31	0	1	0	0	6	0	0	0
West H	Henry		Hull		1906		Armed Services	Juniors (E. Riding)	1	0	0	0	0	0	0	0	0
Wharton PW	Paul	26/06/1977	Newcastle		1995	1997	YTS (Leeds United)	Farsley Celtic	8	3	0	0	0	0	0	0	0
Wheeler P	Paul	03/01/1965	Caerphilly		1989		Cardiff City	Hereford United	0	5	0	0	0	0	0	0	0
White K	Ken	15/03/1922	Selby		1948		Selby Town	Scarborough	1	0	0	0	0	0	0	0	0
White WW	Willie	26/07/1907	Kirkcaldy		1938		Lincoln City	Released	2	0	0	0	0	0	0	0	0
Whitehurst W	Billy	10/06/1959	Thurnscoe		1980	1985	Mexborough Town	Newcastle United	212	17	14	12	16	52	5	6	6
					1988	1989	Sunderland	Sheffield United									
Whitmore TE	Theodore	05/08/1972	Montego Bay (Jam)		1999	2001	Seba United (Jam)	Seba United (Jam)	63	14	8	3	1	9	0	1	1
Whitnall B	Brian	25/05/1933	Doncaster		1954		Juniors (Doncaster)	Scunthorpe United	2	0	0	0	0	0	0	0	0
Whitney JD	Jon	23/12/1970	Nantwich		1998	2000	Lincoln City	Kings Lynn	54	3	2	2	6	3	0	0	0
Whittle JP	Justin	18/03/1971	Derby		1998	2003	Stoke City	Grimsby Town	184	9	10	9	7	2	0	0	1
Whitworth GH	George	14/07/1896	Northampton		1925	1927	Sheffield Wed.	Peterboro' & Flett. U	67	0	5	0	0	31	1	0	0

Name		D.O.B	Place of Birth	Died	First Season	Last Season	Previous Club	Next Club	Appearances					Goals			
									L.Full	L.Sub	FAC	FLC	Oth.	Lge	FAC	FLC	Oth.
Whitworth NA	Neil	12/04/1972	Ince		1998	1999	Kilmarnock	Exeter City	18	1	1	4	0	2	0	0	0
Wicks M	Matthew	08/09/1978	Reading		2001	2002	Brighton & Hove Albion	Released	14	0	0	0	0	0	0	0	0
Wienand G	George 'Toll	27/04/1910	East London, SA		1938		Huddersfield T	Returned To S. Africa	15	0	0	0	0	3	0	0	0
Wigglesworth A	Arthur	26/10/1891	Hull	1974	1919		Goole Town	Doncaster Rovers	7	0	0	0	101	0	0	0	0
Wilbraham AT	Aaron	21/10/1979	Knutsford		2004		Stockport County	Milton Keynes Dons	10	9	1	0	0	2	0	0	0
Wilcox R	Russell	25/03/1964	Hemsworth		1990	1992	Northampton Town	Doncaster Rovers	92	8	5	5	6	7	1	0	0
Wilkinson GJ	Graham	21/10/1934	Hull		1958	1959	Juniors (Hull)	Bridlington Trinity	3	0	0	0	0	0	0	0	0
Wilkinson IJ	Ian	19/09/1977	Ferriby		1995		YTS	Released	8	0	0	0	0	1	0	0	0
Wilkinson J	Jack	13/06/1902	Wath-on-Dearne	1969	1936		Sunderland	Scunthorpe Utd	17	0	1	0	0	2	0	0	0
Wilkinson NF	Norman	16/02/1931	Alnwick		1953		(RAF)	York City	8	0	0	0	0	3	0	0	0
Wilkinson T	Thomas	08/02/1904	Felling		1924	1925	Juniors (Co Durham)	Chester-le-Street	4	0	0	0	0	2	0	0	0
Wilkinson W	Billy	24/03/1943	Stockton	1996	1962	1972	Stockton	Rotherham United	208	15	17	10	2	34	5	2	0
Williams A	Andy	29/07/1962	Birmingham		1995		Rotherham United	Scarborough	33	1	1	2	2	0	0	0	0
Williams E	Emlyn		1903	Aberaman		1929		Clapton Orient	Merthyr Town	1	0	0	0	0	0	0	0	0
Williams GJ	Gareth	12/03/1967	Newport (IOW)		1992		Barnsley (loan)		56	2	1	2	2	4	0	0	1
					1993		Barnsley (loan)										
					1998	1999	Scarborough	Scarborough									
Williams MJ	Mike	23/10/1944	Hull		1962	1965	Apprentice	Aldershot	88	0	6	6	0	0	0	0	0
Williams NJF	Neil	23/10/1964	Waltham Abbey		1984	1987	Watford	Preston NE	75	16	7	7	8	9	1	0	0
Williams RN	Ryan	31/08/1978	Mansfield		2001	2003	Chesterfield	Bristol Rovers	40	12	3	1	6	2	0	0	1
Wilson D	David 'Soldie		1884	Hebburn	1906	1905		Heart of Midlothian	Leeds City	10	0	2	0	0	3	2	0	0
Wilson GG	Gordon	19/06/1904	West Auckland	1947	1925	1930	Scotswood	Luton Town	28	0	0	0	0	1	0	0	0
Wilson H	Henry		1896	Belfast		1920		Glenavon	Charlton Ath.	30	0	5	0	0	2	3	0	0
Wilson SL	Steve	24/04/1974	Hull		1990	2000	YTS	Macclesfield Town	180	1	13	13	12	0	0	0	0
Wilson T	Tom	29/11/1940	Rosewell		1967	1969	Millwall	Goole Town	60	0	5	1	0	1	0	0	0
Windass D	Dean	01/04/1969	Hull		1991	1995	North Ferriby United	Aberdeen	173	3	6	11	12	57	0	4	3
Wiseman S	Scott	09/10/1985	Hull		2003		YTS		2	3	1	0	1	0	0	0	0
Wood AEH	Alf	25/10/1945	Macclesfield		1974	1976	Millwall	Middlesbrough	51	2	5	3	5	10	2	2	0
Wood J	Jamie	21/09/1978	Salford		1999	2000	Manchester United	Halifax Town	15	32	5	5	3	6	1	0	0
Wood JL	James	15/01/1901	Byker	1982	1922		Methley	Released	2	0	1	0	0	2	0	0	0
Woodhead C	Cliff	17/08/1908	Darfield		1930	1938	Denaby United	Goole Town	305	0	18	0	52	0	0	0	0
Woof W	Billy	16/08/1956	Gateshead		1982		Gateshead	Gateshead	9	2	0	0	0	3	0	0	0
Wrack C	Charlie	28/12/1899	Boston	1979	1931		Grimsby Town	Boston FC	3	0	1	0	0	0	0	0	0
Wright D	Dave	05/10/1905	Kirkcaldy	1955	1934		Liverpool	Bradford P.A.	32	0	1	0	0	11	0	0	0
Wright EGD	Gordon	03/10/1884	Earlsfield Green	1947	1905	1912	Corinthians	Emigrated to S. Africa	152	0	16	0	0	14	0	0	0
Wright F	Fred		1908	Ruddington		1930		Grantham Town	Released	2	0	0	0	0	0	0	0	0
Wright GA	George	04/02/1920	Sheffield		1946		Cardiff City	Released	4	0	0	0	0	1	0	0	0
Wright IM	Ian	10/03/1972	Lichfield		1996	1997	Bristol Rovers	Hereford Utd	65	8	4	7	3	2	0	1	1
Wright JB	John	16/11/1922	South Shields		1947		Tyne Dock United	Dartford	1	0	1	0	0	0	0	0	0
Wright TJ	Tommy	29/08/1963	Belfast		1990		Newcastle United (loan)		6	0	0	0	0	0	0	0	0
Wright WJ	William 'Tir		1891	Patrington	1951	1908	1920	Withernsea	Retired	153	0	13	0	78	5	0	0	15
Wyper HTH	Tommy	08/10/1900	Calton, Coatbridge		1926	1927	Accrington Stanley	Arsenal	40	0	0	0	0	2	0	0	0
Yorke RJ	Bob			Dunfermline		1935		Dundee United	Dundee United	9	0	0	0	1	0	0	0	0
Young R	Ron	31/08/1945	Gateshead		1964	1967	Juniors (N.East)	Hartlepool United	24	2	1	1	0	5	0	0	0
Young SR	Stuart	16/12/1972	Hull		1991	1992	(YTS) Arsenal	Northampton Town	11	8	2	1	2	2	0	1	0

Played in FA Cup only:

Name		D.O.B	Place of Birth	Died	First Season	Last Season	Previous Club	Next Club	L.Full	L.Sub	FAC	FLC	Oth.	Lge	FAC	FLC	Oth.
Brooks G	George				1905		Juniors (Hull)	Juniors (Hull)	0	0	1	0	0	0	0	0	0
Carney M	Matthew				1905		East Yorkshire Regt.	Amateur	0	0	1	0	0	0	0	0	0
Cook GW	George				1905		Juniors (Hull)	Amateur	0	0	1	0	0	0	0	0	0
Leiper J	Joe				1904		Motherwell	Aberdare	0	0	2	0	0	0	0	0	0
Pridmore L	Lee	23/04/1978	Rotherham		1995		YTS	Released	0	0	1	0	0	0	0	0	0
Mackrill OW	Oscar				1904		Juniors (Hull)	Amateur	0	0	1	0	0	0	1	0	0
Whitehouse J	James				1904		Third Lanark	Southend United	0	0	2	0	0	0	0	0	0
Wilkinson H	Harry				1904		Manchester United	West Ham	0	0	2	0	0	0	0	0	0
Wolfe F	Fred				1904		Everton	Chelsea	0	0	2	0	0	0	0	0	0

Played in FL Cup and miscellaneous games only

Name		D.O.B	Place of Birth	Died	First Season	Last Season	Previous Club	Next Club	L.Full	L.Sub	FAC	FLC	Oth.	Lge	FAC	FLC	Oth.
Blackburn P	Paul	31/08/1954	Lowestoft		1983		Goole Town (loan)		0	0	0	0	1	0	0	0	0
Chapman L	Liam	17/01/1984	Leeds		2002		YTS	Released	0	0	0	0	1	0	0	0	0
Clubley TR	Ray				1938		Junior Football (Hull)	Junior Football (Hull)	0	0	0	0	2	0	0	0	0
Cockin N	Neil	6/09/1965	North Ferriby		1983		Apprentice	North Ferriby United	0	0	0	1	1	0	0	0	0
Curnow J	Jack	31/10/1910	Lingdale		1939	1944	Tranmere Rovers	Tranmere Rovers	0	0	0	0	55	0	0	0	0
Gilmore HP	Patrick'Mik		1913	Hartlepool		1939	1944	Queen's Park Rangers	Released	0	0	0	0	26	0	0	0	0
Heard J	Jamie	11/08/1983	Sheffield		2002		YTS	Chester City	0	0	0	0	1	0	0	0	0
Hopkin M	Matthew	17/10/1974	Hull		1993		YTS	North Ferriby United	0	0	0	1	0	0	0	0	0
Kerr S	Scott	11/12/1981	Leeds		2002		Bradford City	Scarborough	0	0	0	0	1	0	0	0	0
Olsson P	Paul	24/12/1965	Hull		1983		Apprentice	Exeter City	0	0	0	0	1	0	0	0	1
Smith TF	Thomas		Luncarty		1939		Dundee	Released	0	0	0	0	24	0	0	0	0

Played in abandoned 1939/40 season only

Name		D.O.B	Place of Birth	Died	First Season	Last Season	Previous Club	Next Club									
Lowe RE	Richard	13/07/1915	Cannock		1939		Sheffield United										
Quigley D	Dennis	7/12/1913	St Andrews	1983	1939		Grimsby Town										

Statistical Sections ~ Key and Notes:

Who's Who Section (sheets 1 to 11)

Every player to have played a first team competitive match (from the 1905/06 season to the 2004/05 season) is included, but excluding War-time games and Guest players. All details are complete where known : Surname (with full initials) and given name and/or name most commonly known by; Date (D.O.B.) and place of Birth, plus year of death; the debut season and final season played for Hull City follows, where the year represents the first part of the season (e.g. 1961 = 1961/62 season) - a blank second column for recent seasons indicates the player may still be registered with the club; 'L.Full' refers to the total number of full (or starting) League appearances made for the club, similarly those where appearances as a used substitute are shown ('L.Sub') - in other competitions, the totals are for full and, where used, substitute appearances.

Match Statistics (Reference match statistical section from page 166, also page 163)

All matches (Football League, Friendly matches for the 1904/05 season, principal cup competitions and War-time competitive games) from the club's formation (1904) to the end of the 2004/05 season are included, with line-ups and numbers (see below).

Key: First column shows the (League or Friendly) match number or cup round, e.g. R3 = third round, rep = replay, 1R/2 = 1st leg second round, FN1 = Final - North Section - 1st leg, etc. Second column shows the date of the match. Third column shows the opponents; upper case (capitals) indicates a home match and lower case an away match. Fourth column was the match result (Hull City score first). Fifth column contains the names of the goalscorers and number of goals scored; an own goal is indicated by the goalscorer's name and suffixed (og). The sixth column provides the official or (previous to the 1925/26 season when official attendances were not published) the approximate or generally reported attendance. The players grid that follows shows the shirt number the player wore, or for pre-War matches they relate to the normal position/numbering convention, e.g. 1 = goalkeeper, 3 = left back, 7 = right wing, 10 = inside left, etc. and similar positioning of players/ shirt numbers are used for later seasons (for the most recent seasons this method is continued rather than showing the actual squad numbered shirt worn). Players substituted are underlined, with the substitutes used shown as numbers 12 to 15. Any other notes are self-explanatory.

Players: World War One

Surname	Forename	Date of Birth	Birthplace	Previous Club	Apps	Goals
Adams P*	Peter		Hull	Junior Football (Hull)	1	0
Ainsworth J*	John			Bradford City	2	0
Atkinson W*	William			Goole Town	1	0
Bell A*	Albert			Junior Football (Lancashire)	1	0
Bradbury J*	John			Birmingham	17	4
Brennan T*	Thomas	1890	Cobridge	Portsmouth	1	0
Brown D*	David			Junior Football (Hull)	2	2
Brown J*	John			Bradford City	1	0
Brown W*	William			Goole Town	1	0
Burton E	Edmund	1893	Dunston	Wolverhampton Wanderers	1	1
Chaplin G*	George	26/9/1897	Dundee	Rotherham City	15	0
Charles F*	Frederick			Sunderland	1	0
Christmass J*	John			Junior Football (Hull)	7	4
Coddington AS*	Arthur			Rochdale	1	0
Cookson S*	Samuel	22/11/1896	Manchester	Manchester City	5	3
Crowther H*	Harold			Luton Town	1	0
Cutts E	Ernest			Darlington	2	0
Dick HW*	Harold			Newcastle Utd	1	0
Elvin R*	Robert			Sunderland	2	0
Fairclough S*	Stanley			Derby County	1	0
Fearnley E*	Ernest			Bradford PA	1	0
Ford B*	Bert				30	2
Foss F				Northampton Town	2	0
Gillett JT*	John			Notts County	1	0
Goodfellow S*	Stanley			Bradford PA	3	0
Gordon E	Edward			Junior Football (Hull)	1	0
Grimshaw W*	William	1890	Burnley	Bradford City	18	6
Harrison J	Jack			Junior Football (Hull)	1	0
Hartnell S*	Samuel			Derby County	2	1
Harvey A*				Birmingham	1	1
Hawksworth E*	Ernest	6/12/1894	Rochdale	Bradford PA	1	0
Hawley				Junior Football (Merseyside)	1	0
Haywood				Stockport County	1	0
Higgins A*	Alexander	4/11/1885	Kilmarnock	Newcastle Utd	6	3
Hobson B*	Bert	1890	Tow Law	Sunderland	3	0
Hopkins V*	Victor			Junior Football (Hull)	2	0
Howie D*	David	15/7/1886	Galston	Bradford PA	1	0
Hudson T	Tom			Junior Football (Hull)	1	0
Iremonger A*	Albert	15/7/1884	Wilford	Notts County	1	0
Isherwood R	Robert			Skelmersdale Utd	6	0
Jordan				Prescott Athletic	1	0
Leigh AS*	Sydney	1893	Shardlaw	Goole Town	8	2
Lindley J*	John				1	0
Little TSC	Thomas	27/2/1890	Ilford	Blackheath Town	1	0
Machin E*	Edward				2	0
Malkinson T*	Thomas			Ayr Utd	1	0
Martin H*	Harold			Stalybridge Celtic	2	0
Matthews J*	Jack			Bradford City	1	0
McCourty W*				Preston North End	1	0
McManus T*	Thomas			Worksop Town	9	2
Meynell T*	Thomas			Bradford PA	1	0
Milner A*	Arthur			Bedlington Terriers	1	0

Players: World War Two

Surname	Forename	Date of Birth	Birthplace	Previous Club	Apps	Goals
Adams CL*	Charles			Junior Football (Hull)	3	0
Anderson N*	Norman			Goole Town	0	0
Archer JW*	John	24/07/2008	Wednesbury	Plymouth Argyle	5	0
Armeson LR*	Raymond	28/02/2017	Rotherham	Coventry City	7	1
Beardshaw EC*	Colin	26/11/2012	Crowcroak	Bradford City	14	0
Beeson GW*	William	31/08/2006	Clay Cross	Walsall	20	1
Bircham B*	Bernard	31/08/2024	Philadelphia	Sunderland	1	0
Bradley GJ*	George	07/01/2017	Maltby	Newcastle Utd	11	0
Brailsford T*	Thomas				1	1
Bratley GW*	George	17/01/2009	Rotherham	Rotherham Utd	12	1
Bratton W*	William			Junior Football (Hull)	1	0
Brewer C*	Cyril			Services	3	0
Brown G*	George			Junior Football (Hull)	1	0
Bunting A*	Alan			Birmingham	1	0
Butcher R*	Reginald	13/02/2016	Prescot	Chester	2	0
Clark SD*	Sydney				1	0
Collier T*	Thomas			Halifax Town	5	0
Cottam A*	Alfred			Lincoln City	2	0
Crawford E*	Edmund	31/10/2006	Filey	Clapton Orient	1	0
Crofts EW*	Ernest			Junior Football (Nottm)	2	0
Dawson D	Daniel			Queen of the South	9	3
Dickinson P*	Peter			Junior Football (Hull)	4	0
Dixon JT*	Thomas	10/12/2023	Hebburn-on-Tyne	Aston Villa	1	1
Dowling JR*	Joseph			Services	1	0
Drummond A*	Andrew			Junior Football (Scotland)	1	0
Dyer HR*	Herbert	27/11/2017	Filey	Scarborough	1	0
Eatherington HA*	Harold				2	1
Finch EAR*	Ernest	31/08/2008	Cannock	West Bromwich Albion	3	2
Flinton W*	Walter			Scarborough	16	3
French JL*	John			Junior Football (Hull)	1	0
Galloway A*	Andrew				1	0
Glaister G*	George	15/05/2018	Newcastle	Blackburn Rovers	18	6
Gobey E*	Ernest				1	0
Greaves SW*	William			Junior Football (W. Riding)	1	0
Green R*	Reginald				1	0
Harnby DR*	Donald	20/07/2023	Darlington	Newcastle Utd	1	0
Harris JB*	James			West Ham Utd	34	1
Harvey GK*	George			Junior Football (Hull)	6	0
Heelbeck LW*	Leslie	05/07/2009	Scarborough	Scarborough	3	0
Herdman H*	Henry			Rotherham Utd	1	0
Hewick AE*	Alfred			Services	5	0
Hollis H*	Harold	12/12/2013	Shotton	Chester	8	0
Hope C*	Charles				1	0
Howe LF*	Leslie	04/03/2012	Bengeo	Tottenham Hotspur	9	5
Hutchinson JA*	James	28/12/2015	Sheffield	Sheffield Utd	1	0
Johnson HM*	Herbert				1	1
Johnson J*	Joseph	16/05/2016	South Kirkby	Southport	9	0
Johnson K*					1	0
Jones JT*	John	25/11/2016	Holywell	Northampton Town	1	0
Kingwell LE*	Leonard	31/05/2018	Rosyth	Torquay Utd	2	0
Lamb G*	George			Gateshead	2	0
Landles JAS*	John				1	0

Surname	Forename	Date of Birth	Birthplace	Previous Club	Apps	Goals
Naismith E*				Sheffield Wednesday	3	1
Nevin J*	John	20/2/1886	Lintz	Ayr Utd	14	0
Newton A*	Albert	13/3/1894	Barnsley	Grimsby Town	2	1
Norton H*	Horace			Norwich City	1	0
Osborn F*	Frederick	10/11/1889	Leicester	Bradford PA	14	7
Parr J	Joseph			Junior Football (Edinburgh)	1	0
Peach R*				Bradford PA	1	0
Pepper H*	Harold				1	0
Percival C*	Charles			Grimsby Town	11	3
Priestley J*	Joseph			Junior Football (Hull)	1	0
Rentoul R*	Robert			Junior Football (Hull)	1	1
Riley H	Henry			Leadgate Park Colliery	1	2
Robinson A*					1	0
Saunders J				Junior Football (Hull)	5	2
Shaw P*				Birmingham	8	2
Sheridan J	James			West Stanley	72	2
Simpson A*	Albert				2	0
Slide R	Robert			Cradley Heath	20	7
Smith F*					1	0
Stables A*	Arthur			Aston Villa	1	0
Stevenson T*	Thomas			Bradford PA	1	0
Suddes F*	Frederick			Junior Football (Hull)	5	1
Summers J*	Joseph			Sheffield Wednesday	1	0
Thistleton M*	Mark			Huddersfield Town	3	1
Thorpe T*	Tom	19/5/1881	Attercliffe	Junior Football (Ireland)	1	0
Tickle J*				Junior Football (Hull)	1	0
Veale W*	Walter				1	0
Voase FN	Frank			Junior Football (London)	5	0
Walden H*	Harold	10/10/1889	Manchester	Junior Football (Hull)	25	11
Wale L*	Leslie			Goole Town	2	0
Walters H*				Leicester Fosse	3	0
Wheeldon J*				Derby County	1	0
Whitfield N	Norman	3/4/1896	Prudhoe	Goole Town	3	0
Whittingham H*	Harold			Bradford City	2	0
Wilde R*	Robert		Shipley	Bradford City	2	0
Wilson A*				Notts County	2	0
Woodland A*	Arthur	1889	Liverpool	Birmingham	1	0
Wootton J*	James			Junior Football (Hull)	1	0
Wright J	James			Junior Football (E. Riding)	1	0
Young RT*	Robert	18/2/1894	Brandon	Sunderland	1	0
Totals					**399**	**72**

Surname	Forename	Date of Birth	Birthplace	Previous Club	Apps	Goals
Lucas WH*	William	15/01/2018	Newport	Swindon Town	6	0
McCurdie J*	James			Junior Football (Glasgow)	1	0
McDowell C*	Charles			Services	5	4
Meese AE*	Albert			Junior Football (Yorks)	1	0
Miller D*	David	21/01/2021	Middlesbrough	Middlesborough	16	0
Moore TR*	Roy	18/12/2023	Grimsby	Grimsby Town	1	0
Neary J*	John	14/12/2015	Chorlton	Rochdale	3	0
Porteous JW*				Heart of Midlothian	1	0
Prescott J*	John			Everton	4	0
Prescott JR	John	29/11/2019	Waterloo	Cardiff City	21	16
Pritchard TH*	Thomas				1	0
Raynor G*	George	13/01/2007	Hoyland	Aldershot	1	0
Read S*	Stanley				1	0
Reeve EP*	Eric			Junior Football (Hull)	2	0
Rhodes B*	Brian			Junior Football (Hull)	1	0
Richardson D*	David	08/03/2016	Bishop Burton	Bradford City	2	0
Richardson EW*	Ernest			Aldershot	9	1
Riches W*	William			Junior Football (Hull)	3	0
Robinson J	John	01/04/2013	Leeds	Sheffield Utd	46	0
Rogers W*	William	3/7/1919?	Ulverston	Blackburn Rovers?	1	0
Ross AC*	Albert	09/10/2016	York	Chester	16	0
Rothery H*	Harold			Bournemouth & BA	3	1
Sargent FA*	Frederick	07/03/2012	Islington	Tottenham Hotspur	2	2
Selby WA*	William			Junior Football (Hull)	1	0
Shepherd G*	George			Sheffield Utd	1	0
Sherwood GW*	George	14/03/2017	Selby	Stockport County	7	0
Singleton EA*	Edward	27/11/2019	Hackney	Southend Utd	1	0
Skidmore W*	William	15/03/2025	Barnsley	Wolverhampton Wan	1	0
Smith J*	John				1	1
Smith KR*	Kenneth			Junior Football (E. Riding)	1	1
Spencer E*	Ernest			Services	1	1
Stephenson JE*	Eric	9.1914	Bexleyheath	Leeds Utd	1	0
Stokes E*	Ernest	16/01/2016	West Ella	Southend Utd	10	0
Stone J*	John			Sheffield Utd	6	0
Sullivan MJ*	Maurice	1915	Newport	Mansfield Town	1	0
Sykes H*	Harold				1	1
Symons J	John			Junior Football (Hull)	12	0
Talbot FL*	Leslie	03/08/2010	Hednesford	Cardiff City	7	3
Thomas RW*	Ronald			Services	8	0
Twells D*	Donald			St Mirren	7	0
Vaughan E*	Edward			Junior Football (N. East)	9	1
Vaux E*	Edward	02/09/2016	Goole	Chelsea	2	0
Walker F*	Frederick			Sheffield Wednesday	1	0
Walker FA*	Frederick				3	0
Ward TEG*	Thomas	28/04/2014	Chatham	Mansfield Town	1	0
Waters D*	Dennis			Junior Football (Hull)	1	0
Whitchurch S*	Stanley				4	0
White LS*	Lionel			Junior Football (Hull)	3	0
Wilkinson N*	Norman			Stoke City	1	0
Wilson DM*	David			Junior Football (Scotland)	2	0
Woods C	Cyril	1915	Tinsley	Hartlepools Utd	4	1
Young H*	Harold			Goole Town	1	0
Totals					**486**	**60**

These two lists contain details of players who played for City in the War competitions only. Details of those players who represented the Tigers in peacetime as well as WW1 or WW2 are shown within the Players Section - the appearances are in the Other Competitons category. Those players who were Guests from other clubs are identified by an *

Football League: Seasonal ever-present and leading goalscorers

Season	League Ever-present	Apps	Leading Goalscorer	Goals
1904-05			G. Rushton	29
1905-06	D. Gordon; A. Raisbeck; M. Spendiff	38	P. Howe; J.E. Smith* (16)	12
1906-07	G. Browell; G. Hedley	38	J. Smith	19
1907-08	J.E. Smith; A. Temple	38	J. Smith***	31
1908-09			A. Temple	17
1909-10	A. Browell; E. Roughley	38	J. Smith***	32
1910-11	E. Roughley		T. Browell	16
1911-12			T. Browell; A. Temple	16
1912-13	N. Hendry; J. McQuillan	38	S. Fazackerley	19
1913-14	N. Hendry; S. Stevens	38	S. Stevens	26
1914-15	D. Mercer; W. Wright	38	S. Stevens	24
1915-16 to 1918-19: WORLD WAR ONE				
1919-20			S. Stevens	18
1920-21	W. Mercer	42	C. Flood; H. Sergeaunt* (9)	8
1921-22	W. Mercer	42	C. Flood	17
1922-23	J. Crawford	42	G. Martin	12
1923-24			B. Mills	11
1924-25	T. Bleakley	42	B. Mills	25
1925-26	G. Maddison	42	B. Mills	17
1926-27	G. Martin; W. Taylor	42	G. Whitworth	16
1927-28			G. Martin; A. Nelson	8
1928-29			K. McDonald	23
1929-30			S. Alexander	14
1930-31			S. Alexander	24
1931-32			D. Duncan	19
1932-33	C. Woodhead		W. McNaughton***	41
1933-34	G. Maddison; W. McNaughton	42	W. McNaughton	15
1934-35			A. Duncan	12
1935-36			J. Aquroff	13
1936-37	W. Annables; G. Maddison	42	C. Hubbard	15
1937-38	J. Blyth	42	J. Fryer; H. McNeill* (25)	23
1938-39	A. Cunliffe; D. Davies	42	A. Cunliffe	20
1939-40 to 1945-46: WORLD WAR TWO				
1946-47			B. Lester	15
1947-48			N. Moore	13
1948-49	K. Harrison	42	N. Moore	22
1949-50			H. Carter	16
1950-51	K. Harrison	42	A. Ackerman	21
1951-52	V. Jensen	42	S. Gerrie	24
1952-53	D. Durham; V. Jensen	42	S. Gerrie	13
1953-54			A. Ackerman	17
1954-55			A. Ackerman; R. Crosbie	11
1955-56	A. Davidson	42	W. Bradbury	9
1956-57	J. Stephens	46	W. Bradbury; D. Clarke* (20)	18
1957-58	W. Bradbury; D. Clarke; A. Davidson	46	W. Bradbury	19
1958-59			W. Bradbury	30
1959-60	B. Bulless; A. Davidson	42	R. Shiner	8
1960-61	A. Davidson	46	C. Chilton	19
1961-62	D. Clarke	46	J. McSeveney	14
1962-63	A. Davidson; E. McMillan	46	J. McSeveney	22
1963-64	A. Davidson	46	C. Chilton	22
1964-65	A. Davidson; J. McSeveney	46	C. Chilton	27
1965-66	M. Milner; C. Simpkin; K. Wagstaff	46	K. Wagstaff	27

Seasonal Club Officials

Season	Chairman	Manager	Captain
1904-05	W. Gilyott	J Ramster*	G. Spence
1905-06	A.D. Smith	A. Langley	A. Langley
1906-07	A.D. Smith	A. Langley	E.G.D. Wright
1907-08	A.D. Smith	A. Langley	E.G.D. Wright
1908-09	A.D. Smith	A. Langley	E.G.D. Wright
1909-10	A.D. Smith	A. Langley	E.G.D. Wright
1910-11	A.D. Smith	A. Langley	E.G.D. Wright
1911-12	A.D. Smith	A. Langley	E.G.D. Wright
1912-13	J. Spring	H. Chapman	E.G.D. Wright
1913-14	J. Spring	H. Chapman	D. Gordon
1914-15	J. Spring	F. Stringer	J. Edelston
1915-16 TO 1918-19: WORLD WAR ONE			
1919-20	J. Spring	D.L. Menzies	J. Edelston
1920-21	J. Spring	D.L. Menzies	M. Gilhooley
1921-22	J. Spring	H.P. Lewis	M. Gilhooley
1922-23	J. Spring	W. McCracken	M. Bell
1923-24	J. Spring	W. McCracken	M. Bell
1924-25	J. Spring	W. McCracken	M. Bell
1925-26	J. Spring	W. McCracken	M. Bell
1926-27	Dr. D.C. Pullan	W. McCracken	M. Bell
1927-28	Dr. D.C. Pullan	W. McCracken	M. Bell
1928-29	Dr. D.C. Pullan	W. McCracken	M. Bell
1929-30	Dr. D.C. Pullan	W. McCracken	M. Bell
1930-31	J.W. Barraclough	H. Green	M. Bell
1931-32	J.W. Barraclough	H. Green	W. Newton
1932-33	J.W. Barraclough	H. Green	J. Hill
1933-34	J.W. Barraclough	J. Hill	J. Hill
1934-35	J.W. Barraclough	J. Hill	D. Wright
1935-36	J.W. Barraclough	D.L. Menzies	K. Cameron
1936-37	J.W. Barraclough	E. Blackburn	C. Woodhead
1937-38	J.W. Barraclough	E. Blackburn	C. Woodhead
1938-39	Ald. A. Shepherd	E. Blackburn	C. Woodhead
1939-40 TO 1945-46: WORLD WAR TWO			
1946-47	H. Needler	Maj. F. Buckley	J. Mills
1947-48	H. Needler	Maj. F. Buckley; H.S. Carter	J. Taylor
1948-49	H. Needler	H.S. Carter	H.S. Carter
1949-50	H. Needler	H.S. Carter	H.S. Carter
1950-51	H. Needler	H.S. Carter	H.S. Carter
1951-52	H. Needler	H.S. Carter	H.S. Carter; W. Harris
1952-53	H. Needler	R. Jackson	E. Phillips
1953-54	H. Needler	R. Jackson	T. Berry
1954-55	H. Needler	R. Jackson	N. Franklin
1955-56	H. Needler	B. Brocklebank	T. Berry
1956-57	H. Needler	B. Brocklebank	T. Berry
1957-58	H. Needler	B. Brocklebank	W. Bradbury
1958-59	H. Needler	B. Brocklebank	P. Feasey
1959-60	H. Needler	B. Brocklebank	P. Feasey
1960-61	H. Needler	B. Brocklebank	A. Davidson
1961-62	H. Needler	C.S. Britton	A. Davidson
1962-63	H. Needler	C.S. Britton	A. Davidson
1963-64	H. Needler	C.S. Britton	A. Davidson

Season	League Ever-present	Apps	Leading Goalscorer	Goals
1966-67			K. Wagstaff	21
1967-68			K. Wagstaff	17
1968-69	I. McKechnie; C. Simpkin	42	K. Wagstaff	20
1969-70	I. McKechnie	42	C. Chilton; K. Wagstaff	18
1970-71			C. Chilton	21
1971-72			S. Pearson	15
1972-73	F. Banks; J. McGill	42	S. Pearson	17
1973-74	S. Deere; R. Greenwood;	42	S. Pearson	11
1974-75			K. Wagstaff	10
1975-76	J. Wealands	42	R. Greenwood; A. Wood* (10)	6
1976-77	P. Haigh; J. Wealands	42	P. Daniel; J. Hemmerman; D. Sunley* (7)	6
1977-78			A. Warboys	7
1978-79	B. Bannister; K. Edwards; G. Nisbet	46	K. Edwards	24
1979-80	G. Nisbet	46	K. Edwards	19
1980-81			K. Edwards	13
1981-82			L. Mutrie	27
1982-83	P. Skipper	46	B. Marwood	19
1983-84	R. McNeil; A. Norman; P. Skipper	46	B. Marwood	16
1984-85	W. Askew; A. Norman; P. Skipper	46	W. Whitehurst	20
1985-86	F. Bunn; A. Norman; S. McEwan	42	F. Bunn	14
1986-87	A. Norman	42	A. Saville	9
1987-88	R. Jobson; A. Norman; G. Roberts	44	G. Parker, A. Dyer* (9)	8
1988-89	R. Jobson	46	K. Edwards**	26
1989-90	W. Jacobs	46	A. Payton	17
1990-91			A. Payton	25
1991-92			G. Atkinson; L. Jenkinson* (9)	8
1992-93	G. Atkinson	46	D. Windass	7
1993-94			D. Windass	23
1994-95			D. Windass	17
1995-96			R. Peacock	7
1996-97			D. Darby	13
1997-98			D. Darby	13
1998-99			D. Brown	11
1999-00			J. Eyre	8
2000-01			R. Rowe	6
2001-02			G. Alexander	17
2002-03			S. Elliott	12
2003-04	D. Delaney	46	B. Burgess	18
2004-05			S. Elliott	27

* Denotes those players who were joint top scorers in the League, but who took top spot in the club's scoring list by virtue of Cup goals scored. The total for the season is shown in brackets.

** Leading goalscorer for the division.

*** Leading goalscorer in the Football League

Season	Chairman	Manager	Captain
1964-65	H. Needler	C.S. Britton	A. Davidson
1965-66	H. Needler	C.S. Britton	A. Davidson
1966-67	H. Needler	C.S. Britton	A. Davidson
1967-68	H. Needler	C.S. Britton	C. Chilton
1968-69	H. Needler	C.S. Britton	C. Chilton
1969-70	H. Needler	C.S. Britton	C. Chilton
1970-71	H. Needler	W.T.J. Neill	W.T.J. Neill
1971-72	H. Needler	W.T.J. Neill	K. Knighton
1972-73	H. Needler	W.T.J. Neill	K. Knighton
1973-74	H. Needler	W.T.J. Neill	J. Kaye; J. McGill
1974-75	H. Needler	W.T.J. Neill; J. Kaye	D.Burnett
1975-76	G.H.C. Needler	J. Kaye	D. Roberts
1976-77	G.H.C. Needler	J. Kaye	W. Bremner
1977-78	G.H.C. Needler; R.E. Chapman	J. Kaye; R. Collins; K. Houghton	W. Bremner
1978-79	R.E. Chapman	K. Houghton	S. Croft
1979-80	R.E. Chapman	K. Houghton; M. Smith	G. Nisbet
1980-81	R.E. Chapman	M. Smith	M. Horswill
1981-82	G.H.C. Needler	M. Smith	G. Roberts
1982-83	D. Robinson	C. Appleton	G. Roberts
1983-84	D. Robinson	C. Appleton	G. Roberts
1984-85	D. Robinson	B. Horton	G. Roberts
1985-86	D. Robinson	B. Horton	G. Roberts
1986-87	D. Robinson	B. Horton	G. Roberts
1987-88	D. Robinson	B. Horton	G. Roberts
1988-89	D. Robinson	E. Gray	R. Jobson; P. Skipper
1989-90	D. Robinson; R. Chetham	C. Appleton; S. Ternent	S. Terry; G. Roberts
1990-91	R. Chetham	S. Ternent; T. Dolan	I. Hesford; M. Shotton
1991-92	M.W. Fish	T. Dolan	R. Wilcox
1992-93	M.W. Fish	T. Dolan	D. Norton
1993-94	M.W. Fish	T. Dolan	D. Norton; G. Abbott
1994-95	M.W. Fish	T. Dolan	G. Abbott; R. Dewhurst
1995-96	M.W. Fish	T. Dolan	G. Abbott
1996-97	M.W. Fish	T. Dolan	W. Joyce
1997-98	T. Wilby; D. Lloyd	M. Hateley	G. Rioch; W. Joyce
1998-99	D. Lloyd; T.E. Belton	M. Hateley; W. Joyce	D. D'Auria
1999-00	N. Buchanan	W. Joyce; B. Little	J. Whittle
2000-01	N. Buchanan; A. Pearson	B. Little	J. Whittle
2001-02	A. Pearson	B. Little; J. Molby	J. Whittle
2002-03	A. Pearson	J. Molby; P. Taylor	J. Whittle; I. Ashbee
2003-04	A. Pearson	P. Taylor	I. Ashbee
2004-05	A. Pearson	P. Taylor	I. Ashbee

Tiger Internationals

The following players have all represented their country at various levels whilst also playing for Hull City.

The figures in brackets after their name indicates the number of appearances made. * against the result indicates that the player scored in the game.

Player	Country	Level	Opponents	Date	Venue	F	A
Edgar Ainsworth (2)	England	Am.	Wales	21/01/1933	Torquay	1	0
		Am.	Ireland	18/02/1933	Belfast	3	4
Gerry Bowler (3)	Northern Ireland	Full	Scotland	01/10/1949	Belfast	2	8
		Full	England	16/11/1949	Manchester	2	9
		Full	Wales	08/03/1950	Wrexham	0	0
Peter Daniel (7)	England	U.21	Scotland	27/04/1977	Sheffield	1	0
		U.21	Finland	26/05/1977	Helsinki	1	0
		U.21	Norway	01/06/1977	Bergen	2	1
		U.21	Finland	12/10/1977	Hull	8	1
		U.21	Italy	05/04/1978	Rome	0	0
		U.21	Yugoslavia	19/04/1978	Novi Sad	1	2
		U.21	Yugoslavia	02/05/1978	Manchester	1	1
Ken DeMange (3)	Republic of Ireland	Full	Tunisia	19/10/1988	Dublin	4	0
		U.23	Northern Ireland	11/04/1989	Dublin	3	0
		'B'	England	27/03/1990	Cork	4	2
Stuart Elliott (15)	Northern Ireland	Full	Finland	12/02/2003	Belfast	0	1
		Full	Armenia	29/03/2003	Yerevan	0	1
		'B'	Scotland	21/05/2003	Partick	1	2
		Full	Italy	03/06/2003	Campobass	0	2
		Full	Greece	11/10/2003	Athens	0	1
		Full	Barbados	30/05/2004	Bridgetown	1	1
		Full	St Kitts & Nevis	02/06/2004		2	0
		Full	Trinidad & Tobago	06/06/2004	Barolet, Tobago	3	0
		Full	Switzerland	18/08/2004	Zurich	0	0
		Full	Poland	04/09/2004	Belfast	0	3
		Full	Azerbaijan	09/10/2004	Baku	0	0
		Full	Austria	13/10/2004	Belfast	3	3
		Full	England	26/03/2005	Manchester	0	4
		Full	Poland	30/03/2005	Warsaw	0	1
		Full	Germany	04/06/2005	Belfast	1	4
Alan Fettis (15)	Northern Ireland	Full	Denmark	13/11/1991	Odense	1	2
		Full	Lithuania	28/04/1992	Belfast	2	2
		Full	Denmark	18/11/1992	Belfast	0	1
		'B'	England	10/05/1994	Hillsborough, Sheffield	2	4
		Full	Mexico	11/06/1994	Miami	0	3
		Full	Portugal	07/09/1994	Belfast	1	2
		'B'	Scotland	21/02/1995	Edinburgh	0	3
		Full	Rep of Ireland	29/03/1995	Dublin	1	1
		Full	Latvia	26/04/1995	Riga	1	0
		Full	Canada	22/05/1995	Edmonton	0	2
		Full	Chile	25/05/1995	Edmonton	1	2
		Full	Latvia	07/06/1995	Belfast	1	2
		Full	Portugal	03/09/1995	Porto	1	1
		Full	Liechtenstein	11/10/1995	Eschen	4	0
		Full	Austria	15/11/1995	Belfast	5	3
Mick Gilhooley (1)	Scotland	Full	Wales	04/02/1922	Wrexham	1	2
Ian Goodison (26)	Jamaica	Full	Cayman Islands	24/10/1999	Cayman Island	4	1
		Ful	Uruguay	14/01/2000	Guangshou, China	0	2
		Full	New Zealand	16/01/2000	Guangshou, China	2	1
		Full	Cayman Islands	09/02/2000	Cayman Island	1	0
		Full	Colombia	12/02/2000	Miami, USA	0	1
		Full	Honduras	14/02/2000	Miami, USA	0	2
		Full	Panama	08/05/2000	Kingston, Jamaica	0	1
		Full	Colombia	27/05/2000	East Rutherford, USA	0	3
		Full	Cuba	02/07/2000	Kingston, Jamaica	1	1
		Full	Barbados	05/07/2000	Kingston, Jamaica	5	0
		Full	Trinidad & Tobago	08/07/2000	Trinidad	4	2
		Full	St. Vincent	16/07/2000	St. Vincent	1	0
		Full	Honduras	23/07/2000	Kingston, Jamaica	3	1
		Full	El Salvador	16/08/2000	Kingston, Jamaica	1	0
		Full	St. Vincent	03/09/2000	Kingston, Jamaica	2	0
		Full	Honduras	08/10/2000	Honduras	0	1
		Full	El Salvador	15/11/2000	San Salvador	0	2
		Full	Bolivia	26/01/2001	Miami, USA	3	0
		Full	Bulgaria	28/01/2001	Kingston, Jamaica	0	0
		Full	Trinidad & Tobago	28/02/2001	Kingston, Jamaica	1	0
		Full	Mexico	25/03/2001	Mexico City	0	4
		Full	Honduras	25/04/2001	Kingston, Jamaica	1	1
		Full	Cuba	10/06/2001	Kingston, Jamaica	4	1
		Full	USA	16/06/2001	Kingston, Jamaica	0	0
		Full	Costa Rica	20/06/2001	San Jose, Costa Rica	1	2
		Full	Trinidad & Tobago	30/06/2001	Port of Spain, Trinidad	2	1

Player	Country	Level	Opponents	Date	Venue	F	A
Bill Gowdy (1)	Northern Ireland	Full	Scotland	19/09/1931	Glasgow	1	3
Paul Haigh (1)	England	U.21	Norway	01/06/1977	Bergen	2	1
Bill Halligan (2)	Ireland	Full	Scotland	22/03/1919	Glasgow	1	2
		Full	Scotland	19/04/1919	Belfast	0	0
Alan Jarvis (3)	Wales	Full	Scotland	22/10/1966	Cardiff	1	1
		Full	England	16/11/1966	Wembley	1	5
		Full	Northern Ireland	12/04/1967	Belfast	0	0
Julian Johnsson (3)	Faroe Islands	Full	Yugoslavia	15/08/2001	Belgrade, Yugoslavia	0	2
		Full	Luxembourg	01/09/2001	Totfir, Fl	1	0
		Full	Russia	05/09/2001	Torshavn, Fl	0	3
Danny McKinney (1)	Northern Ireland	Full	Scotland	26/02/1921	Belfast	0	2
Terry Neill (15)	Northern Ireland	Full	Spain	11/11/1970	Seville	0	3
		Full	Cyprus	03/02/1971	Nicosia	3	0
		Full	Soviet Union (USSR)	22/09/1971	Moscow	0	2
		Full	Soviet Union (USSR)	13/10/1971	Belfast	1	1
		Full	Spain	16/02/1972	Hull	1	1
		Full	Scotland	20/05/1972	Glasgow	0	2
		Full	England	23/05/1972	Wembley	1	0
		Full	Wales	27/05/1972	Wrexham	0	0
		Full	Bulgaria	18/10/1972	Sofia	0	3
		Full	Cyprus	14/02/1973	Nicosia	0	1
		Full	Portugal	28/03/1973	Coventry	1	1
		Full	Cyprus	08/05/1973	Fulham	3	0
		Full	England	12/05/1973	Liverpool	1	2
		Full	Scotland	16/05/1973	Glasgow	2	1
		Full	Wales	19/05/1973	Liverpool	0	1
Tony Norman (5)	Wales	Full	Rep of Ireland	26/03/1986	Dublin	1	0
		Full	Uruguay	21/04/1986	Cardiff	0	0
		Full	Canada	10/05/1986	Toronto	0	2
		Full	Malta	01/06/1988	Valletta	3	2
		Full	Italy	05/06/1988	Brescia	1	0
Mick O'Brien (4)	Northern Ireland	Full	England	22/10/1924	Liverpool	1	3
		Full	Scotland	28/02/1925	Belfast	0	3
		Full	Wales	18/04/1925	Wrexham	0	0
		Full	Wales	13/02/1926	Belfast	3	0
Patsy O'Connell (3)	Ireland	Full	Wales	19/01/1914	Wrexham	2	1
		Full	England	14/02/1914	Middlesborough	3	0
		Full	Scotland	14/03/1914	Belfast	1	1
Garry Parker (5)	England	U.21	Italy	09/04/1986	Pisa	0	2
		U.21	Italy	23/04/1986	Swindon	1	1
		U.21	Sweden	09/09/1986	Ostersund	1	1
		U.21	Yugoslavia	11/11/1986	Peterborough	1	1
		U.21	Spain	18/02/1987	Burgos	2	1
Michael Price (6)	Wales	U.21	Armenia	31/08/2001	Merthyr Tydfill, Wales	1	1
		U.21	Norway	04/09/2001	Dramimen, Norway	0	2
		U.21	Belarus	05/10/2001	Cardiff, Wales	1	2
		U.21	Azerbaijan	25/03/2002	Barry	1	0
		U.21	Finland	06/09/2002	Valkeakoski	1	2
		U.21	Azerbaijan	19/11/2002	Baku	1	0
Dave Roberts (11)	Wales	Full	Luxembourg	01/05/1975	Luxembourg	3	1
		Full	Northern Ireland	23/05/1975	Belfast	1	0
		Full	Scotland	06/05/1976	Glasgow	1	3
		Full	Northern Ireland	14/05/1976	Swansea	1	0
		Full	Yugoslavia	22/05/1976	Cardiff	1	1
		Full	England	31/05/1977	Wembley	1	0
		Full	Northern Ireland	03/06/1977	Belfast	1	1
		Full	Kuwait	06/09/1977	Wrexham	0	0
		Full	Kuwait	20/09/1977	Kuwait	0	0
		Full	Scotland	17/05/1978	Glasgow	1	1
		Full	Northern Ireland	19/05/1978	Wrexham	1	0
Johnny Stephens (1)	Wales	U.23	England	23/04/1958	Wrexham	2	1
Dave Stewart (1)	Northern Ireland	Full	Belgium	16/11/1977	Belfast	3	0

Player	Country	Level	Opponents	Date	Venue	F	A
Theodore Whitmore (28)	Jamaica	Full	Uruguay	14/01/2000	Guangshou, China	0	2
		Full	New Zealand	16/01/2000	Guangshou, China	2	1
		Full	Cayman Islands	09/02/2000	Cayman Island	1	0
		Full	Colombia	12/02/2000	Miami, USA	0	1
		Full	Honduras	14/02/2000	Miami, USA	0	2
		Full	Panama	08/05/2000	Kingston, Jamaica	0	1
		Full	Cuba	02/07/2000	Kingston, Jamaica	1	1
		Full	Barbados	05/07/2000	Kingston, Jamaica	5	0
		Full	Trinidad & Tobago	08/07/2000	Trinidad	4	2
		Full	St. Vincent	16/07/2000	St. Vincent	1	0
		Full	Honduras	23/07/2000	Kingston, Jamaica	3	1
		Full	El Salvador	16/08/2000	Kingston, Jamaica	1	0
		Full	St. Vincent	03/09/2000	Kingston, Jamaica	2	0
		Full	Honduras	08/10/2000	Honduras	0	1
		Full	El Salvador	15/11/2000	San Salvador	0	2
		Full	Bolivia	26/01/2001	Miami, USA	3	0
		Full	Trinidad & Tobago	28/02/2001	Kingston, Jamaica	1	0
		Full	Mexico	25/03/2001	Mexico City	0	4
		Full	Honduras	25/04/2001	Kingston, Jamaica	1	1
		Full	Martinique	15/05/2001	Arima, Trinidad	1	0
		Full	Trinidad & Tobago	17/05/2001	Port of Spain, Trinidad	1	2
		Full	Barbados	19/05/2001	Port of Spain, Trinidad	2	1
		Full	Cuba	10/06/2001	Kingston, Jamaica	4	1
		Full	USA	16/06/2001	Kingston, Jamaica	0	0
		Full	Costa Rica	20/06/2001	San Jose, Costa Rica	1	2
		Full	Mexico	02/09/2001	Kingston, Jamaica	1	2
		Full	Honduras	05/09/2001	Tegucigalpa, Honduras	0	1
		Full	USA	07/10/2001	Boston, USA	1	2

Player	Country	Level	Opponents	Date	Venue	F	A
Scott Wiseman (3)	England	U.20	Tunisia	02/06/2005	Toulon	2	0
		U.20	S. Korea	06/06/2005	La Seyne	3	3
		U.20	France	08/06/2005	Toulon	0	0
Jamie Wood (2)	Cayman Islands	Full	Cayman Islands	24/10/1999	Cayman Island	1	4
		Full	Cayman Islands	09/02/2000	Cayman Island	0	1
Gordon Wright (21)	England	Full	Wales	19/03/1906	Cardiff *	1	0
		Am.	Ireland	07/12/1907	Tottenham	6	1
		Am.	France	23/03/1908	Park Royal	12	0
		Am.	Holland	12/04/1909	Amsterdam	4	0
		Am.	Belgium	19/04/1909	Tottenham	11	2
		Am.	Switzerland	20/05/1909	Basle	9	0
		Am.	France	22/05/1909	Paris	11	0
		Am.	Sweden	06/11/1909	Hull	7	0
		Am.	Wales	19/02/1910	Huddersfield	6	0
		Am.	Wales	18/02/1911	Newtown	5	1
		Am.	Belgium	04/03/1911	Crystal Palace	4	0
		Am.	France	23/03/1911	Paris	3	0
		Am.	Germany	14/04/1911	Berlin	2	2
		Am.	Holland	17/04/1911	Amsterdam	1	0
		Am.	Denmark	21/10/1911	Park Royal	3	0
		Am.	Ireland	18/11/1911	Huddersfield	2	0
		Am.	Wales	17/02/1912	Bishop Auckland	3	0
		Am.	Holland	16/03/1912	Hull	4	0
		Am.	Belgium	08/04/1912	Brussels	2	1
		Am.	Finland	02/07/1912	Stockholm	4	0
		Am.	Belgium	09/11/1912	Swindon	4	0

*Although Gordon Wright was registered as a Hull City player with the Football League (the League records show this as taking place on 29th December 1905) his only Full international appearance (as above) is shown in the official FA records as being awarded whilst associated with Cambridge University.

Matches played on a neutral ground

All FA Cup ties involving Hull City. The name of the club hosting the game is shown in brackets:

1926-27	R4 rep2	Feb	7	Everton	Villa Park (Aston Villa)	3-2	Whitworth, Guyan, Martin	16,800
1929-30	SF	Mar	22	Arsenal	Elland Road (Leeds United)	2-0	Howieson, Duncan D	47,549
	SF Rep		26	Arsenal	Villa Park (Aston Villa)	0-1		46,200
1953-54	R3 rep2	Jan	18	Brentford	Belle Vue (Doncaster Rovers)	5-2	Horton (2), Crosbie (2), Ackerman	10,176
1960-61	R2 rep2	Dec	5	Darlington	Elland Road (Leeds United)	1-1	Price	9,801
	R2 rep3		12	Darlington	Belle Vue (Doncaster Rovers)	0-0		5,313
	R2 rep4		15	Darlington	Ayresome Park (Middlesbrough)	3-0	Clarke, Gubbins, King	19,366
1966-67	R3 rep2	Feb	6	Portsmouth	Highfield Road (Coventry City)	1-3	Chilton	18,448
1967-68	R3 rep2	Feb	7	Middlesbrough	Bootham Crescent (York City)	0-1		16,524
1974-75	R3 rep2	Jan	13	Fulham	Filbert Street (Leicester City)	0-1		4,929
1980-81	R2 rep2	Dec	22	Blyth Spartans	Elland Road (Leeds United)	2-1	Norrie, Croft	4,914
1981-82	R1 rep2	Nov	30	Rochdale	Elland Road (Leeds United)	1-0	McClaren	3,268

Abandoned Matches

1905-06	Nov	18	FA Cup	LEEDS CITY	0-0		Game abandoned after 50 minutes (Fog)
1906-07	Jan	17	FA Cup	TOTTENHAM HOTSPUR	0-0		Game abandoned after 100 minutes (Bad light)
1912-13	Jan	4	League	GLOSSOP	0-0		Game abandoned ater 75 minutes (Bad light)
1948/49	Aug	31	League	Oldham Athletic	1-0	Harrison	Game abandoned after 85 minutes (Bad Light)
1953-54	Jan	2	League	Bury	1-4	Ackerman	Game abandoned after 75 minutes (Fog)
1962-63	Jan	19	League	SWINDON TOWN	0-0		Game abandoned after 45 minutes (Snow & Frost)
1970-71	Feb	16	League	BLACKBURN ROVERS	2-0	Neill, Butler	Game abandoned after 45 minutes (Fog)
1993-94	Nov	13	FA Cup	Runcorn	1-0	Atkinson	Game abandoned after 29 minutes (wall collapsed)

Season	Div.	P	HOME					AWAY					TOTAL						Lge Pos	FAC Rd	FLC Rd	Agg Home Attendance	Avg Home Attendance
			W	D	L	F	A	W	D	L	F	A	W	D	L	F	A	Pts	Pos	Rd	Rd		
1905-06	2	38	10	5	4	38	21	9	1	9	29	33	19	6	13	67	54	44	5	1	-	227,645	6,500
1906-07	2	38	11	2	6	41	20	4	5	10	24	37	15	7	16	65	57	37	9	1	-	328,000	7,789
1907-08	2	38	15	1	3	50	23	6	3	10	23	39	21	4	13	73	62	46	8	2	-	310,000	8,289
1908-09	2	38	14	2	3	44	15	5	4	10	19	24	19	6	13	63	39	44	4	1	-	353,500	8,421
1909-10	2	38	13	4	2	52	19	10	3	6	28	27	23	7	8	80	46	53	3	1	-	369,500	9,342
1910-11	2	38	8	10	1	38	21	6	6	7	17	18	14	16	8	55	39	44	5	3	-	311,500	8,000
1911-12	2	38	12	3	4	36	13	5	5	9	18	38	17	8	13	54	51	42	7	1	-	348,500	9,395
1912-13	2	38	12	2	5	42	19	3	4	12	18	37	15	6	17	60	56	36	12	2	-	327,000	7,842
1913-14	2	38	9	5	5	29	13	7	4	8	24	24	16	9	13	53	37	41	7	1	-	402,500	10,000
1914-15	2	38	12	2	5	36	23	7	3	9	29	31	19	5	14	65	54	43	7	QF	-	207,000	4,921
1919-20	2	42	13	4	4	53	23	5	2	14	25	49	18	6	18	78	72	42	11	1	-	504,134	12,671
1920-21	2	42	7	10	4	24	18	3	10	8	19	35	10	20	12	43	53	40	13	QF	-	558,000	10,381
1921-22	2	42	13	5	3	36	13	6	5	10	15	28	19	10	13	51	41	48	5	2	-	492,900	10,233
1922-23	2	42	9	8	4	29	22	5	6	10	14	23	14	14	14	43	45	42	12	1	-	468,000	9,571
1923-24	2	42	8	7	6	32	23	2	10	9	14	28	10	17	15	46	51	37	17	1	-	458,700	9,143
1924-25	2	42	12	6	3	40	14	3	5	13	10	35	15	11	16	50	49	41	10	3	-	474,000	9,286
1925-26	2	42	11	4	6	40	19	5	5	11	23	42	16	9	17	63	61	41	13	3	-	450,884	8,380
1926-27	2	42	13	4	4	43	19	7	3	11	20	33	20	7	15	63	52	47	7	5	-	499,654	10,269
1927-28	2	42	9	8	4	25	19	3	7	11	16	35	12	15	15	41	54	39	14	3	-	458,453	9,049
1928-29	2	42	8	8	5	38	24	5	6	10	20	39	13	14	15	58	63	40	12	3	-	499,836	10,065
1929-30	2	42	11	3	7	30	24	3	4	14	21	54	14	7	21	51	78	35	21	SF	-	403,101	7,771
1930-31	3N	42	12	7	2	64	20	8	3	10	35	35	20	10	12	99	55	50	6	3	-	254,961	6,497
1931-32	3N	40	14	1	5	52	21	6	4	10	30	32	20	5	15	82	53	45	8	3	-	232,263	6,410
1932-33	3N	42	18	3	0	69	14	8	4	9	31	31	26	7	9	100	45	59	1	3	-	347,366	10,097
1933-34	2	42	11	4	6	33	20	2	8	11	19	48	13	12	17	52	68	38	15	4	-	469,573	10,562
1934-35	2	42	9	6	6	32	22	7	2	12	31	52	16	8	18	63	74	40	13	3	-	412,407	7,934
1935-36	2	42	4	7	10	33	45	1	3	17	14	66	5	10	27	47	111	20	22	3	-	350,392	5,713
1936-37	3N	42	13	6	2	39	22	4	6	11	29	47	17	12	13	68	69	46	5	1	-	271,132	7,026
1937-38	3N	42	11	8	2	51	19	9	5	7	29	24	20	13	9	80	43	53	3	3	-	390,171	11,270
1938-39	3N	42	13	5	3	57	25	5	5	11	26	49	18	10	14	83	74	46	7	2	-	270,385	6,327
1946-47	3N	42	9	5	7	25	19	7	3	11	24	34	16	8	18	49	53	40	11	3	-	586,918	19,673
1947-48	3N	42	12	5	4	38	21	6	6	9	21	27	18	11	13	59	48	47	5	3	-	715,028	24,019
1948-49	3N	42	17	1	3	65	14	10	10	1	28	14	27	11	4	93	28	65	1	QF	-	1,135,633	36,522
1949-50	2	42	11	8	2	39	25	6	3	12	25	47	17	11	14	64	72	45	7	4	-	1,449,560	37,324
1950-51	2	42	12	5	4	47	28	4	6	11	27	42	16	11	15	74	70	43	10	5	-	1,213,905	31,771
1951-52	2	42	11	5	5	44	23	2	6	13	16	47	13	11	18	60	70	37	18	4	-	1,135,504	29,210
1952-53	2	42	11	6	4	36	19	3	2	16	21	50	14	8	20	57	69	36	18	4	-	974,794	26,014
1953-54	2	42	14	1	6	47	22	2	5	14	17	44	16	6	20	64	66	38	15	5	-	843,481	20,995
1954-55	2	42	7	5	9	30	35	5	5	11	14	34	12	10	20	44	69	34	19	3	-	811,720	19,793
1955-56	2	42	6	4	11	32	45	4	2	15	21	52	10	6	26	53	97	26	22	3	-	707,504	15,419
1956-57	3N	46	14	6	3	45	24	7	4	12	39	45	21	10	15	84	69	52	8	3	-	467,104	12,056
1957-58	3N	46	15	6	2	49	20	4	9	10	29	47	19	15	12	78	67	53	5	4	-	429,832	10,973
1958-59	3	46	19	3	1	65	21	7	6	10	25	34	26	9	11	90	55	61	2	1	-	578,250	14,375
1959-60	2	42	7	6	8	27	30	3	4	14	21	46	10	10	22	48	76	30	21	3	-	659,370	15,499

			HOME					AWAY					TOTAL						Lge	FAC	FLC	Agg Home	Avg Home
Season	Div.	P	W	D	L	F	A	W	D	L	F	A	W	D	L	F	A	Pts	Pos	Rd	Rd	Attendance	Attendance
1960-61	3	46	13	6	4	51	28	4	6	13	22	45	17	12	17	73	73	46	11	3	1	406,475	8,434
1961-62	3	46	15	2	6	43	20	5	6	12	24	34	20	8	18	67	54	48	10	2	3	333,648	6,887
1962-63	3	46	12	6	5	40	22	7	4	12	34	47	19	10	17	74	69	48	10	3	3	381,595	7,350
1963-64	3	46	11	9	3	45	27	5	8	10	28	41	16	17	13	73	68	49	8	3	3	403,101	8,536
1964-65	3	46	14	6	3	51	25	9	6	8	40	32	23	12	11	91	57	58	4	2	2	561,760	14,628
1965-66	3	46	19	2	2	64	24	12	5	6	45	38	31	7	8	109	62	69	1	QF	1	787,826	22,784
1966-67	2	42	11	5	5	46	25	5	2	14	31	47	16	7	19	77	72	39	12	3	1	877,387	24,730
1967-68	2	42	6	8	7	25	23	6	5	10	33	50	12	13	17	58	73	37	17	3	2	649,388	15,733
1968-69	2	42	10	7	4	38	20	3	9	9	21	32	13	16	13	59	52	42	11	3	2	598,392	14,216
1969-70	2	42	11	6	4	43	28	4	5	12	29	42	15	11	16	72	70	41	13	3	3	552,069	11,230
1970-71	2	42	11	5	5	31	16	8	8	5	23	25	19	13	10	54	41	51	5	QF	2	772,099	19,737
1971-72	2	42	10	6	5	33	21	4	4	13	16	32	14	10	18	49	53	38	12	5	2	589,716	13,974
1972-73	2	42	9	7	5	39	22	5	5	11	25	37	14	12	16	64	59	40	13	5	3	407,520	9,233
1973-74	2	42	9	9	3	25	15	4	8	9	21	32	13	17	12	46	47	43	9	3	4	420,412	8,216
1974-75	2	42	12	8	1	25	10	3	6	12	15	43	15	14	13	40	53	44	8	3	2	451,305	8,573
1975-76	2	42	9	5	7	29	23	5	6	10	16	26	14	11	17	45	49	39	14	4	4	411,023	6,901
1976-77	2	42	9	8	4	31	17	1	9	11	14	36	10	17	15	45	53	37	14	3	2	432,118	7,924
1977-78	2	42	6	6	9	23	25	2	6	13	11	27	8	12	22	34	52	28	22	3	4	407,035	6,835
1978-79	3	46	12	9	2	36	14	7	2	14	30	47	19	11	16	66	61	49	8	2	1	252,742	5,238
1979-80	3	46	11	7	5	29	21	1	9	13	22	48	12	16	18	51	69	40	20	1	1	295,988	5,942
1980-81	3	46	7	8	8	23	22	1	8	14	17	49	8	16	22	40	71	32	24	4	1	240,730	4,193
1981-82	4	46	14	3	6	36	23	5	9	9	34	38	19	12	15	70	61	69	8	3	1	177,409	3,993
1982-83	4	46	14	8	1	48	14	11	7	5	27	20	25	15	6	75	34	90	2	1	1	237,651	6,682
1983-84	3	46	16	5	2	42	11	7	9	7	29	27	23	14	9	71	38	83	4	2	1	318,458	8,128
1984-85	3	46	16	4	3	46	20	9	8	6	32	29	25	12	9	78	49	87	3	3	2	297,482	7,433
1985-86	2	42	11	7	3	39	19	6	6	9	26	36	17	13	12	65	55	64	6	4	2	321,678	7,672
1986-87	2	42	10	6	5	25	22	3	8	10	16	33	13	14	15	41	55	53	14	5	3	307,702	6,674
1987-88	2	44	10	8	4	32	22	4	7	11	22	38	14	15	15	54	60	57	15	3	2	396,367	8,132
1988-89	2	46	7	9	7	31	25	4	5	14	21	43	11	14	21	52	68	47	21	5	2	367,775	6,668
1989-90	2	46	7	8	8	27	31	7	8	8	31	34	14	16	16	58	65	58	14	3	1	415,766	6,518
1990-91	2	46	6	10	7	35	32	4	5	14	22	53	10	15	21	57	85	45	24	3	1	361,592	6,165
1991-92	3	46	9	4	10	28	23	7	7	9	26	31	16	11	19	54	54	59	14	3	2	209,463	4,115
1992-93	ND2	46	9	5	9	28	26	4	6	13	18	43	13	11	22	46	69	50	20	2	1	239,167	4,671
1993-94	ND2	46	9	9	5	33	20	9	5	9	29	34	18	14	14	62	54	68	9	2	1	269,524	5,943
1994-95	ND2	46	13	6	4	40	18	8	5	10	30	39	21	11	14	70	57	74	8	1	1	224,988	4,802
1995-96	ND2	46	4	8	11	26	37	1	8	14	10	41	5	16	25	36	78	31	24	1	2	196,785	3,798
1996-97	ND3	46	9	8	6	29	26	4	10	9	15	24	13	18	15	44	50	57	17	2	1	156,264	3,413
1997-98	ND3	46	10	6	7	36	32	1	2	20	20	51	11	8	27	56	83	41	22	1	3	185,226	4,684
1998-99	ND3	46	8	5	10	25	28	6	6	11	19	34	14	11	21	44	62	53	21	3	2	236,410	6,032
1999-00	ND3	46	7	8	8	26	23	8	6	9	17	20	15	14	17	43	43	59	14	3	2	228,471	5,735
2000-01	ND3	46	12	7	4	27	18	7	10	6	20	21	19	17	10	47	39	74	6	1	1	258,636	6,684
2001-02	ND3	46	12	6	5	38	18	4	7	12	19	33	16	13	17	57	51	61	11	2	2	331,400	9,506
2002-03	ND3	46	9	10	4	34	19	5	7	11	24	34	14	17	15	58	53	59	13	1	1	407,203	12,846
2003-04	ND3	46	16	4	3	50	21	9	9	5	32	23	25	13	8	82	44	88	2	1	1	526,963	16,847
2004-05	Lge1	46	16	5	2	42	17	10	3	10	38	36	26	8	12	80	53	86	2	3	1	626,108	18,027
Totals:		3830	981	510	424	3408	1952	473	502	940	2092	3281	1454	1012	1364	5500	5233	4317					

1904/05 Friendly matches

Player columns (left to right): Abbot H · Alexander R · Andrews M · Bouch C · Brooks G · Brown C · Carney M · Cook GW · Cooper W · Davies HJ · Ford J · Forrester H · Frost WJ · Glaves A · Goodin W · Hay W · Hodson W · Horton V · Howe P · Johnson L · Jones T · Leiper J · Mackrill OW · Manning JT · Martin WTJ · Newman S · Newton R · Raisbeck A · Rushton G · Smith A · Spence G · Thornton W · Turner J · Welsh CT · Whitehouse J · Wilkinson H · Williams T · Wolfe F

#	Date	Match	Score / Scorers	Att	Abb	Ale	And	Bou	Bro	Brn	Car	Coo	Cop	Dav	For	Frr	Fro	Gla	Goo	Hay	Hod	Hor	How	Joh	Jon	Lei	Mac	Man	Mar	Newm	Newt	Rai	Rus	Smi	Spe	Tho	Tur	Wel	Whi	Wil	Wlm	Wol
1	Sep 01	NOTTS COUNTY	2-2 Rushton 2	6000																			9		3	2			4			6	8	10					1	11		5
2	10	EVERTON 'A'	2-0 Howe 2	6000																	8		9		3	2		7	4			6		10					1	11		5
3	19	LEICESTER FOSSE	2-0 Howe, Spence	4000			4																9		3	2		7				6	8	10					1	11		5
4	24	DARLINGTON	5-1 Rushton 4, Wolfe	4000					4														9		3	2		7	5			6	8						1	11		10
5	29	CREWE	1-1 Rushton	2000			2																9		3			7	4			6	8						1	11	10	5
6	Oct 01	Denton	2-1 Howe, Williams	3000			2																9		3				4			6	8		7				1	11	10	5
7	08	SHEFFIELD FC	4-1 Rushton 2, Howe, Martin	3000			2																9		3				4			6	7	8	10				1		11	5
8	12	MIDDLESBROUGH RES	2-2 Smith A 2	2000			2									5									3			7	4			6	9	8	10				1	11		
9	13	DERBY COUNTY	3-2 Rushton, Smith A, Howe	6500	2																		9		3				4			6	7	8	10				1	11		5
10	15	Leeds City	2-0 Smith A, Howe	3000			2																9		3				4			11	7	8	10	6			1			5
11	20	LINCOLN CITY	1-0 Spence	3000	2																	1			3				4			6	7	8	10		5					9
12	22	West Hartlepool	3-1 Rushton, Martin, Jones	1500			2								11							1	9		3				4			6	7	8	10		5					
13	29	STOCKTON	2-2 Rushton, Smith A	2500			2								11								9		3				4			6	7	8	10		5		1			
14	Nov 03	BURTON UTD	3-1 Spence 2, Smith A	2000																			9		3				4			6	7	8	10		5		1	11		2
15	12	BRADFORD CITY	0-2	6000																			9		3				4			6	7	8	10		5		1	11		2
16	17	PORT VALE	1-2 Wolfe	2000		9			2													1	8		3				4					7	10		6			11		5
17	26	GRIMSBY TOWN	4-2 Rushton 2, Howe, Wilkinson	4000					2														9		3				4			6	7	8	10				1	11		5
18	Dec 10	GLOSSOP	2-1 Smith A, Spence	5000					2														9		3				4			6	7	8	10				1	11		5
19	24	LEEDS CITY	3-2 Ridsdale, Wilkinson	2500					2																3				4			6	7	8	10				1	11		5
20	27	Preston NE	2-3 Smith A 2	2000					2														9		3				4			6	7	8	10				1	11		5
21	31	Middlesbrough Res	2-3 Rushton 2	300					2														9		3				4		6		8	7	10				1	11		5
22	Jan 03	Darlington	3-3 Ford 2, Newton	4000					2						11							1	9		3				4		6	8		7	10							5
23	07	Scarborough	2-0 Newton	1000					2						11										3				4		6	8	9	7	10			1				
24	14	WELLINGBOROUGH	3-2 Rushton 2, Howe	2500							1				11								9		3				4		6	8		7	10							5
25	28	CHESTERFIELD	1-2 Howe	5000					6														9		3				4				11	8	7	10	2	1				5
26	Feb 02	DONCASTER ROVERS	3-0 Rushton, Smith A, Howe	3000					2														9		3				4			6	8	7	10				1	11		5
27	04	Manchester C. Res	0-1	5000					2														9		3				4			6	8	7	10				1	11		5
28	11	Gainsborough Trin. Res	1-2 Howe	2000					5														9		3				4			6	8	7	10		2	1			11	
29	18	LIVERPOOL	2-6 Rushton, Doig og	8000					5														9		3				4			6	8	7	10		2	1			11	
30	23	ARMY SERVICE CORPS	5-1 Rushton 2, Spence, Wilkinson, Smith A	2000					5			3		2															4				11	8	10	6		1		9		
31	25	Sheffield FC	3-1 Smith A 2, Brooks	1000					2																3				4			6	7	9	8	5			1	11		
32	Mar 04	Leeds City	5-2 Howe 4, Rushton	5200					2														8		3				4			6	7	10	9	5			1	11		
33	18	SCARBOROUGH	6-0 Howe 2, Smith A 2, Spence, Wilkinson	400					2														10		3				4			6	7	9	8	5			1	11		
34	23	PRINCE OF WALES HUSSARS	1-0 Spence	1500																			8		2				4			6	7	9	10	5			1	11		
35	25	MANCHESTER C. RES	0-0	8000					2														8		3				4			6	7	9	10	5			1	11		
36	Apr 01	COLDSTREAM GUARDS	10-3 *	4000								2							5				10		3				4			6	7	9	8				1	11		
37	05	York Garrison	7-1 **	1000										2									10		3				4			6	7	8	9	5			1	11		
38	08	BARNSLEY	2-1 Wilkinson, Rushton	7000					2														10		3			7	4			6	9	8		5			1	11		
39	15	SHEFFIELD UNITED	3-1 Rushton, Spence, Howe	10000					6					2						8			10		3				4				7	9		5			1	11		
40	21	Grimsby Town	1-2 Howe	3000					5					2									10		3				4			6	7	8	9				1	11		
41	22	Boston Town	4-2 Smith A 2, Martin 2	2000					2					3									10						4			6	7	8	9				1	11		5
42	24	PRESTON NORTH END	2-2 Spence, Raisbeck	8000					2					3									10						4			6	7	8	9	5			1	11		
43	27	EAST RIDING XI	2-2 Howe, Wilkinson	1500			9		2														10						4			6	7	8	5				1	11		3
44	29	GAINSBOROUGH TRIN. RES.	2-3 Rushton 2	3000					3	4							2						10									6	7	9					1	11		5
		Apps			2	1	8	1	24	1	1	2	1	7	5	1	1	1	1	1	1	4	37	1	38	4	5	1	42	3	3	38	41	34	40	14	7	3	38	35	3	26
		Goals			1				1						2								25	1			5				2	3	29	17	15	1				8	1	2

All home matches were played at The Boulevard, except match 33 - at Dairycoates and Match 35 - at The Circle.

One Own Goal

* Goalscorers match 36: Spence (4), Howe (3), Wilkinson, Rushton, Thornton

** Goalscorers match 37: Rushton (3), Spence, Howe, Martin, Wilkinson

McKiernan T played in match no.1 at 7, Robinson E 11 at 11, Ridsdale J 19 at 9, Traynor L 24 at 2, Smith W 30 at 7, Robson F 31 at 10, Patrick A 34 at 3, Sommerscales W 44 at 8

F.A. Cup

	Date	Match	Score / Scorers	Att	How	Jon	Lei	Mac	Mar	Rai	Rus	Smi	Whi	Wil	Wol
P	Sep 17	Stockton	3-3 Howe, Spence, Mackrill	4000	9	3	2	7	4	6	8	10	1	11	5
PR	22	Stockton	1-4 Spence	4000	9	3	2	7	4	6	8	10	1	11	5

1904-05:
Standing: W. Leach (Trainer), F. Wolfe, J. Whitehouse, J. Turner, T. Jones,
Sitting W. Martin, J.E. Smith, G. Spence, P. Howe, A. Raisbeck;
On Ground G. Rushton, H. Wilkinson.

1905-06:
Standing: W. Martin, H. Davis, G. Spence, M. Spendiff, A. Langley (Player-manager), W.S Robinson, D. Gordon;
Sitting: W. Leach (trainer), J. Manning, H. Simmon, D. Wilson, P. Howe, A. Raisbeck;
On Ground: G. Rushton, W. Thornton, J. Smith, P. Lavery.

#	Date	Opponent	Result	Scorers	Att	Browell G	Davies H	Frost W	Goodin W	Gordon DS	Hall E	Hall H	Hedley G	Howe P	Jones T	Langley A	Lavery P	Manning J	Martin W	Raisbeck A	Robinson W	Rushton G	Simmon H	Smith J	Smith JE	Spence G	Spendiff M	Thornton W	Wilson D	Wright G
1	Sep 2	BARNSLEY	4-1	Gordon 2, Spence, Wilson	8000					6				10	3	2			4	11	5	7				8	1		9	
2	9	Clapton Orient	1-0	Howe	3000					6				10	3	2			4	11	5	7				8	1		9	
3	11	Chelsea	1-5	Raisbeck	6000					6				10	3	2			4	11	5	7				8	1		9	
4	16	BURNLEY	1-1	Raisbeck	7000					6				10	3	2			4	11	5	7				8	1		9	
5	23	Leeds City	1-3	Wilson	13654					6				10	3	2				11	5		7	8			1	4	9	
6	30	BURTON UNITED	1-1	Howe	6000	4				6				10	3	2				11	5	7			9		1		8	
7	Oct 11	CHESTERFIELD	3-0	Smith JE, Howe, Raisbeck	4500	4				6				10	3	2				11	5	7			9		1		8	
8	14	GAINSBOROUGH TRIN.	2-0	Wilson, Howe	3500	4				6				10	3	2				11	5	7			9		1		8	
9	21	Bristol City	1-2	Smith JE	6000	4				6				10	3	2				11	5	7			9		1		8	
10	28	MANCHESTER UNITED	0-1		12000	4				6				10	3	2				11	5	7			9	8	1			
11	Nov 4	Glossop	1-3	Smith JE	1500	4				6				10	3	2				11	5	7			9	8	1			
12	11	STOCKPORT COUNTY	3-0	Smith JE 2, Smith J	3000	4				6					3	2		7		11	5			10	9	8	1			
13	25	BRADFORD CITY	5-2	Smith JE 2, Gordon, Robinson, Jones	5000	4	3			10					2			7		6	5	9			11	8	1			
14	Dec 2	West Bromwich Albion	1-1	Gordon	8000	4	2			10					3			7		6	5	9			11	8	1			
15	7	Leicester Fosse	2-1	Raisbeck, Manning	3000	4	2			6				9	3			7		11	5					8	1		10	
16	16	GRIMSBY TOWN	0-1		8000	4	2			10					3			7		6	5	9		8	11		1			
17	23	Lincoln City	4-1	Smith JE, Manning, Rushton, Spence	1500	4	2			10					3			7		6	5	9			11	8	1			
18	25	Burslem Port Vale	3-1	Gordon, Rushton Jones	3000	4	2			10					3			7		6	5	9			11	8	1			
19	26	Burton United	3-0	Gordon 2, Rushton	4000	4				10					3	2		7		6	5	9			11	8	1			
20	Jan 6	CLAPTON ORIENT	3-1	Rushton 2, Manning	3000	4	2			10					3			7		6	5	9			11	8	1			
21	20	Burnley	3-1	Rushton 2, Gordon	2000	4	2			10					3			7		6	5	9		8	11		1			
22	27	LEEDS CITY	0-0		10000	4	2			10					3			7		6	5	9		8	11		1			
23	Feb 10	CHELSEA	4-3	Smith JE 2, Gordon, Rushton	6000	4	2			10					3			7		6	5	9		8	11		1			
24	17	Gainsborough Trinity	1-3	Raisbeck	4000	4	2			10					3			7		6	5	9		8	11		1			
25	24	BRISTOL CITY	0-3		7000	4	2			10					3			7		11	5		6	8	9		1			
26	Mar 3	Manchester United	0-5		14000		2			4				10	3			7		6	5			8	11	9	1			
27	10	GLOSSOP	1-2	Howe	7000		2			4				10	3			7		6	5	9			11	8	1			
28	14	Blackpool	2-1	Smith J, Howe	2000	4	2		5	8	3			10						6				7	11	9	1			
29	17	Stockport County	1-2	Howe	5000	4	2			9	5		3	10						6				7	11	8	1			
30	24	BLACKPOOL	2-2	Howe 2	2000	4	2			9	3			10						6	5			7	11	8	1			
31	31	Bradford City	2-0	Smith J, Hedley	8000	4	2			6			10		3			7		11	5			8	9		1			
32	Apr 7	WEST BROMWICH ALB.	4-0	Smith JE, Gordon, Raisbeck, Wright	7000	4	3			10					2			7		6	5			8	9		1			11
33	13	Chesterfield	2-1	Gordon, Smith J	6000	4	3			6				10	2			7		11	5			8	9		1			
34	14	LEICESTER FOSSE	0-0		10000	4	3			6				10	2			7		11	5			8	9		1			
35	16	BURSLEM PORT VALE	3-2	Howe 2, Browell G	8000	4	3			9				10	2		11	7		6	5			8			1			
36	17	Barnsley	0-2		4000	2		4		10	5				3		9	11	7	6				8			1			
37	21	Grimsby Town	0-1		5000	4	3			10					2	9		7		6	5			8	11		1			
38	28	LINCOLN CITY	2-1	Smith J, Smith JE	6000	4				2	10				3	9		7		6	5			8	11		1			
Apps						31	23	1	1	37	3	1	11	24	27	13	2	24	4	38	35	15	9	20	30	19	38	1	10	1
Goals						1				11			1	12	2			3		5	1	8		5	12	2			3	1

F.A. Cup

#	Date	Opponent	Result	Scorers	Att	Browell G	Davies H	Frost W	Goodin W	Gordon DS	Hall E	Hall H	Hedley G	Howe P	Jones T	Langley A	Lavery P	Manning J	Martin W	Raisbeck A	Robinson W	Rushton G	Simmon H	Smith J	Smith JE	Spence G	Spendiff M	Thornton W	Wilson D	Wright G
Q1	Oct 7	GRIMETHORPE UTD.	8-1	Smith JE 3, Howe 2, Wilson 2, Robinson	2000	4				6				10	3	2				11	5	7			9		1		8	
Q2	28	Denaby United	2-0	Smith J 2	3000		2			6								7	4	11		9		10		8				
Q3	Nov 22	LEEDS CITY	1-1	Raisbeck	3000	4				6					3	2		7		11	5	9		10		8	1			
rep	29	Leeds City	2-1	Rushton, Smith JE	8000	4	3			10					2			7		6	5	9			11	8	1			
Q4	Dec 9	OLDHAM ATHLETIC	2-1	Smith J, Howe	4000	4	2			6				10	3			7		11	5	9		8			1			
R1	Jan 13	READING	0-1		9000	4	2			10					3			7		6	5	9			11	8	1			

Played in Q2: G Cook (at 1), G Brooks (3), M Carney (5)

Matches 10,20,27 played at the Boulevard.
Matches 1,4,6,7,8,12,13,16,22,23,25 and the home F.A. Cup ties played at Anlaby Road Cricket Ground.
Matches 30,32,34,35,38 played at Anlaby Road Football Ground.

		Pl	Home					Away					F.	A.	Pts
			W	D	L	F	A	W	D	L	F	A		(Total)	
1	Bristol City	38	17	1	1	43	8	13	5	1	40	20	83	28	66
2	Manchester United	38	15	3	1	55	13	13	3	3	35	15	90	28	62
3	Chelsea	38	13	4	2	58	16	9	5	5	32	21	90	37	53
4	West Bromwich Alb.	38	13	4	2	53	16	9	4	6	26	20	79	36	52
5	HULL CITY	38	10	5	4	38	21	9	1	9	29	33	67	54	44
6	Leeds City	38	11	5	3	38	19	6	4	9	21	28	59	47	43
7	Leicester Fosse	38	10	3	6	30	21	5	9	5	23	27	53	48	42
8	Grimsby Town	38	11	7	1	33	13	4	3	12	13	33	46	46	40
9	Burnley	38	9	4	6	26	23	6	4	9	16	30	42	53	38
10	Stockport County	38	11	6	2	36	16	2	3	14	8	40	44	56	35
11	Bradford City	38	7	4	8	21	22	6	4	9	25	38	46	60	34
12	Barnsley	38	11	4	4	45	17	1	5	13	15	45	60	62	33
13	Lincoln City	38	10	1	8	46	29	2	5	12	23	43	69	72	30
14	Blackpool	38	8	3	8	22	21	2	6	11	15	41	37	62	29
15	Gainsborough Trinity	38	10	2	7	35	22	2	2	15	9	35	44	57	28
16	Glossop	38	9	4	6	36	28	1	4	14	13	43	49	71	28
17	Burslem Port Vale	38	10	4	5	34	25	2	0	17	15	57	49	82	28
18	Chesterfield Town	38	8	4	7	26	24	2	4	13	14	48	40	72	28
19	Burton United	38	9	4	6	26	20	1	2	16	8	47	34	67	26
20	Clapton Orient	38	6	4	9	19	22	1	3	15	16	56	35	78	21

#		Date	Opponent	Result & Scorers	Att.	Browell G	Dagnall W	Davies H	Dixon E	Gordon DS	Hall E	Hall H	Hedley G	Howe P	Manning J	McQuillan J	Neve E	Pearson F	Raisbeck A	Robinson W	Roughley E	Rushton G	Simmon H	Smith J	Smith JE	Spendiff M	West H	Wright G
1	Sep	1	Wolverhampton Wan.	1-1 Smith J	6000	4	10	3		6			2		7				11	5				8	9	1		
2		8	CLAPTON ORIENT	2-0 Smith J, Martin (og)	5000	3	10			4			2		7	11			6	5				8	9	1		
3		15	Gainsborough Trinity	1-1 Smith J	4000	4		3		10			2		7	11			6	5				8	9	1		
4		22	STOCKPORT COUNTY	3-0 Smith J, Smith JE, Gordon	6000	4		3		10			2		7				6	5				8	9	1		11
5		29	CHESTERFIELD	2-0 Smith J, Wright	8000	4		3		10			2		7				6	5				8	9	1		11
6	Oct	6	Glossop	4-2 Pearson 3, Wright	3000	4		3		10			2		7			9	6	5				8		1		11
7		13	BLACKPOOL	3-0 Smith J 2, Pearson	6000	4		3		10			2		7			9	6	5				8		1		11
8		20	Bradford City	0-1	16000	4		3		10			2		7			9	6	5				8		1		11
9		27	WEST BROMWICH ALB.	0-1	8000	4		3		10			2		7			9	6	5				8		1		11
10	Nov	3	Leicester Fosse	0-3	14000	4	10	3		6			2		7			9		5				8		1		11
11		10	NOTTM. FOREST	1-2 Smith J	8000	4	10	3		6			2		7			9		5				8		1		11
12		17	Lincoln City	1-0 Dagnall	5000	4	10			6			2		7	3	11	9		5				8		1		
13		24	BURTON UNITED	3-0 Wright 2, Pearson	6000	4				6			2		7	3		10		5				8	9	1		11
14	Dec	1	Grimsby Town	3-1 Manning, Pearson, Robinson	7000	4				6			2		7	3		10		5				8	9	1		11
15		8	BARNSLEY	2-0 Wright, Manning	7000	4				6			2		7	3		10		5				8	9	1		11
16		15	Burnley	2-4 Smith JE, Rushton	5000	4				6			2		7	3		10		5		9			8	1		11
17		22	LEEDS CITY	2-1 Smith JE, Rushton	9000	4				6			2		7	3		10		5		9			8	1		11
18		25	CHELSEA	0-1	16000	4				6			2		10	7	3			5		9			8	1		11
19		26	Barnsley	2-4 Rushton 2	4000	4				6	5		2		10							9		7	8	1		11
20		29	WOLVERHAMPTON W.	5-1 Smith JE 2, Manning 2, Rushton	7000	4				6	5		2		7	3	11					9		8	10	1		11
21	Jan	1	Chesterfield	1-3 Smith J	3000	4				6	5		2		7	3	11					9		8	10	1		
22		5	Clapton Orient	1-2 Smith J	7000	4				6			2		7	3				5		9		8	10	1		11
23		19	GAINSBOROUGH TRIN.	2-4 Smith J, Manning	6000	4		3			5		2		7							9		8	10	1	6	11
24		26	Stockport County	1-1 Smith J	6000	4				6			2		7	3				5		9		8	10	1		11
25	Feb	9	GLOSSOP	5-0 Smith J 2, Wright 2, Rushton	7000	4				6			2		7	3				5		9		8	10	1		11
26		16	Blackpool	1-1 Smith J	3000	4				6			2		7	3	11			5		9		8	10	1		11
27	Mar	2	West Bromwich Albion	0-3	10000	4				6			2		7	3			10	5		9		8	7	1		11
28		9	LEICESTER FOSSE	1-1 Hedley	7000	4				6			2		7	3				5		9		10	8	1		11
29		14	BRADFORD CITY	0-3	5000	4				6		8	2		7	3				5				10	9	1		11
30		16	Nottingham Forest	1-2 Neve	12000	4				6			2		10		3		11	5				8	7	1		9
31		23	LINCOLN CITY	1-2 Dagnall	6000	4	10		8	6	5		2				3		11	5					7	1		9
32		29	Chelsea	0-3	60000	4	10		9	6			2				3		11	5				8	7	1		
33		30	Burton United	2-1 Smith J, Robinson	3000	4	10		9	6			2				3		11	5			7	8		1		
34	Apr	1	BURSLEM PORT VALE	4-1 Smith J 2, Browell, Howe	8000	4				6			2		10		3			5	1	9	7	8				11
35		6	GRIMSBY TOWN	4-2 Howe 2, Smith J, Smith JE	10000	4				6			2		10	7	3			5				8	9	1		
36		13	Burslem Port Vale	1-2 Neve	2000	4				6			2		10		3			5			7	8	9	1		
37		20	BURNLEY	1-1 Manning	7000	4				6			2		10	7	3		11	5				8	9	1		
38		27	Leeds City	2-2 Smith JE, Neve	7000	4				6			2		10	7	3		11	5				8	9	1		
			Apps			38	8	11	3	37	5	1	38	8	30	26	13	13	9	33	1	14	3	34	29	37	1	26
			Goals			1	2			1			1	3	6		3	6		2		6		19	7			7

One own goal

F.A. Cup

		Date	Opponent	Result	Att.	Browell G	Gordon DS	Hedley G	Howe P	Manning J	McQuillan J	Neve E	Robinson W	Rushton G	Smith J	Smith JE	Spendiff M	Wright G
R1	Jan	12	Tottenham Hotspur	0-0	28000	4	6	2		7	3		5	9	8	10	1	11
rep		17	TOTTENHAM HOTSPUR	0-0	21795	4	6	2		7	3		5	9	8	10	1	11
rep2		21	Tottenham Hotspur	0-1	20000	4	6	2	9	7	3		5		8	10	1	11

R1 replay a.e.t.

Match 25 played at the Boulevard. All other home games at Anlaby Road football ground.

		Pl	Home					Away					F.	A.	Pts
			W	D	L	F	A	W	D	L	F	A	(Total)		
1	Nottingham Forest	38	16	2	1	43	13	12	2	5	31	23	74	36	60
2	Chelsea	38	18	0	1	55	10	8	5	6	25	24	80	34	57
3	Leicester Fosse	38	15	3	1	44	12	5	5	9	18	27	62	39	48
4	West Bromwich Alb.	38	15	2	2	62	15	6	3	10	21	30	83	45	47
5	Bradford City	38	14	2	3	46	21	7	3	9	24	32	70	53	47
6	Wolverhampton W.	38	13	4	2	49	16	4	3	12	17	37	66	53	41
7	Burnley	38	12	4	3	45	13	5	2	12	17	34	62	47	40
8	Barnsley	38	14	2	3	56	21	1	6	12	17	34	73	55	38
9	HULL CITY	38	11	2	6	41	20	4	5	10	24	37	65	57	37
10	Leeds City	38	10	5	4	38	26	3	5	11	17	37	55	63	36
11	Grimsby Town	38	13	2	4	34	16	3	1	15	23	46	57	62	35
12	Stockport County	38	8	8	3	26	12	4	3	12	16	40	42	52	35
13	Blackpool	38	9	4	6	25	19	2	7	10	8	32	33	51	33
14	Gainsborough Trinity	38	12	3	4	33	20	2	2	15	12	52	45	72	33
15	Glossop	38	10	4	5	32	21	3	2	14	21	58	53	79	32
16	Burslem Port Vale	38	11	5	3	45	26	1	2	16	15	57	60	83	31
17	Clapton Orient	38	9	7	3	25	13	2	1	16	20	54	45	67	30
18	Chesterfield Town	38	10	3	6	36	26	1	4	14	14	40	50	66	29
19	Lincoln City	38	10	2	7	29	24	2	2	15	17	49	46	73	28
20	Burton United	38	7	3	9	24	23	1	4	14	10	45	34	68	23

1906-07
Standing: A. Langley (Manager), G. Browell, M. Spendiff, H. Davis, J.E. Smith, J. Haller (Secretary), W. Leach (Trainer);
Sitting: J. Manning, F. Pearson, E.G.D. Wright, D. Gordon, W. Robinson;
On Ground: G. Hedley, A. Raisbeck.

1907-08
Standing: A. Langley (Manager), G. Hedley, G. Browell, M. Spendiff, D. Gordon, W. Robinson, W. Leach (Trainer);
Sitting: J.E. Smith, J. Smith, E.G.D. Wright, J. Shaw, A. Temple;
On Ground: F. Martin, J. McQuillan.

1907/08 8th in Division Two

						Browell G	Gordon DS	Hedley G	Martin F	McQuillan J	Neve E	Nevins T	Robinson W	Roughley E	Shaw J	Simmon H	Smith J	Smith JE	Spendiff M	Stephenson W	Taylor, John	Temple A	Wright G
1	Sep	2	Clapton Orient	0-1	5000	4	6	2		3	11		5		9		8	7	1			10	
2		3	Fulham	1-0 Smith J	10000	4	6	2		3	11		5		9		8	7	1			10	
3		7	BARNSLEY	2-0 Smith J, Shaw	9000	4	6	2		3	11		5		9		8	7	1			10	
4		14	Chesterfield	2-1 Shaw, Temple	5000	4	6	2		3	11		5		9		8	7	1			10	
5		21	BURNLEY	3-1 Smith J 2, Smith JE	8000		6	2	4	3			5		9		8	7	1			10	11
6		26	CHESTERFIELD	2-0 Smith J, Shaw	5000	4	6	2		3			5		9		8	7	1			10	11
7		28	Oldham Athletic	0-3	15000	4	6	2		3			5		9		8	7	1			10	11
8	Oct	10	CLAPTON ORIENT	5-0 Smith J 4, Robinson	4000	4	10	2		3			5	1		6	8	7				9	11
9		12	Leeds City	2-3 Smith J 2	15000	4	6	2		3			5	1	9		8	7				10	11
10		19	WOLVERHAMPTON W.	2-0 Temple, Robinson	8000	4	10	2		3			5			6	8	7	1			9	11
11		26	Gainsborough Trinity	2-1 Smith JE, Temple	4000	4	10	2		3			5			6	8	7	1			9	11
12	Nov	2	STOCKPORT COUNTY	0-0	8000		10	2	4	3			5			6	8	7	1			9	11
13		9	Glossop	1-5 Smith J	2000		10	2	4	3			5			6	8	7	1			9	11
14		16	LEICESTER FOSSE	3-2 Temple 3	5000	4	6	2		3			5		9		8	7	1			10	11
15		23	Blackpool	1-1 Smith J	2000	4	6	2		3			5		9		8	7	1			10	11
16		30	STOKE	2-1 Smith J, Shaw	7000	4	6	2		3			5	1	9		8	7				10	11
17	Dec	7	West Bromwich Albion	0-1	8000	4	6	2		3	11		5	1	9		8	7				10	
18		14	BRADFORD CITY	0-2	8000	4	6	2		3			5		9		8	7	1			10	11
19		21	GRIMSBY TOWN	4-2 Shaw 2, Temple 2	7000	4	6	2		3			5		9		8	7	1			10	11
20		25	LINCOLN CITY	5-3 Smith J 2, Temple 2, Neve	10000	4	6	2		3	11		5		9		8	7	1			10	
21		26	Lincoln City	1-0 Temple	6000	4	6			3			5		9		8	7	1	2		10	11
22		28	Derby County	1-4 Smith J	12000	4	6	2		3	11		5		9		8	7	1			10	
23	Jan	4	Barnsley	2-4 Smith J, Martin	4000	5	6		4	3					9		8	7	1	2		10	11
24		18	Burnley	0-5	5000			6			11	3	5	1	9		8	7		2		10	
25		25	OLDHAM ATHLETIC	3-2 Smith J 2, Robinson	10000	4			6	3			5		9		8	7	1	2		10	11
26	Feb	8	LEEDS CITY	4-1 Shaw 2, Smith J, Smith JE	9000	4		2	6	3			5		9		8	7	1			10	11
27		15	Wolverhampton Wan.	2-1 Smith J2	10000	4		2	6	3			5		9		8	7	1			10	11
28		22	GAINSBOROUGH TRIN.	0-1	5000	4		2	6	3			5		9		8	7	1			10	11
29		29	Stockport County	3-2 Temple 2, Shaw	5000	4		2	6	3	11		5		9			7	1		8	10	
30	Mar	7	GLOSSOP	3-2 Smith J, Shaw, Temple	8000	4		2	6	3			5		9		8	7	1			10	11
31		14	Leicester Fosse	2-3 Smith J, Shaw	12000	4		2	6				5		9		8	7	1	3		10	11
32		21	BLACKPOOL	3-2 Smith J 2, Temple	6000	4		2	6				5		9		8	7	1	3		10	11
33		28	Stoke	1-1 Smith J	2500	4		2	6		11		5		9		8	7	1	3		10	
34	Apr	4	WEST BROMWICH ALB.	4-2 Temple 2, Smith J, Smith JE	6086	4			6	3			5		9		8	7	1	2		10	11
35		11	Bradford City	1-2 Smith J	16000	4			6	3			5	1	9		8	7		2		10	11
36		18	Grimsby Town	1-1 Temple	6000	4			6	3	11		5	1	9		8	7		2		10	
37		20	FULHAM	1-2 Shaw	14000	4			6	3	11		5	1	9		8	7		2		10	
38		25	DERBY COUNTY	4-0 Shaw 2, Smith J, Smith JE	8000	4			6	3	11		5	1	9		8	7		2		10	

	Apps	35	23	29	19	34	13	1	37	9	33	5	37	38	29	12	1	38	25
	Goals				1		1		3		14		31	5				18	

F.A. Cup

R1	Jan	11	Woolwich Arsenal	0-0	15000	4	6	2	10	3			5				8	7	1			9	11
rep		16	WOOLWICH ARSENAL	4-1 Shaw 2, Temple, Smith J	16000	4		2	6	3			5		9		8	7	1			10	11
R2	Feb	1	Aston Villa	0-3	35000	4		2	6	3			5		9		8	7	1			10	11

		Pl	Home					Away					F.	A.	Pts
			W	D	L	F	A	W	D	L	F	A	(Total)		
1	Bradford City	38	15	2	2	58	16	9	4	6	32	26	90	42	54
2	Leicester Fosse	38	14	2	3	41	20	7	8	4	31	27	72	47	52
3	Oldham Athletic	38	15	4	0	53	14	7	2	10	23	28	76	42	50
4	Fulham	38	12	2	5	50	14	10	3	6	32	35	82	49	49
5	West Bromwich Alb.	38	13	3	3	38	13	6	6	7	23	26	61	39	47
6	Derby County	38	15	1	3	50	13	6	3	10	27	32	77	45	46
7	Burnley	38	14	3	2	44	14	6	3	10	23	36	67	50	46
8	HULL CITY	38	15	1	3	50	23	6	3	10	23	39	73	62	46
9	Wolverhampton W.	38	11	4	4	34	11	4	3	12	16	34	50	45	37
10	Stoke	38	11	5	3	43	13	5	0	14	14	39	57	52	37
11	Gainsborough Trinity	38	9	4	6	31	28	5	3	11	16	43	47	71	35
12	Leeds City	38	9	6	4	33	18	3	2	14	20	47	53	65	32
13	Stockport County	38	9	4	6	35	26	3	4	12	13	41	48	67	32
14	Clapton Orient	38	10	5	4	28	13	1	5	13	12	52	40	65	32
15	Blackpool	38	11	3	5	33	19	0	6	13	18	39	51	58	31
16	Barnsley	38	8	3	8	41	31	4	3	12	13	37	54	68	30
17	Glossop	38	9	5	5	36	26	2	3	14	18	48	54	74	30
18	Grimsby Town	38	8	5	6	27	24	3	3	13	16	47	43	71	30
19	Chesterfield Town	38	6	6	7	33	38	0	5	14	13	54	46	92	23
20	Lincoln City	38	7	2	10	27	28	2	1	16	19	55	46	83	21

1908/09   4th in Division Two

#		Date	Opponent	Score	Scorers	Att.	Browell A	Browell G	Gilberthorpe A	Gordon DS	Martin F	McQuillan J	Morrison J	Neve E	Nevins T	Pace A	Robinson W	Roughley E	Shaw J	Smith J	Smith JE	Smith W	Stephenson W	Storey E	Taylor, John	Temple A	Toward A	Wright G	Wright W
1	Sep	1	Bradford Park Avenue	0-1		15000	4		6			3			11		5	1	9	8	7		2			10			
2		5	CLAPTON ORIENT	3-2	Shaw 2, Smith J	8000	4		6			3			11		5	1	9	8	7		2			10			
3		12	Leeds City	0-2		12000	4		6			3			11		5	1	9	8	7		2			10			
4		14	Bolton Wanderers	0-1		12000		8	6					4	11	3	5	1	9		7		2			10			
5		19	Barnsley	1-2	Temple	7000		8	6					4		3	5	1	9		7		2			10		11	
6		26	TOTTENHAM HOTSPUR	1-0	Smith JE	10000		6		10				4		3	5	1			7		2		8	9		11	
7	Oct	3	BOLTON WANDERERS	2-0	Temple, Gilberthorpe	10000	4	10	6							3	5	1		8	7		2			9		11	
8		10	Derby County	0-0		6000	4	10	6							3	5	1		8	7		2			9		11	
9		17	BLACKPOOL	2-0	Smith J, Temple	8000	4	10	6							3	5	1		8	7		2			9		11	
10		24	Chesterfield	4-0	Smith JE,Temple,Gilberthorpe,Wright W	4000	4	10	6							3	5	1			8		2			9		11	7
11		31	GLOSSOP	0-0		8000	4	10	6							3	5	1			8		2			9		11	7
12	Nov	7	Stockport County	1-3	Gilberthorpe	5000	4	10	6						11	3	5	1			7		2		8	9			
13		14	WEST BROMWICH ALB.	2-2	Smith JE 2	10000	4	10	6							3	5	1	9		7		2			10		11	
14		21	Birmingham	2-1	Gilberthorpe, Gordon	5000	5	4	8	6					11	3		1	9		7		2			10			
15		28	GAINSBOROUGH TRIN.	5-1	Shaw 3, Temple 2	7000	5	4		6					11	3	7	1	9		8		2			10			
16	Dec	5	Grimsby Town	0-0		6000	5	4	8	6		3			11			1	9		7		2			10			
17		12	FULHAM	2-0	Temple 2	10000	5	4	8	6		3						1	9		7		2			10		11	
18		19	Burnley	0-1		5000	5	4	8	6		3			11			1	9		7		2			10			
19		25	BRADFORD PARK AVE.	2-3	Smith J, Shaw	10000	5	4	8	6		3			11			1	9		7		2			10			
20		26	Wolverhampton Wan.	0-3		15000	5	4	10	6		3						1	9	8	7		2					11	
21	Jan	2	Clapton Orient	2-1	Smith J, Gordon	7000	5	4	10	6		3	9					1		8	7		2					11	
22		9	LEEDS CITY	4-1	Smith JE, Gordon, Temple, Wright G	8000		4	10	6		3					5	1		8	7		2			9		11	
23		23	BARNSLEY	4-0	Temple, Toward, Smith J, Browell A	7000	5	4		6		3						1		8	7		2			10	9	11	
24		30	Tottenham Hotspur	0-0		25000	5	4		6		3						1		8	7		2			10		11	
25	Feb	13	DERBY COUNTY	4-0	Taylor 2, Temple, Smith J	8000	5	4		6		3						1		8	7		2		10	9		11	
26		20	Blackpool	3-2	Temple 2, Smith J	5000	5	4		6		3					7	1		8			2		10	9		11	
27		27	CHESTERFIELD	1-0	Temple	6000	5	4		6		3						1		8	7		2		10	9		11	
28	Mar	13	STOCKPORT COUNTY	4-1	Temple 2, Smith JE, Taylor	8000	5	4		6		3						1			7		2	10	8	9		11	
29		20	West Bromwich Albion	0-1		17602	5	4		6		3						1			7		2	10	8	9		11	
30		23	Glossop	1-2	Smith W	1200	5	4		6		3			11			1			7	8	2		10			9	
31		27	BIRMINGHAM	4-1	Smith W 3, Temple	10000	5	4		6		3						1			7	8	2		10	9		11	
32	Apr	3	Gainsborough Trinity	0-2		4000	5	4		6		3						1			7	8	2		10	9		11	
33		10	GRIMSBY TOWN	0-1		12000	5	4			6	3			11			1		8	7		2					9	
34		12	WOLVERHAMPTON W.	0-1		6000	5	4	10	6		3			11			1			7		2		8	9			
35		17	Fulham	3-0	Toward 2, Smith J	15000	5	4		6		3						1		8	7		2			10		9	11
36		24	BURNLEY	3-2	Smith J, Toward, Smith W	6000	5	4		6		3						1		8	7		2			10		9	11
37		27	Oldham Athletic	2-2	Toward, Smith W	3000	5	4		6		3						1		8	7		2			10		9	11
38		29	OLDHAM ATHLETIC	1-0	Smith J	4000	5			6		3						1		8	7	10	2					9	11 4
			Apps				24	35	18	36	1	26	4	13	18	2	14	35	13	23	37	10	28	3	8	36	6	25	3
			Goals				1		4	3									6	10	6	6			3	17	5	1	1

F.A. Cup

		Date	Opponent	Score	Scorers	Att.	Browell A	Browell G	Gilberthorpe A	Gordon DS	Martin F	McQuillan J	Morrison J	Neve E	Nevins T	Pace A	Robinson W	Roughley E	Shaw J	Smith J	Smith JE	Smith W	Stephenson W	Storey E	Taylor, John	Temple A	Toward A	Wright G	Wright W
R1	Jan	16	CHELSEA	1-1	Temple	18100	4	10	6			3					5	1		8	7		2			9		11	
rep		20	Chelsea	0-1		25792	5	4	10	6		3						1		8	7		2			9		11	

		Pl	Home					Away					F.	A.	Pts
			W	D	L	F	A	W	D	L	F	A	(Total)		
1	Bolton Wanderers	38	14	3	2	37	8	10	1	8	22	20	59	28	52
2	Tottenham Hotspur	38	12	5	2	42	12	8	6	5	25	20	67	32	51
3	West Bromwich Alb.	38	13	5	1	35	9	6	8	5	21	18	56	27	51
4	HULL CITY	38	14	2	3	44	15	5	4	10	19	24	63	39	44
5	Derby County	38	13	5	1	38	11	3	6	10	17	30	55	41	43
6	Oldham Athletic	38	14	4	1	39	9	3	2	14	16	34	55	43	40
7	Wolverhampton W.	38	10	6	3	32	12	4	5	10	24	36	56	48	39
8	Glossop	38	11	5	3	35	17	4	3	12	22	36	57	53	38
9	Gainsborough Trinity	38	12	3	4	30	20	3	5	11	19	50	49	70	38
10	Fulham	38	8	4	7	39	26	5	7	7	19	22	58	48	37
11	Birmingham	38	10	6	3	35	21	4	3	12	23	40	58	61	37
12	Leeds City	38	12	3	4	35	19	2	4	13	8	34	43	53	35
13	Grimsby Town	38	9	5	5	23	14	5	2	12	18	40	41	54	35
14	Burnley	38	8	4	7	33	28	5	3	11	18	30	51	58	33
15	Clapton Orient	38	7	7	5	25	19	5	2	12	12	30	37	49	33
16	Bradford Park Ave.	38	9	2	8	30	25	4	4	11	21	34	51	59	32
17	Barnsley	38	11	3	5	36	19	0	7	12	12	38	48	57	32
18	Stockport County	38	11	2	6	25	19	3	1	15	14	52	39	71	31
19	Chesterfield Town	38	10	3	6	30	28	1	5	13	7	39	37	67	30
20	Blackpool	38	9	6	4	30	22	0	5	14	16	46	46	68	29

1908-09
Back Row: E.G.D. Wright, J. McQuillan, E. Roughley, D. Gordon;
Standing: A. Langley (Manager), F. Martin, J. Morrison, G. Browell, G. Lindley, W. Robinson, A. Browell, T. Tildsley, W. Leach (Trainer);
Sitting: J. Taylor, J.E. Smith, J. Smith, J. Shaw, A. Temple, E. Neve, A. Pace;
On Ground: E. Gordon, A. Gilberthorpe, T. Nevins, W. Stephenson, J. Hall.

1909-10
Standing: A. Langley (Manager), G. Browell, J. McQuillan, E. Roughley, A, Temple, W. Leach (Trainer);
Sitting: W.A.B. Glossop (Director), W. Wright, J. Smith, D. Gordon, W. Smith, E. Neve, F.G. Stringer (Director);
On Ground: F. Martin, A. Musgrave, A. Toward.

1909/10 3rd in Division Two

#	Date	Opponent	Score	Scorers	Att	Browell A	Browell G	Gordon Dan	Gordon DS	Martin F	McQuillan J	Musgrave A	Neve E	Nevins T	Pace A	Roughley E	Smith J	Smith JE	Smith W	Stephenson W	Temple A	Toward A	Townend V	Walden G	Wright G	Wright W
1	Sep 2	Barnsley	2-1	Smith W, Neve	5000	5	4		6		3		11			1	8	7	10	2	9					
2	4	LEEDS CITY	3-1	Smith J 3	10000	5	4		6		3		11			1	8	7	10	2	9					
3	6	Burnley	1-0	Temple	7000	5	4		6		3		11	7		1	8		10	2	9					
4	11	Wolverhampton Wan.	2-2	Smith J, Smith JE	7500	5	4		6		3				2	1	8	7	10		9				11	
5	18	GAINSBOROUGH TRIN.	5-1	Smith J 2, Smith W 2, Wright G	10000	5	4		6		3				2	1	8	7	10		9				11	
6	25	Grimsby Town	3-2	Smith J, Smith W, Browell A	10000	5	4		6		3				2	1	8	7	10		9	6			11	
7	Oct 2	MANCHESTER CITY	1-2	Smith J	12000	5	4		6	6	3					1	8	7	10	2	9				11	
8	9	Leicester Fosse	1-3	Temple	12000	5	4		6		3					1	8	7	10	2	9				11	
9	11	BARNSLEY	1-0	Toward	8000	5	4		6		3		11		2	1	8	7	10			9				
10	16	LINCOLN CITY	0-0		8000	5	4		6		3				2	1	8	7				9			11	
11	23	Clapton Orient	0-0		8000	5	4		6		3	8	11		2	1		7	10		9					
12	30	BLACKPOOL	1-2	Smith J	8000	5	4		6		3				2	1	8	7	10		9				11	
13	Nov 6	Bradford Park Avenue	1-0	Walden	14000	5	4		6		3		11			1		7	8	2	10			9		
14	13	Derby County	0-4		8000	5			6		3			7		1	8		10	2			7	9	11	4
15	20	STOCKPORT COUNTY	1-1	Smith J	8000	5	4		6		3		11			1	9		10	2	8		7			
16	27	Glossop	1-2	Smith J	4000	5	4		6		3		11	7		1	9		10	2						
17	Dec 4	BIRMINGHAM	7-0	Temple 3, Smith J 2, Smith W, Browell A	6000	5	4		6		3			7		1	9		10	2	8				11	
18	11	West Bromwich Albion	2-0	Temple, Wright G	6000	5	4		6		3					1	9	7	10	2	8				11	
19	18	OLDHAM ATHLETIC	4-0	Smith J 3, Smith JE	7000	5	4		6		3					1	9	7	10		8				11	
20	25	Fulham	1-3	Smith J	24000	5	4		6		3		11			1	9	7	10	2	8					
21	27	FULHAM	3-2	Smith W 2, Temple	16000	5	4		6		3					1	9	7	10	2	8				11	
22	Jan 1	GRIMSBY TOWN	5-1	Temple 2, Smith W 2, Wright G	8000	5	4		6		3					1	9	7	10	2	8				11	
23	8	Leeds City	1-1	Smith J	10000	5			6	4	3					1	9	7	10	2	8				11	
24	22	WOLVERHAMPTON W.	2-2	Smith J 2	6000	5	4		6		3					1	9	7	10	2	8					
25	Feb 12	Manchester City	0-3		30000	5	4		6		3		11			1	9	7	10	2	8					
26	26	Lincoln City	3-1	Smith J, Temple, Smith W	6000	5	4		6		3		11			1	9	7	10	2	8					
27	Mar 5	CLAPTON ORIENT	3-0	Smith W 3	8000	5	4		6		3					1	9	7	10	2	8				11	
28	12	Blackpool	2-1	Temple 2	4000	5	4		6		3		11			1	9	7	10	2	8					
29	19	BRADFORD PARK AVE.	2-1	Smith J, Smith W	9000	5	4		6		3		11			1	9	7	10	2	8					
30	26	DERBY COUNTY	0-0		8000	5	4		6		3		11			1	9	7	10	2	8					
31	28	BURNLEY	3-2	Smith J, Smith JE, Temple	10000	5	4		6		3		11			1	9	7	10	2	8					
32	Apr 2	Stockport County	5-1	Smith J 3, Smith JE, Temple	5000	5	4		6		3	10	11			1	9	7		2	8					
33	9	GLOSSOP	4-2	Temple 2, Smith J, Smith W	6000	5	4		6		3		11			1	9	7	10	2	8					
34	14	LEICESTER FOSSE	2-1	Smith J, Smith W	8000	5	4	2	6		3		11			1	9	7	10		8					
35	16	Birmingham	2-0	Smith J, Neve	8000	5	4	2	6		3					1	9	7	10		8					
36	20	Gainsborough Trinity	1-0	Neve	2000	5		2	6	4	3		11			1	9	7	10		8					
37	23	WEST BROMWICH ALB.	5-1	Smith J 3, Smith JE, Smith W	15000	5		2	6	4	3		11			1	9	7	10		8					
38	30	Oldham Athletic	0-3		29093	5	4	2	6		3		11			1	9	7	10		8					
		Apps				38	34	5	36	4	36	2	22	20	3	38	35	33	37	15	35	4	2	2	16	1
		Goals				2							3				32	5	17		16	1		1	3	

F.A. Cup

#	Date	Opponent	Score	Scorers	Att	Browell A	Browell G	Gordon DS	McQuillan J	Neve E	Roughley E	Smith J	Smith JE	Smith W	Temple A	Wright G
R1	Jan 15	Chelsea	1-2	Temple	38000	5	4	6	3	2	1	9	7	10	8	11

		Pl	Home					Away					F	A	Pts
			W	D	L	F	A	W	D	L	F	A			(Total)
1	Manchester City	38	15	2	2	51	17	8	6	5	30	23	81	40	54
2	Oldham Athletic	38	15	2	2	47	9	8	5	6	32	30	79	39	53
3	HULL CITY	38	13	4	2	52	19	10	3	6	28	27	80	46	53
4	Derby County	38	15	2	2	46	15	7	7	5	26	32	72	47	53
5	Leicester Fosse	38	15	2	2	60	20	5	2	12	19	38	79	58	44
6	Glossop	38	14	1	4	42	18	4	6	9	22	39	64	57	43
7	Fulham	38	9	7	3	28	13	5	6	8	23	30	51	43	41
8	Wolverhampton W.	38	14	3	2	51	22	3	3	13	13	41	64	63	40
9	Barnsley	38	15	3	1	48	15	1	4	14	14	44	62	59	39
10	Bradford Park Ave.	38	12	1	6	47	28	5	3	11	17	31	64	59	38
11	West Bromwich Alb.	38	8	5	6	30	23	8	0	11	28	33	58	56	37
12	Blackpool	38	7	7	5	24	18	7	1	11	26	34	50	52	36
13	Stockport County	38	9	6	4	37	20	4	2	13	13	27	50	47	34
14	Burnley	38	12	2	5	43	21	2	4	13	19	40	62	61	34
15	Lincoln City	38	7	6	6	27	24	3	5	11	15	45	42	69	31
16	Clapton Orient	38	10	4	5	26	15	2	2	15	11	45	37	60	30
17	Leeds City	38	8	4	7	30	33	2	3	14	16	47	46	80	27
18	Gainsborough Trinity	38	8	3	8	22	21	2	3	14	11	54	33	75	26
19	Grimsby Town	38	8	3	8	31	19	1	3	15	19	58	50	77	24
20	Birmingham	38	7	4	8	28	26	1	3	15	14	52	42	78	23

Match Results

#		Date	Opponent	Score	Scorers	Att
1	Sep	3	WEST BROMWICH ALB.	1-1	Temple	9000
2		10	Bolton Wanderers	1-2	Smith J	10000
3		17	Fulham	1-0	Smith JE	20000
4		24	BRADFORD PARK AVE.	2-2	Smith JE, Temple	10000
5	Oct	1	Burnley	0-0		10500
6		8	GAINSBOROUGH TRIN.	3-2	Smith JE, Neve, Smith W	8000
7		15	Leeds City	0-1		8000
8		22	STOCKPORT COUNTY	4-1	Browell T 3, Temple	5000
9		29	Derby County	3-2	Browell T, Smith W, Temple	9000
10	Nov	5	BARNSLEY	5-1	Browell T 3, Smith W, Gordon DS	7000
11		12	Leicester Fosse	2-0	Smith JE, Browell G	8000
12		19	WOLVERHAMPTON W.	2-2	Browell T, Smith W	9000
13		26	Chelsea	0-2		15000
14	Dec	3	CLAPTON ORIENT	1-2	Browell T	5000
15		10	Blackpool	0-2		4000
16		17	GLOSSOP	1-0	Smith W	3500
17		24	Lincoln City	4-1	Browell T, Smith JE, Smith W, Temple	5000
18		26	BIRMINGHAM	4-1	Browell T 2, Temple, Neve	10000
19		27	BURNLEY	3-0	Browell T, Smith JE, Temple	10000
20		31	West Bromwich Albion	2-0	Browell T 2	12000
21	Jan	2	Huddersfield Town	0-2		4000
22		7	BOLTON WANDERERS	1-1	Temple	10000
23		21	FULHAM	0-0		8000
24		28	Bradford Park Avenue	0-2		15000
25	Feb	11	Gainsborough Trinity	1-1	Smith W	2000
26		18	LEEDS CITY	1-1	Smith W	6000
27	Mar	4	DERBY COUNTY	2-0	Neve, Gordon DS	5000
28		11	Barnsley	1-0	Smith W	5000
29		18	LEICESTER FOSSE	2-2	Smith JE 2	8000
30		25	Wolverhampton Wan.	0-0		5000
31	Apr	1	CHELSEA	1-1	Neve	12000
32		8	Clapton Orient	1-1	Temple	9000
33		14	Birmingham	0-1		10000
34		15	BLACKPOOL	1-1	Temple	11000
35		17	HUDDERSFIELD T	2-2	Houghton, Townend	12000
36		22	Glossop	0-0		1000
37		24	Stockport County	1-1	Houghton	2000
38		29	LINCOLN CITY	2-1	Browell T, Smith JE	5000

Appearances / Goals

	Browell A	Browell G	Browell T	Chapman H	Gordon Dan	Gordon DS	Houghton J	Martin F	McIntosh IB	McQuillan J	Musgrave A	Neve E	Nevins T	Pearce T	Robson W	Roughley E	Smith E	Smith J	Smith JE	Smith W	Temple A	Townend V	Wright G	Wright W
Apps	14	21	32	2	6	32	9	5	30	28	5	26	28	2	6	38	8	7	30	31	29	7	10	12
Goals		1	16			2	2					4						1	9	9	10		1	

F.A. Cup

		Date	Opponent	Score	Scorers	Att
R1	Jan	14	Bristol Rovers	0-0		9666
rep		19	BRISTOL ROVERS	1-0	McQuillan	13000
R2	Feb	4	OLDHAM ATHLETIC	1-0	Temple	17000
R3		25	Newcastle United	2-3	Smith JE 2	46531

R1 replay a.e.t.

Final Table

		Pl	Home W	D	L	F	A	Away W	D	L	F	A	F	A	Pts
1	West Bromwich Alb.	38	14	2	3	40	18	8	7	4	27	23	67	41	53
2	Bolton Wanderers	38	17	2	0	53	12	4	7	8	16	28	69	40	51
3	Chelsea	38	17	2	0	48	7	3	7	9	23	28	71	35	49
4	Clapton Orient	38	14	4	1	28	7	5	3	11	16	28	44	35	45
5	HULL CITY	38	8	10	1	38	21	6	6	7	17	18	55	39	44
6	Derby County	38	11	5	3	48	24	6	3	10	25	28	73	52	42
7	Blackpool	38	10	5	4	29	15	6	5	8	20	23	49	38	42
8	Burnley	38	9	9	1	31	18	4	6	9	14	27	45	45	41
9	Wolverhampton W.	38	10	5	4	26	16	5	3	11	25	36	51	52	38
10	Fulham	38	12	3	4	35	15	3	4	12	17	33	52	48	37
11	Leeds City	38	11	4	4	35	18	4	3	12	23	38	58	56	37
12	Bradford Park Ave.	38	12	4	3	44	18	2	5	12	9	37	53	55	37
13	Huddersfield Town	38	10	4	5	35	21	3	4	12	22	37	57	58	34
14	Glossop	38	11	4	4	36	21	2	4	13	12	41	48	62	34
15	Leicester Fosse	38	12	3	4	37	19	2	2	15	15	43	52	62	33
16	Birmingham	38	10	4	5	23	18	2	4	13	19	46	42	64	32
17	Stockport County	38	10	4	5	27	26	1	4	14	20	53	47	79	30
18	Gainsborough Trinity	38	9	5	5	26	16	0	6	13	11	39	37	55	29
19	Barnsley	38	5	7	7	36	26	2	7	10	16	36	52	62	28
20	Lincoln City	38	5	7	7	16	23	2	3	14	12	49	28	72	24

1910-11
Back Row: T. Nevins, W. Wright, F. Martin, H. Simmon, E. Gordon, T. Browell;
Standing: A. Langley (Manager), E. Roughley, D. Gordon, J. Houghton, A. Browell, J. McIntosh, G. Browell, W. Leach (Trainer);
Sitting: J.E. Smith, A. Temple, T. Pearce, D.S. Gordon, J. Smith, W. Smith, E. Neve;
On Ground: J. McQuillan, A. Musgrave, E. Smith, F. Taylor, N. Hendry

1911-12
Back Row: H. V. Townend, H. Chapman, W. Robson, S. Milner, A. Browell, J. McIntosh, Drewery;
Standing: A. Langley (Manager), H, Simmon, J. McQuillan, J. Houghton, E. Roughley, N Hendry, H. Wilkinson, D. Gordon, W, Leach (Trainer);
Sitting: J.E. Smith, W. Wright, T. Nevins, T. Browell, A. Temple, E. Neve, W. Smith;
On Ground: E. Pearce, E. Smith, C. Best, J. Boland.

1911/12 7th in Division Two

#	Date		Opponent	Score	Scorers	Att	Best C	Browell A	Browell T	Chapman H	Fazackerley S	Fenwick A	Gordon DS	Hedley T	Hendry N	Houghton J	McDonald W	McIntosh IB	McQuillan J	Neve E	Nevins T	Pearce T	Robson W	Roughley E	Shaw F	Smith E	Smith JE	Smith W	Stevens S	Temple A	Townend V	Wright G	Wright W
1	Sep	2	Blackpool	2-3	Browell T 2	10000		5	9	8			6						4	3	11	2		1			7			10			
2		9	GLOSSOP	2-0	Smith JE, Temple	9000		5		8			6						4	3	11	2		1		9	7			10			
3		16	BURNLEY	4-1	Temple 3, Browell T	10000		5	9	8			6							3		2		1			7			10		11	4
4		23	Barnsley	2-1	Browell T, Temple	9000		5	9	8			6							3		2		1			7			10		11	4
5		30	BRADFORD PARK AVE.	5-1	* See below	7000		5	9	8			6							3		2		1			7			10		11	4
6	Oct	7	Fulham	1-0	Temple	10000		5	9	8			6							3		2		1			7			10		11	4
7		14	DERBY COUNTY	0-0		14000		5		8			6							3		2		1			7	9		10		11	4
8		21	Stockport County	1-1	Temple	7000	8	5					6							3	11	2		1			7	9		10			4
9		25	Gainsborough Trinity	3-0	Browell T 3	6000	8	5	9				6							3		2	11	1			7			10			4
10		28	LEEDS CITY	1-0	Temple	12000		5	9	8			6							3		2		1			7			10		11	4
11	Nov	4	Wolverhampton Wan.	0-8		15000		5	9	8			6							3		2		1			7			10		11	4
12		11	LEICESTER FOSSE	4-1	Browell T 4	9000	7	5	9	8			6							3		2		1						10		11	4
13		25	GRIMSBY TOWN	1-0	Chapman	15000	7	5	9				6							3		2		1						10		11	4
14	Dec	2	Nottingham Forest	0-0		12000	7	5	9	8	6									3	11	2		1						10			4
15		9	CHELSEA	1-0	Browell T	15000		5	9	8			6							3	11	2		1						10	7		4
16		16	Clapton Orient	0-4		11000	7		9	8			6			5				3	11		2	1					10				4
17		23	BRISTOL CITY	3-0	Browell T 2, Temple	8000	7	5	9	8			6							3		2		1						10		11	
18		25	BIRMINGHAM	4-0	Chapman 2, Temple, Browell T	10000	7	5	9	8			6							3	11	2		1						10			
19		26	Birmingham	1-5	Temple	10000	8	5	9		4		6							3		2		1				7		10			
20		30	BLACKPOOL	3-0	Browell A 2, Temple	9000	8	5					6							3		2		1				6		10	7	11	4
21	Jan	6	Glossop	1-1	Temple	1000	9	5		8			6							3		2		1						10	7	11	4
22		20	Burnley	1-5	Houghton	14000	8	5					6	9		2				3	11			1			7	10					4
23		27	BARNSLEY	0-0		10000	8	5					10	9						3				1			7	6					4
24	Feb	10	FULHAM	2-3	Temple, Wright G	10000		5		8			6							3				1			7		9	10		11	4
25		17	Derby County	3-2	Chapman 2, Neve	8000		5		8			6			2				3	11			1			7		9	10			4
26		24	STOCKPORT COUNTY	0-2		8000		5		8			6			2				3	11			1			7		9	10			4
27	Mar	2	Leeds City	0-0		8000				8			6			2	7	5	3					1					9	10		11	4
28		9	WOLVERHAMPTON W.	3-0	McDonald, Best, Temple	10000	8			10			6			2	7	5	3					1						9		11	4
29		16	Leicester Fosse	0-3		10000	8			10			6			2	7	5	3		11			1					9				4
30		20	Bradford Park Avenue	1-3	Stevens	3000	8			10			6			2	7	5			11		3	1					9				
31		23	GAINSBOROUGH TRIN.	1-1	Fenwick	4000	8			10		6				2	7	5	3					1					9			11	
32		30	Grimsby Town	0-1		6000	8			10		6				2	7		3				11						5	9			
33	Apr	6	NOTTM. FOREST	2-1	Chapman, Wright W	7000	8			10			6			2	7		3				11	1					5	9			4
34		8	HUDDERSFIELD T	0-1		7000	9						6			2	7	5	3				11	1				8		10			4
35		9	Huddersfield Town	2-0	Best, Shaw	6000	8						6			2	7	5	3					1	11				9	10			4
36		13	Chelsea	0-1		35000	8			10			6			2	7	5	3		11			1			4		9				
37		20	CLAPTON ORIENT	0-2		6000	8			10						2	7	5	3		11			1				6	9				4
38		27	Bristol City	0-0		5000	9			8			6			2	7		3				11	1				5					4
			Apps				24	25	16	30	2	6	30	2	2	16	12	12	35	15	24	1	2	36	4	1	16	13	7	32	3	18	34
			Goals				2	2	16	7		1				1	1	1		1	1						1			16		2	1

Scorers in game 5: Temple, Chapman, Smith JE, Wright G, Browell 1

F.A. Cup

	Date		Opponent	Score	Scorers	Att	Best C	Browell A	Browell T	Chapman H	Fazackerley S	Fenwick A	Gordon DS	Hedley T	Hendry N	Houghton J	McDonald W	McIntosh IB	McQuillan J	Neve E	Nevins T	Pearce T	Robson W	Roughley E	Shaw F	Smith E	Smith JE	Smith W	Stevens S	Temple A	Townend V	Wright G	Wright W
R1	Jan	13	Oldham Athletic	1-1	Best	12000	9	5		8			6							3	11	2		1			7			10			4
rep		16	OLDHAM ATHLETIC	0-1		13112	9	5		8			6							3	11	2		1			7	10					4

		Pl	Home				Away					F.	A.	Pts
			W	D	L	F	A	W	D	L	F	A	(Total)	
1	Derby County	38	15	2	2	55	13	8	6	5	19	15	74	28	54
2	Chelsea	38	15	2	2	36	13	9	4	6	28	21	64	34	54
3	Burnley	38	14	5	0	50	14	8	3	8	27	27	77	41	52
4	Clapton Orient	38	16	0	3	44	14	5	3	11	17	30	61	44	45
5	Wolverhampton W.	38	12	3	4	41	10	4	7	8	16	23	57	33	42
6	Barnsley	38	10	5	4	28	19	5	7	7	17	23	45	42	42
7	HULL CITY	38	12	3	4	36	13	5	5	9	18	38	54	51	42
8	Fulham	38	10	3	6	42	24	6	4	9	24	34	66	58	39
9	Grimsby Town	38	9	6	4	24	18	6	3	10	24	37	48	55	39
10	Leicester Fosse	38	11	4	4	34	18	4	3	12	15	48	49	66	37
11	Bradford Park Ave.	38	10	5	4	30	16	3	4	12	14	29	44	45	35
12	Birmingham	38	11	3	5	44	29	3	3	13	11	30	55	59	34
13	Bristol City	38	11	4	4	27	17	3	2	14	14	43	41	60	34
14	Blackpool	38	12	4	3	24	12	1	4	14	8	40	32	52	34
15	Nottingham Forest	38	9	3	7	26	18	4	4	11	20	30	46	48	33
16	Stockport County	38	8	5	6	31	22	3	6	10	16	32	47	54	33
17	Huddersfield Town	38	8	5	6	30	22	5	1	13	20	42	50	64	32
18	Glossop	38	6	8	5	33	23	2	4	13	9	33	42	56	28
19	Leeds City	38	7	6	6	21	22	3	2	14	29	56	50	78	28
20	Gainsborough Trinity	38	4	6	9	17	22	1	7	11	13	42	30	64	23

1912/13   12th in Division Two

#		Date	Opponent	Score	Scorers	Att	Best C	Boyton J	Briggs J	Edelston J	Fazackerley S	Fenwick A	Goode H	Gordon DS	Hendry N	Hewitson R	Houghton J	Lyon S	McDonald W	McIntosh JB	McQuillan J	Nevins T	O'Connell P	Pattison J	Potts J	Shaw F	Stevens S	Wright G	Wright W
1	Sep	7	BLACKPOOL	4-1	Stevens, Best, Goode, Fazackerley	8000	7				10		8	6	1						5	3	2				9	11	4
2		9	Burnley	0-0		20000	7				10		8	6	1						5	3	2				9	11	4
3		14	Glossop	3-0	Goode 2, Fazackerley	3000	7				10		8	6	1						5	3	2			11	9		4
4		21	CLAPTON ORIENT	2-1	Fazackerley 2	12000	7				10		8	6	1						5	3	2				9	11	4
5		26	BURNLEY	0-0		8000	7				10		8	6	1						5	3	2				9	11	4
6		28	Lincoln City	1-1	Fazackerley	9000	7				10		8	6	1						5	3	2				9	11	4
7	Oct	5	NOTTM. FOREST	2-1	Fazackerley, Best	10000	7				10		8	6	1						5	3	2				9	11	4
8		12	Bristol City	1-1	Fazackerley	20000	7				10	4	8	6	1						5	3	2				9	11	
9		19	BIRMINGHAM	1-2	Fazackerley	10000	7				10	4	8	6	1						5	3	2				9	11	
10		26	Huddersfield Town	2-5	Fazackerley, McIntosh	3000	7				10	4	8	6	1						5	3	2				9	11	
11	Nov	2	LEEDS CITY	6-2	Stevens 4, McDonald, McIntosh	9000	8				10			6	1				7		5	3	2				9	11	4
12		9	Grimsby Town	0-2		8000					10		8	6	1				7		5	3	2			11	9		4
13		16	BURY	2-0	Stevens, Goode	7000					10		8	6	1				7		5	3	2				9	11	4
14		23	Fulham	0-2		20000					10		8	6	1				7			3	2	5			9	11	4
15	Dec	7	Bradford Park Avenue	0-2		10000					10			6	1				7	5		3	2	8			9	11	4
16		14	WOLVERHAMPTON W.	0-1		6000					10	6		1				7	5		3	2	8			9	11	4
17		19	BARNSLEY	0-1		4000					10			1		5		7	6	3	2	8			11	9		4
18		21	Leicester Fosse	2-3	Fazackerley 2	8000		8			9		10	6	1	5			7			3						11	4
19		25	STOCKPORT COUNTY	3-2	Fazackerley 2, Goode	8000					10		11	6	1			9	7		5	3	2	8					4
20		26	Preston North End	0-1		15000					10		8	6	1			9	7		5	3	2					11	4
21		28	Blackpool	2-1	Goode 2	3000		8			10		9	6	1				7		5	3	2					11	4
22	Jan	18	Clapton Orient	1-2	Fazackerley	7000					10		8	6	1				7		5	3	2				9	11	4
23		25	LINCOLN CITY	2-0	Stevens 2	8000		10					8	6	1				7		5	3	2				9	11	4
24	Feb	8	Nottingham Forest	0-5		12000		10					8	6	1				7		5	3	2			11	9		4
25		15	BRISTOL CITY	3-1	Fazackerley, Lyon, McQuillan	7000					10		8	6	1			9	7		5	3	2					11	4
26		22	Birmingham	1-3	Fazackerley	10000		10					8	6	1			9	7		5	3	2					11	4
27	Mar	1	HUDDERSFIELD T	1-3	McDonald	6000							8	6	1			9	7		5	3	2				10	11	4
28		8	Leeds City	0-1		20000		10					9	6	1				7		5	3			2		8	11	4
29		15	GRIMSBY TOWN	5-0	Fazackerley 3, Goode 2	7000					9		8	6	1				7		5	3			2		10	11	4
30		21	Stockport County	3-3	Stevens 2, Goode	7000							8	6	1				7	9	5	3			2		10	11	4
31		22	Bury	0-3		7000							8	6	1				7	9	5	3			2		10	11	4
32		24	PRESTON NORTH END	2-2	Stevens 2	12000			8				9	6	1				7		5	3	2				10	11	4
33		29	Fulham	0-1		7000			8	4			9	6	1				7			3	2				10	11	5
34	Apr	5	Barnsley	1-2	Stevens	6000							8	6	1			9	7		5	3	2				10	11	4
35		12	BRADFORD PARK AVE.	5-0	Stevens 2, Fenwick 2, McQuillan	4000						9	8	6	1				7		5	3	2				10	11	4
36		17	GLOSSOP	2-0	McDonald, Boyton	5000		8				9		6	1		11		7		5	3	2				10		4
37		19	Wolverhampton Wan.	1-0	Fenwick	6000		8		4		9		6	1		11		7		5	3	2				10		
38		26	LEICESTER FOSSE	2-0	Fenwick 2	5000		8		4		9		6	1		11		7		5	3	2				10		
			Apps				11	10	2	3	27	7	28	29	38	1	3	5	28	18	38	33	30	2	4	5	32	31	33
			Goals				2	1			19	5	10						1	3	2	2					15		

F.A. Cup

		Date	Opponent	Score	Scorers	Att	Boyton J	Fazackerley S	Goode H	Gordon DS	Hendry N	McDonald W	McQuillan J	Nevins T	O'Connell P	Stevens S	Wright G	Wright W
R1	Jan	11	Fulham	2-0	Fazackerley, Stevens	10000		10	8	6	1	7	5	3	2	9	11	4
R2	Feb	1	NEWCASTLE UNITED	0-0		18250		10	8	6	1	7	5	3	2	9	11	4
rep		5	Newcastle United	0-3		32278	10		8	6	1	7	5	3	2	9	11	4

League Table

		Pl	Home				Away					F.	A.	Pts
			W	D	L	F	A	W	D	L	F	A	(Total)	
1	Preston North End	38	13	5	1	34	12	6	10	3	22	21	56	33	53
2	Burnley	38	13	4	2	58	23	8	4	7	30	30	88	53	50
3	Birmingham	38	11	6	2	39	18	7	4	8	20	26	59	44	46
4	Barnsley	38	15	3	1	46	18	4	4	11	11	29	57	47	45
5	Huddersfield Town	38	13	5	1	49	12	4	4	11	17	28	66	40	43
6	Leeds City	38	12	3	4	45	22	3	7	9	25	42	70	64	40
7	Grimsby Town	38	10	8	1	32	11	5	2	12	19	39	51	50	40
8	Lincoln City	38	10	6	3	31	16	5	4	10	19	36	50	52	40
9	Fulham	38	13	5	1	47	16	4	0	15	18	39	65	55	39
10	Wolverhampton W.	38	10	6	3	34	16	4	4	11	22	38	56	54	38
11	Bury	38	10	6	3	29	14	5	2	12	24	43	53	57	38
12	HULL CITY	38	12	2	5	42	18	3	4	12	18	37	60	55	36
13	Bradford Park Ave.	38	12	4	3	47	18	2	4	13	13	42	60	60	36
14	Clapton Orient	38	8	6	5	25	20	2	8	9	27	34	47	34	34
15	Leicester Fosse	38	12	2	5	34	20	1	5	13	15	45	49	65	33
16	Bristol City	38	7	9	3	32	25	2	6	11	14	47	46	72	33
17	Nottingham Forest	38	9	3	7	35	25	3	5	11	23	34	58	59	32
18	Glossop	38	11	2	6	34	26	1	6	12	15	42	49	68	32
19	Stockport County	38	8	4	7	32	23	0	6	13	24	55	56	78	26
20	Blackpool	38	8	4	7	22	22	1	4	14	17	47	39	69	26

1912-13
Standing: H. Taylor (Trainer), S. Stevens, N. Hendry, S. Fazackerley, P. O'Connell, A. Langley (Manager);
Sitting: W. Wright, H. Goode, E.G.D. Wright, T. Nevins, D. Gordon;
On Ground: C. Best, J. McQuillan.

1913-14
Standing: W. Cameron, P. O'Connell, N. Hendry, J. Pattison, T. Murray, S. Stevens, H. Taylor (Trainer);
Sitting: J. Edelston, D. Morgan, J. McIntosh, W. Halligan, W. McDonald.

1913/14   7th in Division Two

#	Date		Score		Att	Boyton J	Byrne A	Cameron W	Edelston J	Fenwick A	Gordon DS	Halligan W	Hendry N	Lee J	Lyon J	Lyon S	McCorry H	McDonald W	McIntosh JB	McQuillan J	Melville D	Mercer D	Morgan D	Murray, Thos.	Newins T	O'Connell P	Pattison J	Potts J	Stevens S	Temple A	Wright W
1	Sep 6	Blackpool	2-2	McCorry, Halligan	10000		11		4			9	1				8	7	6				3			5	2		10		
2	13	NOTTM. FOREST	1-0	McCorry	8000		11		4	9			1				8	7	6	3						5	2		10		
3	20	Woolwich Arsenal	0-0		28000		11		4			9	1				8	7	6	3						5	2		10		
4	27	GRIMSBY TOWN	2-1	Lee, McCorry	10000				4			9	1		11		8	7	6	3						5	2		10		
5	Oct 4	Birmingham	1-1	Stevens	9000				4	9			1		11		10	7	6	3						5	2		8		
6	11	BRISTOL CITY	0-1		8000				4				1		11		9	7	6	3						5	2		8		10
7	13	LINCOLN CITY	1-1	Fenwick	5000				4	9			1		11		10	7	6	3						5	2		8		
8	18	Leeds City	2-1	Stevens 2	16000				4				1	11	10			7	6				3			5	2		9		8
9	25	CLAPTON ORIENT	2-0	Wright W, Stevens	8000				4				1	11	10			7	6				3			5	2		9		8
10	Nov 1	Glossop	1-2	McDonald	500				4				1	11	10			7	6				3			5	2		9		8
11	8	STOCKPORT COUNTY	3-0	Stevens 3	6000				4		6	10	1		11		8	7	5				3				2		9		
12	15	Bradford Park Avenue	0-2		10000				4		6	10	1		11		8	7	5				3				2		9		
13	22	NOTTS COUNTY	2-0	Stevens, Lyon J	10000				4		6	10	1		11		8	7	5				3				2		9		
14	29	Leicester Fosse	4-0	Halligan 2, Stevens, Lyon J	11000				4		6	10	1		11		8	7	5				3				2		9		
15	Dec 6	WOLVERHAMPTON W.	7-1	Halligan 4, O'Connell, Stevens, Lee	8000							10	1	11			8	7	6				3			5	2		9		4
16	13	FULHAM	1-1	Stevens	8000							10	1	11			8	7	6				3			5	2		9		4
17	20	Barnsley	2-0	Stevens, Lee	4000				4			10	1	11			8		6				3			5	2		9		7
18	25	Huddersfield Town	3-0	Stevens, Lyon J, Halligan	5000				4			10	1		11		8		6				3			5	2		9		7
19	26	HUDDERSFIELD T	4-1	Stevens 2, Halligan, Lyon J	10000							10	1		11		8	7	6				3			5	2		9		4
20	27	BLACKPOOL	0-0		10000				4			10	1		11		8		6				3			5	2		9		7
21	Jan 3	Nottingham Forest	2-1	Stevens 2	7000				4			10	1		11		8		6				3			5	2		9		
22	17	WOOLWICH ARSENAL	1-2	McCorry	12000				4			10	1		11		8	7	6	3						5	2		9		
23	24	Grimsby Town	3-1	Stevens 2, Halligan	12000						6	11	1				7	10					3			5	2		9	8	
24	Feb 7	BIRMINGHAM	0-0		8000	10			4				1		11		8	7	6				3			5	2		9		
25	14	Bristol City	1-2	Stevens	10000			10	4		6		1		11		8	7	5		2		3						9		
26	21	LEEDS CITY	1-0	Stevens	18000			10	4				1		11			7	6				3	8		5	2		9		
27	28	Clapton Orient	0-3		18000			10	4			11	1					7	6				3	8		5	2		9		
28	Mar 7	GLOSSOP	3-0	Stevens 2, Cameron	9000			8	4		6	10	1	11					7		2		3			5			9		
29	11	Lincoln City	0-0		7000			10	4		6		1		11		8	7			2		3			5			9		7
30	14	Stockport County	1-2	Halligan	6000	11		8	4		6	10	1					7			2		3			5			9		
31	21	BRADFORD PARK AVE.	1-3	Stevens	12000	11		8	4		6	10	1					7			2		3			5	2		9		
32	28	Notts County	1-4	Stevens	26000			8	4		6	10	1		11			7	6				3			5	2		9		
33	Apr 4	LEICESTER FOSSE	0-0		7000			8	4		6	10	1		11			7				5	3				2		9		8
34	10	Bury	0-2		12000			8	4		6	10	1		11							5	3				2		9		7
35	11	Wolverhampton Wan.	0-1		12000			8	4		6	10	1		11								3		7		2		9	5	
36	13	BURY	0-1		8000			8	4		6	10	1		11					3					7		2		9	5	
37	18	Fulham	1-0	Stevens	10000			8	4		6	10	1		11								3	7		5	2		9		
38	25	BARNSLEY	0-1		5000			8	4			10	1		11				6				3		7	5	2		9		
Apps						3	3	13	35	4	14	28	38	22	23	1	10	29	32	16	5	2	23	2	6	28	26	1	38	3	13
Goals								1		1		11		3	4		4	1								1			26		1

F.A. Cup

	Date		Score		Att	Edelston J	Halligan W	Hendry N	Lyon J	McCorry H	McDonald W	McIntosh JB	Morgan D	O'Connell P	Pattison J	Stevens S
R1	Jan 10	BURY	0-0		12000	4	10	1	11	8	7	6	3	5	2	9
rep	14	Bury	1-2	Lee	12808	4	10	1	11	8	7	6	3	5	2	9

		Pl	Home					Away					F.	A.	Pts
			W	D	L	F	A	W	D	L	F	A			(Total)
1	Notts County	38	16	2	1	55	13	7	5	7	22	23	77	36	53
2	Bradford Park Ave.	38	15	1	3	44	20	8	2	9	27	27	71	47	49
3	Woolwich Arsenal	38	14	3	2	34	10	6	6	7	20	28	54	38	49
4	Leeds City	38	15	2	2	54	16	5	5	9	22	30	76	46	47
5	Barnsley	38	14	1	4	33	15	5	6	8	18	30	51	45	45
6	Clapton Orient	38	14	5	0	38	11	2	6	11	9	24	47	35	43
7	HULL CITY	38	9	5	5	29	13	7	4	8	24	24	53	37	41
8	Bristol City	38	12	5	2	32	10	4	4	11	20	40	52	50	41
9	Wolverhampton W.	38	14	1	4	33	16	4	4	11	18	36	51	52	41
10	Bury	38	12	6	1	30	14	3	4	12	9	26	39	40	40
11	Fulham	38	10	3	6	31	20	6	3	10	15	23	46	43	38
12	Stockport County	38	9	6	4	32	18	4	4	11	23	39	55	57	36
13	Huddersfield Town	38	8	4	7	28	22	5	4	10	19	31	47	53	34
14	Birmingham	38	10	4	5	31	18	2	6	11	17	42	48	60	34
15	Grimsby Town	38	10	4	5	24	15	3	4	12	18	43	42	58	34
16	Blackpool	38	6	10	3	24	19	3	4	12	9	25	33	44	32
17	Glossop	38	8	3	8	32	24	3	3	13	19	43	51	67	28
18	Leicester Fosse	38	7	2	10	29	28	4	2	13	16	33	45	61	26
19	Lincoln City	38	8	5	6	23	23	2	1	16	13	43	36	66	26
20	Nottingham Forest	38	7	7	5	27	23	0	2	17	10	53	37	76	23

1914/15 7th in Division Two

#	Mon	Date	Opponent	Score	Scorers	Att	Betts A	Cameron W	Cleland J	Deacey C	Edelston J	Halligan W	Hendry N	Lee J	Lyon J	Medcalf J	Mercer D	Mercer W	Middlehurst J	Morgan D	Pattison J	Stevens S	Turner H	Wright W
1	Sep	3	STOCKPORT COUNTY	1-0	Stevens	4000		8		5	4	10	1			11	7			3	2	9		6
2		5	BLACKPOOL	1-3	Stevens	6000		8		5	4	10	1			11	7			3	2	9		6
3		12	Leeds City	3-2	Stevens, Cameron, Lee	8000	3	8		5	4	10	1	11			7				2	9		6
4		19	CLAPTON ORIENT	0-1		6000	3	8		5	4	10	1	11			7				2	9		6
5		26	Arsenal	1-2	Stevens	20000	3	8		5	4	11	1				7		2	6		9		10
6	Oct	3	DERBY COUNTY	1-0	Halligan	4000	3	8		5	4	10	1				7			11	2	9		6
7		10	Lincoln City	3-0	Cameron 2, Halligan	6000	3	8		5	4	10	1				7			11	2	9		6
8		17	BIRMINGHAM	0-0		7000	3	8		5	4	10	1				7			11	2	9		6
9		24	Grimsby Town	1-1	Stevens	9000	3	8		5	4	10	1				7			11	2	9		6
10		31	Huddersfield Town	0-1		6000	3	8			4	10	1				7			11	2	9	5	6
11	Nov	7	Bristol City	2-5	Stevens 2	8000	3	8			4	10	1				7			11	2	9	5	6
12		14	BURY	3-1	Halligan 2, Stevens	2000	3	8		5		10	1	11			7			4	2	9		6
13		21	Preston North End	1-2	Stevens	4000	3	8		5	4	10	1	11			7				2	9		6
14		28	NOTTM. FOREST	3-1	Lee 2, Halligan	6000	3	8		5	4	10	1	11			7				2	9		6
15	Dec	5	Leicester Fosse	1-1	Halligan	4000	3	8		5	4	10	1	11			7				2	9		6
16		12	BARNSLEY	2-1	Deacy, Stevens	3000	3	8		5	4	10	1	11			7				2	9		6
17		25	WOLVERHAMPTON W.	5-1	Halligan 2, Stevens, Cameron, Mercer D	6000	3	8		5	4	10	1	11			7				2	9		6
18		26	Wolverhampton Wan.	2-1	Lee, Cameron	10000	3	8		5	4	10	1	11			7				2	9		6
19	Jan	1	Stockport County	0-3		5000	3			5	4	10	1	11			7			8	2	9		6
20		2	Blackpool	2-1	Mercer D, Lee	4000	3			5		10	1	11	8		7				2	9	4	6
21		16	LEEDS CITY	2-6	Halligan, Stevens	5000	2	8		5	4	10	1	11			7			3		9		6
22		23	Clapton Orient	3-0	Turner 2, Stevens	2000				5	4	10		11			7	1		3	2	9	8	6
23	Feb	6	Derby County	1-4	Turner	5000				5	4		1	11			7				2	9	10	6
24	Mar	11	LINCOLN CITY	6-1	Stevens 2, Halligan 2, Cameron, Lee	3000	2	8		5	4	10	1	11			7			3		9		6
25		13	BRISTOL CITY	1-1	Lee	4000	2	8		5	4	10	1	11			7			3		9		6
26		16	Glossop	5-0	Stevens 2, Halligan 2, Cameron	500	2	8		5	4	10	1	11			7			3		9		6
27		20	Bury	1-0	Cameron	5000	2	8		5	4	9	1	11			7			3			10	6
28		24	Birmingham	2-2	Cameron, Halligan	5000	2	8		5	4	10	1	11			7			3		9		6
29		27	PRESTON NORTH END	0-1		7000	2	8		5	4	10	1	11			7			3		9		6
30	Apr	2	ARSENAL	1-0	Stevens	8000	2	8		5	4	10	1	11			7			3		9		6
31		3	Nottingham Forest	0-1		4000	2	8		5	4	10	1	11			7			3		9		6
32		5	FULHAM	2-0	Stevens, Mercer D	6000	2	8		5	4	10	1	11			7			3		9		6
33		6	Fulham	1-4	Halligan	2000	2	8		5	4	10	1	11			7			3		9		6
34		10	LEICESTER FOSSE	2-1	Stevens, Halligan	5500		8		5	4	10	1	11			7		2	3		9		6
35		15	HUDDERSFIELD T	0-4		2000	2		8	5	4	10	1	11			7			3		9		6
36		17	Barnsley	0-1		5000	2	8		5	4	10	1	11			7			3		9		6
37		24	GLOSSOP	2-0	Stevens 2	2000	2	8		5	4	10	1	11			7			3		9		6
38		29	GRIMSBY TOWN	4-1	Stevens 2, Mercer D, Halligan	3000	2	8		5	4	10	1	11			7			3		9		6

	Betts A	Cameron W	Cleland J	Deacey C	Edelston J	Halligan W	Hendry N	Lee J	Lyon J	Medcalf J	Mercer D	Mercer W	Middlehurst J	Morgan D	Pattison J	Stevens S	Turner H	Wright W
Apps	34	34	1	36	36	37	37	29	1	2	38	1	2	29	20	37	6	38
Goals		9		1		17		7			4					24	3	

F.A. Cup

#	Mon	Date	Opponent	Score	Scorers	Att	Betts A	Cameron W	Deacey C	Edelston J	Halligan W	Hendry N	Lee J	Mercer D	Morgan D	Pattison J	Stevens S	Wright W
R1	Jan	9	WEST BROMWICH ALB.	1-0	Stevens	13000	3	8	5	4	10	1	11	7		2	9	6
R2		30	NORTHAMPTON TOWN	2-1	Stevens 2	13000	3	8	5	4	10	1	11	7		2	9	6
R3	Feb	20	Southampton	2-2	Cameron, Lee	15607	2	8	5	4	10	1	11	7	3		9	6
rep		27	SOUTHAMPTON	4-0	Stevens 2, Cameron, Lee	11000	2	8	5	4	10	1	11	7	3		9	6
R4	Mar	6	Bolton Wanderers	2-4	Deacy, Stevens	24379	2	8	5	4	10	1	11	7	3		9	6

R3 (first game) a.e.t.

		Pl	Home					Away					F.	A.	Pts
			W	D	L	F	A	W	D	L	F	A	(Total)		
1	Derby County	38	14	3	2	40	11	9	4	6	31	22	71	33	53
2	Preston North End	38	14	4	1	41	16	6	6	7	20	26	61	42	50
3	Barnsley	38	16	2	1	31	10	6	1	12	20	41	51	51	47
4	Wolverhampton W.	38	12	4	3	47	13	7	3	9	30	39	77	52	45
5	Arsenal	38	15	1	3	52	13	4	4	11	17	28	69	41	43
6	Birmingham	38	13	3	3	44	13	4	6	9	18	26	62	39	43
7	HULL CITY	38	12	2	5	36	23	7	3	9	29	31	65	54	43
8	Huddersfield Town	38	12	4	3	36	13	5	4	10	25	29	61	42	42
9	Clapton Orient	38	12	5	2	36	17	4	4	11	14	31	50	48	41
10	Blackpool	38	11	3	5	40	22	6	2	11	18	35	58	57	39
11	Bury	38	11	5	3	39	19	4	3	12	22	37	61	56	38
12	Fulham	38	12	0	7	35	20	3	7	9	18	27	53	47	37
13	Bristol City	38	11	2	6	38	19	4	5	10	24	37	62	56	37
14	Stockport County	38	12	4	3	33	19	3	3	13	21	41	54	60	37
15	Leeds City	38	9	3	7	40	25	5	1	13	25	39	65	64	32
16	Lincoln City	38	9	4	6	29	23	2	5	12	17	42	46	65	31
17	Grimsby Town	38	10	4	5	36	24	1	5	13	12	52	48	76	31
18	Nottingham Forest	38	9	7	3	32	24	1	2	16	11	53	43	77	29
19	Leicester Fosse	38	6	4	9	31	41	4	0	15	16	47	47	88	24
20	Glossop	38	5	5	9	21	33	1	1	17	10	54	31	87	18

1915/16 Midland Section: Principal Competition

						1	2	3	4	5	6	7	8	9	10	11
1 Sep	4	Notts County	0-2		5000	Hendry N	Betts A	McQuillan J	Edelston J	Deacey C	Sheridan J	Mercer D	Bradbury J	Stevens S	Percival C	Lee J
2	11	DERBY COUNTY	4-2	Christmass (2), Bradbury, McQuillan	4000	Bell A	Betts A	McQuillan J	Edelston J	Wright W	Sheridan J	Mercer D	Bradbury J	Christmass J	Percival C	Lee J
3	18	Sheffield Wednesday	4-2	Percival (2), Christmass, Lee	5000	Hendry N	Betts A	McQuillan J	Edelston J	Wright W	Sheridan J	Mercer D	Bradbury J	Christmass J	Percival C	Lee J
4	25	BRADFORD PA	2-0	Christmass, Lee	7000	Hendry N	Betts A	McQuillan J	Edelston J	Wright W	Sheridan J	Mercer D	Bradbury J	Christmass J	Percival C	Lee J
5 Oct	2	Leeds City	1-3	Percival	6000	Hendry N	Betts A	McQuillan J	Edelston J	Deacey C	Wright W	Mercer D	Bradbury J	Christmass J	Percival C	Lee J
6	9	LINCOLN CITY	1-1	Wright W	4000	Hendry N	Betts A	McQuillan J	Edelston J	Wright W	Sheridan J	Mercer D	Bradbury J	Christmass J	Percival C	Lee J
7	16	NOTTINGHAM FOREST	1-3	Lee	4000	Hendry N	Betts A	McQuillan J	Edelston J	Wright W	Sheridan J	Mercer D	Bradbury J	Christmass J	Percival C	Lee J
8	23	Barnsley	1-4	Bradbury	2500	Edelston J	Betts A	McQuillan J	Coddington A	Wright W	Sheridan J	Mercer D	Bradbury J	Stevens S	Percival C	Lee J
9	30	LEICESTER FOSSE	2-2	Stevens, McQuillan	4000	Hendry N	Wilson A	McQuillan J	Edelston J	Wright W	Sheridan J	Mercer D	Bradbury J	Stevens S	Percival C	Lee J
10 Nov	6	Sheffield Utd	0-3		5000	Hendry N	Wilson A	McQuillan J	Edelston J	Wright W	Sheridan J	Mercer D	Bradbury J	Slide R	Percival C	Lee J
11	13	BRADFORD CITY	1-1	Slide	5000	Hendry N	Betts A	McQuillan J	Edelston J	Wright W	Sheridan J	Mercer D	Slide R	Lee J	Bradbury J	Pace A
12	20	Huddersfield Town	0-1		2000	Edelston J	Pattison J	McQuillan J	Jacketts G	Wright W	Sheridan J	Mercer D	Bradbury J	Lee J	Slide R	Pace A
13	27	GRIMSBY TOWN	4-1	Slide (2), Bradbury (2)	3000	Hendry N	Pattison J	McQuillan J	Edelston J	Wright W	Sheridan J	Mercer D	Slide R	Lee J	Bradbury J	Pace A
14 Dec	4	NOTTS COUNTY	3-0	Stevens (3)	1000	Hendry N	Pattison J	Betts A	Edelston J	Wright W	Sheridan J	Mercer D	Slide R	Stevens S	Bradbury J	Lee J
15	11	Derby County	1-3	Lee	1000	Edelston J	Pattison J	Betts A	Pace A	Jacketts G	Sheridan J	Mercer D		Stevens S	Bradbury J	Lee J
16	18	SHEFFIELD WEDNESDAY	1-3	Mercer D	3000	Hendry N	Pattison J	McQuillan J	Edelston J	Wright W	Sheridan J	Mercer D	Pace A	Slide R	Bradbury J	Lee J
17	25	Bradford PA	2-1	Mercer D, Slide	10000	Edelston J	Betts A	McQuillan J	Voase F	Pattison J	Sheridan J	Mercer D	Slide R	Stevens S	Percival C	Lee J
18 Jan	1	LEEDS CITY	0-3		3000	Hendry N	Betts A	McQuillan J	Edelston J	Wright W	Sheridan J	Mercer D	Slide R	Ainsworth J	Saunders J	Lee J
19	8	Lincoln City	1-4	Edelston	4500	Hendry N	Betts A	McQuillan J	Edelston J	Wright W	Sheridan J	Mercer D	Jacketts G	Slide R	Saunders J	Lee J
20	15	Nottingham Forest	1-4	Saunders	5000	Edelston J	Betts A	McQuillan J	Voase F	Pattison J	Sheridan J	Mercer D	Bradbury J	Christmass J	Saunders J	Lee J
21	22	BARNSLEY	1-0	Saunders	3000	Hendry N	Chaplin G	McQuillan J	Edelston J	Wright W	Sheridan J	Mercer D	Simmon H	Slide R	Saunders J	Lee J
22	29	Leicester Fosse	0-4		3000	Edelston J	Chaplin G	McQuillan J	Walters H	Meynell T	Sheridan J	Mercer D	Simmon H	Saunders J	McManus T	Lee J
23 Feb	5	SHEFFIELD UTD	2-0	Stevens, Lee	4000	Edelston J	Chaplin G	Betts A	Walters H	Wright W	Sheridan J	Mercer D	Slide R	Stevens S	Lee J	Ford B
24	12	Bradford City	4-8	Stevens (3), Ford	4000	Edelston J	Chaplin G	Betts A	Walters H	Gordon E	Sheridan J	Mercer D	Slide R	Stevens S	Lee J	Ford B
25	19	HUDDERSFIELD TOWN	2-1	Stevens, Mercer	3000	Hendry N	Chaplin G	McQuillan J	Edelston J	Wright W	Sheridan J	Mercer D	Slide R	Stevens S	Lee J	Ford B
26	26	Grimsby Town	3-2	Lee (3)	2000	Hendry N	Chaplin G	McQuillan J	Edelston J	Wright W	Sheridan J	Mercer D	Cameron W	Slide R	Lee J	Ford B

Subsidiary Cup

1 Mar	4	SHEFFIELD UTD	5-2	Lee 2, Ford, Slade, Sin	3000	Hendry N	Chaplin G	McQuillan J	Edelston J	Wright W	Sheridan J	Mercer D	Simmon H	Slide R	Lee J	Ford B
2	11	Lincoln City	0-7		2000	Hudson T	Pattison J	McQuillan J	Edelston J	Wright W	Sheridan J	Mercer D	Ainsworth J	Simpson A	Lee J	Ford B
3	18	GRIMSBY TOWN	2-5	Slide, Lee	3000	Hendry N	Chaplin G	McQuillan J	Edelston J	Wright W	Sheridan J	Mercer D	Whitfield N	Slide R	Lee J	Ford B
4	25	Sheffield Wednesday	2-0	Naismith, Lee	6000	Hendry N	Chaplin G	McQuillan J	Edelston J	Hall E	Sheridan J	Mercer D	Naismith E	Slide R	Lee J	Ford B
5 Apr	1	Rotherham City	2-4	Slide, Lee	5000	Hendry N	Chaplin G	McQuillan J	Edelston J	Wright W	Sheridan J	Mercer D	Slide R	Simpson A	Lee J	Ford B
6	8	Sheffield Utd	0-2		5000	Hendry N	Wright W	Chaplin G	Edelston J	Hall E	Sheridan J	Mercer D	Whitfield N	Wheeldon J	Lee J	Ford B
7	15	LINCOLN CITY	2-1	Lee 2	3000	Hendry N	Chaplin G	Hobson B	Edelston J	Coverdale R	Sheridan J	Mercer D	Naismith E	Whitfield N	Lee J	Ford B
8	22	Grimsby Town	0-5		4000	Hendry N	Chaplin G	Betts A	Voase F	Edelston J	Sheridan J	Mercer D	Naismith E	Slide R	Lee J	Ford B
9	24	ROTHERHAM COUNTY	4-1	Stevens 2, Lee, Burton	4000	Hendry N	Hobson B	Young R	Voase F	Chaplin G	Jacketts G	Mercer D	Burton E	Stevens S	Lee J	Ford B
10	29	SHEFFIELD WEDNESDAY	1-0	Thistleton	3000	Hendry N	Edelston J	Chaplin G	Voase F	Coverdale R	Sheridan J	Mercer D	Thistleton M	Slide R	Lee J	Ford B

1916/17 Midland Section: Prinipal Competition

						1	2	3	4	5	6	7	8	9	10	11
1 Sep	2	ROTHERHAM COUNTY	0-0		2000	Hendry N	Wigglesworth A	Betts A	Jacketts G	Edelston J	Sheridan J	Mercer D	Simmon H	Lee J	Pace A	Ford B
2	9	Huddersfield Town	1-2	Mercer D	3000	Hendry N	Wigglesworth A	Betts A	Edelston J	Coverdale R	Jacketts G	Mercer D	Simmon H	Veale W	Wright W	Grimshaw W
3	16	LINCOLN CITY	2-1	Mercer D, Simmon	2000	Hendry N	Wigglesworth A	Betts A	Edelston J	Coverdale R	Sheridan J	Mercer D	Higgins A	Grimshaw W	Simmon H	Ford B
4	23	Sheffield Wednesday	1-2	Mercer D	5000	Hendry N	Wigglesworth A	Betts A	Edelston J	Jacketts G	Sheridan J	Mercer D	Simmon H	Grimshaw W	Wright W	Ford B
5	30	BRADFORD PA	1-1	Grimshaw	3000	Hendry N	Wigglesworth A	Betts A	Edelston J	Wright W	Sheridan J	Mercer D	Higgins A	Stevens S	Halligan W	Grimshaw W
6 Oct	7	Birmingham City	2-4	Stevens (2)	16000	Hendry N	Hobson B	Betts A	McCourty W	Deacey C	Sheridan J	Mercer D	Edelston J	Stevens S	Smith J	Grimshaw W
7	14	Chesterfield	0-5		2000	Hendry N	Wigglesworth A	Wright J	Edelston J	Nevin J	Wright W	Mercer D	Simmon H	Howie D	Hawksworth E	Grimshaw W
8	21	NOTTINGHAM FOREST	3-1	Wright W (2), Stevens	2500	Hendry N	Wigglesworth A	Betts A	Edelston J	Nevin J	Sheridan J	Mercer D	Grimshaw W	Stevens S	Wright W	Ford B
9	28	Barnsley	2-8	Grimshaw (2)	2000	Hendry N	Wigglesworth A	Betts A	Edelston J	Nevin J	Sheridan J	Mercer D	Grimshaw W	Atkinson W	Ford B	Fairclough S
10 Nov	4	LEEDS CITY	1-1	Grimshaw	3000	Hendry N	Wigglesworth A	Betts A	Edelston J	Nevin J	Sheridan J	Mercer D	Grimshaw W	Higgins A	Wright W	Ford B
11	11	Sheffield Utd	1-4	Grimshaw	8000	Hendry N	Wigglesworth A	McManus T	Jacketts G	Nevin J	Sheridan J	Mercer D	Grimshaw W	Haywood ?	Wright W	Ford B
12	18	BRADFORD CITY	1-0	Higgins	500	Hendry N	Wigglesworth A	Coverdale R	Jacketts G	Nevin J	Sheridan J	Mercer D	Grimshaw W	Higgins A	Wright W	Ford B
13	24	Leicester Fosse	2-0	Grimshaw, Leigh	2000	Edelston J	Wigglesworth A	Betts A	Jacketts G	Nevin J	Sheridan J	Mercer D	Grimshaw W	Leigh S	Pace A	Ford B
14 Dec	2	GRIMSBY TOWN	2-0	Higgins (2)	3000	Hendry N	Wigglesworth A	Betts A	Wright W	Nevin J	Sheridan J	Mercer D	Grimshaw W	Hawley ?	Higgins A	Ford B
15	9	Rotherham County	1-1	Stevens	2000	Hendry N	Wigglesworth A	Wright W	Brown J	Jacketts G	Sheridan J	Mercer D	Grimshaw W	Stevens S	Leigh S	Ford B
16	16	HUDDERSFIELD TOWN	0-1		1500	Hendry N	Wigglesworth A	Betts A	Edelston J	Jacketts G	Sheridan J	Mercer D	Grimshaw W	Higgins A	Wright W	Lee J
17	23	Lincoln City	1-1	Stevens	1500	Hendry N	Wigglesworth A	Betts A	Edelston J	Jacketts G	Sheridan J	Mercer D	Grimshaw W	Stevens S	Pace A	Ford B
18	25	NOTTS COUNTY	2-0	Stevens, Sheridan	1000	Hendry N	Wigglesworth A	Betts A	Jacketts G	Wright W	Sheridan J	Mercer D	Leigh S	Stevens S	Brown D	Grimshaw W
19	26	Notts County	1-7	Stevens	6000	Hendry N	Wigglesworth A	Betts A	Crowther H	Jacketts G	Sheridan J	Mercer D	Grimshaw W	Stevens S	Leigh S	Ford B
20	30	SHEFFIELD WEDNESDAY	1-0	Mercer D	2000	Hendry N	Wigglesworth A	Betts A	Jacketts G	Wright W	Sheridan J	Mercer D	Edelston J	Thistleton M	Pace A	Ford B
21 Jan	6	Bradford PA	0-4		2000	Hendry N	Wigglesworth A	Betts A	Jacketts G	Edelston J	Sheridan J	Mercer D	Wilde R	Thistleton M	Pace A	Ford B
22	13	BIRMINGHAM CITY	0-1		2000	Hendry N	Wigglesworth A	Betts A	Jacketts G	Wright W	Sheridan J	Mercer D	Edelston J	McQuillan J	Pace A	Ford B
23	20	CHESTERFIELD	3-1	Stevens (2), Leigh	2000	Hendry N	Wigglesworth A	Betts A	Jacketts G	Wright W	Sheridan J	Mercer D	Leigh S	Stevens S	Pepper H	Martin H
24	27	Nottingham Forest	0-3		1000	Iremonger A	Wigglesworth A	Betts A	Jacketts G	Woodland A	Sheridan J	Mercer D	Edelston J	Leigh S	Cutts E	McQuillan J
25 Feb	3	BARNSLEY	0-1		1000	Hendry N	Wigglesworth A	Betts A	Jacketts G	Wright W	Sheridan J	Mercer D	Edelston J	Stevens S	Pace A	McQuillan J
26	10	Leeds City	1-1	Wright W	3000	Hendry N	Wigglesworth A	Betts A	Jacketts G	Wright W	Sheridan J	Mercer D	Edelston J	Dick H	Wilde R	McQuillan J
27	17	SHEFFIELD UTD	1-1	Wright W	1500	Hendry N	Wigglesworth A	Betts A	Jacketts G	Wale L	Sheridan J	Mercer D	Pace A	Wright W	Edelston J	Martin H
28	24	Bradford City	1-3	Lee	2000	Hendry N	Wigglesworth A	Pattison J	Jacketts G	Edelston J	Sheridan J	Mercer D	Pace A	Cleland J	Norton H	Lee J
29 Mar	3	LEICESTER FOSSE	2-1	Mercer D (2)	2000	Hendry N	Wigglesworth A	Betts A	Jacketts G	Wale L	Sheridan J	Mercer D	Leigh S	Osborn F	Edelston J	Wright W
30	10	Grimsby Town	3-2	Osborn (3)	2000	Hendry N	Wigglesworth A	Betts A	Jacketts G	Edelston J	Sheridan J	Mercer D	Cleland J	Osborn F	Cookson S	Isherwood R

Secondary Competition

1 Mar	17	Chesterfield	1-4	Harvey	1500	Hendry N	Wigglesworth A	Matthews J	Pace A	Jacketts G	Sheridan J	Mercer D	Stables A	Cleland J	Harvey A	Isherwood R
2	31	Lincoln City	2-2	Mercer D, Cleland	1500	Hendry N	Wigglesworth A	Betts A	Jacketts G	Edelston J	Sheridan J	Mercer D	Simmon H	Cleland J	Cookson S	Pace A
3 Apr	6	Grimsby Town	1-2	Sheridan	1500	Hendry N	Wigglesworth A	Betts A	Jacketts G	Edelston J	Sheridan J	Mercer D	Robinson A	Cookson S	Simmon H	Isherwood R
4	7	CHESTERFIELD	5-1	Cookson (3), Mercer D, Wright W	2000	Hendry N	Wigglesworth A	Betts A	Jacketts G	Edelston J	Sheridan J	Mercer D	Simmon H	Wright W	Cookson S	Isherwood R
5	9	GRIMSBY TOWN	2-2	Brown D(2)	2000	Hendry N	Wigglesworth A	Betts A	Jacketts G	Edelston J	Sheridan J	Mercer D	Wright W	Brown D	Cookson S	Isherwood R
6	21	LINCOLN CITY	2-1	Mercer D (2)	2000	Hendry N	Wigglesworth A	Betts A	Jacketts G	Edelston J	Sheridan J	Mercer D	Cleland J	Wright W	Pace A	Isherwood R

1915/16

Principal Competition

	P	W	D	L	F	A	Pts
1 Nottingham Forest	26	15	5	6	48	25	35
2 Sheffield United	26	12	7	7	51	36	31
3 Huddersfield Town	26	12	5	9	43	36	29
4 Bradford City	26	12	4	10	52	32	28
5 Leicester Fosse	26	11	6	9	42	34	28
6 Barnsley	26	12	4	10	46	55	28
7 Sheffield Wednesday	26	11	5	10	46	43	27
8 Notts County	26	10	6	10	39	36	26
9 Lincoln City	26	12	2	12	54	54	26
10 Leeds City	26	10	5	11	39	43	25
11 HULL CITY	26	10	3	13	42	58	23
12 Bradford P.A.	26	9	4	13	46	46	22
13 Grimsby Town	26	7	6	13	31	46	20
14 Derby County	26	7	2	17	39	74	16

Subsidiary Cup

	P	W	D	L	F	A	Pts
1 Grimsby Town	10	5	2	3	25	10	12
2 Sheffield United	10	4	3	3	17	11	11
3 Rotherham County	10	5	1	4	20	24	11
4 HULL CITY	10	5	0	5	18	27	10
5 Sheffield Wednesday	10	3	3	4	10	13	9
6 Lincoln City	10	2	3	5	17	22	7

1916/17

Principal Competition

	P	W	D	L	F	A	Pts
1 Leeds City	30	18	10	2	68	29	46
2 Barnsley	30	15	8	7	65	41	38
3 Birmingham	30	14	9	7	56	38	37
4 Huddersfield Town	30	15	6	9	41	31	36
5 Bradford P.A.	30	14	6	10	51	32	34
6 Nottingham Forest	30	14	5	11	57	39	33
7 Notts County	30	13	6	11	47	52	32
8 Bradford City	30	12	7	11	41	41	31
9 Rotherham County	30	12	6	12	53	52	30
10 Sheffield United	30	11	7	12	43	47	29
11 HULL CITY	30	10	7	13	36	57	27
12 Chesterfield Town	30	11	4	15	59	62	26
13 Sheffield Wednesday	30	9	6	15	36	48	24
14 Grimsby Town	30	8	6	16	38	71	22
15 Leicester Fosse	30	6	7	17	29	53	19
16 Lincoln City	30	5	6	19	38	65	16

Subsidiary Competition

	P	W	D	L	F	A	Pts
1 Bradford P.A.	6	3	2	1	10	5	8
2 Sheffield United	6	4	0	2	12	7	8
3 Birmingham	6	3	2	1	17	12	8
4 Leicester Fosse	6	4	0	2	12	12	8
5 Chesterfield Town	6	4	0	2	15	16	8
6 Huddersfield Town	6	3	1	2	6	4	7
7 Leeds City	6	2	2	2	8	7	6
8 Grimsby Town	6	2	2	2	12	11	6
9 HULL CITY	6	2	2	2	13	12	6
10 Sheffield Wednesday	6	2	2	2	12	12	6
11 Barnsley	6	1	3	2	8	9	5
12 Rotherham County	6	2	1	3	9	13	5
13 Lincoln City	6	1	2	3	11	12	[illegible]
14 Nottingham Forest	6	1	2	3	12	14	[illegible]
15 Notts County	6	1	2	3	9	12	[illegible]
16 Bradford City	6	0	3	3	5	13	[illegible]

1917/18 Midland Section Principal Competition

No.	Month	Day	Opponent	Result	Scorers	Att	1	2	3	4	5	6	7	8	9	10	11
1	Sep	1	Birmingham City	1-2	Hughes	8000	Hendry N	Pattison J	Wigglesworth A	Edelston J	Deacey C	Jacketts G	Mercer D	Goodfellow S	Osborn F	Smith J	Hughes R
2		8	BIRMINGHAM CITY	1-2	Hughes	2500	Hendry N	Pattison J	Wigglesworth A	Edelston J	Wright W	Jacketts G	Mercer D	Cleland J	Goodfellow S	Smith J	Hughes R
3		#	Notts County	2-2	Mercer D (2)	3000	Hendry N	Wigglesworth A	Betts A	Pattison J	Edelston J	Jacketts G	Smith J	Mercer D	Goodfellow S	Cleland J	Hughes R
4		#	NOTTS COUNTY	1-2	Hughes	2000	Hendry N	Wigglesworth A	Betts A	Pattison J	Edelston J	Jacketts G	Smith J	Mercer D	Osborn F	Wright W	Hughes R
5		#	Huddersfield Town	2-4	Hughes, Smith J	2000	Hendry N	Wigglesworth A	Betts A	Edelston J	Nevin J	Pattison J	Smith J	Shaw P	Mercer D	Jacketts G	Hughes R
6	Oct	6	HUDDERSFIELD TOWN	3-1	Hughes (2), Smith	2000	Hendry N	Wigglesworth A	Betts A	Jacketts G	Edelston J	Sheridan J	Smith J	Mercer D	Hartnell S	Wright W	Hughes R
7		#	SHEFFIELD WEDNESDAY	3-3	Mercer D, Hartnell, Osborn	1500	Hendry N	Wigglesworth A	Betts A	Edelston J	Wright W	Sheridan J	Smith J	Mercer D	Hartnell S	Osborn F	Hughes R
8		#	Sheffield Wednesday	3-4	Wallis (2), Hughes	5000	Hendry N	Wigglesworth A	Betts A	Edelston J	Nevin J	Jacketts G	Smith J	Mercer D	Wallis H	Wright W	Hughes R
9		#	BRADFORD CITY	5-1	Mercer (3), Hughes, Wallis	2000	Edelston J	Wigglesworth A	Betts A	Jacketts G	Nevin J	Wright W	Smith J	Mercer D	Wallis H	Whittingham H	Hughes R
10	Nov	3	Bradford City	4-2	Hughes (3), Mercer D	2000	Hendry N	Wigglesworth A	Betts A	Jacketts G	Edelston J	Sheridan J	Smith J	Mercer D	Priestley J	Fearnley E	Hughes R
11		#	ROTHERHAM COUNTY	3-1	Mercer, Hughes, Wright W	2000	Edelston J	Wigglesworth A	Betts A	Jacketts G	Wright W	Sheridan J	Smith J	Mercer D	Wallis H	Whittingham H	Hughes R
12		#	Rotherham County	2-1	Wallis (2)	3000	Hendry N	Wigglesworth A	Pattison J	Jacketts G	Edelston J	Elvin R	Smith J	Mercer D	Wallis H	McManus T	Pace A
13		#	LINCOLN CITY	2-0	Mercer D, Hughes	1000	Hendry N	Wigglesworth A	Pattison J	Edelston J	Wright W	Jacketts G	Smith J	Mercer D	Wallis H	McManus T	Hughes R
14	Dec	1	Lincoln City	3-1	Mercer D (3)	2000	Edelston J	Wigglesworth A	Betts A	Pattison J	Wright W	Jacketts G	Smith J	Mercer D	Wallis H	McManus T	Hughes R
15		8	LEICESTER FOSSE	3-1	Mercer D (2), Hughes	2500	Hendry N	Wigglesworth A	Betts A	Pattison J	Edelston J	Jacketts G	Smith J	Mercer D	Wallis H	Wright W	Hughes R
16		#	Leicester Fosse	1-3	Mercer D	2000	Edelston J	Wigglesworth A	Betts A	Jacketts G	Wright W	Pattison J	Smith J	Mercer D	Wallis H	McManus T	Hughes R
17		#	NOTTINGHAM FOREST	3-2	Hughes, Jacketts, Deacy	2000	Hendry N	Wigglesworth A	Betts A	Edelston J	Deacey C	Jacketts G	Smith J	Mercer D	Wallis H	Wright W	Hughes R
18		#	GRIMSBY TOWN	7-1	Hughes (2), Wright W (2), Smith J (2), Mercer D	1000	Hendry N	Wigglesworth A	Betts A	Edelston J	Deacey C	Jacketts G	Smith J	Mercer D	Wallis H	Wright W	Hughes R
19		#	Nottingham Forest	1-5	Mercer D	1500	Hendry N	Edelston J	Wigglesworth A	Leigh S	Deacey C	Jacketts G	Smith J	Mercer D	Wallis H	Shaw P	Hughes R
20	Jan	5	LEEDS CITY	0-2		3000	Edelston J	Wigglesworth A	Betts A	Pattison J	Wright W	Jacketts G	Smith J	Mercer D	Wallis H	McManus T	Hughes R
21		#	Leeds City	3-1	Mercer D, Wright W, Hughes	4000	Hendry N	Wigglesworth A	Betts A	Edelston J	Nevin J	Jacketts G	Smith J	Mercer D	Wallis H	Wright W	Hughes R
22		#	SHEFFIELD UTD	2-4	Hughes, Wright W	3000	Hendry N	Wigglesworth A	Betts A	Edelston J	Nevin J	Jacketts G	Smith J	Mercer D	Wright W	Shaw P	Hughes R
23		#	Sheffield Utd	1-0	Hughes	12000	Hendry N	Wigglesworth A	Betts A	Charles F	Edelston J	Jacketts G	Smith J	Mercer D	Wallis H	Wright W	Hughes R
24	Feb	2	Barnsley	3-1	Riley (2), Wallis	2000	Hendry N	Wigglesworth A	Pattison J	Smith J	Edelston J	Jacketts G	Mercer D	Riley H	Wallis H	Summers J	Hughes R
25		9	BARNSLEY	4-2	Hughes (2), Osborn (2)	3000	Hendry N	Wigglesworth A	Betts A	Pace A	Edelston J	Jacketts G	Smith J	Mercer D	Osborn F	Wright W	Hughes R
26	Mar	2	BRADFORD PA	1-1	Mercer D	2000	Hendry N	Wigglesworth A	Betts A	Edelston J	Wright W	Jacketts G	Smith J	Mercer D	Wallis H	Osborn F	Hughes R
27		3	Bradford PA	3-1	Mercer D, Hughes, Wright W	3000	Edelston J	Wigglesworth A	Betts A	Pattison J	Nevin J	Jacketts G	Smith J	Mercer D	Osborn F	Wright W	Hughes R
28	Apr	#	Grimsby Town	0-0		500	Hendry N	Pattison J	Malkinson T	Jacketts G	Edelston J	Elvin R	Stevenson T	Mercer D	Milner A	Lee J	Hughes R

Secondary Competition

No.	Month	Day	Opponent	Result	Scorers	Att	1	2	3	4	5	6	7	8	9	10	11
1	Feb	#	GAINSBOROUGH TRINITY	4-2	Mercer D (3), Hughes	2000	Hendry N	Wigglesworth A	Betts A	Pace A	Edelston J	Jacketts G	Smith J	Mercer D	Jordan ?	Osborn F	Hughes R
2		#	Gainsborough Trinity	1-0	Jacketts	2000	Hendry N	Brown W	Betts A	Edelston J	Jacketts G	Pace A	Smith J	Mercer D	Wallis H	Osborn F	Hughes R
3	Mar	#	LINCOLN CITY	4-2	Hughes, Mercer D, Wallis, Osborn	2000	Edelston J	Wigglesworth A	Betts A	Jacketts G	Wright W	Pattison J	Smith J	Mercer D	Wallis H	Osborn F	Hughes R
4		#	Lincoln City	1-1	Mercer D	3000	Hendry N	Wigglesworth A	Betts A	Jacketts G	Edelston J	Pattison J	Smith J	Mercer D	Wallis H	Osborn F	Hughes R
5		#	Grimsby Town	0-2		2000	Edelston J	Wigglesworth A	Betts A	Pattison J	Jacketts G	Pace A	Smith J	Mercer D	Wallis H	Osborn F	Shaw P
6	Apr	1	GRIMSBY TOWN	2-2	Mercer D, Shaw	3000	Pattison J	Wigglesworth A	Betts A	Jacketts G	Edelston J	Pace A	Smith J	Mercer D	Wallis H	Shaw P	Hughes R

1918/19 Midland Section Principal Competition

No.	Month	Day	Opponent	Result	Scorers	Att	1	2	3	4	5	6	7	8	9	10	11
1	Sep	7	BRADFORD CITY	2-0	Potter, Lee	4000	Mercer W	Wigglesworth A	Betts A	Jacketts G	Edelston J	Pattison J	Mercer D	Potter C	Hopkins V	Lee J	Hughes R
2		14	Bradford City	0-4		3000	Mercer W	Wigglesworth A	Betts A	Jacketts G	Edelston J	Pattison J	Mercer D	Potter C	Hopkins V	Lee J	Parr J
3		21	SHEFFIELD WEDNESDAY	0-0		4000	Mercer W	Wigglesworth A	Betts A	Jacketts G	Edelston J	Pattison J	Mercer D	Potter C	Pace A	Lee J	Hughes R
4		28	Sheffield Wednesday	1-3	Lee	6000	Thorpe T	Wigglesworth A	Betts A	Edelston J	Jacketts G	Pattison J	Peach R	Mercer D	Machin E	Lee J	Hughes R
5	Oct	5	HUDDERSFIELD TOWN	3-0	Wright W, Hughes, Jacketts	3000	Mercer W	Wigglesworth A	Betts A	Jacketts G	Edelston J	Bleakley T	Mercer D	Potter C	Wright W	Lee J	Hughes R
6		12	Huddersfield Town	0-1		2000	Hendry N	Wigglesworth A	Betts A	Jacketts G	Edelston J	Bleakley T	Mercer D	Tickle J	Machin E	Lee J	Hughes R
7		19	Notts County	0-1		6000	Hendry N	Wigglesworth A	Pace A	Jacketts G	Edelston J	Bleakley T	Mercer D	Potter C	Stevens S	Lee J	Hughes R
8		26	NOTTS COUNTY	1-1	Shaw	4000	Hendry N	Wigglesworth A	Pattison J	Jacketts G	Edelston J	Bleakley T	Mercer D	Charlesworth A	Suddes F	Shaw P	Hughes R
9	Nov	2	Birmingham	1-5	Hughes	10000	Smith F	Wigglesworth A	Pattison J	Jacketts G	Wootton J	Lindley J	Mercer D	Gillett J	Stevens S	Osborn F	Hughes R
10		9	BIRMINGHAM	0-3		4000	Hendry N	Wigglesworth A	Betts A	Jacketts G	Edelston J	Bleakley T	Mercer D	Potter C	Stevens S	Lee J	Hughes R
11		16	Rotherham County	2-2	Hughes, Mercer D	2500	Hendry N	Wigglesworth A	Betts A	Jacketts G	Edelston J	Harrison J	Mercer D	Shaw P	Stevens S	Lee J	Hughes R
12		23	ROTHERHAM COUNTY	4-0	Lee (2), Hughes, Mercer D	3000	Hendry N	Wigglesworth A	Betts A	Jacketts G	Edelston J	Pattison J	Hughes R	Mercer D	Potter C	Shaw P	Lee J
13		30	Lincoln City	2-0	Mercer D, Suddes	3000	Hendry N	Wigglesworth A	Betts A	Jacketts G	Edelston J	Pattison J	Hughes R	Mercer D	Suddes F	Potter C	Lee J
14	Dec	7	LINCOLN CITY	5-1	McManus (2), Potter, Lee, Mercer D	4000	Hendry N	Wigglesworth A	Betts A	Jacketts G	Edelston J	Pattison J	Hughes R	Mercer D	McManus T	Potter C	Lee J
15		14	Leeds City	0-0		6000	Hendry N	Wigglesworth A	Betts A	Jacketts G	Edelston J	Pattison J	Hughes R	Mercer D	Foss F	Potter C	Lee J
16		21	LEEDS CITY	2-1	Mercer D, Stevems	5000	Hendry N	Wigglesworth A	Betts A	Jacketts G	Edelston J	Pattison J	Hughes R	Mercer D	Stevens S	Newton A	Lee J
17		25	Grimsby Town	1-1	Newton	3000	Hendry N	Wigglesworth A	Betts A	Jacketts G	Edelston J	Pattison J	Hughes R	Mercer D	Stevens S	Newton A	Lee J
18		26	GRIMSBY TOWN	2-0	Stevens, Lee	7500	Hendry N	Wigglesworth A	Betts A	Jacketts G	Edelston J	Pattison J	Hughes R	Mercer D	Stevens S	McManus T	Lee J
19		28	Sheffield Utd	0-0		16000	Hendry N	Wigglesworth A	Betts A	Jacketts G	Edelston J	Pattison J	Hughes R	Mercer D	Stevens S	Cutts E	Lee J
20	Jan	11	BRADFORD PA	0-2		6000	Hendry N	Wigglesworth A	Betts A	Jacketts G	Edelston J	Pattison J	Hughes R	Mercer D	Foss F	Potter C	Lee J
21		18	Bradford PA	1-0	Lee	10000	Hendry N	Wigglesworth A	Betts A	Jacketts G	Edelston J	Pattison J	Hughes R	Mercer D	Potter C	Lyon J	Lee J
22		25	COVENTRY CITY	2-0	Lee, Potter	5000	Hendry N	Wigglesworth A	Betts A	Jacketts G	Edelston J	Pattison J	Hughes R	Mercer D	Potter C	Lyon J	Lee J
23	Feb	1	Coventry City	0-3		8000	Hendry N	Wigglesworth A	Betts A	Jacketts G	Edelston J	Bleakley T	Hughes R	Mercer D	Stevens S	Potter C	Lee J
24		8	Barnsley	4-3	Lyon J (2), Hughes, Mercer D	3000	Hendry N	Wigglesworth A	Betts A	Jacketts G	Edelston J	Bleakley T	Hughes R	Mercer D	Potter C	Lyon J	Lee J
25		15	BARNSLEY	1-3	Potter	7000	Hendry N	Wigglesworth A	Betts A	Jacketts G	Edelston J	Bleakley T	Mercer D		Potter C	Lyon J	Lee J
26		22	Leicester Fosse	2-3	Potter, Mercer D	7000	Hendry N	Wigglesworth A	Pattison J	Jacketts G	Edelston J	Wright W	Mercer D	Potter C	Stevens S	Lyon J	Hughes R
27	Mar	1	LEICESTER FOSSE	5-2	Stevens, Hughes, Mercer D, Lyon J, Deacy	8000	Hendry N	Pattison J	Betts A	Edelston J	Deacey C	Jacketts G	Mercer D	Potter C	Stevens S	Lyon J	Hughes R
28		8	Nottingham Forest	1-2	Wallis	14000	Hendry N	Wigglesworth A	Betts A	Jacketts G	Edelston J	Bleakley T	Mercer D	Suddes F	Wallis H	Lyon J	Hughes R
29		15	NOTTINGHAM FOREST	5-0	Lyon J (3), Potter, Wright	10000	Hendry N	Wigglesworth A	Betts A	Edelston J	Deacey C	Wright W	Mercer D	Potter C	Wallis H	Lyon J	Hughes R
30		18	SHEFFIELD UTD	1-1	Rentoul	12000	Hendry N	Wigglesworth A	Betts A	Wright W	Deacey C	Bleakley T	Hughes R	Mercer D	Rentoul R	Lyon J	Lee J

Secondary Competition: Section D

No.	Month	Day	Opponent	Result	Scorers	Att	1	2	3	4	5	6	7	8	9	10	11
1	Mar	22	Lincoln City	2-1	Wallis (2)	4000	Hendry N	Wigglesworth A	Betts A	Wright W	Deacey C	Bleakley T	Mercer D	Little T	Wallis H	Lyon J	Suddes F
2		29	LINCOLN CITY	1-2	Wallis	8000	Hendry N	Wigglesworth A	Betts A	Wright W	Edelston J	Bleakley T	Mercer D	Potter C	Wallis H	Lyon J	Suddes F
3	Apr	5	Coventry City	3-1	Potter, Lee, Morrall	8000	Hendry N	Wigglesworth A	Betts A	Edelston J	Deacey C	Wright W	Mercer D	Lyon J	Potter C	Morrall G	Lee J
4		12	COVENTRY CITY	0-1		7000	Hendry N	Wigglesworth A	Betts A	Edelston J	Deacey C	Wright W	Mercer D	Lyon J	Potter C	Morrall G	Hughes R
5		19	Grimsby Town	2-1	Lyon J, Wright W	7000	Hendry N	Wigglesworth A	Betts A	Edelston J	Deacey C	Jacketts G	Mercer D	Wright W	Lyon J	Bleakley T	Lee J
6		26	GRIMSBY TOWN	3-1	Lee (2), Mercer D	5000	Hendry N	Edelston J	Betts A	Jacketts G	Deacey C	Wright W	Mercer D	Adams P	Lyon J	Brennan T	Lee J

1917/18

Principal Competition

	P	W	D	L	F	A	Pts
1 Leeds City	28	23	1	4	75	23	47
2 Sheffield United	28	20	1	7	66	27	41
3 Birmingham	28	14	6	8	59	38	34
4 HULL CITY	28	15	4	9	67	50	34
5 Nottingham Forest	28	13	4	11	41	28	30
6 Bradford P.A.	28	13	4	11	40	29	30
7 Leicester Fosse	28	13	3	12	52	43	29
8 Huddersfield Town	28	12	2	14	49	46	26
9 Rotherham County	28	8	9	11	42	52	25
10 Notts County	28	7	9	12	43	54	23
11 Sheffield Wednesday	28	9	5	14	45	59	23
12 Grimsby Town	28	5	11	12	24	62	21
13 Bradford City	28	8	4	16	34	55	20
14 Lincoln City	28	7	5	16	25	62	19
15 Barnsley	28	8	2	18	40	74	18

Subsidiary Competition

	P	W	D	L	F	A	Pts
1 Grimsby Town	6	4	1	1	13	3	9
2 Notts County	6	4	0	2	19	9	8
3 Sheffield Wednesday	6	3	2	1	15	8	8
4 HULL CITY	6	3	2	1	12	9	8
5 Leeds City	6	3	2	1	8	6	8
6 Lincoln City	6	3	1	2	11	8	7
7 Huddersfield Town	6	3	1	2	13	11	7
8 Barnsley	6	3	1	2	14	12	7
9 Braford City	6	1	4	1	8	8	6
10 Birmingham	6	2	2	2	6	9	6
11 Sheffield United	6	2	1	3	9	12	5
12 Leicester Fosse	6	2	1	3	6	10	5
13 Nottingham Forest	6	2	1	3	4	7	5
14 Rotherham County	6	1	2	3	4	10	4
15 Bradford P.A.	6	1	1	4	8	12	3
16 Gainsborough Trinity	6	0	0	3	3	19	0

1918/19

Principal Competition

	P	W	D	L	F	A	Pts
1 Nottingham Forest	30	18	6	6	59	31	42
2 Birmingham	30	20	1	9	72	36	41
3 Notts County	30	16	9	5	65	38	41
4 Leeds City	30	17	4	9	55	38	38
5 Bradford P.A.	30	15	7	8	53	41	37
6 Huddersfield Town	30	13	8	9	45	45	34
7 HULL CITY	30	12	7	11	48	42	31
8 Sheffield United	30	12	6	12	56	47	30
9 Coventry City	30	13	4	13	55	59	30
10 Leicester Fosse	30	13	3	14	53	53	29
11 Sheffield Wednesday	30	11	6	13	49	49	28
12 Lincoln City	30	10	4	16	38	59	24
13 Bradford City	30	9	4	17	48	56	22
14 Barnsley	30	9	3	18	45	79	21
15 Grimsby Town	30	7	6	17	40	69	20
16 Rotherham County	30	2	8	20	23	60	12

Subsidiary Competition Section D

	P	W	D	L	F	A	Pts
1 HULL CITY	6	4	0	2	11	7	8
2 Coventry City	6	3	2	1	7	6	8
3 Grimsby Town	6	2	1	3	8	10	5
4 Lincoln City	6	1	1	4	6	9	3

1919/20 11th in Division Two

Player columns (left to right): Barrass J *, Bell M, Betts A, Bleakley T, Charlesworth A, Crawford J, Deacey C, Edelston J, Hendry N, Hughes R, Jacketts G, Johnson W, Lee J, Lyon J, Mason T, Mercer D, Mercer W, Middlehurst J, Morrall G, Needham J, Potter C, Stephenson W, Stevens S, Wigglesworth A, Wright W

#	Date	Opponent	Score	Scorers	Att	Bar	Bel	Bet	Ble	Cha	Cra	Dea	Ede	Hen	Hug	Jac	Joh	Lee	Lyo	Mas	McD	McW	Mid	Mor	Nee	Pot	Ste	StS	Wig	Wri
1	Aug 30	Birmingham	1-4	Stevens	20000			3	6			5	4	1	11						7			10			8	9	2	
2	Sep 1	STOKE	3-0	Stevens, Lyon, Lee	10000			3	6			5	4	1	11			8	10		7							9	2	
3	6	BIRMINGHAM	0-0		10000			3				5	4	1	11			8			7			10					2	6
4	8	Stoke	1-3	Charlesworth	10000			3		4	9	5						8	6		7							10	2	
5	13	Leeds City	2-1	Stevens, Hughes	10000			3		5	9		4	1	11		6				10			7				2	8	
6	20	LEEDS CITY	1-1	Charlesworth	9000			3		5	9		4	1	11		6				10			7				2	8	
7	27	Bury	0-2		8000			3	6			5	4	1	7			11			8					10		9	2	
8	Oct 4	BURY	4-2	Morrall 2, Lee, Mercer D	10000			3	6			5	4	1	7			11			8			10				9	2	
9	11	Nottingham Forest	2-0	Morrall, Stevens	10000		2	3	6			5	4	1	7			11			8			10				9		
10	13	CLAPTON ORIENT	3-1	Stevens, Lee, Mercer D	6000		2	3	6			5	4	1	7			11			8			10				9		
11	18	NOTTM. FOREST	2-0	Mercer D, Deacey	8000		2	3	6			5	4	1	7			11			8			10				9		
12	25	Grimsby Town	1-2	Stevens	6000		2	3	6			5	4	1	7			11			8			10				9		
13	Nov 1	GRIMSBY TOWN	4-1	Mercer D, Charlesworth, Morrall, Lee	9000		2	3	6	9		5	4	1	7			11			8			10						
14	8	Barnsley	3-2	Hughes, Mercer D, Morrall	6000		2	3		9		5	4	1	7			11			8			10						6
15	15	BARNSLEY	3-1	Stevens, Mercer D, Wright W	8000		2	3				5	4	1	7			11			8			10				9		6
16	22	STOCKPORT COUNTY	4-1	Mercer D 2, Morrall, Lee	8000		2		6			5	4	1				11			7			10			8	9		3
17	29	Stockport County	1-3	Stevens	5000		2		6			5	4	1	7			11			8			10				9		3
18	Dec 6	LINCOLN CITY	5-2	Lee 3, Stevens, Mercer D	8000		2	3				5	4	1				11		7	8			10				9		6
19	13	Lincoln City	0-2		4000		2	3				5	4	1	7			11			8			10				9		6
20	20	Wolverhampton W.	2-4	Mercer D, Hughes	12000		2	3				5	4	1	7			11	9		8			10						6
21	25	Tottenham Hotspur	0-4		40008							5	4	1	7			11	9		8			10					3	6
22	26	TOTTENHAM HOTSPUR	1-3	Stevens	28000		2	3	6			5	4	1	7						10			8				9		11
23	27	WOLVERHAMPTON W.	10-3	Mercer D 4, Stevens 3, Morrall 2, Wright W	10000		2		6			5	4	1	7						3			8				9		11
24	Jan 3	South Shields	1-7	Mercer D	19000		2		6			5	4	1				11	3		8			10				9		7
25	17	SOUTH SHIELDS	3-0	Morrall, Stevens, Frith (og)	8000	3			6			5	4		7			11			8	1		10				9	2	
26	24	Leicester City	2-3	Stevens, Mercer D	15000	3			6			5	4		7			11			8	1		10				9	2	
27	Feb 7	Fulham	0-1		18000			3	6			5	4		7			11			8	1		10				9	2	
28	12	LEICESTER CITY	5-1	Morrall 3, Stevens, Deacey	5000	3	2		6			5	4			7		11			8	1		10				9		
29	14	FULHAM	2-0	Lee, Stevens	10000	3	2		6			5	4			7		11			8	1		10				9		
30	21	Coventry City	1-0	Morrall	10000	3			6			5	4		11		7				8	1		10				9		
31	28	COVENTRY CITY	0-1		7000	3			6			5	4		11		7				8	1		10				9		
32	Mar 13	Huddersfield Town	0-2		5000	3			6		11	5									7	1		10		8	2	9		4
33	18	HUDDERSFIELD T	1-4	Mercer D	12000	3			6	9	11	5									7	1		10				8	2	4
34	20	BLACKPOOL	0-1		10000	3			6		7	5		1							8		2	10		4		9		
35	27	Blackpool	1-2	Morrall	4000	3			6		11		5		7						8	1	2	10		4		9		
36	Apr 2	Clapton Orient	2-2	Stevens, Morrall	12000	3		2	6		11	5	4								7	1		10		8		9		
37	3	BRISTOL CITY	0-0		9000	3		2	6		11	5	4				7					1	8	10				9		
38	10	Bristol City	2-2	Crawford, Deacey	12000	3			6		11	5					7					1	2	10	8	4		9		
39	17	WEST HAM UNITED	1-1	Morrall	8000	3			6		11	5					7					1	2	10				9		4
40	24	West Ham United	1-2	Morrall	18000	3			6	9	11		4								5	1	2	10				8		
41	26	ROTHERHAM COUNTY	1-0	Charlesworth	6000	3			6	9		5	4						11		7	1	2	8	10					
42	May 1	Rotherham County	2-1	Charlesworth, Lyon	10000	3			6	9		5							11		7	1	2	8	10	4				
Apps						17	23	17	35	9	9	38	35	25	27	2	5	24	13	1	41	17	7	35	4	10	9	36	7	14
Goals										5	1	3			3			9	2		17			17				18		2

Played in one game: W Clark (34, at 11), E Wadsworth (39, at 8)

One own goal

F.A. Cup

#	Date	Opponent	Score	Scorers	Att	Bar	Bel	Bet	Ble	Cha	Cra	Dea	Ede	Hen	Hug	Jac	Joh	Lee	Lyo	Mas	McD	McW	Mid	Mor	Nee	Pot	Ste	StS	Wig	Wri
R1	Jan 14	Sunderland	2-6	Stevens 2	35586		2	3				5	4	1	7			11			8			10				9		6

* J Barrass was the assumed name of J Lodge

		Pl	Home W D L F A	Away W D L F A	F A (Total)	Pts
1	Tottenham Hotspur	42	19 2 0 60 11	13 4 4 42 21	102 32	70
2	Huddersfield Town	42	16 4 1 58 13	12 4 5 39 25	97 38	64
3	Birmingham	42	14 3 4 54 16	10 5 6 31 18	85 34	56
4	Blackpool	42	13 4 4 40 18	8 6 7 25 29	65 47	52
5	Bury	42	14 4 3 35 15	6 4 11 25 29	60 44	48
6	Fulham	42	11 6 4 36 18	8 3 10 25 32	61 50	47
7	West Ham United	42	14 3 4 34 14	5 6 10 13 26	47 40	47
8	Bristol City	42	9 9 3 30 18	4 8 9 16 25	46 43	43
9	South Shields	42	13 5 3 47 18	2 7 12 11 30	58 48	42
10	Stoke	42	13 3 5 37 15	5 3 13 23 39	60 54	42
11	HULL CITY	42	13 4 4 53 23	5 2 14 25 49	78 72	42
12	Barnsley	42	9 5 7 41 28	6 5 10 20 27	61 55	40
13	Port Vale	42	11 3 7 35 27	5 5 11 24 35	59 62	40
14	Leicester City	42	8 6 7 26 29	7 4 10 15 32	41 61	40
15	Clapton Orient	42	14 3 4 34 17	2 3 16 17 42	51 59	38
16	Stockport County	42	11 4 6 34 24	3 5 13 18 37	52 61	37
17	Rotherham County	42	10 4 7 32 27	3 4 14 19 56	51 83	34
18	Nottingham Forest	42	9 4 8 23 22	2 5 14 20 51	43 73	31
19	Wolverhampton W.	42	8 4 9 41 32	2 6 13 14 48	55 80	30
20	Coventry City	42	7 7 7 20 26	2 4 15 15 47	35 73	29
21	Lincoln City	42	8 6 7 27 30	1 3 17 17 74	44 101	27
22	Grimsby Town	42	8 4 9 23 24	2 1 18 11 51	34 75	25

1919-20

Standing: Mr C. Jordan (Director), J. Lee, A. Wigglesworth, W. Mercer, Mr J. Bielby (Director), N. Hendry,
S. Stevens, A. Betts, Mr J. Locking (Director);
Sitting: Mr D. Menzies (Manager), W. Wright, J. Edelston, D. Mercer, T. Bleakley, J. Lyons, R. Hughes, J. Beck (Trainer);
On Ground: G. Morrell, C. Deacey, G. Jacketts.

1920-21

Back Row: J. Harron, S. Cheetham, M. Bell, W. Smith, C. Deacey, J. Barras, T. Mason;
Standing: D. Menzies (Manager), W. Henzell, C. Flood, W. Mercer, M. Gilhooley, N. Hendry, A. Charlesworth, S. Garrett, J. Beck (Trainer);
Sitting: D. Mercer, W.T. Brandon, J. Collier, W. Wright, G. Davies, R. Hughes, J. Needham, J. Crawford;
On Ground: T. Bleakley, J. Morrall.

1920/21   13th in Division Two

League — Division Two

No	Date	Opponent	Score	Scorers	Att
1	Aug 28	West Ham United	1-1	Henzell	26000
2	30	Birmingham	1-5	Charlesworth	25000
3	Sep 4	WEST HAM UNITED	2-1	Mercer D 2	12000
4	6	BIRMINGHAM	1-0	Charlesworth	13000
5	11	BRISTOL CITY	2-0	Flood, Mercer D	15000
6	18	Bristol City	1-2	Flood	17000
7	25	BARNSLEY	3-0	Crawford, Mercer D, Needham	15000
8	Oct 2	Barnsley	0-0		8000
9	9	ROTHERHAM COUNTY	1-1	Crawford	14000
10	16	Rotherham County	1-1	Wilson	12000
11	23	LEEDS UNITED	0-1		10000
12	30	Leeds United	1-1	McKinney	20000
13	Nov 6	PORT VALE	1-1	Mercer D	15000
14	13	Port Vale	0-4		12000
15	20	South Shields	0-0		18000
16	27	SOUTH SHIELDS	0-2		10000
17	Dec 4	NOTTM. FOREST	0-3		7000
18	11	Nottingham Forest	0-2		12000
19	18	WOLVERHAMPTON W.	0-1		6000
20	25	Clapton Orient	1-1	Crawford	30000
21	27	CLAPTON ORIENT	3-0	Sergeaunt 3	14000
22	Jan 1	Wolverhampton Wan.	3-1	Sergeaunt 2, Wilson	23000
23	15	COVENTRY CITY	1-1	Crawford	8000
24	22	Coventry City	2-3	Sergeaunt, McKinney	18000
25	Feb 3	STOCKPORT COUNTY	1-1	Brandon	6000
26	5	Stockport County	2-2	Cheetham, Sergeaunt	9000
27	12	STOKE	1-1	McKinney	6000
28	26	SHEFFIELD WEDNESDAY	1-1	Mills	9000
29	Mar 12	NOTTS COUNTY	1-1	Sergeaunt	8000
30	19	Notts County	1-4	Mills	12000
31	21	Sheffield Wednesday	0-3		12000
32	25	Bury	0-0		16000
33	26	Blackpool	2-1	Flood 2	12000
34	28	BURY	1-1	Flood	10000
35	Apr 2	BLACKPOOL	2-1	Brandon, Flood,	8000
36	9	Leicester City	0-0		12000
37	11	Stoke	3-1	Flood 2, Mills	5000
38	16	LEICESTER CITY	1-1	Mills	9000
39	23	Cardiff City	0-0		30000
40	30	CARDIFF CITY	2-0	Brandon, Hughes	10000
41	May 2	Fulham	0-3		1000
42	7	FULHAM	0-0		8000

Appearances and goals (summary row)

Player	Apps	Goals
Barrass J *	18	
Bell M	25	
Bleakley T	37	
Brandon T	41	3
Charlesworth A	6	2
Cheetham S	22	1
Collier J	38	
Crawford J	34	4
Davies G	6	
Deacey C	1	
Flood C	14	8
Garratt S	1	
Gilhooley M	38	
Harron J	2	
Henzell W	2	1
Hughes R	12	1
Marshall J	1	
Mason T	2	
McKinney D	19	3
McMurray C	3	
Mercer D	10	5
Mercer W	42	
Mills B	15	4
Morrall G	2	
Needham J	14	1
Ranby S	1	
Ryley H	1	
Sergeaunt H	12	8
Smith J	1	
Stoddart G	7	
Wilson H	30	2
Wright W	5	

F.A. Cup

Rnd	Date	Opponent	Score	Scorers	Att
R1	Jan 8	BATH CITY	3-0	Wilson, Sergeaunt, Crawford	11600
R2	29	Crystal Palace	2-0	Wilson, Crawford	21000
R3	Feb 19	BURNLEY	3-0	Brandon 2, Wilson	26000
R4	Mar 3	PRESTON NORTH END	0-0		27000
rep	10	Preston North End	0-1		32853

F.A. Cup line-ups (all five ties): Mercer W 1, Cheetham 2, Bell 3, Collier 4, Gilhooley 5, Bleakley 6, Crawford 7, Brandon 8, Sergeaunt 9, Wilson 10, Hughes 11.

* J Barrass was the assumed name of J Lodge

Division Two table

		Pl	Home W	D	L	F	A	Away W	D	L	F	A	F	A	Pts
1	Birmingham	42	16	4	1	55	13	8	6	7	24	25	79	38	58
2	Cardiff City	42	13	5	3	27	9	11	5	5	32	23	59	32	58
3	Bristol City	42	14	3	4	35	12	5	10	6	14	17	49	29	51
4	Blackpool	42	12	3	6	32	19	8	7	6	22	23	54	42	50
5	West Ham United	42	13	5	3	38	11	6	5	10	13	19	51	30	48
6	Notts County	42	12	5	4	36	17	6	6	9	19	23	55	40	47
7	Clapton Orient	42	13	6	2	31	9	3	7	11	12	33	43	42	45
8	South Shields	42	13	4	4	41	16	4	6	11	20	30	61	46	44
9	Fulham	42	14	4	3	33	12	2	6	13	10	35	43	47	42
10	Sheffield Wed.	42	9	7	5	31	14	6	4	11	17	34	48	48	41
11	Bury	42	10	8	3	29	13	5	2	14	16	36	45	49	40
12	Leicester City	42	10	8	3	26	11	2	8	11	13	35	39	46	40
13	HULL CITY	42	7	10	4	24	18	3	10	8	19	35	43	53	40
14	Leeds United	42	11	5	5	30	14	3	5	13	10	31	40	45	38
15	Wolverhampton W.	42	11	4	6	34	24	5	2	14	15	42	49	66	38
16	Barnsley	42	9	10	2	31	17	1	6	14	17	33	48	50	36
17	Port Vale	42	7	6	8	28	19	4	8	9	15	30	43	49	36
18	Nottingham Forest	42	9	6	6	37	26	3	6	12	11	29	48	55	36
19	Rotherham County	42	8	9	4	23	21	4	3	14	14	32	37	53	36
20	Stoke	42	9	5	7	26	16	3	6	12	22	40	46	56	35
21	Coventry City	42	8	6	7	24	25	4	5	12	15	45	39	70	35
22	Stockport County	42	8	6	7	30	24	1	6	14	12	51	42	75	30

1921/22 — 5th in Division Two

#	Date	Opponent	Score	Scorers	Att	Bell M	Bleakley T	Blenkinsop E	Brandon T	Cheetham S	Collier J	Coverdale R	Crawford J	Davies G	Doyle D	Eccles T	Flood C	Garratt S	Gilhooley M	Hughes R	Kitchen J	Lodge I *	McKinney D	McMurray C	Mercer W	Mills B	Scorer R	Sergeaunt H	Slater H	Stansfield J
1	Aug 27	SOUTH SHIELDS	1-1	Hughes	14000	3	6		8	2		4	7				9		5	11					1			10		
2	Aug 29	Nottingham Forest	2-3	Flood, Crawford	8000	3	6		8	2		4	7				9		5	11					1			10		
3	Sep 3	South Shields	0-1		18000	3				2		4	7	6			8		5	11					1	9		10		
4	Sep 5	NOTTM. FOREST	0-1		9000	3				2		4	7	6			8		5	11					1	9		10		
5	Sep 10	FULHAM	2-1	Flood 2	10000	3				2		4	7	6			10		5	11	9				1			8		
6	Sep 17	Fulham	0-6		20000					2		4	7	6			8		5	11	9	3			1			10		
7	Sep 24	BLACKPOOL	2-0	Kitchen, Flood	4000		6		2		4	8	7				10		5	11	9	3			1					
8	Oct 1	Blackpool	1-0	Flood	10000		6		2		4	8	7				10		5	11		3			1	9				
9	Oct 8	CLAPTON ORIENT	2-1	Crawford, Flood	12000		6		2		4	8	7				10		5	11		3			1	9				
10	Oct 15	Clapton Orient	2-0	Coverdale, Hughes	18000	3	6		2		4	8	7				10		5	11					1	9				
11	Oct 22	BRISTOL CITY	1-0	Gilhooley	6000	3	6		2		4	8	7				10		5	11					1	9				
12	Oct 29	Bristol City	0-1		12000	3	6		2		4	8	7				10		5	11	9				1					
13	Nov 5	Stoke	0-0		12000	3	6		2		4	8	7				10		5	11					1	9				
14	Nov 12	STOKE	7-1	Mills 4, Flood 2, Coverdale	12000	3	6		2		4	8	7				10		5	11					1	9				
15	Nov 19	LEEDS UNITED	1-0	Flood	12800	3	6		2		4	8	7				10		5	11					1	9				
16	Nov 26	Leeds United	2-0	Mills 2	20000	3	6		2		4	8	7				10		5	11					1	9				
17	Dec 3	BRADFORD PARK AVE.	3-0	Mills 3	16000	3	6		2		4	8	7				10		5	11					1	9				
18	Dec 10	Bradford Park Avenue	1-1	Coverdale	14000	3	6				4	8	7				10		5	11		2			1	9				
19	Dec 17	NOTTS COUNTY	2-0	Flood, Hughes	13000	3	6				4	8	7				10		5	11		2			1	9				
20	Dec 24	Notts County	0-2		10000	3	6				4	8	7				10		5	11		2			1	9				
21	Dec 26	ROTHERHAM COUNTY	0-1		20000	3	6				4	8	7				10		5			2	11		1	9				
22	Dec 27	Rotherham County	0-2		15000		5	3			4		7	6			10			11	9	2	8		1					
23	Dec 31	CRYSTAL PALACE	1-0	Flood	10000		6	3			4	8	7				10		5	11		2			1	9				
24	Jan 14	Crystal Palace	2-0	Mills 2	18000	3	6				4	8	7				10		5	11		2			1	9				
25	Jan 21	PORT VALE	2-0	Flood 2	6000	3	6				4	8	7				10		5	11		2			1	9				
26	Feb 4	WEST HAM UNITED	0-0		8000	3	5				4	6	7				10			11		2	8		1					
27	Feb 11	West Ham United	1-1	McKinney	20000	3	6					4	7				10		5			2	8		1	9				11
28	Feb 13	Port Vale	0-1		10000	3	6					4	7				10		5		9	2	8		1					11
29	Feb 18	BURY	1-1	Hughes	8000	3	6		2		4	8	7				10		5	11			9		1					
30	Feb 25	Bury	0-4		8000	3	6		2		4	8	7				9							10	1		5			
31	Mar 4	LEICESTER CITY	5-2	McKinney 3, Flood 2	7000	3	6				4	8	7				10	5				2	9		1					
32	Mar 11	Leicester City	1-0	Stansfield	10000	3	6				4	8	7				10	5				2	9		1					11
33	Mar 18	Derby County	0-0		7000	3	6				4	8	7				10	5				2	9		1					11
34	Mar 25	DERBY COUNTY	1-1	Crawford	10000	3	6				4	8	7				10	5				2	9		1					11
35	Apr 1	Coventry City	0-2		14000	3	6				4	8	7				10	5				2			1	9				11
36	Apr 8	COVENTRY CITY	2-0	Flood 2	9000	3	6				4	8	7				10				5	2			1	9				11
37	Apr 14	SHEFFIELD WEDNESDAY	0-0		12000	3	6	5			4	8	7				10					2			1	9				11
38	Apr 15	Barnsley	1-4	McKinney	12000		6				8						9	4			5	2	7		1				10	11
39	Apr 17	Sheffield Wednesday	0-0		12000	3	6				4	8	7				10				5	2	9		1					11
40	Apr 22	BARNSLEY	1-3	McKinney	10000	3	6				4	8	7				10				5	2	9		1					11
41	Apr 29	Wolverhampton W.	2-0	Hughes, McKinney	10000	3	6				4		7							11	10	2	8		1	9	5			
42	May 6	WOLVERHAMPTON W.	2-0	McKinney, Eccles	8000	3	6				4		7			9					10	2	8		1		5			11
Apps						36	38	3	15	6	33	39	41	5	1	1	40	6	27	27	13	27	15	1	42	24	2	7	1	12
Goals												3	3			1	17		1	5	1		8			11				1

F.A. Cup

	Date	Opponent	Score	Scorers	Att	Bell M	Bleakley T	Blenkinsop E	Brandon T	Cheetham S	Collier J	Coverdale R	Crawford J	Davies G	Doyle D	Eccles T	Flood C	Garratt S	Gilhooley M	Hughes R	Kitchen J	Lodge I *	McKinney D	McMurray C	Mercer W	Mills B	Scorer R	Sergeaunt H	Slater H	Stansfield J
R1	Jan 7	MIDDLESBROUGH	5-0	Coverdale 2, Mills, Bleakley, Crawford	23000	3	6				4	8	7				10		5	11		2			1	9				
R2	Jan 28	Nottingham Forest	0-3		28000	3	6				4	8	7				10		5	11		2			1	9				

* J Lodge formerly played as J Barrass

		Pl	Home					Away					F.	A.	Pts
			W	D	L	F	A	W	D	L	F	A	(Total)		
1	Nottingham Forest	42	13	7	1	29	9	9	5	7	22	21	51	30	56
2	Stoke	42	9	11	1	31	11	9	5	7	29	33	60	44	52
3	Barnsley	42	14	5	2	43	18	8	3	10	24	34	67	52	52
4	West Ham United	42	15	3	3	39	13	5	5	11	13	26	52	39	48
5	HULL CITY	42	13	5	3	36	13	6	5	10	15	28	51	41	48
6	South Shields	42	11	7	3	25	13	6	5	10	18	25	43	38	46
7	Fulham	42	14	5	2	41	8	4	4	13	16	30	57	38	45
8	Leeds United	42	10	8	3	31	12	6	5	10	17	26	48	38	45
9	Leicester City	42	11	6	4	30	16	3	11	7	9	18	39	34	45
10	Sheffield Wed.	42	12	4	5	31	24	3	10	8	16	26	47	50	44
11	Bury	42	11	3	7	35	19	4	7	10	19	36	54	55	40
12	Derby County	42	11	3	7	34	22	4	6	11	26	42	60	64	39
13	Notts County	42	10	7	4	34	18	2	8	11	13	33	47	51	39
14	Crystal Palace	42	9	6	6	28	20	4	7	10	17	31	45	51	39
15	Clapton Orient	42	12	4	5	33	18	3	5	13	10	32	43	50	39
16	Rotherham County	42	8	9	4	17	7	6	2	13	15	36	32	43	39
17	Wolverhampton W.	42	8	7	6	28	19	5	4	12	16	30	44	49	37
18	Port Vale	42	10	5	6	28	19	4	3	14	15	38	43	57	36
19	Blackpool	42	11	1	9	33	27	4	4	13	11	30	44	57	35
20	Coventry City	42	8	5	8	31	21	4	5	12	20	39	51	60	34
21	Bradford Park Ave.	42	10	5	6	32	22	2	4	15	14	40	46	62	33
22	Bristol City	42	10	3	8	25	18	2	6	13	12	40	37	58	33

1921-22

Left – Right: J. Crawford, R. Hughes, T. Bleakley, S. Cheetham, W. Mercer, M. Bell, C. Flood,
M. Gilhooley, T. Brandon, R. Coverdale, H. Sergeaunt

1922-23

Back Row: S. Garratt, ? , J. Lodge, G. Hall, R. Scorer, ? , E. Blenkinsop, ? ;
Standing: H. Lewis (Manager), T. Eccles, D. Bew, R. Coverdale, A. Briggs, W. Mercer, M. Bell, J. McGee, J. Beck (Trainer);
Sitting: A. Bell (Asst. Trainer) , J. Gibson, J. Crawford, J. Kitchen, B. Mills, T. Bleakley, J. Collier, D. Doyle;
On Ground: D. McKinney, J. Loughran, A. Livingstone, ? .

1922/23 12th in Division Two

#	Date		Opponent	Score	Scorers	Att	Bell M	Bew D	Bleakley T	Blenkinsop E	Briggs A	Collier J	Coverdale R	Crawford J	Doyle D	Eccles T	Gibson J	Hall G	Kitchen I	Lodge J	Loughran J	Martin G	McGee I	McKinney D	Mercer W	Middlemas J	Mills B	Rumney I	Scorer R	Slater H	Thom A	Wood I	Garratt S	Livingstone A
1	Aug	26	Bury	0-1		10000	3	5	6			4		7	11	9	2		10					8	1									
2		28	PORT VALE	3-0	Crawford, Kitchen, Bleakley	6000	3	5	6			4		7		9	2		10					8	1						11			
3	Sep	2	BURY	2-2	Eccles, Kitchen	10000	3	5	6			4		7		9	2		10					8	1						11			
4		4	Port Vale	0-1		10000	3	5	6		1	4		7			2	11	10					8						9				
5		9	Notts County	1-0	Kitchen	12000	3		6			4	8	7	11		2		10					9	1				5					
6		16	NOTTS COUNTY	0-2		10000	3		6			4	8	7	11		2		10					9	1				5					
7		23	FULHAM	1-0	Mills	8000	3		6			4		7					10	2			5	8	1		9				11			
8		30	Fulham	0-0		22000	3		6			4		7					10	2			5	8	1		9				11			
9	Oct	7	Crystal Palace	1-1	Thom	10000	3		6			4		7					10	2			5	8	1		9				11			
10		14	CRYSTAL PALACE	1-1	Bleakley	10000	3		6			4		7					10	2			5	8	1		9				11			
11		21	Rotherham County	1-0	Thom	8000	3	5	6			4	8	7					10	2				9	1						11			
12		28	ROTHERHAM COUNTY	2-3	Martin, McKinney	9000	3	5	6			4		7					10	2		9		8	1						11			
13	Nov	4	Leicester City	1-0	Martin	17000		5		3		4	8	7					10	2		9			1		6				11			
14		11	LEICESTER CITY	1-3	Martin	10000		5		3		4	8	7					10	2		9			1		6				11			
15		18	SHEFFIELD WEDNESDAY	0-0		8000				3		4	10	8			2					9	5	7	1		6				11			
16		25	Sheffield Wednesday	0-1		18000	3		6			4	10	7			2					9	5		1		8				11			
17	Dec	2	Barnsley	0-1		9000			6	3		4	10	7			2					9	5		1		8				11			
18		9	BARNSLEY	2-1	Martin 2	7000			6	3		4		7		10	2					9	5		1		8				11			
19		16	Blackpool	0-0		8000			6	3				7		10	2					9	5		1	4	8				11			
20		23	BLACKPOOL	0-0		8000			6	3			8	7			2					9	5		1	4	10				11			
21		25	SOUTHAMPTON	1-3	Kitchen	14000			6					7			2		10	3		9	5		1		8				11			
22		26	Southampton	1-2	Mills	19000				3				7		8	2		10						1	6	9		5		11		4	
23		30	MANCHESTER UNITED	2-1	Mills, Wood	9000		5	6					7		10	2							3	1	4	8				11	9		
24	Jan	6	Manchester United	2-3	Wood, Thom	15000	3	5	6					7		10	2								1	4	8				11	9		
25		20	Bradford City	1-2	Mills	12000	3		6			4	8	7			2					9	5		1		10				11			
26		27	BRADFORD CITY	0-0		10000	3	5	6				8	7			2								1	4	10	9			11			
27	Feb	3	Clapton Orient	0-2		15000	3	5						7			2					9			1	4	8				11			10
28		10	CLAPTON ORIENT	2-1	Mills, Coverdale	6000	3	5				4	6	7			2					9		8	1		10				11			
29		17	Stockport County	1-1	Martin	11000	3	5				4	6	7			2	8				9			1		10				11			
30		24	STOCKPORT COUNTY	1-0	Hall	6000	3	5				4		7	6		2	8				9			1		10				11			
31	Mar	3	Leeds United	2-2	Martin, Thom	13000	3	5				4	6	7			2	8				9			1		10				11			
32		10	LEEDS UNITED	3-1	Martin, Hall, Bleakley	10000	3	5				4	6	7			2	8				9			1		10				11			
33		17	WEST HAM UNITED	1-1	Mills	14000	3	5				4	6	7			2					9		8	1		10				11			
34		30	Derby County	2-0	Martin, Hall	10000	3	5				4	6	7			2	8				9			1		10				11			
35		31	SOUTH SHIELDS	2-0	Mills, Coverdale	10000	3	5				4	6	7			2	8				9			1		10				11			
36	Apr	2	DERBY COUNTY	4-2	Mills, Martin, Thom, Hall	15000	3	5				4		7	6		2	8				9			1		10				11			
37		7	South Shields	0-0		6000	3	5				4		7		9	2	6	10			8			1						11			
38		9	West Ham United	0-3		18000		5				4		7			2		10	3	6	9		8	1						11			
39		14	WOLVERHAMPTON W.	0-0		6000		5			1	4	6	7			2				3	10					8				11	9		
40		23	Wolverhampton W.	0-3		8000	3	5			1	4	6	7			2				3	10					8				11	9		
41		28	COVENTRY CITY	1-1	Martin	6000	3	5				4	6		11	8	2		10			7			1		9							
42	May	5	Coventry City	1-0	Mills	10000	3	5				4	6	7			2		10					8	1		9				11			
			Apps				30	11	38	8	3	35	23	42	5	8	30	10	17	15	2	27	13	21	39	10	30	1	3	2	35	2	1	1
			Goals						3				2	1		1		4	4			12		1			8				5	2		

Played in one game: S Garratt (22, at 4), A Livingstone (27, 10)

F.A. Cup

#	Date		Opponent	Score	Scorers	Att	Bell M	Bew D	Bleakley T	Blenkinsop E	Briggs A	Collier J	Coverdale R	Crawford J	Doyle D	Eccles T	Gibson J	Hall G	Kitchen I	Lodge J	Loughran J	Martin G	McGee I	McKinney D	Mercer W	Middlemas J	Mills B	Rumney I	Scorer R	Slater H	Thom A	Wood I	Garratt S	Livingstone A
R1	Jan	23	WEST HAM UNITED	2-3	Crawford, Mills	14000	3	5	6				10	7			2								1	4	8				11	9		

		Pl		Home					Away					F.	A.	Pts
			W	D	L	F	A	W	D	L	F	A	(Total)			
1	Notts County	42	16	1	4	29	15	7	6	8	17	19	46	34	53
2	West Ham United	42	9	8	4	21	11	11	3	7	42	27	63	38	51
3	Leicester City	42	14	2	5	42	19	7	7	7	23	25	65	44	51
4	Manchester United	42	10	6	5	25	17	7	8	6	26	19	51	36	48
5	Blackpool	42	12	4	5	37	14	6	7	8	23	29	60	43	47
6	Bury	42	14	5	2	41	16	4	6	11	14	30	55	46	47
7	Leeds United	42	11	8	2	26	10	7	3	11	17	26	43	36	47
8	Sheffield Wed.	42	14	3	4	36	16	3	9	9	18	31	54	47	46
9	Barnsley	42	12	4	5	42	21	5	7	9	20	30	62	51	45
10	Fulham	42	10	7	4	29	12	6	5	10	14	20	43	32	44
11	Southampton	42	10	5	6	28	21	4	9	8	12	19	40	40	42
12	HULL CITY	42	9	8	4	29	22	5	6	10	14	23	43	45	42
13	South Shields	42	11	7	3	26	12	4	3	14	9	32	35	44	40
14	Derby County	42	9	5	7	25	16	5	6	10	21	34	46	50	39
15	Bradford City	42	8	7	6	27	18	4	6	11	14	27	41	45	37
16	Crystal Palace	42	10	7	4	33	16	3	4	14	21	46	54	62	37
17	Port Vale	42	8	6	7	23	18	6	3	12	16	33	39	51	37
18	Coventry City	42	12	2	7	35	21	3	5	13	11	42	46	63	37
19	Clapton Orient	42	9	6	6	26	17	3	6	12	14	33	40	50	36
20	Stockport County	42	10	6	5	32	24	4	2	15	11	34	43	58	36
21	Rotherham County	42	10	7	4	30	19	3	2	16	14	44	44	63	35
22	Wolverhampton W.	42	9	4	8	32	26	0	5	16	10	51	42	77	27

~ 189 ~

1923/24   17th in Division Two

League matches

#	Date	Opponent	Score	Scorers	Att.
1	Aug 25	LEICESTER CITY	1-1	Thom	8000
2	27	Clapton Orient	0-0		18000
3	Sep 1	Leicester City	1-1	Smith T	20000
4	3	CLAPTON ORIENT	2-2	Martin, Thomas	10000
5	8	NELSON	2-1	Rumney 2	9000
6	15	Nelson	1-1	Walker	11000
7	22	LEEDS UNITED	1-2	Smith T	10000
8	29	Leeds United	2-5	Martin, Duffield (og)	14000
9	Oct 6	DERBY COUNTY	0-1		8000
10	13	Derby County	1-4	Rumney	14000
11	20	STOKE	2-0	Rumney, Martin	9000
12	27	Stoke	0-1		10000
13	Nov 3	Crystal Palace	0-0		10000
14	10	CRYSTAL PALACE	2-2	Thom, Feebery (og)	9000
15	17	Sheffield Wednesday	0-1		12000
16	24	SHEFFIELD WEDNESDAY	1-1	Lewis	8000
17	Dec 8	COVENTRY CITY	3-2	Martin 2, Havelock	8000
18	15	Bristol City	0-1		10000
19	17	Coventry City	2-0	Martin, Thom	5000
20	22	BRISTOL CITY	5-0	Mills 3, Thom, Richardson	8000
21	25	Fulham	1-1	Lewis	22000
22	26	FULHAM	4-2	Mills 3, Thomas	13000
23	29	Southampton	0-2		11000
24	Jan 5	SOUTHAMPTON	0-0		11000
25	19	STOCKPORT COUNTY	1-2	Martin	8000
26	26	Stockport County	1-5	Mills	16000
27	Feb 9	Oldham Athletic	0-0		8092
28	14	OLDHAM ATHLETIC	0-0		5000
29	16	SOUTH SHIELDS	1-0	Lewis	9000
30	23	South Shields	1-0	Havelock	8000
31	Mar 1	BURY	0-1		8000
32	8	Bury	0-1		15000
33	15	Manchester United	1-1	Mills	15000
34	22	MANCHESTER UNITED	1-1	Mills	8000
35	29	Barnsley	0-0		5000
36	Apr 5	BARNSLEY	1-2	Lewis	8000
37	12	Bradford City	1-2	Mills	10000
38	18	Blackpool	0-0		16000
39	19	BRADFORD CITY	2-0	Bell, Lewis	10000
40	21	BLACKPOOL	2-1	Thomas 2	10000
41	26	Port Vale	2-2	Martin 2	5689
42	May 3	PORT VALE	1-2	Mills	7000

Appearance grid (shirt numbers)

#	Adey T	Bell M	Bleakley T	Briggs A	Collier J	Coverdale R	Gibson J	Hall G	Hamilton T	Havelock H	Hedley R	Johnson Bill	Lewis H	Lodge J	Loughran J	Martin G	McGee J	Mercer W	Mills B	Mordue T	Richardson GEH	Rumney J	Smith T	Thom A	Thomas A	Walker W
1	5	3	6		4		2									10		1	8			9		11	7	
2	5	3			4		2									10		1	6			9	8	11	7	
3	5	3			4		2									10		1	6			9	8	11	7	
4	5	3			4		2									10		1	6			9	8	11	7	
5	5	3			4		2									10		1	6			9		11	7	8
6	5	3					2						4			10		1	6			9		11	7	8
7	5	3			4		2								6	10		1	9				8	11	7	
8	5	3												2	6	10		1	6				8	11	7	
9	5	3			4									2		10		1	6			9	8	11	7	
10	5	3						7					4	2		10		1	6			9	8	11		
11	5	3						7	2		4	10				8		1	6			9			11	
12	5	3							2		4	10				8		1	6	7		9			11	
13	5	3								2	4	10				8		1	6	7		9			11	
14	5	3								2	4	10				8		1	6	7		9			11	
15	5	3			4		2			7		6				10		1	9					11		
16	5	3			4		2			7		6				10		1	9					11		
17		3	5		4		2			9		6				10		1	8		7			11		
18		3	5		4		2			9		6				10		1	8		7			11		
19		3	5		4		2					6	10			8		1	9		7			11		
20		3	5		4		2					6	10			8		1	9		7			11		
21		3	5		4		2					6	10			8		1	9					11	7	
22		3	5		4		2					6	10			8		1	9					11	7	
23		3	5		4		2					6	10			8		1	9					11	7	
24		3	5		4		2					6	10			8		1	9		7			11		
25		3	5	1	4		2					6	10			8			9					11	7	
26		3	5	1	4		2					6	10			8			9					11	7	
27		3	6							2	4	10				9	5	1		7					11	8
28		3	6							2	4	10				9	5	1		7					11	8
29		3	6						9	2	4	10					5	1		7			8		11	
30		3	6						9	2	4	10					5	1		7			8		11	
31		3	6							2	4	10				9	5	1	8					7	11	
32		3	6							2	4	10	8			10	5	1	9					7	11	
33			5		4					2		6	9			10	3	1	8	7					11	
34		3	6							2	4	10				8	5	1	9	7					11	
35		3	6							2	4	10				8	5	1	9	7					11	
36		3	6			11				2	4	10				8	5	1	9						7	
37		3			4		2					6	10			8	5	1	9					11	7	
38		3	5		4							6	10			8	2	1	9					11	7	
39		3	5		4							6	10			8	2	1	9					11	7	
40		3	5		4							6	10			8	2	1	9					11	7	
41		3	5		4							6	10			8	2	1	9					11	7	
42		3	5		4							6	10			8	2	1	9					11	7	
Apps	16	41	26	2	26	1	24	2	2	6	9	33	31	4	2	39	16	40	41	6	6	12	8	32	32	5
Goals		1								2			5			9			11		1	4	2	4	4	1

Two own goals

F.A. Cup

Rd	Date	Opponent	Score	Scorers	Att.
R1	Jan 12	BOLTON WANDERERS	2-2	Martin, Mills	28603
rep	16	Bolton Wanderers	0-4		40315

Rd	Bell M	Bleakley T	Collier J	Gibson J	Johnson Bill	Lewis H	Martin G	Mercer W	Mills B	Richardson GEH	Thom A
R1	3	5	4	2	6	10	8	1	9	7	11
rep	3	5	4	2	6	10	8	1	9	7	11

Division Two — Final Table

		Pl	Home					Away					F	A	Pts
			W	D	L	F	A	W	D	L	F	A		(Total)	
1	Leeds United	42	14	5	2	41	10	7	7	7	20	25	61	35	54
2	Bury	42	15	5	1	42	7	6	4	11	21	28	63	35	51
3	Derby County	42	15	4	2	52	15	6	5	10	23	27	75	42	51
4	Blackpool	42	13	7	1	43	12	5	6	10	29	35	72	47	49
5	Southampton	42	13	5	3	36	9	4	9	8	16	22	52	31	48
6	Stoke	42	9	11	1	27	10	5	7	9	17	32	44	42	46
7	Oldham Athletic	42	10	10	1	24	12	4	7	10	21	40	45	52	45
8	Sheffield Wed.	42	15	5	1	42	9	1	7	13	12	42	54	51	44
9	South Shields	42	13	5	3	34	16	4	5	12	15	34	49	50	44
10	Clapton Orient	42	11	7	3	27	10	3	8	10	13	26	40	36	43
11	Barnsley	42	12	7	2	34	16	4	4	13	23	45	57	61	43
12	Leicester City	42	13	4	4	43	16	4	4	13	21	38	64	54	42
13	Stockport County	42	10	7	4	32	21	3	9	9	12	31	44	52	42
14	Manchester United	42	10	7	4	37	15	3	7	11	15	29	52	44	40
15	Crystal Palace	42	11	7	3	37	19	2	6	13	16	46	53	65	39
16	Port Vale	42	9	5	7	33	29	4	7	10	17	37	50	66	38
17	HULL CITY	42	8	7	6	32	23	2	10	9	14	28	46	51	37
18	Bradford City	42	8	7	6	24	21	3	8	10	11	27	35	48	37
19	Coventry City	42	9	6	6	34	23	2	7	12	18	45	52	68	35
20	Fulham	42	9	8	4	30	20	1	6	14	15	36	45	56	34
21	Nelson	42	8	8	5	32	31	2	5	14	8	43	40	74	33
22	Bristol City	42	5	8	8	19	26	2	7	12	13	39	32	65	29

1923-24

Back Row: J. Loughran, T. Smith, J. Robson, J. Rumney, G. Martin, F. Walls, W. Johnson;
Standing: W. McCracken (Manager), T. Adey, S. Hamilton, W. Mercer, A. Briggs, W. Walker, G. Hall, J. Beck (Trainer);
Sitting: M. Bell, A. Thomas, T. Bleakley, J. Collier, W. Harris, A. Thom, J. Gibson;
On Ground: T. Mordue, J. McGee, A. Bell (Asst. Trainer), J. Lodge, J. Livingston.

1924-25

Back Row: A. Thomas, J. Robson, S. Hamilton, M. O'Brien, A. Jordan, H. Lewis;
Standing: Mr A. Dixon (Secretary), T. Adey, S. Garrett, G. Maddison, W. Mercer, B. Mills, J. Keen, J. Beck (Trainer);
Sitting: W. Johnson, J. Collier, G. Martin, M. Bell, A. Thom, J. McGee, R. Mitchell;
On Ground: G. Owen, H. Havelock, A. Bell (Asst. Trainer), R. Howarth, J. Gibson.

1924/25   10th in Division Two

League matches

#	Date	Opponent	Score	Scorers	Att.
1	Aug 30	Derby County	0-4		16000
2	Sep 1	BRADFORD CITY	0-0		10000
3	6	BLACKPOOL	1-1	Mills	12000
4	8	Bradford City	1-4	Mills	9000
5	13	Crystal Palace	0-1		15000
6	20	Portsmouth	0-2		20000
7	27	FULHAM	3-0	Mills, Hamilton, Thom	9000
8	Oct 4	Wolverhampton Wan.	1-2	Mills	20000
9	11	BARNSLEY	5-2	Mills 2, Haworth 2, Thom	9000
10	18	Middlesbrough	1-0	Mills	18000
11	25	SOUTHAMPTON	1-1	Haworth	12000
12	Nov 1	Chelsea	0-1		15000
13	8	STOCKPORT COUNTY	3-0	Mills, Haworth, Hamilton	8000
14	15	Manchester United	0-2		29750
15	22	LEICESTER CITY	2-1	Mills 2	10000
16	29	Stoke	0-2		6000
17	Dec 6	COVENTRY CITY	4-1	Mills 2, Martin, Thom	8000
18	13	Oldham Athletic	0-1		5756
19	20	SHEFFIELD WEDNESDAY	4-2	Mills 3, Martin	10000
20	25	Clapton Orient	0-0		17000
21	26	CLAPTON ORIENT	2-1	Haworth, Martin	10000
22	27	DERBY COUNTY	1-1	Mills	10000
23	Jan 3	Blackpool	0-0		7000
24	17	CRYSTAL PALACE	5-0	Martin 2, Hamilton 2, Mills	10000
25	24	PORTSMOUTH	5-0	Mills 2, Martin 2, Hamilton	11000
26	Feb 7	WOLVERHAMPTON W.	0-1		10000
27	9	Fulham	0-4		6000
28	14	Barnsley	2-1	Mills, Haworth	8000
29	28	Southampton	2-2	Hamilton, Mills	7000
30	Mar 7	CHELSEA	1-0	Mills	9000
31	14	Stockport County	2-0	Mills, Haworth	10000
32	19	MIDDLESBROUGH	0-0		7000
33	21	MANCHESTER UNITED	0-1		8000
34	28	Leicester City	0-1		20000
35	Apr 1	South Shields	0-2		9000
36	4	STOKE	0-0		7000
37	10	Port Vale	1-1	Mills	16000
38	11	Coventry City	0-0		12914
39	13	PORT VALE	2-1	Mills, Bleakley	6000
40	18	OLDHAM ATHLETIC	1-0	Hamilton	5000
41	25	Sheffield Wednesday	0-5		12000
42	May 2	SOUTH SHIELDS	0-1		5000

Appearances (shirt numbers)

#	Bell M	Bleakley T	Bown H	Collier J	Gibson J	Goulden J	Hamilton S	Haworth R	Iremonger J	Johnson Bill	Jordan A	Keen J	Lewis H	Maddison G	Martin G	McGee J	Mercer W	Mills B	Mitchell R	O'Brien M	Owen GL	Richardson GEH	Robson JC	Thom A	Thomas A	Wilkinson T
1	3	5		4						6		7	10		8	2	1				9			11		
2	3	5		4						6		7	10		8	2	1				9			11		
3	3	5		4						6		7	10		9	2	1	8						11		
4	3	5		4						6		7	10		8	2	1	9						11		
5	3	6			2	8					4	7			10	5	1	9						11		
6	3	6			2	8	10				4						1	9		5				11	7	
7		6		4	2		8	10								3	1	9		5				11	7	
8		6		4	2		7	8							10	3	1	9		5				11		
9	3	6		4	2		7	8							10		1	9		5				11		
10	3	6		4	2		7	8							10		1	9		5				11		
11	3	6		4	2		7	8							10		1	9		5				11		
12	3	6		4	2		8	10							7		1	9		5				11		
13	3	6		4	2		8	10						1	7			9		5				11		
14	3	6		4	2		8	10						1	7			9		5				11		
15	3	6		4	2			10						1	8			9		5		7		11		
16	3	6		4	2			10						1	8			9		5		7		11		
17	3	6		4	2			10						1	8			9		5		7		11		
18	3	6		4	2			10						1	8			9		5		7		11		
19	3	6		4	2			10	1						8			9		5		7		11		
20		6			2							4	10	1	8	3		9		5		7		11		
21	3	6						10				4		1	8	2		9		5		7		11		
22	3	6		4	2			10						1	8			9		5		7		11		
23	3	6		4	2			10						1	8			9		5		7		11		
24		6	1	4	2		8								10	3		9		5		7		11		
25		6	1	4	2		8								10	3		9		5		7		11		
26	3	6	1	4			8								10	2		9		5		7		11		
27	3	6	1	4				10							8	2		9		5		7		11		
28		6		4	2		8	11						1	10	3		9		5					7	
29	3	6		4	2		8							1	10			9		5				11	7	
30	3	6		4	2		8	11				7		1	10			9		5						
31	3	6		4	2		8	11				7		1	10			9		5						
32	3	6		4	2		8	11				7		1	10			9		5						
33	3	6		4	2		8	11				7		1	10			9		5						
34	3	6		4	2		8	11				7		1				9		5						10
35	3	6		4	2		8	10						1				9		5		7		11		
36	3	6			2		8	10						1				9	4	5		7		11		
37	3	6					8	11		2				1	10			9	4	5		7				
38	3	6					8	10		2				1				9	4	5		7		11		
39	3	6					8	11		2				1	10			9	4	5		7				
40		6		4			8			2				1	10	3		9		5		7		11		
41		6		4			8			2		7		1	10	3		9		5				11		
42		6						10		2	8	7		1		3		9	4	5				11		
Apps	33	42	4	33	31	2	27	30	1	9	3	17	5	25	35	18	12	36	9	33	2	19	1	30	4	1
Goals		1					7	7							7			25						3		

F.A. Cup

Rd	Date	Opponent	Score	Scorers	Att.
R1	Jan 10	WOLVERHAMPTON WAN.	1-1	Mills	22000
rep	15	Wolverhampton Wan.	1-0	Mills	24447
R2	31	CRYSTAL PALACE	3-2	Mills 2, Bleakley	22500
R3	Feb 21	LEICESTER CITY	1-1	O'Brien	27000
rep	26	Leicester City	1-3	Hamilton	19864

R1 replay a.e.t.

Rd	Bell M	Bleakley T	Bown H	Collier J	Gibson J	Hamilton S	Haworth R	Maddison G	Martin G	McGee J	Mills B	O'Brien M	Richardson GEH	Thom A	Thomas A
R1	3	6		4	2		10	1	8		9	5	7	11	
rep		6	1	4	2		10		8	3	9	5	7	11	
R2	3	6	1	4	2	8			10		9	5	7	11	
R3		6		4	2	8		1	10	3	9	5		11	7
rep		6		4	2	8		1	10	3	9	5		11	7

Final table — Division Two

		Pl	Home					Away					F.	A.	Pts
			W	D	L	F	A	W	D	L	F	A	(Total)		
1	Leicester City	42	15	4	2	58	9	9	7	5	32	23	90	32	59
2	Manchester United	42	17	3	1	40	6	6	8	7	17	17	57	23	57
3	Derby County	42	15	3	3	49	15	7	8	6	22	21	71	36	55
4	Portsmouth	42	7	13	1	28	14	8	5	8	30	36	58	50	48
5	Chelsea	42	11	8	2	31	12	5	7	9	20	25	51	37	47
6	Wolverhampton W.	42	14	1	6	29	19	6	5	10	26	32	55	51	46
7	Southampton	42	12	8	1	29	10	1	10	10	11	26	40	36	44
8	Port Vale	42	12	4	5	34	19	5	4	12	14	37	48	56	42
9	South Shields	42	9	6	6	33	21	3	11	7	9	17	42	38	41
10	HULL CITY	42	12	6	3	40	14	3	5	13	10	35	50	49	41
11	Clapton Orient	42	8	7	6	22	13	6	5	10	20	29	42	42	40
12	Fulham	42	11	6	4	26	15	4	4	13	15	41	41	56	40
13	Middlesbrough	42	6	10	5	22	21	4	9	8	14	23	36	44	39
14	Sheffield Wed.	42	12	3	6	36	23	3	5	13	14	33	50	56	38
15	Barnsley	42	8	8	5	30	23	5	4	12	16	36	46	59	38
16	Bradford City	42	11	6	4	26	13	2	6	13	11	37	37	50	38
17	Blackpool	42	8	5	8	37	26	6	4	11	28	35	65	61	37
18	Oldham Athletic	42	9	5	7	24	21	4	6	11	11	30	35	51	37
19	Stockport County	42	10	6	5	26	15	3	5	13	11	42	37	57	37
20	Stoke	42	7	8	6	22	17	5	3	13	12	29	34	46	35
21	Crystal Palace	42	8	4	9	23	19	4	6	11	15	35	38	54	34
22	Coventry City	42	10	6	5	32	26	1	3	17	13	58	45	84	31

1925/26   13th in Division Two

#	Date		Opponent	Score	Scorers	Att	Bell M	Bleakley T	Campbell J	Collier J	Cowan W	Gibson J	Haworth R	Horne A	Johnson, Bill	Jones E	Jordan A	Keers J	Lee P	Maddison G	Martin G	McGee J	Mills B	Mitchell R	Murray J	O'Brien M	Richardson GEH	Swan C	Thom A	Whitworth G	Wilkinson T	Wilson G
1	Aug	29	DERBY COUNTY	0-0		11209	3	6				2			4					1	10		9			5	7	8	11			
2		31	Southampton	2-0	Mills, Richardson	9433	3	6				2			4				10	1			9			5	7	8	11			
3	Sep	5	Bradford City	1-0	Swan	15078	3	6				2							10	1			9	4		5	7	8	11			
4		7	SOUTHAMPTON	4-0	Mills 2, Lee 2	9921	3	6				2							10	1			9	4		5	7	8	11			
5		12	PORT VALE	3-0	Mills 2, Lee	12523	3	6				2							10	1			9	4		5	7	8	11			
6		19	Barnsley	1-2	Thom	3314	3	6				2							10	1			9	4		5	7	8	11			
7		26	CLAPTON ORIENT	2-0	Swan, Mitchell	9695	3	6				2							10	1			9	4		5	7	8	11			
8	Oct	3	Chelsea	0-4		47428	3	6				2							10	1			9	4		5	7	8	11			
9		10	SOUTH SHIELDS	1-3	Mills	10092	3	6				2		7					10	1	8		9	4		5			11			
10		12	NOTTM. FOREST	4-1	Haworth, Cowan, Horne, Thom	4839	3	6			9	2	10	7						1	8			4		5			11			
11		17	Preston North End	0-4		17542	3	6				2	10	7						1			9	4		5		8	11			
12		24	MIDDLESBROUGH	1-2	Wilkinson	10358	3	6				2		7						1	10			4		5		8	11		9	
13		31	Stockport County	1-0	Mills	7445	3	6	4			2		7						1	10	9	8			5			11			
14	Nov	7	FULHAM	1-0	Mills	6992	3	6	4			2		7						1	10	9	8			5			11			
15		14	Swansea Town	0-2		15947	3	6				2	10	8						1			9	4		5	7		11			
16		21	SHEFFIELD WEDNESDAY	0-1		8623	3	6				2			4					1	10		9			5	7		11	8		
17		28	Stoke City	1-3	Thom	7204	3	6				2			4					1	10		9			5	7		11	8		
18	Dec	5	OLDHAM ATHLETIC	1-2	Thom	7747	3					2		7		4	6			1	10		9			5			11	8		
19		12	Portsmouth	2-2	Thom, Mills	15520	3		4			2	10	7			6			1			9			5			11	8		
20		19	WOLVERHAMPTON W.	3-1	Mills 2, Whitworth	6018	3	6				2	10	7						1			9	4		5			11	8		
21		25	Darlington	2-1	Thom, Whitworth	9249	3	6				2						4		1	8		10			5	7		11	9		
22		26	DARLINGTON	1-1	Mills	17422	3	6				2						4		1	8		10			5	7		11	9		
23	Jan	2	Derby County	1-3	Whitworth	12881	3	6				2								1	8		10	4		5	7		11	9		
24		16	BRADFORD CITY	5-0	Mills 2, Martin 2, Whitworth	6836	3	6						7				4		1	8	2	10			5			11	9		
25		23	Port Vale	1-3	Bleakley	7579	3	6						7				4		1	8	2	10			5			11	9		
26		30	BARNSLEY	2-2	Cowan, Whitworth	8478	3	6			9	2		7				4		1	10					5			11	8		
27	Feb	6	Clapton Orient	0-0		14710	3	6	4		9	2		7						1	10					5			11	8		
28		13	CHELSEA	0-1		9464	3	6	4			2								1	8		10			5	7		11	9		
29		27	PRESTON NORTH END	1-1	Martin	8953	3	6	4			2							10	1	7		8			5			11	9		
30	Mar	3	South Shields	3-1	Martin, Mills, Whitworth	5776	3	6	4			2				8		11		1	7		10			5				9		
31		6	Middlesbrough	3-3	Mills	8843	3	6	4			2				8		11		1	7		10			5				9		
32		13	STOCKPORT COUNTY	4-0	Whitworth, Martin, Jones, Keers	6522	3	6	4							8		11		1	7	2	10			5				9		
33		20	Fulham	1-1	Whitworth	14602	3	6	4							10		11		1	7	2				5		8		9		
34	Apr	2	Blackpool	2-2	Whitworth, Wilkinson	13676	3									8	6	11		1	7	2		4		5				9	10	
35		3	Sheffield Wednesday	0-2		29075	3		4							8	6	11		1	7	2				5				9	10	
36		5	BLACKPOOL	1-2	Horne	7365	3							7		8	6	11		1		2	10	4		5				9		
37		10	STOKE CITY	1-0	Martin	4211	3	6				2		7		9		11		1	8	4	10			5						
38		17	Oldham Athletic	1-2	Whitworth	5626	3	6				2		7						1	8	4	10			5			11	9		
39		21	Nottingham Forest	0-4		4706		6				2		7					10	1	8	3		4		5			11	9		
40		24	PORTSMOUTH	1-0	Swan	4559		6				2		7						1	8	3	10	4		5			11	9		
41		26	SWANSEA TOWN	4-2	Haworth 2, Whitworth, Martin	4146		6				2	10	7						1	8	3		4		5			11	9		
42	May	1	Wolverhampton Wan.	1-3	Whitworth	9283		6				2		7					10	1	8			4		5			11	9		3
	Apps						38	37	7	3	4	35	6	21	4	8	6	8	18	42	32	10	27	18	3	41	15	16	34	25	3	1
	Goals							1			2		3	2		1		1	3		7		17	1			1	3	6	13	2	

F.A. Cup

Round	Date		Opponent	Score		Att	Bell M	Bleakley T	Keers J	Maddison G	Martin G	McGee J	Mills B	O'Brien M	Richardson GEH	Thom A	Whitworth G
R3	Jan	9	ASTON VILLA	0-3		26000	3	6	4	1	11	2	8	5	7	10	9

		Pl	Home					Away					F.	A.	Pts
			W	D	L	F	A	W	D	L	F	A	(Total)		
1	Sheffield Wed.	42	19	0	2	61	17	8	6	7	27	31	88	48	60
2	Derby County	42	17	2	2	57	17	8	5	8	20	25	77	42	57
3	Chelsea	42	10	7	4	42	22	9	7	5	34	27	76	49	52
4	Wolverhampton W.	42	15	4	2	55	15	6	3	12	29	45	84	60	49
5	Swansea Town	42	13	6	2	50	16	6	5	10	27	41	77	57	49
6	Blackpool	42	12	6	3	41	16	5	11	5	13	55	76	69	45
7	Oldham Athletic	42	14	4	3	52	24	4	4	13	22	38	74	62	44
8	Port Vale	42	15	3	3	53	18	4	3	14	26	51	79	69	44
9	South Shields	42	11	6	4	50	29	7	2	12	24	36	74	65	44
10	Middlesbrough	42	14	1	6	56	28	7	1	13	21	40	77	68	44
11	Portsmouth	42	12	4	5	48	27	5	6	10	31	47	79	74	44
12	Preston North End	42	17	2	2	54	28	1	5	15	17	56	71	84	43
13	HULL CITY	42	11	4	6	40	19	5	5	11	23	42	63	61	41
14	Southampton	42	11	2	8	39	25	4	6	11	24	38	63	63	38
15	Darlington	42	9	5	7	51	31	5	5	11	21	46	72	77	38
16	Bradford City	42	9	5	7	28	26	4	5	12	19	40	47	66	36
17	Nottingham Forest	42	11	4	6	38	25	3	4	14	13	48	51	73	36
18	Barnsley	42	10	7	4	38	22	2	5	14	20	62	58	84	36
19	Fulham	42	8	6	7	32	29	3	6	12	14	48	46	77	34
20	Clapton Orient	42	8	6	7	30	21	4	3	14	20	44	50	65	33
21	Stoke City	42	8	5	8	32	23	4	3	14	22	54	54	77	32
22	Stockport County	42	8	7	6	34	28	0	2	19	17	69	51	97	25

1925-26

Back Row: W. Cowan, T. Wilkinson, J. Goulden, A. Bell (Asst. Trainer), J. Campbell, J. McGee, J. Hart;
Standing: W. McCracken (Manager), A. Horne, P. Lee, J. Iceton, S. Jarvis, G. Maddison, B. Mills, R. Haworth, J. Beck (Trainer);
Sitting: J. Gibson, G. Martin, T. Bleakley, M. O'Brien, W. Johnson, A. Thom, M. Bell;
On Ground: C. Swan, E. Jones, A. Jordan, G. Richardson, J. Collier, J. Keers.

1926-27

Back Row: J. Gibson, G. Maddison, M. Bell;
Middle Row: W. McCracken (Manager), W. Swan, P. Mooney, S. Dixon, N. Sullivan, H. Scott, J. Beck (Trainer);
Front Row: T. Wyper, T. Bleakley, G. Martin, G. Whitworth, J. Howieson, W. Taylor, A. Jordan.

1926/27 7th in Division Two

#	Date		Opposition	Result	Scorers	Att	Alexander S	Bell M	Bleakley T	Brayson J	Campbell J	Cowan W	Dixon S	Gibson J	Guyan G	Hart I	Horne A	Howieson J	Lee P	Lloyd C	Maddison G	Martin G	McGee J	McLaughlin G	Morris I	Scott H	Sullivan N	Swan C	Taylor W	Whitworth G	Wilson G	Wyper T
1	Aug	28	WOLVERHAMPTON W.	1-0	Whitworth	8321		3	6	11			5	2							1	8		10				4	7	9		
2		30	SOUTH SHIELDS	2-0	Whitworth, McLaughlin	7002		3	6	11			5	2							1	8		10				4	7	9		
3	Sep	4	Notts County	0-1		9629		3	6	11			5	2							1	8		10				4	7	9		
4		11	CLAPTON ORIENT	4-0	Lee 2, Whitworth 2	8235		3	6					2					7	10	1	8	5					4	11	9		
5		15	Reading	1-0	Evans (og)	12078		3	6				5	2					7	10	1	8						4	11	9		
6		18	Middlesbrough	0-2		11618		3	6				5	2					7	10	1	8						4	11	9		
7		20	READING	1-1	Martin	6744			6				5	2	8					10	1	7						4	11	9	3	
8		25	PORT VALE	0-0		7793			6				5		8					10	1	7	2					4	11	9	3	
9	Oct	2	Southampton	1-0	Swan	10890		3	6	4			5								1	7	2	10				8	11	9		
10		9	BRADFORD CITY	4-0	Whitworth 3, Swan	6549		3	6	4			5	2							1	7		10				8	11	9		
11		16	Grimsby Town	1-0	Whitworth	16023		3	6	4			5	2							1	7		10				8	11	9		
12		23	BLACKPOOL	3-0	Swan 2, McLaughlin	11363		3	6				5	2							1	7		10			4	8	11	9		
13		30	Swansea City	0-1		20772		3	6				5	2							1	7		10			4	8	11	9		
14	Nov	6	NOTTM. FOREST	1-2	Lee	7256		3	6				5	2						10	1	7					4	8	11	9		
15		13	Barnsley	2-1	Martin, Dixon	4159		3	6			9	5	2							1	7				8		4	11	10		
16		20	MANCHESTER CITY	3-2	Cowan, Scott, Taylor	11582		3	6			9	5	2							1	7				8		4	11	10		
17		27	Darlington	3-1	Cowan 3	9267		3	6			9	5	2							1	7				8		4	11	10		
18	Dec	4	PORTSMOUTH	2-1	Whitworth, Taylor	13501		3	6			9	5								1	7	2			8		4	11	10		
19		11	Oldham Athletic	1-1	Cowan	14800		3	6			9	5								1	7	2			8		4	11	10		
20		18	FULHAM	2-0	Whitworth, Cowan	11109		3	6			9	5								1	7	2			8		4	11	10		
21		25	Chelsea	0-1		34306		3	6				5		9						1	7	2			8		4	11	10		
22		27	CHELSEA	0-1		23440		3	6				5		9						1	7	2			8		4	11	10		
23	Jan	1	South Shields	1-3	Guyan	9549		3	6				5		9						1	7	2			8		4	11	10		
24		15	Wolverhampton Wan.	2-5	Whitworth, Taylor	16793		3			6	9	5								1	7	2			8	4		11	10		
25		22	NOTTS COUNTY	2-0	Whitworth 2	8891		3	6				5						7		1	10	2			8		4	11	9		
26	Feb	5	MIDDLESBROUGH	3-3	Guyan 2, Wyper	24110		3					5		9						1	10	2			8	6	4	11			7
27		12	Port Vale	0-0		10654		3					5		9			6			1		2			10	4	8	11			7
28		23	Clapton Orient	2-1	Martin, Taylor	4428		3					5		9						1	8	2			6		4	11	10		7
29		26	Bradford City	2-1	Guyan 2	15181		3					5		9						1	8	2	10		6		4	11			7
30	Mar	5	GRIMSBY TOWN	2-3	Guyan 2	22274		3							9			10			1	8	2	5			6	4	11			7
31		12	Blackpool	0-4		9195		3	5						9			10			1	4	2			8	6		11			7
32		14	SOUTHAMPTON	0-0		6912		2	5						9			10			1	8					6	4	11		3	7
33		19	SWANSEA CITY	2-1	Martin, Taylor	13143		3	5						9			10			1	8	2				6	4	11			7
34		26	Nottingham Forest	1-3	Martin	10007		2	5						9			10			1	8					6	4	11		3	7
35	Apr	2	BARNSLEY	5-1	Howieson 2, Martin 2, Whitworth	8671		3	5									10			1	9	2				6	4	11	8		7
36		9	Manchester City	2-2	Whitworth, Martin	21508		3	5					2				10			1	9					6	4	11	8		7
37		16	Preston North End	0-1		17192		3	5					2				10			1	9					6	4	11	8		7
38		16	DARLINGTON	2-1	Howieson, Whitworth	10298		3	5					2				10			1	9					6	4	11	8		7
39		18	PRESTON NORTH END	3-1	Martin 3	12881		3	5					2				10			1	9					6	4	11	8		7
40		23	Portsmouth	0-2		17049		3	5					2				10			1	9					6	4	11	8		7
41		30	OLDHAM ATHLETIC	1-2	Martin	7267	8	3	5									10			1	9	2				6	4	11			7
42	May	7	Fulham	1-3	Sullivan	8910	8	3	5					2							1	9					6	4	11	10		7
			Apps				2	40	36	3	4	7	28	21	12	2	4	12	7	7	42	41	13	8	1	15	22	39	42	33	4	17
			Goals									6	1		7			3	3			12		2		1	1	4	5	16		1

One own goal

F.A. Cup

Rd	Date		Opposition	Result	Scorers	Att	Bell M	Bleakley T	Cowan W	Dixon S	Guyan G	Horne A	Lloyd C	Maddison G	Martin G	McGee J	McLaughlin G	Scott H	Sullivan N	Swan C	Taylor W	Whitworth G
R3	Jan	8	WEST BROMWICH ALB.	2-1	Cowan, Scott	18000	3	6	9	5				1	7	2		8		4	11	10
R4		28	EVERTON	1-1	Martin	22000	3			5		7	7	1	10	2		8	6	4	11	9
rep	Feb	2	Everton	2-2	Guyan, Scott	45000	3			5	9			1	7	2	10	8	6	4	11	
rep2		7	Everton	3-2	Whitworth, Guyan, Martin	16800	3			5	9			1	7	2		8	6	4	11	10
R5		19	Wolverhampton Wan.	0-1		48948	3			5	9			1	7	2		8	6	4	11	10

R4 replay and replay 2 a.e.t.. Replay 2 at Villa Park.

		Pl	Home					Away					F.	A.	Pts
			W	D	L	F	A	W	D	L	F	A	(Total)		
1	Middlesbrough	42	18	2	1	78	23	9	6	6	44	37	122	60	62
2	Portsmouth	42	14	4	3	58	17	9	4	8	29	32	87	49	54
3	Manchester City	42	15	3	3	65	23	7	7	7	43	38	108	61	54
4	Chelsea	42	13	7	1	40	17	7	5	9	22	35	62	52	52
5	Nottingham Forest	42	14	6	1	57	23	4	8	9	23	32	80	55	50
6	Preston North End	42	14	4	3	54	29	6	5	10	20	43	74	72	49
7	HULL CITY	42	13	4	4	43	19	7	3	11	20	33	63	52	47
8	Port Vale	42	11	6	4	50	26	5	7	9	38	52	88	78	45
9	Blackpool	42	13	5	3	65	26	5	3	13	30	54	95	80	44
10	Oldham Athletic	42	12	3	6	50	37	7	3	11	24	47	74	84	44
11	Barnsley	42	13	5	5	56	23	4	4	13	32	64	88	87	43
12	Swansea Town	42	13	5	3	44	21	3	6	12	24	51	68	72	43
13	Southampton	42	9	8	4	35	22	6	4	11	25	40	60	62	42
14	Reading	42	14	1	6	47	20	2	7	12	17	52	64	72	40
15	Wolverhampton W.	42	10	4	7	54	30	4	3	14	19	45	73	75	35
16	Notts County	42	11	4	6	45	24	4	1	16	25	72	70	96	35
17	Grimsby Town	42	6	7	8	39	39	5	5	11	35	52	74	91	34
18	Fulham	42	11	4	6	39	31	2	4	15	19	61	58	92	34
19	South Shields	42	10	8	3	49	25	1	3	17	22	71	71	96	33
20	Clapton Orient	42	9	3	9	37	35	3	4	14	23	61	60	96	31
21	Darlington	42	10	3	8	53	42	2	3	16	26	56	79	98	30
22	Bradford City	42	6	4	11	30	28	1	5	15	20	60	50	88	23

1927/28 14th in Division Two

#	Date	Opponent	Score	Scorers	Att.	Alexander S	Barraclough W	Bell M	Bleakley T	Crozier J	Dixon S	Gibson F	Gibson J	Guyan G	Howieson J	Maddison G	Martin G	Mooney P	Nelson A	Scott H	Starling R	Sullivan N	Swan C	Taylor W	Watson J	Whitworth G	Wilson G	Wyper T
1	Aug 27	Barnsley	1-1	Guyan	10830			3			5		2	9		1	10	4		8		6		11				7
2	29	Preston North End	2-4	Scott 2	21811			3			5		2	9		1	10	4		8		6		11				7
3	Sep 3	WOLVERHAMPTON W.	2-0	Scott, Taylor	11050						5		2	9		1	10	4		8		6		11			3	7
4	5	PRESTON NORTH END	0-0		8915			3			5		2			1	10	4		8	9	6		11				7
5	10	Port Vale	2-1	Scott 2	12169			3			5		2			1	10	4		8		6		11		9		7
6	17	SOUTH SHIELDS	1-0	Martin	10252			3			5		2			1	10	4		8		6		11		9		7
7	24	Leeds United	0-2		21943			3			5		2	9		1	7	4		8		6		11		10		
8	Oct 1	NOTTM. FOREST	2-0	Martin 2	8274			3	6		5		2		10	1	9	4		8				11				7
9	8	Manchester City	1-2	Scott	42038			3	6		5		2		10	1	9	4		8				11				7
10	15	GRIMSBY TOWN	0-1		18862			3	6		5		2		10	1	9			8			4	11				
11	22	Chelsea	0-2		15153			2		11	5				10	1	8	4	9		6	7				3		
12	29	BLACKPOOL	2-2	Nelson, Howieson	9067			3		11	5		2		10	1	8	4	9		6	7						
13	Nov 5	Reading	0-3		9935			3	6		5		2		10	1	8	4				7		11	9			
14	12	CLAPTON ORIENT	2-2	Martin 2	6682			3	6		8		2		10	1	9					4		7		11	5	
15	19	West Bromwich Albion	1-1	Sullivan	8857			3	6		8		2		10	1	9					4		7		11	5	
16	26	SOUTHAMPTON	1-0	Keeping (og)	8081			3	6		8		2		10	1	9					4		11			5	7
17	Dec 3	Stoke City	1-3	Howieson	9638			3	6			1	2		10		9			8		4		11			5	7
18	10	BRISTOL CITY	1-1	Martin	6716			3	6		8	1	2		10		9					4		11			5	7
19	17	Notts County	1-1	Taylor	8758	8		3	6		4	1	2		10		7		9					11			5	
20	24	OLDHAM ATHLETIC	2-2	Nelson, Alexander	6662	8		3	6		4	1	2		10		7		9					11			5	
21	27	FULHAM	3-2	Nelson 3	14050	8		3	6		4	1	2		10		7		9					11			5	
22	31	BARNSLEY	2-1	Alexander, Scott	9569	10		3	6		4	1	2				7		9	8							5	
23	Jan 7	Wolverhampton Wan.	1-1	Nelson	12106			3	6		4		2			1	7		9	8				11			5	
24	21	PORT VALE	1-0	Nelson	7106	8	11	3	6		4		2			1	7		9				10				5	
25	Feb 4	LEEDS UNITED	3-1	Martin 2, Wyper	12520		11	3	6		5		2			1	10		9		4		8					7
26	11	Nottingham Forest	1-1	Swan	6617		11	3	6		5		2			1	10		9		4		8					7
27	22	South Shields	0-1		4322		11	3	6		5		2			1	10		9		4		8					7
28	25	Grimsby Town	1-1	Guyan	15986		11	3	6		5		2	9		1	10			8	4							7
29	Mar 3	CHELSEA	0-2		12679			3	6		5		2	9		1	10			8	4			11				7
30	10	Blackpool	1-2	Sullivan	9988			3	6		5		2		10	1	8		9			4		7		11		
31	17	READING	0-1		6493			3	6		5		2	9	10	1				8		4		7		11		
32	24	Clapton Orient	0-0		8869			3	6		5		2		10	1	9				8	4		11				7
33	26	Fulham	2-0	Nelson, Taylor	7023			3	6		5		2		10	1	9				8	4		11				7
34	31	WEST BROMWICH ALB.	1-1	Howieson	7964			3	6		5		2		10	1	9				8	4		11				7
35	Apr 6	SWANSEA TOWN	0-2		8877			3	6		5		2		10	1	9				8	4		11				7
36	7	Southampton	0-2		11955			3	6		5		2		10	1					8	4		11				7
37	9	Swansea Town	0-2		15732			3	6				2		10	1					8	4		11	5	9		7
38	14	STOKE CITY	1-0	Howieson	4848		11	3	6				2		10	1					8	4	7		5			
39	16	MANCHESTER CITY	0-0		6088		11		6		5		2		10	1						8	4	7		9	3	
40	21	Bristol City	1-0	Whitworth	10198		11		6		5		2		10	1						8	4	7		9	3	
41	28	NOTTS COUNTY	1-1	Whitworth	5284				6	11	5		2		10	1						8	4	7		9	3	
42	May 5	Oldham Athletic	0-5		4936		11		6		5		2		10	1						8	4	7		9	3	
		Apps				6	9	37	33	3	39	6	41	7	27	36	30	11	18	14	15	30	15	34	13	9	6	23
		Goals				2							2	4			8		8	7		2	1	3		2		1

One own goal

F.A. Cup

Round	Date	Opponent	Score	Att.	Alexander S	Bell M	Bleakley T	Dixon S	Gibson F	Gibson J	Howieson J	Martin G	Nelson A	Taylor W	Wilson G
R3	Jan 14	LEICESTER CITY	0-1	23141	8	3	6	4	1	2	10	7	9	11	5

			Pl	Home					Away					F.	A.	Pts
				W	D	L	F	A	W	D	L	F	A		(Total)	
1	Manchester City		42	18	2	1	70	27	7	7	7	30	32	100	59	59
2	Leeds United		42	16	2	3	63	15	9	5	7	35	34	98	49	57
3	Chelsea		42	15	2	4	46	15	8	6	7	29	30	75	45	54
4	Preston North End		42	15	3	3	62	24	7	6	8	38	42	100	66	53
5	Stoke City		42	14	5	2	44	17	8	3	10	34	42	78	59	52
6	Swansea Town		42	13	6	2	46	17	5	6	10	29	46	75	63	48
7	Oldham Athletic		42	15	3	3	55	18	4	5	12	20	33	75	51	46
8	West Bromwich Alb.		42	10	7	4	50	28	7	5	9	40	42	90	70	46
9	Port Vale		42	11	6	4	45	20	7	2	12	23	37	68	57	44
10	Nottingham Forest		42	10	6	5	54	37	5	4	12	29	47	83	84	40
11	Grimsby Town		42	8	6	7	41	41	6	6	9	28	42	69	83	40
12	Bristol City		42	11	5	5	42	18	4	4	13	34	61	76	79	39
13	Barnsley		42	10	5	6	43	36	4	6	11	22	49	65	85	39
14	HULL CITY		42	9	8	4	25	19	3	7	11	16	35	41	54	39
15	Notts County		42	10	4	7	47	26	3	8	10	21	48	68	74	38
16	Wolverhampton W.		42	11	5	5	43	31	2	5	14	20	60	63	91	36
17	Southampton		42	11	3	7	54	40	3	4	14	37	68	91	108	35
18	Reading		42	9	8	4	32	22	2	5	14	21	53	53	75	35
19	Blackpool		42	11	3	7	55	43	2	5	14	28	58	83	101	34
20	Clapton Orient		42	9	7	5	32	25	2	5	14	23	60	55	85	34
21	Fulham		42	12	7	2	46	22	1	0	20	22	67	68	89	33
22	South Shields		42	5	5	11	30	41	2	4	15	26	70	56	111	23

1927-28
Back Row: R. Starling, A. Richards, B. Bradford, N. Sullivan, H. Scott, G. Wilson, E. Mooney, G. Guyan;
Standing: W. McCracken (Manager), C. Swan, R. McKenzie, C. Lloyd, F. Gibson, J. Lodge (asst-Trainer),
G. Maddison, S. Dixon, J. Watson, J. Murray, J. Beck (Trainer);
Sitting: J. Gibson, G. Martin, T. Bleakley, M. Bell, G. Whitworth, J. Howieson, W. Taylor, T. Wyper;
On Ground: J. Alexander, J. Maloney, S. Alexander, J. Crozier.

1928-29
Back Row: K. McDonald, S. Weaver, S. Dixon, G. Maddison, T. Bleakley, N. Sullivan, M. Bell, A. Childs;
Front Row: J. Gibson, S. Alexander, R. Starling, D. Duncan, J. Murray.

1928/29   12th in Division Two

No	Date	Opponent	Score	Scorers	Att	Alexander S	Bell M	Bleakley T	Childs A	Dixon S	Duncan D	Gibson F	Gibson J	Goldsmith G	Hedley F	Maddison G	McDonald K	Nelson A	Prince A	Smith S	Starling R	Sullivan N	Swan C	Taylor W	Turner A	Vickers J	Walsh J	Watson J	Weaver S	Wilson G
1	Aug 25	SOUTHAMPTON	2-2	McDonald, Childs	11232		3		5	4			2			1	9			11	10		6	7			8			
2	27	OLDHAM ATHLETIC	1-0	Smith S	7468				5	4			2			1	9			11	10		6	7			8			3
3	Sep 1	Wolverhampton Wan.	4-2	McDonald 3, Childs	18230			6	5				2			1	9			11	10			7			8		4	3
4	3	Oldham Athletic	1-0	McDonald	10121			6	5		11		2			1	9				10			7			8		4	3
5	8	NOTTS COUNTY	1-1	McDonald	14790		3	6	5				2			1	9			11	10			7			8		4	
6	12	Middlesbrough	1-1	McDonald	15998		3	6	5				2			1	9			11	10			7			8		4	
7	15	Millwall	0-0		23359		3	6	5				2			1	9				10			7	11		8		4	
8	22	PORT VALE	2-0	McDonald, Walsh	11728		3	6	5		11		2			1	9				10			7			8		4	
9	29	Grimsby Town	1-0	Starling	17048		3	6	5		11		2			1	9				10			7			8		4	
10	Oct 6	Tottenham Hotspur	1-4	McDonald	28737		3	6	5		11		2			1	9				10			7			8		4	
11	13	READING	3-0	Walsh 2, McDonald	12657		3	6	5				2		11	1	9				10			7			8		4	
12	20	STOKE CITY	1-3		11919		3	6	5				2		11	1	9				10			7			8		4	
13	27	Clapton Orient	2-0	McDonald, Walsh	9496		3		5	4	11		2			1	9				10			7			8		6	
14	Nov 3	WEST BROMWICH ALB.	4-1	McDonald, Walsh, Starling, Duncan	11301		3		5	4	11		2			1	9				10			7			8		6	
15	10	Bradford Park Avenue	1-5	Walsh	17877		3		5	4	11		2			1	9				10			7			8		6	
16	17	BRISTOL CITY	5-1	McDonald 5	8545	7	3			5	11	1	2				9				10	4					8		6	
17	24	Barnsley	2-2	McDonald 2	4693	7	3			5	11	1	2				9				10	4					8		6	
18	Dec 1	CHELSEA	2-2	McDonald, Walsh	16925	7	3			5	11	1	2				9				10	4					8		6	
19	8	Blackpool	1-2	Duncan	9033	7	3			5	11		2			1	9				10	4					8		6	
20	15	SWANSEA TOWN	1-1	Walsh	10702	7	3			5	11		2			1	9				10	4					8		6	
21	22	Nottingham Forest	1-3	Starling	6758	7	3			5	11		2			1	9				8	4							6	
22	25	PRESTON NORTH END	5-1	McDonald 2, Alexander, Taylor, Smith	17254	7	3		5	4			2			1	9			10	8						11		6	
23	26	Preston North End	0-1		26706	7	3	4	5				2			1	9			10	8						11		6	
24	29	Southampton	2-3	Weaver, Dixon	18384		3	6	5	8				2		1	9						4	7			11		10	
25	Jan 5	WOLVERHAMPTON W.	1-3	Childs	8232	7	3	6	5					2		1	9						4	8			11		10	
26	19	Notts County	0-6		13271	7	3	6	5	8				2		1	9			10							11			
27	Feb 2	Port Vale	1-4	Walsh	6065	7	3	6					2			1	9				8						11	5	10	4
28	9	GRIMSBY TOWN	2-3	Starling, Weaver	10453	7	3	6					2			1	9				8						11	5	10	4
29	23	Reading	0-3		7502	7	3	4					2			1	9				8						11	5	10	6
30	Mar 2	Stoke City	1-1	Taylor	10925	7		6	5							1		9			8	4					11		10	3
31	9	CLAPTON ORIENT	0-0		7916			6	5							1		9			8	4		7	11				10	3
32	16	West Bromwich Albion	0-2		7952		2	6	5							1	9				10	4		7	11		8			
33	23	BRADFORD PARK AVE.	2-3	Taylor	6980		2	6	4		11					1					8			7			9	5	10	3
34	30	Bristol City	0-0		15426		2	6	4		11					1					8			7			9	5	10	3
35	Apr 1	MIDDLESBROUGH	1-1	Wilson	19740		2	6	4		11					1					8			7			9	5	10	3
36	6	BARNSLEY	0-0		6977			6	4		11		2			1					8			7			9	5	10	3
37	13	Chelsea	0-0		9654		2	6	4		11					1					9			7				5	10	3
38	15	TOTTENHAM HOTSPUR	1-1	Weaver	4139		2	6	4			1									9			7	11			5	10	3
39	20	BLACKPOOL	1-3	Weaver	4945		2	6	5		11	1									9			7					10	3
40	22	MILLWALL	4-0	Starling 3, Duncan	3164		2	6	5		11	1									9			7					4	3
41	27	Swansea Town	1-0	McDonald	11242	7	2		5							1	9			10	8					4	11		6	
42	May 4	NOTTM. FOREST	0-1		4294	7	3		5					2		1	9			10	8					4	11		6	

Played in one game: J Murray (21, at 10), A Rodgers (41, at 3).

| | | | | | Apps | 16 | 36 | 28 | 21 | 27 | 20 | 8 | 28 | 5 | 2 | 34 | 32 | 3 | 5 | 14 | 31 | 13 | 3 | 36 | 3 | 2 | 33 | 9 | 37 | 14 |
| | | | | | Goals | 1 | | | 3 | 1 | 3 | | | | | | 23 | | | 2 | 8 | | | 3 | | | 9 | | 4 | 1 |

F.A. Cup

No	Date	Opponent	Score	Scorers	Att	Alexander S	Bell M	Bleakley T	Childs A	Dixon S	Duncan D	Gibson F	Gibson J	Goldsmith G	Hedley F	Maddison G	McDonald K	Nelson A	Prince A	Smith S	Starling R	Sullivan N	Swan C	Taylor W	Turner A	Vickers J	Walsh J	Watson J	Weaver S	Wilson G
R3	Jan 12	BRADFORD PARK AVE.	1-1	McDonald	23000	7	3	6	5	4			2			1	9				8						11		10	
rep	16	Bradford Park Avenue	1-3	McDonald	21072	7	3	6	5	4			2			1	9				8						11		10	

		Pl	Home				Away					F.	A.	Pts
			W	D	L	F	A	W	D	L	F	A	(Total)	
1	Middlesbrough	42	14	4	3	54	22	8	7	6	38	35	92	57	55
2	Grimsby Town	42	16	2	3	49	24	8	3	10	33	37	82	61	53
3	Bradford Park Ave.	42	18	2	1	62	22	4	2	15	26	48	88	70	48
4	Southampton	42	12	6	3	48	22	5	8	8	26	38	74	60	48
5	Notts County	42	13	4	4	51	24	6	5	10	27	41	78	65	47
6	Stoke City	42	12	7	2	46	16	5	5	11	28	35	74	51	46
7	West Bromwich Alb.	42	13	4	4	50	25	6	4	11	30	54	80	79	46
8	Blackpool	42	13	4	4	49	18	6	3	12	43	58	92	76	45
9	Chelsea	42	10	6	5	40	30	7	4	10	24	35	64	65	44
10	Tottenham Hotspur	42	16	3	2	50	26	1	6	14	25	55	75	81	43
11	Nottingham Forest	42	8	6	7	34	33	7	6	8	37	37	71	70	42
12	HULL CITY	42	8	8	5	38	24	5	6	10	20	39	58	63	40
13	Preston North End	42	12	6	3	58	27	3	3	15	20	52	78	79	39
14	Millwall	42	10	4	7	43	35	6	3	12	28	51	71	86	39
15	Reading	42	12	3	6	48	30	3	6	12	15	56	63	86	39
16	Barnsley	42	12	4	5	51	28	4	2	15	18	38	69	66	38
17	Wolverhampton W.	42	9	6	6	41	31	6	1	14	36	50	77	81	37
18	Oldham Athletic	42	15	2	4	37	24	1	3	17	17	51	54	75	37
19	Swansea Town	42	12	3	6	46	26	1	7	13	16	49	62	75	36
20	Bristol City	42	11	6	4	37	25	2	4	15	21	47	58	72	36
21	Port Vale	42	14	1	6	53	25	1	3	17	18	61	71	86	34
22	Clapton Orient	42	10	4	7	29	25	2	4	15	16	47	45	72	32

Player columns (left to right): Alexander S, Bell M, Bleakley T, Bradford B, Cartwright P, Childs A, Dixon S, Duncan D, Fawcett R, Flannigan T, Gibson F, Goldsmith G, Gowdy W, Howieson J, Maddison G, March H, McDonald K, Mills B, Murray J, Rodgers A, Starling R, Surrey T, Taylor W, Turner A, Walsh J, Watson J, Weaver S, Williams E, Wilson G

#		Date	Opponent	Score	Scorers	Att	Ale	Bel	Ble	Bra	Car	Chi	Dix	Dun	Faw	Fla	Gib	Gol	Gow	How	Mad	Mar	McD	Mil	Mur	Rod	Sta	Sur	Tay	Tur	Wal	Wat	Wea	Wil	Wls
1	Aug	31	SWANSEA TOWN	1-0	McDonald	10068		3	4		7	5						2		10	1		9				8			11			6		
2	Sep	2	Southampton	2-2	Starling, Turner	11383		3	4		7	5						2		10	1		9				8			11			6		
3		7	Cardiff City	1-0	McDonald	12664		3	4		7	5					1	2		10			9							11	8		6		
4		14	PRESTON NORTH END	2-0	McDonald, Weaver	10232		3	4		7	5					1	2		10			9							11	8		6		
5		16	SOUTHAMPTON	2-0	McDonald, Howieson	7115		3	6		7	5					1	2		10			9				8			11				4	
6		21	Bristol City	0-4		13154		3	6		7	5					1	2	4	10			9				8			11					
7		23	Wolverhampton Wan.	2-4	McDonald, Howieson	9149			6			5					1	2	4	10			9			3			7	11	8				
8		28	NOTTS COUNTY	0-0		8680	9		6		7	5						2		10	1					3				11	8	4			
9	Oct	5	Reading	1-1	Alexander	15317	9		6		7	5						2		10	1					3	8					4			
10		12	CHARLTON ATHLETIC	0-2		9327	9		6		7	5		11				2		10	1					3	8					4			
11		19	MILLWALL	3-2	Alexander 2, Starling	6404	9	3			7	5						2		10	1						8			11		4	6		
12		26	Oldham Athletic	1-3	Childs	13562	9		6		7	5						3									8		11			2	4	10	
13	Nov	2	NOTTM. FOREST	1-2	Alexander	6182	9		6		3	7	5					2		10	1						8		11				4	10	
14		9	Chelsea	0-3		23416	7	3				5						2	6		1		9				8			11			4	10	
15		16	BURY	1-3	Alexander	4861	9	3			7		5					2			1	10					8			11			4	6	
16		23	Blackpool	2-1	Duncan 2	10364	9	3				5		11			1	2	6	10							8		7			4			
17		30	BARNSLEY	2-0	Duncan, Childs	5706	9					5		11			1	2	6	10						3	8		7			4			
18	Dec	7	Bradford Park Avenue	2-4	Starling, Taylor	6930	9	3				5		11			1	2	6	10							8		7			4			
19		14	WEST BROMWICH ALB.	3-2	Alexander 2, Taylor	4935	9	3				5		11			1	2	6	10							8		7			4			
20		21	Tottenham Hotspur	2-2	Duncan, Taylor	9103	9	3				5		11			1	2	6	10							8		7			4			
21		25	STOKE CITY	3-0	Starling, Duncan, Howieson	10631	9	3				5		11			1	2	6	10							8		7			4			
22		26	Stoke City	1-3	Alexander	17807	9	3				5		11			1	2	6	10							8		7			4			
23		28	Swansea Town	0-2		4555	9	3				5		11			1	2	6			10					8		7			4			
24	Jan	4	CARDIFF CITY	2-2	Alexander, Taylor	11695	8	3				5		11				2	6	10	1				9				7			4			
25		18	Preston North End	2-1	McDonald, Kerr (og)	13475	8	3						11			1	2	6				9				10		7			4	5		
26	Feb	1	Notts County	1-4	Duncan	11747	8	3				5		11			1	2	6				9				10		7			4			
27		8	READING	4-2	Alexander 2, Howieson, Childs	7539						5		11			1	2	6	10			9		3				7			4			
28		22	Millwall	0-0		17544	9							11			1	2	6			10				3	8		7			4	5		
29	Mar	8	Nottingham Forest	1-2	Howieson	11364	9		6						7		1	2		10						3	8			11		4	5		
30		15	CHELSEA	1-3	Starling	4813	9	3							7		1	2	6	10							8			11		4			
31		17	Charlton Athletic	0-4		5996	8					5			7		1		6					11	2		10					4		9	3
32		29	BLACKPOOL	0-3		10113		3	6		7	5		11			1			10					2	8	9					4			
33		31	OLDHAM ATHLETIC	1-0	Murray	5423		3	6		7	5			8	1				10				11	2	9						4			
34	Apr	5	Barnsley	0-3		6243		3			7	5			10	1			6			9		11	2	4	8					4			
35		12	BRADFORD PARK AVE.	0-2		5594		3	5					11			1	2	6	10				9			8		7			4			
36		18	BRADFORD CITY	0-0		8922		3			7			11			1	2	6	10			8	9							4	5			
37		19	West Bromwich Albion	1-7	Mills	6915		3			7			11			1	2	6	10				9			8					4	5		
38		21	Bradford City	1-2	Duncan	14285		2	4		7			11			1			10				9			8						5		3
39		23	Bury	1-2	Dixon	4079		3	4		7		9	11			1							6		2	8				10		5		
40		26	TOTTENHAM HOTSPUR	2-0	Mills, Alexander	6396	8							4	11			2	6	10	1			9		3			7			5			
41	May	1	BRISTOL CITY	0-1		10348	8	3						4	11			2	6	10	1			9					7			5			
42		3	WOLVERHAMPTON W.	2-0	Alexander 2	8208	8							4	11			2	6		1			9		3	10		7			5			

	Ale	Bel	Ble	Bra	Car	Chi	Dix	Dun	Faw	Fla	Gib	Gol	Gow	How	Mad	Mar	McD	Mil	Mur	Rod	Sta	Sur	Tay	Tur	Wal	Wat	Wea	Wil	Wls
Apps	27	29	18	1	20	30	5	24	3	2	28	36	25	28	14	8	9	10	4	15	32	1	23	11	23	22	11	1	2
Goals	14					3	1	7				5		6	2	1		5			4	1					1		

One own goal

F.A. Cup

		Date	Opponent	Score	Scorers	Att	Ale	Bel	Chi	Dun	Fla	Gib	Gol	Gow	How	Mad	McD	Mil	Sta	Tay	Wal
R3	Jan	11	Plymouth Argyle	4-3	Alexander 3, Duncan	28923	8	3	5	11		1	2	6	10			9		7	4
R4		25	BLACKPOOL	3-1	Alexander, Starling, Mills	23000	8	3	5	11		1	2	6				9	10	7	4
R5	Feb	15	Manchester City	2-1	Taylor, Mills	61574	8		5	11		1	2	6	3			9	10	7	4
R6	Mar	1	Newcastle United	1-1	Alexander	63486	9	3	5	11		1	2	6	10				8	7	4
rep		6	NEWCASTLE UNITED	1-0	Howieson	32930	9	3	5	11		1	2	6	10				8	7	4
SF		22	Arsenal	2-2	Howieson, Duncan	47549	7	3	5	11		1	2	6	10			9			4
rep		26	Arsenal	0-1		46200		3	5	11		1	2	6	10			9		7	

SF at Elland Rd Leeds, SF replay at Villa Park, Birmingham

		Pl	Home					Away					F.	A.	Pts
			W	D	L	F	A	W	D	L	F	A	(Total)		
1	Blackpool	42	17	1	3	63	22	10	3	8	35	45	98	67	58
2	Chelsea	42	17	3	1	49	14	5	8	8	25	32	74	46	55
3	Oldham Athletic	42	14	5	2	60	21	7	6	8	30	30	90	51	53
4	Bradford Park Ave.	42	14	5	2	65	28	5	7	9	26	42	91	70	50
5	Bury	42	14	2	5	45	27	8	3	10	33	40	78	67	49
6	West Bromwich Alb.	42	16	1	4	73	31	5	4	12	32	42	105	73	47
7	Southampton	42	14	6	1	46	22	3	5	13	31	54	77	76	45
8	Cardiff City	42	14	4	3	41	16	4	4	13	20	43	61	59	44
9	Wolverhampton W.	42	14	3	4	53	24	2	6	13	24	55	77	79	41
10	Nottingham Forest	42	9	6	6	36	28	4	9	8	19	41	55	69	41
11	Stoke City	42	12	4	5	41	20	4	4	13	33	52	74	72	40
12	Tottenham Hotspur	42	11	8	2	43	24	4	1	16	16	37	59	61	39
13	Charlton Athletic	42	10	6	5	39	23	4	5	12	20	40	59	63	39
14	Millwall	42	10	7	4	36	26	2	8	11	21	47	57	73	39
15	Swansea Town	42	11	5	5	42	23	3	4	14	15	38	57	61	37
16	Preston North End	42	7	7	7	42	36	6	4	11	23	44	65	80	37
17	Barnsley	42	12	7	2	39	22	1	2	18	17	49	56	71	36
18	Bradford City	42	7	7	7	33	30	5	5	11	27	47	60	77	36
19	Reading	42	10	7	4	31	20	2	4	15	23	47	54	67	35
20	Bristol City	42	11	4	6	36	30	2	5	14	25	53	61	83	35
21	HULL CITY	42	11	3	7	30	24	3	4	14	21	54	51	78	35
22	Notts County	42	8	7	6	33	26	1	8	12	21	44	54	70	33

1930/31 6th in Division Three (North)

Results

#	Date	Opponent	Score	Scorers	Att
1	Aug 30	Stockport County	2-3	Mills, Gowdy	12091
2	Sep 2	Nelson	2-0	Alexander, Fairhurst (og)	5128
3	6	GATESHEAD	4-0	Mills 2, Duncan D, Weldon	8644
4	10	Darlington	4-2	Mills, Weldon, Duncan D, Childs	5347
5	13	Doncaster Rovers	2-0	Mills, Duncan D	6238
6	15	DARLINGTON	1-1	Taylor	7426
7	20	CHESTERFIELD	3-1	Alexander, Weldon, Taylor	7937
8	27	LINCOLN CITY	1-3	Childs	12638
9	Oct 4	Hartlepools United	3-1	Alexander 3	6991
10	11	WIGAN BOROUGH	0-0		9335
11	18	Barrow	0-3		5591
12	25	ROTHERHAM UNITED	2-2	Alexander, Duncan D	5805
13	Nov 1	Accrington Stanley	3-1	Longden, Alexander, Turner	2738
14	8	ROCHDALE	3-1	Alexander 2, Barber (og)	7719
15	15	Crewe Alexandra	4-3	Alexander 3, Davin	4947
16	22	WREXHAM	2-3	Duncan D 2	8273
17	Dec 6	CARLISLE UNITED	1-1	Longden	6176
18	13	Tranmere Rovers	0-4		5697
19	20	SOUTHPORT	5-1	Alexander 2, Duncan D 2, Longden	5619
20	25	Halifax Town	1-1	Raleigh	7496
21	26	HALIFAX TOWN	10-0	Raleigh 5, Longden 2, Duncan D 2, Alexander	4022
22	27	STOCKPORT COUNTY	1-1	Raleigh	9557
23	Jan 3	Gateshead	0-1		7450
24	17	DONCASTER ROVERS	8-2	Raleigh 3, Longden 2, Alexander 2, Duncan D	5575
25	24	Chesterfield	4-0	Duncan D, Raleigh, Alexander, Weldon	7708
26	31	Lincoln City	0-3		9737
27	Feb 14	Wigan Borough	1-3	Raleigh	4913
28	21	BARROW	1-1	Speed	6022
29	Mar 7	ACCRINGTON STANLEY	1-1	Duncan D	2834
30	14	Rochdale	0-1		3465
31	18	York City	2-3	Alexander, Speed	3548
32	21	CREWE ALEXANDRA	5-1	Raleigh 2, Alexander 2, Sharpe (og)	4373
33	28	Wrexham	0-2		4723
34	Apr 3	New Brighton	1-1	Duncan D	4524
35	4	TRANMERE ROVERS	1-0	Mills	7516
36	6	NEW BRIGHTON	3-0	Duncan A 2, Alexander	5881
37	11	Carlisle United	5-1	Mills 3, Duncan D 2	4560
38	18	YORK CITY	3-1	Mills, Weldon, Duncan A	4432
39	20	HARTLEPOOLS UNITED	5-0	Mills 2, Weldon, Alexander, Duncan A	3221
40	25	Southport	0-1		2846
41	27	Rotherham United	1-1	Raleigh	2776
42	May 2	NELSON	4-0	Duncan D 2, Speed, Alexander	4542

Appearances / Goals grid

#	Alexander S	Bell M	Childs A	Cooke A	Davin M	Duncan A	Duncan D	Fawcett R	Gibson F	Goldsmith G	Gowdy W	Harris A	Jobson I	Longden E	Maddison G	Mills B	Murray J	Raleigh S	Rodgers A	Speed F	Taylor W	Turner A	Walsh J	Watson J	Weldon A	Wilson G	Woodhead C	Wright F
1	8	3	5				11			2	6				1	9					7	4			10			
2	8	3	5				11			2	6				1	9			3		7	4			10			
3	8	3	5				11			2	6				1	9					7	4			10			
4	8	3	5				11			2	6				1	9	6		2		7	4			10			
5	8	3	5				11			2	6				1	9	10				7	4						
6	8	3	5				11			2	6				1	9	10				7	4						
7	8	3	5				11			2	6				1	9					7	4			10			
8	8	3	5				11			2	6	7			1	9						4			10			
9	9	3	5				11			2		7			1	6		8				4			10			
10	9	3	5				11			2		7			1	6		8				4			10			
11	9	3	5				11			2	6	7			1			8				4			10			
12	9		5				11			2	4	7			1				3	6	8				10			
13	9	3	5				11			2	4			8	1	6					7	10						
14	9	3	5		8		11			2	4			10	1	6					7							
15	9	3	5		8		11			2	4			10	1	6					7							
16	9	3	5		8		11			2	4			10	1	6									7			
17	9	3	5		8		11	7	1	2	4			10		6												
18	7	3	5		8		11		1	2				8		6								4	9			
19	7	3	5				11		1					8		6		9						4	10	2		
20	7	3	5				11		1	2				8		6		9						4	10			
21	7		5				11		1	2	6			8				9	3					4	10			
22	7		5		10		11		1	2	6			8				9	3					4				
23			5				11		1	2	6			8				9	3		7			4	10			
24	7	3	5				11		1					8		6		9	2						10			
25	7	3	5				11		1					8		6		9							10			
26	7	3	5				11		1	2	4			8		6									10			
27	7		5		8					2	4				1	6		9	3		11				10			
28	8	3	5							2	4		11		1	6					7		9		10			
29	8	3	5				11			2	4	7			1	6							9		10			
30	8	3	5				11	7		2	4				1	6							9		10			
31	8	3	5				11	7		2	4				1	6				9					10			
32	7		5				11				4				1	6		9			10				8		3	2
33	7		5	8			11									6		9	3					4	10			2
34	7		5		8		11			2	4			10	1			9	3		6							
35	8		5				11		1	2	4					9	10		3		7		6					
36	9		5			8	11			2						6			3		7			4	10			
37	8		5			8	11			2	4					9			3		7		6					
38	7		5			8	11		1	2	4					9			3				6		10			
39	7		5			8	11		1	2	4					9			3				6		10			
40	7		5			8	11		1	2	4					9			3				6		10			
41	7		5		4	8	11		1	2								9	3				6	10				
42	7		5				11		1	2	4			8					3	9			6		10			
Apps	41	25	23	19	8	7	40	3	18	37	33	5	2	14	24	30	9	15	18	5	17	5	26	3	31	1	1	2
Goals	24		2		1	4	18			1				7		12		15		3	2	1			6			

Three own goals

F.A. Cup

Rd	Date	Opponent	Score	Scorers	Att	Alexander S	Bell M	Childs A	Duncan D	Gibson F	Goldsmith G	Gowdy W	Longden E	Raleigh S	Watson J	Weldon A
R3	Jan 10	BLACKPOOL	1-2	Duncan D	17000	7	3	5	11	1	2	6	8	9	4	10

Division Three (North) table

		Pl	Home W	D	L	F	A	Away W	D	L	F	A	F (Total)	A (Total)	Pts
1	Chesterfield	42	19	1	1	66	22	7	5	9	36	35	102	57	58
2	Lincoln City	42	16	3	2	60	19	9	4	8	42	40	102	59	57
3	Wrexham	42	16	4	1	61	25	5	8	8	33	37	94	62	54
4	Tranmere Rovers	42	16	3	2	73	26	8	3	10	38	48	111	74	54
5	Southport	42	15	3	3	52	19	7	6	8	36	37	88	56	53
6	HULL CITY	42	12	7	2	64	20	8	3	10	35	35	99	55	50
7	Stockport County	42	15	5	1	54	19	5	4	12	23	42	77	61	49
8	Carlisle United	42	13	4	4	68	32	7	1	13	30	49	98	81	45
9	Gateshead	42	14	4	3	46	22	2	9	10	25	51	71	73	45
10	Wigan Borough	42	14	4	3	48	25	5	1	15	28	61	76	86	43
11	Darlington	42	9	6	6	44	30	7	4	10	27	29	71	59	42
12	York City	42	15	3	3	59	30	3	3	15	26	52	85	82	42
13	Accrington Stanley	42	14	2	5	51	31	1	7	13	33	77	84	108	39
14	Rotherham United	42	9	6	6	50	34	4	6	11	31	49	81	83	38
15	Doncaster Rovers	42	9	8	4	40	18	4	3	14	25	47	65	65	37
16	Barrow	42	13	4	4	45	23	2	3	16	23	66	68	89	37
17	Halifax Town	42	11	6	4	30	16	2	3	16	25	73	55	89	35
18	Crewe Alexandra	42	13	2	6	52	35	1	4	16	14	58	66	93	34
19	New Brighton	42	12	4	5	36	25	1	3	17	13	51	49	76	33
20	Hartlepools United	42	10	2	9	47	37	2	4	15	20	49	67	86	30
21	Rochdale	42	9	1	11	42	50	3	5	13	20	57	62	107	30
22	Nelson	42	6	7	8	28	40	0	0	21	15	73	43	113	19

1929-30

Standing: W. McCracken (Manager), M. Bell, F. Gibson, A. Childs, G. Maddison, B. Mills, J. Beck (Trainer);
Sitting: R. Starling, J. Howieson, J. A. Walsh, W. Gowdy, D. Duncan, S. Alexander, A. Rodgers, G. Goldsmith;
On Ground: T. Bleakley, W. Taylor.

1932-33

Back Row: C. Woodhead, B. Mills, A. Rodgers, J. Lodge (Asst Trainer), W. Bell, G. Goldsmith, S. Denby;
Middle Row: F. Forward, T. Gardner, G. Maddison, C. Sargeant, F. Gibson, F. Speed, A. Bullock;
Front Row: J. Beck (Trainer), A. Duncan, W. McNaughton, M. Allen, J. Hill, T. Skelton, G. Stott, H. Green (Manager).

1931/32 8th in Division Three (North)

#		Date	Opponent	Result	Scorers	Att	Alexander S	Allen M	Barley H	Cooke A	Diamond J	Downes P	Duncan A	Duncan D	Gibson F	Goldsmith G	Gowdy W	Havelock H	Hill J	Maddison G	Mills B	Munnings E	Newton W	Raleigh S	Rodgers A	Shelton T	Speed F	Thompson J	Turner RF	Wainscoat R	Woodhead C	Wrack C
1	Aug	29	HALIFAX TOWN	1-0	Raleigh	8503	8		7				10	11	1	2	6							4	9	3						5
2	Sep	5	Walsall	4-1	Duncan D 2, Raleigh, Barley	3655			7	5			8	10	1		4				6	11			9	2					3	
3		7	DARLINGTON	4-1	Raleigh 2, Duncan D, Munnings	5366			7	5			8	10	1			4			6	11			9	3					2	
4		12	GATESHEAD	0-1		9497			7	5			8	10	1			4			6	11			9	3					2	
5		16	Darlington	1-2	Duncan D	3723			7	5			8	11	1			4	10		6				9	3					2	
6		19	New Brighton	2-1	Duncan D 2	3023	8		7	5				10	1	4					6	11			9	3					2	
7		26	BARROW	3-0	Duncan D 2, Raleigh	6991			7	5	9			11	1		4				6	8		10	3						2	
8	Oct	3	Stockport County	0-2		4815	8		7	5				10	1		8				6	11		4	9	3					2	
9		10	Lincoln City	0-1		9492	8		7	5				11	1						10			4		3		9			2	
10		17	ROTHERHAM UNITED	0-1		6645	8		7	5				11	1		6				10			4	9	3					2	
11		24	Tranmere Rovers	2-2	Speed 2	5419				5			10	11	1						6	7	4	8	3		9				2	
12		31	YORK CITY	2-3	Speed 2	7155			7	5					1						6	11	4	8	3		9			10	2	
13	Nov	7	Southport	0-1		4856		7		5					1						6		4		3		9			10	2	
14		14	DONCASTER ROVERS	4-1	Wainscoat 2, Speed, Duncan D	5172		7					8	11	1						6		4		3		9			10	2	5
15		21	Rochdale	6-3	Duncan D 2, Wainscoat, Duncan A, Speed, Munnings	4593							8	11					5	1	6	7	4		3		9			10	2	
16	Dec	5	Carlisle United	1-0	Speed	4674							8	11					5	1	6	7	4		3		9			10	2	
17		19	Accrington Stanley	1-1	Wainscoat	3671			7				8	11		2			5	1	6		4		3		9			10		
18		25	HARTLEPOOLS UNITED	3-1	Wainscoat 2, Speed	13060							8	11		2			5	1	6	7	4		3		9			10		
19		26	Hartlepools United	3-2	Duncan D 2, Wainscoat	5897							8	11		2			5	1	6	7	4		3		9			10		
20	Jan	2	Halifax Town	2-2	Wainscoat, Munnings	4163							8	11		2			5	1	6	7	4		3		9			10		
21		14	CREWE ALEXANDRA	2-4	Speed, Wainscoat	5237							8	11	1	2			5		6	7	4		3		9			10		
22		16	WALSALL	3-0	Mills 3	6287				4			8	11	1				5		9	7			3		6			10	2	
23		23	Gateshead	1-2	Mills	4490				4			8		1				5		9	11	7		3		6			10	2	
24		30	NEW BRIGHTON	4-1	Wainscoat, Mills, Hill, Duncan D	5916							8	11	1				5		9	7	4		3		6			10	2	
25	Feb	6	Barrow	2-0	Duncan D, Raleigh	7251							8	11	1				5			7		9	3		6		4	10	2	
26		13	STOCKPORT COUNTY	4-4	Wainscoat 3, Duncan D	6149							8	11	1				5		4	7	9		3		6			10	2	
27		20	LINCOLN CITY	4-1	Duncan D 2, Duncan A, Wainscoat	13608							8	11	1				5		9	7	4		3		6			10	2	
28		27	Rotherham United	0-2		4039							8	11	1				5		9	7	4		3		6			10	2	
29	Mar	5	TRANMERE ROVERS	3-0	Mills 2, Duncan D	7453							8	11	1	2			5		9	7	4				6			10	3	
30		12	York City	0-0		5012						11	8		1	2			5		9	7	4				6			10	3	
31		19	SOUTHPORT	1-0	Allen	6209		8				11			1	2			5		9	7	4				6			10	3	
32		25	Chester	0-2		13648		8				11			1	2			5		9	7	4				6			10	3	
33		26	Doncaster Rovers	1-2	Mills	4631		8				11			1	2			5		4	7					6			10	3	
34		28	CHESTER	0-2		7914		8				11			1	2			7			9	4				6			10	3	5
35	Apr	2	ROCHDALE	4-1	Mills 2, Munnings 2	3611		8		4		11			1	2			5		9	7					6			10	3	
36		9	Crewe Alexandra	3-4	Wainscoat, Speed, Shelton	4538		8		4		11			1	2			5			7				9	6			10	3	
37		16	CARLISLE UNITED	2-0	Munnings, Downes	2392		8				11			1	2			5		4	7			3	9	6					
38		23	Wrexham	1-2	Brown (og)	2479		8				11			1	2			5		4	7			3	9	6					
39		30	ACCRINGTON STANLEY	3-0	Wainscoat, Munnings, Downes	3535		8				11			1	2			5		4	7				9	6			10	3	
40	May	7	WREXHAM	5-0	Speed 2, Downes, Barley, Mills	3194		8	7			11			1	2			5		6		4								9	3
			Apps				6	10	13	16	1	11	24	27	34	19	7	3	25	6	37	31	24	16	30	4	30	1	1	29	32	3
			Goals					1	2			3	2	19						1	11	7		6			1			12	16	

One own goal

F.A. Cup

	Date	Opponent	Result	Scorers	Att	Duncan A	Duncan D	Gibson F	Goldsmith G	Hill J	Maddison G	Mills B	Munnings E	Newton W	Raleigh S	Rodgers A	Speed F	Wainscoat R	Woodhead C	Wrack C
R1	Nov 28	MANSFIELD TOWN	4-1	Wainscoat 2, Speed, Munnings	10,000	8	11				1	6	7	4		3	9		10	2	5
R2	Dec 12	New Brighton	4-0	Speed 2, Wainscoat, Munnings	5,000	8	11			5	1	6	7	4		3	9		10	2
R3	Jan 9	Stoke City	0-3		22,180		11	1	2	5		6	7	4	8	3	9		10	

League Table

		Pl	Home W	D	L	F	A	Away W	D	L	F	A	F. (Total)	A.	Pts
1	Lincoln City	40	16	2	2	65	13	10	3	7	41	34	106	47	57
2	Gateshead	40	15	3	2	59	20	10	4	6	35	28	94	48	57
3	Chester	40	16	2	2	54	22	5	6	9	24	38	78	60	50
4	Tranmere Rovers	40	15	4	1	76	23	4	7	9	31	35	107	58	49
5	Barrow	40	16	1	3	59	23	8	0	12	27	36	86	59	49
6	Crewe Alexandra	40	15	3	2	64	24	6	3	11	31	42	95	66	48
7	Southport	40	14	5	1	44	15	4	5	11	14	38	58	53	46
8	HULL CITY	40	14	1	5	52	21	6	4	10	30	32	82	53	45
9	York City	40	14	3	3	49	24	4	4	12	27	57	76	81	43
10	Wrexham	40	14	2	4	42	25	4	5	11	22	44	64	69	43
11	Darlington	40	12	1	7	41	27	5	3	12	25	42	66	69	38
12	Stockport County	40	12	3	5	31	15	1	8	11	24	38	55	53	37
13	Hartlepools United	40	10	6	4	47	37	6	1	13	31	63	78	100	37
14	Accrington Stanley	40	14	4	2	56	20	1	2	17	19	60	75	80	36
15	Doncaster Rovers	40	12	3	5	38	27	4	1	15	21	53	59	80	36
16	Walsall	40	12	3	5	42	30	4	0	16	15	55	57	85	35
17	Halifax Town	40	11	6	3	36	18	2	2	16	25	69	61	87	34
18	Carlisle United	40	9	7	4	40	23	2	4	14	24	56	64	79	33
19	Rotherham United	40	10	3	7	41	23	4	1	15	22	49	63	72	32
20	New Brighton	40	8	5	7	25	23	0	3	17	13	53	38	76	24
21	Rochdale	40	4	2	14	33	63	0	1	19	15	72	48	135	11

1932/33   Champions of Division Three (North): Promoted

#		Date	Opponent	Score	Scorers	Att	Ainsworth E	Allen M	Bell W	Bullock A	Denby S	Duncan A	Forward F	Gardner T	Gibson F	Goldsmith G	Hill J	Jordan D	Longden E	Maddison G	McNaughton W	Mills B	Rodgers A	Sargeant C	Speed F	Stott G	Wainscoat R	Woodhead C
1	Aug	27	Walsall	0-1		7067						8			1		5				9	4	3	11	6	7	10	2
2		29	WREXHAM	4-1	Duncan 2, Wainscoat, Sargeant	7476						8			1		5				9	4	3	11	6	7	10	2
3	Sep	3	GATESHEAD	1-1	Wainscoat	10204						8			1		5				9	4	3	11	6	7	10	2
4		7	Wrexham	1-3	McNaughton	7034			2				8	4	1		5				9	6		11		7	10	3
5		10	Stockport County	5-3	Wainscoat 2, McNaughton, Forward, Gardner	7009			2			8	7	4	1		5				9	6		11			10	3
6		17	DARLINGTON	3-1	Wainscoat 2, McNaughton	8147			2			8	7	4	1		5				9	6		11			10	3
7		24	Doncaster Rovers	1-1	Sargeant	5882			2			8	7	4	1		5				9	6		11		8	10	3
8	Oct	1	SOUTHPORT	4-0	McNaughton 3, Sargeant	6061					6	8	7	4		2	5			1	9			11			10	3
9		8	BARNSLEY	5-1	McNaughton 4, Sargeant	7857					6	8	7	4		2	5			1	9			11			10	3
10		15	Hartlepools United	1-0	Sargeant	4553					6	8	7	4		2	5			1	9			11			10	3
11		22	Mansfield Town	1-2	McNaughton	8436						8	7	4		2	5			1	9			11			10	3
12		29	ROTHERHAM UNITED	4-2	McNaughton, Wainscoat, Forward, Duncan	7997						8	7	4		2	5			1	9			11	6		10	3
13	Nov	5	Accrington Stanley	2-1	Duncan, Sargeant	4478						8	7	4		2	5			1	9			11	6		10	3
14		12	NEW BRIGHTON	5-0	Wainscoat 3, McNaughton 2	6792					6	8	7	4		2	5			1	9			11			10	3
15		19	Chester	1-1	Wainscoat	10064					6	8	7	4		2	5			1	9			11			10	3
16	Dec	3	Carlisle United	1-1	McNaughton	4073					6	8	7	4		2	5			1	9			11			10	3
17		17	Crewe Alexandra	1-1	Jordan	4941						8	7	4		2	5	9		1		6		11			10	3
18		24	ROCHDALE	1-1	Wainscoat	10881					6		7	4		2	5		8	1	9			11			10	3
19		26	HALIFAX TOWN	3-1	Sargeant 2, McNaughton	15199		10			6		7	4		2	5		8	1	9			11				3
20		27	Halifax Town	3-1	McNaughton 2, Longden	9311							7	4		2	5		8	1	9	6		11			10	3
21		31	WALSALL	0-0		9803							7	4		2	5		8	1	9	6		11			10	3
22	Jan	7	Gateshead	3-2	McNaughton 2, Sargeant	7723					6	8	7	4		2	5			1	9	10		11				3
23		19	BARROW	3-0	Duncan, Forward, Sargeant	4638					6	8	7	4		2	5			1	9	10		11				3
24		21	STOCKPORT COUNTY	3-0	McNaughton 2, Duncan	8883					6	8	7	4		2	5			1	9	10		11				3
25	Feb	1	Darlington	2-3	McNaughton, Fielden (og)	2211					6	8	7	4		2	5			1	9			11			10	3
26		4	DONCASTER ROVERS	6-1	Duncan 3, McNaughton 2, Sargeant	7985					6	8	7	4		2	5		10	1	9			11				3
27		11	Southport	1-0	McNaughton	4740					6	8	7	4		2	5		10	1	9			11				3
28		18	Barnsley	0-1		7360						8	7	4		2	5		6	1	9			11			10	3
29		25	HARTLEPOOLS UNITED	3-0	McNaughton 2, Wainscoat	5323						8	7	4		2	5		6	1	9			11			10	3
30	Mar	4	MANSFIELD TOWN	4-1	McNaughton 3, Wainscoat	8630				11		8	7	4		2	5		6	1	9						10	3
31		11	Rotherham United	2-3	Longden, Bullock	6861				11		8	7	4		2	5		6	1	9						10	3
32		18	ACCRINGTON STANLEY	4-2	Wainscoat 2, McNaughton, Bullock	9708				11		8	7	4		2	5		6	1	9						10	3
33		25	New Brighton	0-1		4377						8	7	4		2	5		6	1	9			11			10	3
34	Apr	1	CHESTER	2-0	Wainscoat, Forward	20248					6		7	8		2	5			1	9	4		11			10	3
35		8	Barrow	2-0	McNaughton, Wainscoat	5142					6		7	8		2				1	9	4		11	5		10	3
36		14	Tranmere Rovers	0-2		11011					6		7	4		2				1	9	8		11	5		10	3
37		15	CARLISLE UNITED	6-1	* see below	12023					6		7	4		2	5			1	9	8		11			10	3
38		17	TRANMERE ROVERS	3-0	McNaughton 2, Wainscoat	16117					6		7	4		2	5			1	9	8		11			10	3
39		22	York City	2-1	Wainscoat, Forward	8673					6		7	4		2	5			1	9	8		11			10	3
40		29	CREWE ALEXANDRA	3-0	McNaughton, Longden, Hill	8839					6		7	4		2	5		8	1	9			11			10	3
41	May	1	YORK CITY	2-1	McNaughton 2	19233					6		7	4		2	5		8	1	9			11			10	3
42		6	Rochdale	2-3	McNaughton 2	4387	1				6	8	7	4		2	5		10		9			11				3
			Apps				1	1	4	3	23	28	39	39	7	35	36	1	19	34	41	19	3	39	10	4	34	42
			Goals							2		9	6	1			1	1	3		41			13			21	

Scorers in game 37: Sargeant 2, McNaughton, Forward, Wainscoat, Gomm (og)

Two own goals

F.A. Cup

		Date	Opponent	Score	Scorers	Att	Ainsworth E	Allen M	Bell W	Bullock A	Denby S	Duncan A	Forward F	Gardner T	Gibson F	Goldsmith G	Hill J	Jordan D	Longden E	Maddison G	McNaughton W	Mills B	Rodgers A	Sargeant C	Speed F	Stott G	Wainscoat R	Woodhead C
R1	Nov	26	Stalybridge Celtic	8-2	Wainscoat 4, McNaughton, Forward, Sargeant, Hill	6641					6	8	7	4		2	5			1	9			11			10	3
R2	Dec	10	Carlisle United	1-1	Sargeant	10365						8	7	4		2	5			1	9	6		11			10	3
rep		15	CARLISLE UNITED	2-1	Wainscoat, Forward	12000						8	7	4		2	5			1	9	6		11			10	3
R3	Jan	14	SUNDERLAND	0-2		22566					6	8	7	4		2	5			1	9	10		11				3

R2 replay a.e.t.

		Pl	Home					Away					F.	A.	Pts
			W	D	L	F	A	W	D	L	F	A	(Total)		
1	HULL CITY	42	18	3	0	69	14	8	4	9	31	31	100	45	59
2	Wrexham	42	18	2	1	75	15	6	7	8	31	36	106	51	57
3	Stockport County	42	16	2	3	69	30	5	10	6	30	28	99	58	54
4	Chester	42	15	4	2	57	25	7	4	10	37	41	94	66	52
5	Walsall	42	16	4	1	53	15	3	6	12	22	43	75	58	48
6	Doncaster Rovers	42	13	8	0	52	26	4	6	11	25	53	77	79	48
7	Gateshead	42	12	5	4	45	25	7	4	10	33	42	78	67	47
8	Barnsley	42	14	3	4	60	31	5	5	11	32	49	92	80	46
9	Barrow	42	12	3	6	41	24	6	4	11	19	36	60	60	43
10	Crewe Alexandra	42	16	3	2	57	16	4	0	17	23	68	80	84	43
11	Tranmere Rovers	42	11	4	6	49	31	6	4	11	21	35	70	66	42
12	Southport	42	15	3	3	54	20	2	4	15	16	47	70	67	41
13	Accrington Stanley	42	12	4	5	55	29	3	6	12	23	47	78	76	40
14	Hartlepools United	42	15	3	3	56	29	1	4	16	31	87	87	116	39
15	Halifax Town	42	12	4	5	39	23	3	4	14	32	67	71	90	38
16	Mansfield Town	42	13	4	4	57	22	1	3	17	27	78	84	100	35
17	Rotherham United	42	14	3	4	42	21	0	3	18	18	63	60	84	34
18	Rochdale	42	9	4	8	32	33	4	3	14	26	47	58	80	33
19	Carlisle United	42	8	7	6	34	25	5	0	16	17	50	51	75	33
20	York City	42	10	4	7	51	38	3	2	16	21	54	72	92	32
21	New Brighton	42	8	6	7	42	36	3	4	14	21	52	63	88	32
22	Darlington	42	9	6	6	42	32	1	2	18	24	77	66	109	28

1933/34 15th in Division Two

#		Date	Opponent	Res	Scorers	Att	Allen M	Atkinson A	Bullock A	Burdett T	Denby S	Dodds L	Duncan A	Gardner T	Goldsmith G	Hill J	Hubbard C	Jordan D	Lawrance R	Longden E	Lloyd E	Maddison G	McAinsh I	MacKenzie G	McNaughton W	Melville J	Mitchell A	Quantick I	Sargeant C	Shelton T	Speed F	Wainscoat R	Woodhead C
1	Aug	26	NOTTS COUNTY	0-1		13441					6		8	4	2	5						1			9		7		11			10	3
2		30	Bradford City	2-1	McNaughton, Wainscoat	14559					6		8	4	2	5						1			9		7		11			10	3
3	Sep	2	Swansea Town	1-1	McNaughton	9743					6			4	2	5	8					1			9		7		11			10	3
4		9	MILLWALL	3-2	McNaughton, Wainscoat, Sargeant	11618					6			4	2	5	8					1			9		7		11			10	3
5		11	BRADFORD CITY	2-2	McNaughton, Denby	11372					6			4	2	5	8					1			9		7		11			10	3
6		16	Lincoln City	1-2	McNaughton	8820					6		8	4	2	5						1			9		7		11			10	3
7		23	BURY	3-1	McNaughton 2, Duncan	11286					6		10	4	2	5	8					1			9		7		11				3
8		30	Brentford	2-2	Duncan, Sargeant	14570		7			6		10	4	2	5	8					1			9				11				3
9	Oct	7	Fulham	1-1	McNaughton	22836		7			6		10	4	2	5	8					1			9				11				3
10		14	SOUTHAMPTON	1-0	McNaughton	11740					6		8	4	2	5	7					1			9				11			10	3
11		21	BOLTON WANDERERS	1-0	Wainscoat	16167					6		8	4	2	5	7					1			9				11			10	3
12		28	Manchester United	1-4	Gardner	16269					6		8	4	2	5	7					1			9				11			10	3
13	Nov	4	PLYMOUTH ARGYLE	5-4	Wainscoat, Duncan, Longden, Denby, Black(og)	12281					6		8		2	5	7			4		1		11	9							10	3
14		11	West Ham United	1-2	Hubbard	19309		7			6				2	5	8			4		1		11	9							10	3
15		18	NOTTM. FOREST	2-2	McNaughton, Wainscoat	8115		7			6			4	2		8				5	1		11	9							10	3
16		25	Grimsby Town	1-4	McNaughton	16631					6			4	2	5	8					1		11	9		7					10	3
17	Dec	2	BRADFORD PARK AVE.	1-2	McNaughton	9030					6		8	4	2	5						1		11	9		7						3
18		9	Preston North End	0-5		8869					6		10	8	2	5						1			9				11				3
19		16	OLDHAM ATHLETIC	2-0	Sargeant, MacKenzie	8435					6		10	4	2	5						1	7	11	8				9				3
20		23	Burnley	1-3	Duncan	10246			11		6		10	4	2	5						1	7		8				9				3
21		25	Blackpool	0-0		24361			11		6		10	4	2	5						1	7		8								3
22		26	BLACKPOOL	3-0	MacKenzie 2, Denby	15002					6		10	4	2	5						1	7	11	8								3
23		30	Notts County	0-0		9248			11				10	4	2	5						1	7		8			6					3
24	Jan	6	SWANSEA TOWN	0-0		9345			11		6		10	4	2	5						1	7		8								3
25		20	Millwall	0-2		13561					6		8	4	2	5	7			10		1			9				11				3
26	Feb	3	Bury	1-3	Melville	7253					6		8	4	2		7			10		1			9	5			11				3
27		8	LINCOLN CITY	2-0	McNaughton, MacKenzie	6481					6			4	2	5	7			8		1		11	9							10	3
28		10	BRENTFORD	0-1		10566					6			4	2	5	7			8		1		11	9							10	3
29		17	FULHAM	0-0		7928					6			4	2	5	9			10		1	7	11	8								3
30		24	Southampton	1-1	Jordan	7965					6			4	2		7	9		10		1			8	5			11				3
31	Mar	7	Bolton Wanderers	3-3	Jordan 2, Hubbard	5175					6			4	2		7	9		10		1			8	5			11				3
32		10	MANCHESTER UNITED	4-1	McNaughton 2, Jordan, Bullock	5771			11		6			4	2		7	9		10		1			8	5							3
33		17	Plymouth Argyle	1-1	Jordan	6068			11		6			4	2		7	9		10		1			8	5							3
34		24	WEST HAM UNITED	2-0	Jordan 2	7811			11		6			4	2		7	9		10		1			8	5							3
35		30	Port Vale	0-3		10502			11		6			4	2		7	9		10		1			8	5							3
36		31	Nottingham Forest	1-0	Jordan	10105			11		6						7	9		10		1			8	5				2	4		3
37	Apr	2	PORT VALE	2-1	Jordan, Hubbard	13333			11		6				2		7	9		10		1			8	5					4		3
38		7	GRIMSBY TOWN	0-1		20077	4		11		6				2		7	9		10		1			8	5							3
39		14	Bradford Park Avenue	1-3	Jordan	8406	4		11	8	6				2		7	9	3			1			10	5							
40		21	PRESTON NORTH END	0-1		8218	4	9	11		6				2		7			10		1			8	5							3
41		28	Oldham Athletic	0-7		2986	4		11	8	6						7			10		1			9	5		2					3
42	May	5	BURNLEY	0-1		3784			11		6	4			2		7	9		8		1			10	5							3
				Apps			4	5	14	2	39	1	20	27	40	33	34	11	1	23	1	42	7	9	42	14	8	2	21	1	4	16	41
				Goals					1		3		4	1			3	10		1				4	15	1			3			5	

One own goal

F.A. Cup

		Date	Opponent	Res	Scorers	Att	Denby S	Duncan A	Gardner T	Goldsmith G	Hill J	Hubbard C	Longden E	Maddison G	MacKenzie G	McNaughton W	Melville J	Sargeant C	Woodhead C
R3	Jan	13	BRENTFORD	1-0	Hubbard	18000	10	8	4	2	5	7		1	11	9	6		3
R4		27	MANCHESTER CITY	2-2	Hill, Dale (og)	25000		8	4	2	5	7	10	1		9	6	11	3
rep		31	Manchester City	1-4	McNaughton	40000	6	8	4	2	5	7	10	1		9		11	3

		Pl		Home				Away				F.	A.	Pts
			W	D	L	F	A	W	D	L	F	A	(Total)	
1	Grimsby Town	42	15	3	3	62	28	12	2	7	41	31	103 59	59
2	Preston North End	42	15	3	3	47	20	8	3	10	24	32	71 52	52
3	Bolton Wanderers	42	14	2	5	45	22	7	7	7	34	33	79 55	51
4	Brentford	42	15	2	4	52	24	7	5	9	33	36	85 60	51
5	Bradford Park Ave.	42	16	2	3	63	27	7	1	13	23	40	86 67	49
6	Bradford City	42	14	4	3	46	25	6	2	13	27	42	73 67	46
7	West Ham United	42	13	3	5	51	28	4	8	9	27	42	78 70	45
8	Port Vale	42	14	4	3	39	14	5	3	13	21	41	60 55	45
9	Oldham Athletic	42	12	5	4	48	28	5	5	11	24	32	72 60	44
10	Plymouth Argyle	42	12	7	2	43	20	3	6	12	26	50	69 70	43
11	Blackpool	42	10	8	3	39	27	5	5	11	23	37	62 64	43
12	Bury	42	12	4	5	43	31	5	5	11	27	42	70 73	43
13	Burnley	42	14	2	5	40	29	4	4	13	20	43	60 72	42
14	Southampton	42	15	2	4	40	21	0	6	15	14	37	54 58	38
15	HULL CITY	42	11	4	6	33	20	2	8	11	19	48	52 68	38
16	Fulham	42	13	3	5	29	17	2	4	15	19	50	48 67	37
17	Nottingham Forest	42	11	4	6	50	27	2	5	14	23	47	73 74	35
18	Notts County	42	9	7	5	32	22	3	4	14	21	40	53 62	35
19	Swansea Town	42	10	9	2	36	19	0	6	15	15	41	51 60	35
20	Manchester United	42	9	3	9	29	33	5	3	13	30	52	59 85	34
21	Millwall	42	8	8	5	21	17	3	3	15	18	51	39 68	33
22	Lincoln City	42	7	7	7	31	23	2	1	18	13	52	44 75	26

1934/35   13th in Division Two

#	Date		Opponent	Score	Scorers	Att.
1	Aug	29	Plymouth Argyle	4-6	Duncan 3, Dodds	17234
2	Sep	1	Blackpool	1-2	Jordan	18447
3		8	BURY	0-1		12768
4		10	PLYMOUTH ARGYLE	1-1	Jordan	7533
5		15	Southampton	0-3		6273
6		17	WEST HAM UNITED	4-0	Wright, Duncan 2, Dodds	5338
7		22	Nottingham Forest	1-2	Dodds	7696
8		29	BRENTFORD	2-1	Jordan 2	7764
9	Oct	6	Fulham	0-4		20481
10		13	BRADFORD PARK AVE.	2-0	Hutchison, McNaughton	10256
11		20	BOLTON WANDERERS	0-2		12758
12		27	Oldham Athletic	0-5		5725
13	Nov	3	BURNLEY	1-3	Hutchison	5896
14		10	Swansea Town	1-1	Duncan	7741
15		17	MANCHESTER UNITED	3-2	Wright 2, Duncan	6494
16		24	Port Vale	2-1	Duncan, Hubbard	6086
17	Dec	1	BARNSLEY	1-1	Charlton	10311
18		8	Sheffield United	4-3	Duncan 3, Hutchison	12217
19		15	BRADFORD CITY	1-0	Wright	8880
20		22	Notts County	1-1	Acquroff	5673
21		25	Newcastle United	2-6	Duncan, Longden	26943
22		26	NEWCASTLE UNITED	1-1	Hutchison	21788
23		29	West Ham United	2-1	Wright, Hutchison	25344
24	Jan	5	BLACKPOOL	2-2	Acquroff, Wright	10670
25		19	Bury	1-0	Acquroff	7154
26		31	SOUTHAMPTON	0-0		5130
27	Feb	2	NOTTM. FOREST	5-0	Wright 2, Hubbard, Acquroff, Hutchison	6560
28		9	Brentford	1-2	Hutchison	14109
29		16	FULHAM	1-2	Hubbard	5065
30		23	Bradford Park Avenue	2-1	Acquroff, Thorley	6779
31	Mar	6	Bolton Wanderers	2-1	Acquroff, Wright	13715
32		9	OLDHAM ATHLETIC	1-1	Hutchison	5664
33		20	Burnley	3-1	Acquroff 2, Thorley	4256
34		23	SWANSEA TOWN	0-1		4648
35		30	Manchester United	0-3		15358
36	Apr	6	PORT VALE	1-0	Pinkerton	3569
37		13	Barnsley	2-2	Wright, Dodds	9120
38		19	Norwich City	0-3		11927
39		20	SHEFFIELD UNITED	0-3		6876
40		22	NORWICH CITY	1-0	Hubbard	5930
41		27	Bradford City	2-3	Mackie, Acquroff	3512
42	May	4	NOTTS COUNTY	5-1	Thorley 2, Acquroff, Mackie, Wright	2721

Appearances / Goals

Player	Apps	Goals
Acquroff J	25	10
Bullock A	1	
Burdett T	1	
Charlton W	3	1
Denby S	21	
Dodds L	19	4
Duncan A	26	12
Farquharson H	4	
Foster T	2	
Helsby T	22	
Higgins W	5	
Hubbard C	17	4
Hutchison D	38	8
Jordan D	10	4
Lawrance R	3	
Longden E	32	1
Mackie J	7	2
Maddison G	38	
McNaughton W	2	1
Miller A	4	
Moore JE	5	
Pinkerton H	2	1
Quantick J	38	
Simms S	3	
Spivey R	1	
Tabram W	38	
Thomson R	4	
Thorley E	17	4
Woodhead C	42	
Wright D	32	11

F.A. Cup

Round	Date		Opponent	Score	Scorers	Att.
R3	Jan	12	NEWCASTLE UNITED	1-5	Charlton	23000

Division Two — Final Table

		Pl	Home W	D	L	F	A	Away W	D	L	F	A	F (Total)	A	Pts
1	Brentford	42	19	2	0	59	14	7	7	7	34	34	93	48	61
2	Bolton Wanderers	42	17	1	3	63	15	9	3	9	33	33	96	48	56
3	West Ham United	42	18	1	2	46	17	8	3	10	34	46	80	63	56
4	Blackpool	42	16	4	1	46	18	5	7	9	33	39	79	57	53
5	Manchester United	42	16	2	3	50	21	7	2	12	26	34	76	55	50
6	Newcastle United	42	14	2	5	55	25	8	2	11	34	43	89	68	48
7	Fulham	42	15	3	3	62	26	2	9	10	14	30	76	56	46
8	Plymouth Argyle	42	13	3	5	48	26	6	5	10	27	38	75	64	46
9	Nottingham Forest	42	12	5	4	46	23	5	3	13	30	47	76	70	42
10	Bury	42	14	1	6	38	26	5	3	13	24	47	62	73	42
11	Sheffield United	42	11	4	6	51	30	5	5	11	28	40	79	70	41
12	Burnley	42	11	2	8	43	32	5	7	9	20	41	63	73	41
13	HULL CITY	42	9	6	6	32	22	7	2	12	31	52	63	74	40
14	Norwich City	42	11	6	4	51	23	3	5	13	20	38	71	61	39
15	Bradford Park Ave.	42	7	8	6	32	28	4	8	9	23	35	55	63	38
16	Barnsley	42	8	10	3	32	22	5	2	14	28	61	60	83	38
17	Swansea Town	42	13	5	3	41	22	1	3	17	15	45	56	67	36
18	Port Vale	42	10	7	4	42	28	1	5	15	13	46	55	74	34
19	Southampton	42	9	8	4	28	19	2	4	15	18	56	46	75	34
20	Bradford City	42	10	7	4	34	20	2	1	18	16	48	50	68	32
21	Oldham Athletic	42	10	3	8	44	40	0	3	18	12	55	56	95	26
22	Notts County	42	8	3	10	29	33	1	4	16	17	64	46	97	25

1934-35
Standing: J. Beck (Trainer), T. Helsby, J. Quantick, G. Maddison, W. Tabram, C. Woodhead, J. Hill (Manager);
Sitting: A. Duncan, D. Hutchinson, E. Longden, D. Wright, J. Acquroff, E. Thorley.

1935-36
Left to right: G. Maddison, W. Tabram, ? , ? , W. Cuthbert, R. Don, D. Davies, R. Spivey, R. Yorke, J. Acquroff,
J. McPheat, S. Dimbleby, K. Cameron, G. Dreyer, R. Lawrance, C. Hubbard, J. Quantick.

1935/36 Bottom of Division Two: Relegated

	Date	Opponent	Score	Scorers	Att	Acquroff J	Ainsworth E	Bennett R	Cameron K	Campbell A	Cassidy J	Davies D	Denby S	Dimbleby S	Don R	Dreyer G	Dunne L	Farquharson H	Foster T	Holmes M	Hubbard C	Jordan D	Kitchen N	Lawrance R	Mackie J	Maddison G	Martin J	McPheat J	Neish J	Nicol J	Quantick J	Sharp A	Spivey R	Tabram W	Thorley E	Woodhead C	Yorke R
1	Aug 31	FULHAM	1-1	Cameron	11657				10							4	2			9	7				8	1								5	11	3	6
2	Sep 2	Tottenham Hotspur	1-3	Acquroff	25603	9						8	6			4	2			11	7				10	1								5		3	
3	7	Burnley	0-2		10082	9						8	6			4	2			11	7				10	1								5		3	
4	9	TOTTENHAM HOTSPUR	1-0	Acquroff	9616	9						8	6			4	2			11	7				10	1								5		3	
5	14	CHARLTON ATHLETIC	2-4	Holmes, Oakes (og)	7550	9			10			8	6			4	2	1		11									7					5		3	
6	18	Manchester United	0-2		15739	9			10									1						4	8						2		7	5	11	3	6
7	21	Bury	1-3	Cameron	7244	9	1		10															4	8						2		7	5	11	3	6
8	28	Barnsley	1-5	Cameron	9718	9			7											10				4	8	1	11				2			5		3	6
9	Oct 5	PLYMOUTH ARGYLE	2-1	Acquroff, Martin	4990	10			7				6							9				5		1	11	8			2			4		3	
10	12	Bradford City	1-1	Cameron	6844	10			7				6									9		5		1	11	8			2			4		3	
11	19	DONCASTER ROVERS	2-3	Sharp, Acquroff	7213	9			10				6											5		1	11	7			2	8		4		3	
12	26	Blackpool	1-4	Cameron	10624	9			7				6		4									5		1		8			2	10			11	3	
13	Nov 2	NOTTM. FOREST	2-1	Acquroff, Cameron	5526	9			7				6		4									5		1		8			2	10			11	3	
14	9	Norwich City	0-3		11906	9			7				6											5		1		8			2	10		4	11	3	
15	16	SOUTHAMPTON	2-2	Holmes, Sharp	7315	10			7	6										9				5		1					2	8		4	11	3	
16	23	West Ham United	1-4	Cameron	21114	9			7	6														4		1		8			2	10		5	11	3	
17	30	BRADFORD PARK AVE.	1-1	Sharp	5557	9			11	6	10		4								7			5		1					2	8				3	
18	Dec 7	Leicester City	2-2	Cameron, Cassidy	8561	9			11		10		6		4						7			5		1					2	8				3	
19	14	SWANSEA TOWN	3-2	Hubbard, Acquroff, Sharp	4863	9			11		10		6		4						7			5		1					2	8				3	
20	21	Sheffield United	0-7		10413	9			11	6	10		4								7			5		1					2	8				3	
21	26	PORT VALE	1-2	Cameron	5359	9			8	6	10		4				2				7			5		1									11	3	
22	28	Fulham	0-3		13082	9			8	6	10		4								7			5		1									11	3	2
23	Jan 4	BURNLEY	1-2	Hubbard	5811	9			10	6					4						7					1		8						5	11	3	2
24	18	Charlton Athletic	1-4	Acquroff	14222	10				6			4				2				7	9				1						8		5	11	3	
25	Feb 1	BARNSLEY	1-3	Kitchen	4804	9											2				8		7	6		1					4	10	11	5		3	
26	8	Plymouth Argyle	1-0	Acquroff	12604	9													4		8		7	5		1					2	10	11	6		3	
27	15	BURY	2-3	Hubbard, Lawrence	4982	9													4		8		7	5		1					2	10	11	6		3	
28	20	BRADFORD CITY	2-5	Acquroff, Spivey	3750	10				4									8		7			5		1				9	2		11	6		3	
29	22	Doncaster Rovers	1-6	Nicol	10309	10		1							4						7			5				8		9	2		11	6		3	
30	29	LEICESTER CITY	3-3	Acquroff, Cameron, Nicol	2284	10		1	7										6		8			4						9	2			5	11	3	
31	Mar 2	Port Vale	0-4		2669	10			7										6		8			4		1				9	2			5	11	3	
32	7	Southampton	0-1		5476	10			7					6							8			4		1				9	2		11	5		3	
33	14	NORWICH CITY	0-0		3759	10			7					6							8			4		1				9	2		11	5		3	
34	21	Nottingham Forest	0-0		6233	9			7					6							8			4		1					2	10	11	5		3	
35	28	WEST HAM UNITED	2-3	Cameron, Spivey	5038	9			7					6							8			4		1					2	10	11	5		3	
36	Apr 4	Bradford Park Avenue	1-2	Spivey	4746	9			7			8		6										4		1					2	10	11	5		3	
37	10	Newcastle United	1-4	Hubbard	16928	9			7					6							8			5		1					2	10	11			3	4
38	11	BLACKPOOL	0-3		4309	9						10		6							8		7			1					2		11	5		3	4
39	13	NEWCASTLE UNITED	2-3	Acquroff, Thorley	5638	9				6		10	4								8					1					2		7	5	11		3
40	18	Swansea Town	1-6	Acquroff	6264	9				6		10	4					1			8										2		7	5	11	3	
41	30	SHEFFIELD UNITED	2-2	Cameron, Spivey	5411	9		1	10			8	6		4						7										2		11	5		3	
42	May 2	MANCHESTER UNITED	1-1	Acquroff	4540	9			10		8		6		4						7					1					2			5	11	3	
					Apps	41	1	3	30	11	7	9	21	7	8	5	8	3	5	8	29	2	4	30	7	35	4	9	1	6	33	18	17	33	17	41	9
					Goals	13			12		1									2	4		1	1			1			2		4	4		1		

One own goal

F.A. Cup

	Date	Opponent	Score	Scorers	Att	Acquroff J	Ainsworth E	Bennett R	Cameron K	Campbell A	Cassidy J	Davies D	Denby S	Dimbleby S	Don R	Dreyer G	Dunne L	Farquharson H	Foster T	Holmes M	Hubbard C	Jordan D	Kitchen N	Lawrance R	Mackie J	Maddison G	Martin J	McPheat J	Neish J	Nicol J	Quantick J	Sharp A	Spivey R	Tabram W	Thorley E	Woodhead C	Yorke R
R3	Jan 11	West Bromwich Albion	0-2		27505	10							6						4		7	9				1					2	8		5	11	3	

		Pl	Home W	D	L	F	A	Away W	D	L	F	A	F. (Total)	A.	Pts
1	Manchester United	42	16	3	2	55	16	6	9	6	30	27	85	43	56
2	Charlton Athletic	42	15	6	0	53	17	7	5	9	32	41	85	58	55
3	Sheffield United	42	15	4	2	51	15	5	8	8	28	35	79	50	52
4	West Ham United	42	13	5	3	51	23	9	3	9	39	45	90	68	52
5	Tottenham Hotspur	42	12	6	3	60	25	6	7	8	31	30	91	55	49
6	Leicester City	42	14	5	2	53	19	5	5	11	26	38	79	57	48
7	Plymouth Argyle	42	15	2	4	50	20	5	6	10	21	37	71	57	48
8	Newcastle United	42	13	5	3	56	27	7	1	13	32	52	88	79	46
9	Fulham	42	11	6	4	58	24	4	8	9	18	28	76	52	44
10	Blackpool	42	14	3	4	64	34	4	4	13	29	38	93	72	43
11	Norwich City	42	14	2	5	47	24	3	7	11	25	41	72	65	43
12	Bradford City	42	12	7	2	32	18	3	6	12	23	47	55	65	43
13	Swansea Town	42	11	3	7	42	26	4	6	11	25	50	67	76	39
14	Bury	42	10	6	5	41	27	3	6	12	25	57	66	84	38
15	Burnley	42	9	8	4	35	21	3	5	13	15	38	50	59	37
16	Bradford Park Ave.	42	13	6	2	43	26	1	3	17	19	58	62	84	37
17	Southampton	42	11	3	7	32	24	3	6	12	15	41	47	65	37
18	Doncaster Rovers	42	10	7	4	28	17	4	2	15	23	54	51	71	37
19	Nottingham Forest	42	8	8	5	43	22	4	3	14	26	54	69	76	35
20	Barnsley	42	9	4	8	40	32	3	5	13	14	48	54	80	33
21	Port Vale	42	10	5	6	34	30	2	3	16	22	76	56	106	32
22	HULL CITY	42	4	7	10	33	45	1	3	17	14	66	47	111	20

1936/37   5th in Division Three (North)

#	Date		Opponent	Score	Scorers	Att.	Acquroff I	Annables W	Baldry G	Bell E	Best J	Cassidy J	Davies D	Denby S	Dimbleby S	Don R	Edwards E	Foster T	Holmes M	Hubbard C	Llewellyn G	Maddison G	Mayson J	Quantick J	Spivey R	Tabram W	Treanor J	Wilkinson J	Woodhead C	Yorke R
1	Aug	29	Port Vale	3-1	Mayson 2, Spivey	9207	9	2					10		6	4	8						1	7	11	5			3	
2		31	ROTHERHAM UNITED	2-1	Davies, Holmes	9267	9	2					10		6	4	8			11			1	7		5			3	
3	Sep	5	OLDHAM ATHLETIC	2-0	Holmes, Mayson	8710		2					10		6	4	8		9				1	7	11	5			3	
4		7	Rotherham United	0-0		5277		2					10		6		8		9	7	4		1		11	5			3	
5		12	Accrington Stanley	1-0	Holmes	3136		2					10			4	8		9	7	6	11	1			5			3	
6		19	LINCOLN CITY	1-1	Holmes	10462		2					10	6		4	8		9	7		11	1			5			3	
7		26	New Brighton	1-1	Hubbard	4319		2					10			4	8		9	11			1	7		5	6		3	
8	Oct	3	HALIFAX TOWN	0-0		9642	9	2					10			4	8	5		11			1	7			6		3	
9		10	Gateshead	3-2	Treanor, Hubbard, Mayson	8080		2					10			4	8	5		9			1	7			6	11	3	
10		17	Mansfield Town	2-5	Edwards, Davies	9776		3					8			4	10			9			1	7	2	5	6	11		
11		24	CREWE ALEXANDRA	2-0	Acquroff 2	6468	9	3					10		5	4	8						1	7	2		6	11		
12		31	Chester	1-3	Mayson	10235		3			9		8		5	4	10						1	7	2		6	11		
13	Nov	7	ROCHDALE	1-1	Holmes	6963		2			9		8			4			10	8			1	7			6	11	3	
14		14	Barrow	3-2	Best, Wilkinson, Mayson	5323		2			9		8			4			10	8			1	7			6	11	3	
15		21	YORK CITY	1-0	Holmes	7039		2			9		8			4			10	8			1	7			6	11	3	
16	Dec	5	HARTLEPOOLS UNITED	1-0	Wilkinson	5676		2			9		8			4			10	7			1			5	6	11	3	
17		12	Tranmere Rovers	1-2	Best	4338		2		8	9		10	6									1	7		5	4	11	3	
18		19	TRANMERE ROVERS	5-2	Best 4, Bell	4855		2		8	9		10	6									1	7		5	4	11	3	
19		25	WREXHAM	1-0	Davies	9448		2		8	9		10	6									1	7		5	4	11	3	
20		26	PORT VALE	1-1	Bell	14928		2		8	9		10	6									1	7		5	4	11	3	
21	Jan	1	Darlington	2-2	Mayson 2	6297		2		8	9		10	6									1	7		5	4	11	3	
22		2	Oldham Athletic	1-3	Hubbard	7505		2			9		10	6						8			1	7		5	4	11	3	
23		9	ACCRINGTON STANLEY	0-3		6165		2		8	9		10	6						7			1			5	4	11	3	
24		16	Southport	4-1	Davies, Best 2, Hubbard	5717		2			11		10	4				5		9			1	7		8	6		3	
25		21	Carlisle United	1-1	Hubbard	2678		2	7		11		10	4				5		9			1			8	6		3	
26		23	Lincoln City	0-5		5098		2			11		10	4				5		9			1	7		8	6		3	
27		30	NEW BRIGHTON	4-1	Hubbard 2, Tabram 2	2928		2			11		10	4				5	9	7			1			8	6		3	
28	Feb	6	Halifax Town	0-1		8251		2			11		10	4				5	9	7			1			8	6		3	
29		13	Gateshead	3-6	Hubbard, Best, Holmes	2332		2			11	10	8			4		5	9	7			1				6		3	
30		20	MANSFIELD TOWN	3-0	Holmes 2, Best	4249		3		8	11		10	6				5	9	7	4		1		2					
31		27	Crewe Alexandra	1-2	Tabram	2549		3			11		10	4				5	9	7			1			8	6		2	
32	Mar	6	CHESTER	1-1	Bell	7966		3		8	11		10	4					9	7			1		2		5	6		
33		13	Rochdale	0-4		3952		3		8	11		10	4						7			1		2		5	6	11	
34		20	BARROW	3-2	Davies, Hubbard, Quantick	4637		3		8	11		10	4					9	7			1		2		5	6		
35		26	Stockport County	1-3	Foster	13580		3			11		10	4				4	9	7			1		2		5	6		
36		27	York City	1-1	Hubbard	6975		3			11		10	4				5	9	7			1		2	8	6			
37		29	STOCKPORT COUNTY	0-1		11230		3		8	11		10					4	9	7			1		2		6			
38	Apr	3	CARLISLE UNITED	1-1	Davies	4355		3		8	9		10			4					6	1		7	2	5		11		
39		10	Hartlepools United	2-2	Best, Hubbard	4936		3	7		11		10	4				5		9			1		2	8	6			
40		17	SOUTHPORT	3-2	Tabram 2, Hubbard	2003		3	7		11		10	4				5		9			1		2	8	6			
41		19	Wrexham	1-2	Baldry	2100		3	7		11		10	4				5		9			1		2	8	6			
42	May	1	DARLINGTON	4-3	Baldry, Hubbard 2, Annables	3200		3	7		11		10	4				5		9			1		2	8	6			
				Apps			4	42	5	14	31	1	38	20	13	13	10	18	21	32	4	42	23	15	3	35	34	17	27	
				Goals			2	1	2	3	11		6				1	1	8	15			8	1	1	5	1	2		

F.A. Cup

	Date		Opponent	Score	Scorers	Att.	Annables W	Best J	Davies D	Don R	Holmes M	Hubbard C	Maddison G	Quantick J	Tabram W	Treanor J	Wilkinson J	Woodhead C
R1	Nov	28	York City	2-5	Mayson, Hubbard	7700	2	9		4	10	8	1	7	5	6	11	3

Division 3 (North) Cup

	Date		Opponent	Score	Scorers	Att.	Acquroff I	Annables W	Davies D	Edwards E	Hubbard C	Llewellyn G	Maddison/Mayson	Spivey R	Tabram W	Woodhead C	Yorke R
R1	Sep	16	York City	2-3	Hubbard, Edwards	7022	9	2	10	8	7	6	1	11	5	3	4

League Table — Division Three (North)

		Pl	Home					Away					F	A	Pts
			W	D	L	F	A	W	D	L	F	A	(Total)		
1	Stockport County	42	17	3	1	59	18	6	11	4	25	21	84	39	60
2	Lincoln City	42	18	1	2	65	20	7	6	8	38	37	103	57	57
3	Chester	42	15	5	1	68	21	7	4	10	19	36	87	57	53
4	Oldham Athletic	42	13	7	1	49	25	7	4	10	28	34	77	59	51
5	HULL CITY	42	13	6	2	39	22	4	6	11	29	47	68	69	46
6	Hartlepools United	42	16	1	4	53	21	3	6	12	22	48	75	69	45
7	Halifax Town	42	12	4	5	40	20	6	5	10	28	43	68	63	45
8	Wrexham	42	12	3	6	41	21	4	9	8	30	36	71	57	44
9	Mansfield Town	42	13	1	7	64	35	5	7	9	27	41	91	76	44
10	Carlisle United	42	13	6	2	42	19	5	2	14	23	49	65	68	44
11	Port Vale	42	12	6	3	39	23	5	4	12	19	41	58	64	44
12	York City	42	13	3	5	54	27	3	8	10	25	43	79	70	43
13	Accrington Stanley	42	14	2	5	51	26	2	7	12	25	43	76	69	41
14	Southport	42	10	8	3	39	28	2	5	14	34	59	73	87	37
15	New Brighton	42	10	8	3	36	16	3	3	15	19	54	55	70	37
16	Barrow	42	11	5	5	42	25	2	5	14	28	61	70	86	36
17	Rotherham United	42	11	7	3	52	28	3	0	18	26	63	78	91	35
18	Rochdale	42	12	3	6	44	27	1	6	14	25	59	69	86	35
19	Tranmere Rovers	42	10	8	3	52	30	2	1	18	19	58	71	88	33
20	Crewe Alexandra	42	6	8	7	31	31	4	4	13	24	52	55	83	32
21	Gateshead	42	9	8	4	40	31	2	2	17	23	67	63	98	32
22	Darlington	42	6	8	7	42	46	2	6	13	24	50	66	96	30

1936-37

Back Row: R., Yorke, J. Quantick, W, Annables, Pearson, G. Maddison, W. Tabram, A. Simpson, S. Dimbleby;
Middle Row: D. Menzies (Manager), G. Llewellyn, R. Don, T. Foster, C. Woodhead, S. Denby, E. Edwards,
H. Gray, J. Lodge (Asst Trainer), J. Beck (Trainer);
Sitting: G. Baldry, J. Mayson, C. Hubbard, J. Acquroff, M. Holmes, R. Spivey, E. Bell, D. Davies, J. Cassidy;

1937-38

Back Row: G. Salvidge, C. Henderson, C. Robinson, A. Stokes, J. Lodge (Asst Trainer), D. Parker, J. Blyth, W. Mackay, T. Reay;
Middle Row: H. Meens, J. Fryer, G. Dallas, T. Foster, G. Maddison, E. Goodall, J. Treanor, W. Annables, J. Hardy, H. Fowlie;
Sitting: E. Blackburn (Manager), E. Bell, D. Davies, J. Pears, H. McNeill, C. Woodhead, A. Wann, C. Hubbard, J. Beck (Trainer).

1937/38   3rd in Division Three (North)

No	Date		Opponent	Score	Scorers	Att	Annables W	Bell E	Blyth J	Cumner H	Davies D	Fryer J	Goodall E	Hardy J	Hubbard C	Lawrence M	Mackay W	McNeill J	Maddison G	Parker D	Pears J	Robinson C	Treanor J	Woodhead C	Foster T
1	Aug	28	WREXHAM	3-2	Fryer 2, McNeill	8668	2		5		10	8					7	9	1		11	4	6	3	
2		30	Barrow	0-1		5761	2		5		10	8					7	9	1		11	4	6	3	
3	Sep	4	Hartlepools United	2-2	McNeill, Pears	8173	2		5		10	8			6		7	9	1		11	4		3	
4		6	BARROW	4-0	McNeill 3, Fryer	6742	2		5		10	8			6		7	9	1		11	4		3	
5		11	LINCOLN CITY	1-1	Fryer	10615	2		5		10	8			6		7	9	1		11	4		3	
6		15	Crewe Alexandra	1-0	McNeill	3810	2		5		10	8			6		7	9	1		11	4		3	
7		18	Halifax Town	0-1		6142	2		5		10	8			6		7	9	1		11	4		3	
8		25	New Brighton	0-0		5792	2		5		10	8			6		7	9	1		11	4		3	
9	Oct	2	GATESHEAD	3-1	Fryer 2, Davies	11082	2		5		10	8			6		7	9	1		11	4		3	
10		9	Oldham Athletic	1-1	McNeill	10007	2		5		10	8			6		7	9	1		11	4		3	
11		16	CARLISLE UNITED	2-1	McNeill, Fryer	10837	2		5		10	8			6		7	9	1		11	4		3	
12		23	Accrington Stanley	2-0	McNeill, Davies	3198	2		5		10	8	1		6		7	9			11	4		3	
13		30	CHESTER	2-2	McNeill, Hubbard	11383			5		10	8		7	6			9	1	3	11	4		2	
14	Nov	6	Rotherham United	2-2	Hubbard, Fryer	5371			5		10	8		7	6			9	1	3	11	4		2	
15		13	ROCHDALE	4-1	McNeill 2, Fryer 2	8848			5		10	8		7	6			9	1	3	11	4		2	
16		20	Doncaster Rovers	1-2	McNeill	13868			5		10	8		7	6			9	1	3	11	4		2	
17	Dec	4	Bradford City	2-1	McNeill, Davies	3877			5		10	8		7	6			9	1	3	11	4		2	
18		18	Tranmere Rovers	1-3	Hubbard	7455	10		5			8	1	7	6			9		3	11	4		2	
19		25	Darlington	3-1	McNeill, Fryer, Davies	6070			5		10	8	1	7	6			9		3	11	4		2	
20		27	DARLINGTON	4-0	Fryer 2, Pears 2	16783			5		10	8	1	7	6			9		3	11	4		2	
21	Jan	1	Wrexham	1-0	McNeill	8363			5		10	8	1	7	6			9		3	11	4		2	
22		13	SOUTHPORT	10-1	Fryer, Pears 3, Hubbard 2, Davies 2, McNeill 2	5816			5		10	8	1	7	6	4		9		3	11			2	
23		15	HARTLEPOOLS UNITED	4-0	Pears 2, McNeill, Hubbard	8607	10	8	5			8	1	7	6	4		9		3	11			2	
24		22	Lincoln City	1-2	Hubbard	9107			5		10	8	1	7	6	4		9		3	11			2	
25		29	HALIFAX TOWN	0-1		7588			5		10	8	1	7	6	4		9		3	11			2	
26	Feb	5	NEW BRIGHTON	1-1	Hubbard	9337			5		10	8	1	7	6	4		9		3	11			2	
27		12	Gateshead	2-3	McNeill, Fryer	10307			5		10	8	1	7	6	4		9		3	11			2	
28		19	OLDHAM ATHLETIC	4-1	Fryer 2, Hubbard, Milligan (og)	9951			5		10	8	1	7	6	4		9		3	11			2	
29		26	Carlisle United	1-0	McNeill	7525			5		10	8	1	7	6	4		9		3	11			2	
30	Mar	5	ACCRINGTON STANLEY			10343			5		10	8	1	7	6	4		9		3	11			2	
31		12	Chester	3-1	McNeill, Fryer, Cumner	6864		10	5	11		8	1	7	6			9		3		4		2	
32		19	ROTHERHAM UNITED	1-1	Bell	15687		10	5	11		8	1	7	6			9		3		4		2	
33		26	Rochdale	0-0		5761			5	11	10	8	1		6	9	7			3		4		2	
34	Apr	2	DONCASTER ROVERS	2-1	Davies 2	15069	2	10	5	11	7	8	1		9	6				3		4			
35		9	Southport	1-2	Fryer	5581	2	10	5	11	7	8	1		9	6				3		4			
36		15	Port Vale	4-2	Davies, Hubbard, Fryer, Cumner	10984	2		5	11	10	8			6	7	4	9		3					
37		16	BRADFORD CITY	2-2	McNeill, Cumner	14159		8	5	11	10		1		6	7		9		3		4			
38		18	PORT VALE	0-0		13564		8	5	11	10		1		6	7	4	9		3				2	
39		23	York City	1-0	Fryer	9494			5	11		8	1		6	7	10	9		3			4	2	
40		25	YORK CITY	3-1	Fryer 2, Hubbard	15416			5	11		8	1		6	7	10	9		3			4	2	
41		30	TRANMERE ROVERS	0-1		21756			5	11		8	1		6	7	10	9		3			4	2	
42	May	7	CREWE ALEXANDRA	1-1	Cumner	4410			5	11	10	8	1		6	7	4	9		3				2	
			Apps				17	8	42	12	34	40	26	34	31	21	12	39	16	30	30	27	5	38	
			Goals					1		4	9	23			11			23			8				

One own goal

F.A. Cup

	Date		Opponent	Score	Scorers	Att	Blyth J	Davies D	Fryer J	Goodall E	Hardy J	Hubbard C	McNeill J	Parker D	Pears J	Robinson C	Woodhead C
R1	Nov	27	SCUNTHORPE UTD.	4-0	Pears 2, McNeill 2	6,000	5	10	8	1	7	6	9	3	11	4	2
R2	Dec	11	Exeter City	2-1	Hubbard, Fryer	9,000	5	10	8	1	7	6	9	3	11	4	2
R3	Jan	8	Huddersfield Town	1-3	Pears	25,442	5	10	8	1	7	6	9	3	11	4	2

Division 3 (North) Cup

	Date		Opponent	Score	Scorers	Att	Annables W	Bell E	Blyth J	Davies D	Fryer J	Goodall E	Hubbard C	Mackay W	McNeill J	Maddison G	Parker D	Pears J	Robinson C	Woodhead C	Foster T
R1	Oct	21	HARTLEPOOLS UTD.	1-1	Fryer	4,000	2		5	10	8		6	7	9	1		11	4	3	
rep		27	Hartlepools United	0-3		1,600	2	8		10		1	6	7	9		3	11	4		5

		Pl	Home					Away					F.	A.	Pts
			W	D	L	F	A	W	D	L	F	A	(Total)		
1	Tranmere Rovers	42	15	4	2	57	21	8	6	7	24	20	81	41	56
2	Doncaster Rovers	42	15	4	2	48	16	6	8	7	26	33	74	49	54
3	HULL CITY	42	11	8	2	51	19	9	5	7	29	24	80	43	53
4	Oldham Athletic	42	16	4	1	48	18	3	9	9	19	28	67	46	51
5	Gateshead	42	15	5	1	53	20	5	6	10	31	39	84	59	51
6	Rotherham United	42	13	6	2	45	21	7	4	10	23	35	68	56	50
7	Lincoln City	42	14	3	4	48	17	5	5	11	18	33	66	50	46
8	Crewe Alexandra	42	14	3	4	47	17	4	6	11	24	36	71	53	45
9	Chester	42	13	4	4	54	31	3	8	10	23	41	77	72	44
10	Wrexham	42	14	4	3	37	15	2	7	12	21	48	58	63	43
11	York City	42	11	4	6	40	25	5	6	10	30	43	70	68	42
12	Carlisle United	42	11	5	5	35	19	4	4	13	22	48	57	67	39
13	New Brighton	42	12	5	4	43	18	3	3	15	17	43	60	61	38
14	Bradford City	42	12	6	3	46	21	2	4	15	20	48	66	69	38
15	Port Vale	42	11	8	2	45	27	1	6	14	20	46	65	73	38
16	Southport	42	8	8	5	30	26	4	6	11	23	56	53	82	38
17	Rochdale	42	7	10	4	38	27	6	1	14	29	51	67	78	37
18	Halifax Town	42	9	7	5	24	19	3	5	13	20	47	44	66	36
19	Darlington	42	10	4	7	37	31	1	6	14	17	48	54	79	32
20	Hartlepools United	42	10	8	3	36	20	0	4	17	17	60	53	80	32
21	Barrow	42	9	6	6	28	20	2	4	15	13	51	41	71	32
22	Accrington Stanley	42	9	2	10	31	32	2	5	14	14	43	45	75	29

1938/39 7th in Division Three (North)

No	Date	Opponent	Score	Scorers	Att	Annables W	Bly W	Blyth J	Clubley R	Cunliffe A	Darling B	Davies D	Dickinson W	Dowen J	Ellis J	Hardy J	Hubbard C	Huxford H	Lawrence M	McNeill I	Meens H	Richardson G	Robinson C	Salvidge G	Sherwood C	Stokes A	Treanor J	White W	Wienand G	Woodhead C
1	Aug 27	Chester	1-1	Cunliffe	8986			5		11		10		2	1	4	7	9					6						8	3
2	29	OLDHAM ATHLETIC	0-2		7670			5		11		10		2	1		7	9	4				6						8	3
3	Sep 3	BRADFORD CITY	3-2	Hubbard 2, Huxford	4751			5		11		10	8	3	1		7	9	6				4							2
4	5	Barrow	1-3	Cunliffe	4793			5		11		10	8	3	1		7			9			4				6			2
5	10	Carlisle United	2-1	Cunliffe 2	7236			5		11		10		3	1		8						4			7	6			2
6	12	BARROW	4-0	Robinson 2, McNeill, Davies	5195			5		11		10		3	1		8	7		9			4				6			2
7	17	Lincoln City	3-0	Hubbard 2, Cunliffe	5983			5		11		10		3	1	6	8			9			4		7					2
8	24	STOCKPORT COUNTY	4-4	Davies 2, Hubbard, Reid (og)	8652			5		11		10		3	1	6	8			9			4		7					2
9	Oct 1	Accrington Stanley	1-1	McNeill	3799			5		11		10		3	1	6	8			9			4		7					2
10	8	BARNSLEY	0-1		10382			5		11		10		3	1	6	8			9			4	7						2
11	15	DARLINGTON	3-2	Cunliffe, Davies, Salvidge	7613			5		11		10		3	1	6	8			9			4	7						2
12	22	Hartlepools United	3-3	Cunliffe, McNeill, Davies	6189			5		11		10		3	1	6	8			9			4						7	2
13	29	GATESHEAD	1-0	Hubbard	9985			5		11		10		3	1	6	8			9			4						7	2
14	Nov 5	Wrexham	2-4	Hubbard, McNeill	5336			5		11		10		3	1	6	8			9			4						7	2
15	12	YORK CITY	2-0	Cunliffe 2	8159			5		11		10		3	1	6	8			9			4						7	2
16	19	Rochdale	0-4		6690			5		11	1	10		3			8	9		9	6		4							2
17	Dec 3	Doncaster Rovers	0-1		13696					11	1	10		3		6	7			9		8	4					5		2
18	17	Crewe Alexandra	1-0	Hubbard	4231			5		11		10		3	1	6	8	9					4						7	2
19	24	CHESTER	3-0	Cunliffe, Wienand, Davies	5911			5		11		10	9	3	1	6	8						4						7	2
20	26	NEW BRIGHTON	3-0	Hubbard 2, Robinson	8053			5		11		10	9	3	1	6	8						4						7	2
21	27	New Brighton	1-6	Cunliffe	5966			5		11		10	9	3	1	6	8						4						7	2
22	31	Bradford City	2-6	Hubbard 2	8888			5		11		10	9	3	1	6	8						4						7	2
23	Jan 14	CARLISLE UNITED	11-1	* See below	5298			5		11		10	9	3	1	6	7					8	4							2
24	21	LINCOLN CITY	4-2	Davies 2, Dickinson, Hubbard	4962			5		11		10	9	3	1	6	7					8	4							2
25	28	Stockport County	2-2	Hubbard, Richardson	7638			5		11		10	9	3	1	6	7					8	4							2
26	Feb 4	ACCRINGTON STANLEY	6-1	Cunliffe 3, Richardson, Hubbard, Dickinson	5502			5		11		10	9	3	1	6	7					8	4							2
27	11	Barnsley	1-5	Cunliffe	16839			5		11		10	9	3	1	6	7					8	4							2
28	18	Darlington	1-0	Wienand	4304			6		11		10	9	3	1						5	8	4						7	2
29	25	HARTLEPOOLS UNITED	4-1	Richardson 3, Wienand	4565			6		11		10	9	3	1						5	8	4						7	2
30	Mar 4	Gateshead	2-2	Davies 2	4933			6		11		10		3	1		9				5	8	4						7	2
31	9	ROTHERHAM UNITED	0-2		4040			6		11		10			1		9				5	8	4					3	7	2
32	11	WREXHAM	1-1	Davies	4140	3				11		10	9		1	6	7				5	8	4							2
33	18	York City	0-1		5023	3				11		10	9		1	6	7				5	8	4							2
34	25	ROCHDALE	3-3	Richardson 2, Hubbard	3975					11		10	9	3	1	6	7				5	8	4							2
35	Apr 1	Rotherham United	2-0	Richardson 2	5470		1			11		10		3		6	8				5	9	4	7						2
36	7	HALIFAX TOWN	1-1	Davies	10613		1			11		10		3		6	8				5	9	4	7						2
37	8	DONCASTER ROVERS	0-0		8108		1			11		10	9	3		6	7				5	8	4							2
38	10	Halifax Town	0-1		4229		1			11		10	9	3		6	7				5	8	4							2
39	15	Southport	0-4		3805		1			11		10		3		6	8				5	9	4						7	2
40	17	SOUTHPORT	2-1	Cunliffe 2	2335	2	1			11		10		3		6	7	9			5	8	4							
41	22	CREWE ALEXANDRA	2-1	Cunliffe, Hubbard	2948		1			11		10		3		6	9	7			5	8	4							2
42	29	Oldham Athletic	1-4	Lawrence M	3484		1			11		10		3			9	7	6		5	8								2
		Apps				3	8	30		42	2	42	18	39	32	31	40	10	4	13	15	20	41	4	4	1	5	2	15	41
		Goals								20		14	5				19	1	1	4		10	4	1					3	

Scorers in game 23: Dickinson 3, Cunliffe 3, Hubbard 2, Davies 2, Robinson, Richardson

One own goal

F.A. Cup

	Date	Opponent	Score	Scorers	Att	Annables W	Bly W	Blyth J	Clubley R	Cunliffe A	Darling B	Davies D	Dickinson W	Dowen J	Ellis J	Hardy J	Hubbard C	Huxford H	Lawrence M	McNeill I	Meens H	Richardson G	Robinson C	Salvidge G	Sherwood C	Stokes A	Treanor J	White W	Wienand G	Woodhead C
R1	Nov 26	ROTHERHAM UTD.	4-1	Hubbard 2, Cunliffe, Davies	8,000			5		11	1	10		3		6	8	7		9			4							2
R2	Dec 10	Chester	2-2	Davies 2	9,905			5		11		10		3	1	6	7			9		8	4							2
rep	15	CHESTER	0-1		9,000			5		11		10		3	1	6	7			9		8	4							2

Division 3 (North) Cup

	Date	Opponent	Score	Scorers	Att	Annables W	Bly W	Blyth J	Clubley R	Cunliffe A	Darling B	Davies D	Dickinson W	Dowen J	Ellis J	Hardy J	Hubbard C	Huxford H	Lawrence M	McNeill I	Meens H	Richardson G	Robinson C	Salvidge G	Sherwood C	Stokes A	Treanor J	White W	Wienand G	Woodhead C
R2	Feb 22	BRADFORD CITY	0-6		1,678			6	7	11		10	9	3	1						5	8	4							2

		Pl	Home					Away					F.	A.		Pts
			W	D	L	F	A	W	D	L	F	A	(Total)			
1	Barnsley	42	18	2	1	60	12	12	5	4	34	22	94	34		67
2	Doncaster Rovers	42	12	5	4	47	21	9	9	3	40	26	87	47		56
3	Bradford City	42	16	2	3	59	21	6	6	9	30	35	89	56		52
4	Southport	42	14	5	2	47	16	6	5	10	28	38	75	54		50
5	Oldham Athletic	42	16	1	4	51	21	6	4	11	25	38	76	59		49
6	Chester	42	12	5	4	54	31	8	4	9	34	39	88	70		49
7	HULL CITY	42	13	5	3	57	25	5	5	11	26	49	83	74		46
8	Crewe Alexandra	42	12	5	4	54	23	7	1	13	28	47	82	70		44
9	Stockport County	42	13	6	2	57	24	4	3	14	34	53	91	77		43
10	Gateshead	42	11	6	4	45	24	3	8	10	29	43	74	67		42
11	Rotherham United	42	12	4	5	45	21	5	4	12	19	43	64	64		42
12	Halifax Town	42	9	10	2	33	22	4	6	11	19	32	52	54		42
13	Barrow	42	11	5	5	46	22	5	4	12	20	43	66	65		41
14	Wrexham	42	15	2	4	46	28	2	5	14	20	51	66	79		41
15	Rochdale	42	10	5	6	58	29	5	4	12	34	53	92	82		39
16	New Brighton	42	11	2	8	46	32	4	7	10	22	41	68	73		39
17	Lincoln City	42	9	6	6	40	33	3	3	15	26	59	66	92		33
18	Darlington	42	12	2	7	43	30	1	5	15	19	62	62	92		33
19	Carlisle United	42	10	5	6	44	33	3	2	16	22	78	66	111		33
20	York City	42	8	5	8	37	34	4	3	14	27	58	64	92		32
21	Hartlepools United	42	10	4	7	36	33	2	3	16	19	61	55	94		31
22	Accrington Stanley	42	6	5	10	30	39	1	1	19	19	64	49	103		20

1938-39

Back Row: D. Davies, W. Annables, J. Treanor, W. Riches, H. Meens, A. Stokes, J. Hardy, W. White, C. Woodhead;
Middle Row: C. Robinson, H. Huxford, S. Tench, J. Ellis, W. Bly, B. Darling, W. Dickinson, G. Salvidge, J. Lodge (Asst Trainer);
Sitting: E. Blackburn (Manager), M. Lawrence, H. McNeill, J. Blyth, M. Sullivan, B. Duffy,
A. Cunliffe, C. Sherwood, C. Hubbard, J. Beck (Trainer)

1939-40

Back Row: R. Clubley, W. Self, H. Meens, J. Lodge (Asst Trainer), J. Rodger, W. Clark, F. Hall;
Middle Row: J. Robinson, W. Riches, H. Gilmore, W. Bly, J. Curnow, A. Watson, C. Woods, T. Smith;
Sitting: E. Blackburn (Manager), G. Richardson, J. Prescott, A. Cunliffe, D. Davies, C. Woodhead, J. Beck (Trainer);
On Ground: A. Kavanagh, R. Lowe.

1939/40 Division Three (North) - Abandoned after two games

				1	2	3	4	5	6	7	8	9	10	11
Aug	26 LINCOLN CITY	2-2 Lowe, Davies	8696	Curnow J	Woodhead C	Watson A	Robinson C	Meens H	Smith T	Quigley D	Richardson G	Lowe R	Davies D	Cunliffe A
Sep	2 Southport	1-1 Lowe	3711	Curnow J	Woodhead C	Watson A	Gilmore HP	Meens H	Smith T	Quigley D	Richardson G	Lowe R	Davies D	Cunliffe A

North East Regional League

Oct	21 Darlington	0-2	3778	Curnow J	Woodhead C	Watson A	Gilmore HP	Meens H	Smith T	Richardson E	Robinson C	Prescott JR	Davies D	Spivey R
	28 HARTLEPOOLS UTD	2-3 Prescott 2	3000	Curnow J	Woodhead C	Watson A	Gilmore HP	Meens H	Smith T	Robinson J	Davies D	Prescott JR	Crawford E	Richardson E
Nov	4 LEEDS UTD	0-3	3000	Curnow J	Woodhead C	Watson A	Robinson C	Meens H	Smith T	Robinson J	Woods C	Prescott JR	Anderson N	Richardson E
	11 York City	1-3 Woods	3000	Curnow J	Young H	Watson A	Gilmore HP	Meens H	Smith T	Robinson J	Woods C	Prescott JR	Anderson N	Clubley R
	18 HUDDERSFIELD TOWN	1-5 Meens	5000	Curnow J	Woodhead C	Watson A	Gilmore HP	Meens H	Smith T	Robinson J	Woods C	Anderson N	Stephenson E	Richardson E
	25 Bradford PA	1-2 Richardson	1259	Curnow J	Woodhead C	Watson A	Gilmore HP	Meens H	Smith T	Richardson E	Dyer R	Prescott JR	Woods C	Anderson N
Dec	2 MIDDLESBROUGH	3-0 Anderson, Prescott, Meens	3000	Curnow J	Woodhead C	Watson A	Gilmore HP	Meens H	Smith T	Robinson J	Robinson C	Prescott JR	Anderson N	Richardson E
	9 Newcastle Utd	0-3	2500	Curnow J	Woodhead C	Watson A	Gilmore HP	Meens H	Smith T	Robinson J	Davies D	Prescott JR	Anderson N	Richardson E
Jan	6 HALIFAX TOWN	2-0 Prescott, Anderson	1500	Curnow J	Woodhead C	Watson A	Gilmore HP	Meens H	Smith T	Robinson J	Davies D	Prescott JR	Anderson N	Richardson E
Feb	24 Hartlepools Utd	2-3 Prescott 2	1200	Bly W	Woodhead C	Watson A	Robinson J	Gilmore HP	Smith T	Richardson E	Davies D	Prescott JR	Anderson N	Cunliffe A
Mar	9 Bradford City	0-4	1887	Curnow J	Woodhead C	Watson A	Gilmore HP	Meens H	Smith T	Robinson J	Davies D	Prescott JR	Anderson N	Cunliffe A
	16 Huddersfield Town	0-1	2961	Curnow J	Woodhead C	Watson A	Gilmore HP	Meens H	Smith T	Robinson J	Davies D	Prescott JR	Anderson N	Cunliffe A
	23 BRADFORD PA	4-1 Prescott 2, Anderson 2	5000	Curnow J	Woodhead C	Watson A	Gilmore HP	Meens H	Smith T	Robinson J	Davies D	Prescott JR	Anderson N	Cunliffe A
	25 YORK CITY	4-1 Prescott 4	5000	Curnow J	Woodhead C	Watson A	Gilmore HP	Meens H	Smith T	Spivey R	Davies D	Prescott JR	Anderson N	Cunliffe A
	30 Middlesbrough	3-2 Cunliffe, Prescott, Anderson	1500	Curnow J	Woodhead C	Watson A	Gilmore HP	Meens H	Riches W	Robinson J	Davies D	Prescott JR	Anderson N	Cunliffe A
Apr	6 NEWCASTLE UTD	3-1 Davies 2, Prescott	6000	Curnow J	Woodhead C	Watson A	Gilmore HP	Meens H	Smith T	Robinson J	Davies D	Prescott JR	Anderson N	Cunliffe A
May	18 Halifax Town	1-0 Prescott	500	Curnow J	Smith T	Watson A	Gilmore HP	Meens H	Riches W	Robinson J	Davies D	Prescott JR	Anderson N	Cunliffe A
	25 BRADFORD CITY	3-0 Dawson, Cunliffe, Meens	2000	Curnow J	Woodhead C	Watson A	Gilmore HP	Meens H	Smith T	Robinson J	Dawson D	Anderson N	Davies D	Cunliffe A
Jun	1 Leeds Utd	1-3 Anderson	500	Curnow J	Woodhead C	Watson A	Gilmore HP	Meens H	Smith T	Robinson J	Dawson D	Anderson N	Davies D	Spivey R
	8 DARLINGTON	4-4 Anderson 3, Davies	1000	Curnow J	Woodhead C	Watson A	Gilmore HP	Meens H	Smith T	Robinson J	Dawson D	Anderson N	Davies D	Reeve E

Football League War Cup

R	Apr	13 LINCOLN CITY	1-0 Davies	6000	Curnow J	Woodhead C	Watson A	Gilmore HP	Meens H	Smith T	Robinson J	Davies D	Prescott JR	Anderson N	Cunliffe A
1/1		20 York City	1-1 Prescott	4000	Curnow J	Woodhead C	Watson A	Gilmore HP	Meens H	Smith T	Robinson J	Davies D	Prescott JR	Anderson N	Cunliffe A
1/2		27 YORK CITY	1-0 Cunliffe	6000	Curnow J	Woodhead C	Watson A	Gilmore HP	Meens H	Smith T	Robinson J	Davies D	Prescott JR	Anderson N	Cunliffe A
2/1	May	4 Huddersfield Town	1-1 Cunliffe	6000	Curnow J	Woodhead C	Watson A	Gilmore HP	Meens H	Smith T	Robinson J	Davies D	Prescott JR	Anderson N	Cunliffe A
2/2		11 HUDDERSFIELD TOWN	0-1	6500	Curnow J	Woodhead C	Watson A	Gilmore HP	Meens H	Smith T	Robinson J	Davies D	Prescott JR	Anderson N	Spivey R

1939/40 season

		Pl	W	D	L	F	A	Pts
1	Huddersfield Town	20	15	4	1	54	22	34
2	Newcastle United	20	12	1	7	59	42	25
3	Bradford Park Ave. *	19	10	2	7	47	38	22
4	Middlesbrough	20	9	4	7	49	42	22
5	Leeds United *	18	9	3	6	36	27	21
6	Bradford City *	19	8	4	7	41	37	20
7	HULL CITY	20	8	1	11	35	41	17
8	York City	20	8	1	11	36	51	17
9	Darlington *	19	6	3	10	44	56	15
10	Hartlepools United	20	6	1	13	27	47	13
11	Halifax Town *	19	3	2	14	28	53	8

* Full number of games not played

1940/41season (Bottom 10 teams only shown)

		Pl	W	D	L	F	A	Pts
27	Tranmere Rovers	25	9	5	11	67	90	.744
28	Sheffield United	25	6	6	13	44	60	.733
29	Bradford City	29	8	3	18	72	99	.727
30	Rochdale	32	12	5	15	64	92	.695
31	Southport	28	7	2	19	61	88	.693
32	York City	25	7	4	14	49	71	.690
33	HULL CITY	23	8	3	12	44	67	.656
34	Sheffield Wednesday	30	9	6	15	50	78	.641
35	Stockport County	29	9	5	15	54	93	.580
36	Crewe Alexandra	24	2	3	19	32	84	.380

(Final positions determined on goal average) Note: During this (and some other War-time seasons), leagues were formed on a general countrywide regional basis. Fixtures were then played against others on a more local basis, i.e. each club did not play every other on a 'home' and 'away' format within their league (e.g. Hull never played the likes of Wrexham or Bristol City). Consequently the final league tables were on a composite basis. In addition, some matches were 'double-headers' for other competitions.

1940/41

North Regional League

Aug	31 HALIFAX TOWN	4-2 Anderson 2, Davies, Dawson	1500	Curnow J	Gowdy W	Woodhead C	Robinson J	Meens H	Herdman H	Dawson D	Davies D	Burdett T	Anderson N	Cunliffe A
Sep	7 Bradford City	5-4 Burdett 2, Cunliffe, Dawson, Powell(og)	1436	Curnow J	Ross A	Woodhead C	Robinson J	Meens H	Heelbeck L	Dawson D	Davies D	Burdett T	Lucas W	Cunliffe A
	14 York City	1-4 Burdett	2000	Curnow J	Ross A	Woodhead C	Robinson J	Meens H	Rogers W	Dawson D	Davies D	Burdett T	Lucas W	Cunliffe A
	21 BRADFORD PA	2-1 Burdett, Cunliffe	2000	Curnow J	Cottam A	Woodhead C	Robinson J	Meens H	Gowdy W	Dawson D	Davies D	Burdett T	Lucas W	Cunliffe A
	28 YORK CITY	1-3 Cunliffe	1500	Bly W	Ross A	Woodhead C	Cottam A	Meens H	Gowdy W	Robinson J	Davies D	Burdett T	Lucas W	Cunliffe A
Oct	5 ROTHERHAM UTD	0-2	1500	Bly W	Ross A	Woodhead C	Robinson J	Meens H	Heelbeck L	Davies D	Anderson N	Burdett T	Lucas W	Cunliffe A
	12 Doncaster Rovers	2-4 Burdett, Knott	2413	Bly W	Ross A	Woodhead C	Robinson J	Meens H	Heelbeck L	Dawson D	Knott H	Burdett T	Lucas W	Cunliffe A
	19 NEWCASTLE UTD	2-1 Anderson, Barraclough	3000	Bly W	Ross A	Woodhead C	Robinson J	Neary J	Bradley G	Dawson D	Knott H	Anderson N	Davies D	Barraclough W
	26 BRADFORD CITY	5-2 Anderson 3, Knott 2	2000	Bly W	Ross A	Woodhead C	Robinson J	Meens H	Bradley G	Cunliffe A	Knott H	Anderson N	Davies D	Barraclough W
Nov	2 Lincoln City	1-1 Cunliffe	1237	Bly W	Ross A	Woodhead C	Robinson J	Meens H	Bradley G	Cunliffe A	Knott H	Anderson N	Davies D	Barraclough W
	9 Halifax Town	0-3	1000	Bly W	Ross A	Woodhead C	Robinson J	Neary J	Meens H	Cunliffe A	Knott H	Anderson N	Davies D	Barraclough W
	16 DONCASTER ROVERS	5-4 Knott 3, Anderson, Davies	1500	Bly W	Ross A	Woodhead C	Robinson J	Meens H	Bradley G	Cunliffe A	Knott H	Anderson N	Davies D	Barraclough W
	23 Leeds Utd	2-3 Cunliffe, Anderson	3000	Bly W	Ross A	Woodhead C	Robinson J	Meens H	Bratley G	Cunliffe A	Knott H	Anderson N	Davies D	Barraclough W
	30 LINCOLN CITY	1-2 Knott	1000	Bly W	Ross A	Woodhead C	Robinson J	Meens H	Bradley G	Davies D	Knott H	Anderson N	Bratley G	Barraclough W
Dec	7 Newcastle Utd	1-3 Knott	3000	Bly W	Ross A	Woodhead C	Robinson J	Meens H	Bradley G	Spivey R	Knott H	Anderson N	Sullivan M	Reeve E
	14 BARNSLEY	1-2 Knott	500	Bly W	Ross A	Woodhead C	Robinson J	Meens H	Bradley G	McCurdie J	Knott H	Anderson N	Spivey R	Barraclough W
	21 Barnsley	0-5	1595	Bly W	Ross A	Woodhead C	Robinson J	Meens H	Spivey R	Raynor G	Knott H	Anderson N	Cunliffe A	Barraclough W
	25 Grimsby Town	1-1 Knott	4500	Bly W	Green R	Woodhead C	Bradley G	Twells D	Bratley G	Bratton W	Knott H	Anderson N	Spivey R	Barraclough W
Jan	18 LEEDS UTD	4-1 Knott 2, Spivey, Barraclough	1500	Bly W	Bratley G	Woodhead C	Robinson J	Meens H	Bradley G	Cunliffe A	Knott H	Anderson N	Spivey R	Barraclough W
	25 York City	3-3 Anderson 2, Knott	2000	Bly W	Bratley G	Woodhead C	Robinson J	Meens H	Bradley G	Davies D	Knott H	Anderson N	Spivey R	Barraclough W
Mar	22 GRIMSBY TOWN	2-8 Spivey, Bratley	1000	French J	Ross A	Woodhead C	Porteous J	Twells D	Bratley G	Selby W	Sherwood G	Anderson N	Spivey R	Barraclough W
	29 Grimsby Town	1-0 Anderson	1104	Wilson DM	Bradley G	Hewick A	Butcher R	Meens H	Bratley G	Anderson N	Sherwood G	Pritchard T	Spivey R	Barraclough W
Apr	5 MIDDLESBROUGH	0-8	2000	Wilson DM	Twells D	Woodhead C	Butcher R	Meens H	Bratley G	Anderson N	Sherwood G	Knott H	Spivey R	Barraclough W

One own goal

Football League War Cup

Feb	15 LINCOLN CITY	4-1 Knott (4)	2000	Bly W	Twells D	Woodhead C	Robinson J	Meens H	Bratley G	Cunliffe A	Spivey R	Knott H	Davies D	Barraclough W
	22 Lincoln City	2-3 Knott, Cunliffe	1500	Curnow J	Twells D	Woodhead C	Robinson J	Meens H	Bratley G	Cunliffe A	Sherwood G	Knott H	Spivey R	Barraclough W
Mar	1 SHEFFIELD UTD	1-0 Knott	4000	Curnow J	Twells D	Woodhead C	Robinson J	Meens H	Bratley G	Spivey R	Sherwood G	Knott H	Davies D	Barraclough W
	8 Sheffield Utd	1-3 (a.e.t.) Davies	1644	Curnow J	Twells D	Woodhead C	Robinson J	Meens H	Bratley G	Davies D	Sherwood G	Knott H	Spivey R	Barraclough W

1941/42, 1942/43 and 1943/44:

Did not compete

1944/45

Football League North: First Championship

Aug	26	DONCASTER ROVERS	1-8 Sargeant	6980	Wilkinson N	Kingwell L	Prescott J	Archer J	Neary J	Harris J	Sargeant F	Talbot L	Miller D	Bell E	Glaister G
Sep	2	Doncaster Rovers	1-2 Glaister	7000	Curnow J	Beeson G	Prescott J	Montgomery S	Beardshaw C	Harris J	Hubbard C	Richardson G	Singleton E	Miller D	Glaister G
	9	Halifax Town	1-1 Johnson H	5000	Curnow J	Beeson G	Hewick A	Montgomery S	Beardshaw C	Harris J	Bell E	Richardson G	Sherwood G	Johnson H	Brown G
	16	HALIFAX TOWN	2-0 Sargeant, Talbot	7500	Curnow J	Beeson G	Hewick A	Beardshaw C	Montgomery S	Harris J	Sargeant F	Talbot L	Miller D	Glaister G	Bell E
	23	YORK CITY	1-0 Montgomery	5000	Curnow J	Beeson G	Hewick A	Archer J	Beardshaw C	Harris J	Dickinson P	Bell E	Montgomery S	Miller D	Glaister G
	30	York City	0-1	4000	Curnow J	Prescott J	Hewick A	Archer J	Beardshaw C	Harris J	White L	Richardson G	Stone J	Miller D	Glaister G
Oct	7	Leeds Utd	2-5 Glaister, Montgomery	8000	Curnow J	Shepherd G	Prescott J	Archer J	Beardshaw C	Harris J	Bell E	Stone J	Montgomery S	Miller D	Glaister G
	14	LEEDS UTD	0-0	5000	Curnow J	Dickinson P	Harvey G	Montgomery S	Beardshaw C	Harris J	Landles J	Read S	Ward T	Finch R	Glaister G
	21	DARLINGTON	3-2 Montgomery 2, Glaister	5000	Curnow J	Beeson G	Harvey G	Archer J	Beardshaw C	Harris J	Drummond A	Bell E	Montgomery S	Miller D	Glaister G
	28	Darlington	1-7 Glaister	7883	Curnow J	Beeson G	Dowen J	Brewer C	Montgomery S	Harris J	White L	Bell E	Bunting A	Miller D	Glaister G
Nov	4	Newcastle Utd	0-7	8000	Curnow J	Beeson G	Harvey G	Brewer C	Kingwell L	Harris J	Lamb G	Miller D	Gobey E	Hope C	Glaister G
	11	NEWCASTLE UTD	3-6 Smith J, Spencer, Finch	2000	Curnow J	Beeson G	Harvey G	Montgomery S	Thomas R	Harris J	Bell E	Smith J	Spencer E	Finch R	Glaister G
	18	GATESHEAD	1-3 Glaister	5000	Curnow J	Beeson G	Stokes E	Thomas R	Beardshaw C	Harris J	Hubbard C	Bell E	Montgomery S	Miller D	Glaister G
	25	Gateshead	2-5 Finch, Dixon	3000	Bircham B	Beeson G	Harnby D	Brewer C	Richardson D	Harris J	Lamb G	Dixon J	McDowell C	Rhodes B	Finch R
Dec	2	GRIMSBY TOWN	4-3 McDowell 2, Knott, Flinton	4000	Jones J	Dickinson P	Symons J	Johnson J	Thomas R	Harris J	Bell E	Knott H	McDowell C	Richardson G	Flinton W
	9	Grimsby Town	0-0	3604	Moore R	Symons J	Stokes E	Johnson J	Thomas R	Harris J	Bell E	Richardson G	Hubbard C	Dowling JR	Flinton W
	16	BRADFORD PA	0-4	3000	Collier T	Beeson G	Hollis H	Johnson J	Thomas R	Harris J	Hubbard C	Talbot L	McDowell C	Richardson G	Glaister G
	23	Bradford PA	1-6 Beeson	6562	Collier T	Beeson G	Riches W	Johnson J	Thomas R	Harris J	Hubbard C	Talbot L	McDowell C	Richardson G	Cunliffe A

Football League North War Cup (Qualifying)   (Games also counted towards the Second Championship)

Dec	25	York City	1-5 Brailsford	2043	Collier T	Beeson G	Harvey G	Clark S	Hollis H	Gilmore HP	Bell E	Talbot L	Brailsford T	Flinton W	Dickinson P
	30	YORK CITY	6-1 McDowell 2, Talbot 2, Flinton, Bell	4300	Collier T	Beeson G	Stokes E	Johnson J	Beardshaw C	Harris J	Bell E	Talbot L	McDowell C	Flinton W	Cunliffe A
Jan	6	BRADFORD CITY	1-3 Flinton,	4000	Collier T	Beeson G	Harvey G	Galloway A	Beardshaw C	Harris J	Bell E	Talbot L	Thomas R	Glaister G	Flinton W
	13	Bradford City	1-2 Bell	4000	Curnow J	Symons J	Stokes E	Harris J	Beardshaw C	Richardson D	Bell E	Flinton W	Hubbard C	Downie J	Glaister G
	27	Bradford PA	1-2 Glaister	4791	Curnow J	Beeson G	Symons J	Hollis H	Beardshaw C	Armeson L	Bell E	Johnson J	Greaves S	Flinton W	Glaister G
Feb	3	Leeds Utd	1-6 Bell	8000	Curnow J	Beeson G	Symons J	Johnson J	Hollis H	Armeson L	Johnson K	Flinton W	Bell E	Harris J	Glaister G
	10	LEEDS UTD	1-1 Butterworth (og)	4000	Curnow J	Beeson G	Symons J	Harris J	Johnson J	Armeson L	Huxford H	Stone J	Howe L	Vaux E	Glaister G
	17	BARNSLEY	3-0 Howe 2, Armeson	4000	Curnow J	Beeson G	Symons J	Harris J	Johnson J	Armeson L	Bell E	Howe L	Vaux E	Miller D	Flinton W
	24	Barnsley	0-3	7567	Curnow J	Hollis H	Stokes E	Harris J	Vaughan E	Armeson L	Bell E	Howe L	Richardson G	Miller D	Flinton W
Mar	10	BRADFORD PA	0-2	4000	Curnow J	Beeson G	Symons J	Harris J	Vaughan E	Armeson L	Bell E	Walker F	Stone J	Miller D	Flinton W

One own goal

Football League North: Second Championship

Mar	3	GRIMSBY TOWN	3-1 Howe 3	5000	Curnow J	Whitchurch S	Symons J	Harris J	Vaughan E	Armeson L	Bell E	Howe L	Meese AE	Miller D	Flinton W
	17	Grimsby Town	0-4	3000	Adams C	Whitchurch S	Symons J	Hollis H	Vaughan E	Harris J	White L	Stone J	Huxford H	Miller D	Waters D
	24	LINCOLN CITY	1-4 Vaughan	4000	Curnow J	Whitchurch S	Stokes E	Vaughan E	Beardshaw C	Harris J	Bell E	Howe L	Huxford H	Miller D	Flinton W
Apr	2	BRADFORD CITY	3-1 Knott 3	5000	Adams C	Hollis H	Stokes E	Gilmore HP	Vaughan E	Harris J	Bell E	Howe L	Knott H	Walker FA	Flinton W
	7	Lincoln City	2-4 Knott 2	3055	Curnow J	Hollis H	Symons J	Rothery H	Vaughan E	Harris J	Bell E	Knott H	Crofts E	Howe L	Etherington H
	14	Leeds Utd	2-6 Harris, Sykes	2000	Curnow J	Symons J	Stokes E	Rothery H	Vaughan E	Harris J	Bell E	Sykes H	Howe L	Walker FA	Flinton W
	21	ROTHERHAM UTD	2-8 Bell, Rothery	3000	Adams C	Symons J	Skidmore W	Robinson J	Vaughan E	Harris J	Bell E	Rothery H	Howe L	Walker FA	Flinton W
	28	Rotherham Utd	2-1 Smith K, Eatherington	3098	Curnow J	Whitchurch S	Stokes E	Richardson G	Thomas R	Harris J	Smith K	Stone J	Crofts E	Hutchinson J	Eatherington H

First Championship (Bottom 10 teams only)

		Pl	W	D	L	F	A	Pts
45	Accrington Stanley	18	5	2	11	29	46	12
46	Port Vale	18	5	2	11	22	36	12
47	Bury	18	5	2	11	28	48	12
48	Stockport County	18	5	1	12	33	70	11
49	HULL CITY	18	4	3	11	23	60	11
50	Southport	18	3	4	11	32	55	10
51	Lincoln City	18	4	2	12	32	56	10
52	Leicester City	18	3	4	11	23	46	10
53	Tranmere Rovers	18	2	1	15	20	53	5
54	Notts County	18	2	1	15	19	62	5

Second Championship (Bottom 10 teams only)

		Pl	W	D	L	F	A	Pts
51	Middlesbrough	24	6	2	16	40	73	14
52	Walsall	18	5	3	10	24	33	13
53	Swansea Town	20	6	1	13	42	63	13
54	Port Vale	21	5	2	14	27	60	12
55	Mansfield Town	12	5	1	6	22	38	11
56	HULL CITY	18	5	1	12	30	54	11
57	Rochdale	20	4	3	13	17	49	11
58	Southport	22	3	3	16	33	82	9
59	Notts County	21	4	0	17	29	62	8
60	Aberaman	17	2	2	13	36	69	6

Cup (Qualifying) (Bottom 10 teams only)

		Pl	W	D	L	F	A	Pts
51	HULL CITY	10	2	1	7	15	25	5
52	TOranmere Rovers	10	2	1	7	15	28	5
53	Rochdale	10	1	3	6	9	30	5
54	Oldham Athletic	10	2	0	8	19	28	4
55	Sheffield Wed.	10	1	2	7	14	29	4
56	Stockport County	10	2	0	8	14	35	4
57	Covernty City	10	1	1	8	16	35	3
58	Aberaman	10	1	1	8	17	46	3
59	Chester	10	1	1	8	14	39	3
60	Notts County	10	1	0	9	12	33	2

Only top 32 teams qualified

1945/46

Did not compete

1946/47 11th in Division Three (North)

Date	Opponent	Score	Scorers	Att.
Aug 31	LINCOLN CITY	0-0		25586
Sep 2	CREWE ALEXANDRA	2-2	Crawshaw, Sheen	24828
7	Southport	1-3	Crawshaw	5607
9	Crewe Alexandra	0-2		6996
14	ROTHERHAM UNITED	0-2		22187
16	GATESHEAD	1-2	Lester	17770
21	Chester	1-5	Knott	7766
28	YORK CITY	2-2	McGorrighan, Wright G	22249
Oct 5	Tranmere Rovers	3-1	Lester 3	8588
12	DARLINGTON	2-1	Lester, Chadwick	22296
19	HALIFAX TOWN	3-0	Chadwick 2, Lester	23289
26	New Brighton	5-1	Watson 2, Lester 2, Hassall	5005
Nov 2	ROCHDALE	0-1		22616
9	Doncaster Rovers	1-4	Chadwick	17820
16	WREXHAM	1-0	Lester	19081
23	Stockport County	0-2		8586
Dec 7	Bradford City	1-1	Lester	6453
21	Accrington Stanley	0-0		2672
25	Hartlepools United	0-0		8130
26	HARTLEPOOLS UNITED	1-1	Chadwick	30064
28	Lincoln City	3-0	Lester 2, Davidson	10996
Jan 1	Gateshead	0-1		5277
4	SOUTHPORT	4-0	Lester, Peach, Chadwick, Hassall	18800
18	Rotherham United	0-2		16971
Feb 1	York City	0-3		7099
15	Darlington	2-0	Lester 2	6310
Mar 6	CHESTER	1-0	Brown R	10367
8	Rochdale	2-5	Peach, Mills	6565
15	DONCASTER ROVERS	0-1		29579
22	Wrexham	1-0	Brown R	9394
29	STOCKPORT COUNTY	0-3		17209
Apr 4	Carlisle United	2-0	Davidson, Greenhalgh	11704
5	Oldham Athletic	2-1	Davidson 2	9561
7	CARLISLE UNITED	2-0	Davies, Brown R	21854
12	BRADFORD CITY	0-2		21289
19	Barrow	0-1		7400
26	ACCRINGTON STANLEY	3-0	Thompson 3	13023
May 10	TRANMERE ROVERS	1-0	Bell	15562
17	Halifax Town	0-2		4888
24	OLDHAM ATHLETIC	0-1		14954
31	BARROW	1-0	Chadwick	10725
Jun 7	NEW BRIGHTON	1-1	Thompson	9802

	Apps	Goals
Alberry E	1	
Atkinson P	3	
Atkinson T	2	
Bell E	5	1
Bly W	21	
Brown H	22	
Brown R	7	3
Brownsword J	10	
Carter J	5	
Chadwick C	23	7
Cook P	2	
Crawshaw C	2	2
Davidson D	18	4
Davies D	18	1
Durham D	1	
Elliott H	4	
Fowler N	14	
Greenhalgh J	41	1
Hannaby C	13	
Harrison K	2	
Hassall W	14	2
Johnson S	2	
Jones G	7	
Jones J	1	
Knott H	6	1
Koffman J	4	
Lester B	26	15
Major J	3	
McGorrighan F	20	1
Meens H	39	1
Mills J	31	1
Montgomery S	5	
Moore N	3	
Peach J	18	2
Robertson L	2	
Sheen J	5	1
Smith D	15	
Thompson D	5	4
Watson AE	35	2
Wright GA	4	1

Player no. 11: Teasdale T played in match no. 41, Smith A in match no. 6 and Reagan M in match no. 42

F.A. Cup

Date	Opponent	Score	Scorers	Att.
Nov 30	NEW BRIGHTON	0-0		21895
Dec 4	New Brighton	2-1	Lester, Chadwick	7688
14	Darlington	2-1	Lester, Peach	8077
Jan 11	Blackburn Rovers	1-1	Cook	23500
16	BLACKBURN ROVERS	0-3		30501

R1 replay a.e.t.

	Team	Pl	Home W D L F A	Away W D L F A	F A (Total)	Pts
1	Doncaster Rovers	42	15 5 1 67 16	18 1 2 56 24	123 40	72
2	Rotherham United	42	20 1 0 81 19	9 5 7 33 34	114 53	64
3	Chester	42	17 2 2 53 13	8 4 9 42 38	95 51	56
4	Stockport County	42	17 0 4 50 19	7 2 12 28 34	78 53	50
5	Bradford City	42	12 5 4 40 20	8 5 8 22 27	62 47	50
6	Rochdale	42	9 5 7 39 25	10 5 6 41 39	80 64	48
7	Wrexham	42	13 5 3 43 21	4 7 10 22 30	65 51	46
8	Crewe Alexandra	42	12 4 5 39 26	5 5 11 31 48	70 74	43
9	Barrow	42	10 2 9 28 24	7 5 9 26 38	54 62	41
10	Tranmere Rovers	42	11 5 5 43 33	6 2 13 23 44	66 77	41
11	HULL CITY	42	9 5 7 25 19	7 3 11 24 34	49 53	40
12	Lincoln City	42	12 3 6 52 32	5 2 14 34 55	86 87	39
13	Hartlepools United	42	10 5 6 36 26	5 4 12 28 47	64 73	39
14	Gateshead	42	10 3 8 39 33	6 3 12 23 39	62 72	38
15	York City	42	6 4 11 35 42	8 5 8 32 39	67 81	37
16	Carlisle United	42	10 5 6 45 38	4 4 13 25 55	70 93	37
17	Darlington	42	12 4 5 48 26	3 2 16 20 54	68 80	36
18	New Brighton	42	11 3 7 37 30	3 5 13 20 47	57 77	36
19	Oldham Athletic	42	6 5 10 29 31	6 3 12 26 49	55 80	32
20	Accrington Stanley	42	8 3 10 37 38	6 1 14 19 54	56 92	32
21	Southport	42	6 5 10 35 41	1 6 14 18 44	53 85	25
22	Halifax Town	42	6 3 12 28 36	2 3 16 15 56	43 92	22

1947/48 5th in Division Three (North)

#	Date		Opponent	Score	Scorers	Att	Atkinson P	Berry T	Bloomer J	Bloxham A	Bly W	Buchan W	Carter H	Conway A	Cook P	Corbett A	Daley A	Davidson D	Durham D	Fowler N	Gallacher C	Greenhalgh J	Hannaby C	Harrison K	Hassall W	Johnson S	King G	Lester B	McGorrighan F	Meens H	Mellor A	Mills J	Moore N	Murphy G	Peach J	Reagan M	Richardson G	Robertson L	Taylor J	Thompson D	Wright I
1	Aug	23	Lincoln City	3-2	Thompson 2, Gallacher	11116				1					11				7		8	4				2					5	6			10					3	9
2		28	ROCHDALE	0-0		25525				1					11						8	4				2					5	6				7		10		3	9
3		30	ACCRINGTON STANLEY	4-2	Gallacher 2, Thompson 2	23356				1								11			8	4				2					5	6				7		10		3	9
4	Sep	2	Rochdale	0-1		9027				1					11						8	4				2					5	6				7		10		3	9
5		6	Rotherham United	0-0		15205		6		1				7							4					2					5	11	9				10	8	3	
6		11	HALIFAX TOWN	1-2	Moore	21642		3		1												4		11		2					5	6	9			7		10	8		
7		13	Stockport County	0-0		9712		4		1							11				8					2					5	3	6	9			7	10			
8		15	Halifax Town	2-0	Moore, Robertson	8565		4		1							11		2		8										5		6	9					10	7		
9		20	BRADFORD CITY	2-1	Moore, Robertson	22810		4		1									2		11	7									5		6	9					10	8		
10		27	Barrow	2-0	Moore, Richardson	9182				1									2		8			3	11					5	4	6	9			7	10				
11	Oct	4	WREXHAM	1-1	Richardson	32188				1									2		8			3	11					5	4	6	9			7	10				
12		11	HARTLEPOOLS UNITED	5-0	Moore 3, Richardson, Tootill (og)	25414	1	6									11		2		8			3						5	4		9			7	10				
13		18	Gateshead	1-0	Moore	7684	1	6									11		2		8			3						5	4		9			7	10				
14		25	DARLINGTON	0-3		26240	1	6	7								11		2		8			3						5	4						10				
15	Nov	1	Tranmere Rovers	1-2	Moore	9630		6	7										2	8	4		1	11	3					5			9				10				
16		8	OLDHAM ATHLETIC	1-0	Moore	20551		6	11												4	1	8	2						10	5		9			7				3	
17		15	York City	2-2	Lester 2	14125		6	11												4	1	8	2			9		10	5						7				3	
18		22	MANSFIELD TOWN	1-1	Richardson	20677		6	11												4	1	8	2					5		9				7	10			3	
19	Dec	20	LINCOLN CITY	0-1		20923			7	1											8	4		11	2					10	5	6			9					3	
20		25	Southport	2-1	Richardson, Murphy	8223			11	1											4		7	2					3	6		8	9			10			3	5
21		26	SOUTHPORT	1-0	Murphy	25769		5	11	1											8	4		7	2					6			9			10		3		
22	Jan	3	Accrington Stanley	4-2	Murphy 2, Moore, Reagan	7363			11												4		11	2					5	6		8	9		7	10		3		
23		17	ROTHERHAM UNITED	5-3	Murphy 2, Buchan 2, Mellor	29821			11			8					1				4		10	2					5	6		8	9		7			3		
24		24	Carlisle United	0-0		17339		5	11			8					1		6				10	2					3		4	9		7					
25		31	STOCKPORT COUNTY	1-0	Harrison	27410		5	11			8					1		6				10	2					3		4	9		7					
26	Feb	7	Bradford City	0-2		12543		5	11			8					1		6				10	2					3		4	9		7					
27		14	BARROW	0-0		25103		5				8		1	11		6	2	10				7	3						4					9			
28		21	Wrexham	0-1		9522		5	8			10		1	11		6	2					7	3					4					9			
29		28	Hartlepools United	1-3	Murphy	8333		5	7	11	1	8					6	2						3					10	4				9			
30	Mar	6	GATESHEAD	2-3	Murphy, Bloomer	17737		5	7	10		8					1				11	6		2	3						4			9			
31		13	Darlington	0-2		6063		5	7	10		8			1	11							2	3							6	4			9			
32		17	Chester	1-4	Harrison	6087		5		11	1	8					6					7	2	3					4			10	9				
33		20	TRANMERE ROVERS	3-0	Conway 2, Murphy	13558		6		11	1		8					2			4		7							5	10		9			3		
34		26	New Brighton	0-1		7591		6		11	1		8					2			4		7							5	10		9			3		
35		27	Oldham Athletic	0-0		16061		6		1	8								9	2		4		11	7					5	10					3		
36		29	NEW BRIGHTON	3-0	Buchan, Mellor, Hassall	21860		6		1	8								9	2		4		11	7					5	10					3		
37	Apr	3	YORK CITY	1-1	Durham	32466		6		1	10	8							9	2		4		11	7					5					3		
38		10	Mansfield Town	1-1	Buchan	11098		6	11		1	10							9	2		4		7						5		8			3		
39		17	CHESTER	2-1	Moore 2	24138		6	7		1	10	8							11	2		4						5		9			3		
40		22	CREWE ALEXANDRA	2-1	Buchan, Durham	22096		6	7		1	10	8							11	2		4						5		9			3		
41		24	Crewe Alexandra	1-3	Conway	6182		6	7		1	10	8							11	2		4					3	9	5						
42	May	1	CARLISLE UNITED	3-1	Durham 2, Bloomer	25123	3	7			1	10	8							11	2		4					9		5	6						

	Atk	Ber	Blo	Blx	Bly	Buc	Car	Con	Cook	Cor	Dal	Dav	Dur	Fow	Gal	Gre	Han	Har	Has	Joh	Kin	Les	McG	Mee	Mel	Mil	Moo	Mur	Pea	Rea	Ric	Rob	Tay	Tho	Wri
Apps	3	32	4	23	27	18	4	3	3	8	7	4	15	21	18	27	4	20	34	8	2	1	6	35	19	11	24	15	1	17	16	7	20	4	1
Goals		2				5	3						4	3				2	1			2			2		13	9		1	5	2		4	

One own goal

F.A. Cup

#	Date		Opponent	Score	Scorers	Att	Berry T	Bloomer J	Buchan W	Gallacher C	Greenhalgh J	Hannaby C	Harrison K	Hassall W	McGorrighan F	Meens H	Mellor A	Mills J	Moore N	Murphy G	Peach J	Reagan M	Richardson G	Robertson L	Thompson D
R1	Nov	29	SOUTHPORT	1-1	Gallacher	20000	6	11		10	4	1	8	2		9	5					7			3
rep	Dec	6	Southport	3-2	Richardson, Reagan, McGorrighan	11000		11	1	8	4			2	10	5	6					7	9		3
R2		13	CHELTENHAM TOWN	4-2	Richardson 3, Reagan	21000	6	11	1	8	4			3	2	10	5					7	9		3
R3	Jan	10	MIDDLESBROUGH	1-3	Murphy	40179				4	1	11	2			5	6		9	8		7	10		3

R1 (first game) a.e.t.

	Pl	Home						Away						F.	A.	Pts
			W	D	L	F	A	W	D	L	F	A		(Total)		
1	Lincoln City	42	14	3	4	47	18	12	5	4	34	22	81	40		60
2	Rotherham United	42	15	4	2	56	18	10	5	6	39	31	95	49		59
3	Wrexham	42	14	3	4	49	23	7	5	9	25	31	74	54		50
4	Gateshead	42	11	5	5	48	28	8	6	7	27	29	75	57		49
5	HULL CITY	42	12	5	4	38	21	6	6	9	21	27	59	48		47
6	Accrington Stanley	42	13	1	7	36	24	7	5	9	26	35	62	59		46
7	Barrow	42	9	4	8	24	19	7	9	5	25	21	49	40		45
8	Mansfield Town	42	11	4	6	37	24	6	7	8	20	27	57	51		45
9	Carlisle United	42	10	4	7	50	35	8	3	10	38	42	88	77		43
10	Crewe Alexandra	42	12	4	5	41	24	6	3	12	20	39	61	63		43
11	Oldham Athletic	42	6	10	5	25	25	8	3	10	38	39	63	64		41
12	Rochdale	42	12	4	5	32	23	3	7	11	16	49	48	72		41
13	York City	42	8	7	6	38	25	5	7	9	27	35	65	60		40
14	Bradford City	42	10	4	7	38	27	5	6	10	27	39	65	66		40
15	Southport	42	10	4	7	34	27	4	7	10	26	36	60	63		39
16	Darlington	42	7	8	6	30	31	6	5	10	24	39	54	70		39
17	Stockport County	42	9	6	6	42	28	4	6	11	21	39	63	67		38
18	Tranmere Rovers	42	10	1	10	30	28	6	3	12	24	44	54	72		36
19	Hartlepools United	42	10	6	5	34	23	4	2	15	17	50	51	73		36
20	Chester	42	11	6	4	44	25	2	3	16	20	42	64	67		35
21	Halifax Town	42	4	10	7	25	27	3	3	15	18	49	43	76		27
22	New Brighton	42	5	6	10	20	28	3	3	15	18	53	38	81		25

~ 216 ~

1947-48
Back Row: N. Fowler, J. Taylor, W. Bly, T. Berry, H. Meens, J. Greenhalgh;
Insets: G. Murphy, J. Bloomer, A. Corbett, W. Hassall;
Front Row: A. Bloxham, H. Carter (player-manager), N. Moore, W. Buchan, D. Durham.

1948-49
Standing: J. Lodge (Asst. Trainer), J. Greenhalgh, J. Taylor, W. Bly, H. Meens, A. Mellor, J. Berry, G. Lax (Trainer);
Sitting: K. Harrison, V. Jensen, N. Moore, W. Buchan, H. Carter (player-manager).

1948/49 Champions of Division Three (North): Promoted

#	Date	Opponent	Score	Scorers	Att	Berry T	Bloxham A	Bly W	Buchan W	Burbanks E	Carter H	Conway A	Durham D	Fowler N	Greenhalgh J	Harrison K	Jensen V	King G	Meens H	Mellor A	Moore N	Price W	Robinson J	Shepherd E	Taylor J	White K	Wright J
1	Aug 21	Tranmere Rovers	2-1	Moore, Harrison	10107	3		1	10	11	8		6	2	4	7				5	9						
2	26	OLDHAM ATHLETIC	6-0	Carter 2,Harrison,Greenhalgh,Moore 2	32679	3		1		11	8	10	6	2	4	7				5	9						
3	28	MANSFIELD TOWN	4-0	Moore 2, Buchan, Harrison	34075	3		1	10	11	8		6	2	4	7				5	9						
4	Sep 4	Barrow	2-1	Burbanks, Conway	12759	3		1		11	8	10	6	2	4	7				5	9						
5	9	ACCRINGTON STANLEY	3-1	Carter, Conway, Durham	33512	3		1		11	8	10	6	2	4	7				5	9						
6	11	WREXHAM	3-0	Moore 2, Buchan	32075	3		1	10	11	8		6	2	4	7				5	9						
7	18	Halifax Town	4-2	Greenhalgh,Harrison,Burbanks,Moore	18563	3		1	10	11	8		6	2	4	7				5	9						
8	25	BRADFORD CITY	2-0	Carter, Burbanks	36207	3		1	10	11	8		6	2	4	7				5	9						
9	28	Accrington Stanley	2-1	Harrison, Burbanks	13162	3		1	10	11	8		6	2	4	7				5	9						
10	Oct 2	Doncaster Rovers	0-0		37099	3		1	10	11	8				4	7		9	5	6					2		
11	9	Hartlepools United	2-0	Burbanks, Moore,	17118	3		1	10	11	8				4	7			5	6	9				2		
12	16	DARLINGTON	0-1		43801	3		1	10	11	8				4	7			5	6	9				2		
13	23	Rochdale	1-1	Harrison	14967	3		1	10	11	8				4	7			5	6	9				2		
14	30	NEW BRIGHTON	4-1	Moore, Carter, Burbanks, Jensen	31039	3		1		11	10				4	7	8		5	6	9				2		
15	Nov 6	Chester	2-0	Carter, Jensen	13509	3		1		11	10				4	7	8		5	6	9				2		
16	13	SOUTHPORT	5-1	Burbanks 2,Carter,Jensen,Moore	25215	3		1		11	10				4	7	8		5	6	9				2		
17	20	Crewe Alexandra	0-0		11138	3		1		11	10				4	7	8		5	6	9				2		
18	Dec 4	Stockport County	0-0		15049	3		1		11	10				4	7	8		5	6	9				2		
19	25	ROTHERHAM UNITED	3-2	Buchan 2, Bloxham	49655	3	11	1	10		9				4	7	8		5	6					2		
20	27	Rotherham United	0-0		22159	3	11	1	10		9			2	4	7	8		5	6					3		
21	Jan 1	Mansfield Town	1-1	Buchan	11735	3	11	1	10						4	7	8		5	6	9				2		
22	15	BARROW	3-0	Price 2, Carter	26881	3		1	10					11	4	7	8		5	6		9			2		
23	22	Wrexham	2-0	Price, Greenhalgh	18551	3		1	10					11	4	7	8		5	6		9			2		
24	Feb 5	HALIFAX TOWN	6-0	Jensen 3, Buchan 2, Mellor	37114	3		1	10				2	11	4	7	8		5	6		9					
25	19	Bradford City	2-4	Jensen, Harrison	27083	3		1	10					11		7	8		5	6		9			2	4	
26	Mar 5	HARTLEPOOLS UNITED	2-0	Carter, Price	35357	3	11		8		10				4	7			5	6		9	1		2		
27	12	Darlington	1-0	Shepherd	17978	3					10				4	7			5	6		9	1	11	2		
28	19	ROCHDALE	1-1	Price	36509	3					10				4	7	8		5	6		9	1	11	2		
29	23	CARLISLE UNITED	3-0	Carter, Moore, Simpson (og)	36864	3		1		11	10				4	7	8		5	6	9				2		
30	26	New Brighton	0-0		8650	3		1		11	10				4	7	8		5	6	9				2		
31	30	TRANMERE ROVERS	2-0	Harrison 2	33008			1	10	11	8			2	4	7			5	6	9				3		
32	Apr 2	CHESTER	3-2	Jensen, Moore 2	36167			1	10	11				2	4	7	8		5	6	9				3		
33	6	YORK CITY	2-3	Carter, Moore	40002	5				11	10			2	4	7	8			6	9		1		3		
34	9	Southport	0-0		10010	5		1	10		8	6			4	7	2					9		11	3		
35	15	GATESHEAD	2-0	Harrison, Jensen	43795	3		1		11	10	6			4	7	8		5		9				2		
36	16	CREWE ALEXANDRA	5-0	Burbanks, Jensen 2, Moore 2	38089	3		1		11	10	6			4	7	8		5		9				2		
37	18	Gateshead	2-0	Harrison, Moore	17538	3		1		11	10	6			4	7	8		5		9				2		
38	23	York City	3-1	Carter, Moore, Jensen	21010	3		1		11	10	6			4	7	8		5		9				2		
39	26	Oldham Athletic	1-1	Harrison	35200	3		1		11	10	6			4	7	8		5		9				2		
40	30	Stockport County	6-1	Moore 3, Carter 2, Jensen	38192	3		1		11	10				4	7	8		5	6	9			11	2		
41	May 4	DONCASTER ROVERS	0-1		46725	3		1		11	10				4	7	8		5	6	9			11	2		
42	7	Carlisle United	1-1	Jensen	15519	3		1	10						4	7	8		5	6	9			11	2		
		Apps				39	4	38	22	28	39	3	15	14	41	42	27	1	40	27	31	8	4	6	32	1	
		Goals					1		7	9	14	2	1		3	12	14			1	22	5			1		

One own goal

F.A. Cup

Rd	Date	Opponent	Score	Scorers	Att	Berry T	Bloxham A	Bly W	Buchan W	Burbanks E	Carter H	Conway A	Durham D	Fowler N	Greenhalgh J	Harrison K	Jensen V	King G	Meens H	Mellor A	Moore N	Price W	Robinson J	Shepherd E	Taylor J	White K	Wright J
R1	Nov 27	ACCRINGTON STANLEY	3-1	Carter 2, Jensen	21926	3		1		11	10				4	7	8		5	6	9				2		
R2	Dec 11	READING	0-0		29692	3		1	8	11	10				4	7	9		5	6					2		
rep	18	Reading	2-1	Moore 2	21920	3	11	1			10				4	7	8				6	9			2	5	
R3	Jan 8	Blackburn Rovers	2-1	Moore, Buchan	33200	3	11	1	10						4	7	8		5	6	9				2		
R4	29	Grimsby Town	3-2	Moore 2, Carter	26505	3		1	10	11					4	7	8		5	6	9				2		
R5	Feb 12	Stoke City	2-0	Moore, Greenhalgh	46738	3		1	10	11					4	7	8		5	6	9				2		
R6	26	MANCHESTER UNITED	0-1		55019	3		1	10	11					4	7	8		5	6	9				2		

R2 and R3 games a.e.t.

		Pl	Home					Away					F.	A.	Pts
			W	D	L	F	A	W	D	L	F	A			(Total)
1	HULL CITY	42	17	1	3	65	14	10	10	1	28	14	93	28	65
2	Rotherham United	42	16	4	1	47	17	12	2	7	43	29	90	46	62
3	Doncaster Rovers	42	10	8	3	26	12	10	2	9	27	28	53	40	50
4	Darlington	42	10	3	8	42	36	10	3	8	41	38	83	74	46
5	Gateshead	42	10	6	5	41	28	6	7	8	28	30	69	58	45
6	Oldham Athletic	42	12	4	5	49	28	6	5	10	26	39	75	67	45
7	Rochdale	42	14	3	4	37	16	4	6	11	18	37	55	53	45
8	Stockport County	42	13	5	3	44	16	3	6	12	17	40	61	56	43
9	Wrexham	42	12	6	3	35	22	5	3	13	21	40	56	62	43
10	Mansfield Town	42	13	6	2	39	15	1	8	12	13	33	52	48	42
11	Tranmere Rovers	42	8	9	4	23	19	5	6	10	23	38	46	57	41
12	Crewe Alexandra	42	13	4	4	31	18	3	5	13	21	56	52	74	41
13	Barrow	42	10	8	3	27	13	4	4	13	14	35	41	48	40
14	York City	42	11	3	7	49	28	4	6	11	25	46	74	74	39
15	Carlisle United	42	12	7	2	46	32	2	4	15	14	45	60	77	39
16	Hartlepools United	42	10	5	6	34	25	4	5	12	11	33	45	58	38
17	New Brighton	42	10	4	7	25	19	4	4	13	21	39	46	58	36
18	Chester	42	10	7	4	36	19	1	6	14	21	37	57	56	35
19	Halifax Town	42	8	4	9	26	27	4	7	10	19	35	45	62	35
20	Accrington Stanley	42	11	4	6	39	23	1	6	14	16	41	55	64	34
21	Southport	42	6	5	10	24	29	5	4	12	21	35	45	64	31
22	Bradford City	42	7	6	8	29	31	3	3	15	19	46	48	77	29

1949/50 7th in Division Two

#	Date		Opponent	Score	Scorers	Att	Berry T	Bloxham A	Bly W	Bowler G	Burbanks E	Carter H	Durham D	Fowler N	Gibson A	Gibson R	Greenhalgh J	Harris W	Harrison K	Hassall W	Jensen V	Lee, Jimmy	Meens H	Mellor A	Moore N	Neal J	Revie D	Robinson J	Seddon F	Shepherd E	Smith F	Taylor J
1	Aug	20	BURY	3-2	Moore, Carter, Burbanks	42666	3		1	5	11	10					4		7		8				6	9						2
2		22	Blackburn Rovers	2-4	Jensen, Harrison	30982	3		1	5	11	10					4		7		8				6	9						2
3		27	Leicester City	2-1	Carter, Burbanks	37659	3		1	5	11	10					4		7		8				6	9						2
4	Sep	1	BLACKBURN ROVERS	3-1	Moore 2, Harrison	43812	3		1	5	11	10		2			4		7		8				6	9						
5		3	BRADFORD PARK AVE.	3-3	Carter 2, Moore	41624	3		1	5	11	10		2			4		7		8				6	9						
6		5	Cardiff City	0-2		40254			1	5	11	10		2			4		7	3	8				6	9						
7		10	Chesterfield	1-0	Carter	22868			1	5	11	10					4		7	2	8				6	9						3
8		17	PLYMOUTH ARGYLE	4-2	Moore 2, Jensen, Carter	38296	3		1	5	11	10					4		7	2	8				6	9						
9		24	Sheffield Wednesday	2-6	Jensen 2	52403	3		1	5	11	10					4		7		8				6	9						2
10	Oct	1	GRIMSBY TOWN	2-2	Carter, Jensen	46282	3		1		11	10					4		7		8				6	9				5		2
11		8	Queen's Park Rangers	4-1	Carter 2, Jensen, Harrison	28725	3		1	2	11	10					4		7		8				6	9				5		
12		15	PRESTON NORTH END	4-2	Moore 2, Burbanks, Jensen	46179	3		1	2	11	10					4		7		8				6	9				5		
13		22	Swansea Town	2-1	Burbanks, Jensen	22275	3		1	2	11	10					4		7		8			5	6	9						
14		29	LEEDS UNITED	1-0	Jensen	47638	3		1	2	11	10					4		7		8			5	6	9						
15	Nov	5	Southampton	0-5		23275	3		1	2	11	10					4		7		8			5	6	9						
16		12	COVENTRY CITY	2-1	Carter 2	40170	3		1	2	11	10					4		7		9			5	6		8					
17		19	Luton Town	3-0	Carter, Harrison, Mellor	22269	3		1			10					4		7		2			5	6	9	8			11		
18		26	BARNSLEY	2-0	Shepherd, Carter	31521	3		1	5		10					4		7		2				6	9	8			11		
19	Dec	3	West Ham United	1-2	Harrison	29421	3		1	5		10					4		7		2				6	9	8			11		
20		10	SHEFFIELD UNITED	0-4		28853	3		1	5		10				9	4		7		2				6		8			11		
21		17	Bury	0-0		17519	3	11	1	5		10				9			7		4				6		8					2
22		24	LEICESTER CITY	4-0	Moore 2, Harrison 2	35207	3		1	5	11	10							7		4				6	9	8					2
23		26	Brentford	1-3	Carter	33791			1	5	11	10							7		4		3	6	9		8					2
24		27	BRENTFORD	2-0	Jensen, Shepherd	48447			1			10				9	4		7	2	8			5	6					11		3
25		31	Bradford Park Avenue	1-5	Gibson R	27020	3		1			10				9	4		7		8			5	6					11		2
26	Jan	14	CHESTERFIELD	1-0	Harrison	37895	3		1	5							4		7	2	10				6	9	8			11		
27		21	Plymouth Argyle	3-1	Moore, Jensen, Greenhalgh	29535			1	5		11					4		7	2	10				6	9	8					3
28	Feb	4	SHEFFIELD WEDNESDAY	1-1	Jensen	49900	2		1	5	11	9					4		7		10				6		8					3
29		18	Grimsby Town	0-1		26476	2		1	5	11	9					4		7		10				6		8					3
30		25	QUEEN'S PARK RANGERS	1-1	Carter	24586	2		1	5	11	10							7		4				6	9	8	1				3
31	Mar	4	Preston North End	2-4	Harrison, Gibson R	27745	2		1	5	11	10				9			7		4				6			1			8	3
32		11	SWANSEA TOWN	0-0		32873	2		1	5		10				9	4				8				6			1		11	7	3
33		18	Leeds United	0-3		49465			1	5		9			2		4		7		10				6		8	1		11		3
34		25	SOUTHAMPTON	1-2	Gibson R	31937	3		1	5	11	10			2	9	4		7		8				6							
35	Apr	1	Barnsley	1-1	Gibson R	22045	3	11	1	5		10			2	9			7						6		4			8		
36		7	Tottenham Hotspur	0-0		66889	3		1	5	11	10	6		2	9			7								4			8		
37		8	WEST HAM UNITED	2-2	Gibson R, Bloxham	31049	3	11	1	5		10	6		2	9			7								4			8		
38		10	TOTTENHAM HOTSPUR	1-0	Smith	38345	3	11	1	5		10	6			9			7								4			8	2	
39		15	Coventry City	0-2		25518	3	11	1	5			6		2	9	10		7								4			8		
40		22	LUTON TOWN	1-1	Carter	28205		7	1	5		10			2	6			11			9					3	4		8		
41		29	Sheffield United	0-5		29626			1	5		10			2			7	11		6	9					4			8	3	
42	May	6	CARDIFF CITY	1-1	Lee	18213	3		1	5			6		2		4	7	11		10	9					8					
			Apps				34	6	38	38	24	39	5	3	9	12	32	2	41	6	36	3	8	35	23	1	22	4	3	9	9	20
			Goals					1			4	16				5	1		9		12	1			1	11				2	1	

F.A. Cup

	Date		Opponent	Score	Scorers	Att	Bly W	Bowler G	Burbanks E	Carter H	Greenhalgh J	Harrison K	Hassall W	Jensen V	Mellor A	Moore N	Revie D	Taylor J
R3	Jan	7	Southport	0-0		15617	1	5	11	10		7	2	4	6	9	8	3
rep		12	SOUTHPORT	5-0	Moore,Revie,Harrison,Burbanks,Greenhalgh	28018	1	5	11	10	4	7	2		6	9	8	3
R4		28	Stockport County	0-0		26600	1	5		11	4	7	2	10	6	9	8	3
rep	Feb	2	STOCKPORT COUNTY	0-2		24556	1	5	11	10	4	7	2	8	6	9		3

		Pl	Home				Away					F.	A.	Pts
			W	D	L	F	A	W	D	L	F	A	(Total)	
1	Tottenham Hotspur	42	15	3	3	51	15	12	4	5	30	20	81 35	61
2	Sheffield Wed.	42	12	7	2	46	23	6	9	6	21	25	67 48	52
3	Sheffield United	42	9	10	2	36	19	10	4	7	32	30	68 49	52
4	Southampton	42	13	4	4	44	25	6	10	5	20	23	64 48	52
5	Leeds United	42	11	8	2	33	16	6	5	10	21	29	54 45	47
6	Preston North End	42	12	5	4	37	21	6	4	11	23	28	60 49	45
7	HULL CITY	42	11	8	2	39	25	6	3	12	25	47	64 72	45
8	Swansea Town	42	11	3	7	34	18	6	6	9	19	31	53 49	43
9	Brentford	42	11	5	5	21	12	4	8	9	23	37	44 49	43
10	Cardiff City	42	13	3	5	28	14	3	7	11	13	30	41 44	42
11	Grimsby Town	42	13	5	3	53	25	3	3	15	21	48	74 73	40
12	Coventry City	42	8	6	7	32	24	5	7	9	23	31	55 55	39
13	Barnsley	42	11	6	4	45	28	2	7	12	19	39	64 67	39
14	Chesterfield	42	12	3	6	28	16	3	6	12	15	31	43 47	39
15	Leicester City	42	8	9	4	30	25	4	6	11	25	40	55 65	39
16	Blackburn Rovers	42	10	5	6	30	15	4	5	12	25	45	55 60	38
17	Luton Town	42	8	9	4	28	22	2	9	10	13	29	41 51	38
18	Bury	42	10	8	3	37	19	4	1	16	23	46	60 65	37
19	West Ham United	42	8	7	6	30	25	4	5	12	23	36	53 61	36
20	Queen's Park Rgs.	42	6	5	10	21	30	5	7	9	19	27	40 57	34
21	Plymouth Argyle	42	6	6	9	19	24	2	10	9	25	41	44 65	32
22	Bradford Park Ave.	42	7	6	8	34	34	3	5	13	17	43	51 77	31

1949-50
Back Row: V. Jensen, J. Taylor, G. Bowler, W. Bly, T. Berry, A. Mellor;
Front Row: K. Harrison, H. Carter, D. Revie, R. Gibson, A. Bloxham.

1950-51
Back Row: J. Varney, D. Revie, J. Robinson, T. Berry, W. Harris, V. Jensen;
Front Row: G. Lax (Trainer), W. Hassall, K. Harrison, H. Carter (Player-manager), A. Ackerman, S. Gerrie, E. Burbanks.

1950/51   10th in Division Two

#		Date	Opponent	Score	Scorers	Att	Ackerman A	Berry T	Bly W	Burbanks E	Carter H	Durham D	Franklin C	Gaynor L	Gerrie S	Gibson A	Greenhalgh J	Harris W	Harrison K	Hassall W	Inwood G	Jensen V	Meens H	Mellor A	Revie D	Robinson J	Savage J	Smith F	Tarrant E	Varney J
1	Aug	19	West Ham United	3-3	Ackerman 2, Carter	30056	9	3	1	11	10					2		7				4	5	6	8					
2		24	BARNSLEY	3-3	Ackerman, Carter 2	41949	9	3	1	11	10					2		7				4	5	6	8					
3		26	SWANSEA TOWN	2-1	Carter, Revie	35333	9	3	1	11	10					2		7				4	5	6	8					
4		30	Barnsley	2-4	Ackerman, Carter	24583	9	3	1	11	10					2		7				4	5	6	8					
5	Sep	2	GRIMSBY TOWN	2-1	Carter 2	38332	9	3		11	10	6				2	4	7				5			8	1				
6		6	Luton Town	2-1	Ackerman 2	14905	9	5		11	10	6				2	4	7				3			8	1				
7		9	DONCASTER ROVERS	1-2	Carter	40218	9	5		11	10	6				2	4	7				3			8	1				
8		16	BRENTFORD	3-0	Carter 2, Revie	31925	9	5		11	10	6				2	4	7				3			8	1				
9		23	Blackburn Rovers	2-2	Carter, Harrison	28904	9	5		11	10					2	4	7				3			8	1		6		
10		30	SOUTHAMPTON	4-1	Ackerman 2, Harrison 2	22795	9	5		11	10					2	4	7				3			8	1		6		
11	Oct	7	LEICESTER CITY	1-3	Ackerman	33609	9	5		11	10					2	4	7				3			8	1		6		
12		14	Chesterfield	0-0		17486	9		1	11	10							7	2			3	5	6	4			8		
13		21	COVENTRY CITY	0-2		33227		5		7								9	2	11	3			6	4		1	8		
14		28	Manchester City	0-0		45842	9	5			10							4	7	2	11			6	8	1				3
15	Nov	4	BIRMINGHAM CITY	3-2	Carter, Harrison 2	32038	9	5		11	10							4	7	2				6	8	1				3
16		11	Cardiff City	1-2	Harrison	25007	9	5		11	10				8			6	7	2		3			4	1				3
17		18	QUEEN'S PARK RANGERS	5-1	Ackerman 3, Carter, Gerrie	33866	9	5		11	10				8			6	7	2		3			4	1				
18		25	Bury	2-0	Gerrie, Harrison	15239	9	5		11					10	4		6	7	2		3			8	1				
19	Dec	2	PRESTON NORTH END	0-0		37269	9	5		11					8			6	7	2		3			4	1			10	
20		9	Notts County	2-2	Carter, Gerrie,	32708	9	5		11					8			6	7	2		3			4	1			10	
21		16	WEST HAM UNITED	1-2	Burbanks	20623	9	5		11					10			4	7	2		3		6	8	1				
22		23	Swansea Town	0-1		16371	9	5		11					10			4	7	2		3		6	8	1				
23		25	Sheffield United	1-3	Ackerman	34043	9	5										4	7	2	11	3				1		8		
24		26	SHEFFIELD UNITED	1-1	Revie	37145		5		11					9				7	2				6	10	1		8		3
25		30	Grimsby Town	1-1	Carter	20668		5		11	10				9			6	7	2					4	1		8		3
26	Jan	13	Doncaster Rovers	4-2	Ackerman, Carter, Gerrie, Revie	30604	9	5		11	8				10			6	7	2		3			4	1				
27		20	Brentford	1-2	Revie	20523	9	5		11	8				10			6	7	2		3			4	1				
28	Feb	3	BLACKBURN ROVERS	2-2	Gerrie, Ackerman	38786	9			11	8		5		10			6	7	2		3			4	1				
29		17	Southampton	3-2	Carter, Gerrie, Harrison	23710	9			11	8		5		10			6	7	2		3			4	1				
30		24	Leicester City	0-4		35451	9			11	8		5		10			6	7	2		3			4		1			
31	Mar	3	CHESTERFIELD	2-1	Ackerman, Burbanks	30913	9	3		11	8		5		10			6	7	2					4		1			
32		10	Coventry City	1-4	Revie	22650	9	3		11			5		10			6	7	2				4	8		1			
33		17	MANCHESTER CITY	3-3	Carter 2, Harrison	26840		3		11	10		5		9			6	7	2				4	8		1			
34		23	LEEDS UNITED	2-0	Carter, Harrison	46701				11	10		5		9			6	7	2				4	8	1				3
35		24	Birmingham City	1-2	Harrison	27512				11	10		5		9	3		6	7	2				4	8	1				3
36		26	Leeds United	0-3		27889	9			11			5					7	2			4		6	8	1			10	3
37		31	CARDIFF CITY	2-0	Ackerman, Gerrie	20239	11				10		5		9			7	2			4		6	8	1				3
38	Apr	7	Queen's Park Rangers	1-3	Ackerman	14628	11				10		5		9			7	2			4		6	8	1				3
39		14	BURY	4-0	Gerrie 2, Harrison, Revie	25841				11	10		5		9			7	2			3		6	8	1			4	
40		21	Preston North End	0-1		37827	8			11	10		5		9			7	2			3		6	8	1			4	
41		28	NOTTS COUNTY	1-0	Gerrie	24190		5		11	10				9			7	2			3		6	8	1			4	
42	May	5	LUTON TOWN	5-3	Ackerman,Gerrie,Harrison,Revie,Shanks(og)	17478	8			11			5		9			7	2			3		6	10	1			4	
				Apps			34	30	5	38	32	4	14	2	23	12	7	22	42	31	3	35	6	20	41	33	4	8	7	9
				Goals			21			2	19				11				12						8					

One own goal

F.A. Cup

		Date	Opponent	Score	Scorers	Att	Ackerman A	Berry T	Bly W	Burbanks E	Carter H	Durham D	Franklin C	Gaynor L	Gerrie S	Gibson A	Greenhalgh J	Harris W	Harrison K	Hassall W	Inwood G	Jensen V	Meens H	Mellor A	Revie D	Robinson J	Savage J	Smith F	Tarrant E	Varney J
R3	Jan	6	EVERTON	2-0	Carter, Gerrie	36,465	9	5		11	8				10			6	7	2		3			4	1				
R4		27	ROTHERHAM UNITED	2-0	Carter, Harrison	50,040	9	5		11	8				10			6	7	2		3			4	1				
R5	Feb	10	Bristol Rovers	0-3		30,724	9			11	8				10			6	7	2	10	5			4	1				3

		Pl	Home					Away					F.	A.	Pts
			W	D	L	F	A	W	D	L	F	A	(Total)		
1	Preston North End	42	16	3	2	53	18	10	2	9	38	31	91	49	57
2	Manchester City	42	12	6	3	53	25	7	8	6	36	36	89	61	52
3	Cardiff City	42	13	7	1	36	20	4	9	8	17	25	53	45	50
4	Birmingham City	42	12	6	3	37	20	8	3	10	27	33	64	53	49
5	Leeds United	42	14	4	3	36	17	6	4	11	27	38	63	55	48
6	Blackburn Rovers	42	13	3	5	39	27	6	5	10	26	39	65	66	46
7	Coventry City	42	15	3	3	51	25	4	4	13	24	34	75	59	45
8	Sheffield United	42	11	4	6	44	27	5	8	8	28	35	72	62	44
9	Brentford	42	13	3	5	44	25	5	5	11	31	49	75	74	44
10	HULL CITY	42	12	5	4	47	28	4	6	11	27	42	74	70	43
11	Doncaster Rovers	42	9	6	6	37	32	6	7	8	27	36	64	68	43
12	Southampton	42	10	9	2	38	27	5	4	12	28	46	66	73	43
13	West Ham United	42	10	5	6	44	33	6	5	10	24	36	68	69	42
14	Leicester City	42	10	4	7	42	28	5	7	9	26	30	68	58	41
15	Barnsley	42	9	5	7	42	22	6	5	10	32	46	74	68	40
16	Queen's Park Rgs.	42	13	5	3	47	25	2	5	14	24	57	71	82	40
17	Notts County	42	7	7	7	37	34	6	6	9	24	26	61	60	39
18	Swansea Town	42	14	1	6	34	25	2	3	16	20	52	54	77	36
19	Luton Town	42	7	9	5	34	23	2	5	14	23	47	57	70	32
20	Bury	42	9	4	8	33	27	3	4	14	27	59	60	86	32
21	Chesterfield	42	7	7	7	30	28	2	5	14	14	41	44	69	30
22	Grimsby Town	42	6	8	7	37	38	2	4	15	24	57	61	95	28

1951/52 — 18th in Division Two

#	Date	Opponent	Score	Scorers	Att	Berry T	Bly W	Burbanks E	Carter H	Durham D	Duthie J	Fagan F	Franklin C	Gerrie S	Harris W	Harrison K	Hassall W	Jensen V	Linaker J	Meens H	Mellor A	Moore A	Murray T	Nicklas C	Phillips E	Porteous T	Revie D	Robinson J	Robson L	Tarrant E	Todd P
1	Aug 18	BARNSLEY	0-0		37057		1	11	10		9		5		4	7	2	3			6						8				
2	20	Queen's Park Rangers	1-1	Duthie	15809		1	11		6	9		5	10	4	7	2	3									8				
3	25	Sheffield United	1-4	Duthie	34433		1	11		6	9		5	10	4	7	2	3									8				
4	30	QUEEN'S PARK RANGERS	4-1	Gerrie 3, Revie	19661		1	11		6	9		5	10	4		2	3				7					8				
5	Sep 1	WEST HAM UNITED	1-1	Moore	33444		1	11		6	9		5	10	4		2	3				7					8				
6	6	Notts County	0-4		38203		1	11		6	9		5	10	4		2	3				7					8				
7	8	Coventry City	4-1	Moore, Harrison, Gerrie, Revie	25328		1	11					5	9	4	10	2	3				7					8			6	
8	15	SWANSEA TOWN	5-2	Gerrie 3, Revie 2	27947		1	11					5	9	4	10	2	3				7					8			6	
9	20	NOTTS COUNTY	1-3	Gerrie	35499		1	11					5	9	4	10	2	3				7					8			6	
10	22	Bury	1-3	Moore	16869		1					11	5	9	4	10		3			6	7					8			2	
11	29	LUTON TOWN	1-2	Harris	29646		1					11		9	4	10	2	3			6	7					8			5	
12	Oct 6	Southampton	1-1	Gerrie	22823		1			3		11		9	6	7	2	4	5								8				10
13	13	SHEFFIELD WEDNESDAY	0-1		34011		1	11		3				9	6	7	2	4	5								8				10
14	20	Leeds United	0-2		24656		1			3	8			9	6	11	2	4	7	5											10
15	27	ROTHERHAM UNITED	3-3	Gerrie, Harrison, Nicklas	31369	5	1			3				8		11	2	4	7					9		6					10
16	Nov 3	Cardiff City	0-1		23459	5	1	11		3				8			2	4	7					9		6					10
17	10	BIRMINGHAM CITY	0-1		27482	5	1			3		11		9	4			8	7						2	6					10
18	17	Leicester City	0-1		25041	5	1			3				9	8	11	2	4	7							6					10
19	24	NOTTM. FOREST	1-4	Jensen	24924	5	1			3				9		11		4	7						2	6			10		8
20	Dec 1	Brentford	1-2	Robson	26072	5	1			3				9		11		4	7						2				10	6	8
21	8	DONCASTER ROVERS	2-0	Burbanks, Gerrie	28533	5	1	11	8					9	4	7	2	3												6	10
22	15	Barnsley	2-2	Carter, Gerrie	12821	5	1	11	8					9	4	7	2	3												6	10
23	22	SHEFFIELD UNITED	2-1	Gerrie 2	26998	5	1	11	8					9	4	7	2	3												6	10
24	25	Blackburn Rovers	0-1		34077	5	1	11						9	4	7	2	3											10	6	8
25	26	BLACKBURN ROVERS	3-0	Gerrie, Todd, Harrison	36689	5	1	11	8	6				9	4	7	2	3													10
26	29	West Ham United	0-2		19631	5	1	11	8	6				9	4		2	3				7									10
27	Jan 5	COVENTRY CITY	5-0	Gerrie 2, Moore, Carter, Burbanks	25648	5	1	11	8	6				9	4		2	3				7									10
28	19	Swansea Town	0-3		17097	5		11	8	6				9	4	7	2	3										1			10
29	26	BURY	5-0	Gerrie 4, Todd	26744	5		11	8	6				9	4	7	2	3										1			10
30	Feb 9	Luton Town	1-1	Carter	16550	5		11	8	6				9	4		2	3	7									1			10
31	16	SOUTHAMPTON	0-0		26480	5		11	8	6				9	4	7	2	3										1			10
32	Mar 1	Sheffield Wednesday	0-6		41832	5		11	8	6				9	4	7	2	3										1			10
33	8	LEEDS UNITED	3-2	Carter 2, Gerrie	28767	5	1	11	10	6				8	4	7	2	3					9								
34	15	Rotherham United	1-1	Burbanks	19069	5	1	11	10	6		7		8	4		2	3					9								
35	22	CARDIFF CITY	0-0		27009	5	1	11	10	6		7		8	4		2	3					9								
36	29	Birmingham City	2-2	Carter, Harris	14660	5	1	11	10	6				9	8	7	2	4							3						
37	Apr 5	LEICESTER CITY	3-1	Carter, Harrison, Gerrie	24378	5	1	11	10	6				9	8	7	2	4							3						
38	11	Everton	0-5		42980	5	1	11	10	6				9	8	7	2	4							3						
39	12	Nottingham Forest	0-4		26201	5	1	11	8					9	6	7	2	4							3						10
40	14	EVERTON	1-0	Gerrie	30240	5		11	10	6				9	4	7	2	3				8						1			
41	19	BRENTFORD	4-1	Burbanks, Harrison, Duthie, Durham	30891	5		11	10	6	9				4	7	2	3				8						1			
42	26	Doncaster Rovers	1-0	Carter	24476	5		11	10	6				9	4	7	2	3				8						1			
		Apps				26	34	33	22	30	9	6	13	38	38	32	37	42	5	3	3	13	3	6	7	5	13	8	3	11	22
		Goals						4	8	1	3			24	2	5		1				4		1			4			1	2

F.A. Cup

Round	Date	Opponent	Score	Scorers	Att	Berry T	Bly W	Burbanks E	Carter H	Durham D	Duthie J	Fagan F	Franklin C	Gerrie S	Harris W	Harrison K	Hassall W	Jensen V	Linaker J	Meens H	Mellor A	Moore A	Murray T	Nicklas C	Phillips E	Porteous T	Revie D	Robinson J	Robson L	Tarrant E	Todd P
R3	Jan 12	Manchester United	2-0	Harrison, Gerrie	43517	5		11	8	6				9	4	7	2	3										1			10
R4	Feb 2	Blackburn Rovers	0-2		45320	5		11	8	6				9	4		2	3	7									1			10

		Pl	Home					Away					F.	A.	Pts
			W	D	L	F	A	W	D	L	F	A	(Total)		
1	Sheffield Wed.	42	14	4	3	54	23	7	7	7	46	43	100	66	53
2	Cardiff City	42	18	2	1	52	15	2	9	10	20	39	72	54	51
3	Birmingham City	42	11	6	4	36	21	10	3	8	31	35	67	56	51
4	Nottingham Forest	42	12	6	3	41	22	6	7	8	36	40	77	62	49
5	Leicester City	42	12	6	3	48	24	7	3	11	30	40	78	64	47
6	Leeds United	42	13	7	1	35	15	5	4	12	24	42	59	57	47
7	Everton	42	12	5	4	42	25	5	5	11	22	33	64	58	44
8	Luton Town	42	9	7	5	46	35	7	5	9	31	43	77	78	44
9	Rotherham United	42	11	4	6	40	25	6	4	11	33	46	73	71	42
10	Brentford	42	11	7	3	34	20	4	5	12	20	35	54	55	42
11	Sheffield United	42	13	2	6	57	28	5	3	13	33	48	90	76	41
12	West Ham United	42	13	5	3	48	29	2	6	13	19	48	67	77	41
13	Southampton	42	11	6	4	40	25	4	5	12	21	48	61	73	41
14	Blackburn Rovers	42	11	3	7	35	30	6	3	12	19	33	54	63	40
15	Notts County	42	11	5	5	45	27	5	2	14	26	41	71	68	39
16	Doncaster Rovers	42	9	4	8	29	28	4	8	9	26	32	55	60	38
17	Bury	42	13	2	6	43	22	2	5	14	24	47	67	69	37
18	HULL CITY	42	11	5	5	44	23	2	6	13	16	47	60	70	37
19	Swansea Town	42	10	4	7	45	26	2	8	11	27	50	72	76	36
20	Barnsley	42	8	7	6	39	33	3	7	11	20	39	59	72	36
21	Coventry City	42	9	5	7	36	33	5	1	15	23	49	59	82	34
22	Queen's Park Rgs.	42	8	8	5	35	35	3	4	14	17	46	52	81	34

1951-52
Back Row: W. Hassall, V. Jensen, W. Bly, H. Meens, W. Harris, D. Durham;
Front Row: K. Harrison, D. Revie, S. Gerrie, P. Todd, E. Burbanks.

1952-53
Left – Right: D. Durham, E. Phillips, W. Bly, W. Harris, V. Jensen, S. Gerrie, B. Cripsey, J. Linaker, T. Murray, T. Berry, T. Tarrant, K. Horton.

1952/53   18th in Division Two

#	Date	Opponent	Score / Scorers	Att	Berry T	Bly W	Bulless B	Burbanks E	Bursell C	Cripsey B	Davidson A	Durham D	Duthie J	Fagan F	Feasey P	Franklin C	Gerrie S	Harris W	Harrison F	Harrison K	Hassall W	Horton K	Jensen V	Linaker J	Murray T	Neal J	Phillips E	Porteous T	Robinson J	Stephens J	Tarrant E	Todd P
1	Aug 23	Everton	2-0 Jensen 2	43035	3			11				6				5	9	4				2	10	7	8				1			
2	25	WEST HAM UNITED	1-0 Gerrie	35964	3			11				6				5	9	4				2	10	7	8				1			
3	30	BRENTFORD	2-2 Jensen 2	35993	3			11				6				5	9	4				2	10	7	8				1			
4	Sep 1	West Ham United	0-0	19726	3			11				6				5	9	4				2	10	7	8				1			
5	6	Doncaster Rovers	1-3 Jensen	21150	3			11				6				5	9	4				2	10	7	8				1			
6	8	Blackburn Rovers	0-2	21146	3						9	6	7				8	4		5	11	2	10						1			
7	13	SWANSEA TOWN	1-1 Harris	29088	3						9	6					8	4		5	11	2	10	7					1			
8	15	BLACKBURN ROVERS	3-0 Davidson, Harrison K 2	24849	3						9	6				5	8	4			11	2	10	7					1			
9	20	Huddersfield Town	1-1 Gerrie	34411	3						9	6				5	8	4			11	2	10	7					1			
10	27	SHEFFIELD UNITED	4-0 Burbanks, Linaker, Gerrie, Tarrant	32065	3			11				6				5	8	4				2	10	7					1		9	
11	Oct 4	Barnsley	1-5 Jensen	12347	3			11				6					8	4		5		2	10	7					1		9	
12	11	FULHAM	3-1 Burbanks, Gerrie, Jensen	30160	3	1		11				6					8	4		5		2	10	7							9	
13	18	Rotherham United	1-2 Jensen	19929	3	1		11				6						4		5	2	8	10	7							9	
14	25	PLYMOUTH ARGYLE	0-1	31776		1		11				6					10	4		5	2	8	3	7							9	
15	Nov 1	Leeds United	1-3 Todd	25538		1		11				6	5				9	4			2	8	3			7						10
16	8	LUTON TOWN	0-2	22484		1		11				6	5		9			4			2	8	3			7						10
17	15	Birmingham City	3-4 Bursell 2, Durham	17529	5	1			8			6						4	7		11	9			3		2						10
18	22	BURY	0-2	22562	5	1		11	8			6						4	3	7		9					2						10
19	29	Southampton	1-5 Horton	8865		1		11		5		6						4	7		3	8	9				2						10
20	Dec 6	NOTTS COUNTY	6-0 Harrison K, Horton 3, Murray, Fagan	18333						5		6		11			9			7		8	3		10		2	4	1			
21	13	Leicester City	0-5	16466						5		6		11			9			7		8	3		10		2	4	1			
22	20	EVERTON	1-0 Murray	15708	5							6		11			9	4		7		8	3		10		2		1			
23	26	Nottingham Forest	1-4 Jensen	25363	3			11				6					9	4				8	3	7	10		2		1			
24	27	NOTTM. FOREST	3-1 Gerrie 2, Horton	22838	3			11				6					9	4				8	10	7			2		1			
25	Jan 3	Brentford	0-1	16035	3					11		6					9	4		7		8	10				3		1			
26	17	DONCASTER ROVERS	1-1 Horton	28481				11		5		6					9	4			2	8	10	7			3		1			
27	24	Swansea Town	0-3	18323				11		5		6					9	4			2	8	10	7			2		1			
28	Feb 7	HUDDERSFIELD T	0-2	26081	5			11				6						4				9	3	7	8		2		1			10
29	21	BARNSLEY	2-2 Linaker 2	25015		1		11				6			5			4				8	3	7			2			10	9	
30	28	Fulham	2-1 Horton	24991	5	1		11				6					9	4				8	3	7			2			10		
31	Mar 7	ROTHERHAM UNITED	3-2 Gerrie, Murray, Selkirk (og)	25215	5	1		11				6					9	4		7		8	3	7	10		2					
32	14	Plymouth Argyle	2-1 Murray, Horton	19758		1		11				6	5	7			9	4				8	3		10		2					
33	21	LEEDS UNITED	1-0 Harris	25387		1		11				6	5	7			9	4				8	3		10		2					
34	28	Luton Town	2-3 Horton, Gerrie	13747		1		11				6	5	7			9	4				8	3		10		2					
35	Apr 3	Lincoln City	1-2 Gerrie	18445	3	1		11				6	5	7			9	4				8			10		2					
36	4	BIRMINGHAM CITY	2-0 Horton, Murray	23483		1		11				6	5				9	4		7		8	3		10		2					
37	6	LINCOLN CITY	1-1 Gerrie	26802	5			11				6					9	4				8	3		10		2	1	7			
38	11	Bury	1-2 Gerrie	11889	5	1		11				6					9	4		7		8	3		10		2					
39	16	LEICESTER CITY	1-1 Gerrie	16692	5	1		11				6					9	4		7		8	3		10		2					
40	18	SOUTHAMPTON	1-0 Bulless	25312	5	1	11					6					9	4		7		8	3	7	10		2					
41	25	Notts County	0-2	11699	5	1	11					6					9	4		7		8	3		10		2					
42	29	Sheffield United	2-0 Gerrie, Furniss (og)	28114	5	1	11					6	9				10	4		7		8	3				2					
			Apps		29	21	3	20	2	11	11	42	8	8	1	8	35	40	7	17	19	28	42	21	24	1	26	2	21	3	7	5
			Goals				1	2	2		1	1		1			13	2		3		10	9	3	5						1	1

Two own goals

F.A. Cup

Rnd	Date	Opponent	Score / Scorers	Att	Cripsey B	Durham D	Gerrie S	Harris W	Harrison F	Harrison K	Hassall W	Horton K	Jensen V	Murray T	Phillips E	Robinson J	Todd P
R3	Jan 10	CHARLTON ATHLETIC	3-1 Horton, Jensen, Harris	37531	5	6	9	4		7	2	8	10		3	1	
R4	31	GATESHEAD	1-2 Gerrie	37063		6	9	4	5			8	3	7	2	1	10

Final Table (Division Two)

		Pl	Home W	D	L	F	A	Away W	D	L	F	A	F.A. (Total)		Pts
1	Sheffield United	42	15	3	3	60	27	10	7	4	37	28	97	55	60
2	Huddersfield Town	42	14	4	3	51	14	10	6	5	33	19	84	33	58
3	Luton Town	42	15	1	5	53	17	7	7	7	31	32	84	49	52
4	Plymouth Argyle	42	12	5	4	37	24	8	4	9	28	36	65	60	49
5	Leicester City	42	13	6	2	55	29	5	6	10	34	45	89	74	48
6	Birmingham City	42	11	3	7	44	38	8	7	6	27	28	71	66	48
7	Nottingham Forest	42	11	5	5	46	32	7	3	11	31	35	77	67	44
8	Fulham	42	14	1	6	52	28	3	9	9	29	43	81	71	44
9	Blackburn Rovers	42	12	4	5	40	20	6	4	11	28	45	68	65	44
10	Leeds United	42	13	4	4	42	24	1	11	9	29	39	71	63	43
11	Swansea Town	42	10	9	2	45	26	5	3	13	33	55	78	81	42
12	Rotherham United	42	9	7	5	41	30	7	2	12	34	44	75	74	41
13	Doncaster Rovers	42	9	9	3	26	17	3	7	11	32	47	58	64	40
14	West Ham United	42	9	5	7	38	28	4	8	9	20	32	58	60	39
15	Lincoln City	42	9	9	3	41	26	2	8	11	23	45	64	71	39
16	Everton	42	9	8	4	38	23	3	6	12	33	52	71	75	38
17	Brentford	42	8	8	5	38	29	5	3	13	21	47	59	76	37
18	HULL CITY	42	11	6	4	36	19	3	2	16	21	50	57	69	36
19	Notts County	42	11	5	5	41	31	3	3	15	19	57	60	88	36
20	Bury	42	10	6	5	33	30	3	3	15	20	51	53	81	35
21	Southampton	42	5	7	9	45	44	5	6	10	23	41	68	85	33
22	Barnsley	42	4	4	13	31	46	1	4	16	16	62	47	108	18

1953/54   15th in Division Two

No	Date		Opponent	Result	Scorers	Att	Ack	Atk	Ber	Bly	Bul	Cri	Cro	Dur	Fag	For	Fra	Ger	HarW	HarF	HarK	Hor	Jen	Mur	Nea	Phi	Por	Ste	Tar	Tee	Wil
1	Aug	19	Birmingham City	0-2		23846	10	5	1		11				7			9	4	8	3					2	6				
2		22	Oldham Athletic	0-0		22934	10	5	1		11				7			9	4	8	3					2	6				
3		24	EVERTON	1-3	Jensen	26511	10	6	1		11						5	9	4		7	8	3			2					
4		29	BURY	3-0	Gerrie 2, Wilkinson	16295	10	5	1		11							8	4		7		6			3	2				9
5	Sep	2	Everton	0-2		35126	10	5	1						11			8	4		7		6			3	2				9
6		5	Doncaster Rovers	1-4	Jensen	21226		5	1						11			8	4	2	7		10			3			6		9
7		7	NOTTM. FOREST	3-0	Wilkinson 2, Jensen	17288		5	1						11			8	4	2	7	10	6			3					9
8		12	BLACKBURN ROVERS	0-2		23564		5	1						11			8	4	2	7	10	6			3					9
9		16	Nottingham Forest	0-2		13573									11	1		8	4	5	7	10	6			3	2				9
10		19	Derby County	0-2		19175									11	1	5		4	2	7		6	8		3			10		9
11		26	BRENTFORD	2-0	Murray, Fagan	19501									11	1	5	9	4	2	7		6	8		3			10		
12	Oct	3	Bristol Rovers	2-4	Tarrant, Harrison K	25244									11	1	5		4	2	7		6	8		3			10		9
13		10	Luton Town	1-3	Porteous	14754									11	1		9		2	7		6	8		3	4		10		
14		17	PLYMOUTH ARGYLE	2-0	Ackerman, Jensen	24653	10	5	1		11		9					8	4	2	7		6			3					
15		24	Swansea Town	0-1		18925	10	5	1		11		9					8	4	2	7		6			3					
16		31	ROTHERHAM UNITED	1-0	Ackerman	24831	10	5	1				9		11			8	4	2	7		6			3					
17	Nov	7	Leicester City	3-1	Crosbie 2, Jensen	28726	10	5	1				9		11			8	4	2	7		6			3					
18		14	STOKE CITY	1-2	Harris	26581	10	5	1				9		11			8	4	2	7		6			3					
19		21	Fulham	1-5	Ackerman	21716	10	5	1				9		11			8	4	2	7		6			3					
20		28	WEST HAM UNITED	2-1	Horton, Harrison K	21620	10	5	1		11		9	6					4	2	7	8				3					
21	Dec	5	Leeds United	0-0		21070	10	5	1		11		9	6					4	2	7	8				3					
22		12	BIRMINGHAM CITY	3-0	Crosbie, Harrison K, Green (og)	19752	10	5	1		11		9	6					4	2	7	8				3					
23		19	OLDHAM ATHLETIC	8-0	Ackerman 4, Crosbie 2, Horton, Harris	18245	10	5	1		11		9	6					4	2	7	8				3					
24		26	LINCOLN CITY	3-0	Ackerman 2, Cripsey	26476	10	5	1		11		9	6					4	2	7	8				3					
25		28	Lincoln City	0-3		16910	10	5	1		11		9	6					4	2		8			7				3		
26	Jan	16	DONCASTER ROVERS	3-1	Horton 2, Ackerman	23828	10	5	1		11		9	6					4	2	7	8				3					
27		23	Blackburn Rovers	1-3	Ackerman	24196	10	5	1		11			6				9	4	2	7	8				3					
28	Feb	6	DERBY COUNTY	3-0	Horton, Crosbie, Harrison K	23361	10	5	1		11		9	6					4	2	7	8			3						
29		13	Brentford	2-2	Ackerman, Bulless	11522	10	5	1		11		9	6					4	2	7	8				3					
30		27	LUTON TOWN	1-2	Crosbie	21555	10	5	1		11		9			6			4	2		8				3			7		
31	Mar	6	Plymouth Argyle	2-2	Crosbie, Ackerman	18216	10	5	1		11		9						4	2		8				3			6	7	
32		13	SWANSEA TOWN	4-3	Crosbie 2, Ackerman, Cripsey	16619	10	7	5			11	9	6		1			4			8				3		2			
33		20	Rotherham United	2-3	Ackerman, Atkinson	13037	10	7	5			11	9	6		1			4			8				3			6		
34		27	FULHAM	2-1	Crosbie, Crispey	16942	10	7	5			11	9	6		1			4			8				3			6		
35	Apr	3	West Ham United	0-1		13467	10	7				11	9	6		1			5	2		8			3						
36		7	Bury	0-3		8522	10	7				11	9	6		1			5			8			3				4		
37		10	LEICESTER CITY	0-3		19087	10	7	5			11	9	6					4	2		8				3				1	
38		12	BRISTOL ROVERS	4-1	Gerrie 3, Jensen	11543	9	7				11	8				5	10	4	2						3	6			1	
39		16	NOTTS COUNTY	0-2		24031	9	7	5			11	8				4	10		2						3	6			1	
40		17	Stoke City	1-0	Gerrie	17372	10	7				11	9				5	8		2						3	4			1	
41		19	Notts County	1-1	Ackerman	13022	10	7	5			11	9					8		2			6			3	4			1	
42		24	LEEDS UNITED	1-1	Ackerman	18619	10	7	5			11	9					8		2			6			3	4			1	

	Ack	Atk	Ber	Bly	Bul	Cri	Cro	Dur	Fag	For	Fra	Ger	HarW	HarF	HarK	Hor	Jen	Mur	Nea	Phi	Por	Ste	Tar	Tee	Wil
Apps	29	16	35	26	16	16	28	17	12	10	15	23	29	36	26	28	38	5	19	9	9	1	5	6	8
Goals	17	1			1	3	11		1			6	2		4	5	6	1				1		1	3

One own goal

F.A. Cup

Rd	Date		Opponent	Result	Scorers	Att	Ack	Atk	Ber	Bly	Bul	Cri	Cro	Dur	Fag	For	Fra	Ger	HarW	HarF	HarK	Hor	Jen	Mur	Nea	Phi	Por	Ste	Tar	Tee	Wil
R3	Jan	9	Brentford	0-0		15182	10	5	1		11		9	6					4	2	7	8				3					
rep		14	BRENTFORD	2-2	Horton, Crosbie	20126	10	5	1		11		9	6					4	2	7	8				3					
rep2		18	Brentford	5-2	Horton 2, Crosbie 2, Ackerman	10176	10	5	1		11		9	6					4	2	7	8				3					
R4		30	Blackburn Rovers	2-2	Crosbie, Harrison K	33233	10	5			11		9	6			1		4	2	7	8				3					
rep	Feb	4	BLACKBURN ROVERS	2-1	Ackerman, Bulless	23439	10	5	1		11		9	6					4	2	7	8				3					
R5		20	TOTTENHAM HOTSPUR	1-1	Jensen	46839	10	5	1		11		9	6					4	2	7	8				3					
rep		24	Tottenham Hotspur	0-2		52936	10		1		11		9	6			5		4	2		8			7	3					

R3 replay a.e.t.   R3 replay 2 at Belle Vue, Doncaster

	Pl	Home					Away					F.	A.	Pts
		W	D	L	F	A	W	D	L	F	A	(Total)		
1	Leicester City	42	15	4	2	63	23	8	6	7	34	37	97	60	56
2	Everton	42	13	6	2	55	27	7	10	4	37	31	92	58	56
3	Blackburn Rovers	42	15	4	2	54	16	8	5	8	32	34	86	50	55
4	Nottingham Forest	42	15	5	1	61	27	5	7	9	25	32	86	59	52
5	Rotherham United	42	13	4	4	51	26	8	3	10	29	41	80	67	49
6	Luton Town	42	11	7	3	36	23	7	5	9	28	36	64	59	48
7	Birmingham City	42	12	6	3	49	18	6	5	10	29	40	78	58	47
8	Fulham	42	12	3	6	62	39	5	7	9	36	46	98	85	44
9	Bristol Rovers	42	10	7	4	32	19	4	9	8	32	39	64	58	44
10	Leeds United	42	12	5	4	56	30	3	8	10	33	51	89	81	43
11	Stoke City	42	8	8	5	43	28	4	9	8	28	32	71	60	41
12	Doncaster Rovers	42	9	5	7	32	28	7	4	10	27	35	59	63	41
13	West Ham United	42	11	6	4	44	20	4	3	14	23	49	67	69	39
14	Notts County	42	8	6	7	26	29	5	7	9	28	45	54	74	39
15	HULL CITY	42	14	1	6	47	22	2	5	14	17	44	64	66	38
16	Lincoln City	42	11	6	4	46	23	3	3	15	19	60	65	83	37
17	Bury	42	9	7	5	39	32	2	7	12	15	40	54	72	36
18	Derby County	42	9	5	7	38	35	3	6	12	26	47	64	82	35
19	Plymouth Argyle	42	6	12	3	38	31	3	4	14	27	51	65	82	34
20	Swansea Town	42	11	5	5	34	25	2	3	16	24	57	58	82	34
21	Brentford	42	9	5	7	25	26	1	6	14	15	52	40	78	31
22	Oldham Athletic	42	6	7	8	26	31	2	2	17	14	58	40	89	25

1953-54

Standing: Mr R. Jackson (Manager), F. Harrison, A. Ackerman, W. Bly, V. Jensen, D. Durham, W. Harris, J. Mahon (Trainer);
Sitting: E. Phillips, K. Harrison, S. Gerrie, T. Berry, R. Crosbie, B. Bulless, J. Neal.

1955-56

Back Row: T. Porteous, A. Davidson, D. Durham, W. Bly, T. Berry, V. Jensen;
Front Row: J. Major, R. Smith, S. Gerrie, B. Bulless, B. Cripsey.
Inset: S. Mortensen, D. Clarke.

1954/55 _19th in Division Two_

Player columns (left→right): Ackerman A · Atkinson C · Berry T · Bly W · Bulless B · Capewell R · Cripsey B · Crosbie R · Davidson A · Dennison R · Downie J · Dryburgh T · Durham D · Franklin C · Gerrie S · Harrison F · Harrison K · Head M · Horton K · Jensen V · Mannion W · Neal J · Patterson G · Porteous T · Smith R · Teece D · Tulloch R · Whitnall B

#	Date	Opponent	Score	Scorers	Att.	AckA	AtkC	BerT	BlyW	BulB	CapR	CriB	CroR	DavA	DenR	DowJ	DryT	DurD	FraC	GerS	HarF	HarK	HeaM	HorK	JenV	ManW	NeaJ	PatG	PorT	SmiR	TeeD	TulR	WhiB
1	Aug 21	LEEDS UNITED	0-2		32071	10	7		1				9			4	11	6	5	8	2				3								
2	25	Lincoln City	1-0	Ackerman	13827	10	7		1				9			8	11	6	5		2				3				4				
3	28	Nottingham Forest	1-0	Thomas (og)	18805	10			1				9			8	11	6	5		2	7			3				4				
4	30	LINCOLN CITY	4-0	Ackerman, Crosbie, Downie 2	21818	10			1				9			8	11	6	5		2	7			3				4				
5	Sep 4	IPSWICH TOWN	4-2	Crosbie 4	28091	10			1				9			8	11	6	5		2	7			3				4				
6	6	West Ham United	1-1	Crosbie	17615	10			1				9			8	11	6	5		2	7			3				4				
7	11	Birmingham City	0-0		23846	10			1	11			9			8		6	5		2	7			3				4				
8	13	WEST HAM UNITED	0-1		25851	10			1	11			9			8		6	5		2	7			3				4				
9	18	MIDDLESBROUGH	1-0	Brown (og)	26485	10			1	11			9			8		6	5		2	7		4	3								
10	25	Stoke City	0-0		27201	10			1	11			9			8		6	5		2	7		4	3								
11	Oct 2	ROTHERHAM UNITED	1-2	Jensen	31814	10			1				9			8	11	6	5		2	7		4	3								
12	9	Plymouth Argyle	2-1	Ackerman, Crosbie	21466	10			1				9			8	11	6	5		2	7		4	3								
13	16	PORT VALE	2-1	Ackerman, Dryburgh	23892	10			1				9				11	6	5		2	7		8	3				4				
14	23	Swansea Town	0-1		18067	10			1				9				11	6	5		2	7		8	3				4				
15	30	NOTTS COUNTY	5-2	Ackerman 2, Crosbie, Downie, Deans (og)	22995	9			1				7			10	11	6	5		2			8	3				4				
16	Nov 6	Liverpool	1-2	Downie	32595	9		2	1				7			10	11	6	5					8	3				4				
17	13	BRISTOL ROVERS	0-1		19023	11		2	1				9			10		6	5					8	3			7	4				
18	20	Blackburn Rovers	0-4		26873	11						10	9					6	5		2	7			3				4			1	8
19	27	FULHAM	0-0		17869	9										10	11	6	5		2	7		8	3				4			1	
20	Dec 4	Doncaster Rovers	2-2	Horton, Dryburgh	8372	9						10					11	6	5		2	7		8	3				4			1	
21	11	DERBY COUNTY	1-1	Ackerman	16472	10	7					11	9					6	5	8	2				3				4		1		
22	18	Leeds United	0-3		23991	10	7					11	8	9				6	5		2				3				4		1		
23	25	Luton Town	1-1	Downie	15853	11	7						9			8		6	5					4	3	10					1		2
24	27	LUTON TOWN	0-4		39890	11	7						9			8		6	5					4	3	10					1		2
25	Jan 1	NOTTM. FOREST	2-3	Mannion, Jensen	18997		7						9		2	8	11	6	5					4	3	10					1		
26	Feb 5	Middlesbrough	2-1	Ackerman, Dryburgh	32619	9	7		1						2	4	11	6	5					8	3	10							
27	12	STOKE CITY	1-1	Ackerman	10182	9	7		1						2	4	11	6	5					8	3	10							
28	19	Rotherham United	0-2		11447	9	7	5	1						2	4	11	6	8						3	10							
29	26	PLYMOUTH ARGYLE	0-2		14896	9	8	5	1						2	4	11	6					7		3	10							
30	Mar 5	Port Vale	0-3		16658							10	9		2	4	11	6	5				7	8	3						1		
31	12	SWANSEA TOWN	4-3	Ackerman 2, Crosbie 2	12700	10			1	11			9		2			6	5			7		8	3							4	
32	19	Notts County	1-3	Bulless	15103	10			1	11			9		2			6	5			7		8	3							4	
33	26	LIVERPOOL	2-2	Jensen 2	6771				1	8					2	4	11	6	5	9					3	10				7			
34	Apr 2	Bristol Rovers	0-1		17044	8			1	11		10	9		2			6	5						3				4	7			
35	8	Bury	1-4	Crosbie	11381				1	11		10	9		2			6	5						3	8			4	7			
36	9	BLACKBURN ROVERS	1-4	Gerrie	17347				1	11			8		2			6	5	9					3	10			4	7			
37	11	BURY	1-0	Gerrie	13701						1	11		7	2			6	5	9				8	3	10			4				
38	16	Fulham	1-0	Gerrie	13259			5	1						2		11	6	9					8	3	10			4	7			
39	18	Ipswich Town	0-2		11939			5	1	10		7			2		11	6	9					8	3				4				
40	23	DONCASTER ROVERS	1-1	Bulless	12270				1	10		11	7		2				5	9				8	3		6		4				
41	25	BIRMINGHAM CITY	0-3		12848	8			1	10		11			2			6	5	9					3				4	7			
42	30	Derby County	0-3		7766	9			1	10		11			2			6	5					8	3				4	7			

		AckA	AtkC	BerT	BlyW	BulB	CapR	CriB	CroR	DavA	DenR	DowJ	DryT	DurD	FraC	GerS	HarF	HarK	HeaM	HorK	JenV	ManW	NeaJ	PatG	PorT	SmiR	TeeD	TulR	WhiB
	Apps	29	14	6	27	13	1	10	33	2	16	27	23	34	38	11	20	16	3	20	35	16	9	2	32	6	14	3	2
	Goals	11				2			11			5	3			3					1	4	1						

Three own goals

F.A. Cup

	Date	Opponent	Score		Att.	AckA	AtkC	BerT	BlyW	BulB	CapR	CriB	CroR	DavA	DenR	DowJ	DryT	DurD	FraC	GerS	HarF	HarK	HeaM	HorK	JenV	ManW	NeaJ	PatG	PorT	SmiR	TeeD	TulR	WhiB
R3	Jan 9	BIRMINGHAM CITY	0-2		25920	9			1						2	8	11	6	5			7			3	10			4				

		Pl	Home				Away					F.	A.	Pts
			W	D	L	F	A	W	D	L	F	A	(Total)		
1	Birmingham City	42	14	4	3	56	22	8	6	7	36	25	92	47	54
2	Luton Town	42	18	2	1	55	18	5	6	10	33	35	88	53	54
3	Rotherham United	42	17	1	3	59	22	8	3	10	35	42	94	64	54
4	Leeds United	42	14	4	3	43	19	9	3	9	27	34	70	53	53
5	Stoke City	42	12	5	4	38	17	9	5	7	31	29	69	46	52
6	Blackburn Rovers	42	14	4	3	73	31	8	2	11	41	48	114	79	50
7	Notts County	42	14	3	4	46	27	7	3	11	28	44	74	71	48
8	West Ham United	42	12	4	5	46	28	6	6	9	28	42	74	70	46
9	Bristol Rovers	42	15	4	2	52	23	4	3	14	23	47	75	70	45
10	Swansea Town	42	15	3	3	58	28	2	6	13	28	55	86	83	43
11	Liverpool	42	11	7	3	55	37	5	3	13	37	59	92	96	42
12	Middlesbrough	42	13	1	7	48	31	5	5	11	25	51	73	82	42
13	Bury	42	10	5	6	44	35	5	6	10	33	37	77	72	41
14	Fulham	42	10	5	6	46	29	4	6	11	30	50	76	79	39
15	Nottingham Forest	42	8	4	9	29	29	8	3	10	29	33	58	62	39
16	Lincoln City	42	8	6	7	39	35	5	4	12	29	44	68	79	36
17	Port Vale	42	10	6	5	31	21	2	5	14	17	50	48	71	35
18	Doncaster Rovers	42	10	5	6	35	34	4	2	15	23	61	58	95	35
19	HULL CITY	42	7	5	9	30	35	5	5	11	14	34	44	69	34
20	Plymouth Argyle	42	10	4	7	29	26	2	3	16	28	56	57	82	31
21	Ipswich Town	42	10	3	8	37	28	1	3	17	20	64	57	92	28
22	Derby County	42	6	6	9	39	34	1	3	17	14	48	53	82	23

1955/56 22nd in Division Two (Relegated)

#		Date	Opponent	Score	Scorers	Att.	Atkinson C	Berry T	Bly W	Bradbury W	Bulless B	Clarke D	Cripsey B	Davidson A	Dennison R	Duncan J	Durham D	Feasey P	Fisher B	Franklin C	Fraser D	Gerrie S	Harrison F	Jensen V	Kirman H	Major J	Martin T	Mortenson S	Neal I	Patterson G	Peacock T	Porteous T	Smith R	Stephens J	Teece D
1	Aug	20	LEICESTER CITY	2-4	Gerrie, Jensen	20431		5	1		10		11	2				6				9		3			7	4					8		
2		24	Lincoln City	0-2		13391		5	1		10		11	2								9		3			7	4				6	8		
3		27	Liverpool	0-3		38928	8	5					11	2								9					7	4		3		6	10		1
4		29	LINCOLN CITY	2-1	Bulless 2	14810	8	5			10		11	2											6		7	4		3	9				1
5	Sep	3	PLYMOUTH ARGYLE	0-1		17815	8	5			10		11	2								9			6		7	4		3					1
6		5	Leeds United	0-1		17524					10		11	2	8					5							7	4		3	9	6			1
7		10	Stoke City	1-4	Bulless	19965		5	1		10		11	2	8												7	4		3	9	6			
8		17	BRISTOL ROVERS	1-2	Patterson	14014		5	1		10		11	2	8												7	4		3	9	6			
9		24	Doncaster Rovers	0-3		12629		5	1		10		11	4								9		3			7	2	8			6			
10	Oct	1	SHEFFIELD WEDNESDAY	2-2	Bulless, Cripsey	16748		5	1		10		11	4										3			8	2		9		6	7		
11		8	Fulham	0-5		21207	9	5	1		10		11	4										3			8	2				6	7		
12		15	BURY	2-3	Bradbury, Duncan	14042	7			8	10		11	5		9								3			4		2			6			1
13		22	Swansea Town	1-4	Duncan	16648				8	10		11	6		9				5				3			4		2			7			
14		29	MIDDLESBROUGH	2-2	Atkinson, Davidson	14013	8				10	11		2		9			6	5				3			4		2			7			
15	Nov	5	Bristol City	2-5	Cripsey, Jensen	22776				8			11	2		9			6	5				3			4					10	7		
16		12	WEST HAM UNITED	3-1	Bradbury, Mortensen, Clarke	24050	2		1	10		8	6						7	5				3			4	9	1						
17		19	Port Vale	1-0	Mortensen	17778			1	10		8	11	6					7	5				3			4	9	2						
18		26	ROTHERHAM UNITED	0-3		22830			1	10		8	11	6					7	5				3			4	9	2						
19	Dec	3	Barnsley	1-2	Mortensen	14050				10		8		6						5				3			7	4	9	2					
20		10	NOTTS COUNTY	2-0	Bradbury, Stephens	12842		5	1	10		6	8	11						4				3					9	2				7	
21		17	Leicester City	2-1	Bradbury, Mortensen	27013		5	1	10		6	8	11						4				3					9	2				7	
22		24	LIVERPOOL	1-2	Bradbury	19537		5	1	10		6	8	11						4				3					9	2				7	
23		26	Nottingham Forest	1-2	Mortensen	15740		5	1	10		6		11						4				3				8	9	2				7	
24		27	NOTTM. FOREST	0-3		21407		5	1			6	10	11						4				3				8	9	2				7	
25		31	Plymouth Argyle	1-1	Martin	20930	7		1	8	11	10		4		9		5						3				7	2		6				
26	Jan	21	Bristol Rovers	2-4	Clarke 2	23801	7		1	10		6	8	11						4				3				9	2		5				
27	Feb	11	Sheffield Wednesday	1-4	Mortensen	18845		5	1	10		6	8	11						4			2					9	3					7	
28		18	PORT VALE	2-1	Bradbury, Berry	6884		5	1	10		6	8		2				9									7			3			11	
29		25	Bury	2-3	Mortensen, Stephens	10859		5	1	10		6	8		2					11	3							9						7	
30	Mar	3	SWANSEA TOWN	1-4	Mortensen	12943			1	8	10	10		4										3			6	9	2		5				7
31		10	Notts County	2-0	Clarke, Neal	12707			1	8	6	10	11	4				5						3				9	2						7
32		17	BRISTOL CITY	1-3	Jensen	11174			1	8	6	10	11	4				5						3				9	2			7			
33		24	West Ham United	1-1	Smith	12718		5	1		6	10	11	4	8									3				9	2			7			
34		30	Blackburn Rovers	0-2		25327		5	1		6	10	11	4	8									3				9	2			7			
35		31	FULHAM	2-2	Bradbury 2	12683		5		8	6	10	11	4			1				2	3						9				7			
36	Apr	2	BLACKBURN ROVERS	0-3		14135		5		8	6	10	11	4			1				2							9	3			7			
37		7	Rotherham United	2-0	Fraser 2	9619		5		8	6	10		4			1				11	2	3					9				7			
38		10	DONCASTER ROVERS	1-1	Fraser	8155		5		8	6	10		4		9	1				11	2	3									7			
39		14	BARNSLEY	4-1	* see below	8931		5		9	6	10		4			1				11	2	3									7	8		
40		21	Middlesbrough	1-5	Fraser	11190				9	6	10		4			5	1			11	2	3									7	8		
41		28	LEEDS UNITED	1-4	Martin	31123		5		9	6	10		4			1				11	2	3				8					7			
42	May	1	STOKE CITY	3-2	Fraser 2, Clarke	5232		5		9	6	10		4			1				11	2	3				8					7			

Scorers in game 39: Clarke, Bradbury, Smith, Betts (og)

	Atkinson C	Berry T	Bly W	Bradbury W	Bulless B	Clarke D	Cripsey B	Davidson A	Dennison R	Duncan J	Durham D	Feasey P	Fisher B	Franklin C	Fraser D	Gerrie S	Harrison F	Jensen V	Kirman H	Major J	Martin T	Mortenson S	Neal I	Patterson G	Peacock T	Porteous T	Smith R	Stephens J	Teece D
Apps	7	29	26	28	36	26	30	42	3	12	1	4	11	7	6	7	9	35	2	9	25	21	30	5	2	13	17	14	5
Goals	1	1		9	4	6	2	1							2			6	1		3				2	8	1	1	

One own goal

F.A. Cup

		Date	Opponent	Score	Scorers	Att.	Atkinson C	Bly W	Bradbury W	Bulless B	Clarke D	Cripsey B	Davidson A	Jensen V	Martin T	Mortenson S	Porteous T
R3	Jan	7	Aston Villa	1-1	Clarke	32865	7	1	10	6	8	11	4	3	9	2	5
rep		12	ASTON VILLA	1-2	Atkinson	15685	7	1	10	6	8	11	4	3	9	2	5

		Pl	Home W	D	L	F	A	Away W	D	L	F	A	F (Total)	A	Pts
1	Sheffield Wed.	42	13	5	3	60	28	8	8	5	41	34	101	62	55
2	Leeds United	42	17	3	1	51	18	6	3	12	29	42	80	60	52
3	Liverpool	42	14	3	4	52	25	7	3	11	33	38	85	63	48
4	Blackburn Rovers	42	13	4	4	55	29	8	2	11	29	36	84	65	48
5	Leicester City	42	15	3	3	63	23	6	3	12	31	55	94	78	48
6	Bristol Rovers	42	13	3	5	53	33	8	3	10	31	37	84	70	48
7	Nottingham Forest	42	9	5	7	30	26	10	4	7	38	37	68	63	47
8	Lincoln City	42	14	5	2	49	17	4	5	12	30	48	79	65	46
9	Fulham	42	15	2	4	59	27	5	4	12	30	52	89	79	46
10	Swansea Town	42	14	4	3	49	23	6	2	13	34	58	83	81	46
11	Bristol City	42	14	4	3	49	20	5	3	13	31	44	80	64	45
12	Port Vale	42	12	4	5	38	21	4	9	8	22	37	60	58	45
13	Stoke City	42	13	2	6	47	27	7	2	12	24	35	71	62	44
14	Middlesbrough	42	11	4	6	46	31	5	4	12	30	47	76	78	40
15	Bury	42	9	5	7	44	39	7	3	11	42	51	86	90	40
16	West Ham United	42	12	4	5	52	27	2	7	12	22	42	74	69	39
17	Doncaster Rovers	42	11	5	5	45	30	1	6	14	24	66	69	96	35
18	Barnsley	42	10	5	6	33	35	1	7	13	14	49	47	84	34
19	Rotherham United	42	7	5	9	29	34	5	4	12	27	41	56	75	33
20	Notts County	42	8	5	8	39	37	3	4	14	16	45	55	82	31
21	Plymouth Argyle	42	7	6	8	33	25	3	2	16	21	62	54	87	28
22	HULL CITY	42	6	4	11	32	45	4	2	15	21	52	53	97	26

1956/57 8th in Division Three (North)

#		Date	Opponent	Score	Scorers	Att	Berry T	Bly W	Bradbury W	Bulless B	Clarke D	Coates D	Collinson L	Cripsey B	Davidson A	Dennison R	Duncan J	Durham D	Feasey P	Fisher B	Fraser D	Gerrie S	Harrison F	Jensen V	Major J	Martin T	Mortensen S	Nielson N	Rintanen M	Smales K	Smith C	Stephens J
1	Aug	18	Halifax Town	0-1		8402	5	1	8	6				11	4							10	2	3			9					7
2		20	TRANMERE ROVERS	4-1	Mortensen 2, Bradbury, Jensen	12222	5	1	8	6				11	4								2	3			9					7
3		25	ROCHDALE	2-0	Bradbury, Clarke	13089	5	1	9	6	8			11	4							10	2	3								7
4		28	Tranmere Rovers	4-2	Bradbury 3, Clarke	5894	5	1	9	6	8			11	4							10	2	3								7
5	Sep	1	Scunthorpe United	1-1	Bradbury	11004	5	1	9	6	8			11	4								2	3		10						7
6		3	WORKINGTON	0-2		14491	5	1	9	6	8			11	4							10	2	3								7
7		8	CREWE ALEXANDRA	2-0	Bradbury, Jensen	12947	5	1	8	10				11	6								2	3	4	9						7
8		12	Workington	3-4	Mortensen 3	8484	5	1	8	10					6					11			2	3	4	9						7
9		15	Derby County	0-1		20124	5	1	8	6					4					11			2	3			9					7
10		17	Bradford Park Avenue	1-4	Stephens	7102	5		7	6	10				4	2	9									8				1	3	11
11		22	WREXHAM	1-2	Duncan	10667		1	9	6		8			4		10		5				2	3	7							11
12		24	BRADFORD PARK AVE.	2-0	Mortensen, Stephens	8349		1	7	6		8			4		10		5				2	3			9					11
13		29	Gateshead	0-2		5535		1	10	6		8			4		7		5				2	3			9					11
14	Oct	6	York City	1-2	Clarke	10763		1		6	8			11	4				5			10	2	3			9					7
15		13	OLDHAM ATHLETIC	2-1	Clarke, Gerrie	9400				6	8			11					5			10	2	3	4		9				1	7
16		20	Stockport County	2-1	Clarke, Bulless	9272		1		6	8			11	4				5			10	2	3			9					7
17		27	SOUTHPORT	2-1	Mortensen 2	10443		1		6	8			11	4				5			10	2	3			9					7
18	Nov	3	Chesterfield	1-3	Clarke	10610		1		6	8			11	4				5			10	2	3			9					7
19		10	CHESTER	2-0	Bradbury, Stephens	8571		1	10	6	8		4	11				3			5		2				9					7
20		24	BRADFORD CITY	1-0	Currie (og)	11825		1	10	6	8		4	11				3			5		2				9					7
21	Dec	1	Mansfield Town	1-2	Stephens	8809		1	10	6	8		4	11				3	5				2				9					7
22		15	HALIFAX TOWN	3-1	Mortensen, Cripsey, Davidson	9837		1	10	6	8			11	4			3	5				2				9					7
23		25	Darlington	1-1	Clarke	5546		1	10	6	8		4	11				3	5				2				9					7
24		26	DARLINGTON	1-1	Mortensen	9872		1	10	6	8		4	11				3	5				2				9					7
25		29	SCUNTHORPE UNITED	2-2	Bulless, Cripsey	12873		1	10	6	8		4	11				3	5				2				9					7
26	Jan	1	Hartlepools United	3-3	Stephens, Cripsey, Davidson	9768		1	10	6	8		4	11				3	5				2				9					7
27		12	Crewe Alexandra	3-2	Bradbury 2, Edwards (og)	4285		1	10	6	8		4	11				3	5				2				9					7
28		19	DERBY COUNTY	3-3	Clarke 2, Bulless	14543		1	9	10	8		4	11	6			3	5				2									7
29		26	Barrow	2-1	Stephens, Bradbury	7728		1	9	10	8		4	11	6			3	5				2									7
30	Feb	2	Wrexham	2-5	Clarke 2	11841		1	10	11	8		4		6			3	5				2								9	7
31		9	GATESHEAD	1-1	Bradbury	11689		1	10	11	8		4		6			3	5				2								9	7
32		16	YORK CITY	1-1	Bradbury	15697		1	9	10	8		4	11	6			3	5				2									7
33		23	Oldham Athletic	3-1	Stephens 2, Clarke	2500		1	9	10	8		4	11	6			3	5				2									7
34	Mar	2	STOCKPORT COUNTY	5-3	Bradbury 2, Clarke 2, Stephens	12222		1	9	10	8		4	11	6			3	5				2									7
35		5	Rochdale	3-4	Bradbury, Bulless, Collinson	4296		1	9	10	8		4	11	6			3	5				2									7
36		9	Southport	0-1		4439		1	9	10	8		4	11	6			3	5				2									7
37		16	CHESTERFIELD	3-2	Bradbury 2, Collinson	11660		1	9	10	8		4	11	6			3	5				2									7
38		18	BARROW	3-0	Bulless 3	11728		1	9	10	8		4	11	6			3	5				2									7
39		23	Chester	1-1	Cripsey	6272		1	9	10	8		4	11	6			3	5				2									7
40		30	HARTLEPOOLS UNITED	2-0	Bulless, Clarke	13310		1	9	10	8		4	11	6			3	5				2									7
41	Apr	6	Bradford City	1-2	Clarke	9434		1	9	10	8		4	11	6			3	5				2									7
42		9	Carlisle United	3-1	Cripsey, Bulless, Stephens	6297		1	9	10	8		4	11				3	5				2					6				7
43		13	MANSFIELD TOWN	1-2	Stephens	10550		1		10	8		4	11	6			3					2					6	5			7
44		19	ACCRINGTON STANLEY	2-1	Cripsey, Clarke	18304	5	1	9	10	8		4	11				3					2						6			7
45		22	Accrington Stanley	3-0	Davidson 2, Clarke	11400	5	1	9	10	8		4	11	6			3					2									7
46		27	CARLISLE UNITED	0-0		13010		1	9	10	8		4	11	6			3					2						5			7

	Berry T	Bly W	Bradbury W	Bulless B	Clarke D	Coates D	Collinson L	Cripsey B	Davidson A	Dennison R	Duncan J	Durham D	Feasey P	Fisher B	Fraser D	Gerrie S	Harrison F	Jensen V	Major J	Martin T	Mortensen S	Nielson N	Rintanen M	Smales K	Smith C	Stephens J
Apps	12	40	37	45	40	3	26	38	41	3	4	23	36	2	2	9	43	18	1	7	21	2	4	1	2	46
Goals			18	9	18		2	6	4		1					1		2			10					11

Two own goals

F.A. Cup

Rd		Date	Opponent	Score	Scorers	Att	Bly W	Bradbury W	Bulless B	Clarke D	Collinson L	Cripsey B	Davidson A	Durham D	Feasey P	Harrison F	Mortensen S	Stephens J
R1	Nov	17	GATESHEAD	4-0	Mortensen 2, Bradbury, Crispey	12260	1	10	6	8	4	11		3	5	2	9	7
R2	Dec	8	YORK CITY	2-1	Bulless 2	24155	1	10	6	8	4	11		3	5	2	9	7
R3	Jan	5	BRISTOL ROVERS	3-4	Clarke 2, Stephens	22752	1	9	10	8	4	11	6	3	5	2		7

		Pl	Home					Away					F. A.		Pts
			W	D	L	F	A	W	D	L	F	A	(Total)		
1	Derby County	46	18	3	2	69	18	8	8	7	42	35	111	53	63
2	Hartlepools United	46	18	4	1	56	21	7	5	11	34	42	90	63	59
3	Accrington Stanley	46	15	4	4	54	22	10	4	9	41	42	95	64	58
4	Workington	46	16	4	3	60	25	8	6	9	33	38	93	63	58
5	Stockport County	46	16	3	4	51	26	7	5	11	40	49	91	75	54
6	Chesterfield	46	17	5	1	60	22	5	4	14	36	57	96	79	53
7	York City	46	14	4	5	43	21	7	6	10	32	40	75	61	52
8	HULL CITY	46	14	6	3	45	24	7	4	12	39	45	84	69	52
9	Bradford City	46	14	3	6	47	31	8	5	10	31	37	78	68	52
10	Barrow	46	16	2	5	51	22	5	7	11	25	40	76	62	51
11	Halifax Town	46	16	2	5	40	24	5	5	13	25	46	65	70	49
12	Wrexham	46	12	7	4	63	33	7	3	13	34	41	97	74	48
13	Rochdale	46	14	6	3	38	19	4	6	13	27	46	65	65	48
14	Scunthorpe United	46	9	5	9	44	36	6	10	7	27	33	71	69	45
15	Carlisle United	46	9	9	5	44	36	7	4	12	32	49	76	85	45
16	Mansfield Town	46	13	3	7	58	38	4	7	12	33	52	91	90	44
17	Gateshead	46	9	6	8	42	40	8	4	11	30	50	72	90	44
18	Darlington	46	11	5	7	47	36	6	3	14	35	59	82	95	42
19	Oldham Athletic	46	9	7	7	35	31	3	8	12	31	43	66	74	39
20	Bradford Park Ave.	46	11	2	10	41	40	5	1	17	25	53	66	93	35
21	Chester	46	8	7	8	40	35	2	6	15	15	49	55	84	32
22	Southport	46	7	8	8	31	34	3	4	16	21	60	52	94	32
23	Tranmere Rovers	46	5	9	9	33	38	2	4	17	18	53	51	91	27
24	Crewe Alexandra	46	5	7	11	31	46	1	2	20	12	64	43	110	21

~ 229 ~

1956-57
Back Row: L. Collinson, F. Harrison, P. Feasey. W. Bly, D. Durham, A. Davidson;
Front Row: J. Stephens, D. Clarke, W. Bradbury, B. Bulless, B. Cripsey;

1957-58
Back Row: L. Collinson, F. Harrison, B. Fisher, N. Nielson, D. Durham, A. Davidson;
Front Row: J. Stephens, D. Clarke, B. Bradbury, B. Bulless, B. Cripsey.

1957/58 5th in Division Three (North)

#	Date	Opponent	Score	Scorers	Att	Bennion J	Bentley K	Berry T	Bly W	Bradbury W	Bridges B	Bulless B	Clarke D	Coates D	Collinson L	Cripsey B	Cubie N	Davidson A	Dennison R	Durham D	Feasey P	Fisher B	Fraser D	Garvey B	Harrison F	Nielson N	Round L	Smith C	Stephens J
1	Aug 24	YORK CITY	0-1		17671				1	9		10	8		4	11		6	7	3	2				5				
2	26	BARROW	1-1	Dennison	11684	10			1	9		11	8		4			6	7	3	2				5				
3	31	Stockport County	0-1		13091	4				9		10	8			11		6		3	2				5		1		7
4	Sep 2	Barrow	0-0		8681	4				9		10	8			11		6		3	2				5		1		7
5	7	HALIFAX TOWN	5-2	Bradbury, Clarke 4	11593	4				9		10	8		6	11		2		3					5		1		7
6	9	WORKINGTON	3-2	Bradbury, Stephens 2	11433	10				9		11	8		4			6		3	2				5		1		7
7	14	Rochdale	1-2	Bradbury	7612	10				9		11	8		4			6		3	2				5		1		7
8	18	Workington	2-3	Davidson, Stephens	6734			5		9		10	8		4	11		6		3	2						1		7
9	21	CREWE ALEXANDRA	1-0	Cripsey	10966			5		10		6	8		4	11		9		3	2						1		7
10	23	Mansfield Town	3-1	Davidson 2, Stephens	6860			5		10		6	8		4	11	2	9								3	1		7
11	28	Wrexham	0-6		8755					10		6	8		4	11	2	9			5					3	1		7
12	30	MANSFIELD TOWN	1-1	Clarke	7878	6			1	9		10	8		4	11		2		3					5				7
13	Oct 5	SCUNTHORPE UNITED	2-0	Bradbury, Stephens	12009	6			1	9		10	8		4	11		2		3					5				7
14	12	Carlisle United	1-0	Clarke	11178	6			1	9		10	8		4	11		2		3					5				7
15	19	BURY	2-1	Stephens 2	15236	6				9		10	8		4	11		2		3					5		1		7
16	26	Accrington Stanley	0-3		7107	6				9		10	8		4	11		2		3					5		1		7
17	Nov 2	CHESTER	3-0	Bradbury, Cripsey, Clarke	11732	6				9		10	8		4	11		2		3					5		1		7
18	9	Chesterfield	0-0		7922	6				9		10	8		4	11		2		3					5		1		7
19	23	Hartlepools United	1-5	Bradbury	8754	6			1	9		10	8		4	11		2		3					5				7
20	30	BRADFORD PARK AVE.	3-3	Bradbury, Collinson, Perry (og)	11042	4			1	10		6	7	8	9			2		3					5				11
21	Dec 14	SOUTHPORT	3-2	Bradbury, Clarke, Davidson	9148				1	9		11	8		4			6		3	2				5		1		7
22	21	York City	1-3	Clarke	7031	6	10			9		11	8					4		3	5				2		1		7
23	25	GATESHEAD	1-1	Fraser	8950		10					8					4	6		3			11		5	2	1	9	
24	26	Gateshead	1-3	Smith	5148		10					8					4	6		3			11		5	2	1	9	
25	28	STOCKPORT COUNTY	1-0	Bradbury	11719					9	10	8			4			6		3	5	1	11		2				7
26	Jan 11	Halifax Town	2-2	Bradbury, Bulless	5858					9		10	8		4	11		6		2		1			3	5			7
27	18	ROCHDALE	2-1	Clarke, Cripsey	8991					9		10	8		4	11		6		3		1			2	5			7
28	Feb 1	Crewe Alexandra	2-1	Clarke, Cripsey	4370				1	9		10	8		4	11		6		3	5				2				7
29	8	WREXHAM	2-0	Bradbury, Clarke	8241				1	9			8	10	4	11		6		3	5				2				7
30	20	Scunthorpe United	0-2		11408	4			1	9		10	7	8		11		6		3	5				2				
31	22	HARTLEPOOLS UNITED	1-1	Bulless	11926	4			1	9		8	10	8				6		3	5				2				
32	Mar 1	Bury	1-1	Coates	10250	4			1	9		11	8	10				6		3				5	2				7
33	10	DARLINGTON	2-1	Bradbury, Cripsey	6519				1	9		10	8		4	11		6		3	5				2				7
34	15	Chester	1-1	Bradbury	5721				1	9		10	8		4	11		6		3	5				2				7
35	17	TRANMERE ROVERS	0-0		8950				1	9		10	8		4	11		6		3	5				2				7
36	22	CARLISLE UNITED	4-0	Bulless, Davidson, Smith 2	9917				1	8		10	7		4	11		6		3	5				2			9	
37	25	ACCRINGTON STANLEY	1-0	Smith	9382				1	8		10	7		4	11		6		3	5				2			9	
38	29	Tranmere Rovers	4-4	Bradbury, Clarke, Smith, Cripsey	8459				1	8		10	7		4	11		6		3	5				2			9	
39	Apr 5	OLDHAM ATHLETIC	9-0	Bradbury 3, Bulless, Clarke, Cripsey, Smith 3	11007				1	8		10	7		4	11		6		3	5				2			9	
40	7	BRADFORD CITY	1-3	Cripsey	16763				1	8		10	7		4	11		6		3	5				2			9	
41	8	Bradford City	0-1		13789				1	8		10	7		4	11		6		3	5				2			9	
42	12	Bradford Park Avenue	4-4	Clarke, Bulless, Smith 2	5910				1	8		10	7		4	11		6		3	5				2			9	
43	15	Oldham Athletic	1-1	Bulless	6894				1	8		10	7		4	11		6		3	5				2			9	
44	19	CHESTERFIELD	1-0	Bulless	9625				1	8		10	7		4	11		6		3	5				2			9	
45	23	Darlington	2-2	Bradbury, Smith	4056				1	8		10	7		4	11		6		3	5				2			9	
46	26	Southport	2-1	Bradbury, Clarke	1862				1	8		10	7		4	11		6		3	5				2			9	
		Apps				19	4	3	26	46	1	42	46	5	38	35	4	46	2	41	33	3	3	1	25	23	17	13	30
		Goals								19		7	16	1	1	8		5	1				1					11	7

One own goal

F.A. Cup

	Date	Opponent	Score	Scorers	Att	Bennion J	Bentley K	Berry T	Bly W	Bradbury W	Bridges B	Bulless B	Clarke D	Coates D	Collinson L	Cripsey B	Cubie N	Davidson A	Dennison R	Durham D	Feasey P	Fisher B	Fraser D	Garvey B	Harrison F	Nielson N	Round L	Smith C	Stephens J
R1	Nov 16	CREWE ALEXANDRA	2-1	Bradbury, Clarke	10,773	6			1	9		10	8		4	11		2		3					5				7
R2	Dec 7	Port Vale	2-2	Bradbury, Davidson	14,338	10			1	9		11	8		4			6		3	2				5				7
rep	9	PORT VALE	4-3	Bradbury 2, Cleary (og), Carberry(og)	17,403	10			1	9		11	8		4			6		3	2				5				7
R3	Jan 4	BARNSLEY	1-1	Bradbury	21,868					9		10	8		4	11		6		3	5	1			2				7
rep	8	Barnsley	2-0	Bulless, Clarke	20,890					9		10	8		4	11		6		3	5	1			2				7
R4	29	Sheffield Wednesday	3-4	Bradbury, Bulless, Stephens	51,834				1	9		10	8		4	11		6		3	5				2				7

R2 replay a.e.t.

1958/59 2nd in Division Three: Promoted

#	Date	Opponent	Res	Scorers	Att	Bennion J	Bly W	Bowering M	Bradbury W	Bulless B	Clarke D	Coates D	Collinson L	Cripsey B	Davidson A	Duncan J	Durham D	Feasey P	Garvey B	Harrison F	Lord B	Metcalfe V	Milner M	Morris C	Smith C	Wilkinson G
1	Aug 23	PLYMOUTH ARGYLE	1-1	Smith	14318	4	1		8	10	7						6	3	5	2		11			9	
2	27	Swindon Town	0-2		14355	4	1		8	10	7			11			6	3	5	2					9	
3	30	Bradford City	1-2	Bradbury	12165	4	1		8	10	7			11			6	3	5	2					9	
4	Sep 1	SWINDON TOWN	0-0		12035		1	11	8		7	10	4				6	3	5	2				9		
5	6	WREXHAM	1-0	Smith	10898		1	11	8		7	10	4				6	3	5	2					9	
6	11	Notts County	1-1	Bowering	8584		1	7	10	6	8		4	11		9		3	5	2						
7	13	Southampton	1-6	Bradbury	14461		1	7	10	6	8		4	11		9		3	5	2						
8	15	NOTTS COUNTY	5-0	Bradbury, Collinson, Clarke, Smith 2	8521		1		8		7	10	4	11			6	3	5	2					9	
9	20	ACCRINGTON STANLEY	4-2	Bradbury 2, Clarke, Coates	11858		1	11	8		7	10	4				6	3	5	2					9	
10	22	BRENTFORD	3-1	Clarke, Coates, Smith	14172		1	11	8		7	10	4				6	3	5	2					9	
11	27	Halifax Town	2-1	Bradbury, Collinson	7730		1	11	8		7	10	4				6	3	5	2					9	
12	30	Brentford	1-1	Clarke	12441		1	11	8		7	10	4				6	3	5	2					9	
13	Oct 4	NEWPORT COUNTY	2-3	Bradbury, Smith	14753		1	11	8		7	10	4				6	3	5	2					9	
14	6	CHESTERFIELD	3-1	Bowering 2, Bradbury	12305	4		11	8	3	7	10							5	6	1				9	2
15	11	Stockport County	1-2	Bradbury	9521	4	1	11	8		7	10						3	5	6					9	2
16	18	READING	2-0	Bowering, Coates	13955	4	1	11	8		7	10					6	3	5	2					9	
17	25	Colchester United	3-1	Bradbury, Smith, Coates	9277		1	11	8		7	10	4				6	3	5	2					9	
18	Nov 1	BOURNEMOUTH	5-3	Bowering, Coates, Smith 3	14400		1	11	8		7	10	4				6	3	5	2					9	
19	8	Norwich City	1-0	Smith	15929		1	11	8		7	10	4				6	3	5	2					9	
20	22	Rochdale	1-0	Smith	5562		1	11	8		7	10	4				6	3	5	2					9	
21	29	QUEEN'S PARK RANGERS	1-0	Smith	11705		1	11	8		7	10	4				6	3	5	2					9	
22	Dec 6	Bournemouth	0-1		9869		1	11	8		7	10			4		6	3	5	2					9	
23	13	DONCASTER ROVERS	5-1	Bradbury 2, Clarke 2, Smith	10411		1	11	8		7	10			4		6	3	5	2					9	
24	20	Plymouth Argyle	1-1	Smith	20238		1	11	8		7	10			4		6	3	5	2					9	
25	26	MANSFIELD TOWN	5-2	Bradbury 3, Clarke, Smith	20836		1	11	8		7	10			4		6	3	5	2					9	
26	27	Mansfield Town	1-1	Coates	7916		1	11	8		7	10			4		6	3	5	2					9	
27	Jan 1	Chesterfield	1-2	Bradbury	10374		1	11	8		7	10			4		6	3	5	2					9	
28	3	BRADFORD CITY	4-0	Bradbury 3, Coates	14168		1	11	8	3	7	10			4			2	5	6					9	
29	10	SOUTHEND UNITED	3-2	Bradbury, Coates, Smith	12908		1	11	8	3	7	10			4			2	5	6					9	
30	24	Bury	1-2	Smith	7932		1	11	8		7	10			4		6	3	5	2					9	
31	31	SOUTHAMPTON	3-0	Bradbury 2, Clarke	14441		1		8	11	7	10			4	9	6	3	5	2						
32	Feb 7	Accrington Stanley	1-0	Lord (og)	6610		1		8	11	7	10			4	9	6	3	5	2						
33	14	HALIFAX TOWN	4-0	Bradbury, Bulless, Smith 2	13233		1		8	11	7	10			4		6	3	5	2					9	
34	21	Newport County	3-1	Bradbury, Smith, Garvey	6988		1	11	8		7	10			4		6	3	5	2					9	
35	28	STOCKPORT COUNTY	3-1	Bradbury 2, Clarke	16177		1		8	11	7	10			4		6	3	5	2					9	
36	Mar 14	COLCHESTER UNITED	3-0	Davidson, Smith 2	16468		1	11	8	3	7	10			4			2	5	6					9	
37	27	Tranmere Rovers	0-1		15956		1	11	8	3	7	10			4			2	5	6					9	
38	28	NORWICH CITY	3-3	Clarke 2, Smith	24156		1	11	8	3	7	10			4			2	5	6					9	
39	30	TRANMERE ROVERS	1-0	Bradbury	19190		1		10	11	7		8		4	9	3		6	2			5			
40	Apr 4	Southend United	1-1	Coates	12279		1	11	8		7	10			4		6	3	5	2					9	
41	11	ROCHDALE	2-1	Bowering, Clarke	13377		1	11	8		7	10			4		6	3	5	2					9	
42	15	Reading	0-2		13548		1	11	8	10	7				4		6	3	5	2					9	
43	18	Queen's Park Rangers	1-1	Smith	9325		1		8	11	7	10			4		6	3	5	2					9	
44	23	Doncaster Rovers	2-0	Bradbury, Smith	8881		1		8	11	7	10			4		6	3	5	2					9	
45	25	BURY	2-0	Bradbury, Bulless	16447		1		8	11	7	10			4		6	3	5	2					9	
46	29	Wrexham	1-5	Smith	7677		1		8	11	7	10			4		6	3	5	2					9	
		Apps				6	45	33	45	30	45	41	17	5	26	5	39	45	34	44	1	1	1	1	40	2
		Goals						6	30	2	12	9	2		1				1						26	

One own goal

F.A. Cup

#	Date	Opponent	Res	Att	Bly W	Bowering M	Bradbury W	Clarke D	Coates D	Collinson L	Durham D	Feasey P	Garvey B	Harrison F	Smith C
R1	Nov 15	STOCKPORT COUNTY	0-1	17441	1	11	8	7	10	4	6	3	5	2	9

		Pl	Home					Away					F.	A.	Pts
			W	D	L	F	A	W	D	L	F	A		(Total)	
1	Plymouth Argyle	46	14	7	2	55	27	9	9	5	34	32	89	59	62
2	HULL CITY	46	19	3	1	65	21	7	6	10	25	34	90	55	61
3	Brentford	46	15	5	3	49	22	6	10	7	27	27	76	49	57
4	Norwich City	46	13	6	4	51	29	9	7	7	38	33	89	62	57
5	Colchester United	46	15	2	6	46	31	6	8	9	25	36	71	67	52
6	Reading	46	16	4	3	51	21	5	4	14	27	42	78	63	50
7	Tranmere Rovers	46	15	3	5	53	22	6	5	12	29	45	82	67	50
8	Southend United	46	14	6	3	52	26	7	2	14	33	54	85	80	50
9	Halifax Town	46	14	5	4	48	25	7	3	13	32	52	80	77	50
10	Bury	46	12	9	2	51	24	5	5	13	18	34	69	58	48
11	Bradford City	46	13	4	6	47	25	5	7	11	37	51	84	76	47
12	Bournemouth	46	12	9	2	40	18	5	3	15	29	51	69	69	46
13	Queen's Park Rgs.	46	14	6	3	49	28	5	2	16	25	49	74	77	46
14	Southampton	46	12	7	4	57	33	5	4	14	31	47	88	80	45
15	Swindon Town	46	13	4	6	39	25	3	9	11	20	32	59	57	45
16	Chesterfield	46	12	5	6	40	26	5	5	13	27	38	67	64	44
17	Newport County	46	15	2	6	43	24	2	7	14	26	44	69	68	43
18	Wrexham	46	12	6	5	40	30	2	8	13	23	47	63	77	42
19	Accrington Stanley	46	10	8	5	42	31	5	4	14	29	56	71	87	42
20	Mansfield Town	46	11	5	7	38	42	3	8	12	35	56	73	98	41
21	Stockport County	46	9	7	7	33	23	4	3	16	32	55	65	78	36
22	Doncaster Rovers	46	13	2	8	40	32	1	3	19	10	58	50	90	33
23	Notts County	46	5	9	9	33	39	3	4	16	22	57	55	96	29
24	Rochdale	46	8	7	8	21	26	0	5	18	16	53	37	79	28

1958-59

Back Row: F. Harrison, A. Davidson, C. Smith, W. Bly, B. Garvey, D. Durham;
Front Row: D. Clarke, W. Bradbury, P. Feasey, D. Coates, B. Bulless.

1959-60

Back Row: M. Brown, P. Feasey, B. Garvey, A. Davidson, W. Bly, B. Bulless, L. Collinson, A. McLean (Trainer);
Front Row: D. Clarke, R. Shiner, J. Sewell, R. Gubbins, W. Bradbury.

1959/60 21st in Division Two: Relegated

#		Date	Opponent	Score	Scorers	Att.	Bennion J	Bly W	Bowering M	Bradbury W	Brown M	Bulless B	Clarke D	Coates D	Collinson L	Crickmore C	Davidson A	Duncan J	Feasey P	Fisher B	Garvey B	Gubbins R	Harrison F	King D	Lord B	Metcalfe V	Morris C	Sewell J	Shiner R	Smith C	Stocks J	Wilkinson G
1	Aug	22	PLYMOUTH ARGYLE	3-1	Metcalfe 2, Robertson (og)	17319		1		8		3		7	10		4			5	6		2			11				9		
2		24	Sheffield United	0-6		16532		1		8		3		7	10		4			5	6		2			11				9		
3		29	Liverpool	3-5	Coates 2, Metcalfe	35520				8		3		7	10		4	9	1	5	6		2			11						
4		31	SHEFFIELD UNITED	0-2		23168				8		3		7	10		4	9	1	5	6		2			11						
5	Sep	5	CHARLTON ATHLETIC	0-4		17387			11			3		7	10	8	4		1	5	6		2							9		
6		9	Middlesbrough	0-4		28368			11			3		7	10	8	4		1	5	6		2				9					
7		12	Bristol City	1-0	Coates	16427			7	10		3		9	8	11	4		1	5	6		2									
8		14	MIDDLESBROUGH	3-3	Bradbury 2, Bowering	22024			7	10		3		8	4	11	2		1	5	6									9		
9		19	SCUNTHORPE UNITED	0-2		18459			7	10		3		8	4	11	2		1	5	6									9		
10		26	Rotherham United	0-1		11646	1		11	10		3		7	8	4		9		5	6		2									
11	Oct	3	CARDIFF CITY	0-0		14933	4	1	11	9		3		7	10	8				6	5		2									
12		10	LINCOLN CITY	0-5		17170		1	11	8		3		7		4				6	5		2			10				9		
13		17	Leyton Orient	1-3	Bradbury	13002	4	1	7	8		3			9	11				5	6		2			10						
14		24	HUDDERSFIELD T	1-1	Gubbins	15864		1			2	3	7				4	11		5		6	10						8	9		
15		31	Ipswich Town	0-2		12738		1		9	2	3	7				4			5		6	10			11			8			
16	Nov	7	BRISTOL ROVERS	3-1	Bradbury, Shiner 2	16972	4	1	11			3	7				2			5	6	10							8	9		
17		14	Swansea Town	0-0		11886	4	1	11			3	7				2			5	6	10							8	9		
18		21	BRIGHTON & HOVE ALB	3-1	Bradbury, Gubbins, Shiner	17107	4	1	11			3	7				2			5	6	10							8	9		
19		28	Stoke City	1-3	Sewell	12481	4		11			3	7				2		1	5	6	10						8		9		
20	Dec	5	PORTSMOUTH	1-3	Gubbins	14675	4		11			3	7				2		1	5	6	10						8		9		
21		12	Sunderland	3-1	King 2, Shiner	17695		1	11			3	7			6	2			4	5			10				8		9		
22		19	Plymouth Argyle	2-3	Sewell, Shiner	8546		1				3	7			6	2			4	5	11		10				8		9		
23		26	ASTON VILLA	0-1		29399		1	11			3	7			6	2			4	5			10				8		9		
24		28	Aston Villa	1-1	Bradbury	33386		1	11			3	7			6	2			4	5			10				8		9		
25	Jan	2	LIVERPOOL	0-1		18681		1	11			3	7			6	2			4				10				8		9		
26		16	Charlton Athletic	2-3	Bennion, Clarke	11032	4	1	11			3	7			6	2			5				10				8		9		
27		23	BRISTOL CITY	1-1	Clarke	12605	4	1	11			3	7			6	2			5				10				8		9		
28	Feb	6	Scunthorpe United	0-3		10885	4			10		3	11	7						5		2	1					8	9		6	
29		13	ROTHERHAM UNITED	1-0	Smith C	10171			8			3	11			4	6		1	5	10	2				7				9		
30		20	Cardiff City	2-3	Gubbins, Smith C	21580				8		3	11		8	4	6		1	5	10	2				7				9		
31		27	Lincoln City	0-3		10043				8		3	11	8	4	6	7		1	5	10	2								9		
32	Mar	5	LEYTON ORIENT	1-2	Gubbins	10580						6	11			4	2			1	5	10				7			8	9		3
33		12	Huddersfield Town	0-1		12167		1	6			11	4			2	5			3	10					7			8	9		
34		17	STOKE CITY	4-0	Morris 2, Shiner, McCue (og)	11750		1	6			11	4			2	5			3	10					7			8	9		
35		26	Bristol Rovers	0-1		12236		1	6			11	4			2	5			3	10					7			8	9		
36	Apr	2	SWANSEA TOWN	3-1	King, Clarke, Shiner	8691			6			7	4			11	2			5	1	3		10				8	9		
37		9	Brighton & Hove Albion	1-1	King	14318			6			7	4			11	2			5	1	3	9	10					8		
38		15	DERBY COUNTY	1-1	King	13062			6			7	4			11	2			5	1	3	9	10					8		
39		16	SUNDERLAND	0-0		9744			6				4			11	2			5	1	3		10				7	8	9		
40		18	Derby County	3-1	King, Sewell, Shiner	11197			6				4			11	2			5	1	3		10				7	8	9		
41		23	Portsmouth	1-1	Morris	12205			6				4			11	2			5	1	3		10			8					
42		30	IPSWICH TOWN	2-0	Crickmore, King	5719			6				4			11	2			5	1	3		10				7	8	9		
			Apps				10	21	12	22	2	42	34	13	29	11	42	5	35	18	40	22	15	9	3	5	11	27	22	10	1	1
			Goals				1		1	6			3	3		1						5		7		3	3	3	8	2		

Two own goals

F.A. Cup

	Date	Opponent	Score	Att.	Bly W	Bowering M	Bulless B	Clarke D	Crickmore C	Davidson A	Fisher B	Harrison F	King D	Sewell J	Shiner R
R3	Jan 3	Fulham	0-5	22,157	1	11	3	7	6	4	5	2	10	8	9

		Pl	Home					Away					F	A	Pts
			W	D	L	F	A	W	D	L	F	A	(Total)		
1	Aston Villa	42	17	3	1	62	19	8	6	7	27	24	89	43	59
2	Cardiff City	42	15	2	4	55	36	8	10	3	35	26	90	62	58
3	Liverpool	42	15	3	3	59	28	5	7	9	31	38	90	66	50
4	Sheffield United	42	12	5	4	43	22	7	7	7	25	29	68	51	50
5	Middlesbrough	42	14	5	2	56	21	5	5	11	34	43	90	64	48
6	Huddersfield Town	42	13	3	5	44	20	6	6	9	29	32	73	52	47
7	Charlton Athletic	42	12	7	2	55	28	5	6	10	35	59	90	87	47
8	Rotherham United	42	9	9	3	31	23	8	4	9	30	37	61	60	47
9	Bristol Rovers	42	12	6	3	42	28	6	5	10	30	50	72	78	47
10	Leyton Orient	42	12	4	5	47	25	3	10	8	29	36	76	61	44
11	Ipswich Town	42	12	5	4	48	24	7	1	13	30	44	78	68	44
12	Swansea Town	42	12	6	3	54	32	3	4	14	28	52	82	84	40
13	Lincoln City	42	11	3	7	41	25	5	4	12	34	53	75	78	39
14	Brighton & Hove A.	42	7	8	6	35	32	6	4	11	32	44	67	76	38
15	Scunthorpe United	42	9	7	5	38	26	4	3	14	19	45	57	71	36
16	Sunderland	42	8	6	7	35	29	4	6	11	17	36	52	65	36
17	Stoke City	42	8	3	10	40	38	6	4	11	26	45	66	83	35
18	Derby County	42	9	4	8	31	28	5	3	13	30	49	61	77	35
19	Plymouth Argyle	42	10	6	5	42	36	3	3	15	19	53	61	89	35
20	Portsmouth	42	6	6	9	36	36	4	6	11	23	41	59	77	32
21	HULL CITY	42	7	6	8	27	30	3	4	14	21	46	48	76	30
22	Bristol City	42	8	3	10	27	31	3	2	16	33	66	60	97	27

1960/61   11th in Division Three

#	Date	Opponent	Score	Scorers	Att	Bulless B	Chilton C	Clarke D	Collinson L	Crickmore C	Davidson A	Feasey P	Fisher B	Garvey B	Gubbins R	Holah E	King D	Lord B	McMillan E	Milner M	Morris C	Nicholson P	Price D	Sewell J	Stocks J
1	Aug 20	Colchester United	0-4		6713		8		6	11	2	5	1	3			10		4			7	9		
2	22	NEWPORT COUNTY	5-1	Collinson 2, Chilton, Clarke, Morris	9811	6	9	11	4		2	5	1	3			10				7		8		
3	27	GRIMSBY TOWN	2-3	Clarke, McMillan	14252	6	9	11	4		2	5	1	3			10				7		8		
4	29	Newport County	1-3	Clarke	7347	6	9	11	4		2	5		3	10			1	8		7				
5	Sep 3	Southend United	1-3	Chilton	8434	6	9	7	4		2	5	1	3			10				11		8		
6	5	BOURNEMOUTH	2-0	Chilton, King	8496	6	9	7	4		2	5	1	3	11		10						8		
7	10	Reading	4-2	Chilton, Clarke 2, McMillan	7043	6	9	7	4		2	5	1	3	11				10				8		
8	12	Bournemouth	2-2	Price 2	5315	6	9	7	4		2	5	1	3	11				10				8		
9	17	COVENTRY CITY	1-1	Chilton	10374	6	9	7	4		2	5	1	3	11				10				8		
10	19	BARNSLEY	2-0	McMillan, Price	10527	6	9	7	4		2	5	1	3	11				10				8		
11	24	Bristol City	2-1	Price, Gubbins	14899	6	9	7	4		2		1	3	11				10	5			8		
12	28	Barnsley	0-1		4840	6	9	7	4		2	5	1	3	11				10				8		
13	Oct 1	QUEEN'S PARK RANGERS	3-1	Chilton 3	9333	6	9	7	4		2	5	1	3	11				10				8		
14	3	NOTTS COUNTY	3-1	Chilton, Gubbins, Price	12199	6	9	7	4		2	5	1	3	11				10				8		
15	8	BURY	0-1		13164	6	9	7	4		2	5	1	3	11				10				8		
16	15	Walsall	0-1		10125	6	9		4		2	5	1	3	11		10					7	8		
17	22	SHREWSBURY TOWN	3-1	Chilton 2, Sewell	9095	6	9	7	4		2	5	1	3	11								10	8	
18	29	Halifax Town	0-3		6734	6	9	7	4		2	5	1	3	11								10	8	
19	Nov 12	Watford	2-2	Price 2	13746	6	9	7	4		2	5	1	3	11				10				8		
20	19	BRENTFORD	3-0	Chilton, Price, Bulless	7798	6	9	7	4		2	5	1	3	11				10				8		
21	Dec 3	TORQUAY UNITED	2-3	Crickmore, Stocks	6175		9	7	4	11	2	5	1	3			10						8		6
22	10	Port Vale	1-4	Chilton	9006	6	9	7	4		2	5	1	3					10				8		11
23	17	COLCHESTER UNITED	1-1	Sewell	6047	6		7			2	5	1	3	9		11		4				8	10	
24	26	Bradford City	0-0		11450	6		7			2	5	1	3	9		11		4				8	10	
25	27	BRADFORD CITY	3-0	Gubbins, Price, Sewell	13947	6		7			2	5	1	3	9		11		4				8	10	
26	31	Grimsby Town	0-2		12712	6	7				2	5	1	3	9		11		4				8	10	
27	Jan 14	SOUTHEND UNITED	0-1		9744	11		8	6		2	5	1	3	9				4				7	10	
28	28	TRANMERE ROVERS	4-2	Gubbins, Price 2, Sewell	3950	6	9	7	4		2	5	1	3	11				6				8	10	
29	Feb 4	Coventry City	0-4		11160	11	9	7	4		2	5	1	3									8	10	6
30	13	BRISTOL CITY	3-3	Chilton, Clarke, Gubbins	7077	6	9	7	4	11	2	5	1	3	10								8		
31	18	Queen's Park Rangers	1-2	King	12210	6	9		4	11	2	5	1	3			7		10				8		
32	25	Torquay United	2-1	Crickmore, Price	4587	6	9	7	4	11	2	5	1	3					10				8		
33	Mar 4	WALSALL	2-1	Sewell, Clarke	7118	6	9	7		11	2	5	1	3					10					8	4
34	11	Shrewsbury Town	0-0		8698	6	9	7	4	11	2	5	1	3					10					8	
35	18	HALIFAX TOWN	4-2	Chilton 2, Price, Clarke	4997	6	9	7	4	11	2	5	1	3									10	8	
36	24	Tranmere Rovers	0-1		12260	3	9	7	4	11	2	5	1						6				10	8	
37	31	Chesterfield	2-1	Chilton 2	12079	6	9	7	8	11	2	5	1	3					4				10		
38	Apr 1	WATFORD	3-2	Crickmore, Collinson, Holah	7267	3		7	8	11	2	5	1			9			4				10		6
39	3	CHESTERFIELD	2-2	Clarke 2	7162	3	9	7	8	11	2	5	1						4				10		6
40	8	Brentford	2-2	Bulless, Price	6390	6	9	7	8	11	2	5	1	3					4				10		
41	12	Swindon Town	1-1	Crickmore	10877	6	9	7	8	11	2	5	1	3					4				10		
42	15	SWINDON TOWN	0-0		5514	6	9	7	8	11	2	5	1	3					4				10		
43	20	READING	1-0	Davidson	5498	6	8		4	11	2	5	1	3					10	9			7		
44	22	Bury	0-3		10907	6	8		4	11	2	5	1	3					10	9			7		
45	27	Notts County	1-2	King	4941	6	9		4	11	2	5	1	3			8		7						10
46	29	PORT VALE	2-2	King, Chilton	4439	6	9	7	4	11	2	5	1	3			8								10
		Apps				43	41	39	41	19	46	45	45	43	23	1	13	1	37	3	5	1	35	17	8
		Goals				2	19	10	3	4	1			5	1	4	3		1				14	5	1

F.A. Cup

#	Date	Opponent	Score	Scorers	Att	Bulless B	Chilton C	Clarke D	Collinson L	Crickmore C	Davidson A	Feasey P	Fisher B	Garvey B	Gubbins R	Holah E	King D	Lord B	McMillan E	Milner M	Morris C	Nicholson P	Price D	Sewell J	Stocks J
R1	Nov 5	SUTTON TOWN	3-0	Sewell, Price, Gubbins	8482	6	9	7	4		2	5	1	3	11								10	8	
R2	26	Darlington	1-1	Price	8613	6	9	7	4		2	5	1	3	11				10				8		
rep	28	DARLINGTON	1-1	Chilton	18125	6	9	7	4		2	5	1	3	11				10				8		
rep2	Dec 5	Darlington	1-1	Price	9801	6	9	7	4		2	5	1	3					10				8		11
rep3	12	Darlington	0-0		5313	6	9		4	11	2	5	1	3					10				7	8	
rep4	15	Darlington	3-0	Clarke, Gubbins, King	19366	6		7			2	5	1	3	9		11		4				8	10	
R3	Jan 7	BOLTON WANDERERS	0-1		18711	6		7			2	5	1	3	9		11		4				8	10	

R2 replay and replay 3 a.e.t. Rep. 2 abandoned in e.t. Rep. 2 at Elland Rd. Rep. 3 at Belle Vue Doncaster, Rep. 4 at Ayresome Park, Middlesbrough

F.L. Cup

#	Date	Opponent	Score	Scorers	Att	Bulless B	Chilton C	Clarke D	Collinson L	Crickmore C	Davidson A	Feasey P	Fisher B	Garvey B	Gubbins R	Holah E	King D	Lord B	McMillan E	Milner M	Morris C	Nicholson P	Price D	Sewell J	Stocks J
R1	Oct 10	BOLTON WANDERERS	0-0		11980	6	9	7	4		2	5	1	3	11				10				8		
rep	19	Bolton Wanderers	1-5	Gubbins	10781	6	9	7	4		2	5	1	3	11								10	8	

		Pl	Home W D L F A	Away W D L F A	F A (Total)	Pts
1	Bury	46	18 3 2 62 17	12 5 6 46 28	108 45	68
2	Walsall	46	19 4 0 62 20	9 2 12 36 40	98 60	62
3	Queen's Park Rgs.	46	18 4 1 58 23	7 6 10 35 37	93 60	60
4	Watford	46	12 7 4 52 27	8 5 10 33 45	85 72	52
5	Notts County	46	16 3 4 52 24	5 6 12 30 53	82 77	51
6	Grimsby Town	46	14 4 5 48 32	6 6 11 29 37	77 69	50
7	Port Vale	46	15 3 5 63 30	2 12 9 33 49	96 79	49
8	Barnsley	46	15 5 3 56 30	6 2 15 27 50	83 80	49
9	Halifax Town	46	14 7 2 42 22	2 10 11 29 56	71 78	49
10	Shrewsbury Town	46	13 7 3 54 26	2 9 12 29 49	83 75	46
11	HULL CITY	46	13 6 4 51 28	4 6 13 22 45	73 73	46
12	Torquay United	46	8 12 3 37 26	6 5 12 38 57	75 83	45
13	Newport County	46	12 7 4 51 30	5 4 14 30 60	81 90	45
14	Bristol City	46	15 4 4 50 19	2 6 15 20 49	70 68	44
15	Coventry City	46	14 4 5 54 25	2 6 15 26 58	80 83	44
16	Swindon Town	46	13 6 4 41 16	1 9 13 21 39	62 55	43
17	Brentford	46	10 9 4 41 28	3 8 12 15 42	56 70	43
18	Reading	46	13 5 5 48 29	1 7 15 24 54	72 83	40
19	Bournemouth	46	8 7 8 34 39	7 3 13 24 37	58 76	40
20	Southend United	46	10 8 5 38 26	4 3 16 22 50	60 76	39
21	Tranmere Rovers	46	11 5 7 53 50	4 3 16 26 65	79 115	38
22	Bradford City	46	8 7 8 37 36	3 6 14 28 51	65 87	36
23	Colchester United	46	8 5 10 40 44	3 6 14 28 57	68 101	33
24	Chesterfield	46	9 6 8 42 29	1 6 16 25 58	67 87	32

1961/62   10th in Division Three

No	Date		Opponent	Score	Scorers	Att	Bulless B	Chilton C	Clarke D	Collinson L	Crickmore C	Davidson A	Feasey P	Fisher B	Garvey B	Green L	Henderson R	King D	McMillan E	McSeveney J	Milner M	Price D	Shaw A
1	Aug	19	Peterborough United	2-3	Chilton, Crickmore	14730	6	9	7	4	11	2	5	1	3		10					8	
2		21	Port Vale	0-4		11480	6	9	7	4	11	2	5	1	3		10					8	
3		26	NORTHAMPTON T	1-0	Chilton	8027	6	9	7	4	11	2	5	1	3		10					8	
4		31	PORT VALE	3-1	Chilton, Clarke, Crickmore	8095	6	9	7	4	11	2	5	1	3		10			8			
5	Sep	2	Lincoln City	3-0	Chilton, Crickmore, Henderson	6495		9	7	4	11	2	5	1	3		10		6	8			
6		6	Bournemouth	1-1	Crickmore	8370		9	7	4	11	2	5	1	3		10		6	8			
7		9	TORQUAY UNITED	4-0	McSeveney 2, Henderson 2	9535		9	7	4	11	2	5	1	3		10		6	8			
8		16	Swindon Town	1-1	Crickmore	9325	10	9	7	4	11	2	5	1	3				6	8			
9		21	WATFORD	1-0	Chilton	14376	10	9	7	4	11	2	5	1	3				6	8			
10		23	HALIFAX TOWN	1-2	Bulless	13611	10	9	7	4	11	2	5	1	3				6	8			
11		26	Watford	1-1	McSeveney	12406	10	9	7	4	11	2	5	1	3				6	8			
12		30	Queen's Park Rangers	1-1	McSeveney	10076	10	9	7	4	11	2	5	1	3				6	8			
13	Oct	7	Bristol City	1-1	Connor (og)	10088	10	9	7	4	11	2	5	1	3		8		6				
14		11	Portsmouth	1-2	Bulless	14107	10	9	7	4	11	2	5	1	3				6	8			
15		14	BRADFORD PARK AVE.	0-1		12096	10	9	7	4	11	2	5	1	3				6	8			
16		28	SHREWSBURY TOWN	3-1	McSeveney, Henderson, Crickmore	6229	10		7	4	11	2	5	1	3		9		6	8			
17	Nov	11	READING	0-1		6952		9	7	4	11	2	5	1	3		10		6	8			
18		18	Newport County	2-0	Crickmore, Henderson	5089	3	9	7	4	11	2	5	1			10		6	8			
19	Dec	2	Grimsby Town	0-1		6871	3	9	7	4	11	2	5	1			10		6	8			
20		9	COVENTRY CITY	3-1	Henderson, McSeveney, Clarke	3817	3		7	4	11	2	5	1			9		6	10		8	
21		16	PETERBOROUGH UTD.	1-1	Crickmore	6674	3		7	4	11	2	5	1			9		6	10		8	
22		23	Northampton Town	0-2		10203	3		7	4	11	2	5	1			9		6	10		8	
23		26	CRYSTAL PALACE	2-4	Price 2	7559	3		7	4	11	2		1			9		6	10	5	8	
24	Jan	6	PORTSMOUTH	0-1		6454	6	9	7			2	5		3	1	10	4		11		8	
25		13	LINCOLN CITY	1-0	Price	4634	6	9	7			2	5		3	1	10	4		11		8	
26		20	Torquay United	2-4	Clarke, Smith (og)	3176	6	9	7			2	5		3	1	10	4		11		8	
27		27	SOUTHEND UNITED	0-0		4517	6		7			2	5	1	3		9	4		10		8	11
28	Feb	3	SWINDON TOWN	0-1		3729	6		7			2	5	1	3		9	4		10		8	11
29		10	Halifax Town	1-2	King	4124	3		7	4			5	1	2		10	9	6	11		8	
30		16	QUEEN'S PARK RANGERS	3-1	King, Price, McSeveney	3237	3		7	4			5	1	2		10	9	6	11		8	
31		24	BRISTOL CITY	3-2	Price, McSeveney, Henderson	3876	3		7	4			5	1	2		10	9	6	11		8	
32	Mar	3	Bradford Park Avenue	0-1		7736	3		7	4		2	5	1			10	9	6	11		8	
33		10	NOTTS COUNTY	2-1	McSeveney, Henderson	3911			7	4		2	5	1	3		10	9	6	11		8	
34		17	Shrewsbury Town	0-2		4722	3		7	4		2	5	1			10	9	6	11		8	
35		21	Crystal Palace	2-1	Chilton, McSeveney	7041	3	9	7	4		2	5	1				10	6	11		8	
36		24	BRENTFORD	3-0	McSeveney, Price, Clarke	3849	3	9	7	4		2	5	1				10	6	11		8	
37		30	Reading	1-1	Collinson	7210	3	9	7	4		2	5	1				10	6	11		8	
38	Apr	3	Notts County	0-3		3688	3	9	7	4		2	5	1				10	6	11		8	
39		7	NEWPORT COUNTY	4-0	King 3, Chilton	3235		9	7	4		2	5	1	3			10	6	11		8	
40		12	BOURNEMOUTH	2-1	Collinson, King	5289		9	7	4		2	5	1	3			10	6	11		8	
41		14	Southend United	1-2	Price	5354		9	7	4		2	5	1	3			10	6	11		8	
42		20	BARNSLEY	4-0	Price 3, Davidson	6296		9	7	4		2		1	3			10	6	11	5	8	
43		21	GRIMSBY TOWN	2-1	McSeveney, King	12404		9	7	4		2		1	3			10	6	11	5	8	
44		23	Barnsley	0-1		4781		9	7	4		2		1	3			10	6	11	5	8	
45		28	Coventry City	2-0	Price 2	7589			7	4		2		1	3		9	10	6	11	5	8	
46	May	3	Brentford	2-0	McSeveney 2	3583			7	4		2		1	3		9	10	6	11	5	8	
			Apps				33	30	46	41	23	43	40	42	34	4	28	20	42	42	6	30	2
			Goals				2	7	4	2	8	1					8	7		14		12	

Two own goals

F.A. Cup

	Date		Opponent	Score	Scorers	Att	Bulless B	Chilton C	Clarke D	Collinson L	Crickmore C	Davidson A	Feasey P	Fisher B	Garvey B	Green L	Henderson R	King D	McMillan E	McSeveney J	Milner M	Price D	Shaw A
R1	Nov	4	RHYL	5-0	Chilton 2, McSeveney, Henderson, McMillan	7451		9	7	4	11	2	5	1	3		10		6	8			
R2		25	BRADFORD CITY	0-2		10124	3	9	7	4	11	2	5	1			10		6	8			

F.L. Cup

	Date		Opponent	Score	Scorers	Att	Bulless B	Chilton C	Clarke D	Collinson L	Crickmore C	Davidson A	Feasey P	Fisher B	Garvey B	Green L	Henderson R	King D	McMillan E	McSeveney J	Milner M	Price D	Shaw A
R1	Sep	11	BRADFORD PARK AVE.	4-2	Chilton 2, Crickmore, Atkinson (og)	10401	10	9	7	4	11	2	5	1	3				6	8			
R2	Oct	3	Bury	4-3	Chilton 2, Collinson, Clarke	8204	10	9	7	4	11	2	5	1	3				6	8			
R3	Nov	15	Sunderland	1-2	McSeveney	15969	3	9	7	4	11	2	5	1			10		6	8			

		Pl	Home					Away					F.	A.	Pts
			W	D	L	F	A	W	D	L	F	A	(Total)		
1	Portsmouth	46	15	6	2	48	23	12	5	6	39	24	87	47	65
2	Grimsby Town	46	18	3	2	49	18	10	3	10	31	38	80	56	62
3	Bournemouth	46	14	8	1	42	18	7	9	7	27	27	69	45	59
4	Queen's Park Rgs.	46	15	3	5	65	31	9	8	6	46	42	111	73	59
5	Peterborough Utd.	46	16	0	7	60	38	10	6	7	47	44	107	82	58
6	Bristol City	46	15	3	5	56	27	8	5	10	38	45	94	72	54
7	Reading	46	14	5	4	46	24	8	4	11	31	42	77	66	53
8	Northampton Town	46	12	6	5	52	24	8	5	10	33	33	85	57	51
9	Swindon Town	46	11	8	4	48	26	6	7	10	30	45	78	71	49
10	HULL CITY	46	15	2	6	43	20	5	6	12	24	34	67	54	48
11	Bradford Park Ave.	46	13	5	5	47	27	7	2	14	33	51	80	78	47
12	Port Vale	46	12	4	7	41	23	5	7	11	24	35	65	58	45
13	Notts County	46	14	5	4	44	23	3	4	16	23	51	67	74	43
14	Coventry City	46	11	6	6	38	26	5	5	13	26	45	64	71	43
15	Crystal Palace	46	8	8	7	50	41	6	6	11	33	39	83	80	42
16	Southend United	46	10	7	6	31	26	3	9	11	26	43	57	69	42
17	Watford	46	10	9	4	37	26	4	4	15	26	48	63	74	41
18	Halifax Town	46	9	5	9	34	35	6	5	12	28	49	62	84	40
19	Shrewsbury Town	46	8	7	8	46	37	5	5	13	27	47	73	84	38
20	Barnsley	46	9	6	8	45	41	4	6	13	26	54	71	95	38
21	Torquay United	46	9	4	10	48	44	6	2	15	28	56	76	100	36
22	Lincoln City	46	4	10	9	31	43	5	7	11	26	44	57	87	35
23	Brentford	46	11	3	9	34	29	2	5	16	19	64	53	93	34
24	Newport County	46	6	5	12	29	38	1	3	19	17	64	46	102	22

1961-62
Back Row: L. Collinson, P. Feasey; B. Fisher, C. Chilton, B. Garvey, B. Bulless
Front Row: D. Clarke, D. Price, A. Davidson, R. Henderson, C. Crickmore.

1962-63
Back Row: B. Garvey, L. Collinson, M. Williams, C. Chilton, E. McMillan, L. Sharpe;
Front Row: D. Clarke, R. Henderson, A. Davidson, D. King, J. McSeveney.

1962/63 *10th in Division Three*

#	Date	Opponent	Res	Scorers	Att	Bulless B	Chilton C	Clarke D	Collinson L	Cummins G	Davidson A	Feasey P	Fisher B	Garvey B	Granger M	Henderson R	King D	McMillan E	McSeveney J	Milner M	Price D	Sharpe L	Shaw A	Simpkin C	Taylor AM	Wilkinson W	Williams M
1	Aug 18	BRISTOL ROVERS	3-0	McSeveney 2, King	8261	3	9	7	4		2		1				10	6	11	5				8			
2	23	WREXHAM	1-3	Chilton	8535	3	9	7	4		2		1				10	6	11	5				8			
3	25	Brighton & Hove Albion	1-2	Bertolini (og)	16051	3	9	7	4		2		1				10	6	11	5				8			
4	29	Wrexham	0-2		11347	3	9	7	4		2				1		10	6	11	5				8			
5	31	CARLISLE UNITED	3-1	Chilton, McSeveney, Davidson	8325	3	9	7	4		2		1				10	6	11	5				8			
6	Sep 3	Millwall	1-5	Chilton	19619	3	9	7	4		2	5	1				10	6	11					8			
7	8	Swindon Town	0-2		10144	11	9		4		2	5		3	1	8	10	6							7		
8	13	MILLWALL	4-1	Chilton 3, Henderson	7100	3	9	7	4		2			5		8	10	6	11								1
9	15	PETERBOROUGH UTD.	3-2	Henderson 2, McSeveney	8158	3	9	7	4		2			5		8	10	6	11								1
10	20	CRYSTAL PALACE	0-0		9718	3	9	7	4		2			5		8	10	6	11								1
11	22	Barnsley	2-1	Chilton, Henderson	6848	3	9	7	4		2			5		8	10	6	11								1
12	29	NORTHAMPTON T	2-0	Chilton, McSeveney	9536	3	9	7	4		2			5		8	10	6	11								1
13	Oct 6	COLCHESTER UNITED	2-2	Clarke 2	9360	3	9	7	4		2			5		8	10	6	11								1
14	13	Notts County	1-1	McSeveney	9595		9	7	4		2			5		8	10	6	11			3					1
15	20	BOURNEMOUTH	1-1	McSeveney	8702		9	7	4		2			5		8	10	6	11			3					1
16	22	Queen's Park Rangers	1-4	Henderson	18281			7	4		2			5		8	10	6	9			3	11				1
17	27	Coventry City	2-2	Chilton, McSeveney	11821		9	7	4		2			5		8	10	6	11			3					1
18	Nov 10	Watford	2-4	McSeveney 2	7518		9	7	4		2			5		8	10	6	11			3					1
19	17	BRISTOL CITY	4-0	Chilton 3, McSeveney	7367		9	7	4	10	2			5		8		6	11			3					1
20	Dec 1	PORT VALE	0-1		7259		9	7	4		2			5		8	10	6	11			3					1
21	8	Shrewsbury Town	4-1	Chilton 2, Henderson, Cummins	6976		9	7	4	10	2			5		8		6	11			3					1
22	15	Bristol Rovers	5-2	Henderson, Chilton, McSeveney, Clarke, Collinson	5989		9	7	4		2			5		8	10	6	11			3					1
23	22	BRIGHTON & HOVE ALB	2-1	McSeveney, King	8050		9	7	4		2			5		8	10	6	11			3					1
24	26	Southend United	1-0	King	9783		9	7	4		2			5		8	10	6	11			3					1
25	29	SOUTHEND UNITED	1-2	King	9577		9	7	4		2			5		8	10	6				3	11				1
26	Mar 4	Colchester United	3-2	McSeveney 2, Henderson	4143		9	7	4	10	2			5		8		6	11			3					1
27	9	Bournemouth	0-3		6613		9	7	4	10	2			5		8		6	11			3					1
28	13	BRADFORD PARK AVE.	1-0	McSeveney	7635	3	9	7	4	10	2			5		8		6	11								1
29	20	Reading	2-2	McSeveney, King	7167	3	9	7	4		2			5		8	10	6	11								1
30	23	Bradford Park Avenue	1-3	Chilton	7529	3	9	7	4		2			5		8	10	6	11								1
31	25	Peterborough United	3-1	McSeveney 2, Chilton	10193	3	9	7	4	10	2			5		8		6	11								1
32	30	WATFORD	1-0	McSeveney	5462	3	9	7	4	10	2			5		8		6	11								1
33	Apr 6	Bristol City	1-3	McSeveney	8794	3	9	7	4	10	2			5		8		6	11								1
34	12	HALIFAX TOWN	2-0	King, Wilkinson	9831	3	9	7	4	11	2			5			10	6								8	1
35	13	READING	0-1		5978	3	9	7	4	11	2			5			10	6								8	1
36	15	Halifax Town	2-0	Simpkin, Shaw	3633		9	7	4		2			5		8		6				3	11	10			1
37	20	Port Vale	0-1		4673		9	7	4		2			5		8		6				3	11	10			1
38	25	QUEEN'S PARK RANGERS	4-1	Henderson, Clarke, Simpkin, Taylor (og)	5894		9	7	4		2			5		8		6	11			3		10			1
39	27	SHREWSBURY TOWN	2-2	Chilton, Collinson	5607		9	7	4		2			5		8		6	11			3		10			1
40	May 1	Crystal Palace	1-1	Henderson	11210		9	7	4		2			5		8		6				3	11	10			1
41	4	BARNSLEY	0-2		4923		9	7	4		2			5		8		6				3	11	10			1
42	7	COVENTRY CITY	2-0	Cummins, Collinson	5255		9	7	4	10	2			5				6	11					8			1
43	11	Carlisle United	1-2	Simpkin	2519		9	7	4	10	2			5				6	11					8			1
44	18	SWINDON TOWN	1-1	McSeveney	4361		9	7		10	2			5				6	11				4	8			1
45	20	NOTTS COUNTY	1-1	Clarke	4145		9	7		10	2			5				6	11				4	8			1
46	24	Northampton Town	0-3		12110		9	7	4	10	2			5				6	11					8			1

| | | | | | Apps | 21 | 43 | 41 | 44 | 15 | 46 | 8 | 5 | 40 | 2 | 31 | 23 | 46 | 39 | 5 | 11 | 22 | 5 | 17 | 1 | 2 | 39 |
| | | | | | Goals | | 18 | 5 | 3 | 2 | 1 | | | | | 10 | 6 | | 22 | | | | 1 | 3 | 1 | | |

Two own goals

F.A. Cup

	Date	Opponent	Res	Scorers	Att	Chilton C	Clarke D	Collinson L	Davidson A	Garvey B	Henderson R	King D	McMillan E	McSeveney J	Sharpe L	Williams M
R1	Nov 3	CROOK TOWN	5-4	McSeveney 2, Henderson 2, Chilton	9484	9	7	4	2	5	8	10	6	11	3	1
R2	24	WORKINGTON	2-0	McSeveney 2	8686	9	7	4	2	5	8	10	6	11	3	1
R3	Feb 11	Leyton Orient	1-1	Chilton	9752	9	7	4	2	5	8	10	6	11	3	1
rep	19	LEYTON ORIENT	0-2		14214	9	7	4	2	5	8	10	6	11	3	1

R3 replay a.e.t.

F.L. Cup

	Date	Opponent	Res	Scorers	Att	Bulless B	Chilton C	Clarke D	Collinson L	Davidson A	Garvey B	Henderson R	King D	McMillan E	McSeveney J	Price D	Sharpe L	Williams M
R2	Sep 24	MIDDLESBROUGH	2-2	Chilton, Collinson	10640	3	9	7	4	2	5	8	10	6	11			1
rep	Oct 8	Middlesbrough	1-1	Clarke	15612	3	9	7	4	2	5	8	10	6	11			1
rep2	10	MIDDLESBROUGH	3-0	Chilton, Price, McSeveney	11964		9	7	4	2	5	8	10	6	11	3		1
R3	17	FULHAM	1-2	Chilton	20308		9	7	4	2	5	8	10	6	11	3		1

R2 replay and replay 2 a.e.t.

		Pl	Home					Away					F.	A.	Pts
			W	D	L	F	A	W	D	L	F	A	(Total)		
1	Northampton Town	46	16	6	1	64	19	10	4	9	45	41	109	60	62
2	Swindon Town	46	18	2	3	60	22	4	12	7	27	34	87	56	58
3	Port Vale	46	16	4	3	47	25	7	4	12	25	33	72	58	54
4	Coventry City	46	14	6	3	54	28	4	11	8	29	41	83	69	53
5	Bournemouth	46	11	12	0	39	16	7	4	12	24	30	63	46	52
6	Peterborough Utd.	46	11	5	7	48	33	9	6	8	45	42	93	75	51
7	Notts County	46	15	3	5	46	29	4	10	9	27	45	73	74	51
8	Southend United	46	11	7	5	38	24	8	5	10	37	53	75	77	50
9	Wrexham	46	14	6	3	54	27	6	3	14	30	56	84	83	49
10	HULL CITY	46	12	6	5	40	22	7	4	12	34	47	74	69	48
11	Crystal Palace	46	10	7	6	38	22	7	6	10	30	36	68	58	47
12	Colchester United	46	11	6	6	41	35	7	5	11	32	58	73	93	47
13	Queen's Park Rgs.	46	9	6	8	44	36	8	5	10	41	40	85	76	45
14	Bristol City	46	10	9	4	54	38	6	4	13	46	54	100	92	45
15	Shrewsbury Town	46	13	4	6	57	41	3	8	12	26	40	83	81	44
16	Millwall	46	11	6	6	50	32	4	7	12	32	55	82	87	43
17	Watford	46	12	3	8	55	40	5	5	13	27	45	82	85	42
18	Barnsley	46	12	6	5	39	28	3	5	15	24	46	63	74	41
19	Bristol Rovers	46	11	8	4	45	29	4	3	16	25	59	70	88	41
20	Reading	46	13	4	6	51	30	3	4	16	23	48	74	78	40
21	Bradford Park Ave.	46	10	9	4	43	36	4	3	16	36	61	79	97	40
22	Brighton & Hove A.	46	7	6	10	28	38	5	6	12	30	46	58	84	36
23	Carlisle United	46	12	4	7	41	37	1	5	17	20	52	61	89	35
24	Halifax Town	46	8	3	12	41	51	1	9	13	23	55	64	106	30

1963/64 8th in Division Three

Match results

No	Date	Opponent	Score	Scorers	Att
1	Aug 24	Watford	3-3	McSeveney 2, Chilton	9251
2	28	PETERBOROUGH UTD.	0-0		18433
3	31	COLCHESTER UNITED	0-0		11844
4	Sep 7	Millwall	1-0	Henderson	10240
5	9	Peterborough United	1-5	Henderson	12859
6	14	BARNSLEY	2-2	Chilton, Sharpe	8920
7	16	Southend United	1-1	Chilton	11764
8	21	COVENTRY CITY	2-1	McSeveney, Simpkin	12315
9	28	Bournemouth	0-1		11175
10	Oct 2	SOUTHEND UNITED	1-0	Clarke	10706
11	5	WREXHAM	4-2	Chilton 4	8510
12	8	Bristol Rovers	0-4		10681
13	12	Reading	0-2		8214
14	19	SHREWSBURY TOWN	4-2	Chilton 2, Wilkinson 2	7057
15	21	Queen's Park Rangers	2-0	McSeveney, Malcolm (og)	9836
16	26	Bristol City	0-1		10568
17	30	QUEEN'S PARK RANGERS	3-0	Chilton, Henderson, Wilkinson	7932
18	Nov 2	PORT VALE	4-1	Chilton 2, Wilkinson 2	8460
19	23	Crystal Palace	2-2	Wilkinson, Sharpe	16929
20	30	WALSALL	3-1	Wilkinson 3	7578
21	Dec 14	WATFORD	2-2	Chilton, Garvey	8011
22	21	Colchester United	1-1	Wilkinson	3609
23	26	MANSFIELD TOWN	3-1	Chilton, Henderson, Wilkinson	14132
24	28	Mansfield Town	0-2		7790
25	Jan 11	MILLWALL	0-0		10014
26	17	Barnsley	2-2	Henderson 2	8193
27	25	Notts County	1-0	Chilton	9065
28	Feb 1	Coventry City	2-2	Chilton, Davidson	23476
29	8	BOURNEMOUTH	3-4	Rafferty 2, McSeveney	11511
30	15	Wrexham	1-3	Rafferty	5552
31	22	READING	1-1	Chilton	7561
32	26	BRISTOL ROVERS	0-2		3907
33	29	Luton Town	1-2	Henderson	5267
34	Mar 7	BRISTOL CITY	4-4	Wilkinson, Davidson, Garvey, Low (og)	4726
35	11	CREWE ALEXANDRA	2-1	Chilton, Rafferty	3931
36	21	LUTON TOWN	2-0	Henderson, Rafferty	3576
37	27	OLDHAM ATHLETIC	0-1		8696
38	28	Crewe Alexandra	4-1	McSeveney 2, Henderson, Clarke	3335
39	30	Oldham Athletic	1-1	Chilton	7878
40	Apr 4	CRYSTAL PALACE	1-1	McSeveney	6602
41	11	Walsall	1-1	Rafferty	5093
42	13	Port Vale	0-1		6090
43	18	BRENTFORD	0-0		6798
44	22	NOTTS COUNTY	4-1	Chilton 3, McSeveney	5106
45	25	Shrewsbury Town	1-5	Sharpe	3125
46	28	Brentford	3-1	Corner 2, Wilkinson	6818

Appearances (shirt numbers)

No	Brown M	Bulless B	Butler D	Chilton C	Clarke D	Collinson L	Corner N	Cummins G	Davidson A	Feasey P	Garvey B	Henderson R	McMillan E	McSeveney J	Milner M	Rafferty R	Sharpe L	Shaw A	Simpkin C	Summers G	Swan M	Wilkinson W	Williams M
1			3	9	7	4			2		5		6	11		8			10				1
2			3	9	7	4			2		5		6	11		8			10				1
3			3	9	7				2		5		6	11		8		4	10				1
4			3	9	7				2		5	8	6	11				4	10				1
5			3	9	7				2		5	8	6	11				4	10				1
6			3	9	7				2		5	8	6	11				4	10				1
7			3	9	7				2			8	6	11	5			4	10		1		
8			3	9	7				2			8	6	11	5			4	10		1		
9			3	9	7			10	2			8	6	11	5			4			1		
10		11	3	9	7			10	2			8	6		5			4			1		
11		11	3	9	7			10	2			8	6		5			4			1		
12			3	9	7			10	2			8	6	11	5			4			1		
13			3	9	7				2			10	6	11	5						1	8	
14			3	9	7				2	5	4	10	6	11							1	8	
15			3	9	7				2	5	4	10	6	11							1	8	
16			3	9	7				2	5	4	10	6	11							1	8	
17			3	9	7				2	5	4	10					6			11	1	8	
18			3	9	7				2	5	4	10					6			11	1	8	
19			3	9					2	5	4	10			7		6			11	1	8	
20			3	9	7				2	5	4	10					6			11	1	8	
21			3	9					2	5	4	10			7		6			11	1	8	
22			3	9	7	4			2	5		10					6			11		8	1
23			3	9	7	4			2	5		10					6			11		8	1
24			3	9	7	4			2	5		10	6							11		8	1
25			3	9	7	4			2	5		10	6	11								8	1
26			3	9	7	4		11	2	5		10	6									8	1
27			3	9	7	4		11	2	5		10	6									8	1
28			3	9	7	4			2	5		10	6	11								8	1
29			3	9	7	4			2	5		10	6	11		8							1
30				9	7				2	5	3	10	6	11		8	4				1		
31			3	9	7				2	5		10		11		4					1	8	
32			3	9	7				2	5		10	6	11		4					1	8	
33			3	9	7				2			10	6	11	5	4					1	8	
34			3	9	7				2		4	10	6	11	5						1	8	
35			3	9	7				2		4	10	6	11	5						1	8	
36			3	9	7				2		4	10	6	11	5						1	8	
37			3	9	7				2		4	10	6	11	5						1	8	
38			3	9	7				2			10	6	11	5			4			1	8	
39			3	9	7			10	2			10	6	11	5			4			1		
40			3	9	7				2		4	10	6	11	5		8				1		
41			3	9					2		4	10	6	11	5	7	8				1		
42			3	9					2		4	10	6	11	5	7	8				1		
43			3	9	7				2		4	10	6	11	5		8				1		
44				9					2		3	10	6	11	5	7	4				1	8	
45	2			9							3	10	6	11	5	7	4				1	8	
46					7		9		2		3	10	6	11	5		4				1	8	
Apps	1	2	42	45	35	10	1	6	46	19	26	43	25	34	21	14	30	8	21	4	32	27	14
Goals				22	1		2		2		2	9		9		6	4		1			13	

Two own goals

F.A. Cup

Rd	Date	Opponent	Score	Scorers	Att	Butler D	Chilton C	Clarke D	Collinson L	Davidson A	Feasey P	Garvey B	Henderson R	McMillan E	McSeveney J	Milner M	Sharpe L	Summers G	Swan M	Wilkinson W	Williams M
R1	Nov 16	CREWE ALEXANDRA	2-2	Chilton, Shaw	10013	3	9	7		2	5	4	10				6	11	1	8	
rep	20	Crewe Alexandra	3-0	Wilkinson 2, Henderson	7955	3	9			2	5	4	10			7	6	11	1	8	
R2	Dec 7	Wrexham	2-0	Chilton, Henderson	8323	3	9	7		2	5	4	10				6	11	1	8	
R3	Jan 4	EVERTON	1-1	Wilkinson	36478	3	9	7	4	2	5		10	6	11					8	1
rep	7	Everton	1-2	McSeveney	56613	3	9	7	4	2	5		10	6	11					8	1

F.L. Cup

Rd	Date	Opponent	Score	Scorers	Att	Butler D	Chilton C	Clarke D	Cummins G	Davidson A	Garvey B	Henderson R	McMillan E	McSeveney J	Milner M	Shaw A	Swan M	Wilkinson W
R2	Sep 25	EXETER CITY	1-0	Henderson	9313	3	9	7	10	2		8	6	11	5	4	1	
R3	Oct 16	MANCHESTER CITY	0-3		13880	3	9	7		2	5	10	6	11		4	1	8

Final table

		Pl	Home W	D	L	F	A	Away W	D	L	F	A	F. (Total)	A.	Pts
1	Coventry City	46	14	7	2	62	32	8	9	6	36	29	98	61	60
2	Crystal Palace	46	17	4	2	38	14	6	10	7	35	37	73	51	60
3	Watford	46	16	6	1	57	28	7	6	10	22	31	79	59	58
4	Bournemouth	46	17	4	2	47	15	7	4	12	32	43	79	58	56
5	Bristol City	46	13	7	3	52	24	7	8	8	32	40	84	64	55
6	Reading	46	15	5	3	49	26	6	5	12	30	36	79	62	52
7	Mansfield Town	46	15	8	0	51	20	5	3	15	25	42	76	62	51
8	HULL CITY	46	11	9	3	45	27	5	8	10	28	41	73	68	49
9	Oldham Athletic	46	13	3	7	44	35	7	5	11	29	35	73	70	48
10	Peterborough Utd.	46	13	6	4	52	27	5	5	13	23	43	75	70	47
11	Shrewsbury Town	46	13	6	4	43	19	5	5	13	30	61	73	80	47
12	Bristol Rovers	46	9	6	8	52	34	10	2	11	39	45	91	79	46
13	Port Vale	46	13	6	4	35	13	3	8	12	18	36	53	49	46
14	Southend United	46	9	10	4	42	26	6	5	12	35	52	77	78	45
15	Queen's Park Rgs.	46	13	4	6	47	34	5	5	13	29	44	76	78	45
16	Brentford	46	11	4	8	54	36	4	10	9	33	44	87	80	44
17	Colchester United	46	10	8	5	45	26	2	11	10	25	42	70	68	43
18	Luton Town	46	12	2	9	42	41	4	8	11	22	39	64	80	42
19	Walsall	46	7	9	7	34	35	6	5	12	25	41	59	76	40
20	Barnsley	46	9	9	5	34	29	3	6	14	34	65	68	94	39
21	Millwall	46	9	4	10	33	29	5	6	12	20	38	53	67	38
22	Crewe Alexandra	46	10	5	8	29	26	1	7	15	21	51	50	77	34
23	Wrexham	46	9	4	10	50	42	4	2	17	25	65	75	107	32
24	Notts County	46	7	8	8	29	26	2	1	20	16	66	45	92	27

1963-64
Back Row: L. Collinson, D. Butler, M. Williams, E. McMillan, P. Feasey;
Front Row: D. Clarke, W. Wilkinson, A. Davidson, C. Chilton. R. Henderson, J. McSeveney.

1964-65
Back Row: G. Summers, B. Garvey, N. Corner, M. Williams, M. Swan, M. Milner, L. Collinson, G. Cummins;
Middle Row: P. Feasey, C. Chilton, A. Davidson, C. Simpkin, M. Brown, A. Jarvis, T. Heath;
Front Row: D. Clarke, D. Butler, L. Sharpe, R. Henderson, E. McMillan, W. Wilkinson, R. Young, J. McSeveney.

1964/65 4th in Division Three

League — Division Three

#	Date	Opponent	Score	Scorers	Att.
1	Aug 22	Watford	1-2	Clarke	9586
2	26	WALSALL	2-0	Clarke, McSeveney	10605
3	29	WORKINGTON	2-2	McSeveney, Davidson	8725
4	Sep 5	Colchester United	2-1	Wilkinson 2	3310
5	9	SCUNTHORPE UNITED	1-2	McSeveney	8754
6	12	Gillingham	0-1		11144
7	15	Scunthorpe United	1-1	Wilkinson	7525
8	19	BRISTOL CITY	3-2	McSeveney 2, Corner	7485
9	25	Queen's Park Rangers	1-2	Corner	6639
10	30	Barnsley	1-1	Clarke	6940
11	Oct 3	SHREWSBURY TOWN	1-2	McSeveney	6731
12	7	BARNSLEY	7-0	Chilton 4, Henderson 3	7830
13	9	CARLISLE UNITED	1-0	Chilton	10931
14	12	READING	1-0	McSeveney	12107
15	17	Luton Town	3-1	Chilton 2, Young	6020
16	21	Reading	3-3	Chilton 2, Henderson	8582
17	24	MANSFIELD TOWN	1-1	McSeveney	8482
18	27	Brentford	3-1	Chilton 3	12745
19	31	Grimsby Town	0-3		9650
20	Nov 7	PETERBOROUGH UTD.	0-2		8054
21	21	EXETER CITY	3-1	Wagstaff, Chilton, Collinson	11786
22	28	Oldham Athletic	1-2	Wagstaff	8516
23	Dec 12	WATFORD	1-1	Wagstaff	6165
24	19	Workington	3-1	Chilton 2, McSeveney	3851
25	26	Port Vale	3-0	Chilton, Wagstaff, Clarke	6099
26	28	PORT VALE	4-0	Wagstaff 2, Henderson	12468
27	Jan 2	COLCHESTER UNITED	5-1	Wagstaff 2, Chilton, Henderson, McSeveney	16928
28	9	Bournemouth	3-2	Chilton 2, Wagstaff	7515
29	16	GILLINGHAM	1-1	Wagstaff	24426
30	23	Bristol City	2-1	Wagstaff 2	14131
31	30	BRISTOL ROVERS	3-2	Chilton, McSeveney, Wagstaff	28399
32	Feb 6	QUEEN'S PARK RANGERS	3-1	Houghton, Chilton, McSeveney	23574
33	13	Shrewsbury Town	4-0	Chilton, McSeveney, I Butler, Summers	7652
34	20	Carlisle United	0-0		17174
35	27	LUTON TOWN	3-1	Houghton, Wagstaff, Chilton	22986
36	Mar 6	Bristol Rovers	1-1	Chilton	19905
37	13	GRIMSBY TOWN	3-3	Wagstaff 2, McSeveney	26564
38	20	Peterborough United	1-2	Wagstaff	9136
39	27	BOURNEMOUTH	2-1	Houghton 2	18530
40	Apr 3	Exeter City	2-0	McSeveney, Wagstaff	6571
41	6	Walsall	3-3	Wagstaff, Chilton, I. Butler	12097
42	10	OLDHAM ATHLETIC	2-1	Chilton, Wagstaff	19032
43	16	Southend United	1-2	Chilton	11023
44	17	Mansfield Town	1-2	Wagstaff	19500
45	19	SOUTHEND UNITED	0-0		20984
46	24	BRENTFORD	2-1	Houghton, Wagstaff	14924

Appearances (shirt numbers) and summary

#	Butler D	Butler I	Chilton C	Clarke D	Collinson L	Corner N	Davidson A	Feasey P	Garvey B	Heath T	Henderson R	Houghton K	McMillan E	McSeveney J	Milner M	Rafferty R	Sharpe L	Simpkin C	Summers G	Swan M	Wagstaff K	Wilkinson W	Williams M	Young R
1	3		7		4		2			10	9		5	11				6		1		8		
2	3		9	7	4		2			10			5	11				6		1		8		
3	3		9	7	4		2			10			5	11				6		1		8		
4			9	7	4		2		3	10			5	11				6		1		8		
5			9	7	4		2		3	10			5	11				6		1		8		
6	3		9	7	4		2			10			5	11				6		1		8		
7	3		7		4	9	2	5		10				11				6		1		8		
8	3		7		4	9	2	5			10			11				6		1		8		
9	3		7		4	9	2	5			10			11				6		1		8		
10	3		9	7	4		2	5			10			11				6		1		8		
11	3		9	7	4		2	5			10			11				6		1		8		
12			9		4		2		3		10		5	11				6		1		8		7
13			9		4		2		3		10		5	11				6		1		8		7
14			9		4		2		3		10		5	11				6		1		8		7
15			9		4		2		3		10		5	11				6		1		8		7
16			9		4		2		3		10		5	11				6		1		8		7
17			9		4		2		3		10		5	11				6		1		8		7
18			9		4		2		3		10		5	11				6		1		8		7
19			9		4		2		3		10		5	11				6		1		8		7
20	3		9	7	4		2				10		5	11				6		1		8		
21	3		9		4		2				10		5	11				6		1		8	7	
22	3		9		4		2				10		5	11				6		1		8	7	
23	3		9	7	4		2				10		5	11				6		1	8			
24	3		9	7	4		2				10		5	11				6		1	8			
25	3		9	7	4		2				10		5	11				6		1	8			
26	3		9	7	4		2				10		5	11				6	1		8			
27	3	11	9		4		2				10		5	7				6	1		8			
28	3	11	9		4		2					10	5	7				6	1		8			
29	3	11	9		4		2					10	5	7				6	1		8			
30	3	11	9		4		2					10	5	7				6	1		8			
31	3	11	9		4		2					10	5	7				6	1		8			
32	3	11	9		4		2					10	5	7				6	1		8			
33	3	11	9		4		2					10	5	7				6	1		8			
34	3	11	9		4		2					10	5	7				6	1		8			
35	3	11	9		4		2				10		5	7				6	1		8			
36	3	11	9		4		2					10	5	7				6	1			8		
37	3	11	9		4		2					10	5	7				6	1		8			
38	3	11	9		4		2					10	5	7				6	1		8			
39	3	11	9		4		2					10	5	7				6	1		8			
40	3	11	9		4		2					10	5	7				6	1		8			
41	3	11	9		4		2					10	5	7			6		1		8			
42	3	11	9		4		2					10	5	7				6	1		8			
43		11	9		4		2		3			10	5	7				6	1		8			
44		11	9		4		2	5	3			10		7				6	1		8			
45	3	11	9				2	5				10		7			4	6	1		8			
46	3	11	9				2					10		7			4	6	1		8			
Apps	32	20	40	16	42	3	46	5	14	7	25	15	46	41	2	2	4	44	21	25	23	25		8
Goals		2	27	4	1	2	1				6	5		15					1		23	3		1

F.A. Cup

Rd	Date	Opponent	Score	Scorers	Att.	Butler D	Chilton C	Collinson L	Davidson A	Heath T	McMillan E	McSeveney J	Simpkin C	Summers G	Swan M	Wagstaff K	Wilkinson W	Young R
R1	Nov 14	Kidderminster Harriers	4-1	Wilkinson 2, McSeveney, Heath	6619	3	9	4	2	10	5	11	6		1		8	7
R2	Dec 5	LINCOLN CITY	1-1	Summers	10167	3	9	4	2	10	5	11	6	1		8	7	
rep	9	Lincoln City	1-3	McSeveney	8383	3	9	4	2	10	5	11	6	1		8		

F.L. Cup

Rd	Date	Opponent	Score	Scorers	Att.	Butler D	Chilton C	Collinson L	Corner N	Davidson A	Feasey P	Heath T	Henderson R	Houghton K	McSeveney J	Simpkin C	Summers G	Swan M	Wagstaff K	Wilkinson W
R2	Sep 22	SOUTHEND UNITED	0-0		4012	3	7	9	2	5			10	6	11	4		1		8
rep	28	Southend United	1-3	Wilkinson	5089	3		8	9	2	5	4	10		11	6	1			7

Final Table — Division Three

		Pl	Home W	D	L	F	A	Away W	D	L	F	A	F (Total)	A	Pts
1	Carlisle United	46	14	5	4	46	24	11	5	7	30	29	76	53	60
2	Bristol City	46	14	6	3	53	18	10	5	8	39	37	92	55	59
3	Mansfield Town	46	17	4	2	61	23	7	7	9	34	38	95	61	59
4	HULL CITY	46	14	6	3	51	25	9	6	8	40	32	91	57	58
5	Brentford	46	18	4	1	55	18	6	5	12	28	37	83	55	57
6	Bristol Rovers	46	14	7	2	52	21	6	8	9	30	37	82	58	55
7	Gillingham	46	16	5	2	45	13	7	4	12	25	37	70	50	55
8	Peterborough Utd.	46	16	3	4	61	33	6	4	13	24	41	85	74	51
9	Watford	46	13	8	2	45	21	4	8	11	26	43	71	64	50
10	Grimsby Town	46	11	10	2	37	21	5	7	11	31	46	68	67	49
11	Bournemouth	46	12	4	7	40	24	6	7	10	32	39	72	63	47
12	Southend United	46	14	4	5	48	24	5	4	14	30	47	78	71	46
13	Reading	46	12	8	3	45	26	4	6	13	25	44	70	70	46
14	Queen's Park Rgs.	46	15	5	3	48	23	2	7	14	24	57	72	80	46
15	Workington	46	11	7	5	30	22	6	5	12	28	47	58	69	46
16	Shrewsbury Town	46	10	6	7	42	38	5	6	12	34	46	76	84	42
17	Exeter City	46	8	7	8	33	27	4	10	9	18	25	51	52	41
18	Scunthorpe United	46	9	8	6	42	27	5	4	14	23	45	65	72	40
19	Walsall	46	9	4	10	34	36	6	3	14	21	44	55	80	37
20	Oldham Athletic	46	10	3	10	40	39	3	7	13	21	44	61	83	36
21	Luton Town	46	6	8	9	32	36	5	3	15	19	58	51	94	33
22	Port Vale	46	7	6	10	27	33	2	8	13	14	43	41	76	32
23	Colchester United	46	7	6	10	30	34	3	4	16	20	55	50	89	30
24	Barnsley	46	8	5	10	33	31	1	6	16	21	59	54	90	29

1965/66 Champions of Division Three

No	Mon	Date	Opponent	Score	Scorers	Att	Brown M	Butler D	Butler I	Chilton C	Collinson L	Davidson A	Greenwood P	Heath T	Henderson R	Houghton K	Jarvis A	Milner M	Sharpe L	Simpkin C	Summers G	Swan M	Wagstaff K	Wilkinson W	Williams M
1	Aug	21	SCUNTHORPE UNITED	3-2	Wagstaff 2, Houghton	18829		3	11	9		2				10		5		4	6		8	7	1
2		24	Watford	1-1	Chilton	10648		3	11	9		2				10		5		4	6		8	7	1
3		28	Brighton & Hove Albion	2-1	Wagstaff, Henderson	16560		3	11	9		2		7	12	10		5		4	6		8		1
4	Sep	1	SWINDON TOWN	1-0	Wagstaff	23163			11	9		2		7		10		5	3	4	6		8		1
5		4	QUEEN'S PARK RANGERS	1-3	Chilton	20478			11	9		2		7		10		5	3	4	6		8		1
6		11	Mansfield Town	2-1	Chilton, Houghton	14081		3	11	9	4	2			7	10		5		6			8		1
7		18	YORK CITY	1-4	I. Butler	20554		3	11	9	4	2			7	10		5		6			8		1
8		25	READING	3-3	Houghton 2, Chilton	14686		3	11	9		2			7	10		5		4	6		8		1
9	Oct	2	Exeter City	4-1	Houghton 2, Chilton, Wagstaff	7125		3	11	9		2			7	10		5		4	6		8		1
10		6	OLDHAM ATHLETIC	5-1	Chilton 3, Houghton, Wagstaff	17028		3	11	9		2			7	10		5		4	6		8		1
11		9	Swansea Town	2-4	Henderson, I. Butler	7949		3	11	9		2			7	10		5		4	6	1	8		
12		13	Oldham Athletic	2-2	Houghton 2	5883		3	11	9		2			7	10		5		4	6	1	8		
13		16	WALSALL	3-2	Chilton, Henderson, Wagstaff	15931		3	11	9		2			7	10		5		4	6	1	8		
14		22	Workington	0-3		5482		3	11	9		2			7	10	4	5		6		1	8		
15		30	BOURNEMOUTH	3-0	Chilton, Henderson, Wagstaff	12440		3	11	9		2			7	10	4	5		6		1	8	12	
16	Nov	6	Southend United	2-0	Henderson, Bradbury (og)	8088		3	11	9		2			7	10	4	5		6		1	8		
17		20	Shrewsbury Town	2-2	Wagstaff, I. Butler	5316		3	11	9		2			7	10	4	5		6		1	8		
18		24	WATFORD	3-1	Houghton 2, Chilton	15511		3	11	9		2		7	12	10	4	5		6		1	8		
19		27	GRIMSBY TOWN	1-1	Wagstaff	20681		3	11	9		2			7	10	4	5		6		1	8		
20	Dec	11	BRISTOL ROVERS	6-1	Houghton 2, Henderson, I. Butler, Simpkin, Davis (og)	16349		3	11	9		2			7	10	4	5		6		1	8		
21		17	Walsall	4-2	I. Butler (3), Chilton	8617		3	11	9		2			7	10	4	5		6		1	8		
22		27	MILLWALL	1-0	Gilchrist (og)	40231			11	9		2			7	10	4	5	3	6		1	8		
23		28	Millwall	0-3		17184			11	9		2			7	10	4	5	3	6		1	8		
24	Jan	1	SWANSEA TOWN	4-1	Wagstaff 2, Henderson, Chilton	22700		3	11	9		2			7	10	4	5		6		1	8		
25		8	Swindon Town	1-3	Houghton	15875		3	11	9			2		7	10	4	5		6		1	8		
26		15	WORKINGTON	6-0	I. Butler 2, Wagstaff, Houghton, Jarvis, Brown (og)	14704		3	11	9		2			7	10	4	5		6		1	8		
27		29	Scunthorpe United	4-2	Henderson 2, Houghton, Chilton	15570		3	11	9		2			7	10	4	5		6		1	8		
28	Feb	5	BRIGHTON & HOVE ALB	1-0	Wagstaff	25374		3	11	9		2			7	10	4	5		6		1	8		
29		19	Queen's Park Rangers	3-3	Chilton, Houghton, Wagstaff	12327		3	11	9		2		7	12	10	4	5		6		1	8		
30		23	Gillingham	3-0	Chilton, Houghton, Wagstaff	10527		3	11	9		2			7	10	4	5		6		1	8		
31		26	MANSFIELD TOWN	4-0	Wagstaff 2, Henderson, Houghton	28214		3	11	9		2			7	10	4	5		6		1	8	12	
32	Mar	9	GILLINGHAM	1-0	Wagstaff	30122		3	11	9		2			7	10	4	5		6		1	8		
33		12	York City	2-1	Wagstaff, I. Butler	19420		3	11	9		2			7	10	4	5		6		1	8		
34		18	Reading	1-0	I. Butler	14196		3	11	9		2			7	10	4	5		6		1	8		
35	Apr	8	Oxford United	2-0	Houghton, Wagstaff	14359	3		11	9		2			7	10	4	5		6		1	8		
36		9	Brentford	4-2	Wagstaff (4)	9919	3		11	9		2			7	10	4	5		6		1	8		
37		11	OXFORD UNITED	2-1	Chilton, Wagstaff	31992	3		11	9		2			7	10	4	5		6		1	8		
38		16	SHREWSBURY TOWN	2-1	Chilton, Jarvis	24333		3	11	9		2			7	10	4	5		6		1	8		
39		20	EXETER CITY	6-1	Chilton 3, Henderson 2, Houghton	28055		3	11	9		2			7	10	4	5		6		1	8		
40		23	Grimsby Town	0-1		18018		3	11	9		2		10	7		4	5		6		1	8		
41		25	Peterborough United	1-4	Chilton	9547		3	11	9		2			7	10	4	5		6		1	8		
42		30	BRENTFORD	4-1	Chilton, Henderson, Jarvis, Crisp (og)	25039		3	11	9		2			7	10	4	5		6		1	8		
43	May	6	Bristol Rovers	2-1	Chilton, Wagstaff	9234		3	11	9		2		7		10	4	5		6		1	8	12	
44		10	Bournemouth	1-1	I. Butler	7861		3	11	9		2		7	12	10	4	5		6		1	8		
45		17	PETERBOROUGH UTD.	2-1	Houghton, Chilton	28255	3		11	9		2			7	10	4	5		6		1	8		
46		20	SOUTHEND UNITED	1-0	I. Butler	30371	3		11	9		2			7	10	4	5		6		1	8		
			Apps				5	37	45	45	2	45	1	13	39	45	33	46	4	46	11	36	46	4	10
			Goals						13	25					13	22	3			1			27		

5 own goals

F.A. Cup

Rd	Mon	Date	Opponent	Score	Scorers	Att	Brown M	Butler D	Butler I	Chilton C	Collinson L	Davidson A	Greenwood P	Heath T	Henderson R	Houghton K	Jarvis A	Milner M	Sharpe L	Simpkin C	Summers G	Swan M	Wagstaff K	Wilkinson W	Williams M
R1	Nov	13	Bradford Park Avenue	3-2	Houghton, Chilton, I. Butler	11487		3	11	9		2			7	10	4	5		6		1	8		
R2	Dec	8	Gateshead	4-0	Henderson, Wagstaff, Houghton, I. Butler	5935		3	11	9		2			7	10	4	5		6		1	8		
R3	Jan	22	SOUTHAMPTON	1-0	Houghton	28851		3	11	9		2			7	10	4	5		6		1	8		
R4	Feb	12	NOTTM FOREST	2-0	Heath 2	38055	3		11	9		2		10	7	6	4	5				1	8		
R5	Mar	5	SOUTHPORT	2-0	Chilton 2	38871		3	11	9		2			7	10	4	5		6		1	8		
R6		26	Chelsea	2-2	Simpkin	46324		3	11	9		2			7	10	4	5		6		1	8		
rep		31	CHELSEA	1-3	Simpkin	15328		3	11	9		2			7	10	4	5		6		1	8		

F.L. Cup

Rd	Mon	Date	Opponent	Score	Scorers	Att	Brown M	Butler D	Butler I	Chilton C	Collinson L	Davidson A	Greenwood P	Heath T	Henderson R	Houghton K	Jarvis A	Milner M	Sharpe L	Simpkin C	Summers G	Swan M	Wagstaff K	Wilkinson W	Williams M
R1	Sep	22	DERBY COUNTY	2-2	Houghton 2	15601		3	11	9		2			7	10		5		4	6		8		1
rep		29	Derby County	3-4	Chilton, Wagstaff, Simpkin	9645		3	11	9		2			7	10		5		4	6		8		1

League table

	Team	Pl	Home W	D	L	F	A	Away W	D	L	F	A	F (Total)	A	Pts
1	HULL CITY	46	19	2	2	64	24	12	5	6	45	38	109	62	69
2	Millwall	46	19	4	0	47	13	8	7	8	29	30	76	43	65
3	Queen's Park Rgs.	46	16	3	4	62	29	8	6	9	33	36	95	65	57
4	Scunthorpe United	46	9	8	6	44	34	12	3	8	36	33	80	67	53
5	Workington	46	13	6	4	38	18	6	8	9	29	39	67	57	52
6	Gillingham	46	14	4	5	33	19	8	4	11	29	35	62	54	52
7	Swindon Town	46	11	8	4	43	18	8	5	10	31	30	74	48	51
8	Reading	46	13	5	5	36	19	6	8	9	34	44	70	63	51
9	Walsall	46	13	7	3	48	21	7	3	13	29	43	77	64	50
10	Shrewsbury Town	46	13	7	3	48	22	6	4	13	25	42	73	64	49
11	Grimsby Town	46	15	6	2	47	25	2	7	14	21	37	68	62	47
12	Watford	46	12	4	7	33	19	5	9	9	22	32	55	51	47
13	Peterborough Utd.	46	13	6	4	50	26	4	6	13	30	40	80	66	46
14	Oxford United	46	11	3	9	38	33	8	5	10	32	41	70	74	46
15	Brighton & Hove A.	46	13	4	6	48	28	3	7	13	19	37	67	65	43
16	Bristol Rovers	46	11	10	2	38	15	3	4	16	26	49	64	64	42
17	Swansea Town	46	14	4	5	61	37	1	7	15	20	59	81	96	41
18	Bournemouth	46	9	8	6	24	19	4	4	15	14	37	38	56	38
19	Mansfield Town	46	10	5	8	31	36	5	3	15	28	53	59	89	38
20	Oldham Athletic	46	8	7	8	34	33	4	6	13	21	48	55	81	37
21	Southend United	46	15	1	7	43	28	1	3	19	11	55	54	83	36
22	Exeter City	46	9	6	8	36	28	3	5	15	17	51	53	79	35
23	Brentford	46	9	4	10	34	30	1	8	14	14	39	48	69	32
24	York City	46	5	7	11	30	44	4	2	17	23	62	53	106	27

1965-66
Standing: D. Butler, A. Jarvis, A. Davidson, M. Swan, M. Milner, C. Simpkin;
Sitting: R. Henderson, K. Wagstaff, C. Chilton, K. Houghton, I. Butler.

1966-67
Standing: K. Houghton, K. Wagstaff, C. Chilton, I. McKechnie, M. Milner, C. Simpkin, I. Butler;
Sitting: R. Henderson, A. Jarvis, A. Davidson, W. Wilkinson, D. Butler.

League — Division Two

#	Date		Opponent	Result	Scorers	Att.	Beardsley D	Butler D	Butler I	Chilton C	Collinson L	Corner N	Davidson A	Davidson I	Greenwood P	Heath T	Henderson R	Houghton K	Jarvis A	Lees N	Lill D	Lord M	McKechnie I	Milner M	Pettit R	Simpkin C	Swan M	Wagstaff K	Wilkinson W	Young R
1	Aug	20	Coventry City	0-1		27933		3	11	9			2				7	10	4				1	5		6		8		
2		27	BURY	2-0	Wagstaff 2	20438		3	11	9			2			10	7	6	4				1	5				8		
3		31	Norwich City	2-0	Wagstaff, Houghton	14215		3	11	9			2			12	7	10	4				1	5		6		8		
4	Sep	3	Preston North End	2-4	Chilton, Houghton	14959		3		9			2			10	7	6	4				1	5				8	12	11
5		7	Portsmouth	1-0	Chilton	15170	2	3		9	6						7	10	4				1	5				8		11
6		10	ROTHERHAM UNITED	1-0	Houghton	25209	2	3	11	9							7	10	4				1	5				8		
7		17	Millwall	1-2	Houghton	14340	2		11	9	6						7	10	4				1	5		3		8		
8		20	NORWICH CITY	5-0	Chilton 2, Wagstaff, Houghton, I. Butler	24871		3	11	9			2				7	10	4				1	5		6		8		
9		23	NORTHAMPTON T	6-1	Wagstaff 2, Chilton 2, I Butler, Henderson	29122		3	11	9			2				7	10	4				1	5		6		8		
10		28	PORTSMOUTH	2-0	Houghton, Wagstaff	35929		3	11	9			2				7	10	4				1	5		6		8		
11	Oct	1	Plymouth Argyle	1-3	Wagstaff	15776		3	11	9			2				7	10	4				1	5		6		8		
12		8	Cardiff City	4-2	Wagstaff 4	9407		3		9			2				7	10	4				1	5		6		8	12	11
13		15	WOLVERHAMPTON W.	3-1	Chilton, Henderson, I. Butler	32522		3	11	9			2				7	10	4				1	5		6		8		
14		22	Ipswich Town	4-5	Wagstaff 2, Houghton, Henderson	20024		3	11	9	4		2			12	7	10					1	5		6		8		
15		29	BRISTOL CITY	0-2		26630		3	11	9	6		2				7	10	4				1			5		8		
16	Nov	5	Carlisle United	0-2		14157	2	3	11	9	6					12	7	10	4				1	5				8		11
17		12	BLACKBURN ROVERS	2-3	Houghton, Wagstaff	22887	2	3	11	9							7	10	4				1	5		6		8		
18		19	Bolton Wanderers	1-2	Henderson	14950	2	3	11	9							7	10	4				1	5		6		8		
19		26	CHARLTON ATHLETIC	2-2	Chilton, Heath	20383	2	3	11	9						10	7						1	5		6		8		
20	Dec	3	Derby County	3-2	Wilkinson 2, Wagstaff	18793		3	11	9			2				7		4				1	5		6		8	10	
21		10	CRYSTAL PALACE	6-1	Chilton 3, Wagstaff, I. Butler, Wilkinson	21818	12	3	11	9			2				7		4				1	5		6		8	10	
22		17	COVENTRY CITY	2-2	I. Butler 2	25577		3	11	9			2				7		4				1	5		6		8	10	
23		26	HUDDERSFIELD T	2-0	Chilton, Wagstaff	35630		3	11	9			2				7		4				1	5		6		8	10	
24		27	Huddersfield Town	0-1		32268		3	11	9			2				7		4				1	5		6		8	10	
25		31	Bury	2-3	Chilton, Wagstaff	7652		3	11	9			2		4		7						1	5		6		8	10	
26	Jan	7	PRESTON NORTH END	2-2	Wilkinson, Jarvis	22047		3	11	9	12		2			10	7		4				1	5		6			8	
27		14	Rotherham United	1-1	Chilton	17684		3	11	9			2				7		4				1	5		6		8	10	
28		21	MILLWALL	2-0	Simpkin, Jarvis	27189		3	11	9			2				7		4				1	5		6		8	10	
29	Feb	4	Northampton Town	2-2	Houghton, Young	12396		3		9			2				7	10	4				1	5		6		8	12	11
30		11	PLYMOUTH ARGYLE	4-2	Wagstaff, Wilkinson, Chilton, Jarvis	24702		3	11	9			2		12		7		4				1	5		6		8	10	
31		25	CARDIFF CITY	1-0	Wilkinson	23629		3	11	9			2				7		4				1	5		6		8	10	
32	Mar	4	Bristol City	1-2	Chilton	23496		3		9			2				7		4				1	5		6		8	10	
33		18	IPSWICH TOWN	1-1	Jarvis	22775		3	11	9			2			2	7		4				1	5		6		8	10	
34		25	Wolverhampton Wan.	0-4		30991		3		9			2		4		7		10				1	5		6		8		11
35		27	Birmingham City	1-2	Wilkinson	17066		3		9		5	2		2		7					8	1			6			10	11
36		28	BIRMINGHAM CITY	0-2		23122		3		9			2		4	11	7						1	5		6		8	10	
37	Apr	1	CARLISLE UNITED	1-2	Chilton	19029		3	11	9			2		4		7						1	5		6		8		
38		8	Blackburn Rovers	1-4	I. Butler	11622		3	11				2		7	12		4				10	1	5		6		8	9	
39		15	BOLTON WANDERERS	1-1	Simpkin	16480		3	11				2				7		9		10	1		5	6		8		
40		22	Charlton Athletic	3-1	Wilkinson, Lill, Wagstaff	12285		3					2		7		9		11	1		5	6		8	10	
41		27	DERBY COUNTY	1-3	Saxton (og)	19345		3					2		7	10	4		9	11	1		5	6		8	10	
42	May	6	Crystal Palace	1-4	I. Butler	12329	2		11						12			4	3	9	7	1		5	6		8	10	
			Apps				8	41	31	37	7	1	29	1	12	7	40	20	38	1	4	8	41	33	8	36	1	39	22	8
			Goals						8	17						1	4	9	4		1					2		21	8	1

One own goal

F.A. Cup

	Date		Opponent	Result	Scorers	Att.	Butler D	Butler I	Chilton C	Collinson L	Davidson A	Henderson R	Houghton K	Jarvis A	McKechnie I	Milner M	Simpkin C	Wagstaff K
R3	Jan	28	PORTSMOUTH	1-1	Houghton	29381	3	11	9		2	7	10	4	1	5	6	8
rep	Feb	1	Portsmouth	2-2	Houghton, Chilton	33107	3	11	9		2	7	10	4	1	5	6	8
rep2		6	Portsmouth	1-3	Chilton	18448	3	11	9	5	2	7	10	4			6	8

Replay a.e.t. Replay 2 at Highfield Rd. Coventry

F.L. Cup

	Date		Opponent	Result	Att.	Butler D	Butler I	Chilton C	Davidson A	Heath T	Henderson R	Houghton K	Jarvis A	Milner M	Simpkin C	Pettit R	Wagstaff K
R1	Aug	27	Lincoln City	0-1	6238	3	11	9	2	12	7	10	4	5	6	1	8

Division Two final table

		Pl	Home W	D	L	F	A	Away W	D	L	F	A	F (Total)	A	Pts
1	Coventry City	42	17	3	1	46	16	6	10	5	28	27	74	43	59
2	Wolverhampton W.	42	15	4	2	53	20	10	4	7	35	28	88	48	58
3	Carlisle United	42	15	3	3	42	16	8	3	10	29	38	71	54	52
4	Blackburn Rovers	42	13	6	2	33	11	6	7	8	23	35	56	46	51
5	Ipswich Town	42	11	8	2	45	25	6	8	7	25	29	70	54	50
6	Huddersfield Town	42	14	3	4	36	17	6	6	9	22	29	58	46	49
7	Crystal Palace	42	14	4	3	42	23	5	6	10	19	32	61	55	48
8	Millwall	42	14	5	2	33	17	4	4	13	16	41	49	58	45
9	Bolton Wanderers	42	10	7	4	36	19	4	7	10	28	39	64	58	42
10	Birmingham City	42	11	5	5	42	23	5	3	13	28	43	70	66	40
11	Norwich City	42	10	7	4	31	21	3	7	11	18	34	49	55	40
12	HULL CITY	42	11	5	5	46	25	5	2	14	31	47	77	72	39
13	Preston North End	42	14	3	4	44	23	2	4	15	21	44	65	67	39
14	Portsmouth	42	7	5	9	34	37	6	8	7	25	33	59	70	39
15	Bristol City	42	10	8	3	38	22	2	6	13	18	40	56	62	38
16	Plymouth Argyle	42	12	4	5	42	21	2	5	14	17	37	59	58	37
17	Derby County	42	8	6	7	40	32	4	6	11	28	40	68	72	36
18	Rotherham United	42	10	5	6	39	28	3	5	13	22	42	61	70	36
19	Charlton Athletic	42	11	4	6	34	16	2	5	14	15	37	49	53	35
20	Cardiff City	42	9	7	5	43	28	3	2	16	18	59	61	87	33
21	Northampton Town	42	8	6	7	28	33	4	0	17	19	51	47	84	30
22	Bury	42	9	3	9	31	30	2	3	16	18	53	49	83	28

1967/68   17th in Division Two

#	Date	Opponent	Score	Scorers	Att	Banks F	Beardsley D	Butler D	Butler I	Chilton C	Davidson A	Davidson I	Greenwood P	Heath T	Henderson R	Houghton K	Jarvis A	Lees N	Lill D	Lord M	McKechnie I	Milner M	Pettit R	Simpkin C	Swan M	Wagstaff K	Wilkinson W	Wilson T	Young R
1	Aug 19	CARLISLE UNITED	1-0	Simpkin	19123			3	11		2			7		10	4		9			5		6	1	8			
2	Aug 23	Bolton Wanderers	1-6	Houghton	9653			3	11	9	2			7		10	4				1	5		6		8			
3	Aug 26	Blackburn Rovers	0-2		16240	6	3						2	7		10	4	9				5			1	8			11
4	Aug 30	BOLTON WANDERERS	1-2	Simpkin	15776	6		3	11				2	7		10			9			5		4	1	8			
5	Sep 2	BLACKPOOL	0-1		16958	5		3	11	9			2			10	4						7	6	1	8			
6	Sep 4	Birmingham City	2-6	Chilton, Wagstaff	25931	5	7	3	11	9			2			10	4							6	1	8			
7	Sep 9	Millwall	1-1	Wagstaff	11897	5		3		9		2	7			10	4				1			6		8	12		11
8	Sep 16	CRYSTAL PALACE	1-1	I. Butler	15993	5			11				2	7		10	4	3					1	6		8	9		12
9	Sep 23	MIDDLESBROUGH	0-2		17727	5		12			6	2				10	4	3							1	8	7		11
10	Sep 30	Bristol City	3-3	Houghton 2, Chilton	11630			2	11	9						10	4	3					5	6	1	8	12		7
11	Oct 7	Preston North End	2-3	Wagstaff, Chilton	14318	5		3	11	9	2		7										4	6	1	8	10		
12	Oct 14	QUEEN'S PARK RANGERS	2-0	Houghton, Wagstaff	14240	5		3	11	9	2		4			10								6	1	8	7		12
13	Oct 21	Plymouth Argyle	5-2	Houghton,Chilton,Wagstaff,Simpkin,Young	8577	5		3	11	9	2		4			10								6	1	8			7
14	Oct 27	CARDIFF CITY	1-2	Wagstaff	18579	5		3	11	9	2		4			10								6	1	8			7
15	Nov 4	Portsmouth	0-3		17606	5	2	3	11	9			7									12		4	6	1	8	10		
16	Nov 11	NORWICH CITY	0-2		14720	4	12		3	9	2		6		7	10									1	8	11	5	
17	Nov 18	Aston Villa	3-2	Wagstaff, Chilton, Greenwood	19675	12		3		9	2		4		7	10				1				6		8	11	5	
18	Nov 25	DERBY COUNTY	3-0	Wilkinson 2, Chilton	14767	4		3		9			2	12	7	10				1				6		8	11	5	
19	Dec 2	Rotherham United	3-1	Chilton 2, Henderson	15578	2		3	11	9			4		7					1				6		8	10	5	
20	Dec 9	CHARLTON ATHLETIC	1-1	Wagstaff	13967	2		3	11	9			4		7					1				6		8	10	5	
21	Dec 16	Carlisle United	1-1	Wagstaff	9063	2		3	11	9			4		7					1				6		8	10	5	
22	Dec 22	BLACKBURN ROVERS	1-1	I. Butler	18662	2		3	11	9			4		7					1				6		8	10	5	
23	Dec 26	Huddersfield Town	0-2		19739	2		3	11	9			4		7	12				1				6		8	10	5	
24	Dec 30	HUDDERSFIELD T	1-1	I. Butler	17656	2		3	11	9			4		7					1				6		8	10	5	
25	Jan 6	Blackpool	1-3	Chilton	13227	2		3	11	9			4		7					1				6		8	10	5	
26	Jan 13	MILLWALL	1-1	Wagstaff	13669	2		3	11	9			4		7					1				6		8	10	5	
27	Jan 20	Crystal Palace	1-0	Chilton	15431	2		3	11	9			4		7					1				6		8	10	5	
28	Feb 3	Middlesbrough	1-2	Young	16028	2		3			10		4		7	8				1				6			9	5	11
29	Feb 10	BRISTOL CITY	4-2	Wagstaff 3, I Butler	12596	2		3	11	9	10		4		12	7				1				6		8		5	
30	Feb 24	PRESTON NORTH END	1-1	Chilton	14082	2		3	11	9			4		7					1			10	6		8		5	
31	Mar 9	Queen's Park Rangers	1-1	Chilton	17705	2		3	11	9			4		7	6			10	1						8		5	
32	Mar 16	PLYMOUTH ARGYLE	0-2		11948	2		3	11	9			4		7				10	1				6		8		5	
33	Mar 22	Cardiff City	3-2	Henderson 2, Wagstaff	11975	2		3	11	9			4		7		10			1				6		8		5	
34	Mar 30	PORTSMOUTH	1-1	Wagstaff	11490	2			11	9			3		7	10	4			1				6		8		5	
35	Apr 6	Norwich City	2-2	Wagstaff, Chilton	14055	2			11	9			3		7	10	4			1				6		8		5	
36	Apr 13	ASTON VILLA	3-0	Houghton, Wagstaff, Chilton	15965	2			11	9			3		7	10	4			1				6		8		5	
37	Apr 15	IPSWICH TOWN	1-1	Houghton	19558	2			11	9			3		7	10	4			1				6		8		5	
38	Apr 16	Ipswich Town	0-2		24615	2			11	9			3		7	10	4		12	1				6		8		5	
39	Apr 20	Derby County	2-1	I. Butler, Lord	15711	2			11	9			3		7	10	4		12	1				6		8		5	
40	Apr 25	ROTHERHAM UNITED	2-1	Henderson, I. Davidson	20591	2			11	9		8	3		7	10	4			1				6				5	
41	May 4	Charlton Athletic	1-5	Young	10351	2				9	7	4				3	6			1						10	8	5	11
42	May 11	BIRMINGHAM CITY	0-1		10346	2		3	11	9			4				7	6			1					10	8	5	
		Apps				39	4	32	34	37	9	5	39	6	23	31	19	3	3	6	29	4	4	38	13	40	20	27	10
		Goals							5	14	1	1			4	7				1				3		17	2		3

F.A. Cup

Round	Date	Opponent	Score	Scorers	Att	Banks F	Butler D	Butler I	Chilton C	Greenwood P	Henderson R	Houghton K	McKechnie I	Simpkin C	Wagstaff K	Wilkinson W	Wilson T
R3	Jan 27	Middlesbrough	1-1	Chilton	28509	2	3	11	9	4	7		1	6	8	10	5
rep	31	MIDDLESBROUGH	2-2	Wagstaff 2	33916	2	3	11	9	4	7		1	6	8	10	5
rep2	Feb 7	Middlesbrough	0-1		16524	2	3	11	9	4	7	12	1	6	8	10	5

Replay a.e.t. Replay 2 at Bootham Crescent, York

F.L. Cup

Round	Date	Opponent	Score	Scorers	Att	Banks F	Chilton C	Greenwood P	Houghton K	Jarvis A	Lees N	McKechnie I	Simpkin C	Wagstaff K	Wilkinson W	Young R
R2	Sep 12	Queen's Park Rangers	1-2	Wagstaff	16609	5	9	7	10	4	2	1	6	8	3	11

		Pl	Home W	D	L	F	A	Away W	D	L	F	A	F.	A.	Pts (Total)
1	Ipswich Town	42	12	7	2	45	20	10	8	3	34	24	79	44	59
2	Queen's Park Rgs.	42	18	2	1	45	9	7	6	8	22	27	67	36	58
3	Blackpool	42	12	6	3	33	16	12	4	5	38	27	71	43	58
4	Birmingham City	42	12	6	3	54	21	7	8	6	29	30	83	51	52
5	Portsmouth	42	13	6	2	43	18	5	7	9	25	37	68	55	49
6	Middlesbrough	42	10	7	4	39	19	7	5	9	21	35	60	54	46
7	Millwall	42	9	10	2	35	16	5	7	9	27	34	62	50	45
8	Blackburn Rovers	42	13	5	3	34	16	3	6	12	22	33	56	49	43
9	Norwich City	42	12	4	5	40	30	4	7	10	20	35	60	65	43
10	Carlisle United	42	9	9	3	38	22	5	4	12	20	30	58	52	41
11	Crystal Palace	42	11	4	6	34	19	3	7	11	22	37	56	56	39
12	Bolton Wanderers	42	8	6	7	37	28	5	7	9	23	35	60	63	39
13	Cardiff City	42	9	6	6	35	29	4	6	11	25	37	60	66	38
14	Huddersfield Town	42	10	6	5	29	23	3	6	12	17	38	46	61	38
15	Charlton Athletic	42	10	6	5	43	25	2	7	12	20	43	63	68	37
16	Aston Villa	42	10	3	8	35	30	5	4	12	19	34	54	64	37
17	HULL CITY	42	6	8	7	25	23	6	5	10	33	50	58	73	37
18	Derby County	42	8	5	8	40	35	5	5	11	31	43	71	78	36
19	Bristol City	42	7	7	7	26	25	6	3	12	22	37	48	62	36
20	Preston North End	42	8	7	6	29	24	4	4	13	14	41	43	65	35
21	Rotherham United	42	7	4	10	22	32	3	7	11	20	44	42	76	31
22	Plymouth Argyle	42	5	4	12	26	36	4	5	12	12	36	38	72	27

1968/69 — 11th in Division Two

#	Date		Opponent	Score	Scorers	Att	Banks F	Barker G	Beardsley D	Butler D	Butler I	Chilton C	Greenwood P	Houghton K	Jarvis A	Lill D	Lord M	McKechnie I	O'Riley P	Pettit R	Simpkin C	Wagstaff K	Wilkinson W	Wilson T
1	Aug	10	Blackpool	0-2		17364			2	3	11	9	4	10	6			1			5	8	7	
2		17	BLACKBURN ROVERS	1-3	Chilton	13345			3		11	9	2	10	4	12		1		6	5	8	7	
3		21	Fulham	0-0		15072	2		3		11	9	12	10	7			1		4	6	8		5
4		24	Oxford United	1-1	Wagstaff	9637	2		3		11			10	7	12		1	9	4	6	8		5
5		28	Derby County	2-2	Wagstaff, Jarvis	24650	2		3		11	9		10	7			1		4	6	8		5
6		31	MIDDLESBROUGH	3-0	Wagstaff, Simpkin, Jarvis	16838	2		3		11	9		10	7			1		4	6	8		5
7	Sep	7	BRISTOL CITY	1-1	Chilton	12309	2		3		11	9	6	12	7			1		4	6	8		5
8		14	Aston Villa	1-1	I.Butler	17688	2		3		11	9	7	10				1		4	6	8		5
9		18	SHEFFIELD UNITED	1-1	I.Butler	17480	2		3		11	9	7	10				1		4	6	8	12	5
10		21	BOLTON WANDERERS	1-0	Wagstaff	13487			3	2	11	9	7	10				1		4	6	8		5
11		28	Millwall	3-2	Houghton 3	13493	2		3		11	9	7	10				1		4	6	8		5
12	Oct	5	Norwich City	2-1	Houghton, I. Butler	17985	2		3		11	9	7	10	12			1		4	6	8		5
13		9	DERBY COUNTY	1-0	I.Butler	24307			3	2	11	9	5	10	7		7	1			6	8		
14		12	HUDDERSFIELD T	3-0	Houghton 2, Wagstaff	21344			3	2	11	9	5	10	7			1		12	6	8		
15		19	Preston North End	0-1		13864			3		11	9	2	10	4		7	1			5	6	8	
16		26	CARDIFF CITY	3-3	Wagstaff 3	17027			3		11	9	2	10	4		7	1			5	6	8	
17	Nov	4	Carlisle United	0-1		9374	2				11	9	3	10	7			1		12	4	6	8	5
18		8	BURY	3-0	Wagstaff 2 Wilson	13531			3		11	9	2	10	7			1		4	6	8		5
19		16	Charlton Athletic	1-1	Wagstaff	10232	12		3		11	9	2	10	7			1		4	6	8		5
20		23	PORTSMOUTH	2-2	Wagstaff, Lord	14257	2		3		11		6		7		9	1		4	10	8		5
21		30	Birmingham City	2-5	I. Butler, Greenwood	21352	2		3		11		6		7	9		1	12	4	10	8		5
22	Dec	7	CRYSTAL PALACE	2-0	Chilton, I. Butler	13785			3	2	11	9			7	10		1		4	6	8		5
23		14	Huddersfield Town	3-0	Chilton 2, Lill	12418			3		11	9	2		7	10		1		4	6	8		5
24		20	PRESTON NORTH END	1-1	Wagstaff	15976			3		11	9	2		7	10		1		4	6	8		5
25		26	NORWICH CITY	0-1		20312			3		11	9	2		7			1		4	6	8	10	5
26		28	Cardiff City	0-3		24815			3		11		2		7		9	1	12	4	6	8	10	5
27	Jan	11	CARLISLE UNITED	1-2	I. Butler	12389			3		11		2	10	7		8	1		4	6	9	12	5
28		18	Bury	0-0		5659	2		3					7	10			1	11	9	4	6		5
29	Feb	1	CHARLTON ATHLETIC	5-2	I. Butler 2, Wagstaff, Wilkinson, Greenwood	11475	2		3		11		7	10				1		4	6	8	9	5
30		8	Portsmouth	0-1		13960			3	2	11	9	7	10	12			1		4	6	8	9	5
31		22	Crystal Palace	0-2		14172			3	2	11	7		12		10		1		4	6	8	9	5
32	Mar	1	BLACKPOOL	2-2	Lord, I. Butler	10896			3	2	11	7		12		8		1		4	6	10	9	5
33		8	Blackburn Rovers	1-1	Wagstaff	9018			3	2	11	7				8	11	1		4	6	10	9	5
34		14	OXFORD UNITED	0-0		8905			3	2	11	7				8	11	1		4	6	10	9	5
35		22	Middlesbrough	3-5	Wilkinson 2, Jarvis	18330	2		3		11		7	8	4			1			5	6	10	9
36		29	Bristol City	1-1	Jarvis	13105	2		3	12	11		7		4			1			5	6	10	9
37	Apr	5	MILLWALL	2-0	Wilkinson, Jarvis	10786	2	5	3				7		4			1		8	6		10	9
38		7	FULHAM	4-0	Wagstaff 3, Lord	10850	2	5	3				7		4			1		8	6		10	9
39		8	Sheffield United	1-1	Wagstaff	12560	2	5	3				7		4			1		8	6		10	9
40		12	Bolton Wanderers	0-1		5106	2	5	3		11			10			7	1		12	4	6		9
41		15	BIRMINGHAM CITY	1-2	Wagstaff	8702	2	5	3						7	8	11	1			4	6	10	9
42		19	ASTON VILLA	1-0	Wilkinson	10537	2	5	3		11				7	8		1			4	6	10	9
			Apps				23	6	35	17	39	22	34	23	34	10	21	42	3	40	42	39	21	28
			Goals								10	5	2	6	5	1	3				1	20	5	1

F.A. Cup

	Date		Opponent	Score	Scorers	Att	Banks F	Barker G	Beardsley D	Butler D	Butler I	Chilton C	Greenwood P	Houghton K	Jarvis A	Lill D	Lord M	McKechnie I	O'Riley P	Pettit R	Simpkin C	Wagstaff K	Wilkinson W	Wilson T
R3	Jan	4	WOLVERHAMPTON WAN.	1-3	Chilton	27526			3		11	9	2	10	7			1		4	6	8	12	5

F.L. Cup

	Date		Opponent	Score	Scorers	Att	Banks F	Barker G	Beardsley D	Butler D	Butler I	Chilton C	Greenwood P	Houghton K	Jarvis A	Lill D	Lord M	McKechnie I	O'Riley P	Pettit R	Simpkin C	Wagstaff K	Wilkinson W	Wilson T
R1	Aug	14	Halifax Town	3-0	Wagstaff, Wilkinson, Chilton	4493			3		11	9	2	10	4			1		6	5	8	7	
R2	Sep	4	Brentford	0-3		11485	2		3		11	9	6	12	7			1		4	10	8		5

		Pl	Home					Away					F.	A.	Pts
			W	D	L	F	A	W	D	L	F	A	(Total)		
1	Derby County	42	16	4	1	43	16	10	7	4	22	16	65	32	63
2	Crystal Palace	42	14	4	3	45	24	8	8	5	25	23	70	47	56
3	Charlton Athletic	42	11	8	2	39	21	7	6	8	22	31	61	52	50
4	Middlesbrough	42	13	7	1	36	13	6	4	11	22	36	58	49	49
5	Cardiff City	42	13	3	5	38	19	7	4	10	29	35	67	54	47
6	Huddersfield Town	42	13	6	2	37	14	4	6	11	16	32	53	46	46
7	Birmingham City	42	13	3	5	52	24	5	5	11	21	35	73	59	44
8	Blackpool	42	9	8	4	33	20	5	7	9	18	21	51	41	43
9	Sheffield United	42	14	4	3	41	15	2	7	12	20	35	61	50	43
10	Millwall	42	10	5	6	33	23	7	4	10	24	26	57	49	43
11	HULL CITY	42	10	7	4	38	20	3	9	9	21	32	59	52	42
12	Carlisle United	42	10	5	6	25	17	6	5	10	21	32	46	49	42
13	Norwich City	42	7	6	8	24	25	8	4	9	29	31	53	56	40
14	Preston North End	42	8	8	5	23	19	4	7	10	15	25	38	44	39
15	Portsmouth	42	11	5	5	39	22	1	9	11	19	36	58	58	38
16	Bristol City	42	9	9	3	30	15	2	7	12	16	38	46	53	38
17	Bolton Wanderers	42	8	7	6	29	26	4	7	10	26	41	55	67	38
18	Aston Villa	42	10	8	3	22	11	2	6	13	15	37	37	48	38
19	Blackburn Rovers	42	9	6	6	30	24	4	5	12	22	39	52	63	37
20	Oxford United	42	8	5	8	21	23	4	4	13	13	32	34	55	33
21	Bury	42	8	4	9	35	33	3	4	14	16	47	51	80	30
22	Fulham	42	6	7	8	20	28	1	4	16	20	53	40	81	25

1968-69

Standing: D. Butler, F. Banks, I. McKechnie, T. Wilson, M. Swan, K. Houghton, C. Simpkin;
Sitting: P. Greenwood, I. Butler, K. Wagstaff, C. Chilton, W. Wilkinson, A. Jarvis, M. Lord.

1969-70

Standing: D. Butler, D. Beardsley, F. Banks, I. McKechnie, P. Greenwood, T. Wilson, R. Pettit, J. McSeveney (Trainer);
Sitting: A. Jarvis, K. Houghton, K. Wagstaff, C. Chilton, W. Wilkinson, I. Butler, C. Simpkin.

1969/70   13th in Division Two

#	Date		Opponent	Score	Scorers	Att.	Banks F	Barker G	Beardsley D	Blampey S	Butler D	Butler I	Chilton C	Greenwood P	Houghton K	Jarvis A	Lill D	Lord M	McCunnell B	McKechnie I	Pearson S	Pettit R	Simpkin C	Wagstaff K	Wilkinson W	Wilson T
1	Aug	9	Queen's Park Rangers	0-3		15781	2	5			3	11			10	7		12		1			4	6	8	9
2		13	NORWICH CITY	1-0	Houghton	11791	2	5		7	3	11	9		10			12		1			4	6	8	
3		16	BRISTOL CITY	2-0	Chilton, Blampey	10170	2	5		7	3	11	9		10	4				1				6	8	12
4		20	Norwich City	1-2	I. Butler	18158	2	5		7	3	11	9		10	12				1			4	6	8	
5		23	Blackburn Rovers	1-2	I. Butler	11627	2	5			3	11	9		10	7				1			4	6	8	
6		27	BIRMINGHAM CITY	0-0		12242	2	5		7	3		9		10			11		1			4	6	8	
7		29	BLACKPOOL	1-0	Simpkin	9701	2	5		7	3		9		10			11		1			4	6	8	
8	Sep	6	Carlisle United	1-2	I. Butler	10049	2	5		7	3	11			10					1			4	6	8	9
9		13	BOLTON WANDERERS	4-2	Chilton 2, Wagstaff, I. Butler	10646	2	5			3	11	9		10			12		1			4	6	8	7
10		17	Portsmouth	4-1	Wagstaff, Chilton, Houghton, Hand (og)	14786	2	5			3	11	9		10			7		1				6	8	4
11		20	Aston Villa	2-3	Houghton, Chilton	23666	2	5			3	11	9		10			7		1				6	8	4
12		27	CHARLTON ATHLETIC	1-1	Simpkin	10771	2	5		7	3	11	9		10	12	8			1			4	6		
13	Oct	4	Sheffield United	0-3		16246	2	5			3	11	9	12	10		8			1			4	6		7
14		7	Bristol City	1-3	Chilton	18132	2	5			3	11	9	12	10		8			1			4	6		7
15		11	OXFORD UNITED	3-1	Wilkinson, Simpkin, Barker	8176	2	5	3			11		12	10		8			1			4	6	9	7
16		18	Swindon Town	0-1		19013	2	5	3			11		7	10		8			1			4	6	9	
17		25	HUDDERSFIELD T	2-3	Houghton, I. Butler	11375		5	3			11	9	8	2			12		1			4	6	10	7
18	Nov	1	Cardiff City	0-6		20419	2	5	3			11	9	7			8			1			12	6	10	4
19		8	PRESTON NORTH END	3-1	Chilton 2, Wagstaff	7474	2	5			3	11	9	7			8			1				6	10	4
20		15	Middlesbrough	0-1		14235	2	5			3	11	9	7			8			1				6	10	4
21		22	WATFORD	1-1	Chilton	9146	2	5	3			11	9	7			8	12		1				6	10	4
22	Dec	13	Bolton Wanderers	1-2	Chilton	7059	2		3			11	9	8	7				6	1		5	4		10	
23		17	Leicester City	2-2	Chilton, Wagstaff	16059	2	12	3			11	9	8	7					1		5	4	6	10	
24		20	CARLISLE UNITED	2-4	Houghton, Wagstaff	9295	2	5	3			11	9	8	7			12		1			4	6	10	
25		26	BLACKBURN ROVERS	3-0	Houghton, Chilton, I. Butler	11486	2		3			11	9	8	7			12		1		5	4	6	10	
26	Jan	17	Charlton Athletic	4-1	Chilton, Wagstaff, Simpkin, I. Butler	10677	2		3			11	9	8	7					1		5	4	6	10	
27		24	MILLWALL	2-1	Wagstaff, Houghton	11286	2		3			11	9	8	7					1		5	4	6	10	
28		31	SHEFFIELD UNITED	2-3	Wagstaff 2	15551	2		3			11	9	8	7					1		5	4	6	10	
29	Feb	7	Oxford United	0-0		9177	2		3			11	9	8	7					1		5	4	6	10	
30		14	QUEEN'S PARK RANGERS	1-2	Chilton	12698	2		3			11	9	8	7			12		1		5	4	6	10	
31		21	Preston North End	3-3	Chilton, Wagstaff, Simpkin	10038	2		3			11	9	8	7					1		5	4	6	10	
32		28	SWINDON TOWN	1-1	Chilton	10855	2		3			11	9	8	7					1		5	4	6	10	
33	Mar	6	Watford	1-1	Houghton	15470	2		3			11	9	8	7			12		1		5	4	6	10	
34		10	ASTON VILLA	3-1	Wagstaff 2, Houghton	9688	2		3			11	9	8	7			12		1		5	4	6	10	
35		14	LEICESTER CITY	4-1	Chilton, Wagstaff, Simpkin, Nish (og)	11536	2		3			11	9	8	7			12		1		5	4	6	10	
36		18	Blackpool	1-0	Wagstaff	15724			3			11	9	8	2	7		12		1		5	4	6	10	
37		21	Millwall	1-2	Houghton	10350			3			11		8	2	7				1	9	5	4	6	10	
38		28	MIDDLESBROUGH	3-2	Wagstaff 2, Chilton	17434			3			11	9	8	2	7				1		5	4	6	10	
39		30	Huddersfield Town	2-2	Houghton, I. Butler	26046			3			11	9	8	2	7				1		5	4	6	10	
40		31	CARDIFF CITY	1-1	I. Butler	13038			3			11	9	8	2	7				1		5	4	6	10	
41	Apr	4	Birmingham City	4-2	Houghton 3, Wagstaff	13530			3			11	9	8	2	7				1		5	4	6	10	
42		15	PORTSMOUTH	3-3	Houghton 2, Wagstaff	11468			3			11	9	8	2	7				1		9	4	6	10	5
	Apps						34	23	26	7	16	39	36	30	41	25	1	21	1	42	1	22	40	38	34	5
	Goals							1		1		9	18		16								6	18	1	

Two own goals

F.A. Cup

	Date		Opponent	Score	Scorers	Att.	Banks F	Barker G	Beardsley D	Blampey S	Butler D	Butler I	Chilton C	Greenwood P	Houghton K	Jarvis A	Lill D	Lord M	McCunnell B	McKechnie I	Pearson S	Pettit R	Simpkin C	Wagstaff K	Wilkinson W	Wilson T
R3	Jan	3	MANCHESTER CITY	0-1		30271	2		3			11	9	8	7					1		5	4	6	10	

F.L. Cup

	Date		Opponent	Score	Scorers	Att.	Banks F	Barker G	Beardsley D	Blampey S	Butler D	Butler I	Chilton C	Greenwood P	Houghton K	Jarvis A	Lill D	Lord M	McCunnell B	McKechnie I	Pearson S	Pettit R	Simpkin C	Wagstaff K	Wilkinson W	Wilson T
R2	Sep	3	NORWICH CITY	1-0	Wagstaff	10824	2	5		7	3	11	9		10					1			4	6	8	
R3		24	Derby County	1-3	Chilton	31603	2	5			3	11	9		10	12				1			4	6	8	7

		Pl	Home				Away					F.	A.	Pts
			W	D	L	F	A	W	D	L	F	A	(Total)	
1	Huddersfield Town	42	14	6	1	36	10	10	6	5	32	27	68 37	60
2	Blackpool	42	10	9	2	25	16	10	4	7	31	29	56 45	53
3	Leicester City	42	12	6	3	37	22	7	7	7	27	28	64 50	51
4	Middlesbrough	42	15	4	2	36	14	5	6	10	19	31	55 45	50
5	Swindon Town	42	13	7	1	35	17	4	9	8	22	30	57 47	50
6	Sheffield United	42	16	2	3	50	10	6	3	12	23	28	73 38	49
7	Cardiff City	42	12	7	2	38	14	6	6	9	23	27	61 41	49
8	Blackburn Rovers	42	15	2	4	42	19	5	5	11	12	31	54 50	47
9	Queen's Park Rgs.	42	13	5	3	47	24	4	6	11	19	33	66 57	45
10	Millwall	42	14	4	3	38	18	1	10	10	18	38	56 56	44
11	Norwich City	42	13	5	3	37	14	3	6	12	12	32	49 46	43
12	Carlisle United	42	10	6	5	39	28	4	7	10	19	28	58 56	41
13	**HULL CITY**	42	11	6	4	43	28	4	5	12	29	42	72 70	41
14	Bristol City	42	11	7	3	37	13	2	6	13	17	37	54 50	39
15	Oxford United	42	9	9	3	23	13	3	6	12	12	29	35 42	39
16	Bolton Wanderers	42	9	6	6	31	23	3	6	12	23	38	54 61	36
17	Portsmouth	42	8	4	9	39	35	5	5	11	27	45	66 80	35
18	Birmingham City	42	9	7	5	33	22	2	4	15	18	56	51 78	33
19	Watford	42	6	8	7	26	21	3	5	13	18	36	44 57	31
20	Charlton Athletic	42	7	8	6	23	28	0	9	12	12	48	35 76	31
21	Aston Villa	42	7	8	6	23	21	1	5	15	13	41	36 62	29
22	Preston North End	42	7	6	8	31	28	1	6	14	12	35	43 63	28

1970/71   5th in Division Two

#	Date	Opponent	Res	Scorers	Att	Banks F	Barker G	Baxter W	Beardsley D	Butler I	Chilton C	deVries R	Greenwood P	Holbrook S	Houghton K	Jarvis A	Knighton K	Lees N	Lord M	McKechnie I	Neill T	Pearson S	Pettit R	Simpkin C	Wagstaff K	Walters P	Wilkinson W
1	Aug 15	Swindon Town	1-1	Butler	16446				2	11		3			8	12			7	1	5	9		6	10		4
2	22	MIDDLESBROUGH	1-0	Simpkin	20929				2	11	9	3			8				7	1	5			6	10		4
3	29	Watford	2-1	Chilton, Wagstaff	17034				2		9	3			8	11			7	1	5			6	10		4
4	Sep 1	Carlisle United	0-2		8847				2	11	9	3			8				7	1	5			6	10		4
5	5	BOLTON WANDERERS	1-0	Chilton	16290				2	11	9	3			8	12			7	1	5			6	10		4
6	12	Bristol City	3-3	Chilton 2, Butler	12978				2	11	9	3	8						7	1	5	12		6	10		4
7	19	MILLWALL	2-0	Wagstaff, Pearson	15593				2	11		3					8		7	1	5	9		6	10		4
8	26	Norwich City	2-0	Houghton, Wagstaff	16258				2	11	9	3			8				7	1	5			6	10		4
9	Oct 3	BIRMINGHAM CITY	0-1		17582				2	11	9	3			8			12	7	1	5			6	10		4
10	7	Sunderland	1-0	Chilton	18741				2	11	9	3			8				7	1	5			6	10		4
11	10	Orient	1-0	Chilton	9445				2	11	9	3			8				7	1	5			6	10		4
12	16	SWINDON TOWN	2-0	Chilton, Wagstaff	20958				2	11	9	3			8				7	1	5	12		6	10		4
13	21	CHARLTON ATHLETIC	2-0	Chilton, Houghton	17528				2	11	9	3			8	7				1		12	5	6	10		4
14	24	SHEFFIELD UNITED	1-1	Wagstaff	25340	12			2		9	3			8	7					5	11		6	10		4
15	31	Cardiff City	1-5	Barker	21837		11		2	12		3			8	7					5	9		6	10		4
16	Nov 7	LUTON TOWN	0-2		18343	12			2	11	9	3	7		8					1	5			6	10		4
17	14	Oxford United	3-0	Chilton, Wagstaff, Houghton	8850	2				11	9	3	7		8					1	5			6	10		4
18	21	QUEEN'S PARK RANGERS	1-1	Chilton	15606	2				11	9	3	7	12	8					1	5			6	10		4
19	28	Portsmouth	2-2	Chilton, Butler	13360	2			3	11	9		7		8				10	1	5			6			4
20	Dec 5	LEICESTER CITY	3-0	Chilton, Houghton, Butler	21210	2				11	9	3	7		10					1	5			6			4
21	12	Blackburn Rovers	1-0	Chilton	7490	2				11	9	3	7		10					1	5			6			4
22	19	Middlesbrough	0-1		17957	2					9	3	7		10				11	1				6			4
23	26	SHEFFIELD WEDNESDAY	4-4	Chilton 2, Wagstaff, Houghton	24399	2				11	9	3	12		8				7	1	5			6	10		4
24	Jan 9	SUNDERLAND	4-0	Chilton 3, Wagstaff	20532	2				11	9	3	4		8				7	1	5			6	10		5
25	16	Charlton Athletic	1-0	Chilton	9656	2				11	9	3	7		10					1	5			6			4
26	30	PORTSMOUTH	0-1		19958	2				11	9	3	7		12					1	5			6	10		4
27	Feb 6	Leicester City	0-0		31076	2				11	9	3	7		8					1	5			6	10		4
28	20	Queen's Park Rangers	1-1	Wagstaff	13418	2				11	9	3	6		8	12			7	1	5				10		4
29	23	BLACKBURN ROVERS	0-0		23976	2				11	9	3	4		8				7	1	5			6	10		
30	27	CARDIFF CITY	1-1	Carver (og)	25091	2				11	9	3				12			7	1	5	8		6	10		
31	Mar 9	Sheffield United	2-1	Simpkin, Wagstaff	40227			2		11	9	3							8	1	5			6	10		4
32	13	OXFORD UNITED	0-1		26772			2		11	9	3					12		8	1	5			6	10		4
33	20	Luton Town	1-3	Houghton	19566			2	3	11					7		8		9	1	5			6	10		4
34	27	Bolton Wanderers	0-0		8759			2	3		9				11		8		7	1	5			6	10		4
35	Apr 3	WATFORD	1-1	Butler	17199	2			3	11					7		8			1	5	9	4	6	10		4
36	10	Sheffield Wednesday	1-1	Banks	21787	2			3	11	9		12		7		8			1	5			6	10		4
37	12	BRISTOL CITY	1-0	Banks	22178	2			3	11	9		6		7		8			1	5				10		4
38	13	Birmingham City	0-0		33109	2		8			9	3	12		7	11				1	5			6	10		4
39	17	ORIENT	5-2	Chilton 2, Wagstaff 2, Butler	19320	2			3	11	9		4		12	7				1		8	5	6	10		
40	24	Millwall	0-4		10740	2		5	3	11	9		6		7					1		8			10		4
41	28	CARLISLE UNITED	1-2	Butler	14363	2			3	11	9		4		7		6		12	1		8			10		4
42	May 1	NORWICH CITY	1-0	Houghton	11301	2			3	11	9		4		7		6		8						10	1	5
		Apps				24	1	6	26	37	37	32	18	2	37	10	12	1	32	41	35	12	4	37	38	1	39
		Goals				2	1			7	21				7							1		2	12		

One own goal

F.A. Cup

Rd	Date	Opponent	Res	Scorers	Att	Banks F	Barker G	Baxter W	Beardsley D	Butler I	Chilton C	deVries R	Greenwood P	Holbrook S	Houghton K	Jarvis A	Knighton K	Lees N	Lord M	McKechnie I	Neill T	Pearson S	Pettit R	Simpkin C	Wagstaff K	Walters P	Wilkinson W
R3	Jan 2	CHARLTON ATHLETIC	3-0	Wagstaff, Houghton, Butler	19926	2				11	9	3	4		8				7	1	5			6	10		
R4	23	BLACKPOOL	2-0	Wagstaff, Chilton	34752	2				11	9	3	7		12				8	1	5			6	10		4
R5	Feb 13	BRENTFORD	2-1	Houghton, Chilton	29709	2				11	9	3	12		8				7	1	5			6	10		4
R6	Mar 6	STOKE CITY	2-3	Wagstaff 2	41452	2				11	9	3			8				7	1	5			6	10		4

F.L. Cup

Rd	Date	Opponent	Res	Scorers	Att	Banks F	Barker G	Baxter W	Beardsley D	Butler I	Chilton C	deVries R	Greenwood P	Holbrook S	Houghton K	Jarvis A	Knighton K	Lees N	Lord M	McKechnie I	Neill T	Pearson S	Pettit R	Simpkin C	Wagstaff K	Walters P	Wilkinson W
R2	Sep 9	West Ham United	0-1		19264				2		9	3	12		8	11			7	1	5			6	10		4

Watney Cup

Rd	Date	Opponent	Res	Scorers	Att	Banks F	Barker G	Baxter W	Beardsley D	Butler I	Chilton C	deVries R	Greenwood P	Holbrook S	Houghton K	Jarvis A	Knighton K	Lees N	Lord M	McKechnie I	Neill T	Pearson S	Pettit R	Simpkin C	Wagstaff K	Walters P	Wilkinson W
R1	Aug 1	Peterborough United	4-0	Chilton 2, Wagstaff 2	9353				2	11	9	3			8				7	1	5			6	10		4
SF	5	MANCHESTER UNITED	1-1	Chilton	34007				2	11	9	3			8				7	1	5	12		6	10		4

SF lost 3-4 on penalties a.e.t. (N.B. This was the first match in England settled this way)

		Pl	Home					Away					F.	A.	Pts
			W	D	L	F	A	W	D	L	F	A	(Total)		
1	Leicester City	42	12	7	2	30	14	11	6	4	27	16	57	30	59
2	Sheffield United	42	14	6	1	49	18	7	8	6	24	21	73	39	56
3	Cardiff City	42	12	7	2	39	16	8	6	7	25	25	64	41	53
4	Carlisle United	42	16	3	2	39	13	4	10	7	26	30	65	43	53
5	HULL CITY	42	11	5	5	31	16	8	8	5	23	25	54	41	51
6	Luton Town	42	12	7	2	40	18	6	6	9	22	25	62	43	49
7	Middlesbrough	42	13	6	2	37	16	4	8	9	23	27	60	43	48
8	Millwall	42	13	5	3	36	12	6	4	11	23	30	59	42	47
9	Birmingham City	42	12	7	2	30	12	5	5	11	28	36	58	48	46
10	Norwich City	42	11	8	2	34	20	4	6	11	20	32	54	52	44
11	Queen's Park Rgs.	42	11	5	5	39	22	5	6	10	19	31	58	53	43
12	Swindon Town	42	12	7	2	38	14	3	5	13	23	37	61	51	42
13	Sunderland	42	11	6	4	34	21	4	6	11	18	33	52	54	42
14	Oxford United	42	8	8	5	23	23	6	6	9	18	25	41	48	42
15	Sheffield Wed.	42	10	7	4	32	27	2	5	14	19	42	51	69	36
16	Portsmouth	42	9	4	8	32	28	1	10	10	14	33	46	61	34
17	Orient	42	5	11	5	16	15	4	5	12	13	36	29	51	34
18	Watford	42	6	7	8	18	22	4	6	11	20	38	38	60	33
19	Bristol City	42	9	6	6	30	28	1	5	15	16	36	46	64	31
20	Charlton Athletic	42	7	6	8	28	30	1	8	12	13	35	41	65	30
21	Blackburn Rovers	42	5	8	8	20	28	1	7	13	17	41	37	69	27
22	Bolton Wanderers	42	6	5	10	22	31	1	5	15	13	43	35	74	24

1970-71
Back Row: J. McSeveney (trainer), M. Lord, I. McKechnie, P. Greenwood, C. Simpkin;
Middle Row: T. Wilson, G. Barker, F. Banks, I. Butler, R. Pettit, K. Houghton;
Front Row: A. Jarvis, D. Beardsley, K. Wagstaff, T. Neill, C. Chilton, W. Wilkinson.

1971-72
Back Row: K. Knighton, K. Houghton, F. Banks, R. deVries, S. Blampey, P. O'Riley;
Middle Row: I. Butler, P. Greenwood, D. Beardsley, I. McKechnie, P. Walters, R. Pettit, C. Simpkin, T. Docherty (Asst Manager);
Front Row: S. Pearson, K. Wagstaff, T. Neill, M. Lord, W. Wilkinson.

1971/72 12th in Division Two

Match results

No	Date	Opponent	Score	Scorers	Att
1	Aug 14	Charlton Athletic	0-1		9332
2	21	OXFORD UNITED	1-0	Butler	14304
3	28	Cardiff City	1-1	Pearson	17110
4	Sep 1	BIRMINGHAM CITY	1-0	Pearson	16746
5	4	BLACKPOOL	1-0	Pearson	18288
6	11	Bristol City	0-4		16659
7	18	PORTSMOUTH	1-3	Pearson	14363
8	25	Carlisle United	1-2	Wagstaff	9879
9	29	SWINDON TOWN	2-0	Pearson, Lord	10788
10	Oct 2	LUTON TOWN	0-0		13904
11	9	Fulham	0-1		8352
12	16	CHARLTON ATHLETIC	2-3	Clarke (og), Went (og)	9933
13	20	Watford	2-1	Wagstaff, Butler	7983
14	23	BURNLEY	1-2	Pearson	15469
15	30	Preston North End	1-3	Lord	14413
16	Nov 6	NORWICH CITY	1-2	Knighton	11878
17	13	Orient	0-1		6614
18	20	Queen's Park Rangers	1-2	Neill	12627
19	27	MILLWALL	0-0		12505
20	Dec 4	Sheffield Wednesday	1-2	Pearson	20223
21	11	MIDDLESBROUGH	4-3	Kaye 2, Pearson, Banks	13532
22	18	Blackpool	1-1	McGill	9349
23	27	SUNDERLAND	2-3	Pearson, Knighton	26091
24	Jan 1	Portsmouth	0-0		8665
25	8	CARDIFF CITY	0-0		12678
26	22	Swindon Town	1-2	Wagstaff	11796
27	29	WATFORD	4-0	Butler 2, Wagstaff, Pearson	10546
28	Feb 12	Burnley	2-0	Wagstaff, Butler	11751
29	19	PRESTON NORTH END	3-2	Wagstaff 2, Wilkinson	14313
30	Mar 4	ORIENT	1-1	Butler	12845
31	11	FULHAM	4-0	Pearson 2, Wagstaff 2	11112
32	15	Norwich City	0-2		30432
33	18	Oxford United	2-2	Butler, Pearson	7910
34	25	BRISTOL CITY	1-1	Wagstaff	11700
35	Apr 1	Sunderland	1-0	Wagstaff	17621
36	3	CARLISLE UNITED	2-0	Pearson, Butler	16403
37	4	Luton Town	1-0	Knighton	9763
38	8	QUEEN'S PARK RANGERS	1-1	Neill	12830
39	15	Millwall	1-2		15494
40	22	SHEFFIELD WEDNESDAY	1-0	O'Riley	13177
41	25	Birmingham City	0-2		40749
42	29	Middlesbrough	0-3		9539

Appearances (shirt numbers)

Columns: Banks F, Baxter W, Beardsley D, Blampey S, Butler I, Chilton C, deVries R, Green M, Greenwood P, Greenwood R, Holbrook S, Houghton K, Kaye J, Knighton K, Lord M, McGill J, McKechnie I, Neill T, O'Riley P, Pearson S, Pettit R, Simpkin C, Wagstaff K, Walters P, Wealands J, Wilkinson W

No	Bank	Baxt	Bear	Blam	Butl	Chil	deVr	Gree	GrnP	GrnR	Holb	Houg	Kaye	Knig	Lord	McGi	McKe	Neil	O'Ri	Pear	Pett	Simp	Wags	Walt	Weal	Wilk
1			2		11	9	3					8		6	7		1	5					10			4
2			2	8	11	9	3							6	7		1	5	12				10			4
3			2	8			3		4					6	7		1		11	9			10			5
4	2			8			3		4					6	7		1		11	9			10			5
5	2			8			3		12					6	7		1	5	11	9			10			4
6	2						3		5			8		6	7		1		11	9		12	10			4
7	2				11		3		7					6	12		1	5		9	8		10			4
8	2		3		12				4			8		6	11		1	5		9			10			
9	2		3						4	12		10		6	7		1	5		9				8		
10	2		3						4	12		10		6	7		1	5	9	8						
11	2		3		11			12	4			8		6	7		1	5		9			10			
12	2		3		11				4			8		6	7		1	5		9			10			
13	2		3		11				4	12		8		6	7		1	5		9			10			
14	2						3		4	12	7	8		6	11		1	5		9			10			
15	2						3		4	12		8		6	11	7	1	5		9			10			
16	2				11		3		4			8		6	10	7	1	5		9						
17	2				11		3		4	12		8		6	10	7	1	5		9						
18	2				11		3	7	12					6	10	4	1	5		9						
19	2				11		3		4			8		6			1	5		9			10			
20	2			12	11		3		5			8		4	7	6	1			9			10			
21	2				11		3		5				8	4	6	12	1	7		9			10			
22	2				11		3		5				8	4	6	7	1		12	9			10			
23	2				11		3		5				8	4	6	12	1	7		9			10			
24	2				11		3		5					6	8	7	1			9			10			4
25	2				11		3					12		6	8	7	1	5		9			10			4
26	2				11		3							6	8	7	1	5		9			10			4
27	2	12			11		3							6	8	7	1	5		9			10			4
28	2	6			11		3								8	7	1	5	12	9			10			4
29	2	6			11		3								8	7	1	5		9			10			4
30	2	6			11		3								8	7	1	5	12	9			10			
31	2	6			11		3								8	7		5		9			10		1	4
32	2	6			11		3						12		8	7		5		9			10		1	4
33	2	6			11		3								8	7		5		9			10		1	4
34	2				11		3		12				4	6	8	7	1	5		9			10			
35	2	6			11		3						4		8	7	1			9			10			12
36	2	6			11		3						4		8	7	1	5		9			10			12
37	2	6			11		3							7	8		1	5		9			10			4
38	2	6					3		11						8	4	1	5		9			10			12
39	2	6			11		3								8	7	1	5		9			10			
40	2	6					3								8	7	1	5	9				10			4
41	2	6					3								8	4	1	5		9			10			7
42	2	5			11		3		12					6	8	7	1			9			10			4
Apps	38	15	9	6	35	2	37	9	15	7	1	20	13	29	39	24	38	33	17	38	1	4	32	1	3	22
Goals	1				8								2	3	2	1		2	1	15			11			1

Two own goals

F.A. Cup

Rd	Date	Opponent	Score	Scorers	Att
R3	Jan 15	Norwich City	3-0	Wagstaff, Butler, McGill	22044
R4	Feb 5	Coventry City	1-0	Wagstaff	24632
R5	26	Stoke City	1-4	Wagstaff	34558

Rd	Bank	Baxt	Butl	deVr	GrnP	Houg	Kaye	Knig	Lord	McGi	McKe	Neil	O'Ri	Pear	Wags	Wilk
R3	2		11	3				6	8	7	1	5		9	10	4
R4	2	6	11	3					8	7	1	5		9	10	4
R5	2	6	11	3			9		8	7	1	5	12		10	4

F.L. Cup

Rd	Date	Opponent	Score	Att
R2	Sep 7	Liverpool	0-3	31612

Rd	Bank	deVr	GrnP	Houg	Knig	Lord	McKe	O'Ri	Pear	Wags	Wilk
R2	2	3	5	8	6	7	1	11	9	10	4

Division Two final table

Pos	Team	Pl	W	D	L	F	A	W	D	L	F	A	F	A	Pts
				Home					Away				Total		
1	Norwich City	42	13	8	0	40	16	8	7	6	20	20	60	36	57
2	Birmingham City	42	15	6	0	46	14	4	12	5	14	17	60	31	56
3	Millwall	42	14	7	0	38	17	5	10	6	26	29	64	46	55
4	Queen's Park Rgs.	42	16	4	1	39	9	4	10	7	18	19	57	28	54
5	Sunderland	42	11	7	3	42	24	6	9	6	25	33	67	57	50
6	Blackpool	42	12	6	3	43	16	8	1	12	27	34	70	50	47
7	Burnley	42	13	4	4	43	22	7	2	12	27	33	70	55	46
8	Bristol City	42	14	3	4	43	22	4	7	10	18	27	61	49	46
9	Middlesbrough	42	16	4	1	31	11	3	4	14	19	37	50	48	46
10	Carlisle United	42	12	6	3	38	22	5	3	13	23	35	61	57	43
11	Swindon Town	42	10	6	5	29	16	5	6	10	18	31	47	47	42
12	HULL CITY	42	10	6	5	33	21	4	4	13	16	32	49	53	38
13	Luton Town	42	7	8	6	25	24	3	10	8	18	24	43	48	38
14	Sheffield Wed.	42	11	7	3	33	22	2	5	14	18	36	51	58	38
15	Oxford United	42	10	8	3	28	17	2	6	13	15	38	43	55	38
16	Portsmouth	42	9	7	5	31	26	3	6	12	28	42	59	68	37
17	Orient	42	12	4	5	32	19	2	5	14	18	42	50	61	37
18	Preston North End	42	11	4	6	32	21	1	8	12	20	37	52	58	36
19	Cardiff City	42	9	7	5	37	25	1	7	13	19	44	56	69	34
20	Fulham	42	10	7	4	29	20	2	3	16	16	48	45	68	34
21	Charlton Athletic	42	9	7	5	33	25	3	2	16	22	52	55	77	33
22	Watford	42	5	5	11	15	25	0	4	17	9	50	24	75	19

1972/73   13th in Division Two

#	Date	Opponent	Result	Scorers	Att	Banks F	Beardsley D	Blampey S	Butler I	Croft S	deVries R	Green M	Greenwood R	Hawley J	Holme P	Houghton K	Kaye J	Knighton K	Lord M	McGill J	McKechnie I	Neill T	O'Riley P	Pearson S	Wagstaff K	Wealands J	Wilkinson W
1	Aug 12	Millwall	0-2		13203	2					3				10		4	6	8	7	1	5		9			11
2	19	NOTTM. FOREST	0-0		11189	2			11		3				10	12	5	6	7	8	1			9			4
3	26	Sheffield Wednesday	2-4	Pearson 2	19826	2			11		3				10		5	6	7	8	1			9			4
4	29	BRISTOL CITY	2-0	Pearson, Holme	8867	2			11		3				10	12	5	6	7	8	1			9			4
5	Sep 2	ORIENT	2-0	Knighton, Harris (og)	7902	2			11		3				10	12	5	6	7	8				9		1	4
6	9	Preston North End	0-1		8136	2	3						11			12	5	6	7	8		10	9			1	4
7	16	BURNLEY	1-1	Holme	8921	2	3						11	9	10		4	6	7	8		5				1	
8	20	Fulham	0-2		7686	2	3						11	9			4	6	7	8		5		10	12	1	
9	23	Middlesbrough	0-1		9180	2		12	11		3					8	4	6	7			5		9	10	1	
10	26	QUEEN'S PARK RANGERS	4-1	Pearson, Wagstaff, Houghton, Holme	8289	2			11		3					12	8	4	7	6		5		9	10	1	
11	30	SWINDON TOWN	3-2	Butler, Neill, Holme	9131	2			11		3					12	8	4	7	6		5		9	10	1	
12	Oct 7	Brighton & Hove Albion	1-1	Holme	14330	2			11						10	8	4	3	6			5		9	12	1	7
13	14	PORTSMOUTH	5-1	Pearson (4), Holme	9513	2			11						10	8	4	6		7		5		9		1	12
14	21	Luton Town	2-1	Houghton 2	11560	2			11						10	8	4	6		7		5		9		1	12
15	27	OXFORD UNITED	0-1		13426	2	3		11			12			10	8	4	6		7		5		9		1	
16	Nov 4	Queen's Park Rangers	1-1	Pearson	13619	2	3		11						10	8	4	6		7		5		9		1	
17	11	FULHAM	2-2	Pearson, Butler	9405	2	3		11						10	8	4	6		7		5		9		1	
18	18	Sunderland	1-1	Butler	11141	2	3	5	11						10		4	6	8	7				9		1	
19	25	BLACKPOOL	1-2	Butler	8988	2	3	5	11						10	12	4	6	8	7				9		1	
20	Dec 2	Aston Villa	0-2		21213	2	3		11						10	8	4	6		7				9		1	
21	9	CARLISLE UNITED	1-1	Knighton	7075	2	3		11							8	4	6		7		5		9	10	1	
22	16	CARDIFF CITY	1-1	Kaye	5875	2					3					12	8	4	11	7		5		9	10	1	
23	23	Huddersfield Town	3-1	Houghton, Wagstaff, Greenwood	6827	2							11				4	6	3	7	1	5		9	10		
24	26	MIDDLESBROUGH	3-1	Wagstaff, Knighton, Kaye	13580	2			8				11				4	6	3	7	1	5		9	10		
25	Jan 6	SHEFFIELD WEDNESDAY	1-1	Wagstaff	11537	2	3	5	11							8	4	6		7	1			9	10		
26	20	Orient	0-0		3887	2	3		11							8	4	6		7	1	5		9	10		
27	27	PRESTON NORTH END	6-2	*see below	9120	2	3	12	11							8	4	6		7	1	5		9	10		
28	Feb 10	Burnley	1-4	Pearson	13760	2	3		11							8	4	6		7		5		9	1		
29	17	MILLWALL	0-2		9821	2	3	12	11							8	4	6		7		5		9	1		
30	Mar 2	BRIGHTON & HOVE ALB	2-0	Pearson 2	7781	2	3		11						12	8	4	6		7		5		9	10	1	
31	10	Portsmouth	2-2	Holme, Kaye	8139	2	3		11						10	8	4	6		7	1	5		9			
32	13	Nottingham Forest	2-1	Holme	7711	2	3		11						10	8	4	6		7	1	5		9			
33	23	Oxford United	2-5	Holme, Kaye	6727	2	3	12	11						10		4	6	8	7	1	5		9			
34	31	Blackpool	3-4	Houghton, Pearson, Wood (og)	5645	2	3	12	11						10	8	4	6		7	1	5		9			
35	Apr 7	ASTON VILLA	1-2	Banks	8072	2	3		11				9		10	8	4	6	12	7	1	5					
36	10	LUTON TOWN	4-0	Houghton, Knighton, Kaye, Holme	5278	2	3								10	8	4	6	3	7	1	5		9			
37	14	Carlisle United	1-0	Knighton	5870	2			12							8	4	6	3	7	1	5		9			
38	21	SUNDERLAND	0-2		12637	2							11	10		8	4	6	3	7	1	5		9			
39	23	HUDDERSFIELD T	0-0		7480	2							11	10		8	4	6	3	7	1	5		9			
40	24	Swindon Town	1-2	Kaye	8412	2			6		3					11	4	12	8	7	1	5	9		10		
41	28	Bristol City	1-2	Pearson	11066	2					3		11				4	6	8	7	1	5		9	10		
42	May 9	Cardiff City	2-0	Greenwood 2	6235	2				5	3		11					6	8	7	1	4		9	10		

Scorers in game 27: Pearson 2, Houghton, Knighton, McGill, Neill

| | | Apps | | | | 42 | 22 | 9 | 25 | 1 | 13 | 1 | 21 | 2 | 32 | 32 | 41 | 39 | 25 | 42 | 21 | 35 | 3 | 37 | 16 | 21 | 9 |
| | | Goals | | | | 1 | | | 4 | | | | 3 | | 11 | 7 | 6 | 6 | | 1 | | 2 | | 17 | 4 | | |

Two own goals

F.A. Cup

	Date	Opponent	Result	Scorers	Att	Banks F	Beardsley D	Blampey S	Butler I		deVries R		Greenwood R		Holme P	Houghton K	Kaye J	Knighton K		McGill J	McKechnie I	Neill T		Pearson S	Wagstaff K	Wealands J	
R3	Jan 13	Stockport County	0-0		8294	2	3	12	11							8	4	6		7	1	5		9	10		
rep	23	STOCKPORT COUNTY	2-0	Wagstaff, Houghton	13593	2	3	12	11							8	4	6		7	1	5		9	10		
R4	Feb 3	WEST HAM UNITED	1-0	Houghton	32290	2	3		11						10	8	4	6		7	1	5		9			
R5	24	Coventry City	0-3		31663	2	3	12	11						10	8	4	6		7		5		9		1	

R3 replay a.e.t.

F.L. Cup

	Date	Opponent	Result	Scorers	Att	Banks F			Butler I		deVries R				Holme P	Houghton K	Kaye J	Knighton K	Lord M	McGill J			O'Riley P			Wealands J	Wilkinson W
R2	Sep 5	FULHAM	1-0	Knighton	6352	2			11		3				10		12	5	6	7	8			9		1	4
R3	Oct 3	NORWICH CITY	1-2	Holme	11524	2			11		3					12	8	6		7		5		9	10	1	4

Anglo Italian Cup

	Date	Opponent	Result	Scorers	Att	Banks F	Beardsley D		Butler I	Croft S			Greenwood R	Hawley J	Holme P	Houghton K	Kaye J	Knighton K	Lord M	McGill J	McKechnie I	Neill T		Pearson S	Wagstaff K	Wealands J	
Gp	Feb 21	LAZIO	2-1	Knighton, Greenwood	7325	2	3						11		10	8	4	6		7		5		9		1	
Gp	Mar 21	Fiorentina	0-1		4980	2	3		14	11					10	8	4	6	12	7	1	5		9			
Gp	Apr 4	VERONA	2-1	Knighton, Houghton	3965	2	3			5			11		10	8		6	12	7	1	4		9			
Gp	May 2	Bari	0-0		10000	2					3		11	9				6	8	7	1	5			10		

(Did not qualify for semi-finals)

		Pl	Home					Away					F.	A.	Pts
			W	D	L	F	A	W	D	L	F	A			(Total)
1	Burnley	42	13	6	2	44	18	11	8	2	28	17	72	35	62
2	Queen's Park Rgs.	42	16	4	1	54	13	8	9	4	27	24	81	37	61
3	Aston Villa	42	12	5	4	27	17	6	9	6	24	30	51	47	50
4	Middlesbrough	42	12	6	3	29	15	5	7	9	17	28	46	43	47
5	Bristol City	42	10	7	4	34	18	7	5	9	29	33	63	51	46
6	Sunderland	42	12	6	3	35	17	5	6	10	24	32	59	49	46
7	Blackpool	42	12	6	3	37	17	6	4	11	19	34	56	51	46
8	Oxford United	42	14	2	5	36	18	5	5	11	16	25	52	43	45
9	Fulham	42	11	6	4	32	16	5	6	10	26	33	58	49	44
10	Sheffield Wed.	42	14	4	3	40	20	3	6	12	19	35	59	55	44
11	Millwall	42	12	5	4	33	18	4	5	12	22	29	55	47	42
12	Luton Town	42	6	9	6	24	23	9	2	10	20	30	44	53	41
13	HULL CITY	42	9	7	5	39	22	5	5	11	25	37	64	59	40
14	Nottingham Forest	42	12	5	4	32	18	2	7	12	15	34	47	52	40
15	Orient	42	11	6	4	33	18	1	6	14	16	35	49	53	36
16	Swindon Town	42	8	9	4	28	23	2	7	12	18	37	46	60	36
17	Portsmouth	42	7	6	8	21	22	5	5	11	21	37	42	59	35
18	Carlisle United	42	10	5	6	40	24	1	7	13	10	28	50	52	34
19	Preston North End	42	6	8	7	19	25	5	4	12	18	39	37	64	34
20	Cardiff City	42	11	4	6	32	21	0	7	14	11	37	43	58	33
21	Huddersfield Town	42	7	9	5	21	20	1	8	12	15	36	36	56	33
22	Brighton & Hove A.	42	7	8	6	32	31	1	5	15	14	52	46	83	29

1972-73
Back Row: D. Beardsley, R. Greenwood, P. Holme, M. Green, R. Pettit;
Middle Row: K. Wagstaff, K. Houghton, I. McKechnie, S. Pearson, J. Wealands, P. O'Riley, J. Kaye, T. Neill (Player-manager);
Front Row: I. Butler, F. Banks, R. deVries, K. Knighton, W. Wilkinson, J. McGill, M. Lord.

1973-74
Back Row: C. Galvin, S. Blampey, J. Kaye, J. Hawley, D. Beardsley, R. Greenwood;
Middle Row: J. Hemmerman, S. Croft, M. Green, I. McKechnie, J. Wealands, P. Holme, S. Deere, P. O'Riley;
Front Row: F. Banks, R. deVries, J. McGill, T. Neill (Manager), K. Wagstaff, S. Pearson, M. Lord.

1973/74 9th in Division Two

#			Opponent	Score	Scorers	Att	Banks F	Blampey S	Burnett D	deVries R	Deere S	Galvin C	Greenwood R	Grimes V	Hawley J	Hemmerman J	Holme P	Kaye J	Lord M	McGill J	McKechnie I	O'Riley P	Pearson S	Staniforth G	Wagstaff K	Wealands J
1	Aug	25	OXFORD UNITED	0-0		7721	2	12		3	5	6	11					4	8	7			9		10	1
2	Sep	1	Bolton Wanderers	0-1		13065	2	6		3	5		11					4	8	7		12	9		10	1
3		8	PRESTON NORTH END	1-0	Pearson	7009	2	6		3	5		11				10	4	8	7			9			1
4		11	NOTTM. FOREST	0-0		8134	2	6		3	5		11					4	8	7			9		10	1
5		15	Millwall	0-3		7537	2	6		3	5		11			12		4	8	7			9		10	1
6		18	Bristol City	1-3	Pearson	10711	2	6		3	5		11					4	8	7			9		10	1
7		22	WEST BROMWICH ALB.	0-0		7089	2	6		3	5		11		9			4	8	7					10	1
8		29	Cardiff City	3-1	Lord 2, Wagstaff	10522	2	6		3	5		11					4	8	7					10	1
9	Oct	2	BRISTOL CITY	2-1	Wagstaff, Greenwood	7235	2	6		3	5		11			12		4	8	7			9		10	1
10		6	ORIENT	1-1	Pearson	7454	2	6		3	5	12	11		8			4		7			9		10	1
11		13	Middlesbrough	0-1		22135	2	6		3	5	8	11		7			4				12	9		10	1
12		20	PORTSMOUTH	4-1	Wagstaff 2, Greenwood, Hawley	6874	2	4		3	5	6	11		7				8			12	9		10	1
13		23	Nottingham Forest	0-0		10392	2	4		3	5	6	11		7				8				9		10	1
14		27	Luton Town	2-2	Lord, Greenwood	11408	2	4		3	5	6	11		7				8				9		10	1
15	Nov	3	SUNDERLAND	2-0	Hawley, Pearson	17409	2	4		3	5	6	11		7				8				9		10	1
16		10	Carlisle United	0-4		6563	2		4	3	5	6	11		7				8	12			9		10	1
17		17	Aston Villa	1-1	Burnett	23773	2		6	3	5		11		7			4	8				9		10	1
18		24	BLACKPOOL	1-0	Banks	9004	2		6	3	5		11		7			4	8				9		10	1
19	Dec	1	Fulham	0-0		5636	2		6		5		11		7			4	8			3	9		10	1
20		8	CRYSTAL PALACE	3-0	Wagstaff, Greenwood, Deere	7996	2		7		5		11			12		4	8			3	9		10	1
21		15	Notts County	2-3	Wagstaff, Kaye	8574	2		7	12	5	6	11					4	8			3	9		10	1
22		22	CARDIFF CITY	1-1	Greenwood	6826	2		7	3	5		11					4	8			6	9		10	1
23		26	Sheffield Wednesday	1-1	Greenwood	15373	2		7		5		11			12		4	8			6	9		10	1
24		29	Preston North End	0-2		10052	2		7	3	5	4	11						8	6		12	9		10	1
25	Jan	1	BOLTON WANDERERS	0-0		12210	2		6		5	4	11		7				8			3	9		10	1
26		12	MILLWALL	1-1	Lord	5659	2	4	6		5		11		7		10		8			3	9			
27		19	Oxford United	1-1	Burnett	6336	2	4	6	12	5		11		7				8			3	9			1
28		26	Swindon Town	1-1	Greenwood	4605	2		6	3	5		11		7				8	4			9			1
29	Feb	2	NOTTS COUNTY	1-0	Wagstaff	6384	2		6	3	5		11		7			12	8	4			9		10	1
30		16	MIDDLESBROUGH	1-3	Pearson	15287		6	4	3	5		11		7				8	2			9			1
31		23	Orient	1-1	Pearson	9830		6	4	3	5		11		7				8	2		10	9			1
32	Mar	2	SHEFFIELD WEDNESDAY	2-1	Pearson, Greenwood	8193		6	4	3	5		11		7				8	2		12	9		10	1
33		9	LUTON TOWN	1-3	O'Riley	7027		6	4	3	5		11		7	10			8	2		12	9			1
34		16	Portsmouth	1-3	Pearson	9838		6	4	3	5		11	7		10			8	2			9			1
35		19	West Bromwich Albion	3-2	Pearson, Wagstaff, Greenwood	13712	2		4	3	5		11	7					8	6			9		10	1
36		23	CARLISLE UNITED	1-1	Grimes	6137	2		4	3	5		11	7					8	6			9			1
37		30	Sunderland	0-1		20418	2	12	4	3	5		11	7					8	6			9		10	1
38	Apr	6	Blackpool	2-1	Pearson, Hemmerman	8159	2		4	3	5		11	7		10			8	6			9			1
39		13	ASTON VILLA	1-1	Grimes	7810	2	6	4	3	5		11	7		10			8				9			1
40		15	SWINDON TOWN	0-1		5348	2	6	4	3	5		11	6	12	10			8		1		9	7		1
41		20	Crystal Palace	2-0	Greenwood, Hawley	21909	2	6	4		5		11	7	10				8	3			9			1
42		27	FULHAM	2-0	Pearson, Lord	5731	2	6	4		5		11	7	10				8	3			9			1
					Apps		37	26	27	36	42	15	42	9	19	7	6	18	40	33	1	7	41	1	32	41
					Goals		1		2		1		10	2	3	1		1	5			1	11		8	

F.A. Cup

			Opponent	Score	Scorers	Att	Banks F	Blampey S	Burnett D	deVries R	Deere S	Galvin C	Greenwood R	Grimes V	Hawley J	Hemmerman J	Holme P	Kaye J	Lord M	McGill J	McKechnie I	O'Riley P	Pearson S	Staniforth G	Wagstaff K	Wealands J
R3	Jan	5	Bristol City	1-1	Galvin	8968	2		6		5	4	11			7			8	3			9		10	1
rep		8	BRISTOL CITY	0-1		5340	2		6		5	4	11		9	7			8	3					10	1

F.L. Cup

			Opponent	Score	Scorers	Att	Banks F	Blampey S	Burnett D	deVries R	Deere S	Galvin C	Greenwood R	Grimes V	Hawley J	Hemmerman J	Holme P	Kaye J	Lord M	McGill J	McKechnie I	O'Riley P	Pearson S	Staniforth G	Wagstaff K	Wealands J
R2	Oct	8	Leicester City	3-3	Wagstaff, Galvin, Whitworth (og)	9777	2		6		5	8	11		7			4				3	9		10	1
rep		31	LEICESTER CITY	3-2	Pearson, Greenwood, deVries	16003	2		4	3	5	6	11		7				8				9		10	1
R3	Nov	6	Stockport County	4-1	Holme 2, Wagstaff, Banks	13753	2			3	5	6			7		11		8	4		12	9		10	1
R4		27	LIVERPOOL	0-0		19748	2				5	6	11		7			4	8	3			9		10	1
rep	Dec	4	Liverpool	1-3	Lindsay (og)	17120				3	5	6	11		7			4	8	2			9		10	1

Watney Cup

			Opponent	Score	Scorers	Att	Banks F	Blampey S	Burnett D	deVries R	Deere S	Galvin C	Greenwood R	Grimes V	Hawley J	Hemmerman J	Holme P	Kaye J	Lord M	McGill J	McKechnie I	O'Riley P	Pearson S	Staniforth G	Wagstaff K	Wealands J
R1	Aug	11	Mansfield Town	3-0	Galvin, McGill, Greenwood	6340	2			3	5	6	11					4	8	7			9		10	1
SF		14	Bristol Rovers	1-0	Lord	12693	2			3	5	6	11					4	8	7			9		10	1
F		18	Stoke City	0-2		18914	2			3	5	6	11				12	4	8	7			9		10	1

		Pl	Home W	D	L	F	A	Away W	D	L	F	A	F (Total)	A	Pts
1	Middlesbrough	42	16	4	1	40	8	11	7	3	37	22	77	30	65
2	Luton Town	42	12	5	4	42	25	7	7	7	22	26	64	51	50
3	Carlisle United	42	13	5	3	40	17	7	4	10	21	31	61	48	49
4	Orient	42	9	8	4	28	17	6	10	5	27	25	55	42	48
5	Blackpool	42	11	5	5	35	17	6	8	7	22	23	57	40	47
6	Sunderland	42	11	6	4	32	15	8	3	10	26	29	58	44	47
7	Nottingham Forest	42	12	6	3	40	19	3	9	9	17	24	57	43	45
8	West Bromwich Alb.	42	8	9	4	28	24	6	7	8	20	21	48	45	44
9	HULL CITY	42	9	9	3	25	15	4	8	9	21	32	46	47	43
10	Notts County	42	8	6	7	30	35	7	7	7	25	25	55	60	43
11	Bolton Wanderers	42	12	5	4	30	17	3	7	11	14	23	44	40	42
12	Millwall	42	10	6	5	28	16	4	8	9	23	35	51	51	42
13	Fulham	42	11	4	6	26	20	5	6	10	13	23	39	43	42
14	Aston Villa	42	8	9	4	33	21	5	6	10	15	24	48	45	41
15	Portsmouth	42	9	8	4	26	16	5	4	12	19	46	45	62	40
16	Bristol City	42	9	5	7	25	20	5	5	11	22	34	47	54	38
17	Cardiff City	42	8	7	6	27	20	2	9	10	22	42	49	62	36
18	Oxford United	42	8	8	5	27	21	2	8	11	8	25	35	46	36
19	Sheffield Wed.	42	9	6	6	33	24	3	5	13	18	39	51	63	35
20	Crystal Palace	42	6	7	8	24	24	5	5	11	19	32	43	56	34
21	Preston North End	42	7	8	6	24	23	2	6	13	16	39	40	62	31
22	Swindon Town	42	6	7	8	22	27	1	4	16	14	45	36	72	25

1974/75   8th in Division Two

No	Date		Opponent	Result	Scorers	Att	Banks F	Blackburn E	Blampey S	Burnett D	Croft S	Daniel P	deVries R	Deere S	Fletcher P	Galvin C	Greenwood R	Grimes V	Haigh P	Hawley J	Hemmerman J	Lord M	McGill J	Roberts D	Staniforth G	Stewart D	Wagstaff K	Wealands J	Wood A
1	Aug	17	Southampton	3-3	Wagstaff 2, Grimes	16730			2	4			3	5			11	7		8	9	6	12				10	1	
2		20	ASTON VILLA	1-1	Wagstaff	8712			2	4			3	5			11	7		8	9	6					10	1	
3		24	WEST BROMWICH ALB.	1-0	Wagstaff	7864			2	4			3	5	12		11	7		8	9	6					10	1	
4		28	Aston Villa	0-6		18973			2	4			3	5	11	12		7			9	6	8				10	1	
5		31	Bristol Rovers	0-2		11191			2	4	12		3	5	11	8		7			9	6					10	1	
6	Sep	7	NORWICH CITY	0-0		5436			2	4			3	5	9	6	11	7		8							10	1	
7		14	Nottingham Forest	0-4		9427			2	4			3	5	9		11	7		8		12	6				10	1	
8		18	West Bromwich Albion	2-2	Hawley 2	9973				6	12	2	3	5			11	7		9		8	4				10	1	
9		21	OLDHAM ATHLETIC	1-1	Greenwood	6659				4	12	2	3	5		6	11	7		9		8					10	1	
10		24	MILLWALL	1-1	Wagstaff	5997	2			6			3	5		4	11	7		9		8					10	1	
11		28	Cardiff City	2-1	Greenwood, Deere	5648	2			6			3	5		4	11	7		9		8					10	1	
12	Oct	5	Blackpool	2-1	Greenwood, Galvin	8406	2		12	6			3	5		4	11	7		9		8					10	1	
13		12	BOLTON WANDERERS	2-0	Wagstaff 2	7353	2		12	6			3	5		4	11			9		8	7				10	1	
14		19	Sheffield Wednesday	1-2	Lord	11643	2			6			3	5		4	11			9		8	7				10	1	
15		26	SUNDERLAND	3-1	Wagstaff, Hawley, Banks	15010	2		11	6			3	5		4				9		8	7				10	1	
16	Nov	2	Notts County	0-5		9032	2		11	6			3	5		4				9	12	8	7				10	1	
17		9	FULHAM	2-1	Lord, Staniforth	7571	2			6	5		3		12	4				9		8	7		11		10	1	
18		16	Portsmouth	1-1	Wood	9045	2			6	5		3			4				11		8	7				10	1	9
19		23	MANCHESTER UNITED	2-0	Wagstaff, Lord	23287	2			6	5		3			4				11		8	7				10	1	9
20		30	BRISTOL CITY	1-0	Lord	9612	2			6	5		3			4		12		11		8	7				10	1	9
21	Dec	7	Oxford United	1-3	Lord	6751	2			6	5		3			4				11	10	12	8		7			1	9
22		14	SOUTHAMPTON	1-1	Hawley	9004	2			6	5		3			4	11		8	9			7				10	1	
23		21	Orient	0-0		4678	2			6	5		3			4	11			8		10	7					1	9
24		26	NOTTM. FOREST	1-3	Wagstaff	12278	2			6	5		3			4	12			11		8	7				10	1	9
25		28	York City	0-3		10857	2		8	6	5		3			4				11			7				10	1	9
26	Jan	11	OXFORD UNITED	1-0	Galvin	7175	2			6	5		3		9	4		7		11	10	12	8					1	
27		18	Bristol City	0-2		10423	2			6			3	5		4				11	10	8	7					1	9
28	Feb	1	Fulham	1-1	Wood	5739	2			6			3	5		4				11	10	8	7					1	9
29		8	NOTTS COUNTY	1-0	Greenwood	6700	2			6			3	5		4				11	10	8	7					1	9
30		15	Manchester United	0-2		44712	2			10			3	5		4				11		8	7	6				1	9
31		22	PORTSMOUTH	0-0		6919	2			10			3	5	12	4				11	9	8	7	6				1	
32	Mar	1	BRISTOL ROVERS	2-0	Wood, Hawley	6223	2						3	5		4	11			10		8	7	6				1	9
33		8	Millwall	0-2		6918	2						3	5	12	4	11			10		8	7	6				1	9
34		15	CARDIFF CITY	1-1	Lord	5248	2	1			5		3		12	4	11			10		8	7	6					9
35		22	Norwich City	0-1		20724	2				5		3		12	4	11			10		8	7	6				1	9
36		28	Oldham Athletic	1-0	Greenwood	11987	2				5		3			4	11			10		8	7	6				1	9
37		29	ORIENT	0-0		5203	2				5		3			4	11			10		8	7	6				1	9
38		31	YORK CITY	2-0	Hawley, Croft	10095	2				5		3			4	11			8		10	7	6				1	9
39	Apr	5	Sunderland	0-1		29838	2				5		3			4	11			10		8	7	6				1	9
40		12	BLACKPOOL	1-0	Hawley	6027	2				5		3			4				11	10	8	7	6				1	9
41		19	Bolton Wanderers	1-1	Wood	8522	2				5		3			4	11	12		10		8	7	6				1	9
42		26	SHEFFIELD WEDNESDAY	1-0	Fletcher	7652	2	1			5		3		10	4	11	7	6			8			5	12			9
			Apps				33	2	24	19	21	19	25	24	9	34	32	26	1	31	11	37	34	13	2	1	23	40	22
			Goals				1				1			1	1	2	5	1		7		6			1		10		4

F.A. Cup

	Date		Opponent	Result	Scorers	Att	Banks F	Blampey S	Burnett D	Croft S	deVries R	Deere S	Fletcher P	Galvin C	Greenwood R	Grimes V	Hawley J	Hemmerman J	Lord M	McGill J	Wagstaff K	Wealands J	Wood A
R3	Jan	4	Fulham	1-1	Wagstaff	8897	2		6	5	3		12	4	11	7			8		10	1	9
rep		7	FULHAM	2-2	Fletcher, Croft	11850	2		6	5	3		12	9	4	11	7	10	8			1	
rep2		13	Fulham	0-1		4929	2		6		3		5	12	4	11	10		8	7		1	9

Replay a.e.t. Replay 2 at Filbert St. Leicester

F.L. Cup

	Date		Opponent	Result	Scorers	Att	Blampey S	Burnett D	deVries R	Deere S	Fletcher P	Greenwood R	Grimes V	Hawley J	Lord M	McGill J	Wagstaff K	Wealands J
R2	Sep	2	BURNLEY	1-2	Fletcher	7544	2	4	3	5	9	11	7	8	12	6	10	1

		Pl	Home W	D	L	F	A	Away W	D	L	F	A	F.	A.	Pts
													(Total)		
1	Manchester United	42	17	3	1	45	12	9	6	6	21	18	66	30	61
2	Aston Villa	42	16	4	1	47	6	9	4	8	32	26	79	32	58
3	Norwich City	42	14	3	4	34	17	6	10	5	24	20	58	37	53
4	Sunderland	42	14	6	1	41	8	5	7	9	24	27	65	35	51
5	Bristol City	42	14	5	2	31	10	7	3	11	16	23	47	33	50
6	West Bromwich Alb.	42	13	4	4	33	15	5	5	11	21	27	54	42	45
7	Blackpool	42	12	6	3	31	17	2	11	8	7	16	38	33	45
8	HULL CITY	42	12	8	1	25	10	3	6	12	15	43	40	53	44
9	Fulham	42	9	8	4	29	17	4	8	9	15	22	44	39	42
10	Bolton Wanderers	42	9	7	5	27	16	6	5	10	18	25	45	41	42
11	Oxford United	42	14	3	4	30	19	1	9	11	13	32	41	51	42
12	Orient	42	8	9	4	17	16	3	11	7	11	23	28	39	42
13	Southampton	42	10	6	5	29	20	5	5	11	24	34	53	54	41
14	Notts County	42	7	11	3	34	26	5	5	11	15	33	49	59	40
15	York City	42	9	7	5	28	18	5	3	13	23	37	51	55	39
16	Nottingham Forest	42	7	7	7	24	23	5	7	9	19	32	43	55	38
17	Portsmouth	42	9	7	5	28	20	3	6	12	16	34	44	54	37
18	Oldham Athletic	42	10	7	4	28	16	0	8	13	12	32	40	48	35
19	Bristol Rovers	42	10	4	7	25	23	2	7	12	17	41	42	64	35
20	Millwall	42	8	9	4	31	19	2	3	16	13	37	44	56	32
21	Cardiff City	42	7	8	6	24	21	2	6	13	12	41	36	62	32
22	Sheffield Wed.	42	3	7	11	17	29	2	4	15	12	35	29	64	21

1974-75
Back Row: W. Dixon (Asst manager), C. Galvin, G. Staniforth, P. Daniel, V. Grimes, J. Radcliffe (Physio);
Middle Row: A. Davidson (Coach), S. Croft, J. Hawley, S. Deere, J. Wealands, P. Fletcher, D. Burnett, K. Wagstaff, T. Neill (Manager);
Front Row: J. Hemmerman, S. Blampey, J. McGill, J. Kaye, M. Lord, R. deVries, R. Greenwood

1975-76
Back Row: P. Haigh, R. Greenwood, A. Wood, K. Wagstaff, D. Roberts, F. Banks, V. Grimes;
Middle Row: J. Kaye (Manager),R. deVries, P. Fletcher, J. Wealands, C. Galvin, E. Blackburn, D. Stewart, S. Deere, P. Holme (Coach);
Front Row: A. Davidson (Asst Manager), M. Lord, P. Daniel, J. Hemmerman, J. McGill, S. Croft, S. Blampey, G. Staniforth, J. Radcliffe (Physi

1975/76 14th in Division Two

League matches

#	Date		Match	Score	Scorers	Att	Banks F	Blackburn E	Croft S	Daniel P	deVries R	Deere S	Dobson I	Fletcher P	Galvin C	Gibson D	Greenwood R	Grimes V	Haigh P	Hawley J	Hemmerman I	Lord M	Lyall G	McGill I	McIntosh J	Roberts D	Staniforth G	Stewart D	Sunley D	Wagstaff K	Wealands J	Wood A
1	Aug	16	Luton Town	0-2		10389	2		5		3				4		11	7				8				6				10	1	9
2		19	BLACKPOOL	1-0	Galvin	5364	2		5		3				4		11	7				8				6				10	1	9
3		23	BRISTOL CITY	3-1	Greenwood 2, Fletcher	5076	2		5		3			10	4		11	7				8				6		12			1	9
4		30	Oldham Athletic	0-1		6365	2		5		3			10	4		11	7				8				6					1	9
5	Sep	6	ORIENT	1-0	Wood	5194	2		5		3			10	4		11	7				8				6		12			1	9
6		13	Nottingham Forest	2-1	Greenwood, Galvin	12191	2		5		3			10	4		11	7				8				6		12			1	9
7		20	FULHAM	1-2	Grimes	8471	2		5		3			10	4		11	7				8				6					1	9
8		23	NOTTS COUNTY	0-2		8068	2		5		3			10	4		11	7				8				6		12			1	9
9		26	Charlton Athletic	0-1		10319	2		5	7	3				4		11					10				6					1	9
10	Oct	4	SOUTHAMPTON	0-0		6342	2		5	7	3				4		11					10				8				12	1	9
11		11	BRISTOL ROVERS	0-0		5642	2		5		3				12		11					7				8	4			10	1	9
12		18	Portsmouth	1-1	Grimes	8155	2		5		3				4		11	7	9			8				6				10	1	
13		25	BOLTON WANDERERS	2-2	Wagstaff, Lord	7369	2		5		3				4		11	7	9			8				6				10	1	
14	Nov	1	Oxford United	3-2	Wagstaff, Galvin, Grimes	4931	2		5		3				4		11	7	9			8				6				10	1	12
15		4	Blackburn Rovers	0-1		8816	2		5		3				4		11	7	9			8				6				10	1	12
16		8	CHELSEA	1-2	Grimes	9097	2		5		3				4	8	11	7	6			10							9	10	1	
17		15	West Bromwich Albion	0-2		14398			5	2	3				4		11	7	6	10				8							1	9
18		22	PORTSMOUTH	1-0	Galvin	4549				2	3				4	8	11	7	6	9										10	1	5
19		29	PLYMOUTH ARGYLE	4-0	Greenwood 2, Wood, Grimes	5098			5	2	3			10	4	8	11	7				12				6					1	9
20	Dec	6	York City	2-1	Fletcher, Greenwood	7037			5	2	3			10	4	8	11	7				12				6					1	9
21		13	Bristol City	0-3		10361	3		5	2				10	4	8	11	7				12				6					1	9
22		20	LUTON TOWN	1-2	Wood	5449			5	2	3			8		12	11	7	6	4				10						1	9
23		26	Sunderland	1-3	Hawley	35210			5	2							11	7	3	4				10	8	6					1	9
24		27	CARLISLE UNITED	2-3	Hawley, Wood	7056			5								11	8	3	4				10	2	6	7				1	9
25	Jan	10	NOTTM. FOREST	1-0	Wood	6465	3		5	2				12	10			7		4				8		6	11				1	9
26		17	Orient	0-1		3876			5	2	3			12		10		7		4				8		6	11				1	9
27		31	Blackpool	2-2	Wood, Fletcher	4966			5	2	3			10	4								12	8		6			11	7	1	9
28	Feb	6	BLACKBURN ROVERS	0-1		6205			5	2	3			10	4								12	8		6	11		7		1	9
29		18	Chelsea	0-0		10254			5	2	3			10	4			7						8		6			11		1	9
30		21	WEST BROMWICH ALB.	2-1	Fletcher, Lyall	6496			5	2	3			10	4			7						8		6			11		1	9
31		24	Notts County	2-1	Hawley, Sunley	15293			5	2	3				4			7		10				8		6			11		1	9
32		28	Bolton Wanderers	0-1		22592			5	2	3			8	4			7		10	12					6			11		1	9
33	Mar	6	OXFORD UNITED	2-0	Daniel, C Clarke (og)	4820			5	2	3			12	4			7		10				8		6			11		1	9
34		13	Bristol Rovers	1-0	Sunley	6230			5	2	3				10	4			11					8	7	6			9		1	
35		20	Plymouth Argyle	1-1	McIntosh	10631			5	2	3			10	4				11				12	8	7	6			9		1	
36		27	YORK CITY	1-1	Daniel	6306			5	2	3			10	4				11		9	12		8	7	6					1	
37	Apr	3	CHARLTON ATHLETIC	2-2	Hemmerman, Sunley	4656			5	2	3			12	4				11		10	7		8		6			9		1	
38		10	Fulham	1-1	Hemmerman	5624	6		2		3	5		12	4				11		10			8	7				9		1	
39		16	OLDHAM ATHLETIC	3-0	Hemmerman, Sunley, Lyall	5906	6		2		3	5		12	4				11		10			8	7				9		1	
40		17	SUNDERLAND	1-4	Croft	21296	6		2		3	5		12	4				11		10			8	7				9		1	
41		20	Carlisle United	0-0		8185	6		2		3				10	5			11				7	8					9		1	
42		24	Southampton	0-1		18272	6		2		3				10	5		4	11			7		8					9		1	
			Apps				18		41	27	38	3		27	38	7	24	37	7	22	10	10	20	14	6	34	4	3	15	10	42	30
			Goals						1	2				4	4		6	5		3	3	1	2		1				4	2		6

One own goal

F.A. Cup

	Date		Match	Score	Scorers	Att	Banks F	Croft S	Daniel P	deVries R	Deere S	Fletcher P	Galvin C	Greenwood R	Grimes V	Lord M	McGill I	Roberts D	Stewart D	Wealands J	Wood A
R3	Jan	3	PLYMOUTH ARGYLE	1-1	Grimes	6515	2	5				10	4	11	7	8	3	6		1	9
rep		6	Plymouth Argyle	4-1	Wood 2, Hawley, Sutton (og)	20208	3	5	2			10	4	11	7	8		6		1	9
R4	Feb	2	Sunderland	0-1		32320		5	2	3	12	10	7			8		6	11	1	9

F.L. Cup

	Date		Match	Score	Scorers	Att	Banks F	Croft S	deVries R	Galvin C	Gibson D	Greenwood R	Grimes V	Haigh P	Hawley J	Lord M	Roberts D	Staniforth G	Stewart D	Wagstaff K	Wealands J	Wood A
R2	Sep	9	PRESTON NORTH END	4-2	Greenwood 2, Wood, Lord	5095	2	5	3	4		11	7			8	6				1	9
R3	Oct	7	SHEFFIELD UNITED	2-0	Greenwood, Hawley	9536	2	5	3			11	7		7	8	6	4		10	1	9
R4	Nov	11	Doncaster Rovers	1-2	Wood	20476	2	5	3			11	7	6		8	12			10	1	9

Anglo-Scottish Cup

	Date		Match	Score	Scorers	Att	Banks F	Blackburn E	Croft S	Daniel P	deVries R	Fletcher P	Galvin C	Greenwood R	Grimes V	Lord M	Lyall G	Roberts D	Stewart D	Wagstaff K	Wealands J	Wood A
Gp	Aug	2	LEICESTER CITY	1-1	Fletcher	3524	2			3	5	10		11	4	8	7	6			1	9
Gp		6	WEST BROMWICH ALB.	1-2	Wagstaff	3054	2	1		3	5	10		11	7	8	4	6		12		9
Gp		9	Mansfield Town	1-2	Wagstaff	5757	2		6	3	5	9	7	11		8	4			10	1	

Final table — Division Two

		Pl	Home W	D	L	F	A	Away W	D	L	F	A	F (Total)	A	Pts
1	Sunderland	42	19	2	0	48	10	5	6	10	19	26	67	36	56
2	Bristol City	42	11	7	3	34	14	8	8	5	25	21	59	35	53
3	West Bromwich Alb.	42	10	9	2	29	12	10	4	7	21	21	50	33	53
4	Bolton Wanderers	42	12	5	4	36	14	8	7	6	28	24	64	38	52
5	Notts County	42	11	6	4	33	13	8	5	8	27	28	60	41	49
6	Southampton	42	18	2	1	49	16	3	5	13	17	34	66	50	49
7	Luton Town	42	13	6	2	38	15	6	4	11	23	36	61	51	48
8	Nottingham Forest	42	13	1	7	34	18	4	11	6	21	22	55	40	46
9	Charlton Athletic	42	11	5	5	40	34	4	7	10	21	38	61	72	42
10	Blackpool	42	9	9	3	26	22	5	5	11	14	27	40	49	42
11	Chelsea	42	7	9	5	25	20	5	7	9	28	34	53	54	40
12	Fulham	42	9	8	4	27	14	4	6	11	18	33	45	47	40
13	Orient	42	10	6	5	21	12	3	8	10	16	27	37	39	40
14	HULL CITY	42	9	5	7	29	23	5	6	10	16	26	45	49	39
15	Blackburn Rovers	42	8	6	7	27	22	4	8	9	18	28	45	50	38
16	Plymouth Argyle	42	13	4	4	36	20	0	8	13	12	34	48	54	38
17	Oldham Athletic	42	11	8	2	37	24	2	4	15	20	44	57	68	38
18	Bristol Rovers	42	7	9	5	20	15	4	7	10	18	35	38	50	38
19	Carlisle United	42	9	8	4	29	22	3	5	13	16	37	45	59	37
20	Oxford United	42	7	7	7	23	25	4	4	13	16	34	39	59	33
21	York City	42	8	3	10	28	34	2	5	14	11	37	39	71	28
22	Portsmouth	42	4	6	11	15	23	5	1	15	17	38	32	61	25

1976/77 14th in Division Two

Match results

#	Date		Opponent	Result	Scorers	Att
1	Aug	21	Hereford United	0-1		7323
2		24	LUTON TOWN	3-1	Sunley, Hemmerman, Daniel	5499
3		28	SOUTHAMPTON	4-0	Sunley, Stewart, Lyall, Hawley	7774
4	Sep	4	Carlisle United	1-1	Hawley	7530
5		11	Bolton Wanderers	1-5	Stewart	13396
6		17	SHEFFIELD UNITED	1-1	Croft	10494
7		25	Burnley	0-0		10320
8	Oct	2	NOTTM. FOREST	1-0	Bremner	16096
9		9	Charlton Athletic	1-3	Galvin	10345
10		16	WOLVERHAMPTON W.	2-0	Hawley 2	12015
11		23	Fulham	0-0		18671
12	Nov	6	BLACKPOOL	2-2	Daniel, Haigh	9541
13		13	Blackburn Rovers	0-1		8807
14		20	PLYMOUTH ARGYLE	3-1	Hemmerman, Hawley, Staniforth	8161
15		27	Bristol Rovers	0-3		6426
16	Dec	11	Cardiff City	1-1	Daniel	8270
17		18	CHELSEA	1-1	Hemmerman	11774
18		27	Notts County	1-1	Hemmerman	10634
19		28	OLDHAM ATHLETIC	0-1		11149
20	Jan	1	Blackpool	0-0		12508
21		22	HEREFORD UNITED	1-1	Sunley	7819
22		24	Luton Town	1-2	Lyall	8455
23	Feb	5	Southampton	2-2	Sunley 2	20353
24		12	CARLISLE UNITED	3-1	Sunley, Hickton, McDonald (og)	6524
25		15	MILLWALL	0-0		6642
26		19	BOLTON WANDERERS	2-2	Lyall, Daniel	9913
27		26	Sheffield United	1-1	Hemmerman	14174
28	Mar	5	BURNLEY	4-1	Lord 3, Grimes	6636
29		12	Nottingham Forest	0-2		15116
30		19	CHARLTON ATHLETIC	0-0		5575
31		26	Wolverhampton Wan.	1-2	Hemmerman	19598
32	Apr	2	FULHAM	1-0	Daniel	6158
33		8	NOTTS COUNTY	0-1		7225
34		9	Oldham Athletic	0-3		7522
35		12	BLACKBURN ROVERS	1-0	Keeley (og)	4800
36		16	Plymouth Argyle	2-1	Dobson 2	8694
37		19	ORIENT	1-1	Bremner	4494
38		23	BRISTOL ROVERS	0-1		4599
39		30	Millwall	1-2	Moore (og)	5462
40	May	7	CARDIFF CITY	1-2	Daniel	3511
41		14	Chelsea	0-4		43718
42		17	Orient	1-1	Haigh	8397

Appearances / shirt-number grid

#	Bremner W	Croft S	Daniel P	deVries R	Dobson I	Galvin C	Gibson D	Grimes V	Haigh P	Hawley J	Hemmerman J	Hickton J	Lord M	Lyall G	McDonald R	McGifford G	McIntosh J	Nisbet G	Roberts D	Staniforth G	Stewart D	Sunley D	Wealands J	Wood A
1		4	2	3				7	5		12			8						6	11	10	1	9
2		6	2	3			7		4	5	10			8							11	9	1	
3		6	2	3	12		7		4	5	10			8							11	9	1	
4		6	2	3		11	7		4	5	10			8								9	1	
5		6	2	3		12			4	5	10			8				7			11	9	1	
6		6	2	3			7		4	5	10			8				12			11	9	1	
7		6	2	3		12			4	5	10			8				7			11	9	1	
8	4	5	2	3					6	12	10			8				7			11	9	1	
9	4	5	2	3		11			6	8	10							7		12		9	1	
10	4	5	2	3		11			6	9	10			8				7			12		1	
11	4	5	2	3		11			6	9	10			8				7			12		1	
12	4	5	2	3		11			6	9	10			8				7		12			1	
13	4	5	2	3		11			6		10			8				7		9		12	1	
14	4	5	2	3		11			6	9	10			8				7		12			1	
15	4	5	2	3		11			6	9	10			8				7		12			1	
16	4	5	2	3					6	12	10			8			11	7				9	1	
17	4	5	2	3					6	11	10			8				7				9	1	
18	4	5	2	3					6	12	10			8			11	7				9	1	
19	4	5	2	3					6	12	10			8			11	7				9	1	
20	4		2	3	5	11			6		10	12		8				7				9	1	
21	4	5	2	3					6				10	8				7			11	9	1	
22	4	5	2	3					6				10	8			11	7				9	1	
23	4	5	2	3					6		12		10	8			11	7				9	1	
24	4	5	2	3					6		12		10	8			11	7				9	1	
25	4	5	2	3					6		12		10	8			11	7				9	1	
26	4	5	2	3					6		10	12	8				11	7				9	1	
27	4	5	2	3	12				6		10			8			11	7				9	1	
28	4	5	2	3				12	6				10	8			11	7				9	1	
29		5	2	3	3			12	7	4			10	8			11	6				9	1	
30	4	5	2	3					8	6			10				11	7				9	1	
31	4	5	2	3					8	6			10				11	7				9	1	
32	4	5	2	3					8	6			10					7				9	1	
33	4	5	2	3				11	6				10	8				7			12	9	1	
34	4			3	5				6				10	8	2		11	7			12	9	1	
35	4		2	3	5		12		6				10	8				7			11	9	1	
36	4	5	2		10		7		6					8				3			11	9	1	
37	4		5		10		7		3					8				2	6		11	9	1	
38	4		5		10		7		3					8				2	6		11	9	1	
39	4	5	2	3	12	11			10					8				7	6			9	1	
40		5	2	3	11	12			4					8	10			7	6			9	1	
41		5	2	3	11				4					8	10			7	6			9	1	
42		5	3		12	11	7		4					8	10			2	6			9	1	

	Bremner W	Croft S	Daniel P	deVries R	Dobson I	Galvin C	Gibson D	Grimes V	Haigh P	Hawley J	Hemmerman J	Hickton J	Lord M	Lyall G	McDonald R	McGifford G	McIntosh J	Nisbet G	Roberts D	Staniforth G	Stewart D	Sunley D	Wealands J	Wood A
Apps	30	38	41	37	10	14	14	7	42	18	31	6	17	22	4	1	14	38	7	5	14	39	42	1
Goals	2	1	6		2	1		1	2	5	6	1	3	3							1	2		

Three own goals

F.A. Cup

	Date		Opponent	Result	Scorers	Att	Bremner W	Croft S	Daniel P	deVries R	Dobson I	Haigh P	Hawley J	Hemmerman J	Lord M	Lyall G	McGifford G	Nisbet G	Stewart D	Sunley D	Wealands J
R3	Jan	8	PORT VALE	1-1	Nisbet	9694	4	5	2	3		6		10		8	12	7	11	9	1
rep		10	Port Vale	1-3	Hemmerman	10668	4	6	2	3	5	11		10		8		7		9	1

Replay a.e.t.

F.L. Cup

	Date		Opponent	Result	Scorers	Att	Croft S	Daniel P	deVries R	Dobson I	Gibson D	Haigh P	Hawley J	Hemmerman J	Lyall G	Stewart D	Sunley D	Wealands J
R2	Aug	31	Orient	0-1		3578	6	2	3	12	7	4	5	10	8	11	9	1

Anglo-Scottish Cup

	Date		Opponent	Result	Scorers	Att	Bremner W	Croft S	Daniel P	deVries R	Dobson I	Gibson D	Haigh P	Hemmerman J	Lyall G	McDonald R	McGifford G	Nisbet G	Staniforth G	Stewart D	Wealands J	Wood A
R1	Aug	7	Middlesbrough	0-2		6812	4	3			5	7	6	10	8	2	12			11	1	9
R1		10	NEWCASTLE UNITED	0-0		4715	4		2	3	5	7	6	10	8				12	11	1	9
R1		14	SHEFFIELD UNITED	1-0	Lyall	3610			2	3	5	7	6	10	8			4		11	1	9

League table

		Pl	Home					Away					F.	A.	Pts
			W	D	L	F	A	W	D	L	F	A	(Total)		
1	Wolverhampton W.	42	15	3	3	48	21	7	10	4	36	24	84	45	57
2	Chelsea	42	15	6	0	51	22	6	7	8	22	31	73	53	55
3	Nottingham Forest	42	14	3	4	53	22	7	7	7	24	21	77	43	52
4	Bolton Wanderers	42	15	2	4	46	21	5	9	7	29	33	75	54	51
5	Blackpool	42	11	7	3	29	17	6	10	5	29	25	58	42	51
6	Luton Town	42	13	5	3	39	17	8	11	2	28	31	67	48	48
7	Charlton Athletic	42	14	5	2	52	27	2	11	8	19	31	71	58	48
8	Notts County	42	11	5	5	29	20	8	5	8	36	40	65	60	48
9	Southampton	42	12	6	3	40	24	5	4	12	32	43	72	67	44
10	Millwall	42	9	6	6	31	22	6	7	8	26	31	57	53	43
11	Sheffield United	42	9	8	4	32	25	5	4	12	22	38	54	63	40
12	Blackburn Rovers	42	12	4	5	31	18	3	5	13	11	36	42	54	39
13	Oldham Athletic	42	11	6	4	37	23	3	4	14	15	41	52	64	38
14	HULL CITY	42	9	8	4	31	17	1	9	11	14	36	45	53	37
15	Bristol Rovers	42	8	9	4	32	27	4	4	13	21	41	53	68	37
16	Burnley	42	8	9	4	27	20	3	5	13	19	44	46	64	36
17	Fulham	42	9	7	5	39	25	2	6	13	15	36	54	61	35
18	Cardiff City	42	7	6	8	30	30	5	4	12	26	37	56	67	34
19	Orient	42	4	8	9	18	23	5	8	8	19	32	37	55	34
20	Carlisle United	42	7	7	7	31	33	4	5	12	18	42	49	75	34
21	Plymouth Argyle	42	5	9	7	27	25	3	7	11	19	40	46	65	32
22	Hereford United	42	6	9	6	28	30	2	6	13	29	48	57	78	31

1976-77

Back Row: A. Wood, S. Croft, V. Grimes, I. Dobson, J. Wealands, E. Blackburn, P. Haigh, P. Daniel, S. Blampey, G. Staniforth;
Front Row: G. Lyall, J. McIntosh, D. Gibson, D. Stewart, P. Walker, G. McGifford, D. Roberts,
C. Galvin, J. Hawley, M. Lord, J. Hemmerman, D. Sunley.

1977-78

ack Row: D. Stewart, R. McDonald, V. Grimes, P. Daniel, D. Sunley, J. Wealands, E. Blackburn, G. Nisbet, J. Hawley, P. Haigh, I. Dobson;
Front Row: D. Gibson, C. Galvin, G. Lyall, M. Lord, W. Bremner, S. Croft, R. deVries, B. Bannister, D. Hawker.

#		Date	Opponent	Score	Scorers	Att.	Bannister B	Blackburn E	Bremner W	Croft S	Daniel P	deVries R	Dobson I	Galvin C	Gibson D	Grimes V	Haigh P	Hawker D	Hawley J	Hood D	Hoult A	Lord M	McDonald R	Nisbet G	Roberts D	Stewart D	Sunley D	Warboys A	Wealands J
1	Aug	20	SUNDERLAND	3-0	Roberts 2, Bannister	16189	10			5	2	3		12			4		9			8		7	6	11			1
2		23	Sheffield United	0-2		13945			4	5		3		10			7		9			8		2	6	11	12		1
3		27	Crystal Palace	1-0	Hawley	14618	10		4	5		3	11				7		9			8		2	6				1
4	Sep	3	BOLTON WANDERERS	0-0		10106			4	5		3	8	12	7		9							2	6	11	10		1
5		10	Brighton & Hove Albion	1-2	Sunley	20733				5		3		4	12	7						8		2	6	11	10	9	1
6		17	STOKE CITY	0-0		9126	10		4	5		3		8			7							2	6	11		9	1
7		24	Southampton	0-1		18503	10		4	5		3	2	8	11	7									6		12	9	1
8	Oct	1	MANSFIELD TOWN	0-2		6263	10		4			3	5	11		7						8		2	6		12	9	1
9		4	TOTTENHAM HOTSPUR	2-0	Warboys 2	10966	10					3	5	4	8	7								2	6	11		9	1
10		8	Millwall	1-1	Stewart	6506	10					3	5	4	8	7						12		2	6	11		9	1
11		15	BLACKPOOL	2-0	Bannister, Stewart	6800	10		4			3	5	7	8	6								2		11	9		1
12		22	Burnley	1-1	Bremner	8592	10		4		3		5	7	8	6								2		11		9	1
13		29	BLACKBURN ROVERS	0-1		7932	10		4		2	3	5	11	8	6								7				9	1
14	Nov	5	Luton Town	1-1	Bannister	8936	10		4		2	3	5	7	8	6										11		9	1
15		12	CARDIFF CITY	4-1	Stewart 2, Warboys, Dobson	5228	10		4		2	3	5	7	8										6	11		9	1
16		19	Fulham	0-2		6161	10		4	5	2	3		7	8									12	6	11		9	1
17		26	CHARLTON ATHLETIC	0-1		5699	10		4		3		5		7	8								2	6	11	12	9	1
18	Dec	3	Bristol Rovers	1-1	Roberts	5351	10		4		2	3	5		8									7	6	11		9	1
19		10	ORIENT	2-2	Daniel, Dobson	4279	10		4		2	3	5		8	12								7	6	11		9	1
20		17	Cardiff City	0-0		5663	10		4		2	3	5		8							8		7	6	11	9		1
21		26	OLDHAM ATHLETIC	0-1		7270	12				2	3	5		8							4		7	6	11	10	9	1
22		27	Notts County	1-2	Haigh	9486	11				2	3	5	12	8				10			4		7	6			9	1
23		31	SHEFFIELD UNITED	2-3	Dobson, Bannister	8134	10					3	5	4	8	7	9							2	6	11			1
24	Jan	2	Sunderland	0-2		29396	10	1				3	5	4	8	7	9							2	6	11	12		
25		14	CRYSTAL PALACE	1-0	Bremner	5617	10	1	4	6	2	3	5				9					8		7		11			
26		21	Bolton Wanderers	0-1		20244		1	4		2	3	5	11			7	9		10	8			6					
27	Feb	4	BRIGHTON & HOVE ALB	1-1	Hoult	4543	12	1	4		2	3	5	11			6	9		10	8			7					
28		25	Mansfield Town	0-1		7379		1	4		2	3	5		8		6	12		10				7		11		9	
29	Mar	4	MILLWALL	3-2	Warboys 3	5095		1	4		2	3	5		8		7	10			11			6				9	
30		8	Stoke City	0-1		13890		1	4		2	3	5		8		7	10			11			6			12	9	
31		11	Blackpool	0-3		6220		1	4		2	3	5	11			8	10						7	6		12	9	
32		18	BURNLEY	1-3	Hawley	5936		1	4	5	2	3		8			11	10						7	6			9	
33		24	Blackburn Rovers	1-1	Hawley	11561		1	4	5	2	3					11	10			8			7	6		12	9	
34		25	NOTTS COUNTY	1-1	Bremner	5392		1	4		2	3	5				11	10			8			12	6		7	9	
35		27	Oldham Athletic	1-2	Bremner	6614		1	4	5	3	2					11	10			8			7	6			9	
36	Apr	1	LUTON TOWN	1-1	Roberts	4054		1	4	5	3						7	10			8			2	6	11		9	
37		8	Charlton Athletic	1-0	Hawley	7014	10	1	4	5			2				8	7						3	6	11		9	
38		11	SOUTHAMPTON	0-3		7299	10	1	4	5	2		12				8	7						3	6	11		9	
39		15	FULHAM	0-1		3961		1	4	5		3					8	12	7					2	6	11	10	9	
40		22	Orient	1-2	Warboys	5776	10	1		5		3	2				8		7					4	6	11		9	
41		26	Tottenham Hotspur	0-1		36913	10	1		5	2	3					8		7					4	6	11		9	
42		29	BRISTOL ROVERS	0-1		3645	10	1		5	2	3				8			7				9	4	6	11		12	
			Apps				28	19	31	19	26	37	29	23	3	10	38	5	22	4	3	18	1	39	32	28	15	31	23
			Goals				4		4		1		3			1			4		1					4	4	1	7	

F.A. Cup

		Date	Opponent	Score	Scorers	Att.	Ban	Bla	Bre	Cro	Dan	deV	Dob	Gal	Gib	Gri	Hai	Hwk	Haw	Hoo	Hou	Lor	McD	Nis	Rob	Ste	Sun	War	Wea
R3	Jan	7	LEICESTER CITY	0-1		12374	12	1	4			3		5			6	7	9			8		2		11	10		

F.L. Cup

		Date	Opponent	Score	Scorers	Att.	Ban	Bla	Bre	Cro	Dan	deV	Dob	Gal	Gib	Gri	Hai	Hwk	Haw	Hoo	Hou	Lor	McD	Nis	Rob	Ste	Sun	War	Wea
R2	Aug	31	Southport	2-2	Haigh, Bannister	3864	10		4	5		3		11			7		9					2	6	8	12		1
rep	Sep	14	SOUTHPORT	1-0	Southport	4846	10		4	5		3		8			7							2	6	11	9		1
R3	Oct	25	OLDHAM ATHLETIC	2-0	Bannister, Bremner	6923	10		4		3		5	7	8	6								2		11	9		1
R4	Nov	29	Arsenal	1-5	Hawley	25922	10		4			3	5	11	7	8			12					2	6		9		1

Anglo-Scottish Cup

		Date	Opponent	Score	Scorers	Att.	Ban	Bla	Bre	Cro	Dan	deV	Dob	Gal	Gib	Gri	Hai	Hwk	Haw	Hoo	Hou	Lor	McD	Nis	Rob	Ste	Sun	War	Wea
Gp	Aug	6	Notts County	0-1		4020	10				2	3	5		4	6			12			8		7		11	9		1
Gp		9	SHEFFIELD UNITED	0-2		3110	10				2	3	5		4	6			12			8		7		11	9		1
Gp		13	OLDHAM ATHLETIC	1-1	Grimes	1618	10					3	5	8	7	6	9							2	4	11	12		1

		Pl	Home					Away					F.	A.	Pts
			W	D	L	F	A	W	D	L	F	A	(Total)		
1	Bolton Wanderers	42	16	4	1	39	14	8	6	7	24	19	63	33	58
2	Southampton	42	15	4	2	44	16	7	9	5	26	23	70	39	57
3	Tottenham Hotspur	42	13	7	1	50	19	7	9	5	33	30	83	49	56
4	Brighton & Hove A.	42	15	5	1	43	21	7	7	7	20	17	63	38	56
5	Blackburn Rovers	42	12	4	5	33	16	4	9	8	23	44	56	60	45
6	Sunderland	42	11	6	4	36	17	3	10	8	31	42	67	59	44
7	Stoke City	42	13	5	3	38	16	3	5	13	15	33	53	49	42
8	Oldham Athletic	42	9	10	2	32	20	4	6	11	22	38	54	58	42
9	Crystal Palace	42	9	7	5	31	20	4	8	9	19	27	50	47	41
10	Fulham	42	9	8	4	32	19	5	5	11	17	30	49	49	41
11	Burnley	42	11	6	4	35	20	4	4	13	21	44	56	64	40
12	Sheffield United	42	13	4	4	38	22	3	4	14	24	51	62	73	40
13	Luton Town	42	11	4	6	35	20	3	6	12	19	32	54	52	38
14	Orient	42	8	11	2	30	20	2	7	12	13	29	43	49	38
15	Notts County	42	10	9	2	36	22	1	7	13	18	40	54	62	38
16	Millwall	42	8	8	5	23	20	4	6	11	26	37	49	57	38
17	Charlton Athletic	42	11	6	4	38	27	2	6	13	17	41	55	68	38
18	Bristol Rovers	42	10	7	4	40	26	3	5	13	21	51	61	77	38
19	Cardiff City	42	12	6	3	32	23	1	6	14	19	48	51	71	38
20	Blackpool	42	7	8	6	35	25	5	5	11	24	35	59	60	37
21	Mansfield Town	42	6	6	9	30	34	4	5	12	19	35	49	69	31
22	HULL CITY	42	6	6	9	23	25	2	6	13	11	27	34	52	28

1978/79   8th in Division Three

#	Date	Opponent	Score	Scorers	Att	Bannister B	Blackburn E	Croft S	deVries R	Dobson I	Edwards K	Farley J	Galvin C	Haigh P	Hawker D	Hood D	Horswill M	Lord M	McDonald R	Nisbet G	Norrie C	Roberts G	Skipper P	Stewart D	Warboys A	Wealands J
1	Aug 19	CARLISLE UNITED	1-1	Horswill	5062	10		4	3	5	9	11		6			7	8		2					12	1
2	26	Tranmere Rovers	3-1	Edwards, Bannister, Lord	1948	10		4	3	5	9	11		6			7	8	12	2						1
3	Sep 2	CHESTER	3-0	Edwards 3	5325	10		4	3	5	9	11		6			7	8		2					12	1
4	5	Rotherham United	2-0	Bannister, Horswill	6389	10		4	3		9	11		6		5	7	8		2						1
5	9	Brentford	0-1		6528	10			3		9	11		6		5	7	8		2					4	1
6	12	WALSALL	4-1	Edwards 2, Bannister, Lord	6784	10			3		9	11		6		5	7	8	4	2						1
7	16	CHESTERFIELD	1-1	Bannister	7705	10		4	3		9	11		6	8	7	5			2						1
8	23	Exeter City	1-3	Edwards	3733	10		4	3		9	11		6		5	7	8		2					12	1
9	26	Shrewsbury Town	0-1		3777	10		4	3		9		11	6		5		8		2					7	1
10	30	OXFORD UNITED	0-1		5263	10		4	3		9	11		6		5	7	8		2					12	1
11	Oct 7	PETERBOROUGH UTD.	1-1	Lord	4531	10		4	3		9	11	12	6		5	7	8		2						1
12	14	Gillingham	0-2		5460	10			3	5	9	11	7	6	4		8			2						1
13	21	SWANSEA CITY	2-2	Warboys, Haigh	6152	10			3	5	9	11	12	6	4		8			2					7	1
14	23	Southend United	0-3		6894	10			3	5	9	11	7	6	4		8			2				12		1
15	28	Bury	1-1	Bannister	4088	10			3	5	9	11	4	6	7		8			2						1
16	Nov 4	WATFORD	4-0	Bannister 2, Edwards, Nisbet	7739	10			3	5	9	11		6	4		8			2					7	1
17	11	Chester	1-2	Edwards	4467	10			3	5	9	11		6	4		8			2					7	1
18	18	TRANMERE ROVERS	2-1	Edwards, Horswill	4350	10	1		3	5	9	11		6	4		8			2					7	
19	Dec 9	Swindon Town	0-2		5872	12	1	4	3	5	9	11		6		10	8			2					7	
20	26	MANSFIELD TOWN	3-0	Edwards 2, Bannister	4706	10	1	4	3		9	11	7	6		5	8			2				12		
21	Jan 6	Walsall	2-1	Galvin 2	4061	10	1	4	3	5	9	11	7	6			8			2						
22	Feb 3	SHREWSBURY TOWN	1-1	Bannister	5129	10	1		3	5	9	11		6	4		8			2					7	
23	10	Oxford United	0-1		3694	10	1		3	5	9		11	6	4		8			2					7	
24	20	Blackpool	1-3	Warboys	3636	12	1		3	5	9	11		6	4		8	10		2					7	
25	24	GILLINGHAM	0-1		4345	12	1		3	5	9	11	8	6	4			10		2					7	
26	Mar 2	Swansea City	3-5	Bannister 2, Horswill	8919	10	1		3	5	9			6	11		8			2		4			7	
27	6	BRENTFORD	1-0	Edwards	3418	10	1		3	5	9	11		6			8			2		4			7	
28	10	Bury	4-1	Edwards, Bannister, Farley, Skipper	3940	10	1		3		9	11		6	4		8			2		12	5		7	
29	13	COLCHESTER UNITED	1-0	Stewart	4201	10	1	5			9			6	4		8			2		7	3	11		
30	24	ROTHERHAM UNITED	1-0	Hawker	4717	10	1	5			9		12	6	4		8			2		7	3	11		
31	27	Carlisle United	2-2	Edwards, Roberts	6234	10	1	5			9		12	6	4		8		11	2		7	3			
32	31	LINCOLN CITY	0-0		4103	10	1	5			9	11		6	4		8			2		7	3	12		
33	Apr 4	Chesterfield	2-1	Edwards, Galvin	3003	10	1	5			9		11	6	4		8			2		7	3			
34	7	Plymouth Argyle	4-3	Edwards 2, Bannister, Skipper	5816	10	1	5			9		11	6	4	12	8			2		7	3			
35	13	SHEFFIELD WEDNESDAY	1-1	Galvin	10336	10	1	5			9		9	6	4		8		12	2		7	3			
36	14	Mansfield Town	2-0	Edwards, Bannister	5138	10		5			9		11	6	4		8			2		7	3			1
37	16	BLACKPOOL	0-0		6000	10		5			9		11	6	4		8			2		7	3			1
38	21	Colchester United	1-2	Edwards	2762	10		5			9	11		6	4		8			2		7	3			1
39	24	SOUTHEND UNITED	2-0	Edwards, McDonald	3960	10		5			9	11		6	4		8		12	2		7	3			1
40	28	SWINDON TOWN	1-1	Bannister	4980	10					9	11		6	4	12	8	5		2		7	3			1
41	May 1	PLYMOUTH ARGYLE	2-1	Edwards, Horswill	3646	10					9	11	12		4	6	8	5		2		7	3			1
42	5	Lincoln City	2-4	Roberts, Horswill	2532	10			3		9	11		6	4		8	5		2		7				1
43	7	EXETER CITY	1-0	Edwards	4079	10		5			9	11		6	4		8	3		2	12	7				1
44	11	Peterborough United	0-3		1875	10		3		5	9	11		6	4		8		11	2		7				1
45	14	Watford	0-4		26347	10				12	9	11		6	7		8	5		2		3	4			1
46	19	Sheffield Wednesday	3-2	Edwards, Roberts, McDonald	9098	10			3	5	9	11		6		12	8		4	2		7				1
	Apps					46	18	24	29	24	46	32	19	45	22	17	40	24	10	46	1	19	17	5	18	28
	Goals					15					24	1	4	1	1		6	3	2	1		3	2	1	2	

F.A. Cup

#	Date	Opponent	Score	Scorers	Att	Bannister B	Blackburn E	Croft S	deVries R	Dobson I	Edwards K	Farley J	Galvin C	Haigh P	Hawker D	Hood D	Horswill M	Lord M	McDonald R	Nisbet G	Norrie C	Roberts G	Skipper P	Stewart D	Warboys A	Wealands J
R1	Nov 25	STAFFORD RANGERS	2-1	Edwards, Sargeant (og)	5,411	10	1		3		9	11		6	12	5		4	8	2					7	
R2	Dec 16	Carlisle United	0-3		5,335	10	1	4	3		9	11	7	6			8	5		2						

F.L. Cup

#	Date	Opponent	Score	Scorers	Att	Bannister B	Blackburn E	Croft S	deVries R	Dobson I	Edwards K	Farley J	Galvin C	Haigh P	Hawker D	Hood D	Horswill M	Lord M	McDonald R	Nisbet G	Norrie C	Roberts G	Skipper P	Stewart D	Warboys A	Wealands J
R1/1	Aug 12	PETERBOROUGH UTD.	0-1		4,165	10		4	3	5	9	11		6	12		7	8		2						1
R1/2	15	Peterborough United	2-1	Bannister, Haigh	4,387	10		4	3	5	9	11		6			7	8		2						1
rep	22	PETERBOROUGH UTD.	0-1		4,990	10		4	3	5	9	11		6			7	8		2						1

		Pl	Home					Away					F	A	Pts
			W	D	L	F	A	W	D	L	F	A	(Total)		
1	Shrewsbury Town	46	14	9	0	36	11	7	10	6	25	30	61	41	61
2	Watford	46	15	5	3	47	22	9	7	7	36	30	83	52	60
3	Swansea City	46	16	6	1	57	32	8	6	9	26	29	83	61	60
4	Gillingham	46	15	7	1	39	15	6	10	7	26	27	65	42	59
5	Swindon Town	46	17	2	4	44	14	8	5	10	30	38	74	52	57
6	Carlisle United	46	11	10	2	31	13	4	12	7	22	29	53	42	52
7	Colchester United	46	13	9	1	35	19	4	8	11	25	36	60	55	51
8	HULL CITY	46	12	9	2	36	14	7	2	14	30	47	66	61	49
9	Exeter City	46	14	6	3	38	18	3	9	11	23	38	61	56	49
10	Brentford	46	14	4	5	35	19	5	5	13	18	30	53	49	47
11	Oxford United	46	10	8	5	27	20	4	10	9	17	30	44	50	46
12	Blackpool	46	12	5	6	38	19	6	4	13	23	40	61	59	45
13	Southend United	46	11	6	6	30	17	4	9	10	21	32	51	49	45
14	Sheffield Wed.	46	9	8	6	30	22	4	11	8	23	31	53	53	45
15	Plymouth Argyle	46	11	9	3	40	27	4	5	14	27	41	67	68	44
16	Chester	46	11	9	3	42	21	3	7	13	15	40	57	61	44
17	Rotherham United	46	13	3	7	30	23	4	7	12	19	32	49	55	44
18	Mansfield Town	46	7	11	5	30	24	5	8	10	21	28	51	52	43
19	Bury	46	6	11	6	35	32	5	9	9	24	33	59	65	42
20	Chesterfield	46	10	5	8	35	34	3	9	11	16	31	51	65	40
21	Peterborough Utd.	46	8	7	8	26	24	3	7	13	18	39	44	63	36
22	Walsall	46	7	6	10	34	32	3	6	14	22	39	56	71	32
23	Tranmere Rovers	46	4	12	7	26	31	2	4	17	19	47	45	78	28
24	Lincoln City	46	5	7	11	26	38	2	4	17	15	50	41	88	25

1979/80 20th in Division Three

No	Date	Opponent	Score	Scorers	Att	BaB	BeI	BlE	CrS	dVR	DeN	DoI	EdK	FaJ	HaP	HwD	HoD	HoM	MaB	McS	McR	MoP	NiG	NoA	NrC	PhT	RiS	RoD	RoG	SkP	TaM
1	Aug 18	COLCHESTER UNITED	0-2		4463	10		1	5				9		6	4		8				3	2			11				7	12
2	21	Sheffield Wednesday	0-0		14562	10		1		4		5	9		6			8				3	2			11				7	
3	25	OXFORD UNITED	2-2	Phillips, Roberts G	4029	10		1		4		5	9		6			8				3	2			11				7	
4	Sep 1	Mansfield Town	1-1	Haigh	4320			1	6	3		5	9		8	4	12					10	2			11				7	
5	8	SHEFFIELD UNITED	3-1	Edwards, Farley, Moss	9556			1		4		3	5	9	11							8	2			10				7	6
6	15	Bury	1-0	Edwards	3422			1		4		3	5	9	11						12	8	2			10				7	6
7	18	Chesterfield	1-1	Edwards	5034			1		4		3	5	9	11	7						8	2			10					6
8	22	GILLINGHAM	0-0		6142			1		4		3	5	9	11						12	8	2			10				7	6
9	29	Millwall	2-3	Phillips, Tait	6001			1		4		3	5	9	11							8	2			10				7	6
10	Oct 2	CHESTERFIELD	2-1	Moss, Tait	5971			1		4		3	5	9	11						12	8	2			10				7	6
11	6	Swindon Town	0-0		7672			1		4		3	5	9	11							8	2			10				7	6
12	9	SHEFFIELD WEDNESDAY	1-1	Dobson	10306			1		4		3	5	9	11							8	2			10				7	6
13	13	CARLISLE UNITED	2-0	Phillips, Farley	5838	9		1		4		3	5		11							8	2			10				7	6
14	20	Chester	1-2	Tait	3391	9		1		4		3	5		11							8	2			10				7	6
15	23	Rotherham United	1-2	Edwards	5916			1		4		3	5	9	11	12						8	2			10			7		6
16	27	EXETER CITY	2-2	Croft, Dobson	5196			1		4		3	5	9	11	7					12	8	2			10					6
17	Nov 2	Colchester United	1-1	Moss	4466			1		4		3	5	9			11					8	2			10				7	6
18	6	ROTHERHAM UNITED	1-1	Edwards	5899			1		4		3	5	9	11		12					8	2			10				7	6
19	10	Reading	0-3		6909			1				3	5	9	11	4					12	8	2			10				7	6
20	17	BARNSLEY	0-2		8327			1		4			5	9	3	11						8	2						6	7	10
21	Dec 1	WIMBLEDON	1-1	Hawker	3750	10		1	3				5	9	11	4	6					8	2						7		
22	8	Brentford	2-7	Bannister, Farley	6793	10		1	5				9	11	4	6	3					8	2						7		
23	21	BLACKBURN ROVERS	0-1		3720			1	4	3			9				6					8	2		11	10		5	7		
24	26	Blackpool	2-2	Edwards 2	4535			1	4	6			9				3					8	2		10	11		5	7		
25	29	Oxford United	0-3		3888			1	4	6		5	9				8						2		10	11		3	7		
26	Jan 5	Plymouth Argyle	1-5	Norrie	6341			1	4	3			5	9		12	6					8	2		11	10			7		
27	12	MANSFIELD TOWN	3-1	Edwards 2, Moss	4243			1	4	3			5	9			6				12	8	2		11	10			7		
28	19	Sheffield United	1-1	Norrie	14960			1	4	3			5	9			6					8	2		11	10			7		
29	25	Southend United	0-3		3920			1	4	3			5	9			6						2		11	10			7		12
30	Feb 16	MILLWALL	1-0	Edwards	5013	10				4			9		11		6		6			3	2	1				5	7		8
31	23	Carlisle United	2-3	Edwards, Roberts G	4263	10				4		3	9		11		6						2	1				5	7		8
32	Mar 1	CHESTER	1-0	Farley	5771					4		10	9		11		6					3	2	1				5	7		8
33	4	Gillingham	0-1		4161	12				4		10	9		11		6					3	2	1				5	7		8
34	8	Exeter City	2-2	Edwards 2	3771					4		10	9		11		6			12		3	2	1				5	7		8
35	14	SWINDON TOWN	1-0	Moss	5346					4		10	5	9	11		6					3	2	1				7			8
36	22	READING	0-1		4293					4		3	10	9	11		6						2	1				5	7		8
37	25	GRIMSBY TOWN	2-2	Edwards 2	14176							3	10	9	11	4	6						2	1				5	7		8
38	Apr 4	Blackburn Rovers	0-1		14571					4		3	10	9	11		6						2	1				5	7		8
39	5	BLACKPOOL	3-1	Edwards 2, Moss	5425					4		3	10	9	11		6				12		2	1				5	7		8
40	7	Grimsby Town	1-1	Deacy	18360					4	10		9				6						2	1	11			5	7		8
41	12	PLYMOUTH ARGYLE	1-0	Norrie	5369					4	10		9				6				12		2	1	11			5	7		8
42	19	Wimbledon	2-3	Norrie, Roberts D	2046					4	10		9				6				12		2	1	11			5	7		8
43	22	Barnsley	1-3	Cooper (og)	11016	10				4			9				6	8				3	2	1	11			5	7		12
44	26	BRENTFORD	2-1	Edwards, Haigh	5382					4		10	9		6			8				3	2	1	11			5	7		12
45	May 3	SOUTHEND UNITED	1-0	Edwards	3297					4		10	9		6			8				3	2	1	11			5	7		12
46	5	BURY	0-1		6158		5			4		10	9		6			8			6	3	2	1	11				7		12
		Apps				11	1	29	39	34	15	26	41	28	29	8	3	13	6	1	10	36	46	17	15	22	1	13	44	6	33
		Goals				1			1		1	2	19	4	2	1						6			4	3		1	2		3

One own goal

F.A. Cup

	Date	Opponent	Score	Scorers	Att	BaB	BlE	EdK	FaJ	HaP	HwD	HoD	HoM	MoP	NiG	RoG	SkP	TaM
R1	Nov 24	Carlisle United	3-3	Haigh, Tait, Roberts G	4,970		1	5	9	12	3	11	2	8	6	7	4	10
rep	28	CARLISLE UNITED	0-2		6,657	10	1	5	9	11	3	4	2	8	6	7		

F.L. Cup

	Date	Opponent	Score	Scorers	Att	BaB	BlE	CrS	EdK	HaP	HwD	HoM	MoP	NiG	PhT	SkP
R1/1	Aug 11	Sheffield Wednesday	1-1	Edwards	9,134	10	1	5	9	6	4	8	3	2	11	7
R1/2	14	SHEFFIELD WEDNESDAY	1-2	Roberts G	7,059	10	1	5	9	6	4	8	3	2	11	7

		Pl	Home					Away					F.	A.	Pts
			W	D	L	F	A	W	D	L	F	A	(Total)		
1	Grimsby Town	46	18	2	3	46	16	8	8	7	27	26	73	42	62
2	Blackburn Rovers	46	13	5	5	34	17	12	4	7	24	19	58	36	59
3	Sheffield Wed.	46	12	6	5	44	20	9	10	4	37	27	81	47	58
4	Chesterfield	46	16	5	2	46	16	7	6	10	25	30	71	46	57
5	Colchester United	46	10	10	3	39	20	10	2	11	25	36	64	56	52
6	Carlisle United	46	13	6	4	45	26	5	6	12	21	30	66	56	48
7	Reading	46	14	6	3	43	19	2	10	11	23	46	66	65	48
8	Exeter City	46	14	5	4	38	22	5	5	13	22	46	60	68	48
9	Chester	46	14	6	3	29	18	3	7	13	20	39	49	57	47
10	Swindon Town	46	15	4	4	50	20	4	4	15	21	43	71	63	46
11	Barnsley	46	10	7	6	29	20	6	7	10	24	36	53	56	46
12	Sheffield United	46	13	5	5	35	21	5	5	13	25	45	60	66	46
13	Rotherham United	46	13	4	6	38	24	5	6	12	20	42	58	66	46
14	Millwall	46	14	6	3	49	23	2	7	14	16	36	65	59	45
15	Plymouth Argyle	46	13	7	3	39	17	3	5	15	20	38	59	55	44
16	Gillingham	46	8	9	6	26	18	6	5	12	23	33	49	51	42
17	Oxford United	46	10	4	9	34	24	4	9	10	23	38	57	62	41
18	Blackpool	46	10	7	6	39	34	5	4	14	23	40	62	74	41
19	Brentford	46	10	6	7	33	26	5	5	13	26	47	59	73	41
20	HULL CITY	46	11	7	5	29	21	1	9	13	22	48	51	69	40
21	Bury	46	10	4	9	30	23	6	3	14	15	36	45	59	39
22	Southend United	46	11	6	6	33	23	3	4	16	14	35	47	58	38
23	Mansfield Town	46	9	9	5	31	24	1	7	15	16	34	47	58	36
24	Wimbledon	46	6	8	9	34	38	4	6	13	18	43	52	81	34

1978-79
Back Row: K. Edwards, R. McDonald, J. Wealands, W. Boyd, A. Warboys, D. Stewart;
Middle Row: D. Gibson, C. Norrie, G. Nisbet, B. Bannister, D. Sunley, M. Horswill, J. Farley;
Front Row: R. deVries, D. Hood, I. Dobson, S. Croft, M. Lord, P. Haigh, B. Marwood.

1979-80
Back Row: D. Leadbeater, C. Norrie, D. Hood, R. McDonald, P. Skipper, S. Croft, M. Horswill;
Middle Row: T. Phillips, B. Marwood, P. Haigh, W. Boyd, E. Blackburn, I. Dobson, S. McClaren, M. Lord;
Front Row: K. Edwards, D. Hawker, B. Bannister, G. Nisbet, R. deVries, G. Roberts, J. Farley.

1980/81 Bottom of Division Three: Relegated

#	Date		Opponent	Score	Scorers	Att.	Booth D	Croft S	Davies J	Deacy N	Eccleston S	Edwards K	Ferguson B	Flounders A	Haigh P	Hoolickin S	Horswill M	Killgallon M	Kynman D	Marwood B	McClaren S	McNeil R	Moss P	Mutrie L	Nisbet G	Norman A	Norrie C	Richards S	Roberts D	Roberts G	Roberts J	Swann G	Whitehurst W
1	Aug	16	Millwall	1-1	Edwards	3831	4			11		9			6	3							10		2	1	7			8	5		
2		19	BARNSLEY	1-2	McCarthy (og)	6978	4			11		9			6	3		12					10		2	1	7			8	5		
3		23	EXETER CITY	3-3	Edwards, Moss, Deacy	3559	4			11		9			6	3							10		2	1	7			8	5	12	
4		29	Fulham	0-0		4585	4			11		9			6	3				7			10		2	1			12		5	8	
5	Sep	6	WALSALL	0-1		4211	4			11		9			6	3							10		2	1	7				5	8	
6		13	Blackpool	2-2	Haigh 2	6138	4			11		9			6	3						2	10		8	1			12		5	7	
7		16	Burnley	0-2		4933	4			12		9			11	3						2	10		7	1				6	5	8	
8		20	PORTSMOUTH	2-1	Edwards, Swann	4613	4					9			11	3						2	10		7	1				6	5	8	
9		27	Brentford	2-2	Edwards, Swann	6305	4			11		9			6	3						2	10		7	1					5	8	
10		30	BURNLEY	0-0		5497	4			11		9			6	3						2	10		7	1			12		5	8	
11	Oct	4	OXFORD UNITED	0-1		4211	4	6		8		9	12	10			11					3	7		2	1					5		
12		8	Chester	1-4	Edwards	2141	4	6		8		9	12	10			11					3	7		2	1					5		
13		11	Chesterfield	0-1		7546	4			11		9	10	3						8					2	1	12	6	7		5		
14		18	CHARLTON ATHLETIC	0-2		3551	4	6		11			8	3						7		9			2	1	10	12			5		
15		21	CARLISLE UNITED	0-1		3603	4			12		9	8	3						7			10		2	1					5	11	
16		25	Gillingham	0-2		4100	4			11				3					10	7					2	1	12	6			5	8	9
17		28	Colchester United	0-2		2239				11		9		3						7			8		2	1	12			6	5	4	10
18	Nov	1	PLYMOUTH ARGYLE	1-0	Deacy	3367				11		9		3						7			8		2	1				6	5	4	10
19		4	CHESTER	0-0		3335						11			9					7	12	3	8		2	1				6	5	4	10
20		8	Newport County	0-4		5496						11			12					7	9	3	8		2	1				6	4	5	10
21		11	Barnsley	0-5		11628	10					11								7	8	3			2	1				6	4	5	12
22		15	MILLWALL	3-1	Edwards, Marwood, Roberts G	3210						11								7	10	3			2	1				6	4	5	8
23		29	Swindon Town	1-3	Marwood	5518	12					11								7	8	3			2	1	11			6	4	5	10
24	Dec	6	READING	2-0	Edwards, Roberts G	3130		4		11		9								2			7	8			3	1		6	5		10
25		20	Sheffield United	1-3	Edwards	10720		4		11		9								2			7	8	3		1		12		6		10
26		26	ROTHERHAM UNITED	1-2	Edwards	8618		4		11		9	3							2			7	8			10	1			5	6	
27		27	Huddersfield Town	0-5		13240	7	4		11		9	3							2				8			10	1	12	5		6	
28	Jan	10	Charlton Athletic	2-3	Edwards, Roberts J	6493				11		9	3							2			7	6			8	1		4			5	10
29		31	Exeter City	3-1	Mutrie, Marwood, McClaren	5022	3			11		9								2			7	8			10	1		4	6	5	
30	Feb	7	BLACKPOOL	2-1	Edwards, Whitehurst	5315	3		1	11		9								2			7	8			10			4	6	5	12
31		14	Walsall	1-1	Roberts G	3914	3		1	11		9								2			7	8			10			4	6	5	12
32		21	BRENTFORD	0-0		4535	3		1	11		9								2			7	8			10			4	6	5	12
33		28	Portsmouth	1-2	Mutrie	13505	3		1	11		9								2			7	8			10			4	6	5	
34	Mar	7	Oxford United	1-1	Roberts D	3165	3			11		9								2			7	8			10		1	4	6	5	
35		14	CHESTERFIELD	0-0		5488	3			11		9	8							2				10			1	12	4	6	5		7
36		17	COLCHESTER UNITED	0-1		3586	3			11		9	8							2				10			1	12	4	6	5		7
37		21	Carlisle United	0-2		4103	3			11	5									8			2		7	6		1	9	4			12
38		28	GILLINGHAM	2-2	Mutrie, Richards	3309	3			11	5	9	6							2			7	8			10		1	4			12
39	Apr	4	Plymouth Argyle	0-0		4668	3			11	5		4							2			7				10		1	6		8	9
40		7	FULHAM	0-1		3152	3			11	5									2			7	8			10		1	4		12	9
41		14	SWINDON TOWN	0-0		2789	3			11			6							2			7				10	1	12	4	5	8	9
42		18	HUDDERSFIELD T	2-1	Deacy, Marwood	6328	3			11	5	12	6							2			7				10		1	4		8	9
43		20	Rotherham United	1-1	Edwards	11602	3			11	5	9								2	6		7				10	4	1			12	8
44		25	SHEFFIELD UNITED	1-1	Deacy	4895	3			11	5	9								2	6		7				10		1	4			8
45	May	2	Reading	0-2		3399	3				5	9	8							2			7				11		1	4		6	10
46		7	NEWPORT COUNTY	3-1	Mutrie 2, Edwards	2059	3				5	9			6					7				2			10		1	4		8	11

| | | | | | Apps | 37 | 7 | 4 | 42 | 9 | 40 | 13 | 5 | 18 | 22 | 13 | 1 | | 3 | 31 | 20 | 14 | 18 | 20 | 24 | 42 | 14 | 25 | 23 | 20 | 26 | 26 |
| | | | | | Goals | | | | 4 | | 13 | | | 2 | | | | | 4 | 1 | | 1 | 5 | | | | | 1 | 1 | 3 | 1 | 2 |

One own goal

F.A. Cup

	Date		Opponent	Score	Scorers	Att.	Booth	Croft	Deacy	Edwards	Ferguson	Flounders	Haigh	Killgallon	McClaren	McNeil	Moss	Mutrie	Nisbet	Norman	Norrie	Richards	Roberts G	Roberts J	Swann
R1	Nov	22	HALIFAX TOWN	2-1	Edwards 2	4024			11	9	12	3					7	10	2	1	8		6	4	5
R2	Dec	13	BLYTH SPARTANS	1-1	Edwards	6050		4	11	9					3		7	8	2	1	10	6		5	
rep		16	Blyth Spartans	2-2	Edwards, Norrie	5870		4	11	9					3		7	8	2	1	10	6		5	
rep2		22	Blyth Spartans	2-1	Norrie, Croft	4914	2	4	11	9				12	3		7	8		1	10		5	6	
R3	Jan	3	DONCASTER ROVERS	1-0	Deacy	10709		4	11	9	3						7	8	2	1	10	5		6	
R4		24	Tottenham Hotspur	0-2		37432	5		11	9					3		7	8		1	10	4		6	

R2 replay and replay 2 a.e.t. Replay 2 at Elland Rd, Leeds

F.L. Cup

	Date		Opponent	Score	Att.	Booth	Edwards	Haigh	Hoolickin	Moss	Mutrie	McClaren	Nisbet	Norman	Norrie	Richards	Roberts G	Roberts J
R1/1	Aug	9	Lincoln City	0-5	3538	4	9		3		7	12	11	2	1	10	6	8	5
R1/2		12	LINCOLN CITY	0-2	2933	4	9	6	3			12	10	2	1	7		8	5

Played at 11 in R1/2: R. McDonald.

Anglo-Scottish Cup

	Date		Opponent	Score	Scorers	Att.	Booth	Deacy	Edwards	Haigh	Hoolickin	Marwood	McClaren	Moss	Mutrie	Nisbet	Norman	Norrie	Richards	Roberts G	Roberts J	Whitehurst
Gp	Jul	28	GRIMSBY TOWN	1-0	Deacy	5056	4	11	9	6			10		14	2	1	7		5	8	
Gp	Aug	2	Sheffield United	1-2	Moss	5454		11	9	6	3	7		4		2	1	10	14	5	8	12
Gp		5	Chesterfield	1-1	Haigh	4945		11	9	3			8	10	4	2	1	7	6	5		12

Played at 12 in first game: I Bennyworth.

		Pl	Home W	D	L	F	A	Away W	D	L	F	A	F (Total)	A	Pts
1	Rotherham United	46	17	6	0	43	8	7	7	9	19	24	62	32	61
2	Barnsley	46	15	5	3	46	19	6	12	5	26	26	72	45	59
3	Charlton Athletic	46	14	6	3	36	17	11	3	9	27	27	63	44	59
4	Huddersfield Town	46	14	6	3	40	11	7	8	8	31	29	71	40	56
5	Chesterfield	46	17	4	2	42	16	6	6	11	30	32	72	48	56
6	Portsmouth	46	14	5	4	35	19	8	4	11	20	28	55	47	53
7	Plymouth Argyle	46	14	5	4	35	18	5	9	9	21	26	56	44	52
8	Burnley	46	13	5	5	37	21	5	9	9	23	27	60	48	50
9	Brentford	46	7	9	7	30	25	7	10	6	22	24	52	49	47
10	Reading	46	13	6	4	39	22	5	5	13	23	40	62	62	46
11	Exeter City	46	9	9	5	36	30	7	4	12	26	36	62	66	45
12	Newport County	46	11	6	6	38	22	4	7	12	26	39	64	61	43
13	Fulham	46	8	7	8	28	29	7	6	10	29	35	57	64	43
14	Oxford United	46	7	8	8	20	24	6	9	8	19	23	39	47	43
15	Gillingham	46	9	8	6	23	19	3	10	10	25	39	48	58	42
16	Millwall	46	10	9	4	30	21	4	5	14	13	39	43	60	42
17	Swindon Town	46	10	6	7	35	27	3	9	11	16	29	51	56	41
18	Chester	46	11	5	7	25	17	4	6	13	13	31	38	48	41
19	Carlisle United	46	8	9	6	32	29	6	4	13	24	41	56	70	41
20	Walsall	46	8	9	6	43	43	5	7	12	16	31	59	74	41
21	Sheffield United	46	12	6	5	38	20	2	6	15	27	43	65	63	40
22	Colchester United	46	12	7	4	35	22	2	4	17	10	43	45	65	39
23	Blackpool	46	5	9	9	19	28	4	5	14	26	47	45	75	32
24	HULL CITY	46	7	8	8	23	22	1	8	14	17	49	40	71	32

1980-81

Back Row: J.Radcliffe (Physio), N. Deacy, C. Norrie, D. Roberts, S. Richards, J. Davies, A. Norman, I. Bennyworth,
P. Haigh, G. Nisbett, R. McDonald, C. Chilton (Reserves Manager);
Middle Row: B. Brown (Youth Devt.), B. Marwood, M. Horswill, S. McClaren, B. Marwood, M. Horswill, M. Smith (Manager),
C. Lea (Assistant-manager), D. Kynman, P. Moss, G. Roberts, D. Booth, K. Edwards;
Front Row: (Apprentices) J. Gummerson, M. Davies, A. Flounders, A. Hurst, D. Walbank, W. Pate, R. McNeil.

1981-82

Back Row: S. Hoolickin, R. McNeil, B. Ferguson, W. Whitehurst, L. Mutrie, S. Eccleston;
Middle Row: C. Chilton (Coach), D. Roberts, N. Deacy, A. Norman, R. Brown (Coach), J. Davies, S. Richards, C. Norrie, J. Radcliffe (Physio);
Front Row: K. Edwards, D. Kynman, S. McClaren, B. Marwood, M. Horswill, M. Smith (Manager), C. Lea (Assistant-manager), G. Roberts,
D. Booth, P. Moss, G. Swann;   On Ground: A. Hurst, M. Gray, I. Davis, A. Flounders, M. Davies

1981/82 8th in Division Four

#	Date	Opponent	Score	Scorers	Att	Booth D	Davies J	Davis I	Deacy N	Eccleston S	Edwards K	Ferguson B	Flounders A	Hoolickin S	Horswill M	Kymman D	Marwood B	McClaren S	McNeil R	Mutrie L	Norman A	Norrie C	Parkinson K	Richards S	Roberts D	Roberts G	Swann G	Thompson N	Whitehurst W
1	Aug 29	Torquay United	1-2	Mutrie	2780	3			12	5	8	11			6				2	10	1			4		7			9
2	Sep 5	BRADFORD CITY	2-1	Mutrie, Ferguson	4246	3			9	5	8	11		2			7			10	1			4		6			12
3	12	Northampton Town	1-1	Mutrie	1938	3			9	5	8	11		2			7	6		10	1			4					
4	19	SHEFFIELD UNITED	2-1	Edwards, Booth	7397	3				5	8	11		2			12	7		10	1			4		6			9
5	22	PETERBOROUGH UTD.	1-1	Ferguson	3979	3				5	8	11		2				7		10	1			4		6			9
6	26	Blackpool	1-3	Mutrie	4838	3			12	5		11		2	6			7		10	1			4		8			9
7	30	Hartlepool United	2-3	Mutrie, Whitehurst	2654	3			8	5		11		2	6			7		10	1			4					9
8	Oct 3	TRANMERE ROVERS	1-2	Whitehurst	3386	3			8	5		11		2	6		12	7		10	1			4					9
9	10	Mansfield Town	3-3	Mutrie, Marwood, Deacy	3464	3			8					2	6		11	7		10	1			4	5			12	
10	17	WIGAN ATHLETIC	0-2		3803	3			11					2	6			7	12	10	1			4	5	8			
11	20	Scunthorpe United	4-4	Marwood 2, Roberts G, Richards	3575		1		5						3	11	7	8	2	10				4		6			
12	24	ALDERSHOT	1-2	Mutrie	3286		1		12	5					3	11	7	8	2	10				4		6			
13	31	Port Vale	1-2	Mutrie	2591		1		12	5					3	11	7	6	2	10				4		8			
14	Nov 3	YORK CITY	2-0	Marwood, Roberts G	3609	11	1		5						3		7	8	2	10				4		6			
15	7	COLCHESTER UNITED	2-3	Roberts G, Mutrie	3180	11	1		12	5					3		7	8	2	10	1			4		6			
16	14	Hereford United	2-2	Whitehurst 2	2652				5								7	8	2	10	1				4	6			11
17	28	Bury	2-0	McClaren, Roberts G	4488				5								7	8	2	10	1		12		4	6			11
18	Dec 5	CREWE ALEXANDRA	1-0	Mutrie	3420	3			5								7	8	2	10	1				4	6			11
19	Jan 9	Bradford City	1-1	Roberts G	5183	3			5								7	8	2	10	1	9			4	6			11
20	23	TORQUAY UNITED	1-0	Flounders	3293	3	1		5			8	9				7	2							4	6			11
21	30	Sheffield United	0-0		12612	3	1		5			8	12				7	2							4	6			11
22	Feb 6	NORTHAMPTON T	0-1		3627	3	1		5			8	10				7	12	2						4	6			11
23	10	Peterborough United	0-3		3161	3			5				12				7	8	2	10	1				4	6			11
24	13	Tranmere Rovers	2-2	Mutrie 2	1735				11					5			7	8	2	10					4	6	12	3	9
25	20	HARTLEPOOL UNITED	5-2	Mutrie 4, Lowe (og)	3040				11					5			7	8		10					4	6	2	3	9
26	27	MANSFIELD TOWN	2-0	Mutrie, Flounders	5220				11			12	9	5			7	8		10					4	6	2	3	
27	Mar 2	HALIFAX TOWN	2-0	Mutrie, Davis	7288			6	11	12			9				7	8		10	1				4		2	3	
28	6	Wigan Athletic	1-2	Mutrie	6008			6	11					5			7	8		10	1			4			2	3	9
29	9	SCUNTHORPE UNITED	2-0	Mutrie, McClaren	6431	3		6	11					5			7	8		10	1			4		2	12	9
30	12	Aldershot	3-0	Mutrie 2, Marwood	2059	3		6	11								7	8		10	1			4		2	5	9
31	16	York City	3-1	Mutrie, Marwood, Whitehurst	4771	3		6	11								7	8		10	1			4		2	5	9
32	20	PORT VALE	3-1	Mutrie, Deacy, Booth	5719	3		6	11								7	8		10	1			12	4	2	5	9
33	23	Darlington	1-2	Flounders	2651	3		6	11				10				7	8			1			2	4		5	9
34	26	Colchester United	0-2		2193	3		6	11				12	10			7	8			1			2	4		5	9
35	Apr 3	HEREFORD UNITED	2-1	Flounders 2	3984	3		6					9				7	8	2	10	1			11	4		5	
36	6	Rochdale	1-0	Mutrie	1738	3		6					12	9			7	8	2	10	1			11	4		5	
37	10	DARLINGTON	1-3	McClaren	4898	3		6					9				7	8	2	10	1			11	4		5	12
38	12	Stockport County	2-1	Mutrie, McClaren	2240	3		6					9				7	8	2	10	1			11	4		5	
39	17	Crewe Alexandra	1-1	Marwood	1592			6									7	8	2	10	1			11	4	3	5	9
40	20	STOCKPORT COUNTY	0-0		3905	3		12									7	8	2	10	1			11	4	6	5	9
41	24	BURY	3-2	Whitehurst, Mutrie, Roberts G	3892	3		2									7	8		10	1			11	4	6	5	9
42	May 1	Bournemouth	0-1		8055	3		2					9				8	7			10			11	4	6	5	
43	4	BLACKPOOL	1-0	Marwood	3470	3		2				6	9				8	7			10			11	4		5	
44	8	ROCHDALE	2-1	Marwood 2	3411	3		6									8	7			10			11	4	5	2	12	9
45	11	BOURNEMOUTH	0-0		3735	3	1	12									8	7			10			11	4	5	2	9
46	14	Halifax Town	2-2	Marwood 2	2293	3	1	2									8	7			10			11	4	5		6	9
		Apps				37	10	20	30	14	5	15	13	9	18	8	42	37	21	43	36	1	1	29	34	29	20	23	36
		Goals				2		1	2		1	2	5				12	4		27				1		6			6

One own goal

F.A. Cup

Rd	Date	Opponent	Score	Scorers	Att	Booth D	Deacy N	Ferguson B	Marwood B	McClaren S	McNeil R	Mutrie L	Norman A	Norrie C	Richards S	Roberts D	Roberts G	Swann G	Whitehurst W
R1	Nov 21	Rochdale	2-2	Whitehurst, McClaren	2722	3	5		7	8	2	10	1			4	6		11
rep	24	ROCHDALE	2-2	Whitehurst, Swann	4063	3	5		7	8	2	10	1	12		4	6		11
rep2	30	Rochdale	1-0	McClaren	3268	3	5		7	8	2	10	1			4	6		11
R2	Dec 4	HARTLEPOOL UNITED	2-0	Marwood, Mutrie	4975	3	5		7	8	2	10	1	9		4	6		11
R3	Jan 18	Chelsea	0-0		14899	3	5	8											
rep	21	CHELSEA	0-0		13238	3	5	8		12									

R1 replay and replay 2 a.e.t. Replay 2 played at Elland Rd, Leeds

F.L. Cup (Milk Cup)

Rd	Date	Opponent	Score	Scorers	Att
R1/1	Sep 2	Lincoln City	0-3		3498
R1/2	15	LINCOLN CITY	1-1	Ferguson	2702

F.L. Group Cup

Rd	Date	Opponent	Score	Scorers	Att
R1	Aug 15	Bradford City	1-2	Whitehurst	2148
R1	18	ROTHERHAM UNITED	0-1		2205
R1	22	HARTLEPOOL UNITED	1-0	Edwards	1621

	Team	Pl		Home						Away				F.	A.	Pts
			W	D	L	F	A	W	D	L	F	A	(Total)			
1	Sheffield United	46	15	8	0	53	15	12	7	4	41	26		94	41	96
2	Bradford City	46	14	7	2	52	23	12	6	5	36	22		88	45	91
3	Wigan Athletic	46	17	5	1	47	18	9	8	6	33	28		80	46	91
4	Bournemouth	46	12	10	1	37	15	11	9	3	25	15		62	30	88
5	Peterborough Utd.	46	16	3	4	46	22	8	7	8	25	35		71	57	82
6	Colchester United	46	12	6	5	47	23	8	6	9	35	34		82	57	72
7	Port Vale	46	9	12	2	26	17	9	4	10	30	32		56	49	70
8	HULL CITY	46	14	3	6	36	23	5	9	9	34	38		70	61	69
9	Bury	46	13	7	3	53	26	4	10	9	27	33		80	59	68
10	Hereford United	46	10	9	4	36	25	6	10	7	28	33		64	58	67
11	Tranmere Rovers	46	7	9	7	27	25	7	9	7	24	31		51	56	60
12	Blackpool	46	11	5	7	40	26	4	8	11	26	34		66	60	58
13	Darlington	46	10	5	8	36	28	5	8	10	25	34		61	62	58
14	Hartlepool United	46	9	8	6	39	34	4	8	11	34	50		73	84	55
15	Torquay United	46	9	8	6	30	25	5	5	13	17	34		47	59	55
16	Aldershot	46	8	7	8	34	29	5	8	10	23	39		57	68	54
17	York City	46	9	5	9	45	37	5	3	15	24	54		69	91	50
18	Stockport County	46	10	5	8	34	28	2	8	13	14	39		48	67	49
19	Halifax Town	46	6	11	6	28	30	3	11	9	23	42		51	72	49
20	Mansfield Town	46	8	6	9	39	39	5	4	14	24	42		63	81	47
21	Rochdale	46	7	9	7	26	22	3	7	13	24	40		50	62	46
22	Northampton Town	46	9	5	9	32	27	2	4	17	25	57		57	84	42
23	Scunthorpe United	46	7	9	7	26	35	2	6	15	17	44		43	79	42
24	Crewe Alexandra	46	3	6	14	19	32	3	3	17	10	52		29	84	27

1982/83 2nd in Division Four: Promoted

#	Date	Opponent	Res	Scorers	Att	Askew B	Booth D	Davies J	Davis I	Flounders A	Hawley J	Hughes E	Marwood B	McClaren S	McNeil R	Mutrie L	Norman A	Richards S	Roberts D	Roberts G	Skipper P	Swann G	Thompson N	Whitehurst W	Woof W
1	Aug 28	Bristol City	1-2	Flounders	4853	8	6			12		7				10	1	4			5	2	3	9	
2	Sep 4	WIMBLEDON	1-1	Flounders	3674		6			9		7	8	2		10	1		4	11	5		3	12	
3	7	YORK CITY	4-0	Mutrie 2, McClaren, Flounders	3769	3	6			12		7	8	2		10	1		4	11	5			9	
4	10	Stockport County	1-1	Marwood	2252	3	6					7	8	2		10	1		4	11	5			9	
5	18	HARTLEPOOL UNITED	1-1	Roberts G	3913	3	6		1	7			8	2		10			4	11	5			9	
6	25	Aldershot	2-1	McClaren, Roberts G	2345	3	6			10		7	8	2			1		4	11	5			9	
7	28	Colchester United	0-0		3071	3	6			10		7	8	2			1		4	11	5			9	
8	Oct 2	SWINDON TOWN	0-0		3786	3	6					7	8	2		10	1		4	11	5			9	
9	9	TORQUAY UNITED	4-1	Mutrie 2, Roberts D, Skipper	3909	3	6					7	8	2		10	1		4	11	5			9	
10	15	Scunthorpe United	1-0	Mutrie	7483	3	6					7	8	2		10	1		4	11	5			9	
11	20	Hereford United	0-2		2320	3						7	8	2		10	1		4	11	5	6		9	
12	23	NORTHAMPTON T	4-0	Marwood 2, Whitehurst, Flounders	4317	3				10		7	8	2			1	4		11	5	6		9	12
13	30	Tranmere Rovers	1-0	McClaren	1568				6			7	8	2		10	1	4		11	5	3			9
14	Nov 2	BURY	2-1	Marwood, Skipper	6101	6	3					7	8	2		10	1		4	11	5			12	9
15	6	PETERBOROUGH UTD.	4-1	Marwood 2, Woof, Slack (og)	5535		3		6			7	8	2		10	1		4	11	5			12	9
16	13	Port Vale	0-1		5298		3					7	8	2		10	1		4	11	5	6		9	
17	27	CHESTER	2-0	Marwood, McClaren	4606	3	6		1			7	8	2		10			4	11	5			9	
18	Dec 4	Blackpool	1-1	Mutrie	3395	3	6		1		9	7	8	2		10			4	11	5	12			
19	11	COLCHESTER UNITED	3-0	Flounders 2, Hawley	4323	3	6			9	10	7	8	2			1		4	11	5				
20	17	Crewe Alexandra	3-0	Marwood 2, Mutrie	1404	3	6			9		7	8			10	1		4	11	5	2			
21	27	HALIFAX TOWN	1-1	Skipper	9692	3	6			9	7		8			10	1		4	11	5	2			
22	28	Darlington	2-1	Marwood, Askew	2519	3	6	8				7				10	1		4	11	5	2		9	
23	Jan 1	ROCHDALE	2-1	Marwood, Roberts G	9059	3	6					7	8			10	1		4	11	5	2		9	
24	3	Mansfield Town	1-3	Marwood	4517	3	6	1		12		7	8			10			4	11	5	2		9	
25	8	Wimbledon	2-1	Whitehurst, Roberts D	2766	3	6	1				7	8	12		10			4	11	5	2		9	
26	15	BRISTOL CITY	1-0	Mutrie	6835	3	6	1				7	8			10			4	11	5	2		9	
27	22	Hartlepool United	0-0		2295		6	1		9		7			2	10			4	11	5	8	3		
28	29	STOCKPORT COUNTY	7-0	Flounders 3, Mutrie, Roberts G, Skipper, Askew	5901	3	6	8		9		7			2	10	1		4	11	5				12
29	Feb 5	ALDERSHOT	2-2	Mutrie, Flounders	6633	3	6			9		7			2	10	1		4	11	5				
30	15	HEREFORD UNITED	2-0	Whitehurst, Woof	6533	3	6			12		7			2	10	1		4		5	7		9	11
31	19	Torquay United	0-0		2817	3	6		7				8		2	10	1		4		5			9	11
32	26	SCUNTHORPE UNITED	1-1	Marwood	11933		6		12			7	8		2	10	1		4	11	5			9	
33	Mar 1	Bury	3-2	Flounders, Roberts G, Askew	4239	3	6			7	9		8			10	1		4	11	5				
34	5	Northampton Town	2-1	Flounders, Askew	2879	3				7	9		8		2	10	1		4	11	5	6		12	
35	12	TRANMERE ROVERS	0-1		7198	3	6			9		7	8		2	10	1		4	11	5			12	
36	19	Peterborough United	1-1	Mutrie	3805	3	6			9		7				10	1		4	11	5	12		8	
37	26	PORT VALE	1-0	Marwood	14410	3	6				8	7				10	1		4	11	5			9	
38	Apr 2	DARLINGTON	0-0		7459		6					2	7	8		10	1		4	11	5		3	9	
39	4	Halifax Town	2-1	Marwood, Woof	5011							2	7	8		10	1		4	11	5	6	3		9
40	9	BLACKPOOL	3-1	Marwood 2, Bardsley (og)	6972	3						2	7	8		10	1		4	11	5			12	9
41	16	Swindon Town	1-0	Marwood	3937					12		2	7	8			1		4	11	5	6	3	10	9
42	19	York City	0-1		9909							2	7	8	12		1		4	11	5	6	3	10	9
43	23	CREWE ALEXANDRA	1-0	Askew	7041	6				9		2	7	8		10	1		4	11	5	3		12	
44	30	Chester	0-0		2450	6		1				2	7	8		10			4	11	5	3	6	9	
45	May 2	MANSFIELD TOWN	2-2	Flounders, Askew	7875	6		1		9		2	7	8		10			4	11	5	3			
46	14	Rochdale	3-1	Marwood, Mutrie, Roberts G	2730	6		1				7	8	2		10			4	11	5	3			
		Apps				36	34	10	8	23	3	9	40	40	33	40	36	3	43	44	46	25	8	36	11
		Goals				6				13	1		19	4		12			2	6	4			3	3

Two own goals

F.A. Cup

#	Date	Opponent	Res	Scorers	Att	Askew B	Booth D	Davies J	Davis I	Flounders A	Hawley J	Hughes E	Marwood B	McClaren S	McNeil R	Mutrie L	Norman A	Richards S	Roberts D	Roberts G	Skipper P	Swann G	Thompson N	Whitehurst W	Woof W
R1	Nov 20	SHEFFIELD UNITED	1-1	Kenworthy (og)	9152		3					7	8	2		10	1		4	11	5	6		9	
rep	23	Sheffield United	0-2		12232	3	6					7	8	2		10	1		4	11	5			9	

F.L. Cup (Milk Cup)

#	Date	Opponent	Res	Scorers	Att	Askew B	Booth D	Davies J	Davis I	Flounders A	Hawley J	Hughes E	Marwood B	McClaren S	McNeil R	Mutrie L	Norman A	Richards S	Roberts D	Roberts G	Skipper P	Swann G	Thompson N	Whitehurst W	Woof W
R1/1	Aug 31	Sheffield United	1-3	Whitehurst	12236		6			12		7	8	3		10	1		4	11	5	2		9	
R1/2	Sep 14	SHEFFIELD UNITED	1-0	Flounders	7111	3	6		1	7			8	2		10			4	11	5			9	

F.L. Trophy

#	Date	Opponent	Res	Scorers	Att	Askew B	Booth D	Davies J	Davis I	Flounders A	Hawley J	Hughes E	Marwood B	McClaren S	McNeil R	Mutrie L	Norman A	Richards S	Roberts D	Roberts G	Skipper P	Swann G	Thompson N	Whitehurst W	Woof W
R1	Aug 14	Hartlepool United	2-1	Marwood, Whitehurst	962	6			12	14		7	8	2		10	1		4	11	5		3	9	
R1	17	Halifax Town	0-1		1323	6		8				7	12	2		10	1		4	11	5		3	9	
R1	21	BRADFORD CITY	0-0		3202	6		8		12		7	11			10	1		4		5	2	3	9	

		Pl	Home W D L F A					Away W D L F A					F (Total)	A	Pts
1	Wimbledon	46	17	4	2	57	23	12	7	4	39	22	96	45	98
2	HULL CITY	46	14	8	1	48	14	11	7	5	27	20	75	34	90
3	Port Vale	46	15	4	4	37	16	11	6	6	30	18	67	34	88
4	Scunthorpe United	46	13	7	3	41	17	10	7	6	30	25	71	42	83
5	Bury	46	15	4	4	43	20	8	8	7	31	26	74	46	81
6	Colchester United	46	17	5	1	51	19	7	4	12	24	36	75	55	81
7	York City	46	18	4	1	59	19	4	9	10	29	39	88	58	79
8	Swindon Town	46	14	3	6	45	27	5	8	10	16	27	61	54	68
9	Peterborough Utd.	46	13	6	4	38	23	4	7	12	20	29	58	52	64
10	Mansfield Town	46	11	6	6	32	26	5	7	11	29	44	61	70	61
11	Halifax Town	46	9	8	6	31	23	7	4	12	28	43	59	66	60
12	Torquay United	46	12	3	8	38	30	5	4	14	18	35	56	65	58
13	Chester	46	8	6	9	28	24	7	5	11	27	36	55	60	56
14	Bristol City	46	10	8	5	32	25	3	9	11	27	45	59	70	56
15	Northampton Town	46	10	8	5	43	29	4	4	15	22	46	65	75	54
16	Stockport County	46	11	8	4	41	31	3	4	16	19	48	60	79	54
17	Darlington	46	8	5	10	27	30	5	8	10	34	41	61	71	52
18	Aldershot	46	11	5	7	40	35	1	10	12	21	47	61	82	51
19	Tranmere Rovers	46	8	8	7	30	29	5	3	15	19	42	49	71	50
20	Rochdale	46	11	8	4	38	25	0	8	15	17	48	55	73	49
21	Blackpool	46	10	8	5	32	23	3	4	16	23	51	55	74	49
22	Hartlepool United	46	11	5	7	30	24	2	4	17	16	52	46	76	48
23	Crewe Alexandra	46	9	5	9	35	32	2	3	18	18	39	53	71	41
24	Hereford United	46	8	6	9	19	23	3	2	18	23	56	42	79	41

1982-83
Back Row: D.Roberts, B. Whitehurst, L. Mutrie, J. Davies, L. Findlay, T. Norman, S. Richards, I Davis, N. Thompson:
Front Row: D. Booth, S. McClaren, R. McNeil, B. Marwood, G. Roberts, A. Flounders, G. Swann.

1983-84
Back Row: D. Roberts, G. Swann, P. Skipper, A. Norman, W. Whitehurst, J. Davies, R. McNeil, S. Massey, A. Flounders;
Front Row:S. McClaren, D. Booth, J. Vanson (mascot), B. Marwood, W. Askew

1983/84 4th in Division Three

League Matches (Division Three)

#	Date		Opponent	Score	Scorers	Att
1	Aug	27	BURNLEY	4-1	Whitehurst 2, Massey 2	8394
2	Sep	3	Gillingham	2-1	Marwood, Mutrie	2919
3		7	Bradford City	0-0		3510
4		10	MILLWALL	5-0	Mutrie 2, Marwood, Roberts G, McNeill	6537
5		17	Preston North End	0-0		6661
6		24	LINCOLN CITY	2-0	Whitehurst 2	7523
7		27	WIMBLEDON	1-0	Whitehurst	8133
8	Oct	1	Wigan Athletic	1-1	Flounders	4858
9		8	SHEFFIELD UNITED	4-1	Marwood 2, McClaren, Mutrie	14775
10		15	Brentford	1-1	Mutrie	4258
11		18	Bolton Wanderers	0-0		6397
12		22	PLYMOUTH ARGYLE	1-2	McClaren	7707
13		29	Oxford United	1-1	Marwood	8064
14	Nov	1	WALSALL	2-2	Marwood, Askew	7573
15		5	Bournemouth	3-2	Whitehurst, Marwood, Hollifield	4644
16		12	NEWPORT COUNTY	0-0		7235
17		26	ORIENT	2-1	Whitehurst 2	6557
18	Dec	3	Exeter City	1-2	McNeill	3099
19		17	Bristol Rovers	3-1	Roberts G 2, Marwood	5653
20		26	SCUNTHORPE UNITED	1-0	Massey	15461
21		27	Rotherham United	1-0	Skipper	6298
22		31	PORT VALE	1-0	Roberts G	8736
23	Jan	2	Southend United	2-2	Flounders 2	3014
24		28	Millwall	0-1		3996
25	Feb	4	WIGAN ATHLETIC	1-0	Marwood	6341
26		11	Lincoln City	3-1	Swann 2, Marwood	5370
27		25	Plymouth Argyle	0-2		10023
28		28	OXFORD UNITED	0-1		11192
29	Mar	3	BOLTON WANDERERS	1-1	Roberts D	6569
30		6	BOURNEMOUTH	3-1	Flounders, Taylor, McNeill	6897
31		10	Newport County	1-1	Roberts G	2813
32		17	Sheffield United	2-2	Marwood, McClaren	15374
33		24	BRENTFORD	2-0	Marwood, Roberts D	5572
34		27	Walsall	1-2	Flounders	6851
35		31	BRADFORD CITY	1-0	Roberts G	6943
36	Apr	7	Wimbledon	4-1	Flounders, Roberts G, Marwood, McEwan	4495
37		10	PRESTON NORTH END	3-0	Flounders, Taylor, Roberts G	6834
38		14	EXETER CITY	1-0	Taylor	6889
39		17	GILLINGHAM	0-0		7779
40		21	Scunthorpe United	0-2		8286
41		23	ROTHERHAM UNITED	5-0	Flounders 2, Whitehurst, Marwood, Johnson (og)	7712
42		28	Orient	1-3	Whitehurst	3020
43	May	5	SOUTHEND UNITED	2-1	Massey, Roberts G	5900
44		7	Port Vale	0-1		3958
45		12	BRISTOL ROVERS	0-0		9857
46		15	Burnley	2-0	Marwood 2	8051

Appearances and Goals

Player	Apps	Goals
Askew B	33	1
Blackburn P		
Booth D	14	
Cockin N		
Davis I		
Flounders A	30	9
Gill G	1	
Hollifield M	33	1
Marwood B	39	16
Massey S	13	4
McClaren S	40	3
McEwan S	16	1
McNeil R	46	3
Mutrie L	12	5
Norman A	46	
Olsson P		
Roberts D	29	
Roberts G	38	
Saville A	1	
Skipper P	46	
Swann G	41	1
Taylor AD	14	2
Wassell K	1	3
Whitehurst W	37	10

One own goal

F.A. Cup

	Date		Opponent	Score	Scorers	Att
R1	Nov	19	Penrith	2-0	Whitehurst, Roberts G	1828
R2	Dec	10	Rotherham United	1-2	Flounders	6885

F.L. Cup (Milk Cup)

	Date		Opponent	Score	Scorers	Att
R1/1	Aug	30	LINCOLN CITY	0-0		6396
R1/2	Sep	14	Lincoln City	1-3	Skipper	4630

R1/2 a.e.t.

Associate Members Cup

	Date		Opponent	Score	Scorers	Att
R1	Feb	21	York City	2-1	McClaren, Taylor	5837
R2	Mar	13	BURY	1-0	McEwan	4072
R3		20	PRESTON NORTH END	3-0	Roberts G 2, Taylor	4227
QF	May	2	SHEFFIELD UNITED	1-0	Olsson	3680
SF		18	TRANMERE ROVERS	4-1	Taylor 2, Roberts G 2	4678
F		24	BOURNEMOUTH	1-2	McNeill	6197

Final League Table

		Pl		Home					Away					F.	A.	Pts
			W	D	L	F	A	W	D	L	F	A		(Total)		
1	Oxford United	46	17	5	1	58	22	11	6	6	33	28	91	50		95
2	Wimbledon	46	15	5	3	58	35	11	4	8	39	41	97	76		87
3	Sheffield United	46	14	7	2	56	18	10	4	9	30	35	86	53		83
4	HULL CITY	46	16	5	2	42	11	7	9	7	29	27	71	38		83
5	Bristol Rovers	46	16	5	2	47	21	6	8	9	21	33	68	54		79
6	Walsall	46	14	4	5	44	22	8	5	10	24	39	68	61		75
7	Bradford City	46	11	9	3	46	30	9	2	12	27	35	73	65		71
8	Gillingham	46	13	4	6	50	29	7	6	10	24	40	74	69		70
9	Millwall	46	16	4	3	42	18	2	9	12	29	47	71	65		67
10	Bolton Wanderers	46	13	4	6	36	17	5	6	12	20	43	56	60		64
11	Orient	46	13	5	5	40	27	5	4	14	31	54	71	81		63
12	Burnley	46	12	5	6	52	25	4	9	10	24	36	76	61		62
13	Newport County	46	11	9	3	35	27	5	5	13	23	48	58	75		62
14	Lincoln City	46	11	4	8	42	29	6	6	11	17	33	59	62		61
15	Wigan Athletic	46	11	5	7	26	18	5	8	10	20	38	46	56		61
16	Preston North End	46	12	5	6	42	27	3	6	14	24	39	66	66		56
17	Bournemouth	46	11	5	7	38	27	5	2	16	25	46	63	73		55
18	Rotherham United	46	10	5	8	29	17	5	4	14	28	47	57	64		54
19	Plymouth Argyle	46	11	8	4	38	17	2	4	17	18	45	56	62		51
20	Brentford	46	8	6	9	41	30	3	7	13	28	49	69	79		49
21	Scunthorpe United	46	9	9	5	40	31	0	10	13	14	42	54	73		46
22	Southend United	46	8	9	6	34	24	2	5	16	21	52	55	76		44
23	Port Vale	46	10	4	9	33	29	1	6	16	18	54	51	83		43
24	Exeter City	46	4	8	11	27	39	2	7	14	23	45	50	84		33

1984/85 3rd in Division Three: Promoted

						Askew B	Booth D	Brentano S	Flounders A	Hollifield M	Horton B	Jobson R	Massey S	McClaren S	McEwan S	McNeil R	Norman A	Pearson L	Ring M	Roberts D	Roberts G	Saville A	Skipper P	Swann G	Whitehurst W	Williams N
1	Aug	25	Lincoln City	0-0	4139	10					4		7	8	6		1	3		2	11		5		9	
2	Sep	1	BOURNEMOUTH	3-0 Whitehurst, Massey, Ring	4828	10	12						7	4	6		1	3	8	2	11		5		9	
3		8	Bolton Wanderers	0-0	5403	10					11		7	4	6		1	3	8	2			5		9	
4		15	PRESTON NORTH END	1-2 McEwan	5742	10			12				7	4	6		1	3	8	2	11		5		9	
5		18	GILLINGHAM	2-0 Askew 2	5240	10					8		7	4	6		1	3	12	2	11		5		9	
6		22	Burnley	1-1 McEwan	5526	10			12		8		7	4	6		1	3	9	2	11		5			
7		29	READING	0-0	5366	10			12		8		7	4	6		1	3	9	2	11		5			
8	Oct	3	Bradford City	0-2	4446	10			7		8		4	6			1	3		2	11		5		9	
9		6	Plymouth Argyle	1-0 Flounders	5505	10			7		8		4	6			1	3		2	11		5		9	
10		13	DONCASTER ROVERS	3-2 Flounders, McEwan, Skipper	7071	10			7				4	6			1	3		2	11		5	8	9	
11		20	Derby County	1-3 Skipper	13422	10			7	4				6			1	3	11	2			5	8	9	
12		23	SWANSEA CITY	4-1 Whitehurst 2, Skipper, Roberts G	5306	10			7	4				6	2	1	3			11			5	8	9	
13		27	Bristol Rovers	1-1 Whitehurst	5438	10			7	4		11		6	2	1	3						5	8	9	
14	Nov	3	ROTHERHAM UNITED	0-0	6137	10			7	4			8	6	2	1				11			5	3	9	
15		6	CAMBRIDGE UNITED	2-1 Flounders, McClaren	5472	10			7	4		11	8	6	2	1							5	3	9	
16		10	Orient	5-4 Flounders 2, Akew, Massey, McEwan	2365	10			7	4		11	8	6	2	1	12						5	3	9	
17		24	NEWPORT COUNTY	2-0 Whitehurst, McClaren	4809	10			7	4		11	8	6	2	1	3						5		9	
18	Dec	1	Wigan Athletic	1-1 Askew	3743	10			7	4		11	8	6	2	1	3						5	12	9	
19		15	WALSALL	1-0 Whitehurst	6075	10				4		11	8	6	2	1	3	7					5		9	12
20		18	Millwall	2-2 Swann, Smith (og)	5001	10			7				8	6	2	1	3	11					5	4	9	
21		22	BRENTFORD	4-0 Whitehurst 2, McClaren, Askew	6354	10			7				8	6	2	1	3	11					5	4	9	12
22		29	York City	2-1 Flounders, Askew	9565	10			7				8	6	2	1	3	11					5	4	9	12
23	Jan	1	BRISTOL CITY	2-1 Whitehurst, McEwan	9753	10			7				8	6	2	1	3	11					5	4	9	12
24		12	Bournemouth	1-1 Flounders	4454	10			7				9	8	6	2	1	3	11					5	4		12
25	Feb	2	Reading	2-4 Skipper, Hicks (og)	4612	10		2	7		4		12	8	6		1	3					5		9	11
26		9	BURNLEY	2-0 Whitehurst, Massey	6478	10			7	3	4	6	12	8		2	1		11				5		9	
27		16	BRADFORD CITY	0-2	14752	10			7	3	4	6	11	8		2	1				12		5		9	
28		23	Rotherham United	1-1 Whitehurst	7068	10				3	4	6	7	8			1			11		5	2	9	
29		26	Gillingham	0-1	6051	10			12	3		6	7	8			1			11		5	2	9	4
30	Mar	2	BRISTOL ROVERS	2-0 Whitehurst, Flounders	6380	10			7	3			12	8		6	1			11		5	2	9	4
31		5	Swansea City	2-0 McClaren, Williams	4104	10			7	3			8			6	1			11		5	2	9	4
32		9	DERBY COUNTY	3-2 Whitehurst 2, Flounders	9782	10			7	3		12	8			6	1			11		5	2	9	4
33		16	Doncaster Rovers	2-1 Flounders, Williams	5942	10			7	3			8			2	1			11	9	5	6		4
34		19	LINCOLN CITY	1-0 Williams	7029	10			7	3		12	8			2	1			11		5	6	9	4
35		23	PLYMOUTH ARGYLE	2-2 Flounders, Roberts G	6947	10			7	3		12	8	6			1			11		5	2	9	4
36		30	Cambridge United	3-1 Whitehurst, Saville, McEwan	2137	10				3				6	2	1			11	7	5	8	9	4
37	Apr	2	BOLTON WANDERERS	2-2 Whitehurst, McEwan	7863	10			12	3			8	6	2	1					7	5	11	9	4
38		6	MILLWALL	2-1 Flounders, McEwan	10426	10			7				8	6		1	3			11		5	2	9	4
39		8	Bristol City	0-2	11964	10			7		11		8	6		1	3				12	5	2	9	4
40		13	ORIENT	5-1 Whitehurst 3, Flounders, McEwan	7434	10			7				4	8	6		1	3	12	11		5	2	9	
41		20	Newport County	1-0 Swann	1885	10			7		4		9		6	2	1	3		11		5	8		
42		23	Preston North End	4-1 Flounders,Massey,Roberts G,McEwan	4635	10			7		4		9		6	2	1	3		11		5	8		
43		27	WIGAN ATHLETIC	3-1 Whitehurst, McEwan, Massey	8620	10			7				4	8	6		1	3		11		5	2	9	
44	May	4	Walsall	1-0 Skipper	4809	10			7				4	8	6		1	3		11		5	2	9	
45		6	YORK CITY	0-2	15795	10			7			12	4	8	6		1	3		11		5	2	9	
46		11	Brentford	1-2 Swann	4309	10		2	7			3	12	8	6		1			11		5	4	9	
			Apps			46	1	2	39	12	22	8	29	40	37	24	46	31	15	11	29	4	46	32	40	17
			Goals			6			14				5	4	11				1		3	1	5	3	20	3

Two own goals

F.A. Cup

	R						Askew B	Booth D	Brentano S	Flounders A	Hollifield M	Horton B	Jobson R	Massey S	McClaren S	McEwan S	McNeil R	Norman A	Pearson L	Ring M	Roberts D	Roberts G	Saville A	Skipper P	Swann G	Whitehurst W	Williams N
R1	Nov	17	BOLTON WANDERERS	2-1 Massey, Flounders	6424	10			7		4		11	8	6	2	1		3	12			5		9	
R2	Dec	8	Tranmere Rovers	3-0 Ring, McClaren, Skipper	4269	10			7		4		11	8	6	2	1		3	9			5			
R3	Jan	5	Brighton & Hove Albion	0-1	11681	10			7					8	6	2	1		3	11			5	4		9

F.L. Cup (Milk Cup)

						Askew B	Booth D	Brentano S	Flounders A	Hollifield M	Horton B	Jobson R	Massey S	McClaren S	McEwan S	McNeil R	Norman A	Pearson L	Ring M	Roberts D	Roberts G	Saville A	Skipper P	Swann G	Whitehurst W	Williams N
R1/1	Aug	29	Lincoln City	2-0 Whitehurst, McEwan	3465	10	4						7	8	6		1	3		2	11		5		9	
R1/2	Sep	4	LINCOLN CITY	4-1 Whitehurst, Massey, Ring, Strodder(og)	4042	10							7	4	6		1	3	8	2	11		5		9	
R2/1		25	Southampton	2-3 Roberts D, Roberts G	11824	10					8		7	4	6		1	3	9	2	11		5	12		
R2/2	Oct	9	SOUTHAMPTON	2-2 Whitehurst, Flounders	14613	10			7		8			4	6		1	3	12	2	11		5		9	

A.M. Cup (Freight Rover Trophy)

						Askew B	Booth D	Brentano S	Flounders A	Hollifield M	Horton B	Jobson R	Massey S	McClaren S	McEwan S	McNeil R	Norman A	Pearson L	Ring M	Roberts D	Roberts G	Saville A	Skipper P	Swann G	Whitehurst W	Williams N
R1/1	Jan	22	MANSFIELD TOWN	2-2 Whitehurst, Calderwood	2310	10			7				14	8	6	2	1		3	11		12	5	4	9	
R1/2	Feb	6	Mansfield Town	1-2 Askew	2086	10		2	7	3	4		14	8			1			12	6		5		9	11

		Pl	Home				Away				F.	A.	Pts
			W	D	L	F	A	W	D	L	F	A	(Total)	
1	Bradford City	46	15	6	2	44	23	13	4	6	33	22	77 45	94
2	Millwall	46	18	5	0	44	12	8	7	8	29	30	73 42	90
3	HULL CITY	46	16	4	3	46	20	9	8	6	32	29	78 49	87
4	Gillingham	46	15	5	3	54	29	10	3	10	26	33	80 62	83
5	Bristol City	46	17	2	4	46	19	7	7	9	28	28	74 47	81
6	Bristol Rovers	46	15	6	2	37	13	6	6	11	29	35	66 48	75
7	Derby County	46	14	7	2	40	20	5	6	12	25	34	65 54	70
8	York City	46	13	5	5	42	22	7	4	12	28	35	70 57	69
9	Reading	46	8	7	8	31	29	11	5	7	37	33	68 62	69
10	Bournemouth	46	16	3	4	42	16	3	8	12	15	30	57 46	68
11	Walsall	46	9	7	7	33	22	9	6	8	25	30	58 52	67
12	Rotherham United	46	11	6	6	36	24	7	5	11	19	31	55 55	65
13	Brentford	46	13	5	5	42	27	3	9	11	20	37	62 64	62
14	Doncaster Rovers	46	11	5	7	42	33	6	3	14	30	41	72 74	59
15	Plymouth Argyle	46	11	5	7	33	23	4	7	12	29	42	62 65	59
16	Wigan Athletic	46	12	6	5	36	22	3	8	12	24	42	60 64	59
17	Bolton Wanderers	46	12	5	6	38	22	4	1	18	31	53	69 75	54
18	Newport County	46	9	6	8	30	30	4	7	12	25	37	55 67	52
19	Lincoln City	46	8	11	4	32	20	3	7	13	18	31	50 51	51
20	Swansea City	46	7	5	11	31	39	5	6	12	22	41	53 80	47
21	Burnley	46	6	8	9	30	24	5	5	13	30	49	60 73	46
22	Orient	46	7	7	9	30	36	4	6	13	21	40	51 76	46
23	Preston North End	46	9	5	9	33	41	4	2	17	18	59	51 100	46
24	Cambridge United	46	2	3	18	17	48	2	6	15	20	47	37 95	21

1984-85

Back Row: G. Swann, P. Olsson, A. Flounders, L. Pearson, R. McNeill, I. Davis, N. Williams;
Middle Row: C. Chilton (Asst Manager), M. Hollifield, J. Davies, W. Whitehurst, A. Norman, S. McEwan, P. Skipper, D. Booth (Player/Coach);
Front Row: D. Roberts, S. Massey, G. Roberts, B. Horton (Player-Manager), D. Robinson (Chairman),
S. McClaren, W. Askew, J. Radcliffe (Physio).

1985-86

Back Row: A. Flounders, G. Swann, A. Saville, P. Olsson, L. Pearson, A. Tomlinson;
Middle Row: D. Booth (Coach), S. McEwan, P. Skipper, J. Davies, W. Whitehurst, A. Norman, R. Jobson, F. Bunn, J. Radcliffe (Physio);
Front Row: N. Williams, S. Corkain, G. Roberts, B. Horton (Player-Manager), W. Askew, S. Brentano, M. Ring.

1985/86 6th in Division Two

#	Date		Opponent	Score	Scorers	Att	Askew B	Brentano S	Brown N	Bunn F	Doyle R	Flounders A	Heard P	Horton B	Jobson R	McEwan S	Norman A	Parker G	Pearson L	Ring M	Roberts G	Saville A	Skipper P	Swann G	Whitehurst W	Williams N
1	Aug	17	PORTSMOUTH	2-2	Whitehurst, Bunn	8221	10			8					2	6	1		3		11		5	4	9	7
2		24	Leeds United	1-1	Jobson	16731	10			8					2	6	1		3		11		5	4	9	7
3		26	BLACKBURN ROVERS	2-2	Bunn, Rathbone (og)	7288	10			8					2	6	1		3		11		5	4	9	7
4		31	Oldham Athletic	1-3	Whitehurst	4500	10			8	4	12			2	6	1		3		11		5		7	9
5	Sep	7	MIDDLESBROUGH	0-0		7710	10			8	4				2	6	1		3		11		5		7	9
6		14	Bradford City	2-4	Swann, McEwan	4930	10			8	4				2	6	1		3	7	11		5	12		9
7		17	MILLWALL	3-0	Bunn 2, McEwan	6021				8	4			10	2	6	1		3		11		5		7	9
8		21	CARLISLE UNITED	4-0	Whitehurst, Roberts, Swann, Doyle	6117				8	4			10	2	6	1		3		11		5		7	9
9		28	Norwich City	0-2		11945		12		8	4			10	2	6	1		3		11		5		7	9
10	Oct	1	Crystal Palace	2-0	Bunn, McEwan	5226				8	4	11		10	2	6	1		3				5		7	9
11		5	STOKE CITY	0-2		6890				8	4	12		10	2	6	1					3	5		7	9
12		12	Sunderland	1-1	Whitehurst	16613	10			8	4		5		2	6	1			12	11			3	9	7
13		19	HUDDERSFIELD T	3-1	Whitehurst 2, Williams	8128	10		2	8	4		5			6	1				11			3	9	7
14		26	Shrewsbury Town	0-0		3587	10		2	8	4		5			6	1				11	12		3	9	7
15	Nov	2	Sheffield United	1-3	Skipper	13272	10			8	4	12			2	6	1				11		5	3	9	7
16		9	FULHAM	5-0	McEwan 2, Whitehurst, Roberts G, Bunn	5344	10			8	4				2	6	1				11	12	5	3	9	7
17		16	Charlton Athletic	2-1	Bunn 2	4140	10	11		8	4				2	6	1						5	3	9	7
18		23	WIMBLEDON	1-1	McEwan	6576	10	2		8	4					6	1				11		5	3	9	7
19		30	Brighton & Hove Albion	1-3	Saville	8496	10	3		8	4	11			2	6	1			12		9	5			7
20	Dec	7	CRYSTAL PALACE	1-2	Bunn	6058	10	3		8	4				2	6	1			12	11	9	5			7
21		14	Portsmouth	1-1	McEwan	13371	10			8	4				2	6	1				11	9	5	3		7
22		22	LEEDS UNITED	2-1	Bunn, Jobson	11852	10			8	4				2	6	1			12	11	9	5	3		7
23		26	GRIMSBY TOWN	2-0	Askew, Jobson	12824	10			8	4				2	6	1				11	9	5	3		7
24		28	Millwall	0-5		3783	10	11		8	4	12			2	6	1					9	5	3		7
25	Jan	1	Barnsley	4-1	Ring, Doyle, McEwan, Jobson	8363	10			8	4	9		11	2	6	1			7			5	3		
26		11	BRADFORD CITY	1-0	Jobson	9333	10			8	4	9		7	2	6	1				11		5	3		
27		18	OLDHAM ATHLETIC	4-2	Flounders 2, Jobson 2	6909	10			8	4	9		7	2	6	1				11		5	3		
28	Feb	1	Blackburn Rovers	2-2	Bunn, McEwan	5414	10			8	4	9		7	2	6	1			12	11		5	3		
29		25	Huddersfield Town	1-2	Roberts G	4518	10			8	4	9				6	1	7	2		11		5	3		
30	Mar	4	SHREWSBURY TOWN	4-3	Flounders 3, Bunn	6253	10			8	4	9				6	1	7	3		11	12	5	2		
31		8	Stoke City	1-0	McEwan	9112	10			8	4	9				6	1	7	3		11		5	2		
32		11	Carlisle United	1-2	Flounders	3248	10			8	4	9				6	1	7	3		11		5	2		
33		15	SUNDERLAND	1-1	Roberts G	9295	10			8	4	9			2	6	1	7	3		11		5			
34		22	Middlesbrough	2-1	Flounders, Bunn	6227	10			8	4	9			2	6	1	7	3		11		5	12		
35		29	BARNSLEY	0-1		7903	10			8	4	9		12		6	1	7	3		11		5	2		
36	Apr	1	Grimsby Town	1-0	Flounders	9121				8	4	9		10	2	6	1	7			11		5	3		
37		5	SHEFFIELD UNITED	0-0		9645	12			8	4	9		10	2	6	1	7			11		5	3		
38		12	Fulham	1-1	Bunn	2799			12	8	4	9		10	2	6	1	7			11		5	3		
39		19	CHARLTON ATHLETIC	1-1	Askew	7139	11			8	4	9		10	2	6	1						5	3		
40		26	Wimbledon	1-3	Flounders	5171	11			8	4	9		10	2	6	1	7					5	3		
41		29	NORWICH CITY	1-0	Williams	6146				8	4	9		10	2	6	1		11			12	5	3		7
42	May	2	BRIGHTON & HOVE ALB	2-0	Williams, Flounders	5459				8	4	9		10	2	6	1		11			12	5	3		7
			Apps				33	8	1	42	39	25	8	10	36	42	42	12	20	9	33	9	40	39	18	19
			Goals				2			14	2	10			7	10					1	1	1	2	7	3

One own goal

F.A. Cup

	Date		Opponent	Score	Scorers	Att	Askew B	Bunn F	Doyle R	Flounders A	Horton B	Jobson R	McEwan S	Norman A	Ring M	Roberts G	Skipper P	Swann G
R3	Jan	4	PLYMOUTH ARGYLE	2-2	Flounders 2	6776	10	8	4	9		2	6	1	7	11	5	3
rep		7	Plymouth Argyle	1-0	Roberts	13940		8	4	9	7	2	6	1		11	5	3
R4		25	BRIGHTON & HOVE ALB.	2-3	Roberts, McEwan	12228		8	4	9	7	2	6	1		11	5	3

F.L. Cup (Milk Cup)

	Date		Opponent	Score	Scorers	Att	Askew B	Bunn F	Doyle R	Flounders A	Horton B	Jobson R	McEwan S	Norman A	Pearson L	Ring M	Roberts G	Skipper P	Swann G	Whitehurst W	Williams N
R1/1	Aug	20	Halifax Town	1-1	Flounders	820	10	8		9		2	6	1	3		11	5	4		7
R1/2	Sep	3	HALIFAX TOWN	3-0	Bunn 2, Whitehurst	3299	10	8	4			2	6	1	3	12	11	5		7	9
R2/1		24	Queen's Park Rangers	0-3		7021		8	4	12	10	2	6	1	3		11	5		7	9
R2/2	Oct	8	QUEEN'S PARK RANGERS	1-5	Whitehurst	4287	10	8	4			2	6	1			11	5	3	9	7

F.M. Cup (Freight Rover Trophy)

	Date		Opponent	Score	Scorers	Att	Askew B	Brentano S	Brown N	Bunn F	Doyle R	Flounders A	Heard P	Jobson R	McEwan S	Norman A	Ring M	Roberts G	Saville A	Skipper P	Swann G	Whitehurst W	Williams N
R1	Oct	23	BRADFORD CITY	4-1	Bunn 2, McEwan, Whitehurst	2,177	10	2		14	4	8	5		6	1		11	12		3	9	7
SFN	Nov	11	MIDDLESBROUGH	3-1	Whitehurst 2, Bunn	2,637	10			8	4	12		2	6	1		11	14	5	3	9	7
FN1		26	MANCHESTER CITY	2-1	McEwan, Bunn	5,213	10	11		8	4			2	6	1	12		14	5	3	9	7
FN2	Dec	11	Manchester City	0-2		10,180	10			8	4			2	6	1		11	9	5	3		7

SFN a.e.t.

		Pl	Home W	D	L	F	A	Away W	D	L	F	A	F	A (Total)	Pts
1	Norwich City	42	16	4	1	51	15	9	5	7	33	22	84	37	84
2	Charlton Athletic	42	14	5	2	44	15	8	6	7	34	30	78	45	77
3	Wimbledon	42	13	6	2	38	16	8	7	6	20	21	58	37	76
4	Portsmouth	42	13	4	4	43	17	9	3	9	26	24	69	41	73
5	Crystal Palace	42	12	3	6	29	22	7	6	8	28	30	57	52	66
6	HULL CITY	42	11	7	3	39	19	6	6	9	26	36	65	55	64
7	Sheffield United	42	10	7	4	36	24	7	4	10	28	39	64	63	62
8	Oldham Athletic	42	13	4	4	40	28	4	5	12	22	33	62	61	60
9	Millwall	42	12	3	6	39	24	5	5	11	25	41	64	65	59
10	Stoke City	42	8	11	2	29	16	6	4	11	19	34	48	50	57
11	Brighton & Hove A.	42	10	5	6	42	30	6	3	12	22	34	64	64	56
12	Barnsley	42	9	6	6	29	26	5	8	8	18	24	47	50	56
13	Bradford City	42	14	1	6	36	24	2	5	14	15	39	51	63	54
14	Leeds United	42	9	7	5	30	22	6	1	14	26	50	56	72	53
15	Grimsby Town	42	11	4	6	35	24	3	6	12	23	38	58	62	52
16	Huddersfield Town	42	10	6	5	30	23	4	4	13	21	44	51	67	52
17	Shrewsbury Town	42	11	5	5	29	20	3	4	14	23	44	52	64	51
18	Sunderland	42	10	5	6	33	29	3	6	12	14	32	47	61	50
19	Blackburn Rovers	42	10	4	7	30	20	2	9	10	23	42	53	62	49
20	Carlisle United	42	10	2	9	30	28	3	5	13	17	43	47	71	46
21	Middlesbrough	42	8	6	7	26	23	4	3	14	18	30	44	53	45
22	Fulham	42	8	3	10	29	32	2	3	16	16	37	45	69	36

1986/87   14th in Division Two

#	Date	Opponent	Score	Scorers	Att.	Ablett G	Askew B	Brentano S	Buckley N	Bunn F	Corkain S	Curran E	Daniel R	Doyle R	Dyer A	Flounders A	Heard P	Horton B	Jenkinson L	Jobson R	McEwan S	Norman A	Palmer C	Parker G	Payton A	Pearson L	Roberts G	Saville A	Skipper P	Swann G	Williams N
1	Aug 23	WEST BROMWICH ALB.	2-0	Flounders, Roberts	8656					8			10			9	4			2	6	1		7			11		5	3	12
2	26	Millwall	1-0	Bunn	4300					8			10			9	4			2	6	1		7			11		5	3	12
3	30	Oldham Athletic	0-0		5104		10			8						9	4			2		1		7			11	12	5	3	6
4	Sep 2	PORTSMOUTH	0-2		7706		10			8						9	4			2		1		7			11	12	5	3	6
5	6	PLYMOUTH ARGYLE	0-3		6451		10			8						9	4			2		1		7			11	12	5	3	6
6	13	Sunderland	0-1		12911	3	10			8							4			2		1		7			11	9	5	6	12
7	20	BIRMINGHAM CITY	3-2	Roberts 2, Skipper	6851	3				8							4	10		2		1		7			11	9	5	6	
8	27	Leeds United	0-3		13542	3										9	4	10		2		1		7			11	8	5	6	12
9	Oct 4	IPSWICH TOWN	2-1	Saville 2	6872											9	4	10		2		1		7			11	8	5		2
10	11	Derby County	1-1	Pratley (og)	12353	3						9				12	4				6	1		7			11	8	5	10	2
11	18	READING	0-2		5707		12					7				9	3		4		6	1				10	11	8	5		2
12	25	Huddersfield Town	3-1	Saville, Flounders, Skipper	5406		10					7				8	3		4		6	1	12				11	9	5		2
13	Nov 1	Brighton & Hove Albion	1-2	Jobson	7318		10		12			7				9	3		4		6	1	5				11	8			2
14	8	STOKE CITY	0-4		5252		10			8						12	3			2	6	1	4				11	9	5		7
15	15	Blackburn Rovers	2-0	Saville, Corkain	4149						10					9				2	6	1	4		3		11	8	5		7
16	22	BRADFORD CITY	2-1	McEwan, Skipper	6423					12	10					9				2	6	1	4		3		11	8	5		7
17	29	Shrewsbury Town	0-3		2869					12	10					9	3			2	6	1	4				11	8	5		7
18	Dec 6	GRIMSBY TOWN	1-1	McEwan	7217					8	10					9	3	7		2	6	1	4					5			
19	13	Crystal Palace	1-5	Roberts	4839					8	10					9	3	7		2	6	1	4				11				
20	26	Sheffield United	2-4	Flounders, Jobson	11296		10			8						12	3			2	6	1	4				11	9	5		7
21	27	BLACKBURN ROVERS	0-0		5789					8			10			9				2	6	1	4		3		11	12	5		7
22	Jan 1	BARNSLEY	3-4	Bunn, Roberts, McEwan	4879					8			10			9				2	6	1	4		3		11	12	5		2
23	3	Plymouth Argyle	0-4		12064				6	8						9	3	7	10			1	4				11	12	5		2
24	24	West Bromwich Albion	1-1	Jobson	6707		10	2		8						12	9		4		6	1			3		11		5		7
25	Feb 7	OLDHAM ATHLETIC	1-0	Saville	5651		10	2		8						12	6		4			1			3		11	9	5		7
26	14	Portsmouth	0-1		11098		10			8					11	12			4			1	2	6	3			9	5		7
27	28	Birmingham City	0-0		6858		10						8		11		3		4			1	2	6				9	5		
28	Mar 3	SUNDERLAND	1-0	Saville	5713		10			8			6		11		3		4			1	2	7				9	5		
29	7	HUDDERSFIELD T	0-0		5872		10			8			6		11		3		4			1	2	7			12	9	5		
30	14	Reading	0-1		5493		10			12			6		8		3		4			1	2	7			11	9	5		
31	21	DERBY COUNTY	1-1	Saville	9684		10			8						7	3		4			1	2	6			11	9	5		
32	28	Ipswich Town	0-0		10340		10			8						7	3		4			1	2	6			11	9	5		
33	Apr 4	Stoke City	1-1	Bunn	8146		10			8						7	3		4			1	2	6	12		11	9	5		
34	8	LEEDS UNITED	0-0		9531		10			8						7	3		4			1	2	6			11	9	5		
35	14	MILLWALL	2-1	Bunn, Jobson	5327		10			8						7	3		4			1	2	6			11	9	5		
36	18	Barnsley	1-1	Skipper	5607		10			8						7	3		4			1	2	6			11	9	5		
37	20	SHEFFIELD UNITED	0-0		8765		10			8						7	3		4			1	2	6			11	9	5		12
38	25	Bradford City	0-2		10390					8			10			7	3		4			1	2	6			11	9	5		12
39	28	BRIGHTON & HOVE ALBION	1-0	Jobson	5219		10			8			11		9		3		4			1	2	6				5			7
40	May 2	SHREWSBURY TOWN	3-0	Dyer 2, Heard	5114		10			8			11		9		3		4			1	2	6	12			5			7
41	5	Grimsby Town	2-2	Saville 2	6757		10			8			11		9		3		4			1	2	6				12	5		7
42	9	CRYSTAL PALACE	3-0	Dyer 2, Williams N	7656		10			6			11		9		3		4			1	2					8	5		7
		Apps				5	27	2	1	35	5	4	9	4	17	24	37	6		40	17	42	17	38	2	8	35	35	41	9	30
		Goals								4	1				4	3	1			5	3							5	9	4	1

One own goal

F.A. Cup

Rd	Date	Opponent	Score	Scorers	Att.	Askew B	Brentano S	Bunn F	Dyer A	Flounders A	Heard P	Jenkinson L	Norman A	Palmer C	Parker G	Payton A	Roberts G	Saville A	Skipper P	Williams N
R3	Jan 31	Shrewsbury Town	2-1	Bunn, Saville	4130	10	2	8		9	6	4	1			3	11	5		7
R4	Feb 3	Swansea City	1-0	Jobson	8853	10	2	8		9	6	4	1			3	11	5		7
R5	21	Wigan Athletic	0-3		11453	10			8	12		4	1	2	6	3	11	9	5	7

F.L. Cup (Littlewoods Challenge Cup)

Rd	Date	Opponent	Score	Scorers	Att.	Askew B	Buckley N	Curran E	Flounders A	Heard P	Horton B	Jenkinson L	Jobson R	McEwan S	Norman A	Palmer C	Parker G	Payton A	Roberts G	Saville A	Skipper P	Swann G	Williams N
R2/1	Sep 23	GRIMSBY TOWN	1-0	Saville	5,115				9	4	10		2		1		7		11	8	5	6	3
R2/2	Oct 7	Grimsby Town	1-1	McEwan	6,192				9	4			2	6	1		7	3	11	8	5	10	2
R3	28	Shrewsbury Town	0-1		3,077	10	12	7	9	3		4		6	1	5			11	8			2

Full Members Cup

Rd	Date	Opponent	Score	Scorers	Att.	Askew B	Bunn F	Corkain S	Curran E	Flounders A	Heard P	Horton B	Jenkinson L	Jobson R	McEwan S	Norman A	Palmer C	Roberts G	Saville A	Skipper P	Williams N
R1	Oct 21	Grimsby Town	3-1	Flounders 2, Curran	2,460	10			7	9	3		4		6	1		11	8	5	2
R2	Nov 25	Southampton	1-2	Parker	4,158		5	10		9	3	12		2	6		4	11	8	1	7

		Pl	Home W	D	L	F	A	Away W	D	L	F	A	F (Total)	A	Pts
1	Derby County	42	14	6	1	42	18	11	3	7	22	20	64	38	84
2	Portsmouth	42	17	2	2	37	11	6	7	8	16	17	53	28	78
3	Oldham Athletic	42	13	6	2	36	16	9	3	9	29	28	65	44	75
4	Leeds United	42	15	4	2	43	16	4	7	10	15	28	58	44	68
5	Ipswich Town	42	12	6	3	29	10	5	7	9	30	33	59	43	64
6	Crystal Palace	42	12	4	5	35	20	7	1	13	16	33	51	53	62
7	Plymouth Argyle	42	12	6	3	40	23	4	7	10	22	34	62	57	61
8	Stoke City	42	11	5	5	40	21	5	5	11	23	32	63	53	58
9	Sheffield United	42	10	8	3	31	19	5	5	11	19	30	50	49	58
10	Bradford City	42	10	5	6	36	27	5	5	11	26	35	62	62	55
11	Barnsley	42	8	7	6	26	23	6	6	9	23	29	49	52	55
12	Blackburn Rovers	42	11	4	6	30	22	4	6	11	15	33	45	55	55
13	Reading	42	11	4	6	33	23	3	7	11	19	36	52	59	53
14	HULL CITY	42	10	6	5	25	22	3	8	10	16	33	41	55	53
15	West Bromwich Alb.	42	8	6	7	29	22	5	6	10	22	27	51	49	51
16	Millwall	42	10	5	6	27	16	4	4	13	12	29	39	45	51
17	Huddersfield Town	42	9	6	6	38	30	4	6	11	16	31	54	61	51
18	Shrewsbury Town	42	11	3	7	24	14	4	3	14	17	39	41	53	51
19	Birmingham City	42	8	9	4	27	21	3	8	10	20	38	47	59	50
20	Sunderland	42	8	6	7	25	23	4	6	11	24	36	49	59	48
21	Grimsby Town	42	5	8	8	18	21	5	6	10	21	38	39	59	44
22	Brighton & Hove A.	42	7	6	8	22	20	2	6	13	15	34	37	54	39

1986-87
Back Row: S. Corkain, A. Flounders, P. Olsson, N. Brown, L. Pearson, G. Parker, G. Swann, S. Brentano;
Middle Row: A. Saville, S. McEwan, P. Skipper, J. Davies, R. Jobson, A. Norman, F. Bunn, R. Doyle, T. Wilson (Reserve Team manager);
Front Row: D. Booth (Asst. Manager), A. Payton, P. Heard, G. Roberts, B. Horton (Manager), W. Askew, N. Williams, R. Daniel, J Radcliffe (Physio).

1987-88
Back Row: L. Thompson, A. Dyer, P. Heard, L. Jenkinson, N. Buckley, N. Brown, G. Parker, C. Palmer, M. Smith;
Middle Row: T. Wilson (Coach), F. Bunn, G. Kelly, S. McEwan, P. Skipper, A. Norman, R. Jobson, A. Saville, J. Radcliffe (Physio);
Front Row: S. Corkain, N. Williams, G. Roberts, B. Horton, W. Askew, R. Daniel, D. Booth (Asst Manager).

1987/88 — 15th in Division Two

No	Date		Opponent	Score	Scorers	Att	Askew B	Barnes P	Brown N	Bunn F	Daniel R	De Mange K	Dyer A	Edwards K	Heard P	Hotte T	Jacobs W	Jenkinson L	Jobson R	Kelly G	McEwan S	Norman A	Owen G	Palmer C	Parker G	Payton A	Roberts G	Saville A	Skipper P	Thompson L	Williams N
1	Aug	15	BLACKBURN ROVERS	2-2	Bunn, Skipper	6426	10			8			9		3				4		6	1		2	7			11	5		
2		18	Stoke City	1-1	Parker	9139	10			8	11				3				4			1		2	6		7	9	5		
3		22	Crystal Palace	2-2	Parker, Bunn	6688	10			8	11				3				4			1		2	6		7	9	5		
4		29	ASTON VILLA	2-1	Heard, Dyer	8315	10			8	11		9		3				4			1		2	6		7		5		
5		31	Swindon Town	0-0		9600	10			8	11		9		3				4			1		2	6		7		5		
6	Sep	5	BOURNEMOUTH	2-1	Dyer, Askew	5807	10			8	11		9		3				4			1		2	6		7	12	5		
7		12	Leeds United	2-0	Dyer, Parker	18191	10			8	11		9		3				4			1		2	6		7		5		
8		15	SHREWSBURY TOWN	1-1	Roberts	7939	10			8	11		9		3				4			1		2	6		7	12	5		
9		19	OLDHAM ATHLETIC	1-0	Skipper	7083	10			8	11		9		3				4			1		2	6		7	12	5		14
10		29	MANCHESTER CITY	3-1	Bunn 2, Parker	9650	10			8	11				3				4			1		2	6	14	7	9	5		12
11	Oct	3	Sheffield United	1-2	Bunn	10446	10			8					3				4			1		2	6		7	9	5		
12		10	IPSWICH TOWN	1-0	Thompson	6962	10								3				4			1		2	6		7	9	5	8	11
13		17	Barnsley	3-1	Saville, Heard, Askew	7310	10								3				4			1		2	6		7	9	5	8	11
14		20	Huddersfield Town	2-0	Thompson, Parker	8033	10						12		3				4			1		2	6		7	9	5	8	11
15		24	LEICESTER CITY	2-2	Roberts, Williams	8826	10				12		8		3				4			1		2	6		7	9	5		11
16		31	Plymouth Argyle	1-3	Saville	8550	10				12				3				4			1		2	6		7	9	5		11
17	Nov	3	BRADFORD CITY	0-0		15443	10			8					9				4			1		2	6		7		5		11
18		7	BIRMINGHAM CITY	2-0	Williams, Overson (og)	7901	10			8					9				4			1		2	6		7		5		11
19		14	Middlesbrough	0-1		15709	10			8	3		9						4			1		2	6	12	7		5		11
20		21	WEST BROMWICH ALB.	1-0	Askew	7654	10			8	3		9						4			1		2	6		7		5		11
21		28	Millwall	0-2		6743	10			8	3		9						4			1		2	6		7		5		11
22	Dec	5	READING	2-2	Dyer, Parker	5797	10				3		9						4			1		2	6	12	7	8	5		11
23		12	Shrewsbury Town	2-2	Roberts, Saville	2588	10				3		9						4			1		2	6		7	8	5		11
24		19	CRYSTAL PALACE	2-1	Parker, Dyer	6780	10				3		9			11			4			1		2	6		7	8	5		12
25		28	Oldham Athletic	2-1	Heard, Dyer	8092	10				3		9		10	11			4			1		2	6		7		5		8
26	Jan	1	Aston Villa	0-5		19236	10				3		9		11				4			1		2	6	14	7	8	5		12
27		3	LEEDS UNITED	3-1	Payton, Jobson, Dyer	14694	10						9		3			11	4			1		2	12	8	7		5		6
28		16	Blackburn Rovers	1-2	Jobson	9682	10				12		9		3				4			1		2	6	8	7		5		11
29	Feb	6	Bournemouth	2-6	Payton, Dyer	5901	10	14					9		3				4			1		2	6	8	7	12	5		11
30		13	STOKE CITY	0-0		6424	10						9		3				4			1		2	6	8	7	12	5		11
31		27	SHEFFIELD UNITED	1-2	Saville	8832	10				14		9		3		11		4			1		2	6	12	7	8	5		
32	Mar	2	Manchester City	0-2		16040			2		10		9		3				4			1			6		7	8	5		11
33		5	BARNSLEY	1-2	Saville	7622	11	2					10	9	3				4			1	6			12	7	8	5		
34		12	Ipswich Town	0-2		9574	11		6		3		10	9					4			1			12	7	8	5	14	2
35		19	PLYMOUTH ARGYLE	1-1	Parker	5172	11						10	9	3				4			1	6		12	7	8	5		2
36		26	Leicester City	1-2	Edwards	10353	11				12	10		9					4			1		2		6	7	8	5		
37	Apr	2	Birmingham City	1-1	Heard	7059	11				10	9	6	3					4			1		2	12	7	8	5		
38		4	MIDDLESBROUGH	0-0		10752	11				10	9	6	3					4			1		2	8	7	5		
39		9	Bradford City	0-2		13659	11	5			10	9	6	3	14				4			1		2	8	7	12		
40		12	SWINDON TOWN	1-4	Jenkinson	4853	7	2			6	9			3	11	4			1			8	12	14	5	10	
41		23	HUDDERSFIELD T	4-0	Edwards 2, Daniel, Saville	5221	11	2			10			9	3	14			4			1			6	7	8	5	12	
42		30	West Bromwich Albion	1-1	Daniel	8004	11	2			10			9	3	12			4			1			6	7	8	5		
43	May	2	MILLWALL	0-1		10811	11	2			10	12		9	3	14			4			1			6	7	8	5		
44		7	Reading	0-0		6710		2			10			9	3	6	11		4			1			6	7	8	5		
			Apps				30	11	10	18	26	9	28	9	35	4	6	3	44		1	44	3	35	34	21	44	32	43	7	25
			Goals				3			5	2		8	3	4				1						8	2	3	6	2	2	2

One own goal

F.A. Cup

			Opponent	Score	Scorers	Att	Askew B	Brown N	Bunn F	Daniel R	Dyer A	Heard P	Jobson R	Norman A	Palmer C	Parker G	Roberts G	Skipper P	Williams N
R3	Jan	9	Watford	1-1	Roberts	12761	10				9	3	4	1	2	6	8	7	5	11
rep		12	WATFORD	2-2	Williams, Dyer	13681	10				9	3	4	1	2	6	8	7	5	11
rep2		18	Watford	0-1		15261	10	2		14	9	3	4	1			6	8	7	12	5	11

R3 replay a.e.t.

F.L. Cup (Littlewoods Challenge Cup)

			Opponent	Score	Att	Askew B	Bunn F	Daniel R	Heard P	Jenkinson L	Jobson R	Norman A	Palmer C	Parker G	Roberts G	Saville A	Skipper P	Thompson L	Williams N
R2/1	Sep	23	Manchester United	0-5	25041	10	8	11	3		4	1	2	6	7	9	5		12
R2/2	Oct	7	MANCHESTER UNITED	0-1	13586	10			3	14	4	1	2	6	12	7	9	5	8	11

F.M. Cup (Simod Cup)

			Opponent	Score	Scorers	Att	Askew B	Bunn F	Daniel R	Heard P	Jobson R	Kelly G	Palmer C	Parker G	Roberts G	Saville A	Skipper P	Thompson L	Williams N
R1	Nov	10	Charlton Athletic	1-1	Roberts	1338	10		8	12	3	4	1	2	6	7	9	5	14	11

Lost 4-5 on penalties a.e.t.

		Pl	Home					Away					F.	A.	Pts
			W	D	L	F	A	W	D	L	F	A	(Total)		
1	Millwall	44	15	3	4	45	23	10	4	8	27	29	72	52	82
2	Aston Villa	44	9	7	6	31	21	13	5	4	37	20	68	41	78
3	Middlesbrough	44	15	4	3	44	16	7	8	7	19	20	63	36	78
4	Bradford City	44	14	3	5	49	26	8	8	6	25	28	74	54	77
5	Blackburn Rovers	44	12	8	2	38	22	9	6	7	30	30	68	52	77
6	Crystal Palace	44	16	3	3	50	21	6	6	10	36	38	86	59	75
7	Leeds United	44	14	4	4	37	18	5	8	9	24	33	61	51	69
8	Ipswich Town	44	14	3	5	38	17	5	6	11	23	35	61	52	66
9	Manchester City	44	11	4	7	50	28	8	4	10	30	32	80	60	65
10	Oldham Athletic	44	13	4	5	43	27	5	7	10	29	37	72	64	65
11	Stoke City	44	12	6	4	34	22	5	5	12	16	35	50	57	62
12	Swindon Town	44	10	7	5	43	25	6	4	12	30	35	73	60	59
13	Leicester City	44	12	5	5	35	20	4	6	12	27	41	62	61	59
14	Barnsley	44	11	4	7	42	32	4	8	10	19	30	61	62	57
15	HULL CITY	44	10	8	4	32	22	4	7	11	22	38	54	60	57
16	Plymouth Argyle	44	12	4	6	44	26	4	4	14	21	41	65	67	56
17	Bournemouth	44	7	7	8	36	30	6	3	13	20	38	56	68	49
18	Shrewsbury Town	44	7	8	7	23	22	4	8	10	19	32	42	54	49
19	Birmingham City	44	7	9	6	20	24	4	6	12	21	42	41	66	48
20	West Bromwich Alb.	44	8	7	7	29	26	4	4	14	21	43	50	69	47
21	Sheffield United	44	8	6	8	27	28	5	1	16	18	46	45	74	46
22	Reading	44	5	7	10	20	25	5	5	12	24	45	44	70	42
23	Huddersfield Town	44	4	6	12	24	38	2	4	16	21	62	41	100	28

1988/89 21st in Division Two

League Matches

#	Month	Date	Opponent	Score	Scorers	Att	Askew B	Bell D	Brown N	Buckley N	Calvert M	Daniel R	De Mange K	Dyer A	Edwards K	Hesford I	Hotte T	Jacobs W	Jenkinson L	Jobson R	Kelly G	McParland I	Moore J	Mudd P	Murray M	Norman A	Palmer C	Payton A	Roberts G	Saville A	Skipper P	Smith M	Swan P	Terry S	Thompson L	Warren L	Whitehurst W
1	Aug	27	MANCHESTER CITY	1-0	Edwards	11653								7	10			3		2			9		1		12		8	11	3			6		4	
2		29	Oxford United	0-1		5772								7	10			3		2			9		1				8	11	3			6		4	
3	Sep	3	Plymouth Argyle	0-2		8202								7	10			3		2			9		1		12		8	11	3			6		4	
4		10	BARNSLEY	0-0		5654					11	12		7	10			3		5			9		1		2		8					6		4	
5		17	Portsmouth	3-1	Edwards 2, Dyer	11599					11	14		7	10			3		5					1		2		9	8	12			6		4	
6		20	BLACKBURN ROVERS	1-3	Edwards	6681					11	14		7	10					5			12		1		2		9	8				6	3	4	
7		24	Oldham Athletic	2-2	Terry, Milligan (og)	6329						12		7	10					5	1						2		9	8		11		6	3	4	
8	Oct	1	WALSALL	0-0		4805						14		11	10			3		5			12		1		2		9	8				6	7	4	
9		4	LEICESTER CITY	2-2	Edwards, De Mange	5079	7						3	14	11	10				5			9		1		2		8	12				6		4	
10		8	Shrewsbury Town	3-1	Edwards 2, Roberts	3287							3	4	11	10				5			9		1				8	7				6		2	
11		15	SUNDERLAND	0-0		8261								7	4	11	10	3		5			9		1				12	8		14		6		2	
12		22	Crystal Palace	1-3	Dyer	8464								7	11	10		12	3	5					1		2		9			8		6		4	
13		25	CHELSEA	3-0	Edwards 2, Smith	6953								7	12	11		3		5					1		2		9			8		6		4	
14		29	Leeds United	1-2	Palmer	17553								7	12	11		3		5					1		2	14	9			8		6		4	
15	Nov	5	SWINDON TOWN	1-0	Moore	5192								8	11	10	3		5			9		1		2		7					6		4	
16		13	Stoke City	0-4		10505									8			3	11	5			9		1		2	12	7					6		4	
17		19	BIRMINGHAM CITY	1-1	Edwards	5134							3		8	10				5		14	9		1		2	11	7	12				6		4	
18		26	Watford	0-2		10404							3		8	10				5		12			1		2	11	7	9				6		4	
19		29	Bournemouth	1-5	Payton	5420						2	3		8	10				5		9			1			11	7	12				6		4	
20	Dec	3	BRIGHTON & HOVE ALB	5-2	Payton 2, Daniel, Saville, Gatting (og)	5686							3		10				11	5					1		2	7	8	9				6		4	
21		10	West Bromwich Albion	0-2		10094							3		10				11	5					1		2	7	8	9				12		4	
22		26	BRADFORD CITY	1-1	Payton	8791				6			3	10						5					1		2	7	8	9				11		4	
23		31	IPSWICH TOWN	1-1	Whitehurst	7800				6			3	10			1			5							2	7	8	12		11				4	9
24	Jan	2	Barnsley	2-0	Edwards	9879			2	6		11			10		1	3		5									7	8		12				14	9
25		14	BOURNEMOUTH	4-0	Edwards 3, Whitehurst	5690	11		2	6		4			10		1	3		5									7	8							9
26		21	Manchester City	1-4	Edwards	20485	11		2	6		4			10		1	3		5									7	8							9
27	Feb	4	Leicester City	2-0	Edwards 2	9996	11		2	6		4			10		1	3		5									7	8							9
28		11	SHREWSBURY TOWN	3-0	Edwards 2, Whitehurst	11472	11		2	6		4			10		1	3		5									7	8							9
29		25	Sunderland	0-2		14709	11		2	6		4			10		1	3		5									7	8				12			9
30		28	Chelsea	1-2	Roberts	11402	11		2	6				7	4		1	3		5									8								9
31	Mar	4	STOKE CITY	1-4	Whitehurst	5915	7		2	6		11			4		1	3		5									8								9
32		11	Swindon Town	0-1		7090	7		2	6	11						10	1	4	3						14	12	8	9					5			9
33		14	LEEDS UNITED	1-2	Roberts	8887	7								10		1	3	11	5						2	12	8	6					4			
34		18	Blackburn Rovers	0-4		5864						14			10		1	3	11	4						2	12	8	9	7				5	6		
35		25	PLYMOUTH ARGYLE	3-0	Edwards 2, Jobson	5851		11							10		1	3	14	5		7				2	12	8						4			9
36		27	Bradford City	1-1	Edwards	11802		11	2						10		1	3		5		7												4	6	8	9
37	Apr	1	PORTSMOUTH	1-1	Edwards	5325		11	2						10		1	3		5		12				7								4	6	8	9
38		4	OXFORD UNITED	1-2	Swan	6260	8	11	2						10		1	3		5	12					7						11	4	6			9
39		8	Ipswich Town	1-1	Whitehurst	10265	8		2						10		1	3		5		7									11	4	6	12			9
40		11	CRYSTAL PALACE	0-1		5050	8								10		1	3		5		7					12	11					6				9
41		15	Walsall	1-1	Edwards	3935						12			10		1	3		5		7					2		8				4	11	6		9
42		22	OLDHAM ATHLETIC	1-1	McParland	6748	11					12			10		1	3	14	5		7					2		8				4			6	9
43		29	WATFORD	0-3		5225	11				5	8	6	12	10		1	3		2		7											4				9
44	May	1	Brighton & Hove Albion	1-1	Edwards	6750						8	6	11	10			3		2	1	7						12					4	5		9
45		6	Birmingham City	0-1		4686						8	6	11	10					2	1	7		3				9					4	5		
46		13	WEST BROMWICH ALB.	0-1		5217	6					8	3	12	10			11		2					14								7	4	5		9
			Apps				16	4	13	13	5	23	32	15	44	22	1	33	11	46	3	11	14	2	8	21	18	28	35	20	3	12	11	33	7	28	2
			Goals									1	1	2	26					1		1	1				1	4	3	1		1	1	1		1	1

Two own goals

F.A. Cup

Rnd	Month	Date	Opponent	Score	Scorers	Att	Askew B	Brown N	Buckley N	Daniel R	Edwards K	Hesford I	Jacobs W	Jobson R	Roberts G	Saville A	Skipper P	Smith M
R3	Jan	7	Cardiff City	2-1	Brown, Edwards	7128	11	2	6	4	10	1	3	5	7	8		
R4		28	Bradford City	2-1	Whitehurst, Edwards	13748	11	2	6	4	10	1	3	5	7	8		
R5	Feb	18	LIVERPOOL	2-3	Whitehurst, Edwards	20058	11	2	6	4	10	1	3	5		7	8	12

F.L. Cup (Littlewoods Challenge Cup)

Rnd	Month	Date	Opponent	Score	Scorers	Att	Dyer A	Edwards K	Hesford I	Jacobs W	Jobson R	McParland I	Murray M	Palmer C	Roberts G	Saville A	Skipper P	Terry S	Thompson L	Warren L
R2/1	Sep	28	ARSENAL	1-2	Edwards	11450	11	10			5	12	1	2	9	8	7	6	3	4
R2/2	Oct	12	Arsenal	0-3		17885	4	11	10	3	5	9	1	12	8	7		6		2

F.M. Cup (Simod Cup)

Rnd	Month	Date	Opponent	Score	Scorers	Att	Edwards K	Hotte T	Jacobs W	Jenkinson L	Jobson R	Moore J	Murray M	Palmer C	Roberts G	Terry S	Warren L
R1	Nov	8	Portsmouth	1-2	Warren	2784	8	10	3	11	5	9	1	2	7	6	4

Division Two Final Table

		Pl	Home W	D	L	F	A	Away W	D	L	F	A	(Total) F	A	Pts
1	Chelsea	46	15	6	2	50	25	14	6	3	46	25	96	50	99
2	Manchester City	46	12	8	3	48	28	11	5	7	29	25	77	53	82
3	Crystal Palace	46	15	6	2	42	17	8	6	9	29	32	71	49	81
4	Watford	46	14	5	4	41	18	8	7	8	33	30	74	48	78
5	Blackburn Rovers	46	16	4	3	50	22	6	7	10	24	37	74	59	77
6	Swindon Town	46	13	8	2	35	15	7	8	8	33	38	68	53	76
7	Barnsley	46	12	8	3	37	21	8	6	9	29	37	66	58	74
8	Ipswich Town	46	13	3	7	42	23	9	4	10	29	38	71	61	73
9	West Bromwich Alb.	46	13	7	3	43	18	5	11	7	22	23	65	41	72
10	Leeds United	46	12	6	5	34	20	5	10	8	25	30	59	50	67
11	Sunderland	46	12	8	3	40	23	4	7	12	20	37	60	60	63
12	Bournemouth	46	13	3	7	32	20	5	5	13	21	42	53	62	62
13	Stoke City	46	10	9	4	33	25	5	5	13	24	47	57	72	59
14	Bradford City	46	8	11	4	29	22	5	6	12	23	37	52	59	56
15	Leicester City	46	11	6	6	31	20	2	10	11	25	43	56	63	55
16	Oldham Athletic	46	9	10	4	49	32	2	11	10	26	40	75	72	54
17	Oxford United	46	11	6	6	40	34	3	6	14	22	36	62	70	54
18	Plymouth Argyle	46	11	4	8	35	22	3	8	12	20	44	55	66	54
19	Brighton & Hove A.	46	11	5	7	36	24	3	4	16	21	42	57	66	51
20	Portsmouth	46	10	6	7	33	21	3	6	14	20	41	53	62	51
21	HULL CITY	46	7	9	7	31	25	4	5	14	21	43	52	68	47
22	Shrewsbury Town	46	4	11	8	25	31	4	7	12	15	36	40	67	42
23	Birmingham City	46	6	4	13	21	33	2	7	14	10	43	31	76	31
24	Walsall	46	3	10	10	27	42	2	6	15	14	38	41	80	31

1988-89

Back Row: K. De Mange, L. Thompson, W. Jacobs, G. Roberts, W. Askew, T. Hotte, A. Payton, R. Daniel;

Middle Row: T. Wilson (Coach), S. Terry, N. Brown, A. Saville, A. Norman, G. Kelly, L. Jenkinson, J. Moore, R. Jobson, D. Robinson (Chairman), J Radcliffe (Physio);

Front Row: N. Buckley, C. Palmer, D. Booth (Asst Manager), P. Skipper, E. Gray (Manager), A. Dyer, K. Edwards.

1989-90

Back Row: S. Terry, R. Jobson, N. Buckley, W. Whitehurst, P. Swan, L. Jenkinson, L. Warren, P. Mudd;

Middle Row: J. Radcliffe (Physio), D. Roberts (Coach), K. De Mange, A. Payton, M. Murray, G. Kelly, I. Hesford, D. Cleminshaw, P. Waites, N. Brown, M. Smith, S. Ternent (Manager), T. Wilson (Coach);

Front Row: W. Jacobs, S. Doyle, W. Askew, G. Roberts, L. Thompson, I. McParland, M. Calvert.

1989/90 14th in Division Two

#		Date	Opponent	Score	Scorers	Att	Askew B	Atkinson G	Bamber D	Brown N	Buckley N	DeMange K	Doyle S	Edwards K	Hesford I	Hunter P	Jacobs W	Jenkinson L	Jobson R	Kelly G	McParland I	Murray M	Ngata H	Palin L	Payton A	Roberts G	Shaw R	Shotton M	Swan P	Terry S	Thomas G	Warren L	Wheeler P	Whitehurst W	Smith M	Thompson L	Waites P
1	Aug	19	LEICESTER CITY	1-1	Payton	8158	7			12		11		10	1		3		5		14	2			9	8				4	6						
2		26	Bournemouth	4-5	Payton 3, McParland	6454	7			12		11		1	1		3		14		5	9	2		8					4	6					10	
3	Sep	2	WEST HAM UNITED	1-1	Swan	9235	7			9		14	11		1		3	12	6		1	10	2			8				4	5						
4		9	Portsmouth	2-2	Swan 2	6496	7			12			11	10	1		3	2	6		1	9				8				4	5						
5		12	Port Vale	1-1	McParland	6168	7						12	11	1		3	2	6		1	9				8				4	5			10			
6		16	LEEDS UNITED	0-1		11620	7			12			11		1		3	2	6		1	9			14	8				4	5			10			
7		23	Sheffield United	0-0		14969	7			2					1		3	12	6		1	9			11	8				4	5			10			
8		27	Middlesbrough	0-1		16382	7			2	12	14			1		3	11	6		1	9			10	8				4	5						
9		30	NEWCASTLE UNITED	1-3	McParland	9629	7				2	12	11		1		3	14	6		1	9			10	8				4	5						
10	Oct	7	SWINDON TOWN	2-3	Swan 2	5366	7			2			10		1		3	11	6		1	9			12	8				4	5						
11		14	Stoke City	1-1	McParland	9955	7						11		1	1	3	12	6		10					8				4	5	2		9			
12		17	OLDHAM ATHLETIC	0-0		5109	7						11		1	1	3	12	6		10				14	8				4	5	2		9			
13		21	West Bromwich Albion	1-1	Brown	9228	7			2			11		1	1	3	12	6						8					4	5	10		9			
14		28	BRIGHTON & HOVE ALBION	0-2		4756	7			2			11		1	1	3	12	6						8					4	5			9	10		
15		31	Blackburn Rovers	0-0		7678	7			2			10		1	1	3	11	6						12					4	5	8		9			
16	Nov	4	WATFORD	0-0		4718	7			2			10		1	1	3	11	6											4	5	8	12	9			
17		11	Bradford City	3-2	Jobson, Payton, McParland	8540	7			2			10		1	1	3	11	6		14				12					4	5	8		9			
18		18	Oxford United	0-0		4030	7			2			11		1	1	3		4		10				8						5	6	12	9			
19		25	BARNSLEY	1-2	Payton	5715	7			2			11		1	1	3		4		10				8					12	5	6	14	9			
20	Dec	2	Leicester City	1-2	Jacobs	8616				2	12	7	11		1	1	3	10	4						8					9	5	6	14				
21		9	PORT VALE	2-1	Payton, Doyle	4207	7	12		2		8	11		1	1	3		4						10					9	5	6	14				
22		26	Wolverhampton W.	2-1	Brown, Terry	19524	7			2			11		1	1	3	14	4						10	8	6			12	5			9			
23		29	Plymouth Argyle	2-1	Terry, Swan	8588	7			2			11		1	1	3	12	4						10	8	6			9	5						
24	Jan	1	SUNDERLAND	3-2	Jacobs, Payton, Swan	9346	7			2			11		1	1	3	12	4						8	10	6			9	5						
25		13	Bournemouth	1-4	Payton	4673	7			2			14	11	1	1	3	12	4						8	10	6				5			9			
26		20	West Ham United	2-1	Buckley, Payton	16847	10			2	5	6	11		1	1	3		4					12	8	7								9			
27	Feb	3	SHEFFIELD UNITED	0-0		9606	10		9	2	6	11		1	1	3		4						8	7				5							
28		10	Leeds United	3-4	Payton 2, Doyle	30192	10		9	2	6	11		1	1	3		4						8	7				5							
29		17	PORTSMOUTH	1-2	Terry	4883	10		9	2	6	11		1	1	3	14	4					14	8	7				5							
30		24	Barnsley	1-1	Jacobs	8901	10	12	9	2	5	6	11		1	1	3		4					14	8	7				5							
31	Mar	3	OXFORD UNITED	1-0	Payton	4503		10	9	2		6	11		1	1	3		4		12				8	7		5									
32		7	Newcastle United	0-2		20684		10	9	2		10	11		1	1	3		4		14				8	7		5		6							
33		10	MIDDLESBROUGH	0-0		6602	10	11	9	2		6			1	1	3		4		12				8	7		5									
34		17	Swindon Town	3-1	Payton, Bamber, Askew	8123	10	11	9	2		6			1	14	3		4		12				8	7		5									
35		20	STOKE CITY	0-0		6456	10	11	9	2		6			1	14	3		4		12				8	7		5									
36		24	Oldham Athletic	2-3	Jobson, Hunter	11472	12	11	9	2		2			1	14	3		4					10	8	7		5			11						
37		31	WEST BROMWICH ALBION	0-2		5418	11	9				6			1	8	3		4			12	10		2		5	14	7								
38	Apr	6	Brighton & Hove Albion	0-2		6789			9	2		6			1		3	12	4					10	11	7		5			8						
39		10	BLACKBURN ROVERS	2-0	Payton, Bamber	5327			9	2			6		1		3		4					10	8	7		5	12		11						
40		14	Sunderland	1-0	Swan	17455			9	2			6		1	12	3							10	8	7		5	4		11						
41		16	WOLVERHAMPTON W.	2-0	Palin, Bamber	7510			9	2			6		1	12	3		4					10	8	7		5			11						
42		21	Ipswich Town	1-0	Gayle (og)	9430			9	2			6		1		3		4					10	8	7		5	8		11						
43		24	PLYMOUTH ARGYLE	3-3	Swan, Shotton, Hunter	5256		12		2			6		1	14	3		4					10	8	7		5	9		11						
44		28	BRADFORD CITY	2-1	Payton, Swan	6514		12	9	2			6		1	14	3		4						8	7		5	10		11						
45	May	1	IPSWICH TOWN	4-3	Atkinson, Shotton, Swan, Payton	5306		2	9						1		3		4						8	7		5	10		11						
46		5	Watford	1-3	Hunter	9827		12	9				6		1	14	3		4					10	8	7		5	2		11						
					Apps		32	13	19	34	10	21	36	2	38	9	46	22	45	8	20	3	4	9	39	36	4	16	31	29	11	10	5	15	1	1	
					Goals		1	1	3	2	1		2				3	3			2			5	1	17		2	11	3							

One own goal

F.A. Cup

		Date	Opponent	Score		Att																															
R3	Jan	6	NEWCASTLE UNITED	0-1		10743	10			2		6	11		1	1	3	12	4						8	7				9	5				14			

F.L. Cup (Littlewoods Challenge Cup)

		Date	Opponent	Score	Scorers	Att																															
R1/1	Aug	22	GRIMSBY TOWN	1-0	Payton	5045	7			12			11	10	1		3	14	6			9	2			8				4	5						
R1/2		29	Grimsby Town	0-2		6753	7			4			10	12	1		3	11	6		1	9	2			8				14	5						

R1/2 a.e.t.

F.M.Cup (Zenith Data Systems Cup)

		Date	Opponent	Score	Scorers	Att																															
R2	Nov	28	ASTON VILLA	1-2	Jenkinson	2888	7			2		6	12	11		1		3	10	4		14				8				9	5						

		Pl	Home					Away					F.	A.	Pts
			W	D	L	F	A	W	D	L	F	A	(Total)		
1	Leeds United	46	16	6	1	46	18	8	7	8	33	34	79	52	85
2	Sheffield United	46	14	5	4	43	27	10	8	5	35	31	78	58	85
3	Newcastle United	46	17	4	2	51	26	5	10	8	29	29	80	55	80
4	Swindon Town	46	12	6	5	49	29	8	8	7	30	30	79	59	74
5	Blackburn Rovers	46	10	9	4	43	30	9	8	6	31	29	74	59	74
6	Sunderland	46	10	8	5	41	32	10	6	7	29	32	70	64	74
7	West Ham United	46	14	5	4	50	22	6	7	10	30	35	80	57	72
8	Oldham Athletic	46	15	7	1	50	23	4	7	12	20	34	70	57	71
9	Ipswich Town	46	13	7	3	38	22	6	5	12	29	44	67	66	69
10	Wolverhampton W.	46	12	5	6	37	20	6	8	9	30	40	67	60	67
11	Port Vale	46	11	9	3	37	20	4	7	12	25	37	62	57	61
12	Portsmouth	46	9	8	6	40	34	6	8	9	22	31	62	65	61
13	Leicester City	46	10	8	5	34	29	5	6	12	33	50	67	79	59
14	HULL CITY	46	7	8	8	27	31	7	8	3	31	34	58	65	58
15	Watford	46	11	6	6	41	28	3	9	11	17	32	58	60	57
16	Plymouth Argyle	46	9	8	6	30	23	5	5	13	28	40	58	63	55
17	Oxford United	46	8	7	8	35	31	7	2	14	22	35	57	66	54
18	Brighton & Hove A.	46	10	6	7	28	27	5	3	15	28	45	56	72	54
19	Barnsley	46	7	9	7	22	23	6	6	11	27	48	49	71	54
20	West Bromwich Alb.	46	6	8	9	35	37	6	7	10	32	34	67	71	51
21	Middlesbrough	46	10	3	10	33	29	3	8	12	19	34	52	63	50
22	Bournemouth	46	8	6	9	30	31	4	6	13	27	45	57	76	48
23	Bradford City	46	9	6	8	26	24	0	8	15	18	44	44	68	41
24	Stoke City	46	4	11	8	20	24	2	8	13	15	39	35	63	37

League matches

Date	Match	Score	Scorers	Att.
Aug 25	NOTTS COUNTY	1-2	Payton	7385
28	Blackburn Rovers	1-2	Mail	7337
Sep 1	Sheffield Wednesday	1-5	Payton	23673
8	SWINDON TOWN	1-1	Buckley	5240
15	Bristol Rovers	1-1	Swan	4734
19	Millwall	3-3	Payton 2, Palin	9516
22	WEST BROMWICH ALB.	1-1	Payton	5953
29	PORT VALE	3-2	Palin, Payton 2	5185
Oct 2	Watford	1-0	Swan	6448
6	West Ham United	1-7	Hockaday	19519
13	OLDHAM ATHLETIC	2-2	Payton, Palin	8676
20	WOLVERHAMPTON W.	1-2	Payton	7144
24	Brighton & Hove Albion	1-3	Bamber	5354
27	Plymouth Argyle	1-4	Bamber	5039
Nov 3	NEWCASTLE UNITED	2-1	Jacobs, Swan	8375
10	IPSWICH TOWN	3-3	Payton 2, McParland	5294
17	Bristol City	1-1	Finnigan	9346
23	LEICESTER CITY	5-2	Payton 2, Swan 2, Palin	5855
Dec 1	Middlesbrough	0-3		17024
8	BLACKBURN ROVERS	3-1	Payton, Swan 2	4166
15	Notts County	1-2	Swan	5537
22	Charlton Athletic	1-2	Payton	4989
26	OXFORD UNITED	3-3	Payton, Swan 2	5103
29	BARNSLEY	1-2	Palin	7916
Jan 1	Portsmouth	1-5	Payton	8004
12	SHEFFIELD WEDNESDAY	0-1		10907
19	Swindon Town	1-3	Payton	7394
Feb 2	BRISTOL ROVERS	2-0	Buckley, Swan	5302
16	BRISTOL CITY	1-2	Payton	5212
23	Ipswich Town	0-2		9407
Mar 2	MIDDLESBROUGH	0-0		6828
9	Leicester City	1-0	Payton	8386
12	WATFORD	1-1	Wilcox	5815
16	Port Vale	0-0		6103
20	Oldham Athletic	2-1	Payton, Swan	12626
23	WEST HAM UNITED	0-0		9558
30	Oxford United	0-1		4591
Apr 1	CHARLTON ATHLETIC	2-2	Hunter, Payton	5689
6	Barnsley	1-3	Payton	6859
10	West Bromwich Albion	1-1	Payton	10356
13	PORTSMOUTH	0-2		4871
16	MILLWALL	1-1	Payton	4102
20	Wolverhampton Wan.	0-0		9313
27	BRIGHTON & HOVE ALB	0-1		4037
May 4	PLYMOUTH ARGYLE	2-0	Thompson, Hunter	3175
11	Newcastle United	2-1	Walmsley, Thompson	17918

Appearances and goals

	Allison N	Atkinson G	Bamber D	Brown N	Buckley N	Butler L	Calvert M	Dearden K	De Mange K	Doyle S	Finnigan A	Hesford I	Hobson G	Hockaday D	Hunter P	Jacobs W	Jenkinson L	Jobson R	Mail D	McParland I	Ngata H	Norton D	Palin L	Payton A	Roberts G	Shotton M	Smith M	Swan P	Thomas G	Thompson L	Waites T	Walmsley D	Warren L	Wilcox R	Wilson S	Wright T
Aug 25		12	2								6	1		14	3			4	5				10	8	7			9	11							
28		12			5						6	1		14	3			4	5				10	8	7			9	11							
Sep 1		12			5			2			6	1		14	3			4					10	8	7			9	11							
8				2	5						11	6	1		3				4	14			10	8				9	7					12		
15					5						11	6	1		2		3		4				10	8				9	7					12		
19	7		12	5							11		1	2	14				4	9			10	8					3					6		
22	7			5							11	12	1	2	14				4	9			10	8					3					6		
29	7			5							11	1		2					4	12			10	8				9	3					6		
Oct 2				5							3	11	1	2					4				10	8				9	7					6		
6				5							3	11	1	2					4	12	14		10	8				9	7					6		
13		9		4							6	3	1	2						12			10	8		5		11	7					12		
20		9		4							6	3	1	2						12			10	8		5		11	7							
24		9		4							6	3	1	2		14							10	8		5		11						7		
27		9									3	1	2			12		4	11				10	8		5			7					6		
Nov 3											6	7	1	2	3				4	11			10	8		5		9						12		
10		9									6	7	1	2	3				4	12			10	8		5		11								
17		9	2								7	1		3	12				4	11			10	8		5										
23							11					1		2	3	12			4				10	8	7			9		6				5		
Dec 1							11					1		2	14	3	12		4				10	8	7			9		6				5		
8							11					1		2			14		4				10	8	7			9		3	6			5		
15							11					1		2			12		4	14			10	8	7			9		3	6			5		
22				5							12	1		2			11						10	8	7			9	3	4	6					
26				5								1		2			11	6	12				10	8				7	9	3	4					
29				5								1		2	3		12						10	8		6		9	7	4						
Jan 1				5								1		2	14	3	11	12	7				10	8		6		9	4							
12	11			5			1	4						9	3					8	14	2	10			6	7							12		
19	11			5			1	4						7	9	3					14	2	10			6								12		
Feb 2	11			5			1	4							3	12						2	10	8		6	7	9								
16	11			5				4						14	3	7						2	10	8		6		9						12	1	
23	11			5				12						14	3							2		8		6	7	9						10	4	1
Mar 2														7		3	14		5			2	10	8		6		9		12			11	4	1
9														7					5			2	10	8		6		9					11	4	1
12														7			12		5			2	10	8		6		9		3			11	4	1
16							10							7			12		5			2	8			6		9		3			11	4	1
20		10		4	1									7					5			2	8			6		9		3			11		
23		10		4	1									7			12		5			2	8			6		9		3			11		
30		12		4	1									7			10		5	14	2		8			6		9		3			11		
Apr 1		10		4	1									7	14				5	12	2		8			6		9		3			11		
6		10		4									1	7			12		5	14	2		8			6		9		3			11		
10		10		4						1		3	7				12		5		2		8					9					11	6	
13		10		4						1		7				3			5	12			8					9					11	2	
16		12								1	3	2	14			11			5				8			6		9			7			4	
20										1	3	2	9			11			5	14			8			6		9			12	7		4	
27										1	3	2	12			11			5				8			6		9			7			4	
May 4			6			8									2	10			5	9										12		3		7	4	1
11	6		12			8									10	2	11		5										14		3	9	7	4	1
Apps	1	16	9	3	31	4	7	3	6	11	18	31	4	35	18	19	26	2	36	16	10	15	35	43	8	26	6	38	11	20	10	1	15	31	2	6
Goals			2		2						1			1	2	1			1	1			5	25				12		2		1		1		

F.A. Cup

Date	Match	Score	Scorers	Att.
Jan 5	NOTTS COUNTY	2-5	Buckley, McParland	6655

	Buckley N	Finnigan A	Hesford I	Hobson G	Hockaday D	Jenkinson L	Palin L	Payton A	Shotton M	Swan P	Thompson L	Waites T	Wilcox R
Jan 5	5	1	12	3	11	14	10	8	6	9	7	4	2

F.L. Cup (Rumbelows Cup)

Date	Match	Score	Scorers	Att.
Sep 25	WOLVERHAMPTON WAN.	0-0		5250
Oct 9	Wolverhampton Wan.	1-1	Swan	14959
Oct 25	Coventry City	0-3		7780

R2 won on away goals rule a.e.t.

F.M. Cup (Zenith Data Systems Cup)

Date	Match	Score	Scorers	Att.
Nov 20	Middlesbrough	1-3	Waites	8926

a.e.t.

League table

		Pl	Home					Away					F	A	Pts
			W	D	L	F	A	W	D	L	F	A	(Total)		
1	Oldham Athletic	46	17	5	1	55	21	8	8	7	28	32	83	53	88
2	West Ham United	46	15	6	2	41	18	9	9	5	19	16	60	34	87
3	Sheffield Wed.	46	12	10	1	43	23	10	6	7	37	28	80	51	82
4	Notts County	46	14	4	5	45	28	9	7	7	31	27	76	55	80
5	Millwall	46	11	6	6	43	28	9	7	7	27	23	70	51	73
6	Brighton & Hove A.	46	12	4	7	37	31	9	3	11	26	38	63	69	70
7	Middlesbrough	46	12	4	7	36	17	8	5	10	30	30	66	47	69
8	Barnsley	46	13	7	3	39	16	6	5	12	24	32	63	48	69
9	Bristol City	46	14	5	4	44	28	6	2	15	24	43	68	71	67
10	Oxford United	46	10	9	4	41	29	4	10	9	28	37	69	66	61
11	Newcastle United	46	8	10	5	24	22	6	7	10	25	34	49	56	59
12	Wolverhampton W.	46	11	6	6	45	35	2	13	8	18	28	63	63	58
13	Bristol Rovers	46	11	7	5	29	20	4	6	13	27	39	56	59	58
14	Ipswich Town	46	9	8	6	32	28	4	10	9	28	40	60	68	57
15	Port Vale	46	10	4	9	32	24	5	8	10	24	40	56	64	57
16	Charlton Athletic	46	8	7	8	27	25	5	10	8	30	36	57	61	56
17	Portsmouth	46	8	6	7	34	27	4	5	14	24	43	58	70	53
18	Plymouth Argyle	46	10	10	3	36	20	2	7	14	18	48	54	68	53
19	Blackburn Rovers	46	8	6	9	26	27	6	4	13	25	39	51	66	52
20	Watford	46	5	8	10	24	32	7	7	9	21	27	45	59	51
21	Swindon Town	46	8	6	9	31	30	4	8	11	34	43	65	73	50
22	Leicester City	46	12	4	7	41	33	2	4	17	19	50	60	83	50
23	West Bromwich Alb.	46	7	11	5	26	21	3	7	13	26	40	52	61	48
24	HULL CITY	46	6	10	7	35	32	4	5	14	22	53	57	85	45

1990-91

Back Row: M. Smith, L. Jenkinson, R. Jobson, N. Buckley, D. Cleminshaw, I. Hesford, R. Gawthorpe, D. Bamber, P. Swan, D. Mail, A. Pa
Middle Row: M. Docherty (Coach), T. Wilson (Asst Manager), G. Flynn, M. Calvert, S. Doyle, N. Brown, M. Shotton, R. Wilcox,
L. Warren, T. Finnigan, J. Radcliffe (Physio), D. Roberts (Coach);
Front Row: K. De Mange, I. McParland, W. Jacobs, L. Palin, R. Chetham (Chairman), S. Ternent (Manager), M. Fish (Vice-Chairman),
G. Roberts, P. Hunter, L. Thompson, G. Thomas.

1991-92

Back Row: P. Waites, L. Warren, L. Jenkinson, N. Buckley, A. Fettis, P. Swan, N. Brown, L. Palin, A. Payton;
Standing: M. Broughton, L. Said, R. Thompson, B. Ellison (Coach), W. Jacobs, D. Mail, H. Ngata, M. Shotton (Coach),
R. Greenwood, G. Hobson, J. Radcliffe (Physio), N. Allison, K. Morrow, P. Welburn;
Sitting: K. DeMange, M. Calvert, G. Atkinson, J. Lee (Asst Manager), T. Dolan (Manager), R. Wilcox, P. Hunter, S. Young;
On Ground: S. Wilson, M. Hopkin, M. Willingham, S. Knight, S. Fisher, A. Lowthorpe, M. Gallagher,
S. Mulligan, D. Stowe, N. Houghton, M. Shirtliff.

1991/92 14th in Division Three

	Date	Opponent	Res	Scorers	Att	Allison N	Atkinson G	Brown N	Buckley N	Calvert M	De Mange K	Fettis A	France D	Hobson G	Hockaday D	Hunter P	Jacobs W	Jenkinson L	Kelly A	Mail D	Matthews M	Ngata H	Norton D	Palin L	Payton A	Pearson J	Shotton M	Stoker G	Walmsley D	Warren L	Wilcox R	Wilson S	Windass D	Young S
1	Aug 17	Reading	1-0	Jenkinson	4639				5	6		1		12		9	3	11		2	7		10		8				14		4			
2	24	PETERBOROUGH UTD.	1-2	Payton	4806				5	6		1				9	3	11		2			10	7	8				12		4			
3	31	Bournemouth	0-0		5015	5						1		6		9	3	11				12	7	10	8					2	4			
4	Sep 3	BIRMINGHAM CITY	1-2	Palin	4801	5						1		6		9	3	11				12	7	10	8					2	4			
5	7	BURY	0-1		3679	5	12	2				1		6		9	3	11		4		8	7	10					14					
6	14	Wigan Athletic	1-0	Young	2445		7	2	12	14		1		5			3	11				8	10					6			4			9
7	17	Brentford	1-4	Jenkinson	4586	14	7	2	5			1					3	11				8	10					6		12	4			9
8	21	TORQUAY UNITED	4-1	Walmsley 2, Young, Norton	3093	5	3	2		14		1		6				11					10					8	7	12	4			9
9	28	West Bromwich Albion	0-1		11932		3	2				1		6			12	11		5			10					8	7	4				9
10	Oct 5	EXETER CITY	1-2	Jenkinson	3143		3	2						6			12	11		5		7	10					8	14	4		1		9
11	11	Swansea City	0-0		2725		14			6		1					3	11		5			10		8		12	7		4			2	9
12	19	Hartlepool United	3-2	Calvert, Payton 2	2868					7		1					3	11		5	12		10		8		6		14	4			2	9
13	26	DARLINGTON	5-2	Windass, Payton 2, Stoker 2	3514							1				9	3	11		12	4	14	10		8		6	7			5		2	
14	Nov 2	Fulham	0-0		3365							1					3	11		4		9	10		8		6	7			5		2	12
15	5	SHREWSBURY TOWN	4-0	Windass, Payton, Norton, Warren	5025							1					3	11		4		9	10		8		6	7		12	5		2	14
16	9	CHESTER CITY	1-0	Payton	4305							1					3	11		4		9	10		8		6	7		12	5		2	14
17	23	Leyton Orient	0-1		3936		14	8	9			1					3	11		4			10				6	7		12	5		2	
18	30	PRESTON NORTH END	2-2	Walmsley, Brown	4280			9		12		1					3	11		4			10				6	7	8		5		2	
19	Dec 14	Bolton Wanderers	0-1		5273			9				1				8	3	11		4			10	7			6			2	5		12	
20	20	Peterborough United	0-3		7904			9				1				8	3	11		4			10	7			6				5		2	
21	26	BOURNEMOUTH	0-1		4741							1	14			9	3	11		4	12		10	7			6		8		5		2	
22	28	READING	0-1		3661							1	9			14	3	11		4	8		10	7			6	12			5		2	
23	Jan 1	Birmingham City	2-2	France 2	12983							1	9				3	11			8		10	7			6	4			5		2	12
24	11	STOCKPORT COUNTY	0-2		3982							1		5		10	3	11			8		4	7		9	6						2	12
25	18	Bradford City	1-2	Mail	6369					8		1		12			3	11		4			2	7		9	6	10			5			
26	25	STOKE CITY	0-1		4996							1	12				3	11		4			2	7		9	6	8			5		10	
27	Feb 1	HARTLEPOOL UNITED	0-2		3483							1	12	3				11	8				2	7		9	6	4			5		10	
28	8	Darlington	1-0	Windass	3636					12		1	14	3	2			11	8	4			7			9				6	5		10	
29	11	Preston North End	1-3	Wilcox	2932					11		1	14	3	2				8	4			7			9		12		6	5		10	
30	22	Stockport County	1-1	Wilcox	4490		11	3				1			2				8	4			7			9				6	5		10	
31	25	Huddersfield Town	1-1	Atkinson	6003		11	3				1	8		2					4		14	7			9		12		6	5		10	
32	29	HUDDERSFIELD T	1-0	Kelly	5310		11	3				1			2				8	4			7			9				6	5		10	
33	Mar 3	BRADFORD CITY	0-0		4244		11	3				1			2			14	8	4			7			9				6	5		10	
34	7	Stoke City	3-2	Atkinson, Jenkinson 2	13553		8	3				1			2			11		4			7			9				6	5		10	
35	10	Shrewsbury Town	3-2	Wilcox, Atkinson, Jenkinson	1956		8	3				1			2			11		4			7			9		12		6	5		10	
36	14	FULHAM	0-0		3742		8	3				1			2			11		4			7			9				6	5		10	
37	21	Chester City	1-1	Windass	1269		8	3					12		2			11		4			7			9				6	5	1	10	
38	28	LEYTON ORIENT	1-0	Atkinson	3806		8	3		10		1	12		2			11		4	14		7			9				6	5			
39	31	WIGAN ATHLETIC	1-1	Atkinson	3385		8	3				1	9		2			11		4	12		7							6	5		10	
40	Apr 4	Bury	2-3	France, Windass	2245		8	3				1	9	2				11		4	12		7							6	5		10	14
41	11	BRENTFORD	0-3		3770		8	2				1	9	3				11		4	12		7							6	5		10	14
42	14	Torquay United	1-2	Windass	2339		8						9	3				11		4	2		7							6	5	1	10	12
43	20	WEST BROMWICH ALB.	1-0	Jenkinson	4815		8	3				1	9			14		11		4	2		7					12		6	5		10	
44	25	Exeter City	3-0	Atkinson, France, Jenkinson	2772	12	8	3				1	9			14		11		4	2							7		6	5		10	
45	29	BOLTON WANDERERS	2-0	Wilcox, Matthews	3997		8	3				1	9			12		11		4	2		7					10		6	5			
46	May 2	SWANSEA CITY	3-0	Atkinson 2, Matthews	4070	4	8					1		3		9		11			2		7					10		6	5			
					Apps	7	25	25	5	11		43	17	17	12	15	25	42	6	37	16	11	45	13	10	15	17	24	9	31	40	3	32	15
					Goals		8	1		1			4					8	1	1	2		2	1	7			2	3	1	4		6	2

F.A. Cup

	Date	Opponent	Res	Scorers	Att	Allison N	Atkinson G	Brown N	Buckley N	Calvert M	De Mange K	Fettis A	France D	Hobson G	Hockaday D	Hunter P	Jacobs W	Jenkinson L	Kelly A	Mail D	Matthews M	Ngata H	Norton D	Palin L	Payton A	Pearson J	Shotton M	Stoker G	Walmsley D	Warren L	Wilcox R	Wilson S	Windass D	Young S
1	Nov 6	Morecambe	1-0	Wilcox	2853		12		9			1					3	11		4		8	10				6	7	14	2	5			
2	Dec 7	Blackpool	1-0	Hunter	4554			9				1				12	3	11		4			10	7			6	14	8	2	5			
3	Jan 4	CHELSEA	0-2		13580							1	9	12	14		3	11			8		10	7			6	4			5			2

F.L. Cup (Rumbelows Cup)

	Date	Opponent	Res	Scorers	Att	Allison N	Atkinson G	Brown N	Buckley N	Calvert M	De Mange K	Fettis A	France D	Hobson G	Hockaday D	Hunter P	Jacobs W	Jenkinson L	Kelly A	Mail D	Matthews M	Ngata H	Norton D	Palin L	Payton A	Pearson J	Shotton M	Stoker G	Walmsley D	Warren L	Wilcox R	Wilson S	Windass D	Young S
1	Aug 20	Blackburn Rovers	1-1	Payton	6300				5	6		1		7		9	3	11		2			10		8						4			
2	27	BLACKBURN ROVERS	1-0	Jenkinson	3227	5						1		6		9	3	11					7	10	8					2	4			
1	Sep 24	QUEEN'S PARK RANGERS	0-3		4979	5	3	2		12		1		6				11					10		8			9	7		4			
2	Oct 9	Queen's Park Rangers	1-5	Young	5251		12				7			6			3	11		5			10					8	14	4		1	2	9

A.M. Cup (Autoglass Trophy)

	Date	Opponent	Res	Scorers	Att	Allison N	Atkinson G	Brown N	Buckley N	Calvert M	De Mange K	Fettis A	France D	Hobson G	Hockaday D	Hunter P	Jacobs W	Jenkinson L	Kelly A	Mail D	Matthews M	Ngata H	Norton D	Palin L	Payton A	Pearson J	Shotton M	Stoker G	Walmsley D	Warren L	Wilcox R	Wilson S	Windass D	Young S
	Oct 22	BRADFORD CITY	2-1	Matthews, Windass	1218					7		1					3	11		5	4		10		8		6	14	9		12		2	
	Jan 7	HARTLEPOOL UNITED	0-2		1550							1	9		7		3	11		4	8		10	5			6						2	12
	Jan 14	Preston North End	3-2	Windass, Palin, Pearson	2152	5				12		1		6			3	11		4	8		2	7		9							10	
	Feb 4	Crewe Alexandra	0-1		2348		3					1		6	2	14		11		12			8			9				4	5		10	7

Gp3 a.e.t.

		Pl	Home W	D	L	F	A	Away W	D	L	F	A	F. (Total)	A.	Pts
1	Brentford	46	17	2	4	55	29	8	5	10	26	26	81	55	82
2	Birmingham City	46	15	6	2	42	22	8	6	9	27	30	69	52	81
3	Huddersfield Town	46	15	4	4	36	15	7	8	8	23	23	59	38	78
4	Stoke City	46	14	5	4	45	24	7	9	7	24	25	69	49	77
5	Stockport County	46	15	5	3	47	19	7	5	11	28	32	75	51	76
6	Peterborough Utd.	46	13	7	3	38	20	7	7	9	27	38	65	58	74
7	West Bromwich Alb.	46	12	6	5	45	25	7	8	8	19	24	64	49	71
8	Bournemouth	46	13	4	6	33	18	7	7	9	19	30	52	48	71
9	Fulham	46	11	7	5	29	16	8	6	9	28	37	57	53	70
10	Leyton Orient	46	12	7	4	36	18	6	4	13	26	34	62	52	65
11	Hartlepool United	46	12	5	6	30	21	6	6	11	27	36	57	57	65
12	Reading	46	9	8	6	33	27	7	5	11	26	35	59	62	61
13	Bolton Wanderers	46	10	9	4	26	19	4	8	11	31	37	57	56	59
14	HULL CITY	46	9	4	10	28	23	7	7	9	26	31	54	54	59
15	Wigan Athletic	46	11	6	6	33	21	4	8	11	25	43	58	64	59
16	Bradford City	46	8	10	5	36	30	5	9	9	26	31	62	61	58
17	Preston North End	46	12	7	4	42	32	3	5	15	19	40	61	72	57
18	Chester City	46	10	6	7	34	29	4	8	11	22	30	56	59	56
19	Swansea City	46	10	9	4	35	24	4	5	14	20	41	55	65	56
20	Exeter City	46	11	7	5	34	25	3	4	16	23	55	57	80	53
21	Bury	46	8	7	8	31	31	5	5	13	24	43	55	74	51
22	Shrewsbury Town	46	7	7	9	30	31	5	4	14	23	37	53	68	47
23	Torquay United	46	13	3	7	29	19	0	5	18	13	49	42	68	47
24	Darlington	46	5	5	13	31	39	5	2	16	25	51	56	90	37

#	Date	Opponent	Score	Scorers	Att.	Abbott G	Allison N	Atkinson G	Brown L	Calvert M	Carruthers M	Edeson M	Fettis A	France D	Heard P	Hobson G	Hockaday D	Hunter P	Jenkinson L	Jones D	Lund G	Mail D	Miller R	Mohan N	Norton D	Stoker G	Stowe D	Warren L	Wilcox R	Williams G	Wilson S	Windass D	Young S
1	Aug 15	STOKE CITY	1-0	Hunter	9088		8						1	12		3	2	9	11			5	4			7		6				10	
2	22	CHESTER CITY	1-1	Atkinson	4906		8						1	12		3	2	9	11			5	4			7		6				10	
3	28	PLYMOUTH ARGYLE	2-0	Lund, Hockaday	4195		14	8					1	12	3	5	2		11			9	4			7		6				10	
4	Sep 1	SWANSEA CITY	1-0	Hunter	4418			8					1	11	3	5	2	12				9	4			7		6				10	
5	5	Reading	2-1	Lund, Windass	3465			8			14		1	12	3	5	2	11				9	4			7		6				10	
6	12	Stockport County	3-5	Hunter, Carstairs (og), Jenkinson	4216	4	8						1	3		5	2	9	11							7		6				10	
7	15	PRESTON NORTH END	2-4	Jenkinson, Flynn (og)	4463	4	8						1	3	12	5	2	9	11							7		6				10	
8	19	ROTHERHAM UNITED	0-1		4780		8		4				1	12		5	2	9	11							7		14		3		10	
9	26	Leyton Orient	0-0		4951		8						1			5			11			12		6	7	4		2		3		10	9
10	Oct 3	BRADFORD CITY	0-2		5340		8						1			5		12	11					6	7	4		2		3		10	9
11	10	Fulham	3-3	Mohan, Atkinson, Jenkinson	5247		8				14	1						11					4	5	7		6	12	3		10	9
12	17	HUDDERSFIELD T	2-3	Wilcox, Atkinson	4705		8				14	1				12	2	9	11				4		6	7			5			10	
13	24	Bolton Wanderers	0-2		4136		8						1	12			2	9	11				4		6	7	3	5				10	
14	31	WEST BROMWICH ALB.	1-2	Jenkinson,	5443		8						1			5	2	12	11				3		7	4		6				10	
15	Nov 3	Mansfield Town	1-3	Carruthers	3040		8			4	9		1			5	2	12	11				3		7			6				10	
16	7	BURNLEY	0-2		5751		12			4	9			14		5	2	8	11				3		7			6			1	10	
17	21	Port Vale	1-1	Carruthers	6202		8				6					2	9	11					4	3	7					5	1	10	
18	28	BLACKPOOL	3-2	Carruthers, Atkinson, Windass	3906		8				6			12		2	9	11					4	3	7					5	1	10	
19	Dec 12	EXETER CITY	4-0	Atkinson, Carruthers 2, Windass	3167		8				9			6		2		11					4	3	7					5	1	10	
20	19	Bournemouth	0-0		4486	10	8				9					2		11					4	3	7					6	5	1	
21	26	Hartlepool United	0-1		4232	10	8			12	9					2		11					4	3	7					6	5	1	
22	28	BRIGHTON & HOVE ALB	1-0	Hunter	4785	10	8				9					14	2	12	11				4	3	7					6	5	1	
23	Jan 9	Preston North End	2-1	Wilcox, Carruthers	4719	10	8	6			9					2	14	11					4	3	7					5	1	12	
24	16	LEYTON ORIENT	0-0		3897	6	8	11			9					3	2						4		7					5	1	10	
25	26	Plymouth Argyle	0-0		4612	6	8				9					3	2					11	4		7					5	1	10	
26	30	Chester City	0-3		2232	6	8	14			9					3	2					11	4		7			12	5	5	1	10	
27	Feb 6	Stoke City	0-3		15362	6	8	3										11				9	4	12	7				5	1	10	
28	9	Rotherham United	1-0	Lund	3660	8	11	7														9	4	3	2			6	5	1	10	
29	13	READING	1-1	Windass	3593	8	11	7								12						9	4	3	2			6	5	1	10	
30	20	Swansea City	0-1		2656	8	11	7											12			9	4	3	2			6	5	1	10	
31	27	FULHAM	1-1	Atkinson	3645	6	8	7						12				11	9				4	3	2				5	1	10	
32	Mar 6	Bradford City	2-1	Windass, Stapleton (og)	6238	6	8	7						12				11	9				4	3	2				5	1	10	
33	9	WIGAN ATHLETIC	0-0		3394	6	8	7						12				11					4	3	2			9	5	1	10	
34	13	Burnley	0-2		10043	6	5	8	7	10				9		12							4	3	2			14	11	1		
35	20	MANSFIELD TOWN	1-0	Brown	3551	6	5	8	7	11				9					10				4		2			3		1		
36	23	Blackpool	1-5	Abbott	3515	6	11	8						12					9				4		2			3	5			10	
37	27	PORT VALE	0-1		4558	6	12	8	7							14		11	9				4		2			3	5		1	10	
38	Apr 3	Wigan Athletic	0-2		1872	6	14	8	7					12		3		9					4		2			11	5		1	10	
39	6	Exeter City	1-1	Hunter	2415	6		3	7			1						9					11		4			8	5			10	
40	10	HARTLEPOOL UNITED	3-2	Norton, Windass, Jones	3562	6		3	7					1	12			9		11			4	14	2			8	5			10	
41	14	Brighton & Hove Albion	0-2		7776	6	5	3	7					1	12			9		11			4	14	2			8				10	
42	17	BOURNEMOUTH	3-0	Hunter, France 2	3442	6		3	7					1	11			9					4	12	2			8	5			10	
43	24	Huddersfield Town	0-3		6607	6		3	7					1	11			9		12			4	14	2			8	5			10	
44	27	STOCKPORT COUNTY	0-2		4079	6	14	11	7					12					9				4	3	2			8	5		1	10	
45	30	BOLTON WANDERERS	1-2	Windass	8785	6		12	14					7				9					4	3	2			8	5		1	10	
46	May 8	West Bromwich Albion	1-3	France	20122	6	9	11	14					12								7	4	3	2			8	5		1	10	
		Apps				27	11	46	23	7	13	2	20	26	4	21	25	26	26	12	11	39	25	5	45	6	1	36	29	4	26	41	
		Goals				1		6	1		6			3			1	6	4	1	3				2							7	

Three own goals

F.A. Cup

	Date	Opponent	Score	Scorers	Att.	Allison	Atkinson	Carruthers	Fettis	France	Hobson	Hockaday	Hunter	Mail	Miller	Stoker	Wilcox	Williams	Windass
R1	Nov 14	Darlington	2-1	Norton, Atkinson	3132	8				6		2	9	11	4	3	7			5	1	10
R2	Dec 5	Rotherham United	0-1		6118	8				6		2		11	4	3	7		12	5	1	10

F.L. Cup (Coca Cola Cup)

	Date	Opponent	Score	Scorers	Att.
R1/1	Aug 18	ROTHERHAM UNITED	2-2	Hockaday, Atkinson	3226
R1/2	25	Rotherham United	0-1		3565

F.L. Cup (Autoglass Trophy)

	Date	Opponent	Score	Scorers	Att.
Gp	Dec 8	York City	0-0		2253
Gp	15	DONCASTER ROVERS	2-1	Norton, Abbott	1716
R2	Jan 12	CHESTERFIELD	0-1		1833

		Pl	Home					Away					F.	A.	Pt
			W	D	L	F	A	W	D	L	F	A	(Total)		
1	Stoke City	46	17	4	2	41	13	10	8	5	32	21	73	34	9.
2	Bolton Wanderers	46	18	3	2	48	14	9	7	7	32	27	80	41	9
3	Port Vale	46	14	7	2	44	17	12	4	7	35	27	79	44	8
4	West Bromwich Alb.	46	17	3	3	56	22	8	7	8	32	32	88	54	8
5	Swansea City	46	12	7	4	38	17	8	6	9	27	30	65	47	7
6	Stockport County	46	11	11	1	47	18	8	4	11	34	39	81	57	7
7	Leyton Orient	46	16	4	3	49	20	5	5	13	20	33	69	53	7
8	Reading	46	14	4	5	44	20	4	11	8	22	31	66	51	6
9	Brighton & Hove A.	46	13	4	6	36	24	7	5	11	27	35	63	59	6
10	Bradford City	46	12	5	6	36	24	6	9	8	33	43	69	67	6
11	Rotherham United	46	9	7	7	30	27	8	7	8	30	33	60	60	6
12	Fulham	46	9	9	5	28	22	7	8	8	29	33	57	55	6
13	Burnley	46	11	8	4	38	21	4	8	11	19	38	57	59	6
14	Plymouth Argyle	46	11	6	6	38	28	5	6	12	21	36	59	64	6
15	Huddersfield Town	46	10	6	7	30	22	7	3	13	24	39	54	61	6
16	Hartlepool United	46	8	6	9	19	23	6	6	11	23	37	42	60	5
17	Bournemouth	46	7	10	6	28	24	5	7	11	17	28	45	52	5
18	Blackpool	46	9	9	5	40	30	3	6	14	23	45	63	75	5
19	Exeter City	46	5	8	10	26	30	6	9	8	28	39	54	69	5
20	HULL CITY	46	9	5	9	28	26	4	6	13	18	43	46	69	5
21	Preston North End	46	8	5	10	41	47	5	3	15	24	47	65	94	4
22	Mansfield Town	46	7	8	8	34	34	4	3	16	18	46	52	80	4
23	Wigan Athletic	46	6	6	11	26	34	4	5	14	17	38	43	72	
24	Chester City	46	6	2	15	30	47	2	3	18	19	55	49	102	

1992-93
Back Row: L. Jenkinson, N. Allison, D. France, G. Hobson, L. Warren, D. Mail;
Middle Row: D. Hockaday, M. Calvert, S. Young, S. Wilson, A. Fettis, W. Jacobs, D. Cairns, J. Radcliffe (Physio);
Front Row: G. Atkinson, M. Matthews, D. Windass, J. Lee (Asst Manager), M. Fish (Chairman), T. Dolan (Manager),
R. Wilcox, P. Hunter, G. Stoker, D. Norton.

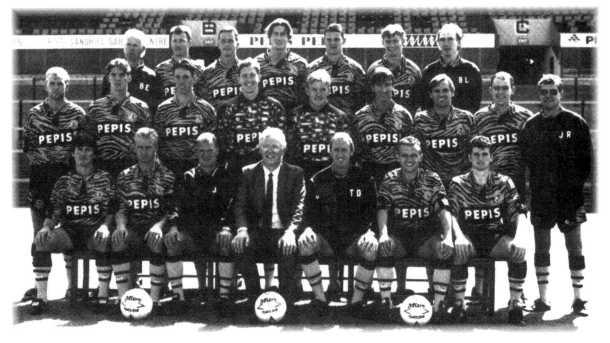

1993-94
Back Row: B. Ellison (Youth Coach), G. Abbott, G. Atkinson, C. Hargreaves, D. Windass, M. Hopkin, W. Legg (Youth Coach);
Middle Row: L. Warren, N. Allison, G. Hobson, A. Fettis, S. Wilson, B. Mitchell, D. Mail, R. Miller, J. Radcliffe (Physio);
Front Row: S. Moran, L. Brown, J. Lee (Asst Manager), M. Fish (Chairman), T. Dolan (Manager), D. Norton, A. Lowthorpe.

1993/94 9th in Division Two

League matches

#	Date		Opponent	Result	Scorers	Att	Abbott G	Allison N	Atkinson G	Bound M	Brown L	Dakin S	Dewhurst R	Fettis A	Hargreaves C	Hobson G	Hopkin M	Lee C	Lowthorpe A	Mail D	Mann N	Miller R	Mitchell B	Moran S	Norton D	Peacock R	Warren L	Williams G	Wilson S	Windass D
1	Aug	14	Barnet	2-1	Abbott, Brown	2129	6	5	11		9				3									2	8	7	4		1	10
2		21	PLYMOUTH ARGYLE	2-2	Brown, Windass	3580	6	5	11		9				3			12						2	8	7	4		1	10
3		28	Cambridge United	4-3	Brown, Windass 3	3861	6	5	11	4	9				3			8						2		7			1	10
4		31	BRENTFORD	1-0	Windass	4517	6	5	11	4	9				3			8						2		7			1	10
5	Sep	4	BRISTOL ROVERS	3-0	Windass 3	5362	6	5	11	4	9				3			8						2		7			1	10
6		11	Cardiff City	4-3	Moran, Bound, Lee 2	7421	6	5	11	4	9				3			8						2		7			1	10
7		14	Wrexham	0-3		4335		5	11	4	9							8				12	3	2	7			14	1	10
8		18	HUDDERSFIELD T	2-1	Brown, Atkinson	7570	6	5	11	4	9				1			3						2		7				10
9		25	Reading	1-1	Brown	6453	6	5	11	4	9				1			3					2	12	7		14			10
10	Oct	2	BRADFORD CITY	3-1	Abbott, Brown, Windass	9492	6	5	11		9				1			3	8	2			12			7		4		10
11		9	Port Vale	1-2	Allison	9459	6	5	11		9				1			3	8	2						7		4		10
12		16	FULHAM	1-1	Peacock	6089	6	5	11		9			1	14	3			8	2					10	7	12	4		10
13		23	Swansea City	0-1		3774	6	5	11		9			1	8	3							2	12	7		4			10
14		30	LEYTON ORIENT	0-1		5246	6	5	11		9			1	8	3		7					2	14			12	4		10
15	Nov	2	Blackpool	2-6	Abbott 2	3968	6	5	11		9			1	7	3		8	14						12		2	4		10
16		6	ROTHERHAM UNITED	4-1	Moran 3, Brown	4860	6	12	11		9		5	1	7			14	3				8	2			4			10
17		20	Bournemouth	2-0	Brown, Atkinson	4124	6	2	11		9		5	1	8			14					3	12	7		4			10
18		27	STOCKPORT COUNTY	0-1		7119	6	2	11		9		5	1	8				3				12	7			4			10
19	Dec	11	Plymouth Argyle	1-2	Windass	6460	6	2	11		9		5		12			3					8	7			4		1	10
20		18	BARNET	4-4	Moran, Windass 3	4115	6	2	11		9		5	12	5			3	13				8	7			4		1	10
21		27	York City	0-0		8481		2					1	9	3			6	5	11			8	7	12	4			10
22		28	HARTLEPOOL UNITED	1-0	Windass	4607					9		5	1	8	3		6	4	11				7	12	2			10
23	Jan	1	Exeter City	1-0	Windass	3547	6		11		9		5	1	8	3		2	4					7		12			10
24		3	BURNLEY	1-2	Abbott	11232	6		11		9		5	1	8	3		2	4					7	14	12			10
25		8	BRIGHTON & HOVE ALB	0-0		5386	6		11		9		5	1	12	3		2	4					7				8		10
26		15	Fulham	1-0	Windass	4407	6				9		5	1		3		2	4					7		11	8		10
27		22	PORT VALE	0-0		6918	6				9		5	1		3		2	4					7	12	11	8		10
28		29	Leyton Orient	1-3	Williams	4355	6						5	1	9	3		2	4					7		11	8		10
29	Feb	5	SWANSEA CITY	0-1		4668	6		12		9		5	1		3		2	4					7		11	8		10
30		12	Brighton & Hove Albion	0-3		8251	6		11		9			1	12	3		2	4				8	7		5	10		
31		19	CAMBRIDGE UNITED	2-0	Atkinson, Windass	4094	6		7					1	9	3		12	4				8	2		5	11		10
32		22	Brentford	3-0	Brown, Windass, Atkinson	4361	6		12		9		5	1	3				4					2		7	11		10
33		26	Bristol Rovers	1-1	Atkinson	5657	6		3		9		5	1				8	4					2		7	11		10
34	Mar	5	CARDIFF CITY	1-0	Windass	4998	6		3		9		5	1	12			8	4					2		7	11		10
35		12	Huddersfield Town	2-0	Dewhurst, Windass	6675	6		3		9		5	1				8	4					2		7	11		10
36		15	WREXHAM	0-0		5749	6		3		9		5	1				8	4					2		7	11		10
37		19	READING	1-2	Windass	7107	6		3		9		5	1	12			8	4					2		7	11		10
38		26	Bradford City	1-1	Williams	9419	6				9	14	5	1	10	3		8	4	12				2		7	11		
39		29	Burnley	1-3	Lee	10574					9	6	5	1	7	3		8	4					2		14	11		10
40	Apr	2	YORK CITY	1-1	Windass	8190	6	4	12		9	7	5	1	11	3		8			14			2					10
41		4	Hartlepool United	1-0	Norton	2448		4	7			2	5	1	9	3		8						6				11	10
42		9	EXETER CITY	5-1	Dewhurst, Norton, Windass, Atkinson 2	4663	6	4	11			12	5	1	9	3		8						6	7				10
43		16	BLACKPOOL	0-0		6211	6	4	11			12	5	1	9	3		8						6	7				10
44		23	Rotherham United	0-1		4941	6	4	11			12	2	5	1	9	3		8	14					7				10
45		30	BOURNEMOUTH	1-1	Abbott	4926	6	4	11			14	2	5	1	9	3		12						7	8			10
46	May	7	Stockport County	0-0		7666	6	4	11			9	2	5	1	8	3		12						7	14			10

	Abbott G	Allison N	Atkinson G	Bound M	Brown L	Dakin S	Dewhurst R	Fettis A	Hargreaves C	Hobson G	Hopkin M	Lee C	Lowthorpe A	Mail D	Mann N	Miller R	Mitchell B	Moran S	Norton D	Peacock R	Warren L	Williams G	Wilson S	Windass D
Apps	40	28	40	7	42	9	27	37	28	36		43	3	24	5	3	9	17	44	11	33	16	9	43
Goals	6	1	7	1	9		2					3						5	2	1		2		23

F.A. Cup

	Date		Opponent	Result	Scorers	Att	Abbott G	Allison N	Atkinson G	Brown L	Dewhurst R	Fettis A	Hargreaves C	Lee C	Miller R	Moran S	Norton D	Peacock R	Warren L	Windass D
R1	Nov	23	Runcorn	2-0	Hargreaves, Brown	1131	6	2	11	9	5	1	8		3		7		4	10
R2	Dec	12	Chester City	0-2		4333	6	2	11	9	5	1	8	12	3		7		4	10

R1 played at Wincham Park, Northwich. Original match (played at Runcorn) was abandoned after a perimeter wall collapsed

F.L. Cup (Coca Cola Cup)

	Date		Opponent	Result	Scorers	Att	Abbott G	Allison N	Atkinson G	Brown L	Hargreaves C	Lee C	Miller R	Moran S	Norton D	Peacock R	Warren L	Wilson S	Windass D
R1/1	Aug	16	Notts County	0-2		3033	6	5	11	9	3			2	8	7	4	1	10
R1/2		23	NOTTS COUNTY	3-1	Abbott, Windass, Atkinson	2222	6	5	11	9	4	14	12	2	8	7	4	1	10

Lost on away goals rule a.e.t.

A.M. Cup (Autoglass Trophy)

	Date		Opponent	Result	Scorers	Att	Abbott G	Allison N	Atkinson G	Brown L	Dewhurst R	Fettis A	Hargreaves C	Hobson G	Lee C	Mail D	Mitchell B	Moran S	Norton D	Peacock R	Warren L	Windass D
Gp	Oct	19	Scunthorpe United	1-1	Abbott	2366	6	5	11	9		1	14	3	12	10		2	8	7	4	
Gp	Nov	9	SCARBOROUGH	0-2		1881	6	12	11		5	1	9		7		3		8	2	4	10

Final table — Division Two

		Pl	Home W	D	L	F	A	Away W	D	L	F	A	F (Total)	A	Pts
1	Reading	46	15	6	2	40	16	11	5	7	41	28	81	44	89
2	Port Vale	46	16	6	1	46	18	10	4	9	33	28	79	46	88
3	Plymouth Argyle	46	16	4	3	46	26	9	6	8	42	30	88	56	85
4	Stockport County	46	15	3	5	50	22	9	10	4	24	22	74	44	85
5	York City	46	12	7	4	33	13	9	5	9	31	27	64	40	75
6	Burnley	46	17	4	2	55	18	4	6	13	24	40	79	58	73
7	Bradford City	46	13	5	5	34	20	6	8	9	27	33	61	53	70
8	Bristol Rovers	46	10	8	5	33	26	10	2	11	27	33	60	59	70
9	HULL CITY	46	9	9	5	33	20	9	5	9	29	34	62	54	68
10	Cambridge United	46	11	5	7	38	29	8	4	11	41	44	79	73	66
11	Huddersfield Town	46	9	8	6	27	26	8	6	9	31	35	58	61	65
12	Wrexham	46	13	4	6	45	33	4	7	12	21	44	66	77	62
13	Swansea City	46	12	7	4	37	20	4	5	14	19	38	56	58	60
14	Brighton & Hove A.	46	10	7	6	38	29	5	7	11	22	38	60	67	59
15	Rotherham United	46	11	4	8	42	30	4	9	10	21	30	63	60	58
16	Brentford	46	7	10	6	30	28	6	9	8	27	27	57	55	58
17	Bournemouth	46	8	7	8	26	27	6	8	9	25	32	51	59	57
18	Leyton Orient	46	11	9	3	38	26	3	5	15	19	45	57	71	56
19	Cardiff City	46	10	7	6	39	33	3	8	12	27	46	66	79	54
20	Blackpool	46	12	2	9	41	37	4	3	16	22	38	63	75	53
21	Fulham	46	7	6	10	20	23	7	4	12	30	40	50	63	52
22	Exeter City	46	8	7	8	38	37	3	5	15	14	46	52	83	45
23	Hartlepool United	46	8	3	12	28	40	1	6	16	13	47	41	87	36
24	Barnet	46	4	6	13	22	32	1	7	15	19	54	41	86	28

1994/95 8th in Division Two

Fixtures

No		Date	Opponent	Score	Scorers	Att
1	Aug	13	Oxford United	0-4		5691
2		20	SWANSEA CITY	0-2		3797
3		27	Leyton Orient	1-1	Brown	3243
4		30	PLYMOUTH ARGYLE	2-0	Mann, Lee	3384
5	Sep	3	CHESTER CITY	2-0	Brown, Windass	3615
6		10	Peterborough United	1-2	Peacock	5044
7		13	Wycombe Wanderers	2-1	Dakin, Brown	4676
8		17	ROTHERHAM UNITED	0-2		4431
9		24	Birmingham City	2-2	Peacock, Windass	12192
10	Oct	1	BOURNEMOUTH	3-1	Dewhurst, Brown, Atkinson	3056
11		8	BLACKPOOL	1-0	Gouk (og)	3829
12		15	Wrexham	2-2	Lawford, Windass	3418
13		22	Shrewsbury Town	3-2	Dewhurst, Peacock, Lawford	3685
14		29	CREWE ALEXANDRA	7-1	Dewhurst, Peacock, Brown 3, Windass 2	4694
15	Nov	1	YORK CITY	3-0	Brown, Windass, Lawford	6551
16		5	Brentford	1-0	Dewhurst	5455
17		19	BRISTOL ROVERS	0-2		4450
18		25	Cardiff City	2-0	Brown, Windass	4226
19	Dec	10	Swansea City	0-2		2903
20		17	OXFORD UNITED	3-1	Windass 2, Fettis	4884
21		26	HUDDERSFIELD T	1-0	Peacock	10220
22		28	Bradford City	0-1		7312
23		31	BRIGHTON & HOVE ALB	2-2	Brown, Windass	5099
24	Jan	2	Cambridge United	2-2	Brown, Windass	3659
25		7	SHREWSBURY TOWN	2-2	Cox, Windass	4369
26		14	Stockport County	0-4		4516
27		21	BRENTFORD	1-2	Joyce	3823
28	Feb	4	CARDIFF CITY	4-0	Joyce, Brown, Ormondroyd 2	3903
29		18	STOCKPORT COUNTY	0-0		4576
30		25	Bournemouth	3-2	Mann, Ormondroyd 2	4345
31	Mar	1	Bristol Rovers	2-0	Brown, Ormondroyd	3694
32		4	BIRMINGHAM CITY	0-0		9854
33		11	LEYTON ORIENT	2-0	Dewhurst, Joyce	4519
34		18	Plymouth Argyle	1-2	Ormondroyd	4839
35		21	PETERBOROUGH UTD.	1-1	Breen (og)	4609
36		25	Rotherham United	0-2		3692
37		28	Chester City	2-1	Abbott, Lund	1191
38	Apr	1	WYCOMBE WANDERERS	0-0		5054
39		4	York City	1-3	Windass	4612
40		8	Brighton & Hove Albion	0-1		6081
41		15	BRADFORD CITY	2-0	Windass 2	2694
42		17	Huddersfield Town	1-1	Dewhurst	12402
43		22	CAMBRIDGE UNITED	1-0	Dewhurst	3483
44		29	WREXHAM	3-2	Dewhurst, Lund, Windass	3683
45	May	2	Crewe Alexandra	2-3	Abbott, Lund	3870
46		6	Blackpool	2-1	Windass, Fettis	4251

Appearances / Goals

	Abbott G	Allison N	Atkinson G	Brown L	Cox P	Dakin S	Dewhurst R	Edeson M	Fettis A	Fewings P	Graham J	Hargreaves C	Hobson G	Joyce W	Lawford C	Lee C	Lowthorpe A	Lund G	Mail D	Mann N	Ormondroyd I	Peacock R	Wallace R	Wilson S	Windass D
1	6	4		12	2	5			1		3	9	14		11	8						7			10
2			12	9		5			1		3	6	4		11	8	2					7			10
3			11	9		5			1		3		4		12	8	2				6	7			10
4			7	9		5			1		3		4		11	8	2				6				10
5	12		7	9		5			1		3		4		11	8	2				6	14			10
6			12	8		5			1		3		4		10	7	2				6	11			9
7	6		11	9	7	5			1		3				8	2		4							10
8	6		11	9	7	5			1		3	14			8	2		4				12			10
9	6		11			5			1		3	9	4		8					2		7			10
10	6		11	9		2	5				3	10	4		7							8	1		
11				9		2	5				3	10	4		11	8					6	7	1		
12				9		2	5				3	10	4		11	8					6	7	1		12
13				9			5				3	12	4		11	8	2				6	7	1		10
14	14			9			5				3	12	4		11	8	2				6	7	1		10
15	12			9			5				3	14	4		11	8	2				6	7	1		10
16				9		2	5				3	12	4		11	8					6	7	1		10
17	12			9		2	5				3	7			11	8			14	6			1		10
18	6			9		2	5				3		4		11	8						7	1		10
19	6	12		9		2	5				3		4		11	8				14		7	1		10
20	6			9	5				12		3		4		11					8		7	2	1	10
21	6			9			5				3		4		11	12				8		7	2	1	10
22	6			9			5				3	14	4		11	8			12			7	2	1	10
23	6			9	5						3		4		11	12						7	2	1	10
24				9	5						3	12	4		11	6				8		7	2	1	10
25				9	5						3	14	4		11	6			12	8		7	2	1	10
26				9	5						3				11	6		4		8		12	2	1	10
27							5	1			3	9	4	7	11	6	2			8					10
28		6		9			5	1			3			4	7	12	2			8	11	14			
29		6		9			5	1			3			4	7	2				8	11				
30		6		9			5	1			3			4	7	2				8	11				
31		6		9			5	1			3			4	7	2				8	11				
32		6		9			5	1			3			4	7	2				8	11	12			
33		6		9			5	1			3			4	7	2				8	11	12			
34		6		9		4	5	1			3				7	12	2			8	11	14			10
35		6		9			5	1			3			7	12	2					11	8			10
36	8	6					12	5			3		4		14	2	9				11	7		1	10
37	8						4	5			3			14	2	12	9	6	7	11					
38	8						5				3			14	2	11	9	6	7	12					
39	8						5	6			3		4	11	7	2	9	12	14						10
40	8						5			6			3	7	2	9	4	11	12						10
41	6					12	5	14				4		3	8	2	9		11			7			10
42	6						4	5				11			8	2	9	3				7			10
43	6						4	5	12			11			8	2	9	3				7			10
44	6	12					4	5				11			8	2	9	3				7			10
45	6		3				4	5				11				2	3	9				7			10
46	6						4	5	12	8	14	11				2	3	9				7		1	10
Apps	26	13	9	33	5	21	41	3	28	2	39	21	36	9	31	45	22	11	14	31	10	37	7	20	44
Goals	2		1	13	1	1	8		2					3	3	1		3			2	6	5		17

Two own goals

F.A. Cup

	Date	Opponent	Score	Att
R1	Nov 12	LINCOLN CITY	0-1	5758

(Abbott 12, Brown 9, Cox 2, Dakin 5, Graham 3, Hargreaves 14, Hobson 4, Lawford 11, Lee 8, Peacock 6, Wallace 1, Windass 10)

F.L. Cup (Coca Cola Cup)

	Date	Opponent	Score	Scorers	Att
R1/1	Aug 16	SCARBOROUGH	2-1	Peacock, Lee	2546
R1/2		23	Scarborough	0-2		2287

R1/1: Abbott 6, Brown 9, Cox 2, Dakin 5, Fettis 1, Graham 3, Hobson 4, Lawford 11, Lee 8, Ormondroyd 12, Peacock 7, Windass 10
R1/2: Atkinson 12, Brown 9, Cox 14, Dakin 5, Fettis 1, Graham 3, Hargreaves 8, Hobson 4, Lawford 11, Lowthorpe 2, Peacock 6, Wallace 7, Windass 10

A.M. Cup (Auto Windscreens Shield)

	Date	Opponent	Score	Att
Gp	Sep 27	DONCASTER ROVERS	0-2	890
Gp	Nov 8	Lincoln City	0-1	1626

Gp Sep 27: Abbott 6, Allison 4, Atkinson 10, Dakin 5, Graham 3, Hargreaves 9, Lawford 11, Lee 8, Mann 2, Ormondroyd 12, Peacock 7, Wallace 1
Gp Nov 8: Abbott 12, Cox 2, Dakin 5, Graham 3, Hargreaves 9, Hobson 4, Lawford 11, Lee 8, Peacock 6, Wallace 7, Wilson 1, Windass 10

League Table

		Pl	Home W	D	L	F	Away W	D	L	F	A	F. (Total)	A.	Pts
1	Birmingham City	46	15	6	2	53	18	10	8	5	31	19	84	37	89
2	Brentford	46	14	4	5	44	15	11	6	6	37	24	81	39	85
3	Crewe Alexandra	46	14	3	6	46	33	11	5	7	34	35	80	68	83
4	Bristol Rovers	46	15	7	1	48	20	7	9	7	22	20	70	40	82
5	Huddersfield Town	46	14	5	4	45	21	8	10	5	34	28	79	49	81
6	Wycombe Wands.	46	13	7	3	36	19	8	8	7	24	27	60	46	78
7	Oxford United	46	13	6	4	30	18	8	6	9	36	34	66	52	75
8	HULL CITY	46	13	6	4	40	18	8	5	10	30	39	70	57	74
9	York City	46	13	4	6	37	21	8	5	10	30	30	67	51	72
10	Swansea City	46	10	8	5	23	13	9	6	8	34	32	57	45	71
11	Stockport County	46	12	3	8	40	29	7	5	11	23	31	63	60	65
12	Blackpool	46	11	4	8	40	36	7	6	10	24	34	64	70	64
13	Wrexham	46	10	7	6	38	27	6	8	9	27	37	65	64	63
14	Bradford City	46	8	6	9	29	32	8	6	9	28	32	57	64	60
15	Peterborough Utd.	46	7	11	5	26	29	7	7	9	28	40	54	69	60
16	Brighton & Hove A.	46	9	10	4	25	15	5	7	11	29	38	54	53	59
17	Rotherham United	46	12	6	5	36	26	2	8	13	21	35	57	61	56
18	Shrewsbury Town	46	9	9	5	34	27	4	5	14	20	35	54	62	53
19	Bournemouth	46	9	4	10	30	34	4	7	12	19	35	49	69	50
20	Cambridge United	46	8	9	6	33	28	3	6	14	19	41	52	69	48
21	Plymouth Argyle	46	7	6	10	22	36	5	4	14	23	47	45	83	46
22	Cardiff City	46	5	6	12	25	31	4	5	14	21	43	46	74	38
23	Chester City	46	5	6	12	23	42	1	5	17	14	42	37	84	29
24	Leyton Orient	46	6	6	11	21	29	0	2	21	9	46	30	75	26

1994-95

Back Row: D. Mail, G. Hobson, C. Hargreaves, S. Wilson, R. Dewhurst, A. Fettis, N. Allison, G. Atkinson, M. Edeson;
Middle Row: W. Legg (Yth Coach), J. Cass, D. Windass, N. Mann, S. Dakin, R. Peacock, J. Graham, B. Mitchell,
B. Ellison (Yth Coach), J. Radcliffe (Physio);
Front Row: S. Moran, L. Brown, G. Abbott, T. Dolan (Manager), J. Lee (Asst Manager), C. Lawford, C. Lee, A. Lowthorpe.

1995-96

Back Row: A. Williams, N. Allison, R. Dewhurst, A. Fettis, S. Wilson, G. Hobson, A. Mason, P. Fewings;
Middle Row: W. Legg (Coach), B. Ellison (Coach), C. Lee, L. Brown, N. Mann, R. Peacock, S. Dakin, G. Haigh,
C. Lawford, A. Lowthorpe, R. Arnold (Coach), J. Radcliffe (Physio);
Front Row: I. Plant, M. Quigley, D. Windass, T. Dolan (Manager), M. Fish (Chairman), J. Lee (Asst Manager),
G. Abbott, J. Graham, D. Chambers.

1995/96 Bottom of Division Two: Relegated

Player columns (in order across the grid):
Abbott G · Allison N · Brown L · Carroll R · Dakin S · Darby D · Davison R · Dewhurst R · Fettis A · Fewings P · Fidler R · Gilbert K · Gordon G · Graham J · Hobson G · Humphries G · Lawford C · Lee C · Lowthorpe A · Mann N · Marks J · Mason A · Maxfield S · Peacock R · Pridmore L · Quigley M · Trevitt S · Watson T · Wharton P · Wilkinson I · Williams A · Wilson S · Windass D

#	Date		Opponent	Result	Scorers	Att
1	Aug	12	SWINDON TOWN	0-1		6525
2		19	Rotherham United	1-1	Windass	3754
3		26	BLACKPOOL	2-1	Brown, Mason	4755
4		29	Brentford	0-1		4535
5	Sep	2	Chesterfield	0-0		4345
6		9	OXFORD UNITED	0-0		4608
7		12	SWANSEA CITY	0-0		3519
8		16	Burnley	1-2	Fewings	10613
9		23	Carlisle United	0-2		5986
10		30	YORK CITY	0-3		5273
11	Oct	7	SHREWSBURY TOWN	2-3	Abbott, Windass	3266
12		14	Bristol City	0-4		5354
13		21	STOCKPORT COUNTY	1-1	Abbott	3496
14		28	Wycombe Wanderers	2-2	Lee, Windass	5021
15		31	Crewe Alexandra	0-1		3609
16	Nov	4	WREXHAM	1-1	Abbott	3515
17		18	Bradford City	1-1	Windass	5820
18		25	PETERBOROUGH UTD.	2-3	Davison, Peacock	3642
19	Dec	9	CARLISLE UNITED	2-5	Peacock 2	3478
20		16	York City	1-0	Fewings	3593
21		23	Bournemouth	0-2		3491
22	Jan	6	Bristol Rovers	1-2	Davison	4276
23		13	ROTHERHAM UNITED	1-4	Abbott	3678
24		20	Swindon Town	0-3		8287
25		23	BRIGHTON & HOVE ALB	0-0		2421
26	Feb	3	Blackpool	1-1	Allison	4713
27		10	BRISTOL ROVERS	1-3	Davison	3311
28		17	Swansea City	0-0		1909
29		24	BURNLEY	3-0	Peacock 2, Davison	4206
30		27	Oxford United	0-2		4650
31	Mar	2	Notts County	0-1		4528
32		5	BRENTFORD	0-1		2284
33		9	BOURNEMOUTH	1-1	Graham	2853
34		12	CHESTERFIELD	0-0		2832
35		16	Brighton & Hove Albion	0-4		4910
36		23	WALSALL	1-0	Abbott	3060
37		26	NOTTS COUNTY	0-0		2589
38		30	Shrewsbury Town	1-1	Peacock	2347
39	Apr	2	BRISTOL CITY	2-3	Mann, Gordon	2641
40		6	WYCOMBE WANDERERS	4-2	* see below	3065
41		8	Stockport County	0-0		5043
42		13	CREWE ALEXANDRA	1-2	Gordon	3497
43		20	Wrexham	0-5		3505
44		23	Walsall	0-3		2740
45		27	Peterborough United	1-3	Allison	6649
46	May	4	BRADFORD CITY	2-3	Gordon, Darby	8965

Scorers in game 40: Wilkinson, Peacock, Abbott, Quigley.

Apps: 31, 35, 23, 23, 6, 8, 11, 16, 7, 25, 1, 13, 13, 24, 29, 12, 31, 28, 19, 38, 5, 20, 4, 45, 13, 25, 4, 9, 8, 34, 19, 16

Goals: Abbott 6, Allison 2, Brown 1, Darby 1, Davison 4, Fewings 2, Gordon 3, Graham 1, Lee 1, Mann 1, Peacock 7, Quigley 1, Wilkinson 1, Windass 4

F.A. Cup

Date		Opponent	Result	Scorers	Att
Nov	4	WREHAM	0-0		3724
	21	Wrexham	0-0		4522

Replay lost 1-3 on penalties a..e.t

F.L. Cup (Coca Cola Cup)

Date		Opponent	Result	Scorers	Att
Aug	15	CARLISLE UNITED	1-2	Windass	2779
	22	Carlisle United	4-2	Windass 2, Allison, Fewings	4250
Sep	20	Coventry City	0-2		8915
Oct	4	COVENTRY CITY	0-1		6929

A.M. Cup (Auto Windscreens Shield)

Date		Opponent	Result	Scorers	Att
Sep	26	Scarborough	2-0	Lawford, Mann	893
Oct	17	PRESTON NORTH END	1-0	Fewings	793
Nov	28	BLACKPOOL	1-2	Windass	1472

League Table — Division Two

		Pl	Home					Away					F.	A.	Pts
			W	D	L	F	A	W	D	L	F	A	(Total)		
1	Swindon Town	46	12	10	1	37	16	13	7	3	34	18	71	34	92
2	Oxford United	46	17	4	2	52	14	7	7	9	24	25	76	39	83
3	Blackpool	46	14	5	4	41	20	9	8	6	26	20	67	40	82
4	Notts County	46	14	6	3	42	21	7	9	7	21	18	63	39	78
5	Crewe Alexandra	46	13	3	7	40	24	9	4	10	37	36	77	60	73
6	Bradford City	46	15	4	4	41	25	7	3	13	30	44	71	69	73
7	Chesterfield	46	14	6	3	39	21	6	6	11	17	30	56	51	72
8	Wrexham	46	12	6	5	51	27	6	10	7	25	28	76	55	70
9	Stockport County	46	8	9	6	30	20	11	4	8	31	27	61	47	70
10	Bristol Rovers	46	12	4	7	29	28	8	6	9	28	32	57	60	70
11	Walsall	46	12	7	4	38	20	7	5	11	22	25	60	45	69
12	Wycombe Wands.	46	9	8	6	36	26	6	7	10	27	33	63	59	60
13	Bristol City	46	10	6	7	28	22	5	9	9	27	38	55	60	60
14	Bournemouth	46	12	6	5	33	25	4	5	14	18	45	51	70	58
15	Brentford	46	12	6	5	24	15	3	7	13	19	34	43	49	58
16	Rotherham United	46	11	7	5	31	20	3	7	13	23	42	54	62	56
17	Burnley	46	9	8	6	35	28	5	5	13	21	40	56	68	55
18	Shrewsbury Town	46	7	8	8	32	29	6	6	11	26	41	58	70	53
19	Peterborough Utd.	46	9	6	8	40	27	4	7	12	19	39	59	66	52
20	York City	46	9	6	9	28	29	5	7	11	30	44	58	73	52
21	Carlisle United	46	11	6	6	35	20	1	7	15	22	52	57	72	49
22	Swansea City	46	8	8	7	27	29	3	6	14	16	50	43	79	47
23	Brighton & Hove A.	46	6	7	10	25	31	4	3	16	21	38	46	69	40
24	HULL CITY	46	4	8	11	26	37	1	8	14	10	41	36	78	31

1996/97 17th in Division Three

Player columns (left to right): Allison N, Brien A, Brown A, Carroll R, Darby D, Davison A, Dewhurst R, Dickinson P, Doncel A, Ellington L, Elliott S, Fewings P, Gilbert K, Gordon G, Greaves M, Joyce W, Lowthorpe A, Mann N, Marks J, Mason A, Maxfield S, Peacock R, Quigley M, Rioch G, Sansam C, Sharman S, Trevitt S, Turner R, Wharton P, Wilson S, Wright I

#	Date		Opponent	Result	Scorers	Att	Apps/line
1	Aug	17	DARLINGTON	3-2	Darby 3	4224	Allison 6, Brien 13, Brown 1, Darby 9, Doncel 5, Gilbert 8, Gordon 11, Joyce 7, Mann 10, Maxfield 12, Peacock 3, Rioch 2, Wright 4
2		24	Carlisle United	0-0		5407	6, 14, 1, 9, 5, 8, 11, 7, 10, 13, 12, 3, 2, 4
3		27	Hereford United	1-0	Darby	2820	6, 1, 9, 5, 11, 7, 10, 12, 13, 8, 3, 2, 4
4		31	BARNET	0-0		4605	6, 14, 1, 9, 5, 11, 7, 10, 12, 13, 8, 3, 2, 4
5	Sep	7	ROCHDALE	1-1	Doncel	3451	6, 12, 1, 9, 5, 10, 7, 13, 8, 11, 3, 2, 4
6		10	Lincoln City	1-0	Peacock	3069	4, 6, 11, 1, 8, 9, 7, 12, 10, 3, 2, 5
7		14	Colchester United	1-1	Gordon	3027	4, 6, 13, 1, 9, 8, 11, 7, 12, 10, 3, 2, 5
8		21	HARTLEPOOL UNITED	1-0	Darby	3886	4, 6, 13, 1, 9, 8, 7, 12, 10, 11, 3, 2, 5
9		28	Swansea City	0-0		2961	4, 6, 14, 1, 9, 8, 10, 7, 12, 11, 3, 2, 5
10	Oct	1	MANSFIELD TOWN	1-1	Gordon	3579	4, 6, 9, 11, 7, 10, 12, 8, 3, 2, 1, 5
11		5	SCUNTHORPE UNITED	0-2		5414	4, 6, 9, 14, 13, 12, 7, 10, 11, 8, 3, 2, 1, 5
12		12	Leyton Orient	1-1	Brien	4499	4, 6, 14, 9, 11, 7, 8, 12, 10, 3, 2, 13, 5
13		15	Scarborough	2-3	Turner 2	3425	4, 6, 1, 9, 12, 5, 7, 10, 11, 3, 2, 8
14		19	FULHAM	0-3		3986	4, 6, 1, 9, 12, 13, 8, 5, 7, 10, 11, 3, 2, 8
15		26	Wigan Athletic	2-1	Peacock, Trevitt	3887	4, 6, 12, 1, 9, 5, 10, 7, 11, 13, 3, 2, 8
16		29	CARDIFF CITY	1-1	Gilbert	2775	4, 1, 9, 5, 10, 12, 7, 11, 13, 3, 2, 8, 6
17	Nov	2	CAMBRIDGE UNITED	1-3	Brown	3563	14, 1, 9, 5, 13, 10, 4, 7, 11, 2, 3, 12, 8, 6
18		9	Chester City	0-0		2085	4, 12, 1, 9, 5, 2, 7, 13, 11, 10, 3, 8, 6
19		20	TORQUAY UNITED	2-0	Darby, Peacock	1775	8, 1, 9, 5, 4, 7, 2, 11, 10, 3, 12, 6
20		23	Exeter City	0-0		3423	8, 14, 1, 9, 5, 4, 7, 12, 11, 10, 3, 13, 6
21		30	WIGAN ATHLETIC	1-1	Doncel	3537	4, 12, 1, 5, 2, 8, 7, 13, 3, 11, 10, 9, 6
22	Dec	3	Northampton Town	1-2	Darby	3519	4, 13, 1, 5, 2, 8, 10, 12, 3, 11, 9, 6
23		14	Brighton & Hove Albion	0-3		3762	4, 9, 1, 5, 12, 8, 7, 10, 2, 11, 13, 3, 6
24		21	DONCASTER ROVERS	3-1	Mason 2, Darby	2830	4, 9, 1, 2, 5, 7, 12, 10, 13, 3, 11, 8
25		26	LINCOLN CITY	2-1	Darby, Mason	4892	4, 9, 1, 12, 5, 7, 2, 10, 11, 3, 8
26	Jan	1	Hartlepool United	1-1	Joyce	1944	4, 9, 1, 12, 8, 5, 7, 2, 11, 10, 3
27		11	SWANSEA CITY	1-1	Mann	2810	9, 1, 4, 10, 5, 7, 13, 11, 12, 8, 3, 2
28		18	Mansfield Town	0-1		2286	9, 1, 4, 10, 5, 7, 13, 2, 11, 12, 8, 3
29		25	Cardiff City	0-2		2328	11, 9, 1, 12, 4, 13, 5, 7, 3, 2, 14, 10, 8
30	Feb	1	CHESTER CITY	1-0	Gordon	2513	12, 1, 9, 4, 7, 11, 5, 10, 2, 8, 3
31		8	Cambridge United	0-1		3160	12, 9, 5, 8, 11, 4, 7, 10, 2, 3, 1
32		15	EXETER CITY	2-0	Joyce, Gordon	2668	13, 1, 9, 5, 12, 8, 4, 7, 2, 11, 10, 3
33		22	Torquay United	1-1	Greaves	2072	9, 1, 5, 12, 8, 4, 7, 2, 11, 10, 3
34		25	Rochdale	2-1	Joyce, Darby	1349	12, 1, 9, 5, 8, 4, 7, 2, 13, 11, 10, 3
35	Mar	1	NORTHAMPTON T	1-1	Darby	3495	14, 1, 9, 5, 4, 8, 12, 7, 2, 11, 3, 10, 13
36		8	Doncaster Rovers	0-0		3274	9, 5, 13, 4, 12, 8, 7, 2, 11, 3
37		15	BRIGHTON & HOVE ALB	3-0	Joyce 2, Darby	3373	12, 9, 5, 4, 8, 7, 2, 11, 10, 3
38		22	CARLISLE UNITED	0-1		3847	8, 9, 5, 4, 12, 7, 2, 11, 10, 3
39		29	Darlington	0-1		3024	8, 9, 5, 4, 14, 12, 7, 2, 11, 10, 13, 3, 1
40		31	HEREFORD UNITED	1-1	Greaves	2818	9, 12, 4, 14, 8, 5, 7, 2, 11, 10, 13, 3, 1
41	Apr	5	Barnet	0-1		1668	12, 11, 9, 4, 14, 8, 5, 7, 2, 10, 3, 13, 1
42		12	Scunthorpe United	2-2	Quigley, Lowthorpe	4257	12, 9, 4, 8, 5, 7, 2, 13, 11, 10, 3, 1
43		15	COLCHESTER UNITED	1-2	Darby	2035	5, 9, 4, 14, 8, 12, 7, 13, 11, 10, 3, 2, 1
44		19	LEYTON ORIENT	3-2	Peacock, Mann, Rioch	2647	5, 14, 9, 6, 8, 12, 7, 11, 10, 4, 3, 13, 2, 1
45		26	Fulham	0-2		10588	6, 9, 5, 12, 8, 7, 11, 10, 4, 3, 2, 1
46	May	3	SCARBOROUGH	0-2		3774	6, 9, 5, 12, 8, 13, 7, 11, 10, 4, 3, 2, 1

	Allison	Brien	Brown	Carroll	Darby	Davison	Dewhurst	Dickinson	Doncel	Ellington	Elliott	Fewings	Gilbert	Gordon	Greaves	Joyce	Lowthorpe	Mann	Marks	Mason	Maxfield	Peacock	Quigley	Rioch	Sansam	Sharman	Trevitt	Turner	Wharton	Wilson	Wright
Apps	11	32	26	23	41	9	22	1	26	2	3	12	19	20	30	45	14	32	10	6	17	40	29	39	3	4	22	5	1	15	
Goals		1	1		13				2				1	4	2	5	1	2		3		4	1	1			1	2			

F.A. Cup

	Date		Opponent	Result	Scorers	Att	
R1	Nov	16	Whitby Town	0-0		3337	6, 8, 1, 9, 4, 7, 12, 2, 11, 10, 3
rep		26	WHITBY TOWN	8-4	Darby 6, Peacock, Mann	2900	4, 8, 9, 5, 12, 14, 7, 13, 2, 3, 11, 10, 1
R2	Dec	7	CREWE ALAXANDRA	1-5	Joyce	3756	4, 9, 5, 2, 7, 10, 11, 6, 3, 14, 1

R1 played at McCain Stadium/Seamer Rd, Scarborough R1 replay a.e.t

F.L. Cup (Coca Cola Cup)

	Date		Opponent	Result	Scorers	Att	
R1/1	Aug	20	SCARBOROUGH	2-2	Rioch, Quigley	2134	12, 6, 14, 1, 9, 5, 8, 11, 7, 10, 13, 3, 2
R1/2	Sep	3	Scarborough	2-3	Rioch, Gordon	2656	6, 1, 9, 5, 13, 7, 10, 12, 11, 8, 3, 2

A.M. Cup (Auto Windscreens Shield)

	Date		Opponent	Result	Scorers	Att	
R1	Dec	10	CHESTER CITY	3-1	Wright, Darby, Joyce	553	4, 9, 1, 5, 13, 8, 7, 10, 2, 12, 3, 11
R2	Jan	28	Carlisle United	0-4		3716	4, 1, 9, 5, 12, 11, 10, 7, 2, 3, 14, 8, 13

		Pl	Home W D L F A	Away W D L F A	F. A. (Total)
1	Wigan Athletic	46	17 3 3 53 21	9 6 8 31 30	84 51
2	Fulham	46	13 5 5 41 20	12 7 4 31 18	72 38
3	Carlisle United	46	16 3 4 41 21	8 9 6 26 23	67 44
4	Northampton Town	46	14 4 5 43 17	6 8 9 24 27	67 44
5	Swansea City	46	13 5 5 37 20	8 3 12 25 38	62 58
6	Chester City	46	11 8 4 30 16	7 8 8 25 27	55 43
7	Cardiff City	46	11 4 8 30 23	9 5 9 26 31	56 54
8	Colchester United	46	11 9 3 36 23	6 8 9 26 28	62 51
9	Lincoln City	46	10 8 5 35 25	8 4 11 35 44	70 69
10	Cambridge United	46	11 5 7 30 27	7 6 10 23 32	53 59
11	Mansfield Town	46	9 8 6 21 17	7 8 8 26 28	47 45
12	Scarborough	46	9 9 5 36 31	7 6 10 29 37	65 68
13	Scunthorpe United	46	11 3 9 36 33	7 6 10 23 29	59 62
14	Rochdale	46	10 6 7 34 24	4 10 9 24 34	58 58
15	Barnet	46	9 9 5 32 23	5 7 11 14 28	46 51
16	Leyton Orient	46	11 6 6 28 20	4 6 13 22 38	50 58
17	HULL CITY	46	9 8 6 29 26	4 10 9 15 24	44 50
18	Darlington	46	11 5 7 37 28	3 5 15 27 50	64 78
19	Doncaster Rovers	46	9 7 7 29 23	5 3 15 23 43	52 66
20	Hartlepool United	46	8 6 9 33 32	6 3 14 20 34	53 66
21	Torquay United	46	9 4 10 24 24	4 7 12 22 38	46 62
22	Exeter City	46	6 9 8 25 30	6 3 14 23 43	48 73
23	Brighton & Hove A.	46	12 6 5 41 27	1 4 18 12 43	53 70
24	Hereford United	46	6 8 9 26 25	5 6 12 24 40	50 65

1996-97

Back Row: P. Wharton, S. Maxfield, S. Trevitt, A. Mason, S. Wilson, R. Carroll, J. Marks, D. Darby, M. Quigley, K. Gilbert;
Middle Row: R. Arnold (Coach), A. Doncel, M. Greaves, I. Wilkinson, A. Brown, N. Allison, G. Gordon, I. Wright, P. Fewings, J. Radcliffe (Physio), W. Legg (Coach);
Front Row: G. Rioch, A. Lowthorpe, W. Joyce, T. Dolan, (Manager), M. Fish (Chairman), J. Lee (Asst Manager), A. Brien, N. Mann, R. Peacock.

1997-98

Back Row: G. Gordon, I. Wright, R. Dewhurst, A. Brown, S. Thompson, A. Brien, M. Greaves, R. Peacock, P. Fewings;
Middle Row: M. McGurn (Fitness Coach), W. Kirkwood (Asst Manager), S. Sharman, S. Trevitt, G. Rioch, S. Wilson, N. Mann, A. Doncel, J. Marks, D. Darby, J. Radcliffe (Physio), R. Arnold (Coach);
Front Row: P. Dickinson, S. Maxfield, A. Lowthorpe, M. Hateley (Player-Manager), M. Quigley, P. Wharton, C. Baxter, W. Joyce.

1997/98 22nd in Division Three

League Matches (Division Three)

No	Date		Opponent	Score	Scorers	Att
1	Aug	9	Mansfield Town	0-2		4627
2		16	NOTTS COUNTY	0-3		7412
3		23	Peterborough United	0-2		5701
4		30	SWANSEA CITY	7-4	Darby 3, Rioch, Mann 2, Hodges	5198
5	Sep	2	ROTHERHAM UNITED	0-0		6127
6		5	Chester City	0-1		2271
7		13	LINCOLN CITY	0-2		4736
8		20	Rochdale	1-2	Lowthorpe	2085
9		27	Scunthorpe United	0-4		4905
10	Oct	4	TORQUAY UNITED	3-3	Peacock, Greaves, Gordon	5139
11		11	SCARBOROUGH	3-0	Peacock, Rocastle, Quigley	5315
12		18	Barnet	0-2		2315
13		21	Cambridge United	1-0	Greaves	2388
14		25	BRIGHTON & HOVE ALB	0-0		5686
15	Nov	1	Darlington	3-4	Joyce, Rioch, Gordon	2893
16		4	EXETER CITY	3-2	Joyce, Ellington 2	3837
17		8	SHREWSBURY TOWN	1-4	Rioch	4758
18		18	Cardiff City	1-2	Darby	2509
19		22	Macclesfield Town	0-2		2508
20		29	DONCASTER ROVERS	3-0	Rioch(p), Hocking, Gore(og)	4721
21	Dec	2	Hartlepool United	2-2	Joyce, Hodges	1933
22		13	COLCHESTER UNITED	3-1	Dewhurst, Rioch (p), Darby	3896
23		20	Leyton Orient	1-2	Wright	4020
24		26	CHESTER CITY	1-2	Dewhurst	6807
25		28	Rotherham United	4-5	Darby 2, Hodges 2	5995
26	Jan	10	MANSFIELD TOWN	0-0		4440
27		17	Swansea City	0-2		2899
28		20	Notts County	0-2		4017
29		24	PETERBOROUGH UTD.	3-1	Darby 2, Joyce	4669
30		31	Lincoln City	0-1		4067
31	Feb	7	ROCHDALE	0-2		4031
32		14	Torquay United	1-5	Bettney	2793
33		21	SCUNTHORPE UNITED	2-1	Dewhurst, McGinty	4920
34		24	BARNET	0-2		3313
35		28	Scarborough	1-2	Boyack	3831
36	Mar	3	Shrewsbury Town	0-2		1523
37		7	DARLINGTON	1-1	Wright	3616
38		14	Exeter City	0-3		3052
39		21	CARDIFF CITY	0-1		3408
40		28	MACCLESFIELD TOWN	0-0		3677
41	Apr	4	Doncaster Rovers	0-1		2597
42		11	HARTLEPOOL UNITED	2-1	Brown D 2	3343
43		13	Colchester United	3-4	Boyack, McGinty, Darby	4762
44		18	LEYTON ORIENT	3-2	Mann, Boyack, Lowthorpe	3744
45		25	Brighton & Hove Albion	2-2	Darby 2	3888
46	May	2	CAMBRIDGE UNITED	1-0	Darby	4930

Appearances / Goals (totals)

	Bettney C	Boyack S	Brien A	Brown A	Brown D	Darby D	Dewhurst R	Dickinson P	Doncel A	Edwards M	Ellington L	Fewings P	Gage K	Gordon G	Greaves M	Hateley M	Hocking M	Hodges G	Joyce W	Lowthorpe A	Mann N	Maxfield S	McGinty B	Morley B	Peacock R	Quigley M	Rioch G	Rocastle D	Thomson S	Trevitt S	Tucker D	Wilson S	Wright I	Wharton P
Apps	30	12	15	3	7	29	24	3	12	21	7	18	10	5	25	9	31	18	45	23	34	14	21	8	27	9	39	10	9	4	7	37	33	
Goals	1	3			2	13	3				2				2	2			1	4	4	2	3			2	1	5	1					2

One own goal

F.A. Cup

	Date		Opponent	Score	Scorers	Att
R1	Nov	15	HEDNESFORD TOWN	0-2		6091

F.L. Cup (Coca Cola Cup)

	Date		Opponent	Score	Scorers	Att
R1/1	Aug	12	Macclesfield Town	0-0		2249
R1/2		26	MACCLESFIELD TOWN	2-1	Peacock, Joyce	3376
R2/1	Sep	16	CRYSTAL PALACE	1-0	Darby	9323
R2/2		30	Crystal Palace	1-2	Wright	6407
R3	Oct	15	Newcastle Utd	0-2		35832

R2 won on away goals rule.

A.M. Cup (Auto Windscreens Shield)

	Date		Opponent	Score	Scorers	Att
R1	Dec	6	SCARBOROUGH	2-1	Darby, Atkin (og)	1518
R2	Jan	6	Grimsby Town	0-1		4778

Final Division Three Table

		Pl	Home W	D	L	F	A	Away W	D	L	F	A	F (Total)	A
1	Notts County	46	14	7	2	41	20	15	5	3	41	23	82	43
2	Macclesfield Town	46	19	4	0	40	11	4	9	10	23	33	63	44
3	Lincoln City	46	11	7	5	32	24	9	8	6	28	27	60	51
4	Colchester United	46	14	5	4	41	24	7	6	10	31	36	72	60
5	Torquay United	46	14	4	5	39	22	7	7	9	29	37	68	59
6	Scarborough	46	14	6	3	44	23	5	9	9	23	35	67	58
7	Barnet	46	10	8	5	35	22	9	5	9	26	29	61	51
8	Scunthorpe United	46	11	7	5	30	24	8	5	10	26	28	56	52
9	Rotherham United	46	10	9	4	41	30	6	10	7	26	31	67	61
10	Peterborough Utd.	46	13	6	4	37	16	5	7	11	26	35	63	51
11	Leyton Orient	46	14	5	4	40	20	5	7	11	22	27	62	47
12	Mansfield Town	46	11	9	3	42	26	5	8	10	22	29	64	55
13	Shrewsbury Town	46	12	3	8	35	28	4	10	9	26	34	61	62
14	Chester City	46	12	7	4	34	15	5	3	15	25	46	60	61
15	Exeter City	46	10	8	5	39	25	5	7	11	29	38	68	63
16	Cambridge United	46	11	8	4	39	27	3	10	10	24	30	63	57
17	Hartlepool United	46	10	12	1	40	22	2	11	10	21	31	61	53
18	Rochdale	46	15	3	5	43	15	2	4	17	13	40	56	55
19	Darlington	46	13	6	4	43	28	1	6	16	13	44	56	72
20	Swansea City	46	8	8	7	24	16	5	8	10	22	29	64	55
21	Cardiff City	46	5	13	5	27	22	4	10	9	21	30	48	52
22	HULL CITY	46	10	6	7	36	32	1	2	20	20	51	56	83
23	Brighton & Hove A.	46	3	10	10	21	34	3	7	13	17	32	38	66
24	Doncaster Rovers	46	3	3	17	14	48	1	5	17	16	65	30	113

1998/99 21st in Division Three

Player columns (left to right): Alcide C · Bolder A · Bonnor M · Brabin G · Brown D · Darby D · D'Auria D · Dewhurst R · Dudley C · Edwards M · Ellington L · Faulconbridge C · French J · Gage K · Gibson P · Greaves M · Harrison GR · Hateley M · Hawes S · Hocking M · Joyce W · Mann N · McGinty B · Morley B · Oakes A · Peacock R · Perry J · Rioch G · Saville A · Swales S · Whitney J · Whittle J · Whitworth N · Williams G · Wilson S

League (Division Three)

#	Date	Opponent	Result	Scorers	Att.
1	Aug 8	Rotherham United	1-3	D'Auria	5447
2	15	DARLINGTON	1-2	Whitworth	5217
3	23	Chester City	2-2	Brown, Hateley	2577
4	29	PETERBOROUGH UTD.	1-0	Hateley	4636
5	31	Hartlepool United	0-1		3277
6	Sep 5	BRENTFORD	2-3	Hocking, Whitworth	4058
7	8	ROCHDALE	2-1	Peacock, Brown	3433
8	12	Barnet	1-4	Peacock	2025
9	19	HALIFAX TOWN	1-2	McGinty	4719
10	26	Mansfield Town	0-2		2603
	Oct 3	CAMBRIDGE UNITED	0-3		3882
	9	CARDIFF CITY	1-2	Brown	8594
	17	Scarborough	2-1	Mann, Hateley	2760
	20	Exeter City	0-3		2101
	24	SOUTHEND UNITED	1-1	McGinty	3551
	31	Plymouth Argyle	0-0		4285
	Nov 7	LEYTON ORIENT	0-1		5288
	10	BRIGHTON & HOVE ALB	0-2		4433
	21	Scunthorpe United	2-3	Dudley, Brown	5633
	28	CARLISLE UNITED	1-0	Dudley	4452
	Dec 12	Torquay United	0-2		2033
	19	SWANSEA CITY	0-2		4208
	26	CHESTER CITY	1-2	D'Auria	6695
	28	Shrewsbury Town	2-3	D'Auria, Joyce	2879
	Jan 9	ROTHERHAM UNITED	1-0	Bonner	5575
	23	HARTLEPOOL UNITED	4-0	Brown 2, McGinty 2	5808
	26	Peterborough United	1-1	Wittney	4405
	30	SHREWSBURY TOWN	1-1	Gayle (og)	7331
	Feb 6	Brentford	2-0	Alcide, Brown	5086
	12	Rochdale	0-3		5374
	16	Darlington	1-0	Brabin	3107
	20	BARNET	1-1	Whittle	6823
	27	Halifax Town	1-0	Brown	4455
	Mar 6	MANSFIELD TOWN	0-0		6692
	9	Cambridge United	0-2		4948
	13	Leyton Orient	2-1	Brabin, Brown	5481
	20	PLYMOUTH ARGYLE	1-0	Brabin	6294
	26	Southend United	1-0	D'Auria	4176
	Apr 3	SCARBOROUGH	1-1	Brabin	13949
	5	Cardiff City	1-1	Alcide	8252
	10	EXETER CITY	2-1	Williams, Alcide	5836
	13	Carlisle United	0-0		3743
	17	SCUNTHORPE UNITED	2-3	Joyce, Brown	9835
	24	Brighton & Hove Albion	0-0		3481
	May 1	TORQUAY UNITED	1-0	Brown	7789
	8	Swansea City	0-2		9266

Apps: 17 · 1 · 1 · 21 · 42 · 8 · 42 · 8 · 7 · 30 · 6 · 10 · 15 · 3 · 4 · 25 · 8 · 12 · 19 · 26 · 29 · 20 · 32 · 12 · 19 · 14 · 8 · 13 · 3 · 22 · 21 · 24 · 18 · 25 · 23

Goals: 3 · · · 1 · 4 · 11 · · 4 · · 2 · · · · · · · · · 3 · · 1 · 2 · 1 · 4 · · · 2 · · · · · · · 1 · 1 · 2 · 1

One own goal

F.A. Cup

Date	Opponent	Result	Scorers	Att.
Nov 14	Salisbury City	2-0	Rioch, McGinty	2573
Dec 5	Luton Town	2-1	Morley, Dewhurst	5021
Jan 2	Aston Villa	0-3		39217

F.L. Cup (Worthington Cup)

Date	Opponent	Result	Scorers	Att.
Aug 11	Stockport County	2-2	Brown, McGinty	3134
18	STOCKPORT COUNTY	0-0		3480
Sep 15	Bolton Wanderers	1-3	Brown	7554
22	BOLTON WANDERERS	2-3	Brown, Rioch (p)	4226

R1 won on away goals rule.

A.M. Cup (Auto Windscreens Shield)

Date	Opponent	Result	Scorers	Att.
Dec 22	Notts County	1-0	D'Auria	1109
Jan 5	WREXHAM	1-2	Williams	2331

Final Table

		Pl	Home W	D	L	F	A	Away W	D	L	F	A	F (Total)	A	Pts
1	Brentford	46	16	5	2	45	18	10	2	11	34	38	79	56	85
2	Cambridge United	46	13	6	4	41	21	10	6	7	37	27	78	48	81
3	Cardiff City	46	13	7	3	35	17	9	7	7	25	22	60	39	80
4	Scunthorpe United	46	14	3	6	42	28	8	5	10	27	30	69	58	74
5	Rotherham United	46	11	8	4	41	26	9	5	9	38	35	79	61	73
6	Leyton Orient	46	12	6	5	40	30	7	9	7	28	29	68	59	72
7	Swansea City	46	11	9	3	33	19	8	5	10	23	29	56	48	71
8	Mansfield Town	46	15	2	6	38	18	4	8	11	22	40	60	58	67
9	Peterborough Utd.	46	11	6	6	41	29	7	8	8	31	27	72	56	66
10	Halifax Town	46	10	8	5	33	25	7	7	9	25	31	58	56	66
11	Darlington	46	10	6	7	41	24	8	5	10	28	34	69	58	65
12	Exeter City	46	13	5	5	32	18	4	7	12	15	32	47	50	63
13	Plymouth Argyle	46	11	6	6	32	19	6	4	13	26	35	58	54	61
14	Chester City	46	6	12	5	28	30	7	6	10	29	36	57	66	57
15	Shrewsbury Town	46	11	6	6	36	29	3	8	12	16	34	52	63	56
16	Barnet	46	10	5	8	30	31	4	8	11	24	40	54	71	55
17	Brighton & Hove A.	46	8	3	12	25	35	8	4	11	24	31	49	66	55
18	Southend United	46	8	6	9	24	21	6	6	11	28	37	52	58	54
19	Rochdale	46	9	8	6	22	21	4	7	12	20	34	42	55	54
20	Torquay United	46	9	9	5	29	20	3	8	12	18	38	47	58	53
21	HULL CITY	46	8	5	10	25	28	6	6	11	19	34	44	62	53
22	Hartlepool United	46	8	7	8	33	27	5	5	13	19	38	52	65	51
23	Carlisle United	46	8	8	7	25	21	3	8	12	18	32	43	53	49
24	Scarborough	46	8	3	12	30	39	6	3	14	20	38	50	77	48

1998-99

Back Row: D. Brown, B. McGinty, M. Greaves, R. Dewhurst, N. Whitworth, M. Edwards;

Middle Row: W. Kirkwood (Asst Manager), D. Tucker, G. Rioch, M. Baker, S. Wilson, M. Hocking, W. Joyce, M. Hateley (Manager);

Front Row: R. Peacock, J. French, S. Hawes, S. Sharman, K. Gage, D. D'Auria, N. Mann, L. Ellington.

1999-2000

Back Row: S. Swales, J. Perry, J. Schofield, J. Whittle, J. Whitney, M. Edwards, J. Harris, M. Greaves, G. Brabin;

Middle Row: J. Davies (Coach), M. Matthews (Physio), N. Mann, S. Morgan, S. Wilson, L. Bracey, G. Williams, C. Alcide, R. Arnold (Coach), W. Russell (Coach);

Front Row: D. D'Auria, B. Morley, S. Harper, W. Joyce (Player-Manager), J. McGovern (Asst Manager), D. Brown, J. Wood, J. Eyre.

1999/2000   14th in Division Three

#	Date		Opponent	Score	Scorers	Att.
1	Aug	07	Exeter City	0-1		3834
2		14	LINCOLN CITY	1-1	Greaves	7046
3		21	Cheltenham Town	0-1		4426
4		28	MACCLESFIELD TOWN	2-3	Alcide, Brown	6222
5		31	Brighton & Hove Alb.	0-3		5856
6	Sep	03	CHESTER CITY	2-1	Eyre 2	6137
7		11	Torquay United	1-0	Eyre	2466
8		18	SWANSEA CITY	2-0	Brown, Wood	5871
9		25	YORK CITY	1-1	Eyre	8293
10	Oct	02	Barnet	0-0		3449
11		09	Hartlepool United	0-2		3114
12		16	NORTHAMPTON TOWN	0-1		6467
13		19	PLYMOUTH ARGYLE	0-1		4727
14		23	York City	1-1	Williams	5109
15	Nov	02	Rochdale	2-0	Harper, Whitmore	2265
16		06	ROTHERHAM UNITED	0-0		7045
17		13	Southend United	2-1	Greaves, Brabin	4940
18		23	HALIFAX TOWN	0-1		6047
19		27	Shrewsbury Town	0-3		2577
20	Dec	04	EXETER CITY	4-0	Edwards, Harper (3)	5683
21		18	CARLISLE UNITED	2-1	Wood, Eyre	4727
22		26	Darlington	0-0		7058
23		28	MANSFIELD TOWN	2-0	Greaves, Joyce	7215
24	Jan	03	Leyton Orient	0-0		5169
25		08	PETERBOROUGH Utd	2-3	Brown, Eyre	5898
26		15	Lincoln City	1-2	Brown	4687
27		22	CHELTENHAM TOWN	1-1	Whitmore	4691
28		29	Macclesfield	2-0	Eyre (2)	1900
29	Feb	05	BRIGHTON & HOVE ALB	2-0	Harris (2)	5167
30		12	Chester City	0-0		2802
31		19	SHREWSBURY TOWN	0-0		5100
32		22	Peterborough Utd	1-2	Brabin	6668
33		26	Swansea City	0-0		6137
34	Mar	04	TORQUAY UNITED	0-0		4668
35		07	Hartlepool United	0-3		4881
36		11	ROCHDALE	2-2	Wood (2)	4219
37		18	Halifax Town	1-0	Wood	2519
38		21	SOUTHEND UNITED	0-0		4150
39		25	DARLINGTON	0-1		5617
40	Apr	01	Carlisle United	4-0	Prokas (og), Harris (2), Morgan	3495
41		08	LEYTON ORIENT	2-0	Whitney, Brown	4422
42		15	Mansfield Town	1-0	Wood	2213
43		21	Northampton Town	0-1		6758
44		24	BARNET	1-3	Brabin	4883
45		29	Plymouth Argyle	1-0	Wood	4233
46	May	06	HARTLEPOOL UNITED	0-3		7620

Apps: 12, 2, 2, 19, 37, 10, 12, 45, 4, 4, 12, 40, 24, 18, 38, 38, 29, 3, 19, 1, 2, 19, 1, 1, 3, 25, 20, 17, 21, 38, 1, 13, 27, 32

Goals: 1, 3, 6, 1, 8, 3, 4, 4, 1, 2, 1, 1, 6

One own goal

F.A. Cup

Date		Opponent	Score	Scorers	Att.
Oct	30	Macclesfield Town	0-0		2401
Nov	09	MACCLESFIELD TOWN	4-0	Eyre (2), Greaves, Brown	4844
Nov	20	Hayes	2-2	Watts (og), Edwards	2749
Nov	30	HAYES	3-2	Brown, Edwards, Wood	5945
Dec	11	CHELSEA	1-6	Brown	10249

F.L. Cup (Worthington Cup)

Date		Opponent	Score	Scorers	Att.
Aug	10	Rotherham United	1-0	Eyre	3294
Aug	24	ROTHERHAM UNITED	2-0	Alcide, Brown	4373
Sep	14	LIVERPOOL	1-5	Brown	10034
Sep	21	Liverpool	2-4	Eyre, Alcide	24318

A.M. Cup (Auto Windscreens Shield)

Date		Opponent	Score	Scorers	Att.
Aug	10	York City	1-0	Morgan	1005
Aug	24	CHESTER CITY	2-0	Joyce, Morgan	1680
Sep	14	Rochdale	0-0		1745

Rochdale win 5-4 on Penalties

		Pl	Home						Away						F. A.		Pts
			W	D	L	F	A	W	D	L	F	A		(Total)			
1	Swansea City	46	15	6	2	32	11	9	7	7	19	19	51	30			85
2	Rotherham United	46	13	5	5	43	17	11	7	5	29	19	72	36			84
3	Northampton Town	46	16	2	5	36	18	9	5	9	27	27	63	45			82
4	Darlington	46	13	9	1	43	15	8	7	8	23	21	66	36			79
5	Peterborough Utd.	46	14	4	5	39	30	8	8	7	24	24	63	54			78
6	Barnet	46	12	6	5	36	24	9	6	8	23	29	59	53			75
7	Hartlepool United	46	16	1	6	32	17	5	8	10	28	32	60	49			72
8	Cheltenham Town	46	13	4	6	28	17	7	6	10	22	25	50	42			70
9	Torquay United	46	12	6	5	35	20	7	6	10	27	32	62	52			69
10	Rochdale	46	8	7	8	21	25	10	7	6	36	29	57	54			68
11	Brighton & Hove A.	46	10	7	6	38	25	7	9	7	26	21	64	46			67
12	Plymouth Argyle	46	12	10	1	38	18	4	8	11	17	33	55	51			66
13	Macclesfield Town	46	9	7	7	36	30	9	4	10	30	31	66	61			65
14	HULL CITY	46	7	8	8	26	23	8	6	9	17	20	43	43			59
15	Lincoln City	46	11	6	6	38	23	4	8	11	29	46	67	69			59
16	Southend United	46	11	5	7	37	31	4	6	13	16	30	53	61			56
17	Mansfield Town	46	9	6	8	33	26	7	2	14	17	39	50	65			56
18	Halifax Town	46	7	5	11	22	24	8	4	11	22	34	44	58			54
19	Leyton Orient	46	7	7	9	22	22	6	6	11	25	30	47	52			52
20	York City	46	7	10	6	21	21	5	6	12	18	32	39	53			52
21	Exeter City	46	8	6	9	27	30	3	5	15	19	42	46	72			44
22	Shrewsbury Town	46	5	6	12	20	27	7	2	12	20	40	40	67			40
23	Carlisle United	46	6	8	9	23	27	3	4	16	19	48	42	75			39
24	Chester City	46	5	5	13	20	36	5	4	14	24	43	44	79			39

2000/01 6th in Division Three

League Matches

No	Date	Opponent	Score	Scorers	Att
1	Aug 12	Blackpool	1-3	Edwards	5862
2	Aug 19	PLYMOUTH ARGYLE	1-1	Whitmore	5431
3	Aug 26	Macclesfield Town	0-0		1795
4	Aug 28	LINCOLN CITY	1-1	Brown	5780
5	Sep 02	CHELTENHAM TOWN	0-2		4750
6	Sep 09	Leyton Orient	2-2	Whitmore (2)	5177
7	Sep 12	Mansfield Town	1-1	Brightwell	2629
8	Sep 16	SHREWSBURY TOWN	1-0	Brown	4775
9	Sep 23	Barnet	1-1	Marcelle	2109
10	Sep 30	CARDIFF CITY	2-0	Gabbidon (og) Greene (og)	5503
11	Oct 06	BRIGHTON & HOVE ALB	0-2		6225
12	Oct 14	Halifax Town	2-0	Whitmore Marcelle	3003
13	Oct 17	Exeter City	1-0	Greaves	2470
14	Oct 21	SOUTHEND UNITED	1-1	Eyre	6701
15	Oct 24	HARTLEPOOL UNITED	0-0		5294
16	Oct 28	York City	0-0		5493
17	Nov 04	DARLINGTON	2-0	Brabin, Whitmore	5344
18	Nov 11	Chesterfield	0-1		5659
19	Nov 25	CARLISLE UNITED	2-1	Brown, Goodison	4677
20	Dec 02	Scunthorpe United	1-0	Brightwell	6101
21	Dec 16	TORQUAY UNITED	1-2	Greaves	4708
22	Dec 23	KIDDERMINSTER HARR.	0-0		5472
23	Dec 26	Rochdale	0-1		4327
24	Jan 06	MACCLESFIELD TOWN	0-0		6217
25	Jan 13	Lincoln City	0-2		4600
26	Jan 16	BLACKPOOL	0-1		4450
27	Jan 27	Kidderminster Harr	2-2	Brown, Francis	3029
28	Feb 03	Cheltenham Town	1-0	Francis	3360
29	Feb 10	LEYTON ORIENT	1-0	Rowe	8782
30	Feb 17	Shrewsbury Town	2-0	Rowe, Francis	3004
31	Feb 20	MANSFIELD TOWN	2-1	Francis, Rowe	7248
32	Feb 24	BARNET	2-1	Eyre (2)	7268
33	Mar 03	Cardiff City	0-2		10074
34	Mar 06	HALIFAX TOWN	1-0	Philpott	6167
35	Mar 10	Brighton & Hove Alb	0-3		6823
36	Mar 13	Plymouth Argyle	1-1	Elliott (og)	5482
37	Mar 17	EXETER CITY	2-1	Burrows (og), Rowe	7536
38	Mar 27	ROCHDALE	3-2	Brabin, Edwards, Rowe	7365
39	Mar 31	Torquay United	1-1	Holt	2779
40	Apr 07	SCUNTHORPE UNITED	2-1	Whitney, Holt	10881
41	Apr 14	Hartlepool United	1-0	Eyre	4364
42	Apr 16	YORK CITY	0-0		11820
43	Apr 21	Darlington	2-0	Jeannin (og), Eyre	4998
44	Apr 28	CHESTERFIELD	3-1	Edwards, Francis, Rowe	11337
45	May 01	Southend United	1-1	Edwards	3573
46	May 05	Carlisle United	0-0		8194

Appearances (Apps) / Goals totals by player

Player	Apps	Goals
Atkins M	8	
Brabin G	37	2
Bracey L	10	
Bradshaw G	2	
Brightwell D	27	2
Brown DA	37	4
Brumwell P	4	
Edwards M	42	4
Eyre J	28	5
Fletcher G	5	
Francis KMD	22	5
Goodison I	36	1
Greaves MA	30	2
Harper S	27	
Harris I	9	
Holt A	10	2
Mann N	13	
Marcelle C	23	2
Matthews R	8	
Morley B	2	
Musslewhite P	37	
Perry J	6	
Philpott L	42	1
Rowe RC	21	6
Swales SC	26	
Whitmore T	26	5
Whitney JD	15	1
Whittle JP	38	
Wood I		

Five own goals

F.A. Cup

Rd	Date	Opponent	Score	Att
R1	Nov 18	Kettering	0-0	2831
R1R	Nov 28	KETTERING	0-1	3858

F.L. Cup (Worthington Cup)

Rd	Date	Opponent	Score	Scorer	Att
R1/1	Aug 22	NOTTS COUNTY	1-0	Eyre	2675
R1/2	Sep 05	Notts County	0-2		1907

R1/2 a.e.t.

A.M. Cup (Auto Windscreens Shield)

Rd	Date	Opponent	Score	Att
R1	Dec 05	Chester City	0-1	770

Division Three Play-Offs

Rd	Date	Opponent	Score	Scorer	Att
SF/1	May 13	LEYTON ORIENT	1-0	Eyre	13310
SF/2	May 16	Leyton Orient	0-2		9419

SF/2 a.e.t.

Final Division Three Table

Pos		Pl	Home W	D	L	F	A	Away W	D	L	F	A	F (Total)	A	Pt
1	Brighton & Hove A.	46	19	2	2	52	14	9	6	8	21	21	73	35	9-
2	Cardiff City	46	16	7	0	56	20	7	6	10	39	38	95	58	8-
3	Chesterfield	46	16	5	2	46	14	9	9	5	33	28	79	42	8-
4	Hartlepool United	46	12	8	3	40	23	9	6	8	31	31	71	54	7-
5	Leyton Orient	46	13	7	3	31	18	7	8	8	28	33	59	51	7-
6	HULL CITY	46	17	4	2	47	18	7	10	6	20	21	47	39	7-
7	Blackpool	46	14	4	5	50	26	8	2	13	24	32	74	58	7-
8	Rochdale	46	11	8	4	36	25	7	9	7	23	23	59	48	7-
9	Cheltenham Town	46	12	5	6	37	27	6	9	8	22	25	59	52	6-
10	Scunthorpe United	46	13	7	3	42	16	5	4	14	20	36	62	52	6-
11	Southend United	46	10	8	5	29	23	5	10	8	26	30	55	53	6-
12	Plymouth Argyle	46	13	5	5	33	17	2	8	13	21	44	54	61	5-
13	Mansfield Town	46	12	7	4	40	26	3	6	14	24	46	64	72	5-
14	Macclesfield Town	46	10	5	8	23	21	4	9	10	28	41	51	62	5-
15	Shrewsbury Town	46	12	5	6	30	26	3	5	15	19	39	49	65	5-
16	Kidderminster H.	46	10	6	7	29	27	3	8	12	18	34	47	61	5-
17	York City	46	9	6	8	23	26	4	7	12	19	37	42	63	5
18	Lincoln City	46	9	9	5	36	28	3	6	14	22	38	58	66	5
19	Exeter City	46	8	9	6	22	20	4	5	14	18	38	40	58	5
20	Darlington	46	10	6	7	28	23	2	7	14	16	33	44	56	4
21	Torquay United	46	8	9	6	30	29	4	4	15	22	48	52	77	4
22	Carlisle United	46	8	8	7	26	26	3	7	13	16	39	42	65	4
23	Halifax Town	46	7	6	10	33	32	5	5	13	21	36	54	68	4
24	Barnet	46	9	8	6	44	29	3	1	19	23	52	67	81	4

2000-01

Back Row: J. Perry, J. Whittle, M. Edwards, D. Brightwell, I. Goodison, T. Whitmore, M. Greaves, G. Brabin, J. Harris, J. Whitney;
Middle Row: M. Matthews (Physio), R. Arnold (Coach), N. Mann, J. Wood, S. Wilson, L. Bracey, J. Eyre,
P. Brumwell, W. Russell (Coach), J. Davies (Coach);
Front Row: B. Morley, D. Brown, S. Swales, D. Moore (Asst Manager), B. Little (Manager),
K. Smith (Asst Manager), S. Harper, L. Philpott, G. Bradshaw.

2001-02

Back Row: M. Bloomer, B. Petty, N. Mohan, M. Edwards, T. Whitmore, J. Whittle, I. Goodison, M. Greaves, G. Alexander, A. Holt, L. Dudfield;
Middle Row: W. Russell (Coach), R. Arnold (Coach), R. Rowe, R. Matthews, M.
Glennon, J. Johnsson, P. Musselwhite, D. Lee, N. Mann, A. Little (Scout), M. Matthews (Physio);
Front Row: S. Kerr, B. Morley, R. Williams, J. Davies (Coach), D. Moore (Asst. Manager), A. Pearson (Chairman),
B. Little (Manager), K. Smith (Asst. Manager), L. Philpott, D. Beresford, M. Price.

2001/02 11th in Division Three

#	Date		Opponent	Score	Scorers	Att.
1	Aug	11	Exeter City	3-1	Whitmore, Greaves, Dudfield	4,677
2		18	PLYMOUTH ARGYLE	0-0		10,755
3		25	Carlisle United	0-0		3,695
4		27	KIDDERMINSTER HARR	2-1	Alexander (2)	8,835
5	Sep	08	YORK CITY	4-0	Mohan, Dudfield, Alexander, Lee	9,737
6		15	Macclesfield Town	0-0		2,740
7		18	ROCHDALE	3-1	Alexander (2), Dudfield	10,213
8		22	SWANSEA CITY	2-1	Dudfield, Johnsson	10,440
9		25	Mansfield Town	2-4	Alexander, Reddy	5,702
10		29	HALIFAX TOWN	3-0	Dudfield, Reddy (2)	9,572
11	Oct	06	Shrewsbury Town	1-1	Alexander	5,010
12		13	TORQUAY UNITED	1-0	Reddy	9,102
13		20	Rushden & Diamonds	3-3	Alexander, Hunter (og) Rowe	4,676
14		23	LEYTON ORIENT	1-1	Alexander	9,843
15		27	Darlington	1-0	Alexander	5,163
16	Nov	03	CHELTENHAM TOWN	5-1	Banks (og), Dudfield, Alexander, Whitmore, Beresford	9,435
17		06	Hartlepool United	0-4		3,183
18		10	Lincoln City	1-2	Alexander	4,950
19		20	Luton Town	1-0	Matthews	7,214
20		24	BRISTOL ROVERS	0-0		9,680
21	Dec	01	OXFORD UNITED	3-0	Matthews, Dudfield, Alexander	9,552
22		15	Scunthorpe United	1-2	Dudfield	6,479
23		22	SOUTHEND UNITED	0-0		8,678
24		29	Kidderminster Harr	0-3		3,962
25	Jan	12	Plymouth Argyle	0-1		9,134
26		15	CARLISLE UNITED	0-1		8,526
27		19	EXETER CITY	2-0	Johnsson, Alexander	8,459
28		23	Southend United	0-2		3,341
29		26	SHREWSBURY TOWN	3-0	Williams, Dudfield, Edwards	8,534
30		29	York City	1-2	Rowe	6,495
31	Feb	02	Halifax Town	1-0	Johnsson	3,400
32		05	HARTLEPOOL UNITED	1-1	Williams	8,419
33		09	RUSHDEN & DIAMONDS	2-1	Alexander, Van Blerk	8,825
34		16	Torquay United	1-1	Alexander	2,403
35		23	MACCLESFIELD TOWN	0-1		8,431
36	Mar	01	Swansea City	0-1		5,006
37		05	MANSFIELD TOWN	4-1	Philpott, Bradshaw, Norris, Johnsson	9,158
38		09	SCUNTHORPE UNITED	0-1		12,529
39		16	Oxford United	0-1		5,952
40		23	Leyton Orient	0-0		4,265
41		30	DARLINGTON	1-2	Alexander	8,642
42	Apr	01	Cheltenham Town	0-1		5,546
43		06	LUTON TOWN	0-4		9,379
44		09	ROCHDALE	2-3	Dudfield (2)	3,433
45		13	Bristol Rovers	1-4	Matthews	6,340
46		20	LINCOLN CITY	1-1	Dudfield	11,890

Apps: 43 41 3 3 4 38 39 1 26 16 26 30 40 11 4 15 27 3 20 6 27 11 1 5 6 14 22 2 10 34 36 14
Goals: 17 1 1 12 1 1 1 4 1 3 1 1 1 4 2 1

Two own goals

F.A. Cup

	Date		Opponent	Score	Scorers	Att.
R1	Nov	17	Northwich Victoria	5-2	Johnsson, Matthews, Dudfield, Alexander, Barnard (og)	2,285
R2	Dec	08	Oldham Athletic	2-3	Dudfield, Alexander	9,422

F.L. Cup (Worthington Cup)

	Date		Opponent	Score	Scorers	Att.
R1	Aug	21	Wrexham	3-2	Whitmore, Greaves, Alexander	1,761
R2	Sep	12	Derby County	0-3		11,246

A.M. Cup (Auto Windscreens Shield)

	Date		Opponent	Score	Scorers	Att.
R2	Oct	30	Leigh RMI	3-0	Alexander (3)	5,226
NQF	Dec	04	Port Vale	2-1	Whittle, Whitmore	5,326
NSF	Jan	07	Huddersfield Town	0-1		7,248

		Pl	Home W D L F A	Away W D L F A	F. A. (Total)	Pt
1	Plymouth Argyle	46	19 2 2 41 11	12 7 4 30 17	71 28	102
2	Luton Town	46	15 5 3 50 18	15 2 6 46 30	96 48	97
3	Mansfield Town	46	17 3 3 49 24	7 4 12 23 36	72 60	79
4	Cheltenham Town	46	11 11 1 40 20	10 4 9 26 29	66 49	78
5	Rochdale	46	13 8 2 41 22	8 7 8 24 30	65 52	78
6	Rushden & Diamonds	46	14 5 4 40 20	6 8 9 29 33	69 53	73
7	Hartlepool United	46	12 6 5 53 23	8 5 10 21 25	74 48	71
8	Scunthorpe United	46	14 5 4 43 22	5 9 9 31 34	74 56	71
9	Shrewsbury Town	46	13 4 6 36 19	7 6 10 28 34	64 53	70
10	Kidderminster H.	46	13 6 4 35 17	6 3 14 21 30	56 47	66
11	HULL CITY	46	12 6 5 38 18	4 7 12 19 33	57 51	61
12	Southend United	46	12 5 6 36 22	3 8 12 15 32	51 54	58
13	Macclesfield Town	46	7 9 7 23 25	8 6 9 18 27	41 52	60
14	York City	46	11 5 7 26 20	5 4 14 28 47	54 67	57
15	Darlington	46	11 6 6 37 25	4 5 14 23 46	60 71	56
16	Exeter City	46	9 7 7 25 32	7 4 12 23 41	48 73	55
17	Carlisle United	46	11 5 7 31 21	1 11 11 18 35	49 56	52
18	Leyton Orient	46	10 10 7 37 25	3 6 14 18 46	55 71	55
19	Torquay United	46	8 6 9 27 31	4 9 10 19 32	46 63	51
20	Swansea City	46	7 8 8 26 26	6 4 13 27 51	53 77	51
21	Oxford United	46	8 7 8 34 28	3 7 13 19 34	53 62	47
22	Lincoln City	46	8 4 11 25 27	2 12 9 19 35	44 62	46
23	Bristol Rovers	46	8 7 8 28 28	3 5 15 12 32	40 60	45
24	Halifax Town	46	5 9 9 24 28	3 3 17 15 56	39 84	36

~ 296 ~

2002/03 13th in Division Three

#		Date	Opponent	Score	Scorers	Att	Alexander G	Anderson J	Appleby RD	Ashbee I	Bradshaw G	Branch PM	Burgess B	Burton S	Delaney D	Donaldson C	Dudfield L	Edwards M	Elliott S	Fettis AW	Forrester JM	Glennon M	Greaves MA	Green S	Holt A	Jevons P	Johnson S	Joseph M	Keates DS	Melton S	Musselwhite P	Otsemobor J	Price M	Reeves ML	Regan	Smith GS	Strong G	Walters J	Webb D	Whittle IP	Williams RN
1	Aug	10	SOUTHEND UNITED	2-2	Green, Elliott	10449	5			4							8	2	7			1		9	10										3	6				11
2		13	Bristol Rovers	1-1	Johnson	7501		5		4	9						8	2	7			1	11	10			14							12		3	6			15	
3		17	Exeter City	1-3	Green	4257	9	5		4							8		7			1		10			12							11		2	3	6		14	15
4		24	BURY	1-1	Johnson	8804	9	5			15						14					1	6	10			11							12		2	3			4	
5		26	Hartlepool United	0-2		4236	9	5		4	12						8					1		10			11	7								3				6	14
6		31	LEYTON ORIENT	1-1	Keates	7684	9	5		4	11						12					1		10		8									2	3			6	7
7	Sep	07	Cambridge United	2-1	Whittle, Smith	4258	9	5		4									14			1			10	7	8								2	3			6	11
8		14	CARLISLE UNITED	4-0	Alexander (3), Dudfield	8461	9	5		4							12	14				1		10	8	15	7								2	3			6	11
9		17	MACCLESFIELD TOWN	1-3	Green	8703	9	5		4							12					1		10	8	14	7								2	3			6	11
10		21	Oxford United	0-0		5445	9	5		4							12							10	8	14	7		1						2	3			6	11
11		28	SWANSEA CITY	1-1	Jevons	8070	9	5		4							14	12						10	8	15	7		1						2	3			6	11
12	Oct	05	Kidderminster Harr	0-1		3787		5		4		9					14	3	11					10	8	15	7		1						2	12			6	
13		12	ROCHDALE	3-0	Jevons, Branch (2)	9057	14	5		4		9	3						11					10	8	15	7		1						2				6	12
14		19	Torquay United	4-1	Ashbee, Jevons, Anderson, Green	3607	14	5		4		9	15	3					11					10	8		7		1						2				6	12
15		26	RUSHDEN & DIAMONDS	1-1	Green	10659	9	5		4	14		15	3					11					10	8		7		1						2				6	12
16		29	Shrewsbury Town	1-1	Elliott	3086	9	5		4			12	3					11					10	14		7		1						2				6	8
17	Nov	02	SCUNTHORPE UNITED	2-0	Branch, Alexander	11885	9	5		4		14	3						12					10	8		7		1						2				6	11
18		09	Lincoln City	1-1	Alexander	6271	9	5				8	3	4					12					10	14		7		1						2				6	11
19		23	BOSTON UNITED	1-0	Delaney	9460	9	5				8	3						12					10	14		7	11	1						2				6	
20		30	Wrexham	0-0		4412	9	5		4		8	3											10	12		14	7	11	1					2				6	
21	Dec	14	DARLINGTON	0-1		14162	9	5		4							12							10	8		6	7	11	1					2	3		15	14	
22		21	AFC Bournemouth	0-0		6098	12	5		4					3		9							10	8		6	7	11	1					2					
23		26	HARTLEPOOL UNITED	2-0	Keates, Green	22319	9	5		4					3		15		10					8		12	6	7	11	1					2				14	
24		28	York City	1-1	Keates	7856	9	5		4					3		12							14	15	8	2	7	11	1					10				6	
25	Jan	01	Bury	0-3		4290	14	5		4					11		12		9					8	3		2		10	1					7				6	
26		04	BRISTOL ROVERS	1-0	Alexander	14913	9	5		4					3		8		11					10	14		6		7	1					2	12		15		
27		11	EXETER CITY	2-2	Elliott (2)	13667	9	5		4					6		14		11					7	3				8	1					2			10		12
28		18	Leyton Orient	0-2		5125	9	5		4					6		15		11					7	3		2		8	1					14			10		12
29		25	YORK CITY	0-0		18437		5		4					8			9		10				3			6		12	1					2			15	14	11
30	Feb	01	Southend United	0-3		4534	15								14	6		9	1	10				7	3		4		8						2			12	5	11
31		08	LINCOLN CITY	0-1		13728	5			4					3	14	8		12	1	9						2	7										10	6	11
32		15	Scunthorpe United	1-1	Forrester	6284				4					8		15	12	1	9				5	7	14								2	3			10	6	11
33		22	CAMBRIDGE UNITED	1-1	Forrester	15670	5	8							3		9		11	1	10				15		2	7	4					14					6	12
34	Mar	01	Carlisle United	5-1	Walters (2), Elliott (2), Forrester	4678		5	8								12		11	1	10						2	7	4					14	3		9	15	6	
35		04	Macclesfield Town	1-0	Elliott	2229		5	8	4									11	1	10						2	7								12	3	9		6	
36		08	OXFORD UNITED	0-0		17404		5	8	4					3				11	1	10						2	7	14				12			15		9		6	
37		15	Rushden & Diamonds	2-4	Otsemobor, Walters	4713		5	8						3				11	1	10						7	14		2		4				12		9		6	
38		18	TORQUAY UNITED	1-1	Elliott	13310		5	8						3				11	1	10		14				7	12		2		4						9		6	
39		22	SHREWSBURY TOWN	2-0	Otsemobor, Keates	13253		5							14	3			11	1	10					12	6	7	8	2		4	15				9				
40	Apr	05	WREXHAM	1-2	Otsemobor	15002		5				9	12	3			11	1					14		4	7	8	2		6				10						15
41		12	Boston United	1-0	Elliott	3782		5				9		8	12		11	1							2	4						7	3			10		6			
42		19	AFC BOURNEMOUTH	3-1	Walters, Elliott (2)	15816		5				9		8			11	1							2	4		14		12		15	7	3			10		6			
43		21	Darlington	0-2		3487		5				9		8			10	1						12	2	4		11		3			7	14				6			
44		26	KIDDERMINSTER HARR	4-1	Burgess (3), Walters	14544						9	12	3			11	1							5	4	8		2			7				10	15	6			
45		29	Rochdale	1-2	Burgess	2225		5				9	14	3			11	1							4	8		2		12	7					10	15	6			
46	May	03	Swansea City	2-4	Elliott, Reeves	9585						9	14	8			10	1						5	4	11		2		7			3			14	6			

	Apps	25	43	6	31	5	7	7	11	30	2	21	6	36	17	11	9	3	28	6	24	12	23	36	25	20	9	3	8	38	22	3	11	12	39	23
	Goals	6	1		1		3	4		1		1		12		3			6		3	2		4						3	1		1	5		1

Russell S played at 14 in match 44, Philpott L at 12 in 1, Peat N 12 in 7, Morrison O at 8 in 4 and 14 in 6, Petty B at 7 in 4 and 2 in 5

F.A. Cup

R1	Nov	17	MACCLESFIELD TOWN	0-3		7803	9	5		4			3	8					14					7		10						1			2	15			6	11

Peat N played at 12

F.L. Cup (Worthington Cup)

R1	Sep	11	LEICESTER CITY	2-4	Alexander, Ashbee	7061	9	4	8	6												1				10	12		11					14		2	3			5	7

a.e.t. 1-1 at 90 minutes

A.M. Cup (LDV Vans Trophy)

R1	Oct	23	Port Vale	1-3	Donaldson	2621	9					10		4		12																1		3						11

Chapman L played at 5, Fry R at 15, Heard J at 2 and Kerr S at 7, Peat N at 8

		Pl	Home				Away					F.	A.	Pts
			W	D	L	F	A	W	D	L	F	A	(Total)	
1	Rushden & Diamonds	46	16	5	2	48	19	8	10	5	25	28	73 47	87
2	Hartlepool United	46	16	5	2	49	21	8	8	7	22	30	71 51	85
3	Wrexham	46	12	7	4	48	26	11	8	4	36	24	84 50	84
4	Bournemouth	46	14	7	2	38	18	6	7	10	22	30	60 48	74
5	Scunthorpe United	46	11	8	4	40	20	8	7	8	28	29	68 49	72
6	Lincoln City	46	10	9	4	29	18	8	7	8	17	19	46 37	70
7	Bury	46	8	8	7	25	26	10	8	5	32	30	57 56	70
8	Oxford United	46	9	7	7	26	20	10	5	8	31	27	57 47	69
9	Torquay United	46	9	11	3	41	31	7	7	9	30	40	71 71	66
10	York City	46	11	9	3	34	24	6	6	11	18	29	52 53	66
11	Kidderminster H.	46	8	8	7	30	33	8	7	8	32	30	62 63	63
12	Cambridge United	46	10	7	6	38	25	6	6	11	29	45	67 70	61
13	HULL CITY	46	9	10	4	34	19	5	7	11	24	34	58 53	59
14	Darlington	46	8	10	5	36	27	4	8	11	22	32	58 59	54
15	Boston United	46	11	6	6	34	22	4	7	12	21	34	55 56	54
16	Macclesfield Town	46	8	6	9	29	28	6	6	11	28	35	57 63	54
17	Southend United	46	12	1	10	29	23	5	2	16	18	36	47 59	54
18	Leyton Orient	46	9	6	8	28	24	5	5	13	23	37	51 61	53
19	Rochdale	46	9	6	8	28	24	5	10	8	33	40	63 70	52
20	Bristol Rovers	46	7	7	9	25	27	5	8	10	25	30	50 57	51
21	Swansea City	46	9	6	8	28	25	3	7	13	20	40	48 65	49
22	Carlisle United	46	5	5	13	26	40	8	5	10	26	38	52 78	49
23	Exeter City	46	7	7	9	24	31	4	8	11	26	33	50 64	48
24	Shrewsbury Town	46	5	6	12	34	39	4	8	11	28	53	62 92	41

2002-03

Back Row: B. Petty, N. Mohan, M. Edwards, J. Anderson, S. Wicks, G. Strong, M. Greaves, G. Alexander, A. Holt, L. Dudfield;

Standing: R. Arnold (Coach), M. Bloomer, I. Ashbee, M. Glennon, J. Whittle, P. Musselwhite, S. Burton,

N. Mann, G. Barnet (Asst. Manager), M. Matthews (Physio);

Sitting: S. Kerr, G. Bradshaw, R. Williams, S. Smith, S. Elliott, J. Molby (Manager), L. Philpott, R. Appleby, N. Peat, S. Green, M. Price.

2003-04

Back Row: A. Thelwell, R. Hinds, J. Whittle, D. Allsopp, D. Delaney, B. Burgess, C. Donaldson, J. Anderson, J. Price, I. Ashbee;

Standing: W. Russell (Coach), R. Arnold (Coach), S. Butler (Coach), A. Dawson, S. Burton, M. Joseph, D. Webb, P. Musselwhite, A. Fettis,

Holt, C. Regan, S. Smith, S. Melton, C. Murphy (Asst-Manager), S. Maltby (Physio), N. Mann (Coach);

Sitting: J. Forrester, D. Keates, R. Fry, S. Elliott, J. Holmes (Director), M. Brannigan (Director), P. Taylor (Manager), A. Pearson (Chairman),

Hough (Secretary), R. Appleby, S. Green, N. Peat, R. Williams.

2003/04 2nd in Division Three: Promoted

Date	Result	Scorers	Att	Allsop D	Ashbee I	Burgess B	Burton S	Dawson A	Delaney D	Donaldson C	Elliott S	Fettis AW	Forrester JM	France R	Fry R	Green S	Hinds RP	Holt A	Joseph M	Keates DS	M. Kuipers	Lewis K	Marshall LK	Melton S	Musslewhite P	Myhill G	Peat N	Price J	Regan CA	Smith GS	Strong G	Thelwell A	Walters J	Webb D	Whittle JP	Williams RN	Wiseman S
Aug 09 DARLINGTON	4-1	Burgess, Price, Thelwell, Allsopp	14675	10	6	9		3			11	1	15			8	4	5	14									7				2			12		
16 Oxford United	1-2	Allsopp	6618	10	6	9		3			11	1	12			8	4	5									13	7				2					
23 CHELTENHAM TOWN	3-3	Elliott, Price, Allsopp	12522	10	6	9		3			11	1	15			8	4	5	12								1	7				2				14	
25 Cambridge United	2-0	Price, Allsopp	4571	10	6	9		3			11						4	14	8				12				1	7				2				5	
30 BOSTON UNITED	2-1	Elliott, Green	13091	10	6	9		3			11		12			8	4		14				15				1	7				2					
Sep 08 Doncaster Rovers	0-0		7132	10	6	9		3	4		11					8	2		7	1								12						14		5	
13 SOUTHEND UNITED	3-2	Allsopp, Dawson, Elliott	12545	10	6	9		3	4		11					8	2	12		1		14						7								5	
16 Leyton Orient	1-1	Burgess	3728		6	9		3	4		11		10			7	2		8	1			12											14		5	
20 Rochdale	2-0	Green, Burgess	4215		6	9		3	4		11					7	2	12	8								1									5	
27 KIDDERMINSTER HARR	6-1	Burgess (2), Allsopp, Dawson, France, Green	13683			9		3	4		11		14	15		8	2	12	6								1	7								5	
30 SWANSEA CITY	1-0	Elliott	20903	10	6	9		3	4		11					8	2	12									1	7								5	
Oct 04 Northampton Town	5-1	Elliott, Allsopp, Price, Burgess, Forrester	6011	10	6	9		3	4		11		14			8	2	12	15								1	7								5	
12 CARLISLE UNITED	2-1	Burgess, Forrester	19050	10	6	9		3	4		11		12	15		8	2	11									1	7				14				5	
18 Torquay United	1-1	Elliott	3720	10	6	9		3	4		11		14	12		8	15										1	7				2				5	
21 Bury	0-0		3896	10	6	9		3	4				15	14		12	11	8									1	7				2				5	
25 LINCOLN CITY	3-0	Holt, Allsopp, Green	17453	10	6	9		3	4				12			8	15	11	8								1	7				2				14	
Nov 01 MACCLESFIELD TOWN	2-2	Hinds, Allsopp	15053	10		9		3	4		11		12			8	6	14	2								1	7								5	
15 Huddersfield Town	1-3	Forrester	13893	10	6	9		3	4		11	1	12	14		8	2	5										7									
22 YEOVIL TOWN	0-0		14367		6	9		3	4		11		10	12		8	2	5										7								14	
29 Bristol Rovers	1-2	Burgess	6331		6	9		3	4		11			7		8	2	14	5	12								10									
Dec 06 BURY	2-0	Price, Burgess	11308		6	9		3	4		11					8	2	12	5	7								10									
13 Scunthorpe United	1-1	Elliott	6426		6	9		3	4		10			12		14	2	11	5	8								7									
20 MANSFIELD TOWN	0-1		15005	12	6	9		3	4		10			14		8	2	15	5	11								7									
26 York City	2-0	Burgess, Forrester	7923		6	9		3	4		11		10			8	2	12	5								1	7									
28 DONCASTER ROVERS	3-1	Price (3)	23006	12	6	9		3	4		11		10	15		8	2	5									1	7				14					
Jan 03 CAMBRIDGE UNITED	2-0	Elliott (2)	14271	12	6	9		3	4		11		10	15		8	2	5									1	7				14					
10 Darlington	1-0	Elliott	6847	12	6	9		3	4		11		10			8	14	5									1	7				2					
17 OXFORD UNITED	4-2	Burgess, Allsopp (2), Crosby (og)	21491	10	6	9		3	4		11		15			8	2	14	5								1	7							12		
24 Cheltenham Town	2-0	Allsopp, Burgess	4536	10	6	9		3	4		11			7		8	2	12	5			14					1										
Feb 07 YORK CITY	2-1	Allsopp, Walters	19099	10	6	9		3	4		11			7		8	4	14	15	5				2			1						12				
14 Carlisle United	1-1	Green	7176	10		9		3	4		11					8	7	15	5			2	14				1						12		6		
21 TORQUAY UNITED	0-1		15222			9			4		11		15	12		8	7	3	5				6				1			14			2	10			
28 Lincoln City	0-2		7069			9			4		11		14			8	7	15	5		6	2					1	12					3	10			
Mar 06 Mansfield Town	0-1		6859		6	9			4		11		15	14			12	11	5		8	2					1						3	10			
13 SCUNTHORPE UNITED	2-1	Burgess (2)	19076	12	6	9			4		11						5			8	2						1						3	10			
16 LEYTON ORIENT	3-0	Elliott, Burgess, France	15531	12	6	9			4					15	14		5			8	2						1						3	10			
27 ROCHDALE	1-0	Delaney	16050		6	9			4			14		12			5			8	2						1						3	15			
31 Boston United	2-1	Elliott, Allsopp	4741	10		9			3		11		12			8	4	5			6	7					1						2	14			
Apr 03 Kidderminster Harr	1-1	Burgess	3853			9			4		11		7			8	5			6	2						1						3	14			12
10 NORTHAMPTON TOWN	2-3	Elliott, Dawson	18017	10	6	9		12	3		11		7			8	5	4									1						2	15			14
12 Swansea City	3-2	Allsopp, Burgess (2)	5993	10	6	9		3	4		11			12		7	15	5		8							1						2	14			
17 Macclesfield Town	1-1	Joseph	3801	10	6	9		3	4		11			14		7		5	8								1						2	12			
20 Southend United	2-2	Lewis, Ashbee	5389	10	6	9		3	4		11			14		7	12	5	8								1						2	15			
24 HUDDERSFIELD TOWN	0-0		23495	10	6	9		3	4		11			12		7		5	8								1						2	14			
May 01 Yeovil Town	2-1	Green, Ashbee	8760	10	6			3	4		9			7		11	2	5	8								1					14		12			
08 BRISTOL ROVERS	3-0	Price, Delaney, Elliott	22562	10	6			3	4		9		14	7		11	2	5	8								1	12						15			
Apps				36	39	44		33	46		42	3	21	28		42	39	25	32	14	3	13	11	5		18	23	1	33				26	16	4	18	2
Goals				15	2	18		3	2		14		4	2		6	1	1	1			1						9						1		1	

One own goal

F.A. Cup

Date	Result	Scorers	Att	Ashbee	Burgess	Dawson	Delaney	Elliott	Forrester	Green	Hinds	Holt	Joseph	Price	Williams
Nov 08 Cheltenham Town	1-3	Price	3624	6	9	3	4	12	14	8	7	11	2	10	5

F.L. Cup (Carling Cup)

Date	Result	Scorers	Att	Allsop	Ashbee	Burgess	Dawson	Elliott	Fettis	Green	Hinds	Joseph	Marshall	Price	Thelwell	Williams
Aug 12 Wigan Athletic	0-2		3295	10	6	9	3	11	1	8	4	14	12	7	2	5

A.M. Cup (LDV Vans Trophy)

Date	Result	Scorers	Att	Burgess	Dawson	Delaney	Forrester	France	Holt	Joseph	Price	Regan	Smith	Strong	Thelwell	Williams	Wiseman
Oct 14 Darlington	3-1	France, Forrester, Williams	1578	5	12	1	10	7	6		8	14	2	3	4	9	11
Nov 04 SCUNTHORPE UNITED	1-3	Webb	6656		15	1	10	12	2	6	8		3	7	5	9	4

		Pl		Home					Away					F.	A.	Pts
			W	D	L	F	A	W	D	L	F	A	(Total)			
1	Doncaster Rovers	46	17	4	2	47	13	10	7	6	32	24	79	37	92
2	HULL CITY	46	16	4	3	50	21	9	9	5	32	23	82	44	88
3	Torquay United	46	15	6	2	44	18	8	6	9	24	26	68	44	81
4	Huddersfield Town	46	16	4	3	42	18	7	8	8	26	34	68	52	81
5	Mansfield Town	46	13	5	5	44	25	9	4	10	32	37	76	62	75
6	Northampton Town	46	13	4	6	30	23	9	5	9	28	28	58	51	75
7	Lincoln City	46	9	11	3	36	23	10	6	7	32	24	68	47	74
8	Yeovil Town	46	14	3	6	40	19	9	2	12	30	38	70	57	74
9	Oxford United	46	14	8	1	34	13	4	9	10	21	31	55	44	71
10	Swansea City	46	10	7	6	37	26	6	6	11	22	35	59	62	61
11	Boston United	46	11	7	5	35	21	5	4	14	15	33	50	54	59
12	Cambridge United	46	6	7	10	26	32	8	7	8	31	35	57	67	56
13	Bury	46	10	7	6	29	26	5	4	14	25	38	54	64	56
14	Bristol Rovers	46	9	7	7	29	28	5	6	12	21	35	60	63	55
15	Kidderminster Harr	46	9	5	9	28	29	5	8	10	17	30	45	59	55
16	Cheltenham Town	46	11	4	8	37	38	3	9	11	20	34	57	72	55
17	Southend United	46	8	4	11	27	29	6	8	9	24	34	51	63	54
18	Darlington	46	10	4	9	30	28	4	7	12	23	33	53	61	53
19	Leyton Orient	46	8	9	6	28	27	5	3	13	20	38	48	65	53
20	Macclesfield Town	46	8	9	6	28	25	5	4	14	26	44	54	69	52
21	Rochdale	46	7	8	8	28	26	5	6	12	21	32	49	58	50
22	Scunthorpe United	46	7	10	6	36	27	4	6	13	33	45	69	83	49
23	Carlisle United	46	8	5	10	23	27	4	4	15	23	42	46	69	45
24	York City	46	7	6	10	22	29	3	8	12	13	37	35	64	44

2004/05 2nd in League One (Formerly Division Two): Promoted

#	Date	Opponent	Score	Scorers	Att	Allsop D	Angus S	Ashbee I	Barmby N	Burgess B	Cort L	Dawson A	Delaney D	Duke M	Edge R	Elliott S	Ellison K	Facey D	Fagan C	France R	Fry R	Green S	Hessenthaler A	Hinds RP	Joseph M	Keane MJT	Lewis K	Myhill G	Price J	Stockdale R	Thelwell A	Walters J	Wilbraham A	Wiseman S
1	Aug 07	AFC BOURNEMOUTH	1-0	Green (p)	17569	10		4	8		14	3	5			11						7		2	6			9	1				12	15
2	Aug 10	Torquay United	3-0	Green, Elliott (2)	3973	10		4	8		6	3	5			11			15			7		2				9	1				12	14
3	Aug 14	Port Vale	2-3	Barmby, Elliott	6736	10		4	8		6	3	5			11		15	12			7		2				9	1				14	
4	Aug 21	OLDHAM ATHLETIC	2-0	Allsopp, Green	16916	10		4	8		6	3	5	13		11		15				7			2			9	1				12	
5	Aug 28	Barnsley	2-1	Elliott, Keane	13175	15		4	8		6	3	5			11			12			7			2	14		9	1				10	
6	Aug 31	BRADFORD CITY	0-1		16865	14		4	8		6	3	5			11		15				7			2			9	1				12	10
7	Sep 05	Huddersfield Town	0-4		13542	10		4	8		6	3										7		2	5			9	1	12			14	11
8	Sep 11	BLACKPOOL	2-1	Green, Elliott	15568	10		4	8		6	3	5			11						7	9	2					1	14			12	
9	Sep 18	Peterborough Utd	3-2	Elliott (2), Cort	5745	10		4			6	3				11						7		2	8	5			1	14		12	15	9
10	Sep 25	STOCKPORT COUNTY	0-0		16182	10		4			6	3				11						7	12		8	5			1	14	2	15	9	
11	Oct 02	Hartlepool United	0-2		5768	10		4				3	6	1		11		15	12			7			8	5				14	2		9	
12	Oct 09	CHESTERFIELD	1-0	Green	15500			4			5	3	6					14	2			11		12	8		9	1	7				10	
13	Oct 16	Bristol City	1-3	Facey	12011	12					5	3	6			11	9		7			10		2	8		4	1	14					
14	Oct 19	MILTON KEYNES D	3-2	Green (2), Keane	14317	14			8			3	6			11	9		7			10			5	12	4	1	15					2
15	Oct 23	LUTON TOWN	3-0	Elliott (2), Facey	18575	12			8		5		6		3	11	9					10			2	14	4	1	7				15	
16	Oct 30	Wrexham	2-2	Cort, Facey	5601	14			8		5	3	6		12	11	9					7		2			10	1	15					
17	Nov 06	WALSALL	3-1	Barmby, Elliott, Lewis	16010	10		4	8		5	3	6			11						7		2	12	9	1	15				14		
18	Nov 20	Swindon Town	2-4	Walters, Elliott	6348	14		4	8		5	3	6			11						7		2	10	9	1					12		
19	Nov 27	BRENTFORD	2-0	Elliott (2)	15710			4	8		5	3	6			11		12	15			7		2	14	10	1					9		
20	Dec 08	Sheffield Wed	4-2	Keane, Barmby (2), Allsopp	28701	12		4	8		5	3	6			11	9	7						2	10	15	1						14	
21	Dec 11	Colchester United	2-1	France, Elliott	4046	14		4	8		5	3	6			11	9	7						2	10	12	1						15	
22	Dec 18	TRANMERE ROVERS	6-1	Ashbee, Elliott (3), Barmby, Allsopp	20064	12		4	8		5		6		3	11	9	7				10		2	14		1						15	
23	Dec 26	Blackpool	2-0	Elliott (2)	8774	14		4	8		5		6		3	11	9					7		2	10		1	15				12		
24	Dec 28	DONCASTER ROVERS	2-1	Allsopp, Elliott	24117	9	14	4	8		5		6		3	11						7		2	10		1	12				15		
25	Jan 01	HUDDERSFIELD TOWN	2-1	Elliott, Wilbraham	22291		2	4			5	3	6			11	9					7			10	15	1	14				8	12	
26	Jan 03	Stockport County	3-1	Wilbraham, Price, Allsopp	6670	10		4			5	3	6		11			14						2	12	8	1	7					9	15
27	Jan 15	PETERBOROUGH Utd	2-2	Barmby, Green	16149	12		4	8		5	3	6				11	9	7			10		2	14	15	1							
28	Jan 22	Doncaster Rovers	0-1		9633	12		4	8		5	3	6				11	9	7			14	2		10		1	15						
29	Feb 01	Chesterfield	1-1	Lewis	5517				8		5	3	6				11	11	14			15	4			10	1	7	2			9		
30	Feb 05	BRISTOL CITY	1-1	Barmby	17637	12			8		5		6		3		11	15	7			10	14			4	1		2			9		
31	Feb 12	Luton Town	0-1		9500			4	8		5		6		3		12					7	10			11	1	14	2			9		
32	Feb 19	WREXHAM	2-1	Allsopp (2)	15995	10		4	8		5	3	6			11						7					1	9	2					
33	Feb 22	Milton Keynes D	1-1	Facey	4407	10		4	15		5		6				3	14	11	9		12	7	8			1		2					
34	Feb 26	COLCHESTER UNITED	2-0	Cort, Barmby	16484			4	8		5	3	6			11	9		7			10				12	1	14	2					
35	Mar 05	Tranmere Rovers	3-1	Ellison, Price, Fagan	12684			4	8		5		6		3	9	11		12	14					10	1	7	2						
36	Mar 08	HARTLEPOOL UNITED	1-0	Elliott	17112			4	8		5		6			11	12	9	7			10			14	1		2						
37	Mar 12	TORQUAY UNITED	2-0	Fagan, Elliott	17147			4	8		5		6		3	11	14	9	7				2		10	1	12					15		
38	Mar 19	AFC Bournemouth	4-0	France, Elliott (2), Delaney	8895			4	8		5		6		3	11		9	7	15					10	1	14	2				12		
39	Mar 26	PORT VALE	2-2	Cort, Fagan	17678			4	8		5	3	6			11		9	7	10					14	1	12	2				15		
40	Mar 28	Oldham Athletic	0-1		8562			4	8		5	3	6		3	11		9	7				2		10	1	14					12	15	
41	Apr 02	BARNSLEY	2-1	Cort, Fagan	19341			4	8		5	3	6			11	15	9	7	10			2		4	1	14	12						
42	Apr 10	Bradford City	2-0	Elliott, Barmby	13631			4	8		5	3	6			11		9	7				2		10	1		12						
43	Apr 16	SWINDON TOWN	0-0		23125			4	8		5	3	6			11	14	9	7			15			10	1	12	2						
44	Apr 23	Walsall	0-3		7958			4	8		5	3	6			11	12					14	2		10	1						7	15	
45	Apr 30	SHEFFIELD WED	1-2	Elliott	24277			4	8	15	5		6		3	11	7	9				12			14	10	1		2					
46	May 07	Brentford	1-2	Cort	9604			4	8	15	5	3	6			11	7		9		10					14	1	12	1					
	Apps					28	2	40	39	2	44	34	43	2	14	36	16	21	12	31	1	29	10	6	29	20	39	45	27	14	3	21	19	
	Goals					7		1	9		6	1				27	1	4	4	2		8				3	2		2				1	2

F.A. Cup

#	Date	Opponent	Score	Scorers	Att	grid
R1	Nov 13	MORECOMBE	3-2	Green, Keane, Walters	10129	Allsop 10, Ashbee 4, Barmby 8, Cort 5, Dawson 3, Delaney 6, Elliott 11, Fagan 12, Green 7, Hinds 2, Keane 9, Myhill 1, Wilbraham 14
R2	Dec 04	MACCLESFIELD TOWN	4-0	France, Facey (2), Elliott	9831	Ashbee 4, Barmby 8, Cort 5, Dawson 3, Delaney 6, Elliott 11, Facey 9, Fagan 7, Hinds 2, Joseph 10, Keane 14, Lewis 15, Myhill 1, Wilbraham 12
R3	Jan 08	COLCHESTER UNITED	0-2		14027	Allsop 12, Angus 2, Cort 5, Dawson 3, Delaney 6, Facey 9, France 15, Green 7, Joseph 8, Keane 4, Myhill 1, Price 11, Wiseman 10

F.L. Cup (Carling Cup)

#	Date	Opponent	Score	Scorers	Att	grid
R1	Aug 24	WREXHAM	2-2	Keane, France	6079	Ashbee 4, Cort 5, Dawson 12, Delaney 6, Duke 1, Edge 3, Elliott 14, Facey 9, France 11, Fry 15, Hinds 2, Joseph 8, Lewis 7, Wilbraham 10

a.e.t. lost 3-1 on penalties

A.M. Cup (LDV Vans Trophy)

#	Date	Opponent	Score	Scorers	Att	grid
R1	Sep 28	Hartlepool United	3-3	Price, Green, Elliott	1535	Ashbee 4, Dawson 12, Delaney 3, Duke 15, Elliott 9, Green 8, Hinds 5, Joseph 11, Keane 6, Lewis 1, Myhill 7, Wilbraham 2, Wiseman 10

a.e.t. lost 4-1 on penalties

2004-05

Back Row: C. Donaldson, D. Allsopp, L. Cort, D. Delaney, A. Wilbraham, K. Lewis, S. Wiseman, D. Facey, R. Hinds;

Middle Row: R. Arnold (Coach), S. Butler (Coach), R. France, M. Joseph, B. Burgess, B. Myhill, M. Duke, J. Walters,
J. Price, A. Thelwell, C. Murphy (Asst. Manager), S. Maltby (Physio);

Front Row: M. Keane, N. Barmby, R. Fry, S. Elliott, P. Taylor (Manager), A. Pearson (Chairman), I. Ashbee, S. Green, A. Dawson, R. Edge

And Finally.......Hull City versus the rest
Summary of results against every opponent in the Football League

Opponent	P	W	D	L	F	A
Accrington Stanley	24	17	5	2	51	23
AFC Bournemouth	40	18	11	11	70	56
Aldershot	4	2	1	1	8	5
Arsenal	4	1	1	2	3	4
Aston Villa	16	5	5	6	20	28
Barnet	12	2	5	5	12	20
Barnsley	88	33	20	35	144	133
Barrow	22	14	4	4	40	16
Birmingham City	50	14	15	21	69	76
Blackburn Rovers	44	9	11	24	46	71
Blackpool	90	37	26	27	125	124
Bolton Wanderers	36	8	13	15	35	47
Boston Utd	4	4	0	0	6	2
Bradford City	70	26	16	28	93	95
Bradford P.A.	34	10	6	18	51	65
Brentford	48	23	9	16	82	59
Brighton & H.A.	38	11	10	17	37	53
Bristol City	68	22	17	29	96	112
Bristol Rovers	42	16	10	16	60	51
Burnley	42	14	10	18	57	63
Burton Utd	4	3	1	0	9	2
Bury	62	23	10	29	83	85
Cambridge Utd	16	10	2	4	24	18
Cardiff City	46	15	17	14	60	60
Carlisle Utd	70	30	20	20	113	71
Charlton Athletic	30	7	8	15	40	58
Chelsea	26	4	5	17	17	45
Cheltenham Town	8	3	2	3	12	9
Chester City	42	17	13	12	54	49
Chesterfield	34	20	9	5	52	26
Colchester Utd	26	10	7	9	40	35
Coventry City	28	13	7	8	45	35
Crewe Alexandra	32	19	5	8	66	38
Crystal Palace	32	14	10	8	50	36
Darlington	48	25	9	14	81	59
Derby County	40	15	13	12	58	59
Doncaster Rovers	40	17	9	14	70	55
Everton	6	3	0	3	5	10
Exeter City	32	19	6	7	66	37
Fulham	76	27	24	25	86	94
Gainsborough Trinity	14	7	3	4	27	18
Gateshead	22	8	4	10	34	34
Gillingham	14	4	4	6	11	12
Glossop	20	11	3	6	41	23
Grimsby Town	46	17	12	17	71	61
Halifax Town	42	23	7	12	80	39
Hartlepool Utd	48	24	13	11	83	57
Hereford Utd	8	3	3	2	9	8
Huddersfield Town	46	17	10	19	61	67
Ipswich Town	18	6	6	6	25	28
Kidderminster Harriers	8	3	3	2	15	10
Leeds Utd	56	21	12	23	76	85
Leicester City	56	23	17	16	97	84
Leyton Orient	86	35	30	21	119	86
Lincoln City	66	30	14	22	101	80
Liverpool	6	0	1	5	7	15
Luton Town	34	12	7	15	49	52
Macclesfield Town	12	2	6	4	9	12
Manchester City	12	3	4	5	15	21
Manchester Utd	16	4	3	9	17	30
Mansfield Town	46	17	13	16	72	58
Middlesbrough	36	9	11	16	40	58
Millwall	50	19	14	17	66	68
Milton Keynes Dons *	10	4	4	2	17	14
Nelson	4	3	1	0	9	2
New Brighton	18	9	6	3	38	17
Newcastle Utd	8	2	1	5	11	21
Newport County	12	7	2	3	24	14
Northampton Town	16	6	3	7	27	20
Norwich City	22	9	4	9	23	24
Nottingham Forest	52	19	7	26	60	81
Notts County	58	18	15	25	71	85
Oldham Athletic	70	27	19	24	103	91
Oxford Utd	42	12	14	16	44	48
Peterborough Utd	30	7	8	15	40	58
Plymouth Argyle	62	26	17	19	95	89
Port Vale	62	27	13	22	87	80
Portsmouth	42	11	15	16	58	62
Preston North End	42	12	10	20	64	72
Queens Park Rangers	30	12	10	8	57	41
Reading	38	11	12	15	41	50
Rochdale	44	20	9	15	72	64
Rotherham Utd	66	22	19	25	81	87
Rushden & Diamonds	4	1	2	1	8	9
Scarborough	6	2	1	3	9	9
Scunthorpe Utd	30	11	7	12	41	46
Sheffield Utd	40	8	15	17	47	79
Sheffield Wednesday	36	6	14	16	38	67
Shrewsbury Town	40	17	13	10	72	56
South Shields	18	7	3	8	17	22
Southampton	40	11	15	14	50	59
Southend Utd	32	11	12	9	34	38
Southport	22	15	1	6	51	24
Stockport County	70	26	23	21	120	97
Stoke City	44	14	13	17	51	60
Sunderland	24	10	5	9	29	26
Swansea City	62	21	14	27	78	94
Swindon Town	40	8	15	17	32	49
Torquay Utd	28	12	8	8	45	33
Tottenham Hotspur	14	5	4	5	13	18
Tranmere Rovers	32	18	4	10	63	40
Walsall	26	13	7	6	42	29
Watford	26	10	10	6	39	36
West Bromwich Albion	38	13	12	13	50	50
West Ham Utd	32	8	13	11	39	47
Wigan Athletic	12	4	5	3	12	12
Wigan Borough	2	0	1	1	1	3
Wolverhampton Wanderers	46	21	8	17	84	70
Workington	8	3	1	4	19	17
Wrexham	38	14	7	17	54	68
Wycombe Wanderers	4	2	2	0	8	5
Yeovil Town	2	1	1	0	2	1
York City	50	20	15	15	69	59
TOTALS	3830	1454	1012	1364	5500	5233

* Formerly Wimbledon

~ Advanced Subscribers ~

Stephen Clark - Doncaster

Steph Clark - Doncaster

Gary Sutton - Beverley

David R. Taylor. Hull

Dean Barber, Etton

Colin Malin

Peter F. Lincoln

Patrick & Simon Bromwich, Beverley

Matt Wales & Family (West Ardsley)

Mike Ford, Warsash, Hampshire

Mike Armstrong

Graham Charles Tomlinson

Zoe & Bill Shirley

John Charles Trever

Great Fans With Jo

Russ Mein

Ian Beadle (Hull)

Paul Fowler, Hull

Phil Warriner, Hull

Roger Cass, Portland, Oregon

Victor Markham Thatcham (formerly Hessle)

Paul Atkin - Bedford

Michael Charles, Leeds

Nicholas Brown - Kelfield, York

David Rae, Kettering, Northants

Trevor Haylock, East Hull

David "Slick" Lickiss, Hedon

Eddie Heelas, Willerby, Hull

Carl & Jane Mortimer, Chesterfield

Beryl Gunderson, Hull

Michael Ayre

Andy Haylock, Beverley

Stephen Maddison, Hull

Michael Randerson, West Hull

Paul Atkin, Hull

David Jepson, Hessle

Mike Parsons, Hull

Colin Leslie, Lancaster

John R. Wood, Hull

Alastair And Nicholas Cliffe

Mark Fisher - Hull

Dave Windley, Hull

Dean Banyard - Cottingham

Iain Poplett, South Croydon

Frederick Ronald Charlton, Bradford

David & Bryony Lovell, Birmingham

Thomas Burns - Northallerton

George Burns - Edinburgh

Dave Ponton-Brown, Norton

Adam Fairbank - Barrow

John Kelly, Keyingham

Jack Kelly, Keyingham

John Whiting, Hull, East Yorkshire

Mark Flower, Whiteley

James Flower, Whiteley

Scott Solway, Hull

Mark Alexander, Swanland

Rachel Alexander, Swanland

Sean Pidd, Hull

Mike Leighton

Bryan Leighton

Ron Lithgow, Hessle

James Lithgow, Sheffield

Martin Wacholder, Barnet

Clare J Weston, Beverley

Colin R Weston, Beverley

Richard H Johnson, Rawtenstall, Lancs

The McAllister Family, Hull

Sue Leighton, Hull

Kibibi And Cleome Felstead

James Senior, Filey

Alan Moor

Ray Tupling

Trevor Bugg

In memory of Jim Bugg

John Wilson

Matthew Wilson

Nick Turner

Chris Elton

Steve Sands

Brian Sands

Paul Gilliland

Joseph Gilliland

Doug Saunders

Graham Jackson

Tony Brown

Jim Creasey

Dave Lofthouse

Dominic Love

Alan Mabbutt

Peter Miles, Southend United

Derek Hyde

Colin Cresswell

P.Cogle, Aberdeen

Geoff Allman

David Jowett, Keighley

Allan Grieve, Tillicoultry

Richard Stocken

Gordon Macey (QPR Historian)

David Paul Smith, Liverpool

David Keats, Thornton Heath

John Ringrose

Richard Owen, Portsmouth FC Historian

Graham Spackman

Terry Frost, Football Historian

George Mason

Phil Hollow, Plymouth Argyle

Jonny Stokkeland, Kvinesdal, Norway

Fred Lee, The Pilgrims

Gareth A. Evans

David Brealey, Chesterfield

Richard Shore

Christer Svensson, Sweden

Thomas Leleux

Robert Lilliman

Keith Kieron Coburn

D. E. Griffiths

John Newman

Gary Smith

Arran & Nicholas Matthews

Yore Publications

(Established 1991 by Dave Twydell)

We specialise in football books (only), normally with an historic theme.

Especially: Comprehensive **Football League club histories**, over 30 to date, including: Bolton Wanderers, Partick Thistle, Rochdale, Scunthorpe United, Reading, etc.

Also players '**Who's Who**' books, recent clubs include: Oldham Athletic, Portsmouth, Queens Park Rangers, Notts County etc. (The highly successful Hull City - 'Tiger Tales' is now out of print)

Other titles of a more unusual nature include: '**The Ultimate Directory of English and Scottish Football League Grounds**" (An encyclopaedia detailing every ground on which a League match has been played - updated to 2005)

'**Through The Turnstiles Again**' (A history of football related to attendances)

'**Rejected F.C.**' (A series of books providing the histories of former Football League clubs.

Plus non-League - The '**Gone But Not Forgotten**' series (histories of defunct non-League clubs and former grounds)

Free newsletters (for details of these and many other titles) are issued biannually, for your first copy please send a s.a.e. to: **Yore Publications, 12 The Furrows, Harefield, Middx. UB9 6AT** (website: www.yore.demon.co.uk)